Praise For Midnight Murders on Rock Cut Road

Dr. Krell has written the definitive history of the murders of Mickey Schwerner, James Chaney, and my brother, Andy Goodman. His 2-volume history of the murders and the pursuit of justice is thoroughly researched and documented.

Most importantly for me, his forensic examination is very much appreciated. For years, I have lived with the haunting rumor that my brother was buried alive. The forensic analysis using forensic science and soils science clearly dispels that rumor. I am relieved.

David Goodman

==

"Stunning...the most complete factual history of the tragic events that became the seminal moment in the struggle for civil rights in the U.S. Dr. Krell takes the reader from the dark dirt roads of 1964 Mississippi to the current effort of many local citizens to seek a long-delayed redemption. This is the whole story."

Dick Molpus
Neshoba County native
Mississippi Secretary of State - 1984 to 2006

==

"We, the Featherston family, have worked for years to exonerate any claims of wrongdoing in the autopsies of Schwerner, Chaney and Goodman by Dr William Featherston, our father.

In his first version, Dr. Krell's forensic analysis clearly proved that Bill Featherston acted honestly with integrity and accurately described the cause of death of the trio. He additionally proved that claims of misconduct by others were without foundation. His forensic analyses were confirmed by doctors who reviewed the analyses.

In this revised version, Dr. Krell presents additional proof that further confirms the integrity of Dr. Featherston and the accuracy of the autopsy conducted. We are relieved that the world finally sees the truth about our father and the autopsies – he performed an accurate autopsy without regard to race or color, as his Hippocratic oath required."

Becky Featherston Chamberlain, daughter of Dr. William Featherston
William Featherston, Jr., son of Dr. William Featherston

===

"The definitive work on the 1964 Freedom Summer murder of three Civil Rights workers in Mississippi, with expert forensic analysis and previously unpublished material. Answers many questions that have gone unanswered for decades. A must-read for twenty-first century understanding of race relations today."

Lawrence Primeaux
Chancery Court Judge, Twelfth District of Mississippi

===

"This book is amazing you worked very hard on it. It is extremely accurate and factual. I find it very hard to put it down even with my hectic schedule THANKS"

Pete Talley
Former President, Neshoba County NAACP

===

At first, I had reservations when I was contacted about providing guidance for this project. After Bruce and I discussed what information he was seeking, my boss and I decided it was a good idea. Bruce needed landform and soil interpretation information to correlate the sequence of events of the "Midnight Murders on Rock Cut Road". What makes the book even more interesting was his focus on soils and soil types to sort out and validate prior evidence at and collected from the crime scenes. It took me a while to read through the book myself, but when I finished, I had a whole different opinion of this and other devastating crimes committed in Mississippi. I totally recommend reading the book. I bet it will cause you to have a different perspective about Mississippi history.

Delaney B. Johnson, MS State Soil Scientist, Retired, USDA-NRCS

==

"This is the first book to capture the historical details of the local events in Neshoba County that led to the trial of Edgar Ray Killen in 2005. Dr. Krell has certainly done his homework. Historical details starting in 1966 and ending in 2004 with the Demand for Justice by the Philadelphia Coalition are extremely well documented. He has also taken great care to present the perspectives of individuals involved in the process. A large range of information has been collected into a coherent, readable whole document. Well worth the time to read."

Susan M. Glisson, PhD
Former Director, the William Winter Institute for Racial Reconciliation
Cofounder and Partner, Sustainable Equity

==

"It is always arresting when an author takes a highly charged and widely discussed and written about event like the murder of three young civil rights workers in Neshoba County, Mississippi in 1964, and produces what will be the definitive work on this pivotal episode. What Dr. Bruce Krell accomplishes here is quite unique. He grabs prospective readers and draws them in through a vivid and exhaustive series of parallel narratives, intricately illustrated, lucidly written in digestible chunks, of the historical context of the crime.

Then follows analysis of the building of the case against the killers through forensic detective work and cutting through hostile political terrain. He brings the drama of the long journey to justice ending in the arrest and incarceration of the aging Klansman Edgar Ray Killen in 2005. This is a saga that will simultaneously grip and dazzle the serious reader and affirms that in our rugged and often unforgiving world, persistent people can still assemble daunting puzzles that give us hope that making pure evil risky is still possible."

Frederick L. Shiels
Prof. History and Political Scientist
Cornell University, Baruch and Mercy Colleges.

==

"The heinous murders of three young civil rights volunteers just before the start of Mississippi Freedom Summer, 1964 are among those events of American history that will never be forgotten. We know that those murders, committed with the collaboration of law enforcement, the Mississippi White Knights of the Ku Klux Klan and a lay preacher helped motivate the American public to begin the long and ongoing fight to end the deep-seated racism that has plagued us since the founders mistake to allow the continuance of chattel slavery. But many of the details of how and why this happened and how justice for the martyrs and those falsely accused evolved are yet to be told. Dr. Bruce Krell's spectacular detective work and excellent writing now fills in many of the long missing historical gaps about this sordid event and what has followed from it. All Americans who await the swing of the pendulum toward justice will want to read both volumes of *Midnight Murders on Rock Cut Road*."

Richard D. deShazo, MD

Billy S. Guyton Distinguished Professor and Professor Emeritus
The University of Mississippi Medical Center, Jackson, MS

==

Midnight Murders On Rock Cut Road

Murder

Racism, Terrorism Forensics, Reconstruction

BRUCE E. KRELL, PHD

The Past Is Never Dead, It's Not Even The Past

Requiem For A Nun, William Faulkner, Oxford, MS, 1951

(Revised, 2023)

Front Cover Images

Top:

Photos Of Schwerner, Chaney, and Goodman

FBI Missing Persons Poster, June 29, 1964

Bottom:

Location of Murders on Rock Cut Road, June 21, 1964

FBI FOIA Request, 1-49 Photo 36

Author Contact Information

Bruce E. Krell, PhD

www.SWArchitects.com

BKrell@swarchitects.com

Midnight Murders on Rock Cut Road

Series Titles

Murders: Racism, Terrorism, Forensics Reconstruction

(Revised 2023)

Justice: Partial Justice, Silence, Redemption, Final Justice

Midnight Murders On Rock Cut Road

Murder

Racism, Terrorism Forensics, Reconstruction

BRUCE E. KRELL, PHD

(Revised, 2023)

Copyright ©2020-2023 Bruce Krell, BM Krell Trust

All Rights Reserved. No part of this book may be reproduced in any form or by any electronic or mechanical means, including information storage and retrieval systems, without permission in writing from the author and copyright holder above, except by a reviewer who may quote brief passages in a review. Scanning, uploading, and electronic distribution of this book or any part of this book or the facilitation of such without the permission of the author and copyright holder is prohibited. Please purchase only authorized electronic versions, and do not participate in or encourage electronic piracy of copyrighted materials. Your support of the rights of the author and copyright holder is greatly appreciated.

(Color Version)

ISBN-13: **978-0-9966250-4-3**

Library of Congress Control Number: **2023901744**

Printed in the United States   Revised: January 30, 2023

Bruce Krell, BM Krell Trust

Beverly Hills, CA

Table of Contents
(Revised, 2023)

Preface To The Revised Edition 1

Racism, Terrorism 3

Partial Justice, Silence, Redemption, Final Justice 5

Shooting Incident Reconstruction 7

Legal Analysis And Interpretation 7

MS Burning And The Dignity Of Mankind 9

Preface 11

Reasons For This Book 13

Introduction 19

A Note On Sources 21

The Importance of Prehistory 25

The Value Of Quotes 25

Part 1: Introduction And Background 27

Chronology At A Glance 29

Mississippi Burning: Philadelphia, MS, 1964 31

Part 2: Hatred And Violence Resisted By Dignity 57

Racist, Segregationist Organizations Involved 59

Civil Rights Organizations Involved 69

MS Religions and Blacks and Jews 87

Part 3: Murder And Search 129

People and Events Prior To The Murders 131

The Murders On Rock Cut Road 183

The Search, The Autopsies, And The Funerals 225

Effects of the Murders on Freedom Summer 319

Part 4: Forensic Evidence Analysis 321

A Word Of Caution 323

Forensic Evidence Analysis 325

Claims About The Murders Over The Years 367

James Chaney -- What Really Happened 395

Forensic Analysis Conclusions 411

Part 5: Foundations Of Visual Reconstruction 417

Location Analysis and Identification 419

Murder Sequence Specification 469

Part 6: Detailed Shooting Incident Reconstruction 475

Visual Reconstruction Prerequisites 477

Detailed Timeline Analysis 489

Visual Reconstruction Of Murders 495

Ill-Fated Decisions By Chaney 609

Summary and Conclusions 613

Part 7: The Past Is Never Dead 615

A Dark Cloud Over Neshoba County 617

A Final Warning 625

Endnotes 627

Part 8: References. Audio, Video, Newspapers 683

Part 9: Appendices 701

Appendix A: Autopsy By William Featherston, MD 703

Appendix B: Chaney Autopsy By David Spain, MD 712

Appendix C: Radiology Report By James Packer, MD 713

Appendix D: Condition Of Body, Chaney, FBI 715

Appendix E: Complete Passenger List 716

Appendix F: Specific Locations, June 21, 1964 717

Appendix G: SNCC Incident Tabulation 720

Dedications To The Heroes

Mickey Schwerner, James Chaney, and Andy Goodman, who gave their lives trying to make the world a better place.

Rita Schwerner Bender, Steve Schwerner, Ben Chaney, Barbara Chaney, and David Goodman, the survivors, who suffered by being alive and knowing what happened to their loved ones.

John Doar, who persisted in obtaining some measure of justice despite resistance from a segregationist Federal judge.

Gov. William Winter who moved the state of MS forward, setting the conditions for justice.

Dick Molpus, who initiated and increased public pressure to hold public officials accountable to bring about justice.

Stan Dearman, Pete Talley, and David Vowell, the earliest Philadelphia citizens who began the public call for justice in the murders.

Leroy Clemons, Jim Prince, Susan Glisson, and all 30 members of the Philadelphia Coalition, whose Call for Justice proved that good still triumphs over evil and that mankind is still capable of redemption.

MS AG Jim Hood and Neshoba County DA Marc Duncan, who finally obtained a large measure of justice for the murders through a trial in the Neshoba County Courthouse.

Dr. William Featherston, whose Autopsy Report proved to be sufficient to reconstruct the actual shooting sequence on Rock Cut Road.

Jerry Mitchell, Investigative Reporter, *Clarion Ledger*, whose persistence and articles shined a bright light on the absence of justice and the final delivery of justice.

Taylor Branch, whose definitive histories of the Civil Rights Movement, demonstrated the feasibility of a 1000-page book containing breadth and detail on the Civil Rights Movement.

Acknowledgements

MS Gov William Winter, for his kind permission to use his photograph of the Boys of Spring, his staff in 1982.

Dick Molpus, former MS Secretary of State, for his unwavering support, encouragement, interviews, and excellent insights into the calls for prosecution in MS.

Steve Kilgore, Neshoba County District Attorney, for providing a copy of the original autopsy of Schwerner, Chaney, and Goodman by Dr. William Featherston.

Larry Primeaux, for his permission to use his photo of the Meridian CORE building and willingness to read my forensic drafts.

Richard DeShazo, MD, MACP, former staff member at the University of MS Medical Center, and author of *The Racial Divide in American Medicine: Black Physicians and the Struggle for Justice in Health Care*, for his input during editing of the forensic analysis results.

Orrin Terry, MD, FACS, for his generation of the autopsy diagrams from the Featherston autopsy and his careful review of my analyses.

Michael Weinstein, Deputy Federal Public Defender, for his detailed and accurate explanations of the Federal habeas corpus appeals process and for taking the time to review my process descriptions.

Delaney Johnson, State Soil Scientist for MS, USDA-NRCS, for his patient introductions to soil science, his maps and data about soils at the murder and burial locations, and his review of my soil analyses.

Dean Forbes, retired Deputy Sheriff, Harris County, TX, worked for Naval Intelligence and at the Navy Forensic Lab in San Diego, former student and longtime friend, for proofreading drafts of the book and evaluating the forensic analysis from the perspective of law enforcement.

Jim Adcock, PhD, cold case investigation expert, for his reviews of the forensic analysis and the visual shooting incident reconstruction.

MS Band of Choctaw Indians, for providing video footage of the 40th Anniversary Commemoration in 2004 and for its permission to use frames from the video.

William Winter Institute for its permission to use frames from the 40th Anniversary Celebration after-party.

Susan Glisson, for her insights, documentation, and memories regarding the Philadelphia activities of the Winter Institute for Racial Reconciliation and the activities of the Philadelphia Coalition.

Pete Talley, from Philadelphia, who reviewed my coverage of his 1989 lawsuit that resulted in the Black 5th voting district in Philadelphia.

Charles Brown, from Philadelphia, who patiently worked with me to uncover the Civil Rights Movement in Neshoba County from 1964-1967.

Eva Tisdale, also from Philadelphia, who also patiently shared her memories with me regarding the Movement in Neshoba from 1964-1967.

Micki Dickoff, for her kind permission to use original images from her film *Neshoba: The Price of Freedom*, available at www.neshobafilm.net.

Michael Wenger, for the link to his paper to President Bill Clinton on the President's Council on Racial Reconciliation.

Ally Mellon, Director of Library Services, MS Department of Archives and History, for her much-appreciated facilitation of research requests and for her excellent research skills in finding obscure documents.

John Gibson, Director of Television, MS Public Broadcasting, for locating and releasing DVDs of the 2005 trial of Edgar Ray Killen and for his permission to use frames and images from the trial videos.

Maria Merkle, MS Legislative Reference Bureau, for scanning high resolution digital images of various MS Legislators.

Andrea' R. Barnes, Staff Attorney, MS Department of Corrections, for servicing the FOIA request to release the incarceration records of Edgar Ray Killen.

Mike Moore, my Civil Air Patrol friend from my early days and fellow Tulane student, for his careful proofreading of the drafts of this book.

Jane Hearn, for her generous licensing of the Jim Lucas photo of the burnt ruins at Mt. Zion Methodist Church.

Steve Schapiro, for his permission to use his photograph of Mickey and Rita Schwerner at Freedom Summer Training in Ohio.

Aaron Brudenell, Forensic Scientist, for his permission to use his photo of the 38 Smith and Wesson Ballistic Gel Test.

Darrel Wayne Thomas, for his permission to use the photo of the Longhorn Drive-In in Meridian, MS.

Rick Shiels, PhD, friend and fellow member of the 1967 Hattiesburg High School graduating class, for his encouragement to write MS History and his review of draft materials.

Midnight Murders On Rock Cut Road
Bruce E. Krell, PhD

Just before midnight during the last few minutes of June 21, 1964, 3 young kids with good hearts were murdered. Mickey Schwerner, James Chaney and Andy Goodman were brutally murdered in a remote area of Neshoba County, MS. These murders committed between 11:35 pm - 11:45 pm are the ***Midnight Murders***.

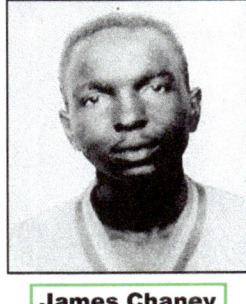

(FBI Missing Poster, June 29, 1964)

These heinous murders were performed on a remote road called ***Rock Cut Road***. This road was given the name because the road was cut from the local bedrock in the area. Currently, the road is named Road 515.

Rock Cut Road   Dam On Old Jolley Farm
(FBI 1-49 Photos 36)   (FBI 1-50 Photos 43)

After the murders, the bodies were buried in an unmarked grave that was a dam under construction on Old Jolly Farm, owned by an abettor.

If We Can Crack Mississippi ...

MS is the stronghold of the whole vicious system of segregation. If we can crack MS, we will likely be able to crack the system in the rest of the country.

John Lewis, Chairman, Student Non-Violent Coordinating Committee[1]

US Representative (D-GA, 5th District) 1987- 2020

On June 21, 1964, Mickey Schwerner, James Chaney and Andy Goodman were brutally murdered in Neshoba County, MS. These murders have been called the "Pearl Harbor" of the Civil Rights movement.

On December 7, 1941, the Japanese attacked Pearl Harbor. This attack awakened the sleeping giant called the US. In response, the US conducted a multi-year war that resulted in the defeat of Japan and the end of WWII.

On June 21, 1964, the White Knights attacked/murdered Schwerner, Chaney, and Goodman. These murders awakened the sleeping giant called the US. In response, the US conducted a multi-year war on MS that resulted in the end of extremist racist violence and segregation, ultimately in the whole US.

These deaths forced the nation to dedicate extensive resources to crack racist violence and segregation in MS. Just like WWII, this war in MS was a multi-year war. Ku Klux Klan controls over MS and the remainder of the US were decimated.

Members of the White Knights perpetrated the murders as a warning to stop the MS Freedom Summer Project and to warn the nation to stay out of MS. Ironically, these heinous murders had the opposite effect. Exposure of the murders increased national pressure for civil rights for Blacks in MS. Under this pressure, the Federal government mobilized national resources into MS. MS was changed forever.

For the most part, ...

---

[1] Atwater, James. "If We Can Crack Mississippi," *The Saturday Evening Post*, July 25, 1964, p. 21

Mickey Schwerner, James Chaney, Andy Goodman

White Knights Imperial Wizard Sam Bowers ordered the *Elimination* of Schwerner, called *Goatee* and *Jew Boy* in late May, 1964. On Father's Day, Sunday, June 21, 1964, at about 3:30 pm, Mickey Schwerner, James Chaney, and Andy Goodman were arrested on false charges. Neshoba County Deputy Sheriff Cecil Price, who arrested the trio, was a member of the Philadelphia Klavern of the White Knights of the KKK.

Cecil Price held the trio in Jail for 7 hours. During that time, Edgar Ray Killen, , White Knights Kleagle (recruiter and organizer), arranged a conspiracy of 19 members of the Meridian and Philadelphia Klaverns. This conspiracy was to kidnap, to murder, and to bury Schwerner, Chaney, and Goodman. After arrangements were made, Price freed the trio. This freedom gave them hope of returning to Meridian alive. As the trio was driving slowly south on Highway 19, Price and a car of White Knights cruelly kidnapped the trio, after giving them hope of escape.

Between 11:30 - 11:45 pm, 9 of the Klansman participated in the murders of Schwerner, Chaney and Goodman. These murders were conducted on Rock Cut Road, 9.5 miles south of Philadelphia, MS. Just over an hour later, the trio was buried in a dam under construction on Old Jolley Farm. This farm was owned by Olen Burrage, also one of the White Knights.

After a statewide search and extensive national publicity, the bodies of Schwerner, Chaney and Goodman were found on August 4, 1964, 44 days later. Olen Burrage himself informed the FBI about the burial location for a substantial reward of $30,000. Burrage used these funds to build a successful trucking company and became rich.

Some perpetrators were convicted of denying civil rights of the trio. Ultimately, Edgar Killen was convicted of the manslaughters of the trio.

Murder convictions were never obtained for the cruel deaths!

Schwerner, Chaney and Goodman were cruelly and brutally murdered by a conspiracy of 19 cowards and thugs. Yet, the trio died with dignity – no screaming, no crying, no begging, just quiet dignity. Mickey Schwerner even expressed empathy for the White Knights Klansman who was about to murder him: *Sir, I know just how you feel.*

Midnight Murders Historical Timeline

A period of 81 years (1939 – 2020) is involved in the prehistory, history, and ramifications of the murders of Schwerner, Chaney and Goodman. All of these years are covered in great detail in this 2-volume history. Some portions of this history have been covered in reasonable details in other books. Other portions have been partially discussed. Several of these areas have not been addressed at all in other books.

With all the new materials available, 2 volumes are necessary to cover the 81 years and the additional forensic analysis performed by the author. *Murder* covers all the conditions and events leading up to the murders, the murders themselves, and the forensic analyses. *Justice* includes the local Neshoba Civil Rights Movement, federal prosecution, prosecution in MS, and all of the resultant appeals.

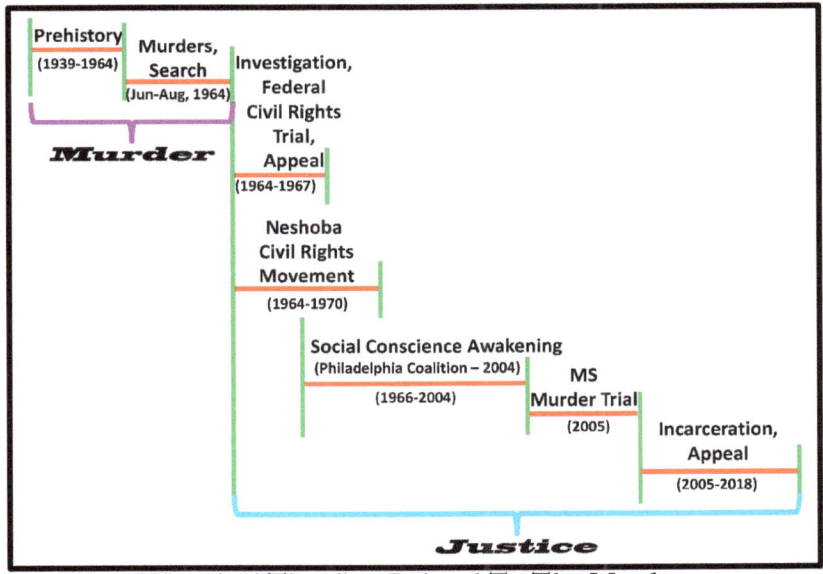

Historical Timeline Related To The Murders

Prehistory Mickey Schwerner was born in 1939. From the time of his birth until the day of his death, existing civil rights organizations were expanded. New organizations were also born. These organizations included the NAACP, CORE, SCLC, SNCC and COFO. During that same time, racist and segregationist groups grew and flourished. Included in these groups were multiple Ku Klux Klan organizations, Citizens Councils, and state, county, and city governments. White Southern Baptist and white Methodist religious denominations created moral conditions that enabled the murders of Schwerner, Chaney and Goodman without remorse.

Murders, Search On June 21, 1964, 19 members of the White Knights of the Ku Klux Klan murdered Schwerner, Chaney and Goodman. Two days later pm June 23, 1964, the burned 1963 Ford Fairlane Ranch Wagon driven by the trio was found. A 44-day manhunt for the bodies of the trio was conducted throughout the state of MS. FBI investigators participated in the search for the bodies. Nationwide news organizations covered search activities. Local leaders and governmental representatives claimed the disappearance was a hoax. On August 4, 1964, the bodies were found buried in a dam on Old Jolly Farm. This farm was owned by Olen Barrage, an abettor after the fact. An autopsy was conducted by Dr. William Featherston, an independent pathologist, on August 5, 1964.

Investigation, Federal Civil Rights Trial, Appeal After the bodies were found, an extensive investigation was conducted by the FBI. Local residents did their best to obstruct the investigation. Ultimately, Jim Jordan and Doyle Barnette, two White Knight participants in the murders, gave detailed confessions. In 1964, only white males served on state and local juries. These all white juries would never convict white Klansmen for the murders of Schwerner, Chaney and Goodman. John Doar, Assistant US Attorney General, charged 19 Klansmen from Meridian and Philadelphia with civil rights violations. These charges were dismissed by Harold Cox, a segregationist Federal court judge. An appeal to the US Supreme Court (US vs Price) reinstated the charges. A Federal jury drawn from Southern Mississippi convicted 8 of the 19 perpetrators. Those convicted spent between 2 and 6 years in Federal prisons. Most people did not consider these convictions as sufficient for the brutal murders.

Neshoba Civil Rights Movement Immediately after the bodies were found, a local civil rights movement emerged in Neshoba County. Local Black leaders wanted to ensure that the deaths did not go unappreciated. COFO established a Neshoba County office. Outside volunteers worked with local Black leaders to begin extensive civil rights activities. Voter registration Freedom Days were conducted. Local leaders became more and more vocal. Martin Luther King Jr marched with local Black residents on the first anniversary of the murders. Schools were integrated. Despite the ongoing federal trials, local Klan members continued to engage in violent acts against local Blacks participating in civil rights activities. Integration of Black students into local schools was accomplished. Local white leaders and white residents resisted these integration efforts. Federal Headstart programs were established in Neshoba County to provide economic support for poor Black children.

Social Conscience Awakening

Within several years after the bodies were found, local white leaders began to develop a social conscience regarding the murders. Efforts to pressure the state of MS to obtain justice for the murders began in 1966 with editorials published by Stan Dearman, editor of *The Neshoba Democrat*. Other state officials, such as Dick Molpus, a Philadelphia resident who was MS Secretary of State, began to speak out about the need for local prosecution of the murders. Neshoba County suffered economically due to the stain of the murders. Something had to be done. Despite all the published and vocal pressure over the years, MS AG Mike Moore slow walked the efforts to bring prosecution. Finally, the Philadelphia Coalition, a group of 30 local white, Black and Choctaw residents, began publishing formal demands for prosecution in 2004.

MS Murder Trial

In 2005, MS AG Jim Hood was newly elected to the office. Hood, along with MS 8th Circuit DA Mark Duncan brought murder charges against Edgar Ray Killen. By this time, Killen was the only remaining participant in the murders who could be prosecuted. Rev. Killen was a self-proclaimed white Southern Baptist preacher who had been the organizational brains behind the conspiracy to commit murder. A well-publicized trial ensued in 2005. In an amazingly shortsighted decision, the jury convicted Killen on three counts of the lesser charge of manslaughter. Judge Marcus Gordon sentenced Killen to 3 consecutive prison terms. Each term was for 20 years. Since he was 80 at the time of his conviction, these sentences amounted to life imprisonment for Killen.

Incarceration, Appeal

Once incarcerated, Edgar Ray Killen continued his racist activity towards Blacks. Killen was regularly disciplined for his racially abusive behavior towards Black prison guards and administrators. While imprisoned, Killen conducted an extensive appeal for a writ of habeas corpus in the Federal courts. If granted, this writ would have given Killen a new trial. The District Court, the Circuit Court of Appeals, both of the US 5th Circuit, and the US Supreme Court, all refused to even hear any motions for a writ. Killen died at Parchman Prison in MS in 2018. A Federal Public Defender participated in preparing the summary discussion of the habeas corpus process that introduces this part of the history.

Murder convictions were never obtained for the cruel deaths!

Midnight Murders Forensic Investigation

When a murder occurs, a forensic investigation usually follows. After the bodies were discovered, the FBI did perform an investigation. This investigation was adequate for the times. However, in general, the FBI examination was woefully inadequate. This inadequacy was further exacerbated because the state of MS refused to release an official autopsy.

In ***Murder***, a thorough forensic investigation is performed. All aspects of this forensic investigation were performed with high professional standards by an experienced forensic scientist (the author). Results are founded on science and on the evidence. Where appropriate, alternate theories are formulated and investigated. Complete reviews were accomplished by a doctor with gunshot wound experience, a soil scientist, a forensic scientist, an expert in cold case reconstruction, and a criminal courts judge.

This investigation consists of four components: a forensic analysis, location identification, rumor analysis, and a visual reconstruction.

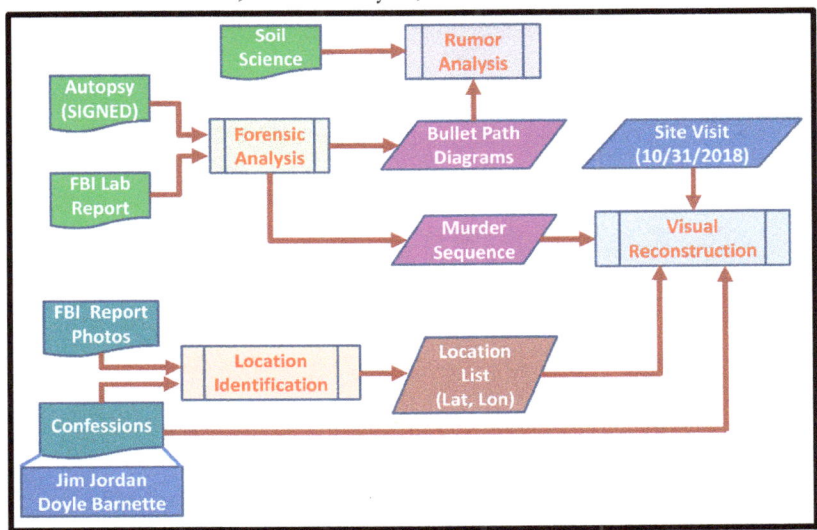

Forensic Investigation Process, Inputs And Outputs

At the core of this investigation is the autopsy performed by Dr. William Featherston. **An actual signed copy of the autopsy is included in the**

Appendices. At this time, this copy appears to be the only published copy of the signed autopsy.

As the first step, a forensic analysis is performed using the signed Autopsy Report and the FBI Lab Report. This analysis produces 2 outputs: bullet path diagrams and a detailed murder sequence on Rock Cut Road. Bullet path diagrams were not created and published with the original Autopsy Report. Using the bullet path diagrams and principles of soils science, outstanding rumors about the murders are dispelled in a Rumor Analysis.

On the day of the murders, 35 locations in Neshoba County and Meridian were involved. Exact geographical coordinates for some of these locations were missing. A Location Analysis was performed to determine geographical coordinates for these missing locations. FBI pictures taken during the investigation and detailed descriptions from the two confessions were used. An accurate list of geographic coordinates for all 35 locations was created.

A Visual Reconstruction consists of a series of visual images and diagrams that characterize everything that happened at each of the 35 locations. This series is presented in the order in which actual activities took place on the day of the murders. Each visual image has a background. Background photos were collected in a site visit to the Neshoba County and Philadelphia area on October 31, 2018. Background photos, murder sequence, location list, and confession details form the basis of the visual reconstruction that appears in this book.

These murders of Schwerner, Chaney and Goodman were premeditated with intent. The visual reconstruction shows the complexity of activities on the day of the murders. Activities this complex would not have succeeded in such remote settings if the activities were not well planned and intentional.

Preface To The Revised Edition

On October 14, 2020, I released the 2 volume series *Midnight Murders on Rock Cut Road*. I sent some copies out to interested parties who had been involved in the aftermath of the murders and were still alive.

Two of the interested parties were Becky Featherston Chamberlain, daughter of Dr. William Featherston, and William Featherston, Jr., son of Dr. William Featherston. After a short period, I received an e-mail from one of them containing the file of Dr. William Featherston, their father. In this file, I found letters from the other doctors who had watched both the Featherston autopsies and the Spain autopsy. These contained some informative and revealing information about the Spain autopsy.

More importantly, I found a post autopsy radiology report performed by Dr. James Packer, a radiologist from Jackson. Featherston sent the x-rays to Packer, requesting that he perform an analysis using those x-rays. Featherston received the results of this analysis by Packer on August 28, 1964, about 3 weeks after his own autopsy and a few weeks after the Spain autopsy.

I was astounded. After 3 years of research and writing and interviews, I had never encountered any reference to an independent radiology analysis performed by Packer. I read this radiology report carefully. After reading the report, I was convinced that I needed to perform a detailed analysis of the Packer post autopsy report. I also needed to compare the radiology report by Packer with the original autopsy by Featherston. This revised version of *Volume I: Murder* contains the Packer post autopsy radiology report, an analysis of this report, and acomparison of the Packer report and Featherston autopsy.

After generating my analysis and comparison of the Packer post autopsy report, I sent a copy of my work to Dr. Rick DeShazo and Dr. Orrin Terry. This pair had reviewed the original autopsy sections that I wrote in the first version. They were kind enough to read and review the new autopsy report and my analysis and comparison. Thanks to both of them for their interest.

This post autopsy report by Packer confirms the same findings as presented by Featherston. Moreover, the Packer findings further confirm that James **Chaney was NOT beaten. All damage to the body of Chaney was caused by the decomposition of the body for 60 days and the destructive nature of the Featherston autopsy.** I made these same conclusions in the previous version. These conclusions are significantly strengthened by the Packer post autopsy report.

While the medical analysis and review were ongoing, I was contacted by Dr. Jim Campbell. Dr. Campbell is the Edgar E. Robinson Professor in United States History at Stanford University. Jim had read my book and suggested some clarifications and corrections. More importantly, Jim provided some additional and important information regarding the activities of Edgar Ray Killen on the day of the murders. He kindly offered me that information, which has been incorporated into this revised version. This information proves beyond a shadow of a doubt that **Killen was NOT at the funeral home at the time of the murders**, as he later claimed.

Finally, after the first version of Volume 1: Murders was distributed, some interested parties provided additional endorsements. These endorsements have been included.

Bruce Krell, PhD   Los Angeles, CA   January 20, 2023

Racism, Terrorism

Mickey Schwerner, a Jew, James Chaney, a Black, and Andy Goodman another Jew, were simply trying to make the world a better place for Blacks in rural Mississippi.

Racism: a propaganda campaign of ignorance and hatred

Until 1970, Blacks and Jews in MS lived in a world of **Racism**. Uneducated, ignorant whites in MS and in Neshoba County hated Blacks and Jews.

Many of these whites organized into a domestic terror group called the White Knights of the Ku Klux Klan. White Knights ruled the state and the County through violence. Rural Neshoba County typified the most ignorant and violent members of the White Knights.

The White Knights conducted a propaganda campaign of hatred throughout the state of MS. This campaign was based on a number of core principles.

Anti-Semitism was an underlying principle ... *these people have been permitted to gain financial control over America ... the savage Kike lust for money is destroying Christian Civilization* ... Inferiority of Blacks was assumed.... *the Black man is one of his creatures under His Protection except for social equality and integration with the White Man* ...

Any form of violence was justified to maintain control of Jews and Blacks. *As MILITANTS, we are disposed to the use of physical force against our enemies*. Physical force included cross burning, whipping, bombing, and elimination.

A military hierarchy with strong discipline insured member compliance. *an act of violation of the Klan law ... shall be tried by his Klavern and all penalties shall be final*. Penalties included expulsion from the Klan and even burning, whipping, bombing, and elimination of the offending member.

Terrorism: a brutal, morally reprehensible murder

Schwerner, Chaney, and Goodman refused to be intimidated. **Terrorism** was used to stop these freedom fighters on June 21, 1964. A conspiracy of 19 members of the White Knights from Philadelphia and Meridian accomplished the murders. This conspiracy included members of law enforcement, such as Neshoba County Deputy Sheriff Cecil Price. These murders were brutal and morally reprehensible.

In addition, the murders were accomplished with extreme cruelty. Schwerner, Chaney and Goodman were arrested. After about 7 hours, the trio was released. This release gave them hope. After being released, law enforcement and several cars filled with White Knights chased them down. All hope of escape was immediately lost when the trio saw the lights, sirens, and lynch mob overtaking them in the dark night. Giving and then removing hope of escape was cruel.

Partial Justice, Silence, Redemption, Final Justice

Partial Justice: convictions on civil rights violations

When the perpetrators were identified in the Fall of 1964, murder prosecutions and convictions by a MS jury were unlikely. So, the US Department of Justice assumed the lead. Perpetrators were charged with conspiracy to deny civil rights. Segregationist Federal judges then conspired to prevent prosecution. An appeal to the US Supreme Court finally allowed Federal prosecution to proceed.

Partial justice was accomplished by conviction for conspiracy to deny civil rights in 1967. However, only 8 of 19 perpetrators were convicted. All of the perpetrators served 6 years or less in prison. The key conspirator, Edgar Ray Killen, was not convicted. These results were unsatisfying to most people in the US. A black cloud descended over the reputation of Neshoba County.

Silence: frustrated attempts by local residents to pursue justice

For years afterwards from 1967 until 1989, residents of Neshoba County were silent about the murders. Most residents hoped that the murders could be swept under the rug and would disappear. This **silence** by the community discouraged the MS Attorney General and the Neshoba County District Attorney from pursuing any prosecutions for murder under MS statutes. Murder prosecutions would lead to stiffer penalties such as life without parole.

As a result of the black cloud of guilt hanging over Neshoba County, economic growth and expansion opportunities were limited in Neshoba County. Furthermore, many residents felt guilty about the murders and the failure of prosecution. Local pressure to pursue prosecution of the murders began slowly. From 1989 until 2004, the MS Attorney General and the Neshoba County District Attorney paid lip service to the possibility of a prosecution for murder. Local pressure through public demands increased for a murder prosecution. These pressures grew greater and greater.

Redemption: Neshoba County residents demand prosecution

Redemption came to the residents of Neshoba County in 2004. In that year, the Philadelphia Coalition, a group of Black, white, and Choctaw residents, publicly apologized to the survivors for the murders of their loved ones. This group also publicly demanded prosecution for the murders in the MS courts. Legal authorities in MS could no longer ignore the demands for prosecution.

Final Justice: a murder trial conducted in Neshoba County

MS Attorney General Jim Hood and Neshoba County DA Marc Duncan finally filed murder charges in 2005. Edgar Ray Killen, the chief conspirator, was charged with murder for the deaths of Schwerner, Chaney, and Goodman. **Justice** was **finally** achieved on June 21, 2005, the anniversary of the murders. Killen was convicted of three counts of manslaughter, to be served sequentially.

On January 11, 2018, Edgar Ray Killen died in Parchman Prison in MS. Killen was 92 years old at the time of his death.

Shooting Incident Reconstruction

History and shooting incident reconstruction have a lot in common.

History consists of a series of events. Some of these events occur in sequence over time. Other events occur at the same time. History describes each event in order by answering the questions who, what, when, where, how, and why. A historian uses documents and interviews as his sources to create a history.

Shooting incidents consist of a series of events. Some of these events occur in sequence over time. Other events occur at the same time. A shooting incident reconstruction describes each event in order by answering the questions who, what, when, where, how, and why. A shooting incident reconstruction expert uses documents, such as investigation reports and confessions, math, science, physics, and experiments as his sources to create a shooting incident reconstruction.

In both of these situations, the reader encounters a story.

Legal Analysis And Interpretation

Much of the aftermath of the murders of Schwerner, Chaney, and Goodman deals with the legal pursuit for justice. During and after the 1967 Federal Civil Rights trial of 19 defendants, appeals were pursued. After the 2005 trial and conviction of Edgar Ray Killen in Neshoba County, appeals and a civil case were conducted.

Understanding all of this legal activity yields important insights into the aftermath and the implications of the murders. Legal techniques and approaches that worked to prohibit prosecution in 1967 did not work in 2005. The legal basis for appeals changed between 1964 and 2005, as the country as a whole become intolerant of racist and segregationist behavior. In 1967, criminal appeals were used by defense attorneys in an attempt to prevent and to overturn convictions. After the 2005 trial, criminal appeals and a civil case were used by defense attorneys in an attempt to overturn the convictions.

Simply repeating the legal historical events is insufficient. Some understanding of the arguments made and the responses offered are important. Arguments for legal action by defense attorneys reveal that the major strategy used in both 1967 and 2005 convictions was essentially the same. Despite being dressed in legal technicalities, the underlying assumption was that the guilt of the perpetrators should be overlooked or excused. Perpetrators engaged in a conspiracy to commit the murders because those murders were essentially sanctioned by the community at the time.

In 1967, thinly disguised arguments about community support worked somewhat. Local MS and Federal circuit court judges were hard core segregationists and sometime racists. By 2005, judges at all levels were not buying the thinly disguised arguments. Despite extensive legalese used to disguise the community support argument, filings and motions were harshly rejected by all courts involved. Legal pleadings relied more and more upon obscure legal technicalities. Delving into the details of pleadings and dependence on technicalities helps to reveal the desperation of the defense attorneys.

In a trial, witnesses give testimony under oath. An attorney asks questions. A response is given by the witness. Sometimes the statements by the witness need further explanation. After a witness completes testimony, understanding the testimonial effect on proving or disproving the case is important. I have attempted to provide further explanations and the testimonial effect as part of the history.

In the US, every case has a docket. A docket is a brief list of all proceedings, filings, and possibly deadlines in a case.[1] Using the docket, a historical record of the case is created. Proceedings are generally documented by a transcript. Filings consist of motions, memoranda and authorities, responses, more memoranda and authorities, orders, and rulings. These documents are written by judges and attorneys. Often the documents are written in perfect legal terms as may actually be required for the legal action supported by the document. Many of these documents are just poorly written.

Since the legal activity involved in the 55-year aftermath of the murders is an important part of the history, I have attempted to translate legal documents into layman's terms. The general concepts expressed in the legal document are simply stated. Small but targeted portions of the document are then used to illustrate the expressed arguments. Each portion is accompanied by a plain English overview of the targeted portion of the document.

Potential problems do exist with explaining legal pleadings in layman's terms. Oversimplification can miss important nuances of the legal point being expressed. Interpretations of the meaning can be correct, partially incorrect or even completely wrong.

As an expert in the criminal and civil courts over a decade, I have become sensitive to expressing legal concepts in layman's terms. I have testified in cases where I actually had to simply express legal concepts for a judge or for a jury. In this history, I worked hard to express legal issues in understandable terms. I also tried to relate all of the ongoing legal activities to the historical context of the murders and to the Neshoba County community. I alone am responsible for any errors of omission or commission in summarizing and interpreting legal documents. My goal was to communicate with the reader.

MS Burning And The Dignity Of Mankind

By 1964, a large portion of the residents of Neshoba County were fueled by hatred for Blacks and hatred for Jews. With the murders of Schwerner, Chaney, and Goodman, this community morally hit rock bottom. After 40 years, leaders in Neshoba County publicly apologized for the murders in 2004. These leaders also publicly demanded prosecution for the murders by a Neshoba County Court. With the apology and the call for justice, the community of Neshoba County achieved a large measure of redemption. After 41 years, a jury from Neshoba County convicted Edgar Ray Killen of 3 counts of manslaughter for the murders. Justice was finally obtained.

Falling to rock bottom, obtaining redemption, and achieving justice is an aspect of the dignity of mankind. Only humans have the dignity and the freedom of choice to obtain redemption. Humans have a moral compass. A moral compass is what enables mankind to take the necessary actions to obtain redemption and justice. Animals do not possess a moral compass.

Please do not take this optimistic outlook as forgiveness for the murders. These murders cannot be forgiven. Despite the redemption of Neshoba County, residents need to be vigilant to ensure that the hatred and violence do not rise again. After all, Neshoba County is part of east central MS. Human history shows that history often repeats in cycles.

Now, I don't mean to say that there is any kind of utopia now in Neshoba County; there is still anger, hate, and evil. I don't know that it will ever change ...[2]

Dick Molpus, "History Is Lunch", **June 18, 2014**

Preface

I grew up in Hattiesburg, MS, about 125 miles south of Philadelphia, MS, where Mickey Schwerner, James Chaney, and Andy Goodman lost their lives. At the time, the summer of 1964, I was 15 years old, a young Jewish kid growing up in one of the most deep South cities of the deep South. Both Schwerner and Goodman were Jewish. This murder sent an ominous signal to all of us MS Jews living in small towns.

During those years, I experienced everything bad that you could experience being a Jew in that small city in the deep South. Hattiesburg was one of the worst cities in the South for hatred and cruel behavior towards Blacks and Jews.

During the fall of 1965, I met both Robert Shelton, Imperial Wizard of the United Klans of America and Sam Bowers, Imperial Wizard of the White Knights of the KKK.

On October 28, 1965, the United Klans of America held a rally in a field next to the Leaf River, near Petal, MS, just outside Hattiesburg. Out of curiosity, I attended that rally. At the end, I introduced myself to Shelton. He indicated that he knew who I was, knew who my father was, and that my Dad and other Jewish merchants were being targeted. The Klan hated Jews. The Klan did not like the Jewish merchants giving credit to Blacks. My Dad and other Jewish merchants did extend credit to Blacks.

In mid-December, 1965, I visited Albert Brown, a Jewish friend in Laurel. As we were standing outside his father's store, the Diamond Shop, Bowers came up to us. In his comments, Bowers made a friendly threat that us "Kikes" would be targeted if we did not behave. FBI informant records show that Albert's house and his Dad's store had been targeted for cross burnings. Bowers knew my friend and his Dad personally as he had participated in the planning for the cross burnings.

In addition to being a hated Jew, I was also vocal about being in favor of integration. And, I committed the ultimate sin in the view of the White Knights. I had friends who were Black.

I was 16 years old and had been warned of violence against me and my friends personally by both Imperial Wizards. (Details of these stories will be told elsewhere in a different book.) So, I am totally familiar with the sense of fear that a Black or a Jew felt when going outside during the years of the White Knights. I personally faced that fear every day I left my house. That fear was that a car would pull up, a group of thugs would get out and kidnap me, and then seriously hurt or murder me.

Based on what happened to Mickey Schwerner, a Jew, and his associates Chaney and Goodman, also a Jew, that fear was clearly very real.

    Bruce E. Krell, PhD   Beverly Hills, CA   2018

Reasons For This Book

The Past Is Never Dead, It's Not Even The Past
Requiem For A Nun, **William Faulkner, Oxford, MS, 1951**

Why Now?

Interest in specific historical events cycles every 20-30 years. More information sources become available. Succeeding generations lose insight into historical incidents. Now is the time to revisit the murders of Schwerner, Chaney, and Goodman.

As I researched another book on MS during the civil rights era, I discussed the murders of Schwerner, Chaney and Goodman with people younger than me. I was shocked at how several generations were unaware of the murders and their implications. New generations need to be informed of the ultimate sacrifices of Schwerner, Chaney, and Goodman for civil rights often taken for granted by current generations.

A need exists for a documented history that updates the story to include recent events. While the murders were performed in 1964, a number of recent events have occurred related to those murders. In 2005, conspirator Edgar Ray Killen was convicted of manslaughter in a local MS/Neshoba County trial. Killen died in Parchman Prison in 2018.

This book contains a complete history of the murders, from beginning to end. The murders of Schwerner, Chaney, and Goodman were the nexus of the direct conflict between civil rights organizations and segregationist and racist organizations in MS. So, this history begins with the formations of the violent and racist White Knights of the Ku Klux Klan and the segregationist MS Sovereignty Commission. Histories of the major civil rights organizations, the NAACP, CORE, SCLC, SNCC, and COFO, are also provided. Historically, the story and ramifications of the murders ends in 2018, with the death of chief conspirator Edgar Ray Killen in Parchman Prison.

In recent years, additional information sources have become available. These sources reveal further details regarding the murders and their aftermath. Complete unredacted confessions by James Jordan and Doyle

Barnette, two participants in the murders, were finally published in 2010. Redacted versions of the FBI MIBURN files are available. MIBURN was the FBI code name for the murder investigation. Actual transcripts from the October, 1967 Federal trials reveal additional details. In 2016, the FBI submitted a report to Jim Hood, MS Attorney General, containing a history and status of the murders. A lawsuit by the ACLU forced the state of MS to make the records of the MS Sovereignty Commission available to the public. All of these sources shed additional light on the murders and their consequences.

The redacted FBI MIBURN files contained a large number of photos taken during the investigations in the Summer of 1964. These photos were useful but highly degraded. I filed a Freedom of Information Act (FOIA) request for high resolution, digital copies of all the photos. In response, the FBI provided all of the digitally scanned photos. Included in the FOIA response were digital, high-resolution scans of an aerial survey of the various involved areas around Philadelphia, MS. These aerial photos do not appear to be anywhere else on the web. Many of these photos appear in this history.

Back issues of local newspapers appear in online digital archives. These back issues close to the time period provide detailed dates and events. Extensive quotes appear in these back issues. Quotes provided at the time of the events yield great insight into the events and the perspectives of the people involved. Providing these perspectives adds a human element to the history.

After all these years, a better understanding exists of the implications and the role of the murders in society. Most Constitutional law courses discuss US vs Price, the Supreme Court case that affirmed that the due process clause of the Constitution applies to state actors as well as those who participate with state actors. This case and its implications are discussed in terms that are meaningful and understandable for an average citizen who is not an attorney.

A large number of sources today distort major details regarding the murders and their ramifications. I clean up these distortions by reliance on mostly original sources and by extensive footnoting. Authors on the web often borrow from other web pages, then restate in their own terms. Restating introduces distortions. Others then restate these distortions, introducing other distortions. Worse yet, most web authors do not footnote or attribute their sources. I provide accurate footnoted statements from primary sources to eliminate distortions.

Why Me?

I grew up Jewish in that area of southern MS. I was born in and lived in Hattiesburg, MS, about 125 miles south of Philadelphia, MS. I was personally physically threatened in a face-to-face meeting with Robert Shelton, Imperial Wizard of the United Klans of America. I was also personally physically threatened in a face to face meeting with Sam Bowers, Imperial Wizard of the White Knights. A local member of the Forrest County Klavern of the White Knights shot at me with a handgun. He went around town telling people how he was going to get the "Jew boy." I knew life as faced by Mickey Schwerner, a Jew, as he tried to improve the lives of Blacks in MS.

During the past ten years, I have served as an expert in shooting incident reconstruction in the criminal courts. I know the techniques and scientific principles and the proper approaches to use them. Most importantly, I understand the issues and shortcomings in dealing with eyewitness testimony. I know the means used to overcome the shortcomings of eyewitness testimony. Most of the real evidence in the Schwerner, Chaney, and Goodman murders is in the form of eyewitness testimony.

While not an attorney, I have extensive criminal legal experience. As an expert, I have to understand the legal requirements for my testimony to qualify for presentation to the jury.

In this history, I apply my extensive actual investigative experience to this history of the murders. I reconstructed over 100 shooting incidents and testified in 10 trials regarding these incidents.

What Value Is Added?

This book adds value to the existing knowledge regarding the murders of Schwerner, Chaney, and Goodman.

An extremely thorough, detailed, documented, and footnoted reconstruction of the history is provided. Murders, legal activities, and consequences to the perpetrators are all covered in detail. Pictures, testimony, newspaper quotes are integrated in-line with the text. These pictures are provided by the FBI, the Library of Congress, and various newspapers and wire services. As you read, you see the pictures as part of the narrative. This integration helps to make the people and the events seem alive.

Legal issues and maneuvering by both the prosecution and the defense attorneys are discussed in a reader-digestible format. A reader does not have to be an attorney to understand all the legal aspects.

Extensive emphasis is given to the more human side. Using testimony, writings, and newspaper articles, direct statements give insight into the feelings and reactions of people involved in the incidents.

Growing up Jewish in the area gives me insight into the motivations and behaviors of the White Knights. My own experiences as a Jew with the White Knights enables me to select and to present information that clearly elucidates their motivations and behavior.

Growing up in that society in the area also guides me in the selection of materials that best illustrate the manner in which residents in that area behaved. Decisions were often made by leaders who acted in concert through telephone calls and not through legal mechanisms.

My experience as a shooting reconstruction expert has enabled a far more detailed analysis of the incidents on June 24, 1964. Thirty-five (35) locations in the Philadelphia, MS, and Meridian area were involved during that day. Over the years, some exact locations had been lost. Using clues in the primary source documents and photos provided by the FBI, I found all 35 locations by latitude and longitude. For example, authors regularly state that the second arrest occurred on Highway 492 West. Using clues in the primary source documents and photos provided by the FBI, the actual location of the arrest which was determined by latitude and longitude.

When I perform a reconstruction, I go to the actual locations involved. With all 35 locations in hand, I visited the actual locations in Philadelphia, MS, on October 31, 2018, took photos, and confirmed the locations. Using these photos and some Google Maps street views, I constructed a visual, step-by-step tour of the sequence of events on June 24, 1964.

<u>As you view the visual reconstruction, you will see exactly what the perpetrators saw as they participated in the conspiracy and the murders.</u>

This visual reconstruction presents the real trial exhibits I would use if I were to testify in the actual trial. These trial exhibits have never been produced by other authors. I was able to add this value to the history because of my real investigative and trial experience as a shooting reconstruction expert.

<u>As you view the visual reconstruction, you will see exactly what the jury would see as an expert testifies in a trial of the conspirators for the murderers.</u>

Introduction

For the past 10 years, I have been an expert witness in the criminal and civil courts. As an expert, I had over 200 cases, testifying in 26 of those cases. Over 100 of those cases examined real shooting incidents. I testified in 10 of those shooting incidents. I used math, science, physics, testimony and evidence to evaluate those shooting incidents.

First and foremost, the murder of Schwerner, Chaney, and Goodman is a shooting incident. As an expert in shooting incidents, my goal is to answer the questions of who, what, when, where, how, and sometimes why. In most cases, answering why is not possible. In this case, significant evidence exists that enables a reconstruction to explain why.

In performing my incident reconstruction, I am required to meet a very strict standard. Any statement that I make when I testify must be justified and have a foundation based on evidence, testimony, math, science, and physics. Every statement that I make must be accurately source referenced.

In my analysis, sometimes a sentence can have multiple footnotes as references. A footnote can refer to a single word, a phrase, a whole sentence, or a paragraph in an original source. Clearly, some reading between the lines is necessary. Furthermore, I have to be prepared and often am required to testify under oath.

Clear foundation, detailed and accurate source referencing, and testifying under oath are far stricter and difficult criteria than are faced by historians and journalists.

An important requirement of shooting incident reconstruction is to consider alternative theories of the incident. In the case of Schwerner, Chaney, and Goodman, only one possible alternate theory has been offered. And, that alternate theory only describes the manner in which James Chaney was murdered. This theory will be evaluated based on the documented evidence and testimony.

One of the biggest problems with non-professional analysis of these types of incidents is an assumption that just because a different theory can be formulated, then anything is possible. In real shooting incident reconstruction by professional experts, every interpretation must be justified by a foundation of evidence, testimony, math, science, and physics.

In these cases, a lot of evidence is gathered. As a reconstruction expert, I have to distill all the evidence and emphasize the essential elements of the incident. I try to be as simple, clear and as precise as possible. Furthermore, I often have to resolve conflicting pieces of evidence, especially with eyewitness testimony.

This book begins with an overview of the people and groups involved in the incident. A short prehistory of events leading up to the murder is provided. All events on the day of the murder are described, including who, what, when, where, how and why. The aftermath involving finding the burned vehicle and uncovering the bodies is covered. These explanations consist of the sequence of events and participants that were presented by the prosecution. The detailed legal history of the prosecution of the perpetrators is presented. Several controversial issues surrounding the murders are discussed. One of these issues involves conflicting sequences of actions at the actual murder site.

A forensic analysis is performed that identifies 35 locations involved on the day of the murders. A visual representation of the complete sequence of events on the day of the murder is provided. ***This visual representation is the actual exhibits I would create to testify in a criminal trial.*** This representation is based on an actual trip to Philadelphia, MS, and a series of photos taken at those locations. You will see the actual location and sequence of events at the murder site, among other photographs. Finally, a clear statement identifies the statements that I can make under oath as part of testimony in a trial.

A Note On Sources

Primary sources are those sources, often documents, created by persons involved in an incident around the time of the incident. Confessions by perpetrators, reports by FBI investigators, newspaper interviews with members of the community and jurors, and trial transcripts all qualify as primary sources. Since these sources were created close in time to the incident, the details are still fresh in the mind of the creator of the source. Therefore, these sources provide the most accurate information.

Of course, some persons who were involved may distort the details in a self-serving manner. For this reason, corroboration across multiple sources is the best approach.

In recent years, a number of primary sources have become newly available:

- the redacted FBI MIBURN investigation files;
- the FBI Ku Klux Klan investigation files;
- the FBI Klan leader investigation files;
- high resolution digital scans of all investigation photos taken by the FBI, provided by the FBI;
- the House Un-American Activities Committee Klan investigation transcripts and evidence appendices;
- the October, 1967 Federal conspiracy trial transcripts;
- unredacted confessions of James Jordan and Doyle Barnette;
- an extensive number of investigative articles by Jerry Mitchell from the *Clarion Ledger* newspaper;
- online digital archives of *The Neshoba Democrat* newspaper;
- online digital archives of the *Hattiesburg American* and the *Laurel Leader Call* newspapers;
- online digital archives of newswire services such as the Associated Press;
- oral histories dictated by various participants such as Klan leaders Sam Bowers and Eddie McDaniel;
- online digital archives of the MS Sovereignty Commission, , hosted by the MS Department of Archives and History;

- civil rights repository web sites, such as the Civil Rights Movement Veterans website, crmv.org;
- the trial transcript of the 2005 Neshoba County trial of Edgar Ray Killen, provided by the MS Department of Archives and History;
- the video of the public testimony portion of the 2005 Neshoba County trial of Edgar Ray Killen, provided by the MS Public Broadcasting System; and
- a copy of the actual autopsy of Schwerner, Chaney, and Goodman generated by Dr. William Featherston, provided by Steve Kilgore, Neshoba County District Attorney.

An even larger number of secondary sources are available. Secondary sources are based on interpretation of primary sources or are far in time from the events. A secondary source often references undiscovered primary sources that are useful. Many recollections may still be fairly accurate despite the distance in time from the actual incident. Academic historians often collect material from primary sources and provide extremely illuminating interpretations and insights.

However, some of these secondary sources are often extremely biased in their interpretations. Some secondary sources claim that James Chaney was beaten and was screaming loudly in pain. Some sources also claim that Chaney was castrated. These claims are incendiary interpretations by the author. Primary sources are investigated to determine the validity of the claims.

As a criminal court expert and as a historian, I take great care when using secondary source information. A court would likely disallow the statement regarding Chaney's screams as hearsay or lacking foundation. Therefore, that statement would not be allowed during a jury trial.

So, secondary source interpretations and insights have to be used with great care when reconstructing a murder.

Perhaps the best-known secondary source is Wikipedia. As a historical reference source, Wikipedia entries demonstrate all of the issues with secondary sources. Wikipedia entries can be very useful. Facts are often available that have been carefully linked to primary sources. However, some claims are stated without reference.

Some secondary sources include, but are not limited to:

- books by historians that are documented and footnoted;
- peer reviewed articles that are documented and footnoted; and,
- civil rights organization web sites.

Civil rights organization web sites can be very valuable. Generally, information is provided on civil rights web sites without footnote and reference. However, the information presented serves as an excellent guide to direct historical research efforts. Some web sites regarding civil rights organizations also contain original documents for review.

The Importance of Prehistory

Every history possesses a prehistory. History consists of an event conducted by participants at one or more locations over a specific time period. This information answers the questions who, what, when, where, and how.

However, a good history also attempts to answer the question why. Why did Mickey Schwerner go to Meridian and Neshoba County? Why did Imperial Wizard Sam Bowers order the murder of Mickey Schwerner? Why did Deputy Sheriff Price and the gang of 20 follow those orders? Why was John Doar forced to pursue Federal charges for violation of civil rights? Why did residents of Neshoba County demand a prosecution for murder in Neshoba County? Why did the MS AG finally succumb to those demands?

These questions are answered by the prehistory of the persons involved and the conditions at the time of historical event. For instance, a short biography of Mickey Schwerner clearly explains why Schwerner felt the need to actually go South.

The Value Of Quotes

Quotes add to the understanding of why. A direct quote from a person generally gives insight into the thought processes and feelings of that person at the time of the quote. Direct quotes from a document generally explain why a particular document was created. Since documents are created by people, a document can provide further insight into why the author wrote the document in the first place. Quotes from newspapers near the time of an event explain the context and details of the event, provided prehistory, history, and supporting the answer to why.

Most books place quotes between a double quote mark. "This is a quote." But, this book uses a different mechanism. Quotes are presented in italics *This is a quote*. Quotes are also surround by white space before and after. This additional approach provides greater emphasis to the quote.

Part 1: Introduction And Background

This part provides a frame of reference for the remainder of the book.

Essential information is presented. This information provides an overview of the complete history and consequences of the murders of Schwerner, Chaney, and Goodman.

In a summary form, various aspects of the murders are provided from beginning to end of the history.

Summaries are presented that include the chronology/overall timeline of activities from beginning to end, the participants, the locations, the events, and some detailed timelines.

Phases of activity include the events leading up to the murders, the activities on the day of the murders, subsequent Federal legal actions and defense maneuvers, and final MS legal actions.

Extensive details are provided in subsequent parts.

Chronology At A Glance

Activities surrounding the murders of Schwerner, Chaney, and Goodman began on 1/19/1964. At 5:00 pm, on that date, Mickey and Rita Schwerner arrived in Meridian to open an office for CORE.

Date	Event
1/16/1964	Mickey, Rita Schwerner Arrived In Meridian To Open CORE Office
6/16/1964	Beatings, Burning At Mt Zion Methodist Church
6/21/1964	Arrest, Incarceration, Arrest, Murders, Burial, Burning Of Vehicle
6/23/1964	Charred Ranch Wagon Vehicle Discovered
7/10/1964	FBI Reopens Jackson Division Office
8/4/1964	Bodies Found Buried In Dam On Old Jolly Farm
8/5/1964	Autopsies Performed At University of MS Medical School
9/13/1964	First Break: Paid Informant Wallace Miller, Meridian PD
1/15/1965	First Indictment, US Southern District of MS Section 241, Conspiracy To Deprive Rights Section 242, Deprive Rights Under Color of Law
2/24/1965	Charges Dismissed, Judge Harold Cox, Southern District of MS
3/28/1966	Dismissal Reversed, US vs Price, US Supreme Court
2/27/1967	Second Indictment, Section 241, More Representative Grand Jury
10/20/1967	Federal Trial, US Southern District of MS Section 241, Conspiracy To Deprive Rights, 8/20 Guilty
12/29/1967	Sentencing And In Forma Pauperous Hearing, Judge Harold Cox
7/17/1969	Appeal Ruling, Convictions Upheld, 5th Circuit Court of Appeals
3/19/1970	Incarceration Of All Federally Convicted White Knights Begins
5/26/2004	Philadelphia Coalition Demands MS Prosecution
6/21/2005	MS/Neshoba County Murder Trial Edgar Ray Killen Guilty Of 3 Counts Manslaughter
11/5/2006	Sam Bowers Dies, Parchman Prison, Dahmer Murder
4/12/2007	Killen Appeals Ruling, Convictions Upheld, MS Supreme Court
1/11/2018	Edgar Ray Killen Dies, Parchman Prison

Ramifications of the murders lasted until January 11, 2018. On this date, Edgar Ray Killen, chief organizer of the murders, died in Parchman Prison in MS. Killen was the only participant convicted of the murders by a MS prosecutor. Killen was convicted on 3 counts of manslaughter.

Mississippi Burning: Philadelphia, MS, 1964

That savage Kike[3] Schwerner is a "thorn in the side of everyone living, especially the white people. He needs to be taken care of."[4] Sam Bowers, Imperial Wizard of the White Knights, was talking to James Jordan, a member of the Meridian Klavern. Sam was giving his permission as Imperial Wizard of the White Knights to "eliminate" Schwerner. This meeting was in Laurel, MS, in May, 1964.[5] Pete Harris and Earl Akin, also members of the Meridian Klavern of the White Knights, were at this meeting.[6]

As he had made clear in his bulletin from WASP, Inc., Bowers hated Jews. He blamed the "savage Kike lust" for money as the cause of the Civil Rights Movement.[7] When Bowers received the request from the Meridian Klavern to terminate Schwerner, a trouble-making Jew, he had approved the request for a Number 4 "elimination" solution for Schwerner.[8] Bowers did not have any qualms or moral dilemmas about issuing such an order for "elimination".

Michael "Mickey" Schwerner, a Jew, was the assassination target of the Mississippi Burning incident. Mickey had arrived in Meridian on January 19, 1964, a short four months earlier. And now he was being targeted for murder by the White Knights. James Chaney and Andy Goodman just happened to be in the wrong place at the wrong time. Worse yet, Andy Goodman had only been in the state of MS for about 24 hours when he was murdered! All three deaths were horrific, barbarous and cruel.

The Victims

Michael "Mickey" Schwerner was born in New York City. His parents were Nathan[9] and Anne[10] Schwerner.

Michael "Mickey" Schwerner
(FBI, *Missing Persons Poster*, June 29, 1964)

When Mickey was eight years old, his parents moved from New York City to Pelham, NY.[11] As a youngster, Schwerner played baseball in a local North Pelham Little League team. Schwerner attended Pelham Memorial High School in Pelham. During his high school years, Schwerner was extremely active in extra-curricular activities. Schwerner played high school football and other sports. He was in the orchestra and band. Mickey performed plays as a member of the Sock-n-Buskin drama club. In May 1967, Mickey Schwerner graduated from Pelham High School.[12]

**Mickey Schwerner
(Pelham High School Yearbook, 1957)**

After graduating from High School, Schwerner initially attended Michigan State University for 1 year. Then, Mickey Schwerner transferred to Cornell University.[13] In May, 1961, Schwerner graduated from the College of Agriculture at Cornell University, with a major in rural sociology. Upon graduation, he continued his studies at the School of Social Work at Columbia University.[14]

Mickey spent the 1961-1962 school year in graduate studies at Columbia.[15] In the summer of 1962, Mickey Schwerner applied for a job at the Hamilton-Madison House, a settlement house, in the Alfred E. Smith Public Housing Project[16] Mickey was hired as a group worker with teens.[17]

As he worked at the House, Mickey became increasingly motivated to participate full-time in the civil rights movement. In June of 1963, Mickey was accepted into CORE.[18] One of his first tasks for CORE was to establish a CORE office in the same area of New York City as the Smith Housing Project, the Two Bridges Neighborhood[19]

But, Mickey was becoming impatient. Working in an office did not really satisfy his inner need to participate. Direct involvement was needed.

A demonstration for integration was organized at Gwynn Oak Park in Baltimore, MD. Over the course of the protest, 283 people were arrested and charged with trespassing outside the park. Mickey Schwerner was among the group arrested.[20] A short time later, the arrested protesters were released.

Later in July, 1963, both Mickey and his wife Rita participated in another demonstration. This activity targeted a building project in Manhattan. After ten days, the protesters were arrested and given a jail sentence. Mickey drew a sixty-day sentence. All demonstrators were released on appeal. Ultimately, the case was continued indefinitely.[21]

The March on Washington, being led by Reverend Martin Luther King, Jr., was scheduled for August 28, 1963. Mickey Schwerner and 90 young Blacks from the Hamilton-Madison House participated in the March on Washington on August 28, 1963.[22]

Mickey and Rita applied to work with CORE in MS. The couple received notification of acceptance into the CORE Task Force on Thanksgiving, 1963.[23]

Robert Moses of COFO assigned Mickey and Rita to the Meridian office. The couple was to organize a Community Center, similar to a settlement house.[24] Mickey and Rita Schwerner were the first white civil rights workers to be based outside of the MS state capitol of Jackson.[25]

About 5 P.M. on Sunday, January 19, 1964, the couple arrived in Meridian. Five months later, Mickey would enter the cold, empty space of death.

James Chaney was born May 30, 1943, in Meridian, Mississippi. His parents were Ben and Fannie Lee Chaney.

James Chaney
(FBI, *Missing Persons Poster*, June 29, 1964)

Chaney was the eldest son in a family of five children. His mother, a domestic servant, was protective. His father, a plasterer, left his mother when James was in his mid-teens.

Chaney first encountered problems at the Catholic school for Blacks that he attended. In 1959, when he was sixteen. Chaney was suspended for a week. He refused to remove a yellow paper NAACP "button." The next year he was expelled from school for fighting.

Chaney tried to join the US Army. His asthma resulted in a 4-F disqualification. Unemployed and restless, Chaney joined the Negro plasterer's union as an apprentice to his father. His work as a plasterer ended in 1963 after a fight with his father.

Chaney had begun volunteer work at the new CORE office in Meridian in October, 1963. A girlfriend had introduced Chaney to Matt Suarez, the Meridian office's first director. Chaney soon became Suarez's chief aide, guide, and companion. His work ranged from constructing bookshelves at the community center to traveling to rural counties to arrange meetings.

When Mickey Schwerner arrived in January, 1964, to assume direction of the Meridian office, Chaney became their most willing volunteer.

Since he was Black, Chaney was able enter places that were dangerous to white volunteers. Mississippi whites viewed Chaney to be "as inconspicuous as an alley cat."[26]

Andrew "Andy" Goodman was born on November 21, 1943, and raised in New York City in an intellectual and socially-aware family. He was one of three sons of Robert and Carolyn Goodman.

**Andy Goodman
(FBI, *Missing Persons Poster*, June 29, 1964)**

Goodman attended the progressive Walden School, widely known for its anti-authoritarian approach to learning. An activist from the age of 15, while a high school sophomore at Walden, Goodman traveled to Washington, D. C. to participate in the "Youth March for Integrated Schools." As a senior, he and a classmate visited a depressed coal mining region in West Virginia to prepare a report on poverty in America.

After graduating from the Walden School, Goodman then attended the University of Wisconsin for a year. Then, he transferred to Queens College, New York City. At Queens College, one of his classmates was the musician, Paul Simon.

Goodman enrolled at Queens College in part because of its strong drama department. With some brief experience as an off-Broadway actor, he originally planned to study drama. Soon, however, his longing for commitment led him away from his interest in drama and back to politics. So, he switched to an anthropology major.

During the winter of 1964, Goodman protested U.S. President Lyndon Johnson's presence at the opening of that year's World's Fair.

In April 1964, Goodman applied for and was accepted into the Mississippi Summer Project. Although not seeing himself as a professional reformer, Goodman knew that his life had been somewhat sheltered and thought that the experience would be educational and useful.

As part of his Freedom Summer preparation, Goodman was attending the class in developing civil rights protest strategies at Western College for Women [now part of Miami University] in Oxford, Ohio when he met Mickey Schwerner. When Schwerner decided to return to Meridian, Goodman chose to go along and start his Freedom Summer service working with Schwerner and Chaney.[27]

The Perpetrators

A total of 20 members of the White Knights of the Ku Klux Klan conspired to murder Schwerner, Chaney, and Goodman.

Members of the White Knights of the KKK from three cities in MS were involved in these murders.

Sam Bowers, Imperial Wizard
(FBI, Booking Photo, December 4, 1964)

At the head of the conspiracy was Sam Bowers, a businessman, from Laurel, MS.[28] Sam was Imperial Wizard of the White Knights.

Nine members of the Meridian Klavern of the White Knights participated in the conspiracy.

| Wayne Roberts | James Jordan | Doyle Barnette | Jimmy Arledge | Jimmy Snowden |

Meridian Klavern Members
(FBI, Booking Photo, December 4, 1964)

- Alton Wayne Roberts: a salesman;
- James Jordan: a construction worker,

- HD (Doyle) Barnette: a salesman;
- Jimmy Arledge: truck driver;

Travis Barnette   Frank Herndon   Pete Harris   Bernard Aiken

- Jimmy Snowden: a truck driver;

More Meridian Klavern Members
(FBI, Booking Photo, December 4, 1964)

- Travis Barnette: a garage operator;
- Frank Herndon: a restaurant operator;
- Pete Harris: a truck driver; and,
- Bernard Aiken: a salesman. [29]

In addition, ten members of the Philadelphia Klavern of the White Knights also participated.

Cecil Price   Billy Posey   Herman Tucker   Olen Burrage   Edgar Killen

Philadelphia Klavern Members
(FBI, Booking Photo, December 4, 1964)

- Cecil Price: Deputy Sheriff, Neshoba County;
- Billy Wayne Posey: a service station operator;
- Herman Tucker: a contractor and bulldozer operator;
- Olen Burrage: a truck company and garage operator;

- Edgar Ray Killen: a preacher and sawmill operator;

Lawrence Rainey   Richard Willis   Jerry Sharpe   Jimmy Townsend   Otha Burkes

**More Philadelphia Klavern Members
(FBI, Booking Photo, December 4, 1964)**

- Lawrence Rainey: Sheriff, Neshoba County;
- Richard Willis: a Patrolman, Philadelphia Police Department;
- Jerry Sharpe: a pulpwood supply manager;
- Jimmy Townsend: a service station attendant; and,
- Otha Burkes: a Patrolman, Philadelphia Police Department. [30]

Ethel Glen "Hop" Barnette, a former Neshoba County Sheriff and a member of the Philadelphia Klavern of White Knights, was also charged in the murders.[31] A picture of Barnette is not available.

All of the non-law enforcement participants were either business operators, equipment operators, or manual laborers. Professionals, such as doctors, lawyers, and teachers were not involved in the murders.

Perhaps most surprising was the heavy involvement of law enforcement officers. Rainy, Price, Willis, and Burkes were either directly involved or were complicit is some ways, despite the absence of a conviction. So, 20% (4 out of 20) of the participants involved in these murders were in law enforcement!

Perpetrator Roles

Murder is a crime under MS state law, not under Federal law. An indictment for murder could only be brought by a local county prosecutor. In 1964, the prosecutor in Neshoba County, where the murders occurred, would not bring murder charges against local white residents. The Neshoba County prosecutor also would not indict local law enforcement officers such as Price, Rainey, Willis, and Burkes.

So, the US Department of Justice brought charges under Title 18, Section 241 of the US Code. This Code Section defines participation in a conspiracy to deprive civil rights of a citizen as a Federal crime. Conviction of this crime carries a maximum of 10 years incarceration in a Federal prison and a fine up to $5,000.

Title 18 Section 371 of the US Code defines a criminal conspiracy as an agreement between two or more people to commit an illegal act, along with an action by at least one of the people to achieve the goal of the agreement.

John Doar, Assistant Attorney General, U.S. Department of Justice, Civil Rights Division,[32] was the Lead Prosecutor in the Federal conspiracy trial of the murderers in October, 1967. Doar identified the various roles that would be observed by participants in the conspiracy.

In the execution of a conspiracy, there are members of the conspiracy who play different parts. There are master planners, there are organizers, there are lookout men, there are killers, there are clean-up and disposal people, and there are the protectors. Each of the defendants played one or more parts in this conspiracy.[33]

Wayne Roberts was the participant who actually pulled the trigger to murder Mickey Schwerner and James Goodman. James Jordan was the participant who actually pulled the trigger that caused the death of James Chaney.

All of the other 18 participants played one or more parts in the conspiracy. The parts played by the various participants appears in the table below.

Count	Name	Activity
1	Sam Bowers	Ordered Schwerner Level 4 "Elimination"
2	Wayne Roberts	Murdered Schwerner, Goodman
3	James Jordan	Murdered Chaney, Confessed, Testified
4	Doyle Barnette	Present At Murders, Drove A Car With WK
5	Jimmy Arledge	Present At Murders, Drove Ranch Wagon

6	Jimmy Snowden	Present At Murders
7	Bernard Aiken	Present When Herndon Recruited Team
8	Frank Herndon	Recruited Meridian Participants
9	Pete Harris	Recruited Meridian Participants
10	Travis Barnette	Maybe Present At Murders
11	Cecil Price	Arrested Trio, Took To Murder Location
12	Billy Posey	Present At Murders, Drove Bodies To Dam
13	Richard Willis	Told Waiting Klansmen Where To Find Trio
14	Herman Tucker	Buried Bodies, Drove Vehicle For Dumping
15	Olen Burrage	Owned Farm Where Buried,
		Drove Escort Truck
16	Edgar Killen	Recruited Philadelphia Participants
17	Lawrence Rainey	Hired Price,
		Warned Participants Not To Talk
18	Jerry Sharpe	Maybe Present At Murders
19	Jimmy Townsend	Remained With Posey's Disabled Vehicle
20	Otha Burkes	Not Involved In Activities

Both of the actual murderers were from the Meridian Klavern of the White Knights. A strategy of the White Knights was to have the violence performed by members of a different Klavern, rather than by members of the closest Klavern. This approach enabled the members of the local Klavern to deny any part in the violence.

Location of Events

Two counties were involved in the "elimination" of Schwerner, Chaney, and Goodman. Half of the participants were from Meridian and were members of the Meridian Klavern of the White Knights. Meridian is in Lauderdale County. Remaining participants were from Philadelphia. Philadelphia is in Neshoba County.[34] All of the activity surrounding these murders took place around Philadelphia in Neshoba County.

Both counties are in the center of the state of MS. Neshoba County is northwest of Lauderdale County. Philadelphia is 39 miles from Meridian. MS State Highway 19 is the road that connects Philadelphia and Meridian.

This two-lane travels extremely 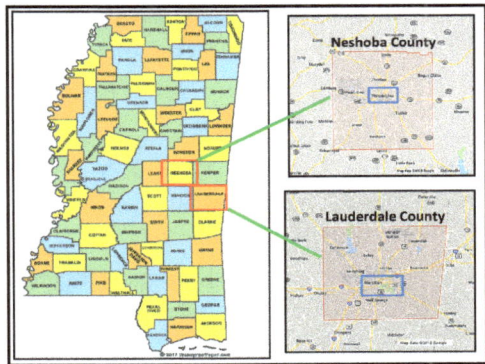 Highway is a highway that through rural areas.

Neshoba and Lauderdale Counties
(State: Digital Topo Maps, Counties: Google Maps)

Neshoba County, MS, was and is a small rural community in the center of the state. Population statistics in the community show the composition of the community residents.

A larger white majority of residents dominated a significantly smaller Black minority. The ratio of whites to Blacks in the area was 3 to 1.

District	Area	White	Black	Total
District 1	Philadelphia	7441	2379	9820
District 2	North Bend	1097	599	1696
District 3	Mogulusha	2114	330	2444
District 4	Dixon and Waldo	2740	808	3548
District 4	Riley	1634	670	2304
Total		15026	4786	19812
Percent		75.8	24.2	100

Population In Neshoba County, MS, 1960 US Census[35]

In 1960, 75% of the population was white, 25% of the population was Black. Philadelphia itself appears to present that same percentage break down. Literally, whites ruled both Neshoba County and Philadelphia.

Schwerner, Chaney, and Goodman were murdered south of Philadelphia on Road 515, locally called Rock Cut Road. Rock Cut Road heads west off Highway 19 between Philadelphia and Meridian. At the time of the murders, Rock Cut Road was a dirt road, mostly red clay.

**Murder Location On Rock Cut Road
(FBI-MBI, p. 251; FBI FOIA Image, 1-49 Photo 36)**

Selection of this location on Rock Cut Road was deliberate and preplanned. This location is too remote and too well protected from view to have been selected on the spur of the moment. This location was less than 1 mile from the home of Edgar Ray Killen, conspirator in chief, who planned, organized, and participated in the murders.

Rock Cut Road was the location of the actual murders of Schwerner, Chaney, and Goodman. A total of 35 locations were involved in the events surrounding the murders on June 21, 1964. Each of these locations is specified by latitude and longitude in Appendix A.

Sequence of Events

Most people familiar with the murders know the core events associated with the murders. These events were the first arrest, incarceration, the second arrest, murder, burial, destruction of the vehicle driven by the victims.

However, a larger number of events occurred both before and after the actual murders of Schwerner, Chaney, and Goodman on June 21, 1964.

- investigation of the burned ruins at Mt. Zion Methodist Church;[36]
- arrest heading west past the intersection of Beacon and Main Streets;[37]
- incarceration on fake charges at the Old Neshoba County Jail;[38]
- arrest notification to members of Meridian, Philadelphia Klaverns;[39]
- staging of Klan members a few blocks northwest from the Jail;[40]
- release of the three volunteers about 10:30pm;[41]
- Deputy Price taking lead at Standard Service Station on Hwy 19;[42]
- Posey vehicle stopping with engine trouble on Hwy 19 near House;[43]
- arrest on Highway 492, several miles west of Hwy 19[44];
- Posey vehicle passengers loading into Ranch Wagon on Hwy 19;[45]
- shooting on Road 515, about 350 yards west of Hwy 19;[46]
- traveling cross country with bodies in victims' Ranch Wagon;[47]
- retrieving the bulldozer operator 1 mile north of the dam;[48]
- burying the bodies at the dam on Old Jolly Farm;[49] and,
- destroying the victims' Ranch Wagon on Hwy 21 near Hwy 491.[50]

In fact, 35 events took place at 35 individual locations on that day. These events and locations are described in detail in the text and summarized in a table in Appendix A.

Timeline of Events

Activities surrounding the murders started about 11 am when Schwerner, Chaney and Goodman departed the Meridian COFO office for Mt. Zion Methodist Church.

Time	Event	Event Number	Source
11:00 AM	Trio Departs Meridian for Mt. Zion		Documented
12:00 PM	Trio Arrives At Mt. Zion	1	Approximate Based On Distance
1:30 PM	Trio Visits 4 Homes Steele, Lewis, Rushing, Cole	-	Documented
2:20 PM	Trio Visits Ernest, Frank Kirkland	-	Documented
3:00	Poe, Wiggs Receive Radio Call For Help	10	Documented

PM			
3:30 PM	Trio Delivered To Lockup	11	Documented
10:30 PM	Trio Released	13	Documented
11:30 PM	Second Arrest	18	My Recorded Time
12:00 AM	Arrive At Murder Site/Murder	22	My Recorded Time
12:45 AM	Arrive At Burial Site	25	My Recorded Time, Partial Doc
1:45 AM	Station Wagon Arrives At Garage	29	Documented
2:00 AM	Barnette Meets Rainey, Price, Burkes		Documented
2:30 AM	Drivers Notice Burning Car On Hwy 21	31	Documented (About 2 AM)
3:00 AM	Escort Truck Returns To Garage	32	My Recorded Time
3:30 AM	Barnette Arrives At Home In Meridian	33	Drops Other WK At Home

By 4 am on June 22, 1964, all of the activities had been completed. The bodies were buried. The COFO Ranch Wagon was burned. All participants had dispersed.

This timeline was determined by a number of methods. Some times are documented in the FBI investigation results and in the Federal trial transcripts. Other times were determined from a time log maintained as the author traveled to all the locations involved in the murders

Legal Maneuvering

Convicting the conspirators was to be a difficult process.

Start Date	Entity	Result
9/9/1964	Fed Grand Jury, Biloxi	Members Selected
9/21/1964	Neshoba Grand Jury	No True Bills
9/21/1964	Fed Grand Jury, Biloxi	True Bills, Civil Rights Violations
10/3/1964	FBI Arrests	Civil Rights Violations By Accused
12/4/1964	FBI	Arrests of 19, Meridian, Philadelphia
12/4/1964	FBI	Arrest, James Jordan, Gulfport

12/4/1964	FBI	Arrest, Doyle Barnette, Bossier City
		Prelim Hearing Never Scheduled
12/10/1964	Commissioner, Meridian	Dismisses All Charges
12/11/1964	Commissioner, Gulfport	Dismisses Charges, Jordan
1/1/1965	Fed Grand Jury, Jackson	Civil Rights Violations Sections 241, 242, 371
1/13/1965	FBI	Arrests, Meridian, Philadelphia
1/18/1965	FBI	Arrest, Barnette, Shreveport
1/18/1965	FBI	Surrender, Jordan, Atlanta
1/25/1965	Fed Trial Judge Cox, Meridian	9 Pretrial Motions Filed
1/27/1965	Fed Trial Judge Cox, Meridian	All Defendants Arraigned, Bond
2/24/1965	Fed Trial Judge Cox, Jackson	All Motions To Dismiss Section 241 Granted
2/25/1965	Fed Trial Judge Cox, Jackson	Some Motions To Dismiss Sections 242, 371 Granted
3/3/1965	Appeal Filed With US Sup Ct	Request Expedited Hearing
11/9/1965	US Supreme Court, US vs Price	Indictments Reinstated
2/27/1967	Rabinowitz vs US	New Federal Jury Issues True Bills Section 241 Only

The local Federal judiciary was against prosecution and issued biased rulings. Only the best defense attorneys were involved. These defense attorneys caused the judicial process to take several years.

Federal prosecutors knew that a local MS prosecutor would never bring murder charges against any of the White Knights. A Federal prosecution was necessary. Charges were pursued under Title 18 USC Section 241: conspiracy to deprive citizens of their civil rights and Title 18 USC Section 242: prevention of exercise of civil rights using a weapon under color of law. Section 241 carried a maximum incarceration of ten years. A maximum 1 period of incarceration could be assigned under Section 242.

An initial Grand Jury was called in September of 1964. Indictments were issued. By the end of 1964, all of the indictments returned by this Grand Jury had been dismissed by Federal Commissioners.

A second attempt to convict the conspirators was initiated in January, 1965. This attempt was thwarted by Judge Harold Cox of the Southern District of MS, 5th Circuit.

**Judge Harold Cox
(Associated Press, ©1964, 10/22/1964)**

Cox was a staunch and aggressive segregationist with years of anti-civil rights rulings. He dismissed all indictments under Section 241. All indictments under Section 242 were dismissed against the non-law enforcement participants in the murders. Judge Cox claimed that the term "color of law" applied only to law enforcement officers.

These dismissals ultimately led to a Supreme Court ruling in US vs. Price in March, 1966. All charges were reinstated. The murderers denied the victims due process of law. Due process of law was a civil right protection under Section 241. Non-law enforcement participants in the murder had leveraged the powers of law enforcement as a tool to perform the murders. The term "color of law" included direct action by law enforcement officers and leveraging the powers of law enforcement as a tool. The case was remanded back to Judge Cox for trial.

US vs Price has become and remains a central case in Constitutional Law courses in law schools to this day.

In January, 1967, a Supreme Court ruling in Rabinovitz vs US declared that the jury pool selection process could not exclude major groups such as Blacks. So, a third attempt to convict the murderers was initiated. A new jury pool was selected. From this pool, a new Grand Jury was selected. Indictments of all conspirators were issued by the Grand Jury. However, this time, charges were only brought against Title 18 USC Section 241: conspiracy to deprive citizens of their civil rights. This charge brought a maximum penalty of ten years of incarceration.

US DOJ was going for broke.

Trial Results

John Doar, Assistant Attorney General, U.S. Department of Justice, Civil Rights Division,[51] was the Lead Prosecutor in the Federal conspiracy trial of the murderers in October, 1967.

John Doar, AAG
(Associated Press, ©1966, 9/1/1966)

Doar was assisted by Robert Hauberg, a US DOJ attorney assigned to the Jackson Division of the Southern District of MS[52], and Robert Owen, an Attorney from the Civil Rights Division of the US DOJ.[53]

Twenty (20) members of the White Knights were charged under Title 18 Section 241 of the US Code: conspiracy to deprive citizens of their civil rights. A maximum sentence of ten years incarceration could be imposed.

A trial was held at the Federal Courthouse for the Southern District of MS in Meridian. This trial went from October 9, 1967 until October 20, 1967. Verdicts were announced on October 20, 1967.

Count	Klavern	Name	Verdict	Sentence
1	Imperial Wizard	Sam Bowers	Guilty	10 Years
2	Meridian	Wayne Roberts	Guilty	10 Years
3		James Jordan	Plea	4 Years
4		Doyle Barnette	Guilty	3 Years
5		Jimmy Arledge	Guilty	3 Years
6		Jimmy Snowden	Guilty	3 Years
7		Bernard Aiken	Acquitted	
8		Frank Herndon	Acquitted	
9		Pete Harris	Acquitted	
10		Travis Barnette	Acquitted	
11	Philadelphia	Cecil Price	Guilty	6 Years
12		Billy Posey	Guilty	6 Years
13		Richard Willis	Acquitted	
14		Herman Tucker	Acquitted	
15		Olen Burrage	Acquitted	
16		Edgar Killen	Mistrial	
17		Lawrence Rainey	Acquitted	
18		Jerry Sharpe	Mistrial	
19		Jimmy Townsend	Not Charged	
20		Otha Burkes	Dismissed	

Seven out 20 participants were found guilty. James Jordan had accepted a plea deal before the trial in exchange for this testimony. Two of the defendants received ten-year sentences. Two defendants received six-year sentences. Three defendants received three-year sentences. James Jordan plead to a four-year sentence. Acquittals were obtained by eight of the defendants. Two mistrials were obtained. One defendant was actually not charged. One defendant had the charges dismissed.

Of the four law enforcement officers charged, only Deputy Sheriff Cecil Price was convicted. Rainey and Willis were acquitted. Charges against Otha Burkes were dismissed.

While the primary perpetrators were held accountable, the others should have been convicted. These others were part of the conspiracy.

Pursuit of Appeals

In December 1967, Judge Cox issued sentences to those who had been convicted. Defense attorneys immediately began the appeals process.

12/29/1967	Fed Court, US vs Price	Sentences Awarded, 3 - 10 Years
5/26/1969	Fifth Circuit Court of Appeals	Start Oral Argument On Appeals
7/17/1969	Fifth Circuit Court of Appeals	Appeals Denied
2/27/1970	US Supreme Court	Appealed Conviction, Turned Down
3/19/1970	Appeals Exhausted	Sentenced Defendants Enter Fed Prison

An appeal to the Fifth Circuit Court of Appeals was denied. Defense attorneys then appealed to the US Supreme Court. This Court refused to hear the case. Refusal left the sentences in the jurisdiction of the Fifth Circuit for enforcement.

All of the convicted murderers served six years and less. All were released early for good behavior based on Federal release standards. After release, all of the convicted murders could only find low paying, mostly manual labor jobs.

Assessment of the Convictions

Penalties for murder should be life without parole or the death penalty. These light sentences and short incarcerations were slaps on the wrist.

However, this trial was the first time in history that an all white, MS jury had convicted racists for murder. These convictions were to be the beginning of the end for the White Knights.

Edgar Ray Killen obtained a mistrial. Killen was the chief conspirator. Killen received the phone call from Price that Schwerner, Chaney, and

Goodman were in custody. He initiated the phone calls to the Klan members in Meridian and Philadelphia that result in the murders.

Philadelphia Promotes Action

Murder does not have a statute of limitations.

Many local residents in Philadelphia were dissatisfied that Neshoba County had never convicted anyone for the murders. Pressure from Philadelphia residents, both Black and white, to bring murders charges grew over the years.

Date	Event
1/27/1989	*Mississippi Burning* Released Nationwide
Jan, 1989	Dearman Contacts Molpus About A Citywide 25th Commemoration
Feb. 1989	25th Anniversary Planning Committee Formed in Philadelphia
4/25/1989	Philadelphia Mayors Formalize Philadelphia-Philadelphia Project
4/26/1989	Dearman Publishes Interview With Carolyn Goodman
6/17/1989	MS AG Mike Moore Begins To Investigate
6/21/1989	25th Anniversary Commemoration Held
6/21/1989	Molpus Apologizes For Murders
12/27/1998	AG Reads About Bowers Interview On January 30, 1984 Implicating Killen
2/25/1999	MS AG Mike Moore Officially Opens Case
3/29/1999	State Grants Philadelphia Permission To Establish Tourism Council
5/3/2000	Dearman Publishes Call For Justice In Neshoba Democrat
2/19/2004	Molpus Addresses Strategic Planning Task Force At Lake Tiak-O'Khata
3/15/2004	Steering Committee Organized To Plan 40th Anniv Commemoration
3/15/2004	Clemons, Prince Elected Co-Chairs, Task Force
3/29/2004	Clemons, Prince Convene Task Force
4/21/2004	Task Force Publicly identified As Philadelphia Coalition
5/26/2004	Philadelphia Coalition Publicly Demands MS Prosecution
6/20/2004	Coalition Hosts 40th Anniversary Commemoration
6/20/2004	Philadelphia Coalition Publicly Demands MS Prosecution AGAIN
9/14/2004	MS AG Hood Meets With Philadelphia Coalition

False starts were begun by MS Attorney General Mike Moore in 1989 and 1999. Neither Moore nor Neshoba County District Attorney Ken Turner brought murder charges against anyone. Turner regularly expressed concern over the potential backlash from local residents who wanted to let the memory of the murders simply disappear.

In 2004, a group of concerned local citizens formed the Philadelphia Coalition. Members of the Coalition included Leroy Clemons, head of the Neshoba County NAACP, James Young, President of the Neshoba County Board of Supervisors, Dick Molpus, former Secretary of State of MS, and Jim Prince, editor and publisher of The Neshoba Democrat. Both Clemons and Young are Black. This group publicly pressured local officials to pursue murder charges under MS statutes.

Leroy Clemons
(Neshoba, 34183)

James Young
(City Of Philadelphia)

On May 26, 2004, and again on June 20, 2004, the Philadelphia Coalition published and publicly read demands for justice in the MS Courts.

MS Finally Acts

Finally, Neshoba County District Attorney Mark Duncan indicted Edgar Ray Killen for three counts of murder in the deaths of Schwerner, Chaney, and Goodman. Killen was the chief conspirator. He received a phone call from Deputy Cecil Price informing that the trio was in custody. In response, Killen called members of the Philadelphia and Meridian Klaverns of the White Knights to gather to perform the murders.

**Edgar Ray Killen At 2005 Murder Trial
(MS Public Broadcasting)**

In June 2005, the trial was held in the Neshoba County Courthouse in Philadelphia. MS AG Jim Hood and MS 8th Circuit District Attorney Marc Duncan presented evidence that Killen activated the Klansmen. He told the Klansmen where to wait for notification of release of the trio from jail. A murder location was selected very near his home. Then Edgar Ray Killen insured he had a convenient alibi for the time of the murders. All those actions demonstrate intent. Despite this evidence, on June 21, 2005, exactly 41 years to the day of the murders, Edgar Ray Killen was convicted of three counts of manslaughter. Jury members claimed that the prosecution failed to convince that Killen acted with intent to cause death. Manslaughter is a lesser charge with less incarceration. Killen was the only participant to be convicted in a MS state court. Manslaughter convictions were disappointing to many.

Date	Event
1/6/2005	AG and DA Present Case To Grand Jury
1/6/2005	Grand Jury Indicts Edgar Ray Killen At Age 80, Killen Arrested
6/21/2005	Neshoba County Jury Convicts Killen, 3 Charges of Manslaughter
6/23/2005	Judge Marcus Gordon Sentences 3 Consecutive 20 Year Terms
6/27/2005	Killen Incarcerated, Central MS Correctional Facility
6/5/2006	MS Supreme Court Appeal Filed
4/12/2007	MS Supreme Court Affirms Killen Sentences
6/17/2008	New Trial Filed Against Epps, US 5th Circuit, Southern District of MS
2/24/2010	Damages Suit Filed Against Hood, US 5th Circuit, Southern District of MS
6/25/2010	Killen Transferred To MS State Penitentiary, Parchman
3/23/2011	US 5th Circuit Dismisses Damages Lawsuit With Prejudice

3/31/2012	US 5th Circuit Dismisses Motion For New Trial With Prejudice
4/10/2012	Killen Appeals Dismissal of New Trial
11/14/2012	US 5th Circuit Denies Request To Pursue Appeal
11/29/2012	5th Circuit Dismissal Forwarded to 5th Circuit Court of Appeals
5/6/2013	US 5th Circuit Court of Appeals Denies Killen Appeal
7/24/2013	Killen Applies To USSC For Writ Of Certiorari
11/4/2013	US Supreme Court Rejects Killen Writ Of Certiorari

While incarcerated, Killen pursued relief in the courts. Killen filed a lawsuit for relief and damages against Hood, Doar, and the FBI in the Southern District of MS of the US 5th Circuit. He was charged with multiple violations of his Constitutional right to a fair trial and asked for a declaration that his Constitutional rights were violated and for monetary damages. This lawsuit was dismissed with prejudice.

Killen filed a motion for a new trial with the MS Supreme Court. This motion was overturned. Killen then filed a separate petition for a writ of habeas corpus (motion for a new trial) with the Southern District of MS of the US 5th Circuit. This petition for a writ was denied.

Once his petition for a writ of habeas corpus was denied, Killen filed multiple motions to obtain permission to file an appeal of his dismissed petition. His motions for permission to file an appeal were rejected by the Southern District of MS of the US 5th Circuit, by the US 5th Circuit Court of Appeals and twice by the US Supreme Court. All 3 of these Federal courts refused to let him file an appeal of his dismissed petition for a writ of habeas corpus.

Edgar Ray Killen was regularly disciplined in prison. Killen was an unrepentant racist. Most of his disciplinary actions were verbal abuse of Black prison guards and employees.

Edgar Ray Killen died in Parchman Prison on January 11, 2018.

The White Knights and Hattiesburg

Bowers and the White Knights were not finished. On January 10, 1966, the White Knights firebombed the house of Vernon Dahmer in Hattiesburg, MS. Dahmer died from smoke inhalation.

Vernon Dahmer
(Randall Collection, M351, ID #134)
(University of Southern MS)

Dahmer was the former President of the Forrest County Chapter of the NAACP. He had been a dynamic leader in voter registration efforts. Vernon Dahmer supported Freedom Summer activities in Hattiesburg during the summer of 1964.

Bombed Out Ruins
(Moncrief Collection)
(No 71408, ID 510)
(MS Dept of Archives and History)

As Imperial Wizard, Bowers also ordered the Level 4 "Elimination" of Vernon Dahmer. Ultimately, Bowers would be held accountable for this murder also. He was convicted in 1998 by a jury of MS residents in the Forrest County Courthouse in Hattiesburg, MS. Billy Roy Pitts, a member of the White Knights who participated in the bombings, served as an informant in the trial. Dickie McKenzie, a local Hattiesburg native, was the judge in that trial.

Just like Killen, Sam Bowers died in Parchman Prison.

Loyalty appears to have been absent in the White Knights. Participants served as informants and testified in both the Schwerner, Chaney, and Goodman murder trials and the Vernon Dahmer murder trials.

Conclusions

The murders of Mickey Schwerner, James Chaney, and Andy Goodman were brutal, senseless, and extremely cruel.

Mickey, Jim, and Andy were simply trying to make the world a better place for Blacks in MS. No justification exists for murder as a response for these well-intentioned actions by the trio.

These murders were perpetrated with extreme cruelty. After seven hours of detention, the trio was released. This release gave the trio hope of a safe return to Meridian. As the trio proceeded down Highway 19 south towards Meridian, a Neshoba County Sheriff's vehicle overtook them at 60 mph with lights shining and sirens blasting. Overtaking the trio by law enforcement in this manner clearly informed the trio they had no hope of survival. This offering and abrupt removal of hope constituted the cruelty of the murders.

As they were being overtaken, that removal of hope must have resulted in a sinking feeling in the guts of each member of the trio.

Prosecuting and convicting Edgar Ray Killen by a jury in Neshoba County was a major accomplishment in obtaining justice for these brutal, cruel, reprehensible murders. Officials and residents of the state do get full credit for that accomplishment.

The state of MS and Neshoba County failed to hold the perpetrators fully accountable. A single conviction for three counts of manslaughter simply does not suffice or satisfy. All of the perpetrators should have served sentences of life imprisonment without parole for the heinous nature of these murders.

Part 2: Hatred And Violence Resisted By Dignity

White Knights hated Jews, Blacks, applied violence to control minorities.

Citizens Councils of businessmen, applied economic pressure.

Sovereignty Commission state organization spied on troublemakers.

Poll taxes and literacy tests targeted poor, uneducated Blacks.

Civil rights organizations developed different approaches to change.

NAACP filed lawsuits in courts, all the way to US Supreme Court.

CORE conducted protests, marches and boycotts.

SCLC energized local activists through Black churches.

SNCC conducted voter registration, education in MS Black communities.

COFO coordinated activities, shared limited resources in MS.

White Southern Baptists promoted racist violence using vigilantes.

White Southern Methodists organized for *separate but equal* segregation.

White Southern Presbyterians actively obstructed civil rights support.

Racist, Segregationist Organizations Involved

The White Knights of the Ku Klux Klan

The White Knights were the largest Klan group operating in the state of Mississippi during the Civil Rights period. In addition, this organization was the most violent of the KKK organizations operating in the state and possibly in the whole United States.

As an organization, the White Knights followed a number of core principles. These principles made the organization extremely effective as a terrorist organization.

Anti-Semitism:. . . *these people have been permitted to gain financial control over America . . . the savage Kike lust for money is destroying Christian Civilization . . .*

Inferiority of Blacks:. . . . *the Black man is one of his creatures under His Protection except for social equality and integration with the White Man . . .*

Any form of violence: *As MILITANTS, we are disposed to the use of physical force against our enemies.* Physical force included cross burning, whipping, bombing, and elimination.

Military hierarchy with strong discipline: *an act of violation of the Klan law . . . shall be tried by his Klavern and all penalties shall be final.* Penalties included expulsion from the Klan and even burning, whipping, bombing, and elimination.

Samuel Holloway Bowers, Jr., was the Imperial Wizard of the White Knights. He was born on August 6, 1924, in the city of New Orleans, LA. His parents were Samuel Bowers Sr., a salesman from Gulfport, MS., and Evangeline Peyton. Bowers was the product of educated, affluent families, who could be called MS royalty. One grandfather, Eaton J. Bowers, was a four-term Congressman from MS. Another grandfather was a wealthy Southern planter.[1]

In the eighth grade, Sam started to attend Bailey Jr. High.[2] At this school, he met Bill Thompson. Sam and Bill became fast friends. Sam and Bill attended Central High School in Jackson together after attending Bailey

Jr. High.[3] At both Bailey and Central, Sam and Bill participated in what can best be described as guerilla hit and run tactics against the teachers.

These undetected and unpunished activities taught the young Sam Bowers what could be done to authority by a conscious guerilla group.[4] **Secret guerilla hit and run tactics were to be the hallmark of the operations strategy for the conscious guerilla group that would come to be known as the White Knights of the Ku Klux Klan.**

Ten days after Pearl Harbor, on December 17, 1941, Sam enlisted in the US Navy.[5] Sam remained on active duty in the Navy for exactly four years, leaving the Navy on December 17, 1945.[6] Sam's Navy service was to have a major impact on the development and operation of the White Knights.

According to the oral interview in 1983, Sam stated that he gained a number of *important insights from his Navy experience*:

- the sense of belonging that is achieved from membership in a purposeful community;[7]
- the increased ability to obtain those purposes with a central authority that rules the individuals and a hierarchical, top down chain of command;[8]
- the strength of community that derives from a symbiotic defensive relationship between the community members and the community; and[9]
- having members simultaneously protect themselves and the community when the community engages in dangerous activities.[10]

All of these principles were to be utilized in organizing and operating the White Knights.

In December, 1947, Sam moved to Laurel to work in the pinball business. During the years, 1947-1950, he was immersed in building his pinball business.[11] Initially, in Laurel, Bowers had no interest in the question of racial segregation. His attitude was "loose and liberal" towards this issue as a result of his 18 months in California.[12]

After some time in Laurel, Sam met an older local man, Walter Johnson. According to Walter, a good Southerner did not go out of the way to mistreat Blacks. However, *if a Black got out of line, then he had to be put down.* These misguided principles would become guidelines for all future behavior by Bowers towards local Blacks.[13]

Initially, the Klan in Mississippi was actually the Mississippi Realm within the Original Knights of the KKK, headquartered in Bogalusa, LA. On February 15, 1964, 200 Klansmen who were members of the Mississippi Realm of the Original Knights met in Brooklyn, MS. These men assembled because of a disagreement over the misappropriation of funds by J.D. Swenson, one of the leaders of the Mississippi Realm.[14]

These Klansmen agreed to form the White Knights of the Ku Klux Klan of Mississippi. The avowed aims of the White Knights were to promote white supremacy and to maintain the segregation of the races. Activities were limited to the state of Mississippi.[15]

Six days later, on February 21, 1964, an organization meeting of the White Knights was held. At this meeting, Sam Bowers was elected to be Imperial Wizard of the White Knights. Another organization meeting was held on February 23, 1964. At this meeting, a special constitution and bylaws were created for the White Knights.[16]

Raleigh, MS, was the location of a secret state meeting attended by 300 members of the White Knights on June 7, 1964. All state officers were present. A status report indicated that 62 Klaverns had been organized in the 82 counties of Mississippi.[17] In four months, the White Knights had grown from 200 original members to 62 Klaverns across the state.

The guiding principle of the White Knights was hatred. Two groups were the target of this hatred -- Blacks and Jews.

In the Preamble to the Constitution, Bowers clearly states the primary goal of the White Knights:

> *to Promote the Purity and Integrity of the Separate Races of Mankind . . .*[18]

Every candidate for membership in the White Knights had to take an oath. Parts of this oath stated in Article XII, Section 6 of the Constitution define member obligations:

> *I . . . do hereby pledge, swear, and dedicate, my mind heart and body to the Holy Cause of preserving Christian Civilization . . . I will die in order to preserve Christian Civilization . . .*[19]

Unfortunately, the Constitution fails to define the term Christian Civilization. However, *The Klan Ledger*, does clearly define this term:

> *. . . we recognize that the Black man is one of his creatures, and is therefore under His Protection. This Divine Protection does not extend to social equality and integration with the White Man as the Scriptures clearly show.(See Genesis 49, 1-33, and I Cor. 15-39, which shows clearly that there are many species within the "one flesh."*[20]

Each member of the White Knights promises to maintain separation of Blacks and Whites, even if his death is required. Implied in this oath is a hatred for Blacks as an inferior race.

Bowers diplomatically tiptoed around his hatred of Blacks. He always sanitized his racial animus towards Blacks behind lofty and honorable appeals to Christianity. He generally does not use the derogatory N-***** in his writing, preferring the more respectful Negro. With Jews, however, Bowers was outright hostile and dripping with hate.

A more vitriolic and direct hatred for Jews was expressed in an undated bulletin produced by Bowers under the organization name WASP, Inc.

> *The Supreme Tragedy is that these people have been permitted to gain financial control over America . . . to the savage Kike, money reacts in the same manner as does alcohohol [sic] to the Alcohoholic [sic]. He is a fanatic about it. He is ruled by it. He must have more and more of it to sustain his lust . . . he must feed his savage ego by exploiting Christians and destroying Christian Civilization.*[21]

According to Bowers, the savage Kike's lust for money is driving him to destroy the separation between Blacks and Whites ("Christian Civilization").

The tone of this screed is pure hatred towards the Jews. Bowers even uses the derogatory term "Kike" to refer to a Jewish person. He modifies this reference with the term savage, indicating that Jews are animals!

The constitution of the White Knights made clear that the Imperial Wizard maintained absolute control over the organization at all levels. Sam Bowers clearly made sure that this was the situation.

Article II, Section 8 clearly and unambiguously ensures that Bowers as Imperial Wizard possesses complete control:

> *The Imperial Wizard shall direct the Political, Educational, and other activities of the Klan and shall have the necessary powers to initiate action and issue orders to accomplish the purposes of the Klan ...The Imperial Wizard shall enjoy the right of secrecy and his own, private council for his private deliberations ...*[22]

As Sam Bowers had learned from his service in the Navy, one key to organizational success involved a central authority. Clearly, the Imperial Wizard was the central authority for the White Knights.

Bowers did not disappoint in this regard.

A chain of command is clearly defined in Article II Section 24:

> *The Administration of the Klan shall consist of three levels of command, which shall be known as the Klan Chain of Command.*

This article continues on to define the three levels of command: Klan level, Province Level, Klavern Level.[23]

Article 25 of the Constitution of the White Knights describes the mechanisms of communications across the chain of command:

> *The Province officers shall be the connecting link between the Klavern and the Klan level officers . . . The Klavern Exalted Cyclops shall use the Province officer most convenient to him for transmission of administrative problems through the Chain of Command.*[24]

A Province was a group of Klaverns. Typically, several counties were included in a Province.

Generally, a problem and recommended solution was identified at the Klavern or Province level. Some solutions had to be decided by Bowers, the Imperial Wizard. If approved the Province or Klavern was delegated the authority to accomplish the solution. Other solutions could be decided at the Province level by the Province Giant (President).

Klan investigators at all levels were used to identify problems. A **problem** was clearly any issue within the sphere of interest of the Klan investigator. Most often the problem was persons or organizations engaged in promoting civil rights.

Four **solutions** were used by the White Knights:

    1: cross burning;

    2: strapping (whipping);[25];

    3: bombing;

    4: elimination (meaning assassination).[26]

Only the Imperial Wizard could approve using a solution 3 or a solution 4 on a problem.[27] A Provincial Giant (President) could approve using solution 1 or a solution 2 on a problem.[28]

Citizens Councils[29]

The first Citizens' Council was formed in Indianola, MS, on July 11, 1954,[30] following the ruling in Brown v. Board of Education by the US Supreme Court. This ruling struck down segregation in public schools. Other chapters were formed around the state. Soon, the Association of Citizens' Councils of MS, was founded in Winona, MS. By 1956, the state Association claimed 80,000 members in MS. The Citizens' Councils of America was formed on April 7, 1956.[31]

Revenue from membership dues and grants from the publicly funded Mississippi Sovereignty Commission supported group operations. The Citizens' Council officially denounced violence as a strategy. However, many Council members privately condoned the violent tactics used by the Ku Klux Klan. Council members used their connections to influence lawmakers, editors, business owners and operators, and state officials to enact pro-segregation legislation. Economic pressure was exerted on supporters of civil rights activities. Intimidation was directed at Blacks who attempted to register to vote.

Publicity was created and distributed/broadcast for anti-integration viewpoints. *The Citizen*, a national magazine, was published. *Forum*, a weekly telecast, was produced and broadcast on WLBT-TV in Jackson.

Mississippi Sovereignty Commission[32]

The Mississippi State Sovereignty Commission was created on March 29, 1956,[33] by Chapter 365 of the Laws of MS.[34]

Its objective was explicitly stated in the law: *do and perform any and all acts and things deemed necessary and proper to protect the sovereignty of the state of Mississippi, and her sister states from encroachment thereon by the Federal Government or any branch, department or agency thereof; to resist the usurpation of the rights and powers reserved to this state and our sister states by the Federal Government or any branch, department or agency thereof."*

Extensive investigative capabilities were granted to the Commission in order to exercise this loosely defined objective.

This small agency possessed a staff consisting of a director, a public relations director, investigators, and clerical staff. Throughout its existence, the Commission used both paid and unpaid informants to supplement its investigation team. Private detective agencies were also used to conduct investigations. Its first 2-year budget was $250,000 ($2,388,952 in 2020).[35]

Activities performed by the commission were wide and deep. Leaders and investigators spied on civil rights workers, acted as a clearinghouse for information on civil rights activities and legislation from around the nation, funneled money to pro-segregation causes, and distributed right-wing propaganda.

Erle Johnston was associated with the Commission from 1960. He served as director from 1963 – 1968. In 1956, the Commission hired Leonard Hicks as its first investigator. Zack Van Landingham became an investigator in 1958. Investigators R.C. "Bob" Thomas, State Representative Hugh Boren, Andy Hopkins, and Tom Scarbrough were hired in 1960. Other principal investigators for the Sovereignty Commission were Virgil Downing, Leland Cole, Fulton Tutor, Edgar C. Fortenberry, and James "Mack" Mohead.[36]

The MS Constitution

In 1890, a new MS state Constitution was approved. This new Constitution possessed several sections specifically designed to discriminate against Blacks.

Article 12: Franchise

Sec. 241. Every male inhabitant of this State ... who has paid, ... all taxes which may have been legally required of him ... for the two preceding years, ... is declared to be a qualified elector; ...

Sec. 243. A uniform poll tax of two dollars ... is hereby imposed on every male inhabitant of this State between the ages of twenty-one and sixty years, except persons who are deaf and dumb or blind, or who are maimed by loss of hand or foot; ...

Sec. 244. ... every elector shall, in addition to the foregoing qualifications, be able to read any section of the constitution of this State; or he shall be able to understand the same when read to him, or give a reasonable interpretation thereof.

Sections 241 and 243 combined require that a MS resident paid an annual poll tax of $2.00 to qualify to vote. The poll tax had to be paid for each of the 2 years before an election.

Section 244 required passing a literacy test to qualify as a voter.

Both poll tax and literacy test were discriminatory against Blacks.

Almost all Blacks in MS were extremely poor. These poor Blacks did not have $2.00 in cash, even in 1964. Black schools were neglected in MS. Black schools generally only went through the 8th grade. Most Blacks could not read and write.

Worse yet, this provision was generally abused by county registrars. Registrars had discretion over which Constitutional section was to be interpreted. Whites were asked to interpret a section that was a single line. Blacks were asked to interpret long, convoluted, obscure sections. Some registrars even went so far as to ask irrelevant questions that really did not have an answer.

Cooperation Among Organizations

The Klan, Citizens Councils, and the Sovereignty Commission regularly conspired to help each other obtain their individual objectives.

The Commission was an official investigative agency of the state of MS. Investigators could go anywhere and talk to anyone. Investigators did not have any legal obligation to maintain privacy over the results of ongoing investigations. Rumors could and were passed to other racist and segregationist organizations.

Extensive examples exist throughout the Sovereignty Commission records that demonstrate the interactions of the organizations. Citizens Council members publicly denounced violence. Yet, Council members often gave information about civil rights troublemakers to Klan members. Then, Klan members did the dirty work of directing violence at the troublemaker. If Klan members identified troublemakers, this identification was passed to the local Citizens Council. Council members then delivered economic repercussions to the troublemaker.

In the middle of all this interaction was the Sovereignty Commission. Commission investigators both initiated the flow of information and acted as a transfer agent of information.

This network of agencies was supported by the power of the state government of MS through the involvement of the Sovereignty Commission.

Civil Rights Organizations Involved

NAACP, The National Association of Colored People

On February 12, 1909, the NAACP was formed by a group of mixed-race individuals. White founders included Mary White Ovington, Oswald Garrison Villard, William English Walling, and Dr. Henry Moscowitz. W.E.B. Dubois, Ida B. Wells-Barnett, and Mary Church Terrell were among the Black founders of the Association. Some 60 people were among the founders.[37]

Actual incorporation was accomplished on June 9, 1911. Original signers of the charter included W.E.B. DuBois, John Haynes Holmes, Oswald Garrison Villard, Walter E. Sachs, and Mary White Ovington. The NAACP Corporate Charter was approved by the Supreme Court of the State of NY. Judge Daniel F. Cohalan of the First Judicial District signed the charter on behalf of the Supreme Court of the State of NY. Dr. DuBois was to be the intellectual leader. Listed among the initial members of the Board of Directors was the Rev. A Clayton Powell from New York City, NY. [38,39]

According to the Articles, the objectives of the NAACP included:[40]

> That the principal objects for which the corporation is formed are voluntarily to promote equality of rights and eradicate caste or race prejudice among the citizens of the United States; to advance the interest of colored citizens; to secure for them impartial suffrage; and to increase their opportunities for securing justice in the courts, education for their children, employment according to their ability, and complete equality before the law.

This statement of objectives clearly reveals the main approach that would be used by the NAACP to obtain all of the other objectives. *"Securing justice in the courts* would be the primary method for changing society.

In 1938, Thurgood Marshall was appointed as special counsel for the NAACP. Marshall founded the NAACP Legal Defense Fund in 1940. The objective of the LDF was to end segregation by legally overturning the "separate but equal" doctrine from Plessy vs. Ferguson(1896).[41] From 1948 until 1954, the NAACP LDF conducted a series of cases that established the foundation to challenge the "separate but equal" doctrine at the Supreme Court level.[42] Thurgood Marshall was involved in some of these cases. Howard Hamilton Houston was involved in other cases. Other NAACP LDF attorneys represented the plaintiffs in some of these cases.

Over a 4-year period, the NAACP LDF, with Thurgood Marshall at the helm, successfully navigated the legal hurtles associated with Brown vs the Board of Education:

- February 28, 1951: Brown v. Board of Education filed in US District Court, in Kansas;
- June, 1951: District Court trial begins, Brown v. Board of Education;
- August, 1951: US District Court ruling, Brown vs Board of Education: "*no willful, intentional or substantial discrimination*" existed in Topeka's schools;
- October, 1952: bundling of the Brown v. Board cases;
- December 9th – 11th, 1952: first round of arguments, Brown vs. Board;
- December 7th – 9th, 1953: second round of arguments, Brown vs. Board;
- May 17, 1954: first ruling, Brown vs Board, racial segregation in the schools violates the Equal Protection Clause of the Fourteenth Amendment;
- April, 1955: third round of arguments, concerning remedies, Brown vs. Board; and,
- May 31, 1955: second ruling, Brown vs. Board, desegregation to occur with *all deliberate speed*.[43]

During the Civil Rights Movement, litigation and Youth Council activity were to be the primary means of NAACP participation.

CORE, The Congress of Racial Equality

In May, 1942,[44] an interested group of Black and white members of the Fellowship of Reconciliation (FOR), many of whom lived around the University of Chicago, decided to try an experiment in non-violent, direct actions. Members of the group had heard that Jack Spratt Coffee House on East 47th Street at Kimbark Avenue in the Kenwood neighborhood of Chicago refused to serve Blacks. In order to dissuade Blacks from asking for service, the counterman would ask any Black customer to wait. After a long wait, the counterman would charge the Black customer a dollar for a donut. White customers only paid 5 cents for the same donut.[45]

The group decided to do a large-scale sit-in at Jack Spratt, occupying all available seats. Twenty-eight persons entered Jack Spratt in groups. Each group had at least one black person. All group members would NOT eat until all Blacks were served. Any white person would give their plate to the nearest Black person who had not been served. Other customers, already in the diner, did the same. The manager offered to serve the Black customers in the basement. This offer was unacceptable and declined by the group. A second offer was for the Blacks to sit in the back corner to be served, Again, the group declined. Finally, the manager called the police. Upon arrival, the police refused to eject the group. All patrons were served. Afterward, tests were regularly performed at Jack Spratt to ensure that the diner's policy had changed.[46]

This direct action was the first, race relations sit-in in the United States.[47] This incident proved that a non-violent, direct action approach could obtain immediate results. Costs were only transportation and food. Enforcement by an Executive organization was not needed.

As a result of the success of this test sit-in, the first CORE chapter was formed in Chicago.[48] Originally, 50 members joined that first chapter. Of these volunteers, 28 were men and 22 were women. Roughly one-third were Black and two-thirds were white.[49] Many of these original members were from the Chicago Branch of the Fellowship of Reconciliation. Members of the first chapter included James L. Farmer, George Houser, Bernice Fisher, James R Robinson, Joe Guinn, Homer Jack, and Samuel E. Riley. Bayard Rustin, a Field Director of the Fellowship of

Reconciliation, was not a member of CORE but was an active supporter.[50]

CORE was initially organized as a non-hierarchical, decentralized organized. Voluntary contributions by its members entirely funded the organization. Initial leaders were James Farmer, a Black, and George Houser, a white.[51]

Initially, CORE chapters were centered in the North. Emphasis was placed on non-violent, direct action and concentrated on public accommodations.[52] In 1942, CORE expanded nationally. James Farmer traveled the country with Bayard Rustin, a field secretary with FOR, and recruited activists at FOR meetings. CORE's early growth consisted almost entirely of white middle-class college students from the Midwest.[53]

In its Constitution, CORE clearly stated its purpose and nature:[54]

> The purpose for which this organization has been formed and for which it exists is to abolish discrimination based upon Skin Color, Race, Religion or National Origin, stressing non-violent, direct action methods.

According to the mission of CORE, three types of power are inherent to nonviolent direct action:

1. the power of active goodwill and non-retaliation;

2. the power of public opinion against injustice; and,

3. the power of refusing to be a party to injustice, as illustrated by boycotts and strikes.[55]

Once organized and operational, CORE had a large number of successes between 1942 and 1961. Techniques employed included sit-ins, picketing, boycotts, passing out leaflets, voter registration training committees, and pressure campaigns. During this time period, CORE was the only organization taking these direct actions.[56]

CORE and the Fellowship of Reconciliation decided to work together to test enforcement of this ruling. A two-week Journey of Reconciliation was planned. This Journey was to involve 8 Black and 8 white riders using public interstate transportation through Virginia, North Carolina,

Tennessee, and Kentucky. These states were all in the upper South.[57] George Hauser, Executive Secretary of CORE, and Bayard Rustin of FOR led this group.[58] Actual travel on the Journey of Reconciliation was during the period April 9-23, 1947.[59] All travel was performed on two interstate carriers: Greyhound and Trailways Bus Lines.[60]

On December 5, 1960, the Supreme Court issued a ruling in Boynton vs. Virginia.[61] Simply stated, segregation was prohibited on interstate transportation by motor carrier and in terminals and restaurants.[62] The first 1961 Freedom Ride would test the seating aboard buses and the use of the terminal restaurants.[63]

CORE Director James Farmer and 13 Freedom Riders (7 Black, 6 white) boarded Greyhound and Trailways buses out of Washington, DC, on May 4, 1961. Most of the Riders were members of CORE.[64] This first Freedom Ride conducted by CORE lasted from May 4-17, 1961. These Riders were unable to complete the Ride. Both Greyhound and Trailways drivers refused to man the buses containing Freedom Riders. More than 60 Freedom Rides crossed the South between May and November of 1961. CORE members heavily participated in these rides, along with SNCC members.

CORE activities seemed to work well. Targeted non-violent direct actions could obtain results, sometimes within hours. However, availability of CORE participants was limited. CORE operations required extensive time for planning, organizing, and conducting events. Generally, activities were conducted by interested outsiders. Participants in the First Freedom Ride were from various geographic locations, not from the local communities where the activities were conducted.

SCLC, The Southern Christian Leadership Conference

On December 1, 1955, Rosa Parks was arrested for refusing to give up here bus seat in Montgomery, AL. Bus boycotts were started all over the South in response to her arrest. Many groups were involved in these boycotts. A regional organization was needed to coordinate future civil rights activities across these groups. Representatives of these groups met at the Ebenezer Baptist Church at 407 Auburn Avenue in Atlanta[65] on January 10 – 11, 1957.[66] Reverend Martin Luther King, Jr., was the Pastor at this Baptist Church.[67]

As a result of this meeting, this organization issued a written statement entitled *A Statement to the South and Nation*. This statement was authored by Rev. Martin Luther King, Jr., Rev. Fred Shuttlesworth, and Rev. Charles K. Steele.[68] King was Pastor of Ebenezer Baptist Church in Atlanta.[69] Shuttlesworth was Pastor of Bethel Baptist Church in Birmingham.[70] Steele was Pastor at Bethel Baptist Church in Tallahassee, FL.[71] Noticeably, all authors were ministers. All founders had participated in boycott activities in their communities.

In this document, the ministers made important statements that would guide the activity of the SCLC. *No matter how great the obstacles and suffering, we urge all Negroes to reject segregation ... We advocate non-violence in words, thoughts, and deeds ... Not one hair of one head of one white person shall be harmed.*[72]

A mass meeting was held on August 17, 1957, in Montgomery. Over 2000 attendees were present. At this meeting, the name of the organization was shortened to Southern Christian Leadership Conference.[73] This name was chosen to reflect a vision and goal of mobilizing the inherent power of Black churches around social causes such as voting rights, fighting segregation, opposing economic exploitation and alleviating poverty.[74]

On January 9, 1958, Ella Baker, Director of Branches of the NAACP,[75] arrived in Atlanta to assume the full-time position of Associate Director of the SCLC. Her immediate tasks were to open the Atlanta Headquarters and to organize and to launch the upcoming voter registration campaign.[76]

As its first national activity, SCLC announced its *Crusade for Citizenship*. Objectives of this program were to stimulate Blacks to vote and to help Blacks to obtain the right to vote where that right did not exist. With this program, SCLC wanted to double the registered Black voters in the South.[77] Public meetings were held all in over 20 cities throughout the South. All speakers were ministers in various churches, sometimes from out of town, sometimes from local churches.[78] These meetings were held on February 12, 1958,[79] and were well attended. Attendees were enthusiastic. However, voter registration applications did not significantly increase after the meetings.[80]

On May 22, 1958, the SCLC published a flyer that clearly revealed the plan to use the churches in leading the Civil Rights Movement. This flyer was titled *Some Reasons Why Churches Should Take The Lead In Registration and Voting*.[81] Nine reasons were provided. The most important reasons were: *Churches are located in practically every community ... The church membership meets weekly ... Churches have the resources and techniques for motivating people to service.* Instinctively, King recognized that he had a large army of leaders, the Black ministers, who could motivate and lead local residents.

SCLC had an unrealized problem with local Black churches as affiliate organizations. King and the other ministers were asking a Black minister to put his life on the line. King really did not understand the extent to which local white racists would respond with violence. Ministers generally worked at motivating congregation members towards single person actions -- accepting salvation and living a Christian life.

From April 3 – May 10, 1963, the SCLC conducted the Birmingham Campaign. This campaign of nonviolent direct action was led by Martin Luther King Jr., James Bevel, Fred Shuttlesworth and others. Despite its non-violent intent, the campaign culminated in widely publicized confrontations between young Black students and white civic authorities. Dr King was jailed. From his jail cell, King wrote his famous *Letter From Birmingham Jail*.[82]

King and the SCLC were leaders in the Selma to Montgomery marches. On February 26, 1965, activist and deacon Jimmie Lee Jackson died after being shot several days earlier by AL state trooper James Fowler. This shooting was during a peaceful march in nearby Marion, AL. James Bevel, an SCLC activist, called for a march of dramatic length from Selma to the state capital of Montgomery. This march was to demonstrate the desire of Black citizens to exercise their Constitutional right to vote.

On March 7, 1965, Bloody Sunday, the first march took place. Marchers were beaten by AL State Troopers at the Edmund Pettus Bridge in Selma at the beginning of the march. A second march was attempted on March 9, 1965. Dr. King was convinced to turn the march around before crossing the Pettus in Selma. A final third march was conducted from March 21 – March 24, 1965. This march successfully covered the 54 miles between Selma and Montgomery. On March 25, 1965, marchers demonstrated in front of the AL State Capital Building.[83]

SNCC, Student Nonviolent Coordinating Committee

Ella Baker began her involvement in the civil rights movement by joining the NAACP in 1940. Baker worked as a Field Secretary and then served as Director of Branches from 1943 until 1946. In 1957, she moved to Atlanta to help organize the Southern Christian Leadership Conference (SCLC). After moving to Atlanta, Ella Baker became the Executive Director of the SCLC.[84],[85] After the Greensboro lunch counter sit-ins on February 21, 1960, Ella felt that her next objective should be to assist the new student activists. Ella viewed young, emerging activists as a resource and an asset to the movement. She decided she would have to leave the SCLC in order to form a youth-based organization.[86]

Speaking on February 16, 1960 at the White Rock Baptist Church in Durham, North Carolina, Rev. Martin Luther King, Jr. acknowledged the emerging importance of young people. *What is new in your fight is the fact that it was initiated, fed, and sustained by students.*[87]

On Easter weekend (April 15-17) in 1960[88] at Shaw University in Raleigh, North Carolina, Ella brought sit-in leaders from all over the South together for the first time. This conference was attended by 126 student delegates from 58 sit-in centers in 12 states from 19 northern colleges. Students also represented the Southern Christian Leadership Conference (SCLC), the Congress of Racial Equality (CORE), the Fellowship of Reconciliation (FOR), the National Student Association (NSA), and Students for a Democratic Society (SDS).[89]

Unlike other adult leaders at the conference, Baker encouraged the budding activists to form their own organization dedicated fully to the Black Freedom Struggle. Attendees embraced her suggestion. The Student Nonviolent Coordinating Committee (SNCC) was formed.[90]

Founding members were all students, as the name of the organization indicated. Many of these founders would become well-known leaders in SNCC and in the Civil Rights Movement: Diane Nash, Marion Barry, and John Lewis, from Fisk University in Nashville; James Bevel and Bernard Lafayette, from American Baptist Theological Seminary; James Lawson, from Vanderbilt University; Charles F. McDew, from South Carolina State University; J. Charles Jones, from Johnson C. Smith University;

Julian Bond from Morehouse College, Atlanta; and Stokely Carmichael from Howard University, Washington, D.C.[91]

The first meeting of SNCC was held on May 13-14, 1960, at Atlanta University in Atlanta, GA. Marion Barry of Fisk University was elected as the first Chairman of SNCC.[92]

Some student activists who were members of SNCC began to drop out of school to become full-time organizers. One of these student organizers was Robert Moses. Bob Moses was a native of Harlem, New York, who had come to Atlanta as an SCLC volunteer in the summer of 1960. Ella and Jane Stembridge sent Moses on a journey through the Deep South to recruit students to participate in a SNCC conference being planned for October 1960, in Atlanta.[93]

Amzie Moore, the local NAACP President from Cleveland, MS, in the Delta area, had initially presented the concept of a voter registration project to SNCC.[94] During the period October 8-10, 1961, members of the diverse communities within SNCC met at a SNCC Staff Meeting. These members worked with Ella Baker to formulate a structure for initiating long range programs. This structure included both voter registration and statewide non-violent direct activities.[95]

Direct activities meant working with local Blacks in their communities to actively address violations of civil rights by local leaders... *it is imperative that we look into the possibility of engaging in political activity on all levels, local, state, and federal. This means that we let politicians know forcefully how we feel about issues which are of vital importance to us.*[96] At the heart of direct action was an obligation to get arrested. *There are not enough jails to accommodate the movement ... If one or two of us are arrested, the rest must non-violently seek arrest ... This is one of the best ways to immobilize repercussive police apparatus.*[97]

On May 4, 1961, CORE conducted the first Freedom Rides. This group consisted of 7 Blacks, 6 whites, and was led by CORE director James Farmer. A bus trip across the south was begun from Washington, DC. Travelling on interstate buses, the group was brutally attacked by mobs of Ku Klux Klansmen in Anniston, AL, on May 14, 1961. Local police stood by and watched. This group was also assaulted on in Birmingham,

AL, an hour later on the same day. Under pressure from the Kennedy Administration, CORE discontinued this initial Freedom Ride.

SNCC leaders were undeterred. Diane Nash, from Nashville SNCC, called for new riders. Oretha Castle Haley, Jean C. Thompson, Rudy Lombard, James Bevel, Marion Barry, Angeline Butler, Stokley Carmichael, and Joan Trumpauer Mulholland, joined John Lewis and Hank Thomas, the two young SNCC members of the original Ride. This new group continued the rides on May 20, 1961, travelling from Nashville, TN, to Jackson, MS. A savage beating was delivered to the group in Montgomery, AL. In Jackson, MS, the group was arrested. This group was confined in the Maximum Security (Death Row) Unit of the infamous Mississippi State Penitentiary--*Parchman Farm*.[98]

James Foreman, a teacher and Black journalist from Chicago, participated in a number of civil rights activities during the period 1958 - 1961. In August 1961, Foreman was arrested protesting segregated facilities in Monroe, NC. He was jailed with Freedom Riders This episode brought Forman into contact with Robert F. Williams of the NAACP. Williams won Forman's admiration. After his sentence was suspended, Forman agreed to become Executive Secretary of SNCC. The most important lesson Foreman brought into SNCC was a *hands-off* approach to SNCC's organizing work in the field.[99]

After the SNCC structure was defined, Bob Moses was originally sent to Amzie Moore in the Delta area of MS to conduct a voter registration project. Unfortunately, Amzie was not ready for Bob. So, Amzie sent Bob Moses to Curtis Conway "C.C." Bryant, leader of the McComb NAACP. In late 1961, Bob Moses initiated a voter registration project in McComb.

Moses was unsuccessful in getting Blacks to register to vote. Most Black residents were simply afraid. After all, McComb, Hattiesburg, and Laurel were the home of some of the most violent Klaverns in the United Klans of America and the White Knights.[100] However, this activity did reap some positive benefits.

Local young people were excited just by the presence in town of Bob Moses and other incoming SNCC workers. These local young Blacks felt that *Freedom Riders* had come to their town. Young Blacks wanted to be part of the Movement that had only heard about. Some began working with Moses, canvassing the Black community for those willing to put their lives on the line to try to register to vote. Other young people began organizing their own student protest movement.

The other effect of the McComb project was to bring SNCC's work to the attention of Black leaders in the surrounding counties. Soon, residents *out in the rural* came to McComb and asked SNCC to begin projects in their counties.[101] By summer, 1963, extensive SNCC operations were being conducted throughout dangerous areas such as MS, southwest GA, central AL, eastern AK, and southern VA. Over 150 Field Secretaries initiated and participated in direct action campaigns in 49 cities in 13 states.[102]

In June, 1963, SNCC conducted one of its regular meetings. At that meeting, John Lewis was elected 3rd Chairman of SNCC. Lewis was only 23 years old. In November, 1959, Lewis became involved in the Civil Rights Movement in Nashville, TN. He had been arrested 32 times since that beginning. Lewis was savagely beaten in Montgomery, AL, when participating in the Freedom Ride.[103]

SNCC was the primary organization that conducted activities in MS during Freedom Summer, 1964. Most of the volunteers came to MS from SNCC during that summer. Direct action at the local Black community level was the objective. Freedom Summer activities by SNCC consisted of voter registration, Freedom Schools, establishment of libraries, and Community Center cultural activities.

Cooperation Among Organizations

Each of the civil rights organizations conducted its civil rights activities in different spheres. NAACP addressed civil rights issues in the courts. CORE was the leader in sit-ins, demonstrations, and boycotts. SCLC worked through the Black churches in the South. SNCC provided leadership to local Blacks to obtain civil rights such as voter registration and education. However, all of these groups had one thing in common. All of the groups wanted civil rights for Black citizens of the US.

These civil rights organizations needed to demonstrate their unanimity on the issue of civil rights and to push for passage of a civil rights bill in Congress. Two national Black leaders had been agitating for a March on Washington for many years. A. Philip Randolph was President of the Brotherhood of Sleeping Car Porters, President of the Negro American Labor Council, and Vice President of the AFL-CIO. Bayard Rustin was Race Relation Secretary of the Fellowship of Reconciliation. Rustin and Martin Luther King, Jr, organized the Southern Christian Leadership Conference (SCLC).[104]

King, Randolph, and Rustin joined forces to organize a united march. On July 2, 1963, Randolph and King convened a summit meeting of the *Big Six* in New York City to plan a united march in Washington for *Jobs and Freedom*. Attending this summit were: A. Phillip Randolph, Jim Farmer (CORE), Dr. King (SCLC), John Lewis (SNCC), Roy Wilkins (NAACP), and Whitney Young (Urban League). Wilkins and Young were undecided about the march. Randolph, Farmer, King, and Lewis, the direct-action wing of the Movement, refuse to cancel.

A date was selected for the march, Wednesday, August 28, 1963, in just 8 weeks. Everyone at the July 2nd meeting knew that Bayard Rustin was the best man for the job — perhaps the only one who could organize the march in such a short time.

Wilkins and Young opposed appointing Rustin to head the march. Rustin, a Quaker, served prison time during WWII as a Conscientious Objector. That classified Rustin as a *draft dodger*. As s publicly avowed socialist, Rustin was political poison. Rustin was also a homosexual who had once been arrested on a *morals* charge. Wilkins and Young viewed Rustin as a social pariah, fearing that opponents will use Rustin's past as a basis to smear the march.

Randolph, King, and Farmer defended Rustin Both Randolph and King had worked successfully with Rustin on the Montgomery Bus Boycott, Prayer Pilgrimage to DC for Civil Rights, and the two Youth Marches for Integrated Schools. Debate was hot and bitter. Finally, a compromise was reached. Randolph would be the titular head of the march. Rustin would be his *deputy*. Cleveland Robinson, of the Negro American Labor Council, would be Administrative Chairman. Everyone understood that Rustin would lead the actual work of organizing the march.

After extensive negotiations among representatives of the Big 6, a set of demands was created for the march.

1. Comprehensive and effective civil rights legislation from the present Congress, without compromise or filibuster, to guarantee civil rights to all Americans: access to all public accommodations, decent housing, adequate and integrated education, and the right to vote.
2. Withholding of federal funds from all programs in which discrimination exists.
3. Desegregation of all school districts in 1963.
4. Enforcement of the Fourteenth Amendment, reducing Congressional representation of states where citizens are disfranchised.
5. A new Executive Order banning discrimination in all housing supported by federal funds.
6. Authority for the Attorney General to institute injunctive suits when any Constitutional right is violated.
7. A massive federal program to train and place all unemployed workers, Black and white, on meaningful and dignified jobs at decent wages.
8. A national minimum wage act that will give all Americans a decent standard of living. Government surveys showed that anything less than $2.00 an hour was insufficient for a decent standard of living.
9. A broadened Fair Labor Standards Act to include all areas of employment which are presently excluded.
10. A federal Fair Employment Practices Act barring discrimination by federal, state, and municipal governments, and by employers, contractors, employment agencies, and trade unions.

On August 28, more than 2,000 buses, 21 chartered trains, 10 chartered airliners, and uncounted cars converged on Washington. All regularly scheduled planes, trains, and buses were also filled to capacity. Nearly 250,000 march, including 60,000 white participants.

Representatives from the sponsoring organizations addressed the crowd from a podium of the Lincoln Memorial. A. Philip Randolph – March Director; Walter Reuther – UAW, AFL-CIO; Roy Wilkins – NAACP;

John Lewis – SNCC; Daisy Bates – Little Rock, Arkansas; Dr. Eugene Carson Blake – United Presbyterian Church and the National Council of Churches; Floyd McKissick –CORE; Whitney Young – National Urban League; several smaller speeches, including Rabbi Joachim Prinz – American Jewish Congress, Mathew Ahmann – National Catholic Conference, Josephine Baker – actress; Dr. Martin Luther King Jr. – SCLC. Closing remarks were given by A. Philip Randolph and Bayard Rustin, March Organizers, leading with The Pledge and list of demands. Each speaker was limited to 7 minutes for his speech.

Dr. King's address became famous as the *I Have a Dream speech*. But the dream section was not part of his original draft. Originally, King was to end his speech with the metaphor of the bounced check and the echo of Amos that ... *we will not be satisfied until justice rolls down like waters, and righteousness like a mighty stream*. As he neared the end of his speech, King sensed that something more had to be said. Dr. King felt that the march itself required some summing up, some articulation of the vision that moved the Movement. Listeners needed to hear some expression of the aspirations, pride, determination, and courage of not just these marchers, but the Freedom Movement as a whole.

Legend says that Mahalia Jackson, sitting near Dr. King, leaned forward and whispered, *Tell them about the dream, Martin*. Jackson had heard King speak about the dream at recent rallies. With that suggestion, King continued beyond the 7-minute limit and off his prepared text. His words soared, speaking from the soul of the struggle to the heart of oppressed people everywhere.

Go back to Mississippi, go back to Alabama, ... go back to the slums and ghettos of our northern cities ... Let us not wallow in the valley of despair ... And so even though we face the difficulties of today and tomorrow, I still have a dream. I have a dream that one day this nation will rise up and live out the true meaning of its creed: We hold these truths to be self-evident that all men are created equal ... I have a dream that my four little children will one day live in a nation where they will not be judged by the color of their skin but by the content of their character. I have a dream today! ... Free at last, free at last. Thank God Almighty, I'm free at last.

These remarks were deeply rooted in the Old Testament and the unfulfilled promise of the American creed, two cherished gospels. This 19-minute address indelibly positioned the Civil Rights Freedom Movement in faith and history.

COFO, the Council of Federated Organizations

In 1961, the Council of Federated Organizations was founded. Its initial objective was to support jailed Freedom Riders.[105]

At the initiative of MS NAACP State President Aaron Henry, COFO was revived in 1962[106]. Its new purpose was to coordinate voter registration activities in the state of MS across all the organizations: NAACP, SCLC, CORE, and SNCC. Aaron Henry became President. Bob Moses was appointed the COFO Program Director. David Dennis of CORE was to be Assistant Program Director. SNCC and CORE field secretaries became COFO staff.[107]

As a coalition, COFO was designed to be a coordinating body meant to avoid inter-organizational political wrangling and to facilitate the flow of funds into Mississippi for voter education and registration. Equally as important, the COFO umbrella was also meant to protect and nurture grassroots activism in the state.[108]

COFO's voter registration program involved three basic steps to break the fear and political apathy of local white power structures. Door-to-door canvassing was the primary means of meeting and talking with community members. Workshops were conducted to prepare local residents for the actual registration attempt, including voter education. Actual registration attempts were made, which required a direct confrontation with the hostile local power structure.[109]

COFO's financial support was divided according to MS Congressional Districts. SNCC financially supported offices and projects in the First, Second, Third, and Fifth MS Congressional Districts. In the Fourth Congressional District, COFO offices and projects were financially supported by CORE. Both Meridian and Canton are in the Fourth MS Congressional District. A COFO Office in Meridian or Canton would be staffed by members of CORE, because CORE was paying all the expenses for the office.[110]

NAACP and Meridian

Over time, local branches were established within the states. The first local branch in MS was in Vicksburg. This branch was chartered in 1918 and then rechartered on April 8, 1940. In 1945, members of branches from across the state came together to charter the Mississippi State Conference of Branches.[111] Two well known members of the Conference were Aaron Henry and Medger Evers. Aaron Henry was State Conference President for 33 years and was perhaps the chief architect of integration in MS. Medger Evers served as Executive Secretary of the Conference until his untimely death on June 12, 1963.[112]

A branch of the NAACP was organized in Meridian in March, 1935. First Branch President was Roy L. Young. In that month, Young wrote a letter to Roy Wilkins, Executive Secretary of the NAACP. Young told Wilkins, *Our people have decided to take a stand, whatever the cost may be ...We must show and prove to you that we mean business.* By the end of March, 1935, Wilkins had publicly announced the formation of the Meridian branch. *A branch of the association has been organized in Meridian with 126 charter members. This is the first active unit in the state of MS in many years.*[113]

In the early 1950s, Charles Darden served as President of the Meridian branch. From 1955 - 1965, Darden served as President of President of the Mississippi State Conference of Branches. In the fall of 1960, Darden was replaced by Aaron Henry as President of the State Conference.[114]

Darden was well acquainted with James Chaney, the local Black who was part of the murdered trio. In 1959, Darden was charged with disturbing the peace at Harris Junior College, a black school in Meridian. The college suspended a group of students after the students wore badges commemorating the fifth anniversary of the Supreme Court's *Brown v. Board of Education* decision. This group of students included Darden's sons as well as James Chaney. Darden spoke with the principal. Then, he photographed the students leaving the school following the suspensions. When he arrived home, local police confiscated the film. Darden was fined fifty dollars for disturbing the peace by encouraging the students' protest.[115]

During Freedom Summer, the summer of 1964, Darden was instrumental in organizing an NAACP Youth Council in Meridian.[116] During that summer, Roscoe Jones, Sr., was President of the Youth Council. Roscoe also volunteered in the COFO office. He worked with Schwerner, Chaney, and Goodman to encourage voter registration by Blacks in Meridian.[117] Members of the Meridian NAACP Youth Council were heavily involved with the COFO activity.

COFO and Meridian

In January 1964, COFO (Council of Federated Organizations) began to establish a headquarters and strong presence in Meridian. Acquisition of the office space was accomplished by Matteo Suarez and Albert Jones. Suarez was the COFO coordinator for Mississippi's Fourth Congressional District. Jones was one of Meridian's wealthiest and most prominent black real estate owners. Working together, Suarez and Jones were able to acquire a space at 2505 1/2 Fifth Street above Fielder & Brooks Drug Store. Dr. Alvin L. Fielder's assistance came with the rented space. This space consisted of five rooms on the second floor.

Someone was still needed to run the Meridian COFO office and to build COFO activity in the Meridian area. Since CORE would be financially supporting the Meridian office of COFO, this COFO office would be led by two white CORE members from New York City, Michael and Rita Schwerner.

MS Religions and Blacks and Jews

MS is part of an area commonly called the Bible Belt. This area encompasses most of the southeast quarter of the US. In this area, the Christian religion is dominant. A large percentage of residents are of some denomination of Christianity. All Christians use the Holy Bible as their foundational document.

In the US, MS is one of the most religious states. By far, the largest denomination in MS is that of the Southern Baptists. As of 2017, Southern Baptists had 2132 churches in MS. This denomination was followed by the United Methodists. Methodists possessed about 987 churches in MS in 2017.[118]

Religion	Number Places	Percent	Cumulative
Southern Baptist	2132	47.7	47.7
United Methodist	987	22.1	69.9
Church of Christ	364	8.2	78.0
Missionary Baptist	300	6.7	84.7
Pentecostal	191	4.3	89.0
Presbyterian	121[119]	2.7	91.7
Catholic	98	2.2	93.9
Episcopalian	89	2.0	95.9
Seventh Day Adventist	80	1.8	97.7
Jehovah's Witness	42	0.9	98.6
Mormon	38	0.9	99.5
Islamic	12	0.3	99.8
Jewish	11[120]	0.2	100.0
Total	4465	100.0	

Almost 48% of the houses of worship in MS are generally Southern Baptist. Another 22% of the religious entities are Methodist. Those two denominations alone represent a whopping 70% of the religious houses of worship in the state of MS! Southern Baptist churches included both white Southern Baptist churches and Black Southern Baptist churches.

Racists believed that violence should be used to suppress Blacks and Jews. Segregationists felt that the legal system and governments were less violent and should be used for suppression. In the 1950s and 1960s, most racists who believed in violence to control Blacks and Jews were Southern Baptists. However, some Southern Baptists were segregationists. Most segregationists were attracted to the Methodist denomination, willing to use the legal system and governments to keep Blacks and Jews separate. However, some Methodists were racist. Segregation of Jews usually translated into keeping Jews out of local white only country clubs and participation in white only groups such as the Masons.

This difference in attitude by Southern Baptists and Southern Methodists towards Blacks and Jews developed for a number of reasons. Important differences between the two religions controlled the attitudes of congregants towards Blacks and Jews: the history of white supremacy and the Christian churches, core beliefs on salvation, organizational structure, and educational qualifications of clergy.

A History of White Supremacy

White supremacy actually began in Europe in the 1400s. This concept was the ideological driver of the European colonial projects and U.S. colonial projects. Superiority of whites was used to rationalize unjust rule of people and lands, theft of land and resources, enslavement, and genocide. In the United states, the principle of Manifest Destiny assumed that whites should rule over indigenous peoples.

In the interest of trade and location of raw materials, white Europeans explored the world. As part of these explorations, colonies controlled by whites were created in India, Africa, and the Americas. White Europeans maintained control over indigenous non-white natives.

Early European explorers easily and subconsciously exerted white supremacy over rustic natives. Every aspect of the existence and interaction between the explorers and the natives confirmed the supremacy of the white explorers. Natives were often dark skinned, undeveloped, and undernourished. Groups of natives were hunters and gatherers of fruits and vegetables that grew wild. Clothing was made from skin and plants such as vines. One day, something appeared on the horizon of the sea. Eventually, that something grew larger and anchored off the coast. This big unknown object disgorged a bunch of white people. These people used a small boat to come ashore.

Imagine that first meeting. Undernourished, poorly clothed, uneducated, dark skinned natives faced well nourished, well clothed and clad, somewhat educated, white skinned people. Given these differences in the two groups of people, the whites subconsciously felt far superior to the dark-skinned natives. Dark skinned natives subconsciously felt inferior. Inferiority came from the lack of education and the attitude of control exerted by the whites.

This subconscious superiority of the whites directed all aspects of the interactions with the dark-skinned natives. At best, the whites took control of the land. A colony was created. Whites began to develop the land. At worst, the whites imprisoned the dark-skinned natives. These imprisoned natives were treated as property, taken by the whites, and sold to other whites for farm labor.

Whites possessed technology that enabled enforcement of white superiority and control. That technology was the firearm. Around the late 14th century (1370s) in Italy, small, portable hand-cannons or *schioppi* were developed. These cannons were the first smoothbore personal "rifle". Rifles allowed a person to hurt or kill another person from a distance. By the middle 15th Century (1450s), rifles were common in Europe. European explorers carried rifles as new areas were subjugated by the white European explorers.[121]

White European explorers also used protective armor. Protective armor had been around since before the time of the Romans.

Rifles combined with protective armor made the white Europeans invincible relative to the dark-skinned natives. At the time, smoothbore rifles only had a range of 7 feet or so. When combined with protective armor, that range was sufficient for white European explorers to subjugate dark skinned races. A local native wearing a breech cloth of animal skin and holding a sharpened wooden spear faced a white European protected by armor and holding a rifle at 7 feet away. Superior whites always won the exchange.

Initial European exploration and colonization is known as the Age of Discovery. During the early Age of Discovery (ca. 1420-92), Portugal initiated the global naval era by exploring the coast of Africa in hopes of finding a way around Africa to India. Several Atlantic islands were colonized. African trading posts were established which fostered a booming trade with West Africa in gold, ivory, and slaves. Henry the

Navigator, a Portuguese prince, was the leading patron of these voyages[122] During the late Age of Discovery (ca. 1492-1520), Spain joined Portugal as a nation of global exploration and conquest. This period began with the arrival of Columbus in the Americas and concluded with the circumnavigation of the globe by the voyage of Ferdinand Magellan.[123]

Soon after Christopher Columbus landed in the New World (1492), Spain and Portugal signed the Treaty of Tordesillas. This treaty divided the world using a longitudinal line. Jurisdiction over exploration and colonization west of the line was given to Spain. Portugal had all jurisdiction over the east of the line. This jurisdiction by Portugal included the exclusive right to pursue trade routes around Africa.[124] A similar agreement, the Treaty of Saragossa, was later reached for a line dividing the other side of the world. As a result of these treaties, Spain and Portugal each claimed authority over half the planet.

These two treaties assumed that European whites were superior to all other non-white and indigenous peoples in the world.

After the American Revolution, the original 13 colonies began to expand westward from the eastern seaboard of the newly created US. At the time, westward movement was accomplished using a simple approach. White Americans moved into an area. Indigenous residents were forcefully ejected. White civilians were erected. These actions of forceful removal were disputed by some Americans at the time.

On August 1, 1837, William Channing wrote a letter to Henry Clay in the US Congress regarding the *Annexation of Texas to the US*. In this letter, Channing questioned the morality of this expansion by a white population. From his comments, Channing clearly was questioning the assumed superiority of whites over indigenous peoples.

Some crimes, by their magnitude, have a touch of the sublime; and to this dignity the seizure of Texas by our citizens is entitled. Modern times furnish no example of individual rapine on so grand a scale. It is nothing less than the robbery of a realm [p. 20] ... It is from a free, well-ordered, enlightened Christian country that hordes have gone forth in open day, to perpetrate this mighty wrong [p. 21]. Already it has been proclaimed, that the Anglo Saxon race is destined to the sway of this magnificent realm, [p. 25] by a like necessity, the Indians have melted before the white man, and the mixed, degraded race of Mexico must melt before the Anglo Saxon. Away with this vile sophistry. There is no necessity for crime. [p. 28][125]

In the proposed annexation of Texas, whites were assumed superior to Indians and to Mexicans. White superiority allows whites to mow down these indigenous peoples with impunity. This assumption and behavior should not stand.

A response to this criticism was published a few years later, specifically to promote the annexation and admission of Texas. John O'Sullivan was editor of *The United States Magazine and Democratic Review*, a publication that was an advocate for the Democratic Party. In the issue published in July/August, 1845, O'Sullivan wrote an article on the necessity of annexing of Texas. In this article, he discussed the inevitability of American expansion.

... other nations have undertaken to intrude themselves ... in a spirit of hostile interference against us, for the avowed object of thwarting our policy and hampering our power, limiting our greatness, checking the fulfillment of our manifest destiny to overspread the continent allotted by Providence for the free development of our yearly developing millions.[126]

Developing meant those citizens that were attempting to grow their economic future. At the time, the only developing millions were mostly white.

On December 27, 1845, O'Sullivan expanded on the idea of manifest destiny in an article in the *New York Morning News*.

... the right of our manifest destiny to over spread and to possess the whole of the continent which Providence has given us for the development of the great experiment of liberty and right of development of self government entrusted to us. It is right such as that of the tree to the space of air and the earth suitable for the full expansion of its principle and destiny of growth.[127]

Providence has given us had a specific meaning. Whites(*Us*) possessed a God given(*Providence*) right to expand and take over the remaining geographic area of the US. Whites were superior to all of the other indigenous races being displaced.

As the colonies expanded westward during 1800-1850, religious believers targeted settlers in those areas for proselytizing. At the beginning of the 1800s, both Baptists and Methodists were small groups. In order to mount a missionary program, each denomination had to evolve.

A <u>theological change</u> was made in how followers obtained salvation. <u>Specific methods</u> were developed that reached out to potential new believers to convert to the denomination. Disassociated churches combined in order to utilize shared resources. Each religion created <u>specific organizations</u> for conducting missionary programs. Religions showed relevance to current issues. As the early 1800s passed, slavery was the most important issue effecting the country. <u>Biblical support</u> was identified for both pro-slavery and abolitionist positions towards slavery.

Theological Shift In Salvation

In religion, salvation is the saving of the soul from evil acts and sin and its consequences.[128] Both Baptists and Methodists believed in salvation as the key to entering heaven after death despite any evils committed in life. Until the early 1800s, Baptists and Methodists believed that salvation came from God. A person prayed. God may or may not deliver salvation for whatever mysterious reason motivated God. This notion was based on the teachings of John Calvin. At the turn of the century, in the early 1800s, a new theological concept of salvation emerged. Humans could take actions that led to salvation by a living faith. Humans had the ability to obtain their own salvation through moral action. Baptists and Methodists differed in the manner in which a believer could obtain salvation.[129]

Conversion was necessary to obtain salvation. A potential penitent first had to face the terror of eternal damnation from his own sinful actions. Experiencing deep fear over the prospect of eternal damnation led to the conclusion that the penitent was justly condemned for his/her sins and deserved eternal damnation. Repentance and unconditional surrender to God and to Christ lead to conversion.[130]

Specific Methods of Conversion

As the nation grew, frontier communities were formed. These communities did not have church buildings yet. A method was developed that enabled the churches to bring the conversion experience to those frontier communities.

During the Second Great Awakening, revivals were used by religions to proselytize on the actual frontier. Itinerant ministers traveled to actual camp locations on the frontier, conducting camp meetings.[131]

Camp meetings used different techniques for soliciting spiritual conversion. Ministers preached for multiple days at a camp meeting. Emotional exhortations were used. Sermons focused on the torments of hell, fire and brimstone, faced by those without salvation. Brimstone was an archaic term for sulfur.[132] Lightning strikes give off an acrid odor. Lightning was understood as divine punishment. Participants became so emotionally involved that physical collapse resulted. People were convinced they were experiencing a visitation of the Holy Spirit.[133]

Hearing a fire and brimstone sermon was like going to a horror movie today. At the heart of this sermon was the use of fear and emotion. Delivery techniques include Bible beating, loud yelling, and physical antics such as jumping up and down. These techniques worked very well with the poor and the uneducated frontier settlers. Basically, preachers "scared the hell" out of the settlers. Fear of eternal damnation in Hell was the equivalent of watching the Exorcist in 1973.

Scary Biblical descriptions of Hell existed throughout both the Old Testament and the New Testament.[134]

Old Testament descriptions include:
• Everlasting burning *(Isaiah 33:14)*
• A devouring fire *(Isaiah 33:14)*

New Testament descriptions include:
• A lake of fire *(Revelation 20:15)*
• A bottomless pit *(Revelation 20:1)*
• A furnace of fire *(Matthew 13:41,42)*

- A place of torment *(Luke 16:23)*
- A place of filthiness *(Revelation 22:11)*
- A place where they can never repent *(Matthew 12:32)*
- A place of everlasting punishment *(Matthew 25:46)*
- A place they do not want their loved ones to go to *(Luke 16:28)*
- A place of murderers and liars *(Revelation 21:8)*

One of the first fire and brimstone sermons was delivered on July 8, 1741, by Jonathan Edwards of the Church of Christ in Northampton.[135] This sermon clearly describes Hell and applies pressure to convert.

According to the New Testament, anyone who is not converted is condemned to eternal Hell.

"He that believeth not is condemned already" [New, John, 3.18] So that every unconverted Man properly belongs to Hell. [page 6] ...

Hell is full of fire and brimstone waiting to consume those not immediately converted. Only the tolerance of God stands between a person and eternal Hell.

... the Pit is prepared, the Fire is made ready, the Furnace is now hot, ready to receive them, the Flames do rage and glow ... the Pit hath opened her Mouth under them [page 7] ... the Devil is waiting for them, Hell is for them, the Flames gather and flash about them, and would fain lay hold on them, and swallow them up... That World of Misery, that Lake of burning Brimstone is extended abroad under you. There is the dreadful Pit of the glowing Flames of the Wrath of God; there is Hell's wide gaping Mouth open; and you have nothing to stand upon, not any Thing to take hold of: there is nothing between you and Hell but the Air; 'tis only the Power and mere Pleasure of God that holds you up [page 12] ...

Hell is waiting for if a person does not convert. God can drop a person into Hell at anytime.

O Sinner! Consider the fearful Danger you are in: 'Tis a great Furnace of Wrath, a wide and bottomless Pit, full of the Fire of Wrath, that you are held over in the Hand of that God, whose Wrath is provoked and incensed as much against you as against many of the Damned in Hell: You hang by a slender Thread, with the Flames of divine Wrath flashing about it, and ready every Moment to singe it, and burn it asunder; and you have no Interest in any Mediator, and nothing to lay hold of to save yourself, nothing to keep off the Flames of Wrath, nothing of your own, nothing that you ever have done, nothing that you can do, to induce God to spare you one Moment. [page 16] ...

Time is of the essence. A limited window of opportunity is available to convert.

But this is the dismal Case of every Soul in this Congregation, that has not been born again, however moral and strict, sober and religious they may otherwise be. [page 22] ... And now you have an extraordinary Opportunity, a Day wherein Christ has flung the Door of Mercy wide open, and stands in the Door calling and crying with a loud Voice to poor Sinners [page 23] ...

If conversion is today, right now, the conversion will hold.

God seems now to be hastily gathering in his Elect in all Parts of the Land; and probably the bigger Part of adult Persons that ever shall be saved, will be brought in now in a little Time, ... the Election will obtain, and the rest will be blinded. [page 25]

Reading all of this exhortation seems really mild by the standards of today. However, imagine the impact of a highly emotional delivery on a person who is poor, uneducated, and actually believes in witchcraft, magic, and higher beings. An injection of adrenaline into the body results. Image the first time a person saw The Exorcist in 1973.

Organizations for Missionary Activities

At the beginning of the 1800s, the Baptists were a small group. On May 18, 1814, separate Baptist groups across the US combined to form the General Missionary Convention of the Baptist Denomination in the United States of America for Foreign Missions.[136] This Convention met every 3 years and became known as the Triennial Convention. Its primary objective was to combine resources and coordinate activities in support of Baptist missionary activities.[137] One of the major issues that this group had to resolve was the Baptist outlook on slavery.

In 1792, Methodist churches across the US began conducting a General Conference every 4 years.[138] From its earliest days, Methodists debated the issue of slavery. At issue was the relationship the church should have to the peculiar institution in a country where slavery was legal, and in some parts of the country, widely supported. Methodist conferences even before the first General Conference spoke out against slavery. Conferences suggested that clergy who held slaves should promise to set them free. Several General Conferences struggled with the issue. Traveling elders were pressed to emancipate their slaves. Eventually, pressure to emancipate was withdrawn in states where the laws did not permit manumission. By 1808, the General Conference threw up its hands, finding the subject unmanageable Each Annual Conference was given the right to enact its own rules relative to slaveholding.[139]

Biblical Support For Slavery

By the period 1800-1850 in the US, slavery was growing throughout the South. States in the south were generally agrarian economies, based on farming, lumber gathering, and sawmilling. White supremacy was at the heart of these economies. White owners used Black slaves as a low-cost form of labor. States in the north were generally industrial economies. Northerners generally abhorred slavery.

Religious adherents in the South believed in slavery. Religions are based on documents, such as the Bible. The Bible is interpreted through the lens of human eyes. A human interpreting the Bible picks and chooses what he wants to justify based on a predisposed attitude. Religious interpretations of the Bible that supported slavery needed to be made in order to evangelize farmers and workers in the South.

On December 24, 1822,[140] Richard Furman, the first President of the Baptist Triennial Convention,[141] wrote an *Exposition of the Views of the Baptists Relative to the Coloured[sic] Population* to the Governor of South Carolina. In this exposition, Furman precisely expressed the Biblical support for white enslavement of Blacks.[142]

> ... *for the right of holding slaves is clearly established by the Holy Scriptures, both by precept and example. In the Old Testament, ... it is declared, that the persons*

*purchased were to be their "bond-men forever;" and an "inheritance for them and their children." ... *[See Leviticus XXV. 44, 45, 46, &c.]* [P6]

In the New-Testament, the Gospel History, or representation of facts, presents us a view... The powerful Romans had succeeded, in empire, the polished Greeks; and under both empires, the countries they possessed and governed were full of slaves ... In things purely spiritual, they appear to have enjoyed equal privileges; but their relationship, as masters and slaves, was not dissolved. ... The masters are not required to emancipate their slaves; ... [P. 7]

Had the holding of slaves been a moral evil, it cannot be supposed, that the inspired Apostles, who feared not the faces of men, and were ready to lay down their lives in the cause of their God, would have tolerated it, for a moment, in the Christian Church. [P. 8]

Both the Old Testament and the New Testament supported slavery.

Abolitionist arguments had also been published by prominent Baptist ministers. On August 27, 1807,[143] David Barrow, Pastor of the First Baptist Church in Mount Sterling, KY,[144] had published a pamphlet on *Slavery Examined on the Principles of Nature, Reason, Justice, Policy, and Scripture.*

it is not merited bondage, servitude or slavery or that which is voluntary or that that which may be for a term of time ... but it is unmerited, involuntary, perpetual, absolute hereditary bondage, servitude or slavery that I object to ... [page 28]

He that stealeth a man, and sellith him, or if he be found in his hand, he shall surely be put to death. [Exodus, xxi: 16]. And the Apostle Paul, ranks "men stealers," with and among the most atrocious culprits [1 Tim. i: 9, 10] [page 33].

And our Savior, comprehends the whole of the moral law, under two heads, namely -- "Thou shalt love the Lord thy God with all they heart," "and they neighbor as thyself". [page 43].

Barrow also felt that slavery was inconsistent with the principles upon which the United States was founded.

The United States of America have declared unanimously in favour of the Rights of Man ... And what a pity it is, that we have virtue enough in general, to give those principles their full scope. The friends of slavery, plead their right of enslaving the Africans from the sacred scriptures; but it appears to me that George the third, can support the doctrine of kingly government, and his right over America as a king, on much better scripture ground, than they can support unmerited &c. slavery. [page 48].

This important difference in opinion among Baptists was not resolved. On May 8, 1845, about 293 Baptist leaders of the South gathered at the First Baptist Church, in Augusta, Georgia, representing over 365,000 Baptists. A new organization, called the Southern Baptist Convention, was created on May 10, 1845. Representatives wanted to retain final authority with local churches rather than take direction from a central authority. An association form of organization was adopted. This Convention adopted the position that slavery was justified in the Bible.[145]

Surprisingly, Southern Baptist churches in the south were integrated from the beginning. However, this form of integration was a method of control over Blacks, based on the principal of white superiority. A Black person was only admitted under two conditions. The person was a slave. The owner attended. Blacks sat in balconies specifically allocated to Blacks. Blacks and whites were admitted together, gave oral evidence of their conversion together, baptized together, and dismissed together. But Blacks did not vote on church matters.[page 297] Blacks did not criticize whites. Slavery was not mentioned in the sermons.[page 298].[146]

In these Baptist churches, Blacks were under control of the superior white race at all times. All control activities, such as voting on church matters and criticizing of whites, were reserved strictly to whites. White superiority was the underlying principle of governance.

These integrated situations in the Baptist Church tended to be in larger cities only. In rural areas, such as Philadelphia, MS, Blacks did not have churches available during the ante-bellum days before the Civil War.

Methodists had a different approach to slavery from the beginning. John Wesley, the founder of the Methodist denomination, publicly denounced slavery. In 1774, Wesley wrote and published the pamphlet *Thoughts Upon Slavery.*[147]

I strike at the root of this complicated villainy. I absolutely deny all slave-holding to be consistent with any degree of even natural justice. [page 34] ... *I strike at the root of this complicated villainy.* [page 35] ... *I deny that villainy is ever necessary. It is impossible that it should ever be necessary, for any reasonable creature to violate all the laws of justice, mercy and truth. No circumstances can make it necessary for a man to burst in sunder all the ties of humanity. It can never be necessary for a rational being to sink himself below a brute. A man can be under no necessity, of degrading himself into a wolf. The absurdity of the supposition is so glaring, that one would wonder any one can help seeing it.* [page 38] ... *Freedom is unquestionably the birth right of all mankind; Africans as well as Europeans: to keep the former in a state of slavery, is a constant violation of that right, and therefore also of justice.* [page 79].

On February 24, 1791, six days before his death, Wesley wrote his last letter to William Wilberforce. Wilberforce was a member of the British Parliament and a leader of the movement to abolish the slave trade.[148]

Go on, in the name of God and in the power of his might, till even American slavery (the vilest that ever saw the sun) shall vanish away before it.[149]

Methodist churches initially began to grow in the north-eastern and mid-western part of the US. These Methodist churches were integrated. Whites and Blacks attended services together. Slaves and free Blacks were especially attached to the condemnation of slavery. Generally, these churches were against slavery and conducted integrated services with Blacks and Whites. As the nation grew across the South, Methodist churches were developed that supported slavery and for that reason conducted mostly white only services.

Northern churches allowed Blacks and whites to attend the same services. However, races were segregated inside the church. As the number of Black members increased, Blacks were made to sit in a separate gallery built in the church. Groups of these Blacks began to splinter into their own Black only, Methodist churches. On April 9, 1816, these Black churches formed the African Methodist Episcopal Church in Philadelphia, PA.[150]

Blacks initiated the segregation. Whites tolerated the segregation. Black Methodist churches had their own religious leaders. Black church members voted on matters relative to church governance. Whites did not have any influence or control over these Black churches. In essence, Methodists enabled the "separate but equal" method of Black segregation.

At the Methodist General Conference beginning on May 1, 1844, the difference in attitudes on slavery was the main topic of debate. James Osgood Andrew, a Bishop and high-ranking Methodist, inherited slaves. After extensive negotiations, the Conference voted to suspend Andrew from exercising his office until he freed his slaves. Differences between Methodist Churches in the South and the North about slavery could not be resolved.[151]

Immediately after the General Conference, members of the Methodist church in Raleigh Station, NC, sent a resolution to the North Carolina delegates. *We believe an immediate division of the Methodist Episcopal Church is indispensable to the peace, prosperity, and honor of the Southern portion thereof, if not essential to her continued existence...we regard the officious, and unwarranted interference of the Northern portion of the Church with the subject of slavery alone, a sufficient cause for a division of our Church.*[152] On May 1, 1845, Methodist churches in the South formed the Methodist Episcopal Church, South.[153]

Prior to the Civil War, Southern Baptist churches were integrated Black and white churches strictly governed based on white supremacy. During that time, a number of "separate but equal" Black Methodist churches were operating in the South in Maryland, Kentucky Missouri, Louisiana, and South Carolina.[154]

Post Civil War Evolution of Denominations

After the Civil War, significant changes occurred in religious participation in the South and in MS.

Blacks deserted the Southern Baptist Church in large numbers. By 1890, churches in the Southern Baptist Convention were 100% white.[155]

Black Baptists simply formed their own denominations: the Baptist Foreign Mission Convention(1880), the American National Baptist Convention (1886), and the National Baptist Education Convention (1893). On September 24, 1895, at the Friendship Baptist Church in Atlanta, the three groups combined into the National Baptist Convention of the USA.[156] Initially, this Convention had 3 Boards: foreign missions, home missions, and education. Each of the founding Conventions became one of the Boards of the new Convention.

Slavery was transitioned into white superiority by the Southern Baptist Convention and the Methodist Annual Conference. Features of the Southern Baptist religion determined by the SBC enabled local white preachers to channel white superiority into white supremacy, racism, and Jim Crow. Features of the Methodist religion strengthened denominational support for white supremacy through an organization structure supporting "separate but equal" segregation.

After the Civil War, the Southern Baptist Convention had a real dilemma. In the Southern Baptist religion, Biblical inerrancy, was a key principle: scripture is truth, without any mixture of error. The Southern Baptist Convention now faced a theological crisis. Biblical authority was used to justify the practice of slavery. Slavery was now both illegal and immoral. Implicit in the concept of slavery is belief that one race is superior to another race.

The Southern Baptist Conference supported white Supremacy through its mission, its publications, and an education system of organized colleges. All of these activities informed Baptists how to be and act like Baptists in the South. White supremacy enforced by violence was the key concept.

Increasingly, preachers in the Southern Baptist Conference adopted revival-based evangelism. Fear worked well on the poor and uneducated people in the South. Self ordained preachers delivered fire and brimstone sermons that enforced the belief that poor whites were superior to Blacks. Superiority of poor whites over Blacks was appealing to the poor whites. In 1859, the Southern Baptist Theological Seminary was founded by the Southern Baptist Convention. John Broadus, one of its more practical faculty members, published *The Preparation and Delivery of Sermons* in 1870.[157] With the publication of this document, the Seminary established its role as the intellectual and theological foundation of the Convention. Writings that originated from the Seminary were disseminated throughout the churches in the Convention. Newsletters and sermons in churches regularly featured statements from and philosophies expressed in the writings published by the Seminary faculty.

Publication and sermons by the Seminary faculty were contradictory. Seminary leaders regarded blacks as equal in human nature and dignity. God created all humanity from one person. Pastors were exhorted to save the eternal souls of Blacks and whites. Despite this spiritual equality, Seminary faculty asserted white superiority and defended racial inequality. Belief in white supremacy that undergirded slavery also undergirded new forms of racial oppression.[158]

The seminary's founding faculty all held slaves ... and defended the righteousness of slaveholding ... After emancipation, the seminary faculty opposed racial equality ... In the Reconstruction era, the faculty supported the restoration of white rule in the South ... Before the 1940s, the seminary faculty generally approved the Lost Cause mythology ... In the nineteenth and early twentieth centuries, the seminary faculty appealed to science to support their belief in white superiority.[159]

During the period 1850-1900, most whites in the South envisioned a social order in which Blacks were inferior. Blacks should be driven away. Those Blacks that remained should be limited in economic opportunity, serving as laborers or servants. Whites generally opposed the education of Blacks.[160]

Blacks began the Reconstruction area in charge in most states in the South. Republican rule was upheld by the large voting population of freed slaves, and federal and state office holders included many blacks. Tensions between Blacks and whites were high. Seminary faculty members believed and promoted political control by whites was necessary to resolve racial tensions. Whites used terror and disenfranchisement to revert governmental control back to whites.[161]

In 1866, Edward Pollard, an author and Editor of the Richmond Examiner, published *The Lost Cause: A New Southern History of the War of the Confederates*.[162]

This Lost Cause myth asserted that Southerners did not fight for slavery or independence. The South went to war for the sake of honor and for the principle of sacred state rights over federal tyranny. Southerners had full knowledge that the North would prevail in a contest of arms with the South. Hence, the Civil War was a lost cause from the start.

God intended the South's sufferings to perfect the nation. One form of suffering was the vast grief from lost sons, husbands, and fathers. Another form of suffering was the shattering economic privation of the loss of investment in slaves and destruction to property. Suffering the grief from the corrupt and despotic rule of Radical Republican carpetbaggers and freedmen was the final source. Purified by suffering, Southern whites emerged from this crucible to re-establish white rule based on the superiority of the white race.[163]

Plantation life of the ante-bellum South was the ideal environment for Blacks.

The Legend of the Lost Cause began as mostly a literary expression of the despair of a bitter, defeated people over a lost identity. It was a landscape dotted with figures drawn mainly out of the past: the chivalric planter; the magnolia-scented Southern belle; the good, gray Confederate veteran, once a knight of the field and saddle; and obliging old Uncle Remus. All these, while quickly enveloped in a golden haze, became very real to the people of the South, who found the symbols useful in the reconstituting of their shattered civilization. They perpetuated the ideals of the Old South and brought a sense of comfort to the New.[164]

Embedded in this golden view of the antebellum South was a blatant assumption of White Supremacy. Blacks generally lacked the capacity for learning, literature, and self-governance. Whites must regain control.

In its conclusion, The Lost Cause clearly identified that white supremacy should be maintained in the South after the Civil War.

She [the South] must submit fairly and truthfully to "what the war has properly decided". But the war properly decided only what was put in issue: the restoration of the Union and the exclusion of slavery; ... But the war did not decide negro [sic] equality; it did not decide negro [sic] suffrage; it did not decide State Rights, ... And these things which the war did not decide, the Southern people will still cling to, still claim, and still assert in them their rights and views.[165]

The Lost Cause myth gained acceptance in the North and South. Companion ideals, such as support for white supremacy, gained cultural authority based on that acceptance.

Elections starting in 1876 in South Carolina began the trend of returning control of state governments to whites. Edwin Dargan, a faculty member at the Seminary, commented on the harassment and intimidation techniques used against Blacks by whites in the election.

The methods of obtaining and keeping this ascendancy have been partly unobjectionable, but not wholly so. No doubt more people have practiced both fraud and intimidation upon ignorant voters. The better elements of society have not done the dirty work, but they have enjoyed the fruits of it, and have connived at it as a sad choice of evils.[166]

This publication provided Southern Baptists a theological excuse for congregants to exercise violence to suppress Blacks in the South. Local pastors surely read and heard about this position by the respected Seminary faculty.

A Baptist minister took the next step that led to Southern Baptist support for racist violence. Thomas Dixon was born in Shelby, North Carolina, the son of Thomas Jeremiah Frederick Dixon II and Amanda Elvira McAfee, daughter of a planter and slave-owner from York County, South Carolina. He was one of eight children, of whom five survived to adulthood.[167]

Dixon was ordained as a Baptist minister on October 6, 1886. He initially served as a Parson at two churches in NC.[168] Eventually, Dixon became pastor of the Twenty-third Street Baptist Church in New York City His audiences soon outgrew the church. Dixon was forced to hold services in a neighboring YMCA until a new People's Temple could be built.[169] Thousands were turned away.[170]

In 1895, Dixon resigned his position. *For reaching of the non-church-going masses, I am convinced that the machinery of a strict Baptist church is a hindrance. I wish for a perfectly free pulpit.*[171] Thomas Dixon became a lecturer and a novelist. Dixon wrote The Klan Trilogy, 3 books that became the heart and soul of racism in the Southern Baptist church and modern America.

The Clansman (1905) presents the true story of the 'Ku Klux Klan Conspiracy,' which overturned the Reconstruction regime. This book displays Dixon's faith in the enduring spirit of the South in the face of economic and social hardship. *The Leopard's Spots* (1902) offers a historical outline of the conditions from the enfranchisement of the Negro to his disfranchisement. *The Traitor* (1907) transpires amid the Klan's decline. In addition to dramatizing the woeful story of life in the Reconstruction South, Dixon offers energetic testimony to the gallant, courageous, and transformative spirit of the South and its people.[172]

In his novel, *The Leopard's Spots*, Thomas Dixon promoted two concepts regarding subordination of Blacks in the South: white supremacy and suppression using violent vigilantes.[173]

Rev John Durham, pastor of the fictional Baptist church, explains the concept of white supremacy to Col Charles Gaston, Democratic candidate for Governor.

"My boy, the future American must be an Anglo-Saxon or a Mulatto! We are now deciding which it shall be. The future of the world depends on the future of this Republic. This Republic can have no future if racial lines are broken, and its proud citizenship sinks to the level of a mongrel breed of Mulattoes. The South must fight this battle to a finish. Two thousand years look down upon the struggle, and two thousand years of the future bend low to catch the message of life or death!"

He could see now his drawn face with its deep lines and his eyes flashing with passion as he said this. These words haunted Gaston now with strange power as he walked along the silent streets. [page 198]

A Baptist minister was explaining the concept of white supremacy.

Rev Durham also endorsed the use of violence to suppress Black voters.

Major Stuart Dameron, the chief of the Klan in Campbell county, [page 152] *was attending a service being conducted by the Rev. John Durham.*

Two days before the election, the prayer meeting was held at eight o'clock in the Baptist church at Hambright. It was the usual mid-week service, but the attendance was unusually large.

After the meeting, the Preacher, Major Dameron, and eleven men quietly walked back to the church and assembled in the pastor's study.

"Gentlemen," said Major Dameron, "I've asked you here to-night to deliver to you the most important order I have ever given, and to have Dr. Durham as our chaplain to aid me in impressing on you its great urgency."

"We're ready for orders, Chief," said young Ambrose Kline, the deacon's son.

"You are to call out every troop of the Klan in full force the night before the election. You are to visit every negro in the county, and warn every one as he values his life not to approach the polls at this election. Those who come, will be allowed to vote without molestation. All cowards will stay at home. Any man, black or white, who can be scared out of his ballot is not fit to have one. Back of every ballot is the red blood of the man that votes. The ballot is force. This is simply a test of manhood. It will be enough to show who is fit to rule the state. As the masters of the eleven township lodges of the Klan, you are the sole guardians of society to-day. When a civilized government has been restored, your work will be done."

"We will do it, sir," cried Kline. [page 160]

"Let me say, men," said the Preacher, "that I heartily endorse the plan of your chief. See that the work is done thoroughly, and it will be done for all time ... "You are asked to violate for the moment a statutory law. There is a higher law. You are the sworn officers of that higher law." [page 161]

The group of leaders left the church with enthusiasm and on the following night they carried out their instructions to the letter. The election was remarkably quiet. Thousands of soldiers were used at the polls by Hogg's orders. But they seemed to make no impression on the determined men who marched up between their files and put the ballots in the box. [page 161]

A Baptist preacher was endorsing the use of violent vigilantes to suppress Blacks from exercising their rights to vote.

Colonel Charles Gaston wanted to be Governor of the fictional state. Gaston gave a speech about the party platform at the Democratic Convention explaining white supremacy. He echoed the words conveyed to him by Rev Durham.

When Gaston rose to offer and defend his minority report, a sudden hush fell on the sea of eager faces. A few men in the convention had heard him speak. All had heard he was an orator of power, and were anxious to see him ...

"Mr. Chairman and Gentlemen of the Convention:" he began with a deliberate clear voice which spoke of greater reserve power than the words he uttered conveyed--*"I move to substitute for this document of meaningless platitudes the following resolution on which to make this campaign."* [page 433]

You could have heard a pin fall, as in ringing tones like the call of a bugle to battle he read, "Whereas, it is impossible to build a state inside a state of two antagonistic races, And whereas, the future North Carolinian must therefore be an Anglo-Saxon or a Mulatto, Resolved, that the hour has now come in our history to eliminate the Negro from our life and re-establish for all time the government of our fathers." [page 434]

"We grant the Negro the right to life, liberty and the pursuit of happiness if he can be happy without exercising kingship over the Anglo-Saxon race, or dragging us down to his level. But if he cannot find happiness except in lording it over a superior race, let him look for another world in which to rule. There is not room for both of us on this continent!" [page 438-439]

"This is a white man's government, conceived by white men, and maintained by white men through every year of its history, -- and by the God of our Fathers it shall be ruled by white men until the Arch-angel shall call the end of time! [page 442]

Government leaders took their cues from leading Baptist preachers.

The Baptist Argus, a privately published newspaper in Louisville, KY, published information on the activities of the Baptist church. Its masthead motto was *Watch and Pray*. This newspaper covered missionary appointments, changes in pastoral guidance at the local level, and major actions of the statewide conferences. Since the Southern Baptist Theological Seminary had moved to Louisville in 1877, this newspaper was likely to have all the real inside scoop on activities. Due to the physical proximity of the Seminary, theological positions offered by faculty at the Seminary were regularly published.[174] Any theological article published by a faculty member of the Seminary became part of the Baptist gospel for local preachers.

Professor Archibald Robertson was one of the most accomplished and influential scholars at the Baptist Theological Seminary. On April 10, 1902, Robertson authored a review of *The Leopard's Spots* in *The Baptist Argus* entitled "The Problem of the Negro".[175] This review of *The Leopard's Spots* became the formal theological blessing of the principles expounded by Thomas Dixon.

There is so much to commend that criticism is largely drowned. Every thoughtful American citizen ought to read this book ... He makes a trumpet call to the Anglo-Saxon race to maintain the supremacy now regained in the South. This book is brilliant and powerful, realistic and tragic, inspirational and sorrowful. The dominance of the white race now seems certain in the South, but the cloud still rests of the fate of the Negro ... we must do our duty by the Negro, Christianize and civilize him, and save him from going down the vortex if we can. We will do more by looking at facts, and Mr. Dixon's book will make us all do that.

Robertson could not find anything substantive to criticize.[176] White supremacy was a foregone conclusion. Superior whites had an obligation to civilize Blacks. Robertson referred to a trumpet call. This trumpet call was the use of violent vigilantes to civilize Blacks.

A nationally respected faculty member of the Seminary publicly blessed white supremacy and violence by vigilantes to suppress Blacks in the South. Self-proclaimed, poorly educated white Baptist preachers in the South incorporated these topics into their sermons at churches and at revivals.

These books by Dixon were huge bestsellers. Dixon licensed *The Clansman* to D W Griffith for $10,000 ($254,661 in 2019)[177] and then 25% interest in the picture.[178] On January 1st and 2nd, 1915, the silent film called *The Clansman* premiered at the Loring Opera House in Riverside, CA. During the first days of February, 1915, Dixon suggested that the name be changed to *Birth of A Nation*.[179]

On Wednesday, March 3, 1915, *The Clansman* opened at the Liberty Theater in NYC. This 12-reel, 3-hour long film[180] was shown in 2 acts. A short intermission took place between the 2 acts. During the intermission, Thomas Dixon himself spoke to the audience. *I would have allowed none but the son of a Confederate soldier to direct the film version of "The Clansman."*[181] This film was directed by D. W. Griffith. Griffith was born on a farm in Oldham County, Kentucky, the son of Jacob Wark "Roaring Jake" Griffith, a Confederate Army Colonel in the Civil War who was later elected as a Kentucky state legislator.[182]

Thomas Dixon became rich due to the unprecedented success of the film. Dixon's proceeds were the largest sum any author had received [up to 2007] for a motion picture story and amounted to several million dollars.[183] ($3,000,000 in 1915 equals $76,398,415)[184]

In those days, racism and vigilante violence sold all over the nation, especially in the South. After the movie was successfully played throughout the US, the rebirth of the Ku Klux Klan occurred. On Thanksgiving Eve 1915, William Joseph Simmons took 15 friends to the top of Stone Mountain, near Atlanta. Simmons built an altar on which he placed an American flag, a Bible and an unsheathed sword. Simmons also set fire to a crude wooden cross. He muttered a few incantations about a "practical fraternity among men". William Simmons then declared himself Imperial Wizard of the Invisible Empire of the Knights of the Ku Klux Klan.[185]

The modern Ku Klux Klan was reborn thanks in large part to the film. Klan activities flourished nationwide in the 1920's through the 1940's. Klaverns sprang up in urban areas of the Midwest and West and especially throughout the South.

Simmons presented a ministerial public persona. However, in private, he was described as a foulmouthed racist, decrying "N-*****, Catholics, and Jews."[186]

The initial corporate charter from the state of Georgia was dated December 4, 1915.[187] Simmons developed a secret book of oaths and rituals, known as the Kloran. This book was supposed to be kept secret. But Simmons registered this book for a copyright with the Library of Congress in 1917.

Southern Methodists further incorporated the "separate but equal" segregation into the organizational DNA of the denomination in 1939.

In the US, the United Methodist Church is hierarchically organized into Conferences. The Annual Conference is the primary unit of denominational government. Each Annual Conference generally includes the churches in a geographical area, such as a state, and is under the management of a Bishop.[188] Mississippi has an Annual Conference.[189]

Annual conferences within a region are members of a Jurisdictional Conference. A total of 15 Annual Conferences are in the Southeastern Jurisdictional Conference. The Mississippi Annual Conference is a member of the Southeastern Jurisdictional Conference.[190]

Every four years, the United Methodist Church conducts a General Conference. This Conference sets the rules and establishes procedures for virtually every aspect of the life of the Church.[191] Each Annual Conference selects a number of delegates to attend the General Conference. Number of delegates representing an Annual Conference is determined by a formula. This formula depends upon the number of clergy members and the number of local church members in the Annual Conference.[192]

Only the General Conference can speak for the Church.[193] All approved legislation becomes part of the *Book of Resolutions* used to govern the Methodist Church.[194] Over the years, General Conferences had addressed a number of social issues, such as slavery, female clergy, education, and Global Health.[195]

Previously, on April 9, 1816, Black Methodist churches had formed the African Methodist Episcopal Church in Philadelphia, PA.[196] This denomination would never be incorporated back into the United Methodist Church.

In 1939, the jurisdictional organization did not exist. Three Methodist denominations did exist: the Methodist Episcopal Church, the Methodist Episcopal Church, South, and the Methodist Protestant Church. A large number of Black churches existed in the Methodist Episcopal Church. A *Uniting Conference* was held in Kansas City, MO, during the period April 26, 1939 - May 10, 1939.[197]

One of the major obstacles to unification was raised by white ministers from the Methodist Episcopal Church, South. Delegates from these all white churches opposed the possible appointment of Black bishops in their own Annual Conferences. For instance, a large number of Black ministers and Black congregants could end up electing a Black bishop as head of the MS Annual Conference. In order for the Uniting Conference to succeed, an organizational structure was needed that would prevent this situation.

On May 8, 1939, the Uniting Conference adopted Report Number 8.[198] This report created the Jurisdictional Conferences. Section II of this Report identified the Jurisdictional Boundaries. A Southeastern Jurisdiction included the state of MS. A Central Jurisdiction was defined in this Section.

Central: The Negro [sic] Annual Conferences, the Negro [sic] Mission Conferences and Missions in the United States of America.[199]

This Jurisdiction consisted of all the Black Methodist Churches in the US at the time of creation of the Central Jurisdiction. All other Jurisdictions were defined strictly by geographic boundaries. This Jurisdiction was defined strictly to race: Negro [sic]. "Separate but equal" segregation was now officially integrated into the organizational DNA of the Methodist Church.

Adding insult to injury, Report Number 9 was also adopted by the Uniting Conference on May 10, 1939.[200] This Report identified Central Conferences *in territory outside the United States of America.*[201] The Central Jurisdiction was acknowledged as part of territory outside the US. Black Methodist Churches were separate outside the white church Jurisdiction boundaries. This section went further and defined the authority of the Central Jurisdiction and the Central Conferences to define their own bishops and ministers. Now, the Central Jurisdiction was equal with all of the other church Jurisdictions.

When the Uniting Conference adopted Report Numbers 8 and 9, "separate but equal" segregation was incorporated into the organizational structure of the Methodist Church. From this point forward, "separate but equal" segregation became the official position of the Methodist

Church. Methodist ministers in the South would deliver sermons supporting "separate but equal" segregation without fear of discipline from the governing hierarchy.

Black members were less than 5% of the Methodist Church in 1939. Due to this small percentage, opposition to creation of the Central Jurisdiction by Black Methodists failed to block merger of the northern and southern halves of the Church. Black Methodist churches remained within the Church. These churches had invested a great deal in the Church. Staying in the Church enabled these Black Churches to support the mission of being a witness against racism and injustice.[202]

In 1954, the US Supreme Court issued the decision in Brown vs. Board of Education. This decision called for the integration of public schools *with all deliberate speed*.[203] Brown raised the possibility that the government might integrate secular society faster than churches desegregated their own structures. Equal access to schools might come before access to Methodist churches. Methodists and Methodist leaders felt pressure to desegregate.[204] Desegregation required dismantling the Central Jurisdiction.

Numerous attempts were made within the Methodist Church to dismantle the Central Jurisdiction. A first attempt was to allow churches to voluntarily transfer from the Central Jurisdiction to a jurisdiction in the same geographical area. Voluntarism as a strategy for integration grew out of two myths.

The "Great Myth," suggested that African Americans were generally treated well, that communication across racial lines was clear, and that existing institutions could resolve any racial disputes. The second, or "Southern," myth was prevalent in the most conservative circles. It asserted that segregation was Christian and even natural and that changes in race relations might occur with negotiations between the existing white power structure and moderate Black leaders, but not through outside coercion.[205]

Voluntarism was created at the 1956 General Conference in Minneapolis, MN. In the morning session, on Wednesday, May 2, 1956, the General Convention approved Amendment 9 to the Methodist Constitution.[206]

This amendment governed transfer of a Church between two Annual Conferences and an Annual Conference between two Jurisdictions.

Members of the church had to cast a 2/3 majority for transfer. Then, members of the leaving Annual Conference had to cast a 2/3 majority for transfer, Finally, members of the receiving Annual Conference. had to cast a 2/3 majority to approve the transfer.[207] A similar process was created for an Annual Conference to transfer between Jurisdictions. Annual Conference, leaving Jurisdiction and receiving Jurisdiction had to each approve the transfer by a 2/3 majority. Jurisdictional voting was accomplished at the individual Annual Conferences, not at the Jurisdictional Conference.[208]

Once all of the Annual Conferences in the Central Jurisdiction were transferred by this process, the Central Jurisdiction was dissolved.[209] Just like the US Constitution, Amendment 9 had to be ratified. According to the Methodist Constitution at the time, a 2/3 majority of all of the Annual Conferences had to approve. Each member Annual Conference had to cast a 2/3 majority for approval by that individual Conference. After the votes were counted, 137 of 139 Annual Conferences approved. Affirmative votes by delegates across all the Conferences numbered 21,142. Total negative votes were 1,623. Only the AL-West FL Conference and the North MS Conference failed to pass Amendment 9.[210]

This amendment accomplished very little towards desegregation of the Methodist churches. A Black Methodist Church needed 2/3 majority approval of the receiving white dominated Annual Conference to transfer. A Black Methodist Annual Conference needed 2/3 majority of the approval of the receiving white dominated Jurisdiction to transfer. Not surprisingly, this transfer process did not really happen very often in the south and the Southeast. A target date for transfer was not stated. While supportive of voluntarism, Methodist leaders wanted to wait and see if voluntarism would result in desegregation.

Voluntarism failed to achieve desegregation of the Methodist Church. A Commission of Seventy was appointed to study the problem of desegregation. This Committee reported to the 1960 General Conference on Jan 6, 1960. While making some recommendations, this Committee recommended continued reliance on voluntarism. A proposed amendment to set a target date for elimination and merger of the Central Jurisdiction was rejected by the General Conference.[211]

Extensive efforts were conducted by the Methodist Church in the 1960s to eliminate segregation in the Methodist Church. The Central Jurisdiction and segregated Black Annual Conferences and Black churches all needed to be eliminated.[212]

On April 23, 1968, the United Methodist Church was created in Dallas, TX. The Evangelical United Brethren Church (represented by Bishop Reuben H. Mueller) and The Methodist Church (represented by Bishop Lloyd Christ Wicke) joined hands at the constituting General Conference in Dallas, Texas. Mueller and Wicke pronounced the words, *Lord of the Church, we are united in Thee, in Thy Church and now in The United Methodist Church.*[213] UBC representatives insisted that the Central Jurisdiction be removed for the merger to be approved. In the new UMC, only five regional jurisdictions were created.[214,215]

By 1972, mergers of the remaining segregated Black Conferences were completed under the watchful eye of the Commission on Religion and Race of the now United Methodist Church.[216]

Southern Baptists and Modern Revivals

By the 1950s and 1960s, a half century later, white supremacy and racist violence was ingrained into the psyche of the Southern Baptist congregant. As part of the gospel in the South, these principles passed on from generation to generation. Self-proclaimed, poorly educated, white Baptist preachers in the South transferred these principles to the next generation of self-ordained Baptist preachers.

As the white Southern Baptist congregations approached the 1950s and 1960s, both church and self-proclaimed preachers began to depend more and more on the campfire revival method. Hundreds of these Southern Baptist revivals were conducted yearly in the South.

In the 1950s and 1960s, revivals exhorting racism were commonplace in the South, especially in MS. Racism with vigilante violence appealed to poor whites. Poor whites were jealous that Blacks performed many skilled and unskilled labor jobs for less money. Poor whites felt good because they were better than someone else, despite being poor. Elevation of poor whites over Blacks allowed the poor whites to mistreat the Blacks with some religious justification.

Blacks did not voluntarily perform jobs at lower cost. White employers used intimidation tactics of white supremacy to force Blacks to perform jobs at a lower cost. A Black who asked for more money would likely be visited by a member of the Ku Klux Klan. A lot of the white employers were Southern Baptist. Many times, these whites were the prime benefactor for a small Southern Baptist church. Economic leverage over the church was used to pressure the Baptist preacher of the church to keep the poor whites riled against Blacks. Poor whites were too uneducated to recognize being manipulated by the preacher at the pressure of the white patron.

Southern Baptist revivals with fire and brimstone sermons were conducted regularly in MS in the 1950s and 1960s. Heated emotions combined with white supremacy and racist violence led to a need for physical actions by attendees against Blacks. Membership in the White Knights was not a prerequisite for application of violence against Blacks. However, these pent-up emotions of hatred had to be released.

Southern Baptist preachers were involved in a group called the Americans for Preservation of the White Race. This group was formed in May 1963 by nine white men at a gas station outside Natchez. By 1964, the group had more than twenty chapters, primarily in central and southwestern Mississippi.[217] Since white Southern Baptist ministers were involved, preaching and sermons were a part of the program of every meeting.

A meeting of the group was conducted in Brookhaven, MS, in July 1964. White Southern Baptist Minister C O Stegall was the evangelist who delivered the sermon at the meeting. Stegall was Pastor/Preacher at several white Southern Baptist Churches in MS at the time. [Ephesus Primitive Baptist Church, Purvis[218]; and Elmo Baptist Church, Roxie[219]] About 150 small-business owners, farmers, mechanics, and their wives attended the meeting/sermon.

The preacher built up momentum slowly, hissing and gasping in the sweltering heat, arms waving until the sweat covered his glasses and face. He continually punctuated his exhortations with the phrase "God bless your soul." In a hoarse voice, he declared that *he was proud to be a white man, that he had never had any trouble with n-*****s but would never let one in his church.*[220]

This message was clearly mild, promoting segregation rather than violence. But plenty of sermons promoted the use of violence with vigilantes and individual participation.

In late Spring, 1966, a Southern Baptist revival was conducted on the banks of the Leaf River between Hattiesburg and Petal in MS.[221] About 50 congregants were in attendance. Most of the attendees were poor whites. A <u>self-proclaimed</u> preacher led the activities.

In the first half of the revival, some congregants were Baptized by immersion. Some of the congregants who were going to be Baptized wore white robes, some did not wear white robes. The congregant laid back in the arms of the preacher. The preacher asked: *Do you believe in Jesus Christ as your savior and that he died on the cross for your redemption from sin?* When the worshipper applied in the affirmative, the preacher pushed the worshipper backwards into the water. While holding the worshipper under the water, the preacher exclaimed: *I Baptize you in the name of the Father, the Son and the Holy Spirit.* After a few seconds, the preacher pulled the worshipper back out of the water. *You have been accepted in Christ and have been redeemed forever from sin.* No matter what sin this Baptized person committed, he was forgiven forever.

After some congregants were Baptized by immersion, the revival moved to a giant tent in a field right next to the immersion location at the river. The self-ordained Baptist preacher then delivered a sermon. Much of this sermon was full of fire and brimstone and the tortures of Hell. Then, the preacher switched to all of those races that would never be admitted to forgiveness of sin. *The existence of the n-***** is an abomination and a sin. The n-***** needs to be civilized to prevent rape of white women and mongrelizing of the races. Civilization of the n-***** should be accomplished by whatever means necessary, including violence.* A young Jewish kid about age 17 was in the audience. This preacher had been warned. He looked straight at the Jewish kid. *The Kike was attempting to bring down Christian civilization. The Kike was a spawn of the devil. Kikes had horns and a tail that could easily be exposed. The Kike needed to be taught that white folk would not tolerate destruction of Christian civilization for money.*

People in the audience were emotionally aroused. *You tell it, preacher. You tell them n-***** and them Jews.* Some of the attendants at this revival were local members of the White Knights of the Ku Klux Klan.[222] These congregants could hardly have missed the message.

By the 1950s and 1960s, a quarter century later, "separate but equal" segregation was ingrained into the psyche of the Methodist congregant. The Center Jurisdiction was still alive and well. Ministers in the South regularly delivered sermons exhorting this principle to Methodist congregants. Many of these congregants were local government officials and local business and community leaders. Segregation was a concept blessed by the official liturgy of the Methodist church. Barriers to integration were erected at all levels: state, county, and local governments and activities.

Sadly, both the white Southern Baptist Church and the white Methodist Church were engaged in extreme hypocrisy. Christian principles such as the Golden Rule and the Ten Commandments were being preached but not being applied to the relationship between whites and Blacks. These principles were also not being applied to the relationship between whites and Jews.

Southern Presbyterians and Segregation

White Baptists and white Methodists are 70% of the population in MS. However, most of the other religions also participated in the white superiority behavior, especially towards Blacks. Another large religion in MS is the Presbyterians. In the early years of the US, Presbyterians were actually pro-slavery.

Numerous arguments were presented by Churchmen to explain or to justify why the ideals of the Declaration of Independence were not applicable to Blacks ... Africans, in general, were believed [by most Presbyterians] to be irresponsible, immoral, and vicious. Most churchmen were convinced that the slave-master relationship ... was the most satisfactory arrangement for the two races to live together in the same society.[223]

At the 1818 Presbyterian General Assembly, delegates declared slavery to be unacceptable to Christians.

We consider the voluntary enslaving of one part of the human race by another as a gross violation of the most precious and sacred rights of human nature; as utterly inconsistent with the law of God, which requires us to love our neighbor as ourselves ... it is manifestly the duty of all Christians ... to obtain the complete abolition of slavery throughout Christendom ... [224]

This statement was a clear call for all Presbyterian slave owners to free their own slaves. Apparently, this order was easily ignored.

This demand by the General Assembly was also provided with an inconsistent excuse for ignoring the order.

... we cannot indeed urge that we should add a second injury to the first, by emancipating them in such manners as that they will be likely to destroy themselves or others. [225]

This statement is a clear example of white supremacy. If freed, Blacks would immediately become animals, hurting themselves and others.

In 1817, the American Colonization Society was formed. This Society wanted to send free Blacks back to Africa. In 1822, the Society established a colony on the west coast of Africa to receive these Blacks. In 1847, this colony became the independent nation of Liberia.[226]

In this same General Assembly of 1818, delegates voted to advise Presbyterians throughout the nation to patronize and to encourage this Society.[227] These sentiments were echoed in sermons throughout the South. Local congregations were urged to aid the designs of the Colonization Society.[228]

During the 1950s and 1960s, Southern Presbyterians were some of the most strenuous and ardent segregationists in the state of MS. Presbyterian leaders in Hattiesburg actively obstructed attempts by outside Presbyterian ministers to help local Blacks in the exercise of civil rights.

On January 22, 1964, civil rights organizations COFO, SNCC, and CORE conducted Hattiesburg Freedom Day. This activity was an attempt to register Blacks to vote in Forrest County. About 50 ministers from other states came to MS to help conduct demonstrations outside the Forrest County Courthouse.[229]

Only one minister was officially commissioned by the Mattoon Presbytery of the United Presbyterian Church to attend the demonstrations. That minister was , Rev Robert Moore, Chaplain of Millikin University, a United Presbyterian Church School. Several other ministers from the Presbytery unofficially took part in the demonstration in Hattiesburg. Committees of the Mattoon Presbytery requested a report by Rev Moore who had officially attended the demonstrations in Hattiesburg. On the afternoon of Sunday, February 23, 1964, 500 members of the Mattoon Presbytery attended a report meeting in the First Presbyterian Church of Charleston, IL. Presbyterian laymen in churches in east-central Illinois had considerable opposition to ministers participating in demonstrations.[230]

Presbyterians from Hattiesburg were invited to address the meeting. Five Hattiesburg Presbyterians attended: Rev W J Stanway, Pastor of First Presbyterian Church, Rev Newton Cox, Pastor of Westminster Presbyterian Church, Rev Ed Jussely of Bay Street Presbyterian Church, attorney Frank Montague, Jr, Elder of Westminster Presbyterian Church, and Leonard Lowrey, Elder of First Presbyterian Church and Editor of the local newspaper, the *Hattiesburg American*.[231]

After Rev Moore gave his report, Rev W J Stanway read a joint statement to the meeting prepared by the three ministers and the ruling elders.

We find no justification in the Word of God nor in the Presbyterian standards for the invasion of our community by relays of ministers from various from parts of the county intent upon participating in daily picket line marches ... Such activities by ministers serve to inflame frictions between the races, and to disgust many who have had a genuine concern for improved race relations ... [232]

After the long speech by Rev Stanway, Elder Frank Montague addressed the meeting on behalf of the Presbyterian lay persons in Hattiesburg.

Citizens and leaders of Hattiesburg are doing the best they can to solve their problems with gradualism and thorough education and evolution ... We question the necessity, the ethics, and effectiveness of the demonstrations and deplore their tactics ... There is a constant and growing concern among both races that a constructive solution can never be reached if picket lines and demonstrations continue. We believe real progress could, is, and will be made without picketing and demonstrations ... I doubt, from my personal acquaintance with Theron Lynd, that he has ever personally discriminated against anyone.[233]

At this time, Theron Lynd, Forrest County Circuit Court Clerk, was under supervision by the US 5th Circuit Court of Appeals for failing to register Blacks. As an attorney, Montague had to know that this last statement to the Presbyterian meeting was an outright lie.

These two statements were a clear message from the Presbyterian ministers and lay Presbyterians of Hattiesburg to the whole United Presbyterian Church. We will solve our problems gradually. Blacks are not ready for equality so rights have to be extended gradually. Stay out of Hattiesburg. Active participation by outside Presbyterian ministers will create more problems with local Blacks. We have our Blacks under control. Local Blacks are satisfied with the progress being made.

Presbyterian leaders in Hattiesburg actively obstructed attempts by outside Presbyterian ministers to help local Blacks in the exercise of civil rights.

Two forms of white supremacy were now being utilized by the primary religious denominations in the South. Racism incorporating violence was predominantly rooted in the white Southern Baptist churches. "Separate but equal" segregation was an implicit assumption in the creation of Black Southern Baptist denominations and white and Black Methodist churches. Racism using violence was enforced by the White Knights of the Ku Klan and the United Klans of America. Allegedly, "separate but equal" segregation in MS was enforced through the laws and through government administration at all levels.

Denominational Features Supporting White Superiority

Both Southern Baptist and Methodist denominations had features that enabled preachers and ministers to promote their individual approaches to white superiority. These features included the means of salvation, the organizational structure, and the criteria for entrance into the clergy.

Features of the Southern Baptist denomination enabled incorporation of racist violence. A core principle of the religion was one of the features. *All true believers endure to the end. Those whom God has accepted in Christ, and sanctified by His Spirit will never fall away from the state of grace, but shall persevere to the end.*[234] This *Once Saved, Always Saved* principle allowed a penitent to be saved once and then to commit any sin with forgiveness. Further church attendance was not even necessary to renew their salvation.

Several methods are available to obtain salvation. Baptism by immersion, Baptism by public declaration at a service and saying the Sinner's Prayer are common approaches. Baptism by immersion is accomplished by a public ceremony at a creek or river. Public declaration of faith generally is accomplished at a service in a church. Saying the Sinner's Prayer can be accomplished anywhere, without any witnesses. Baptist belief is that this prayer on the one prayer always and immediately answered by God. In response, God plants the Holy Spirit in the believer.

A standard Sinner's Prayer does not seem to exist. Any prayer of repentance that meets certain criteria is acceptable. Admission of being a sinner and asking for forgiveness are the main criteria. This prayer can be prayed silently, aloud, read from a suggested model, or repeated after someone modeling the prayer role. An example from the Billy Graham web site demonstrates a Sinner's Prayer.

Dear God, I know I'm a sinner, and I ask for your forgiveness. I believe Jesus Christ is Your Son. I believe that He died for my sin and that you raised Him to life. I want to trust Him as my Savior and follow Him as Lord, from this day forward. Guide my life and help me to do your will. I pray this in the name of Jesus. Amen[235]

On Wednesday, June 20, 2012, delegates at the Southern Baptist Convention in New Orleans passed a resolution that affirmed the Sinner's Prayer.

RESOLVED, That we affirm that repentance and faith involve a crying out for mercy and a calling on the Lord (Romans 10:13), often identified as a "sinner's prayer," as a biblical expression of repentance and faith; ... [236]

Steve Gaines, Pastor of Bellevue Baptist Church in Cordova, TN, expressed an opinion that represented the majority of delegates.

I believe the biblical pattern is you hear the Gospel, you repent of your sins, you believe in the Lord Jesus and you call upon his name and at that split-second, that nano-second you're saved and forevermore you belong to Jesus.

This resolution passed by a majority vote of around 80 percent.[237]

Once Saved, Always Saved was easily distorted by white Southern Baptists, self ordained ministers and their congregants. Obtain salvation by a private prayer. All sins from that point are forgiven, without constraint, Any violence committed against a Black or a Jew was immediately forgiven.

Another contributing factor that enabled incorporation of racist violence was the organization of the Southern Baptist Church. *A New Testament church of the Lord Jesus Christ is an autonomous local congregation of baptized believers, associated by covenant in the faith and fellowship of the gospel, ... Each congregation operates under the Lordship of Christ through democratic processes. In such a congregation each member is responsible and accountable to Christ as Lord.*[238] Southern Baptist Churches were autonomous entities. Each Church was democratic, free to interpret the gospel in any way desired by the local congregation. Beliefs were not held accountable to a hierarchy which could bring pressure on the local Church leadership to enforce certain interpretations of the gospel.

Qualifications of religious leaders also created conditions that helped to incorporate violent racism into the Southern Baptist religion. *Every ... Southern Baptist church is autonomous and decides individually whether or not to ordain an individual, or whether to require ordination of its pastor or ministry staff ... Some cooperating churches may require seminary training from an SBC seminary prior to ordination, while others may not; such a requirement is entirely up to the church.*[239]

Degrees were not needed to become a Southern Baptist Preacher. Especially in rural communities in MS, any person who met three requirements were admitted as preachers. First, a person had to experience a "calling" from Christ to preach the gospel. Second, sermons delivered by the person had to use Bible-beating, intense physical activity and fanatical theatrics of hellfire[240] and dangers of hell spawn. Third, the person needed charisma. His personal charm and ability to connect with congregants while preaching was necessary to spread the gospel. With this low bar for admission, preachers were drawn from the local community of poor whites who attended the Church.

Preachers and congregants in a rural Southern Baptist church were all poor. Generally, preachers in these churches were unpaid, part-time participants in the church. All had to earn a real living outside the church. These poor preachers were hired by local employers. These same employers were financial patrons for operating expenses of the local Southern Baptist church. In exchange for financial support, employers consciously or subconsciously demanded that preachers enforce the inferiority and separation of Blacks and Jews to insure low wages to both groups. Poor preachers were willing to and free to comply, distorting the message of the gospel This distortion of the gospel then became ingrained into the daily behavior of the congregants. Employers were pleased as this kept the poor whites and the poor Blacks separate. Their economic profits were preserved.

Sam Bowers, Imperial Wizard of the White Knights, was a devout Baptist. After ordering the murders of Schwerner, Chaney and Goodman and of Vernon Dahmer in Hattiesburg, Bowers joined the Hillcrest Baptist Church in Laurel. As part of his participation, Bowers taught an adult men's Sunday School class.[241] Edgar Ray Killen was a part-time, self-proclaimed Southern Baptist preacher. Killen regularly preached at Baptist churches in Neshoba County, such as the Pine Grove Baptist Church in House, MS.[242]

Many Southern Baptists, such as politicians, publicly appeared as segregationists. This position towards race allowed them to appear more reasonable to the nation in regard to white superiority. Gov Ross Barnett and Gov Paul Johnson were Southern Baptists who publicly declared as segregationists. But these positions were a lie. Barnett and Johnson hid behind Citizens Councils. These Councils were typically composed of white businessmen. Council leaders had direct connection to the White Knights. Moreover, the state of MS operated the MS Sovereignty Commission, a spy agency with direct connections to the White Knights. This Commission reported to the MS Governor and took orders from the Governor. Gubernatorial orders to the White Knights were often transmitted through the Commission.

Methodists believe differently from Southern Baptists regarding salvation. Core principles for Methodists are described by 3 simple rules: *Do Good. Do No Harm. Abide.*[243] These principles are practical guidelines to be followed every day of your life. According to the Methodist Articles of Faith: *We believe all men stand under the righteous judgment of Jesus Christ, both now and in the last day. We believe in the resurrection of the dead; the righteous to life eternal and the wicked to endless condemnation.*[244] Methodists do good every day. At the end of your life, Christ decides whether you obtain salvation and go to heaven. Salvation is only obtained after a life of doing good. *Once Saved, Always Saved* is not part of the core principles for Methodists, as with Southern Baptists.

Oddly, Methodists in MS in the 1950s and 1960s felt that segregation did no harm! If interpreted in a very narrow, short term sense, this interpretation was correct. Assuming that harm equated to physical violence, removing racist violence against Blacks certainly did no harm. That assumption justified segregation as doing no physical harm. But segregation was extremely harmful to Blacks. Segregated schools prevented Black children from obtaining an education. Segregation justified denial of voting rights and other civil rights.

Methodist churches existed within a rigid hierarchy. Methodists have bishops. A Bishop assigns a pastor in a District to a congregation in that District after consultation with the congregation.[245] A pastor is answerable to the Bishop for his approach to preaching the gospel.[246] Judicial proceedings for removal may be brought against a pastor who *disseminates doctrines contrary to the established standard doctrines of the United Methodist Church.*[247] Gospel preaching in Methodist churches conformed to the dictates of the 3 rules and the Articles of Faith. Failure of a pastor to adhere to these constructs have future consequences, such as removal from the clergy. This adherence was completely different from Southern Baptist preaching that conformed to local standards of interpretation.

Under these circumstances, a local patron has very little leverage over a Methodist pastor to control the interpretation of the gospel. Of course, the pastor did have to maintain a delicate balance between the Methodist hierarchy and his local congregants. In the 1950s and 1960s, both the hierarchy and the local congregants were willing to accept segregation as doing no harm. Therefore, this position relative to Blacks and Jews was satisfactory to all.

Educational requirements for Methodist pastors are fairly high. At the time, a minimum of a high school degree was needed. Pastoral training is also required. This training requires five years of diligent study. Local residents cannot simply walk off the street into the church and start Bible thumping, like the Southern Baptists. Extensive qualification requirements have to be satisfied before a candidate gets anywhere near a pulpit in front of a congregation.

Violence towards Blacks and Jews was regularly committed by Christians in the South. Adult Christians, especially white Southern Baptists, regularly participated in lynchings. NAACP leader Walter White commented on the relationship between Christianity and lynching.

It is exceedingly doubtful if lynching could possibly exist under any other religion than Christianity. No person who is familiar with the Bible-beating, acrobatic, fanatical preachers of hell-fire in the South, and who has seen the orgies of emotion created by them, can doubt for a moment that dangerous passions are released which contribute to emotional instability and play a part in lynching.[248]

Usage of the phrase *Bible-beating* by White clearly implicates the Southern Baptist religion.

Racist Behavior Supported By Churches

In southern MS, religion was a critical part of life. All whites attended church on Sundays. Many attended prayer meetings mid-week, typically Wednesdays. Any white high school student who failed to attend church services on Sundays was looking for trouble, from his parents.

Disregard for the human worth of Blacks and Jews started at an early age in MS. White Southern Baptist preachers delivered sermons full of vitriol and hatred for Blacks and for Jews. White United Methodist ministers delivered sermons about the inferiority of Blacks and Jews. Young white children were warned of the dangers of hell for fraternizing with the animals -- Blacks and Jews. Jews were depicted as devil spawn with horns and tails. Sunday school teachers further indoctrinated this racist and segregationist hatred into the minds of youth under the guise of teaching the gospel strictures. Selected passages from the Bible were used to provide a theological foundation for racism and segregationism.

Massive indoctrination of young minds by spiritual leaders about the inferiority of Jews and Blacks had consequences. White youth regularly directed vitriol and even violence towards Jews and Blacks. These youth felt that this behavior towards Jews and Blacks was doing God's work. Religious leaders knew that this behavior was ongoing. Many leaders suggested and applauded this behavior. Since these leaders often were born and raised in these communities, the clergy had likely engaged in this behavior themselves in their youth.

Worse yet, adult white male Southern Baptists often provided a role model for white male teenage Southern Baptists. Adult white male Southern Baptists regularly perpetrated violence against Blacks and Jews. Lynching and beating of Blacks by adult white males were common occurrences in the deep South.

At this time, life in the rural South was pretty boring for most teenagers. Public dancing was often prohibited by strict Southern Baptist clergy and parents. With the implicit and sometimes explicit approval of spiritual leaders and parents, poorly education white teenagers turned to violence against Blacks and Jews as a form of entertainment!

In the 1950s and 1960s, *n-****-knocking* was a common entertainment for white male teenagers. *N-****-knocking* was standard practice once the sun went down. This disgusting entertainment took a specific form. Usually, this activity was conducted at night. Some form of projectile was selected. A group of 4 white male teenagers jumped in a car. That group drove over to the Black quarter (commonly called n-**** town). Any unlucky Blacks on the streets were targets. As the car drove by the Black person(s), the projectiles were directed at the Black person from the moving vehicle. After launching the projectiles at the target Blacks, car occupants whooped and laughed as the car sped away.[249]

Choice of projectile determined the extent of violence delivered to the target. In its mildest form, balloons filled with water were used as projectiles. Sometimes water was mixed with urine in the balloons or rocks were used as the drive-by projectile. Rocks delivered more damage to the target. Clay pots were easier to throw accurately. Even if a pot missed, a loud sound upon impact further terrified the victim. Dozens of loud popping sounds of crashing clay pots sounding like a fusillade of gunfire. A more violent projectile used radio antennas to whip a Black on the back as the vehicle drove past.[250] In its most harsh and violent form, Blacks were taken to remote areas, then beaten, and sometimes brutally tortured.[251]

Sheriff Lawrence Rainey was born in and grew up in Neshoba County. Deputy Sheriff Cecil Price was born in and grew up in Flora, MS. Flora was about 70 miles from Philadelphia. Both were white and likely Southern Baptist. Both Price and Rainey were indoctrinated into the racist belief that Blacks and Jews had no human value. Very likely, both Rainey and Price participated in Saturday night n-****-knockings as high school teenagers. Early in life, the pair came to be desensitized to the effects of violence applied to Blacks and Jews. When each became members of law enforcement, this desensitization enabled them to commit violence against Blacks and Jews, up to and including murder. On the Sunday following the murders, June 28, 1964, Price and Rainey went to church and prayed to Jesus. After all, each had been saved once. *Once Saved, Always Saved!*

Part 3: Murder And Search

Schwerner, Chaney, and Goodman Are Murdered By The White Knights

Their Burned Ranch Wagon Is Found In 2 Days

A 44 Day Search Is Conducted Before The Bodies Are Found

An Autopsy Is Performed By Dr. William Featherston

An Independent Autopsy Is Performed By Dr. David Spain

Dr. Spain Questions The Accuracy Of the Featherston Autopsy

The FBI Re-Opens A Field Office In Jackson

A Post Autopsy Radiology Report Is Performed By Dr. James Packer

People and Events Prior To The Murders

Mississippi Burning

When the investigation into the Schwerner, Chaney, and Goodman murders was opened by the FBI, the Bureau nicknamed the case "Mississippi Burning." This choice of nickname was to represent the burned 1963 Ford Ranch Wagon of Schwerner, Chaney, and Goodman found on June 23, 1964.

On July 10, 1964, the FBI re-opened its Jackson Field Office. This office had been closed since 1946. Schwerner, Chaney, and Goodman had last been seen on June 21, 1964. In response to increasing pressure on the Federal government to get involved, the FBI had re-opened the Field Office. Its primary purpose was to search for the missing workers. Additionally, the government realized that the issues of denial of civil rights were becoming national issues. So, the secondary purpose of the Field Office was to more effectively address the growing civil rights conflicts in the state.[1]

Since the FBI office was formed on July 10, 1964, the number of bombing/arson events from April 1, 2018 until July 10, 1964, is of interest. In comparison, the number of bombing/arson events after the opening of the Jackson office is also of interest. The period July 11, 1964 until December 31, 1964, is an appropriate time period for comparison. Determining the number of bombing/arson events before opening the office indicates the validity of calling the case Mississippi Burning. Comparing the number of bombing/arson events before and after opening the office reveals the effectiveness of opening the Jackson office in curtailing the bombing/arson events.

Three sources are available for counting bombing/arson events (as well as other types of events). Documented hearings by the House Un-American Activities Committee (HUAC) identifies a list of violent events in Jones County for the period May 10, 1965 until October 26, 1965.[2] During Freedom Summer, 1964, the Council of Federated Organizations (COFO) maintained a Running List of Incidents in MS during the period June 16, 1964 until August 26, 1964.[3] A more extensive list of violent incidents throughout the US from March 4, 1954 until June 15, 2004.[4] Bombing/arson incident counts for the two time periods can be determined from these sources. Of course, these lists contain some overlap. So, overlapping incidents were not multiply counted.

Source	April 1 - July 10	July 11 - Dec 31
HUAC	0	0
COFO	11	24
Other Source	9	21
Total	20	45

Bombing/Arson Incidents Before/After FBI Office

Prior to opening the FBI Jackson office on July 10, 1964, MS experienced 20 bombing/arson incidents. So, MS was indeed burning. However, after opening the office, 45 bombing/arson incidents occurred in MS prior to the end of 1964. The number of bombing/arson incidents actually increased after the opening of the FBI Jackson office. Opening the Jackson office did not have any deterrence effect on the ongoing bombing and arson activities.

After the FBI found the burned-out Ranch Wagon driven by Schwerner, Chaney, and Goodman on June 23, 1964, the FBI labeled the investigation with the title **Mississippi Burning (MIBURN)**[5]. This label was in honor of the burnt-out Ranch Wagon and not the increasing number of bombing/arsons that let to fires.

Extensive investigations were performed by the FBI regarding these, 65 bombing/arson incidents that happened during 1964 in Mississippi. Yet, charges were never brought against anyone for any of them.

Edgar Ray Killen, Baptist Preacher

Edgar Ray Killen
(FBI, Booking Photo, December 4, 1964)

Edgar Ray Killen was born on January 17, 1925, in the House Community[6] near Philadelphia, MS. His parents were Lonnie Ray Killen and Etta Hitt Killen. Killen was one of 8 children.[7] Family members farmed, hauled pulpwood, cut timber, or did any work that could raise money. Killen was able to complete high school. A lot of his education was obtained through home schooling.[8]. Killen earned his living as a farmer[9] and sawmill operator.[10]

At age 17, Edgar Ray Killen first "got the call" to preach. Killen resisted that call for a long time.[11] He became a self-proclaimed, Freewill [fundamentalist] Baptist Minister, He explained his call to be a preacher. *God knocked me on my butt and woke me up.*[12]

Over the course of 60 years, from ages 20 until 80, Edgar Ray Killen served as a part-time preacher.[13] Killen preached in over 18[14] local churches in Neshoba County. He also conducted weddings and funerals. Often, Killen preached strong fire and brimstone[15] sermons favoring racial segregation.[16] Killen also had a radio program, in which he gave sermons and advice to locals.[17] As a volunteer, part-time preacher, Killen never accepted any fees or payments for his work as a preacher.[18]

The earliest published reference to Killen operating as a preacher was in 1954. On February 7, 1954, Killen provided a home devotional service at the Golden Wedding Anniversary of Mr. and Mrs. J. W. Duett.[19] Killen was 29 years old at the time of the service. Some of the churches at which Killen provided pastoral services were the Ephesus Baptist Church,[20] the Duffee Baptist Church,[21] the Mt Carmel Baptist Church,[22] the Pleasant Grove Baptist Church,[23] the Zion Hill Baptist Church,[24] the Enon Baptist Church,[25] the Golden Grove Baptist Church,[26] the Salem Baptist Church,[27] and the Greenland Baptist Church.[28]

MS Governors maintain a list of honorary colonels on the staff of the Governor.[29] An aristocratic tinge attaches to the social usage of the honorary title of colonel. This honorific designates a southern gentleman. MS Governors award this honorary title to political heavyweights, usually big campaign donors. On January 17, 1960, Chief of Staff William Goodman released the list of honorary colonels on the staff of MS Gov Ross Barnett. This list was an extremely long list. Twenty (20) colonels were honored from Neshoba County alone. Edgar Ray Killen was on the list from Neshoba County.[30]

By his own admission, Edgar Ray Killen was a staunch segregationist. Killen believed that segregation was the teaching and the will of God. He also believed in the inferiority of Blacks.

He made the races different and, therefore, each race was meant to be with its own kind.[31] *... it is 100% impossible for a Negro to have morals. The quicker the Black race know and accept this, the faster this country can heal and move forward.*[32] *... N-****s are smart but have no morals. Values were never meant for a n-****. At best, you are the animal in a circus. You follow orders well.*[33] *...*

Just like his mentor Sam Bowers, Edgar Ray Killen firmly hated Jews. Killen vocally proclaimed those views in his letters and statements over the years. Blacks were not the real problem. Jews were the real problem.

*It really ain't because of the n-****s that I am treated so badly ... It's all propaganda distributed by the communist Jews who own most of the American news media. Jews who buy and support our failed and corrupt MS judicial system ... That's all it is to them, money ... They are scum ...*[34]

*The two white Jew n-****s were communist Jews, ... according to their morals and teachings, there was no God.*[35]

To all you fine Caucasian Christians, I tell you, fight the communist Jews who pour destruction on our children and nation ... The communists and the Jews do their all to oppose our Lord, out Constitution and our American way.[36]

In 1964, Edgar Ray Killen ran against Lawrence Rainey to be Sheriff of Neshoba County.[37] Rainey won. Despite his loss to Rainey, Edgar Ray Killen had a very high opinion of Lawrence Rainey. *Rainey did not have much formal education, but he was the best Sheriff Neshoba County every had.*[38]

Lawrence Rainey, Sheriff, Neshoba County

**Lawrence Rainey
(FBI, Booking Photo, December 4, 1964)**

Lawrence Rainey was born on March 2, 1923, in Neshoba County.[39] His parents were John and Bessie Rainey. John Rainey, his father, was a farmer. This family was likely poor sharecroppers during the Great Depression. Rainey had a younger brother who died at a young age.

Rainey was raised on the farm in Neshoba County. He attended school through the eighth grade.[40] Like most poor families in rural MS, a son had to leave school early to work on the farm. As he grew older, Rainey found work as a mechanic.[41]

After a while, Lawrence Rainey was hired as an officer for the Philadelphia Police Department.[42] During his tenure with the Philadelphia PD, Rainey shot and killed a Black man.

Philadelphia Police Chief Bill Richardson and Officer Lawrence Rainey were on patrol[43] on Sunday, October 25, 1957. The pair came upon Luther Jackson and Hattie Thomas in a wrecked car sitting in a ditch off the side of the road. Rainey helped the couple out of the car. After helping, Rainey decided that the couple was drunk. He tried to arrest Jackson. Jackson yelled *No white SOB policeman is going to arrest me.* Then, the burly Jackson attacked Rainey. Jackson tried to choke Rainey. Rainey first shot Jackson in the stomach. After being shot, Jackson backed off. Jackson advanced the attack again. At that point, Rainey shot Jackson until he was dead. After Jackson was killed, Hattie Thomas attacked Rainey. Rainey subdued Thomas. Thomas was arrested and jailed on charges of assault and battery. A coroner's inquest returned a verdict of justifiable homicide.[44]

This description of events was told to reporters by Philadelphia Police Chief Bill Richardson. Since this event was the murder of a Black man by a police officer in rural MS, local residents did not think much of the killing. However, the NAACP was dissatisfied with the explanation. Hattie Thomas signed affidavits that the explanations by Rainey and Richardson were untrue. This affidavit was forwarded by the NAACP to the US DOJ with a request to investigate the death of Jackson. On Monday, November 9, 1959, the FBI announced that an investigation into the death of Luther Jackson was being initiated.[45] Charges were never brought against Rainey for this killing.

After his stint with the Philadelphia Police Dept, Lawrence Rainey was hired as Deputy Sheriff by Neshoba County Sheriff EG "Hop" Barnette. Rainey was appointed Deputy Sheriff by Barnette around January 1, 1960, when Barnette assumed his position as Neshoba County Sheriff.
Rainey was involved in another shooting of a Black after assuming his duties as Deputy Sheriff. On May 24, 1962, Sheriff Barnette and Deputy

Sheriff Rainey were taking Willie Otis Nash, a Black, to the mental hospital at Whitfield. Nash was in the back seat of the Sheriff's cruiser. As the trio were traveling on Hwy 16 just outside Philadelphia, Nash *went wild.*[46]

Nash struck Rainey, then jumped into the front seat of the car. After getting into the front seat, Nash grabbed a gun from the glove compartment. Nash fired several times. Most of the shots discharged by Nash went through the back window of the vehicle. Barnette, who was driving, stopped the car near a trailer court. After stopping, Barnette drew his pistol and fired several times. Nash was stricken by 3 or 4 of the discharges by Barnette. Nash died. Neither Barnette nor Rainey were wounded. Several persons along the side of the road near the trailer court witnessed the shooting. A coroner's jury was quickly assembled. This jury ruled that the shooting was justifiable homicide. [47]

Supposedly, both shooting incidents were self-defense killings.

In MS at the time, a Sheriff could not succeed himself. Lawrence Rainey chose to run for Sheriff in August, 1963. This year was the end of the term of office of Hop Barnette. Rainey made his position clear on the role of Blacks in Neshoba County. *I believe in our Southern way of life and will strive to keep it that way.*[48] Rainey appeared at meetings all over Neshoba County. *I'm Lawrence Rainey and if you elect me Sheriff, I'll take care of things for you.*[49] Rainey was actually saying quite clearly: *Elect Rainey and leave the n-****s and the n-****-lovers to him.*[50]

Since Rainey had killed at least two Blacks, Black residents of Neshoba County were afraid of Rainey.

One night, Rainey walked into the light at a Black county fair attended by 300 men. He stood there without saying a word. Gradually, the crowd began to thin until every Black was gone. Rainey was left alone on the grounds. The fair was over.[51]

White residents had a completely different and rose-colored view of Lawrence Rainey. Jack Tannahill, Editor of *The Neshoba Democrat*, described Rainey in far more generous terms. *I'll tell you what kind of man he is. When he sees a drunk n-**** on the street, instead of just grabbing him, Lawrence will say "Now, boy, you get on home now 'fore [sic] I have to run you in." That's the kind of man Lawrence Rainey is.*[52]

A Philadelphia banker provided another gentler description of Lawrence Rainey. *This n-**** woman was trying to cash a forged check. I told the teller to call for the Sheriff. The n-**** grabbed the check and started to run. Rainey caught up with her at the corner. She resisted and was slamming him [Rainey] up against a building when I arrived. I don't believe in police brutality, but I told the Sheriff "Take that club and knock hell out of her out of her. He didn't do it.*[53]

Lawrence Rainey was over 6 feet tall, weighed more than 250 pounds, chewed tobacco, carried a blackjack on his belt, and wore a holster with a large 44 magnum revolver.[54] With this height and weight, a woman would not be able to slam Rainey against a wall, whether the woman was Black or white. This description by the banker was just so much rose-colored fluff. Whites generally wanted to provide excuses for Rainey. Rainey and his violence towards Blacks protected whites from their race problem.

In the 1963 election, Lawrence Rainey ran against Leland Kilgore. Voting was conducted on Tuesday, August 27, 1963. Rainey collected 2943 votes. His opponent, Kilgore, only received 2347 votes.[55] In a small, rural county like Neshoba County, this difference was a comfortable margin.

If Leland Kilgore had won this election, the murders of Schwerner, Chaney, and Goodman might never have happened. Descendants of Kilgore played a big role in obtaining justice for the murders and maintaining equitable justice in Neshoba County today. Kilgore had a son, Don Kilgore. Don Kilgore, a Philadelphia attorney, became a member of the Philadelphia Coalition. This Coalition successfully pressured MS officials to prosecute Edgar Ray Killen, the conspirator in chief of the murders, in 2005. Steven Kilgore, the current MS 8th Circuit Court District Attorney, is the grandson of Leland Kilgore.[56] This participation by the descendants of Leland Kilgore suggests that Kilgore was not an extreme violent racist like Lawrence Rainey.

Lawrence Rainey assumed office as Neshoba County Sheriff on January 1, 1964.[57] The gregarious sheriff wore a Stetson hat, cowboy boots, and a loaded six-shooter. As a rural county Sheriff, Rainey wielded considerable discretionary power in Neshoba County Whites who were not labor organizers or civil rights workers were treated in a friendly manner by Rainey. According to one Rainey supporter, "He had a grin, a wave, and a good word for every friend he met." .[58]

In Neshoba County, a Sheriff was elected to his position. However, the Sheriff appointed his own Deputy. Any Sheriff needed to carefully pick his Deputy. A Deputy must be willing to enforce all of the policies and orders of the Sheriff. Deputies were paid directly by the Sheriff. So, an appointed Deputy must be highly active. Sheriffs and Deputy Sheriffs were tax collectors. A Sheriff was paid a percentage of the taxes his office collected. A complicated and lucrative fee system also helped to pay the Sheriff who paid the Deputy. A lazy, ineffective Deputy would not earn more than he was paid.[59]

Lawrence Rainey hired Cecil Price as his Deputy Sheriff. Price had a reputation for controlling Blacks using violence.

Cecil Price, Deputy Sheriff, Neshoba County

**Cecil Price
(FBI, Booking Photo, December 4, 1964)**

Cecil Ray Price, Jr., was born on April 15, 1938, Flora, MS. His parents were Cecil Price, Sr., and Lucille Davis Price.[60]

Prior to his being elected Deputy Sheriff, Price had been a dairy supplies salesman and a Fire Chief.[61]

Price was appointed Deputy Sheriff of Neshoba County, MS, by Lawrence Rainey on January 9, 1964.[62] He was 25 years old.

Rainey picked his man well. Rainey and Price were definitely birds of a feather. This pair ruled Blacks in the County through violence and intimidation.

Not long after assuming office, Rainey and Price engaged in a beating of a local Black man. On January 26, 1964, Kirk Culberson, a lumberyard worker, was arrested for drunkenness by Sheriff Rainey and his Deputy Price. Culberson was beaten and struck on the head with a blackjack. As a result of the beating, Culberson was hospitalized for 5 weeks.[63]

Sam Henry Germany, a Black man, was arrested on cow stealing charges in October, 1962. Arresting officers were Rainey, Philadelphia Police officers Otha Burkes and Richard Willis, and former Sheriff Ethal Glen Barnette. Germany was incarcerated. While incarcerated, Germany was stripped of his clothing and whipped with leather straps.[64] He was forced to make self-incriminating admissions and confessions.[65] All 4 arresting officers - Rainey, Barnette, Burkes, and Willis participated in the whipping.[66]

Four other Blacks were subjected to the same treatment in October, 1962. Cleo Jack Nichols, Harvey Nichols, Earl Tisdale, and Earnest Kirkland, were all arrested for cow theft. Sheriff Rainey and Philadelphia PD officer Richard Willis performed the arrest. This group was taken to the Neshoba County Jail and incarcerated. At the jail, all 4 were stripped to the waist. Rainey, Price, Willis, and Barnette proceeded to beat the 4 Blacks with leather straps.[67]

Using his discretionary powers, Sheriff Rainey imposed a curfew on Blacks. A Black person had to be off the street by 10 pm. If you were caught outside after the curfew, Rainey and Price would literally run you home. A spotlight was shined on the offending Black. Then, the order was given *Run, n-****, run*. As the Black person ran, Rainey and Price would drive their car, chasing after the running Black. Whites did not face any curfew or limitations.[68]

Price seemed to derive great pleasure from terrorizing Neshoba County Blacks. One night, Price showed up at a roadhouse popular with young Blacks. He drew his revolver and shouted, "All you n-**** men get your hands on the wall, and all you n-**** women do the Dog!"[69]

Black students held dances in a community center dedicated for activities by Blacks only. On a regular basis, Rainey and Price showed up unannounced at a dance. Rainey and Prince entered the dance area with the apparent objective of intimidating participants. Music and dancing stopped. Attendees stood still and quiet in the almost dark center. Rainey and Prince scanned the group using their flashlights. Several minutes of scanning passed while everyone stood quietly. Rainey and Price departed. Immediately upon departure, music and dance resumed.[70]

Lawrence Rainey and Cecil Price were uneducated thugs using intimidation and violence to control Blacks residing in Neshoba County. At the time, law enforcement positions did not require any education or training. In the South and in MS pretty much everywhere, police and sheriff positions were filled by the same kinds of people as Rainey and Price. Just like Rainey and Price, many of these officers throughout MS were uneducated racists and members of the White Knights.

Mt Zion Methodist Church Leaders

Mt Zion United Methodist Church was used by the White Knights as a trap to draw Mickey Schwerner back to Neshoba County. Leaders of the Church were brutalized and badly beaten.

J R *Bud* Cole: a member of the Finance Committee at the Mt Zion United Methodist Church.

Beatrice Cole: wife of Bud Cole, also a member of the Finance Committee at the Mt Zion United Methodist Church.

James *Jim* Cole: brother of Bud Cole, Sunday School teacher, Steward, and member of the Finance Committee at Mt Zion United Methodist Church.

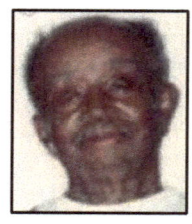

Georgia Rush: a member of the congregation and a leader at Mt Zion United Methodist Church.

John Thomas Rush, Jr: son of Georgia Rush and a member of the congregation at the Mt Zion United Methodist Church.

Cornelius Steele: a member of the Finance Committee at the Mt Zion United Methodist Church.

Mable Steele: wife of Cornelius Steele, and also a member of the Finance Committee at the Mt Zion United Methodist Church.

T J Miller: a member of the Finance Committee at the Mt Zion United Methodist Church.

Earnest Kirkland: a local Black activist and member of the Mt Zion United Methodist Church.

White Domination Of Neshoba County

Prior to the start of the Civil Rights Movement, life for Blacks in Mississippi was bad. A combination of racist violence and segregation was used to control Blacks. In Neshoba County, extreme violence was exercised against Black residents, perhaps more so than any other county in MS. Any white person could exert violence against any Black person with total impunity. Blacks were ruled by whites with blatant, extreme, unjustified cruelty.[71] Life for Blacks in Neshoba County was pure hell.

Law enforcement officers regularly harassed Blacks simply to keep them in a state of fear. One time, Sheriff Lawrence Rainey conducted intimidation activities against Fred Black. Rainey drove up in a truck, not his normal police cruiser. Black was ordered into the back of the truck. With Fred Black in the back of the truck, Rainey drove around the community. This activity frightened Fred Black. Rainey had a reputation for being rough with Blacks. Black did not know what was in his future as he was driven around in the truck. Rainey was also delivering a clear warning to the rest of the Black community. *Look, this can happen to you too.* Such a history of intimidation caused many Blacks to be reluctant to join the Civil Rights Movement once started.[72]

Blacks in Neshoba County were often beaten for no particular reason. A young Black man with a light complexion was seen dating a young darker Black woman. Local whites reacted mercilessly. These whites beat the young Black man with the light complexion senseless. As a result of the beating, the Black man was mentally retarded for the rest of his life.[73] Neshoba County was a small lightly populated area. These whites knew that the young man was really Black. His offense was impersonating a white person in public. This young man could not help his physical coloring. Worse yet, his lighter complexion was likely the result of the rape of a female ancestor by a white man.

Another arbitrary beating was the result of a fender bender. A young Black man was driving down the street. He had to stop suddenly. As a result of the sudden stop, the car behind lightly tapped the rear bumper of the Black man. The young Black man exited the car to inspect the damage to his rear bumper. White passengers in the car behind also exited their car. One of the white passengers carried a bat. Using the bat, the young Black man was savagely beaten. A week later, this young man died from the beating.[74]

No one was charged or prosecuted in either of these brutal beatings.

Murders were a regular occurrence. A young Black man was found floating in a creek. This victim was castrated. His private parts were stuffed in his mouth. These mutilation killings never were reported in the news.[75]

No one was charged or prosecuted in this horrendous murder.

During the 1950s and early 1960s, lynchings were conducted using a special technique. At the time, electrical power was not widely distributed around the Philadelphia area. Black sections especially were without power. Every so often a *blackout* would take place. All of the power in the city was turned off. Turning off the power was not difficult since the power distribution grid was small. After the power returned, a Black man would be found hanging by a rope. A lynching had been conducted under cover of darkness so that witnesses could not identify perpetrators. Of course, whites told everyone that the Black had hung himself.[76]

No one was charged or prosecuted for these lynchings.

White men raped Black women regularly without any criminal repercussions. Even worse sexual acts by whites against Blacks were tolerated. In 1955, a white man named Hicks raped 3 ½ year old Lynn Brown. Murray Brown, her mother had gone to work, leaving Lynn, and brothers Charles and Ronnie at home. While Murray was gone, Hicks came into the house. He raped 3 ½ year old Lynn. Hicks committed this rape right in front of her brothers. After completing the rape, Hicks took Lynn and left the house.

When she returned home, Murray was upset that daughter Lynn was missing. Brothers Charles and Ronnie told her what Hicks had done. Murray immediately started driving to look for Lynn. After a short distance, Lynn came walking down the road. Hicks had released Lynn.

Murray Brown complained to the white power structure about the rape of her daughter by Hicks. This complaint was so horrendous that the complaint could not be ignored. Hicks was charged and arraigned. A trial was actually held. Of course, an all-white jury unanimously found Hicks to be not guilty.[77]

Brutal violence committed by a white person against a Black person was totally acceptable to the white community in Neshoba County. Even the brutality of the rape of a 3 ½ year old innocent girl was acceptable.

Extensive economic discrimination was practiced against Blacks in the County, just as elsewhere in MS. Several national industries operated factories in Neshoba County. Among them, US Electrical Motors, Inc., a division of Emerson Electric Co employed a work force of 200 people. Only 4 of these employees were Black. Two of the employees were janitors. Two actually worked on the factory floor. Plans were made to significantly expand operations at the plant, increasing the workforce. Hiring of more Blacks was not expected.[78]

A Black person applied for a job. An application was taken. But the Black person was told that no jobs were available. White persons would often apply right behind the Black person. Many times, whites would be hired immediately after a Black person was rejected.[79]

Helen Tention, a Black woman with 4 children, had to provide for herself and the children. Helen received a welfare payment of $10 per week per child. She was able to find a job as a maid working in the house of a white person. For working as a maid, Helen was paid another $10 per week. Combining both sources of income gave Helen a monthly budget of $200 ($1742[80] per month in 2020 dollars) to raise her family. These funds had to cover rent, food, utilities, and clothes and all other family expenses.[81]

White merchants in downtown Philadelphia discouraged Blacks from buying in their stores. Several techniques were used by the merchants. Since Blacks were generally extremely poor, white merchants would charge much higher prices when Black customers tried to pay. Often, if a white merchant saw a Black person approaching the store, a closed sign was quickly posted. The door was temporarily locked. Efforts by the Black person to gain entry by knocking on the door were simply ignored. Eventually, the Black customer gave up and walked away.[82]

Voter registration was equally discouraged. Prior to the Civil Rights Movement in Neshoba County, a Black who tried to register was simply arrested on some trumped-up charge. At the time, MS required payment of a poll-tax and passing of a literacy test. Sympathetic voter registrars sometimes allowed Blacks in Neshoba to fill out the application and take the test. Black registrants were told that they would be informed of the results. Of course, results were never forthcoming. Black registrants were subject to hoses and harassment. Water hoses were used to direct high pressure water streams at any Blacks attempting to register as a group. Barking, snarling dogs were often used to discourage any Blacks who tried to register to vote. During the summer, another trick was used to discourage Black registrants. Heaters were turned up full strength making the atmosphere in the County Clerk's office physically intolerable.[83]

Basic goods and services were denied or delivered with ugliness towards Blacks. Blacks had a difficult time receiving the mail. Many Black areas were unpaved. Local postmaster J L Posey and Assistant Postmaster J H Carter refused to deliver mail to unpaved Black areas. Paved streets were required before mail delivery was established.[84]

Blacks who lived on paved streets were subjected to indignity when the mail was delivered. Postmen threw the mail on the ground in front of the house rather than placing the mail into the mailbox. Black resident Helen Tention experienced this behavior firsthand. Tention filed a complaint against the postman who repeatedly threw her mail on the ground. Ultimately, the local postmaster intervened. After an apology from the postman, Tention withdrew the complaint. From that time onward, the postman placed her mail into the postbox in front of her house, as he did with mail deliveries to whites.[85]

Local violence against Blacks was ongoing throughout MS before the Civil Rights Movement. White governmental leaders all over MS downplayed any issues with Blacks and civil rights in their communities. Neshoba County leaders participated in the denial of any issues with Blacks. On April 2, 1959, Zack Van Landingham, an investigator for the MS Sovereignty Commission visited Philadelphia to assess the status of local race relations. Landingham talked with Philadelphia Police Officer HB Holley. *Everything is quiet in Philadelphia as far as racial matters are concerned. Excellent relations exist between the white and colored races.* This declaration completely misstates the situation. Blacks in Philadelphia were indeed quiet. Speaking out or attempting to assert rights could easily get a black person murdered by local law enforcement.[86]

Despite this denial, evidence was beginning to emerge showing that Blacks in Neshoba County were becoming restless in the denial of their rights. In early August 1961, Philadelphia Black Earthy and Francis Culberson complained to the FBI about abuses by Neshoba County Sheriff E G Hop Barnett and Deputy Sheriff Lawrence Rainey. In the complaint, the Culbersons accused Barnett and Rainey of beating, kicking, and mistreating the Culbersons. Barnett was interviewed by Mississippi Sovereignty Commission investigator AL Hopkins on August 10, 1961.

Of course, Barnett claimed that the Culbersons were the problem. *Earthy Culberson is a known bootlegger of long standing in Philadelphia. Earthy Culberson* has a record of 19 convictions for misdemeanors since 1953. Francis Culberson was arrested on July 8, 1961. Officers were attempting to confiscate whiskey that was concealed in the bathroom of her home. While trying to destroy the whiskey, Francis scuffled with the officers. She was charged with resisting arrest.

Francis Culberson was interviewed after the interview with Sheriff Barnett. Francis had a different explanation. She claimed that she went into the bedroom to see if her husband had left any whiskey in the room. She found an empty jar without any whiskey. As she was leaving the room with the jar, Culberson was met by the Sheriff and the deputies. Officers knocked Earthy down several times, just after the search was completed. Barnett took the empty jar and left. A few days later, Barnett returned and arrested Culberson. At the time of the trial, the jar did have whiskey. Clayton Lewis, Culberson's attorney, claimed that the whiskey spelled like fresh bootleg whiskey, declaring that Barnett had placed fresh whiskey into the jar just before trial.

In his report, Hopkins completely exonerated Barnett and the deputies. *The sheriff and his deputies appear to be doing a good job and there is no evidence that they have mistreated anyone.*[87]

Yet, cracks were beginning to show in the calm in Neshoba County. Benny Stennis, a Black male, was employed as a porter at the Citizens Bank. Several times a day Stennis would go back-and-forth to the Post Office on behalf of the bank. An American Oil service station was located on the corner of Church and Main St, directly across the street from the Post Office. When he had to urinate, Stennis went behind the Service Station to hide himself from view and to urinate. Bathrooms at the service station were only for white males and white females. Eventually, the view obstructing objects were removed. On October 1, 1963 Stennis found himself in the unenviable position of having to urinate without any objects to obstruct the view. So, in an act of desperation, Benny Stennis did the unforgivable. Stennis used the bathroom reserved and identified for white males only.

As he exited the toilet, Stennis noticed that Mrs. W H Holland, wife of the operator, was seated at her desk in the corner of the service station preparing monthly statements. Stennis removed his hat. He bowed his head and asked her pardon for entering the white male only toilet. Benny Stennis explained to Mrs. Holland that he was in a bad situation and had no choice but to use the toilet. Then, Stennis went to Mr. Holland and apologized for being in a position of having to use the toilet immediately. Benny Stennis assured Mr. Holland he would never use the toilet for *white* men only again if any way existed for some other convenience.

Holland did not say anything about the incident to anyone. As far as Holland was concerned, the incident was closed. Yet, on October 15, 1963, Virgil Downing, an investigator for the MS Sovereignty Commission, arrived at the AMOCO service station. Holland described the incident to Downing.[88] Benny Stennis did not face any repercussions for this failure to know his place. However, this incident demonstrates the attitude of white residents of Neshoba County towards its Black citizens. A Black man was forced to urinate outside behind a building, just like any other dog or animal. Blacks were not entitled to privacy or consideration. Any misbehavior by a Black was most certain to be spotted and reported to the white authorities. Consequences for the misbehaving Black person could be deadly.

The Environment In Neshoba County

An extremely dangerous situation existed in Neshoba County in Spring 1964. A highly active White Knights group had a stranglehold on the community. Business leaders fell mostly into two groups: active members of the Klan and supporters of the objectives of the Klan. An exceedingly small minority of businessmen and local leaders were supportive of civil rights for Blacks. This group generally did not speak out in public in fear of retaliation by the White Knights.

On the evening of April 5, 1964, 12 crosses were burned throughout Neshoba County. These cross burnings were the first to occur on a widescale basis throughout the state of MS. A statewide showing of cross burnings by the White Knights did not occur until later in the month on Friday, April 24, 1964.[89]

Six crosses were burned inside the city limits of Philadelphia. Five of these crosses were burned in Independence Quarters, the Black section of town. Another cross was actually burned on the lawn in front of the Neshoba County Courthouse. Another 6 crosses were burned out in Black areas of the county.[90]

Sheriff Lawrence Rainey commented on the cross burnings in the *Neshoba Democrat*. *It is believed that outsiders came through this area and burned the crosses and were gone before anybody could see them. I definitely feel that the burning was not done by local people and it that it was an attempt by outside groups to disrupt the good relations enjoyed by all races in this county.*

Jack Tannehill, the Editor of the *Neshoba Democrat*, also commented on the cross burnings. *We deplore the burning of the crosses in this community last Saturday night and can only hope that someday the guilty persons will be found out and get the judges book thrown at them. All races here enjoy the very best of relationships, and many of us count our Negro citizens as true and loyal friends. We hope our status quo remains, and feel that others do too, regardless of race. Outsiders who come in here and try to stir up trouble should be dealt with in a manner they won't forget.*[91]

Some readers claimed that this statement by Tannehill was a justification for potential violence against civil rights workers.

Sheriff Rainey certainly exaggerated the situation. His statements were just plain bald-faced lies that contradicted other ongoing activities by the White Knights in Neshoba County, as future Klan activity clearly showed.

White Knights In Neshoba County Continue Activities

Around May 10 – 12, 1964, circulars were distributed to every house in the white community of Philadelphia. This circular listed 20 reasons for joining the White Knights of the Ku Klux Klan of Mississippi.[92]

5. Because it is a very secret organization and no one will know that you are a member.
11. Because the goals of the KKK are the total segregation of the races and the total destruction of communism in all its forms.
17. Because one of the goals of the KKK is States' Rights and complete State Sovereignty.[93]

A critical message was written across the bottom of the page in bold letters. *This article was refused to be printed by our local paper. Can 91,000 Mississippians be wrong?* A copy of the circular was deposited in the front door of the office of the *Neshoba Democrat*. A penciled note was written across the back of the circular. *Whose side are you on Mr. Editor: NAACP or segregation?*[94]

Jack Tannahill, Editor of the *Neshoba Democrat*, replied to the handwritten note and an editorial published on May 14, 1964.

I will not run an advertisement about secret organizations to which no one will sign his name. From past news stories and editorials, we don't think it's any secret where we stand. But again, we don't believe in a secret organization that takes the law in its own hands in any instance.

No doubt we will be involved to some extent this summer by some segments of the NAACP, core, and other pressure groups, but it is our belief that the agitation will come from outsiders moving into our city and County and doing everything possible to stir up our citizenry. Cool heads in a firm stand by those responsible for keeping the peace will go a long way in preserving our dignity and putting our invaders to flight.

We believe all possible steps should be taken to preserve our southern way of life and maintaining the separate identity of the races. But we don't believe intimidation and coercion of those who believe in and have always believed in the principle of segregation is the solution.[95]

After a close reading, this editorial appears to be contradictory. On one hand, possible agitation is placed squarely on the shoulders of outside agitators. After admitting potential involvement with the outsiders, the editorial then supports segregation and the separate identity of the races.

Aggressive recruiting efforts by the White Knights grew the membership significantly in Neshoba County. Conditions were ripe for extensive violence during the upcoming Freedom Summer invasion.

The Making of a Civil Rights Activist

Michael "Mickey" Schwerner was born on November 6, 1939, in New York City. His parents were Nathan[96] and Anne[97] Schwerner.

When Mickey was eight years old, his parents moved from New York City to Pelham, NY. Pelham is somewhat north of the Bronx.[98] As a young boy, he protected other young boys from bullies. One young boy whom he protected from bullies was Robert Reich. Reich eventually became US Secretary of Labor.[99] Schwerner attended Pelham Memorial High School in Pelham, NY.[100]

After graduating high school in 1957, Mickey completed three terms of pre-veterinary study at Michigan State University. In September, 1958, Mickey transferred to Cornell University. At Cornell, he entered the College of Agriculture. His intention was to become a Doctor of Veterinary Medicine. At some point, during his undergraduate studies, Mickey became interested in working with people. He switched his major to rural sociology.[101]

While an undergraduate at Cornell, Schwerner was initiated into the Jewish fraternity Alpha Epsilon Pi. Mickey was instrumental in efforts that led to the admission of the first Black member of the fraternity. This Black fraternity brother went on to become the vice-president of the student government at Cornell.[102]

In May, 1961, Schwerner graduated from the College of Agriculture at Cornell with a major in rural sociology. Upon graduation, he continued his studies at the School of Social Work at Columbia University.[103]

Mickey spent the 1961-1962 school year in graduate studies at Columbia.[104] Mickey met Rita Levant during the school year in 1961. Mickey was a student at Columbia. Rita was a student at Queens College. The pair were introduced by a high school friend working at a location where Mickey also worked.[105] In 1962, Mickey and Rita were married. Mickey was 22. Rita was 20.[106]

In the summer of 1962, Mickey Schwerner applied for a job at the Hamilton-Madison House of the Alfred E. Smith Public Housing Project. This Project is in the Two Bridges Neighborhood, between the approaches and abutments to the Manhattan and Brooklyn Bridges.[107] At the time, the Hamilton-Madison House was located at 50 Madison Street, on the lower east side of Manhattan.[108]

**Hamilton-Madison House, Uses Three Floors
(Google Maps, Street View)**

Hamilton-Madison House was a settlement house. The settlement house provided educational, recreational, and other social services to the residents of the Housing Project. Three floors of one of the buildings in the Project hosted the facilities of the House. Facilities included club rooms, game rooms, classrooms, machine shops, a darkroom, a gym, an auditorium, a library, and a music room. A paid, professional staff of sixty men and women operated the facilities. Staff members included group workers and case workers, and specialists in diverse areas including art education, recreation, music, and dance.[109]

Mickey applied for a job as a group worker to work with teen-agers. He was interviewed by House Executive Director Geoffrey R. Weiner. Wiener was impressed by Mickey's commitment to working with people. After an investigation into his background, Mickey was hired as a group worker with teens.[110]

A typical day for Mickey started at noon and ended about midnight. His activities included writing records, visiting homes of troubled teens, accompanying teens to court, working with a group of teens, and discussing problem teens in his group with other group workers. Teen group activities included discussing problems, studying current events, playing games, and helping one another with homework.[111]

As he worked at the House, Mickey became increasingly motivated to participate full-time in the civil rights movement. Ed Pitt, a Black social worker from the South, at the House, was Mickey's best friend. In an interview, Pitt commented on Mickey's inner need to participate.

He thought the civil rights movement was the essential domestic conflict of our time, and wanted to be identified with problem-solving solutions. He wasn't satisfied with sporadic activity; he wanted full-time participation.[112]

But Mickey was impatient for participation in the civil rights movement itself. In June of 1963, Mickey Schwerner applied to join Downtown CORE.[113] In his application, Schwerner stated:

My vocation for the rest of my life is and will be to work for an integrated society.

That same month, Mickey was accepted into Downtown CORE.[114] This CORE chapter had only recently been formed in March, 1963.[115]

One of Mickey's first tasks for Downtown CORE was to establish a CORE office in the same area of New York City as the Smith Housing Project, the Two Bridges Neighborhood. Schwerner established the CORE office at 64-66 Delancey Street[116], in a rotting, rat-ridden loft.[117]

**Downtown CORE Uses Loft
(Google Maps, Street View)**

Once the office was established, Mickey would rise at 6 am. He would spend the morning working for CORE. After working for CORE, Mickey proceeded to his day job at the Hamilton-Madison House.[118]

But Mickey was becoming impatient. Working in an office did not really satisfy that inner need to participate. Direct involvement was needed. So, during the summer, Mickey and his wife Rita became activists.

A demonstration for integration was organized at Gwynn Oak Park in Baltimore, MD. This Park contained rides such as a roller coaster and a Ferris wheel. Admission to the Park was limited to whites only. The event was organized by the local chapter of the Congress of Racial Equality, Maryland Council of Churches and the New York headquarters of Campus Americans for Democratic Action. Participants included respected, highly placed, local and national Catholic, Protestant and Jewish clergymen -- white and black.[119]

On Thursday, July 4, 1963, demonstrators initially gathered at Metropolitan Methodist Church in West Baltimore before boarding buses to the Park. Protesters arrived at the main gate to the Park about 3:00 pm. Baltimore County Police Chief Robert Lally and 560 police offers met the protestors. Lally ordered the protesters arrested. Quietly, orderly and accompanied by freedom songs, the protesters boarded county school buses and were driven to the Woodlawn police station.[120]

Over the course of the protest, 283 people were arrested and charged with trespassing outside the park. The demonstration remained peaceful, as many arrested were clerics from all over the East Coast. Two members of the Episcopal Church's National Council staff, Bishop Daniel Corrigan and Father Daisuke Kitagawa, Executive Secretary of the Division of Domestic Missions, were among the group arrested.[121] Mickey Schwerner was among the group arrested.[122] A short time later, the arrested protesters were released.

Both Mickey and Rita participated in another demonstration on July 13, 1963, at the Rutgers Houses at 65 Pike Street in NYC. This demonstration was part of the 1963 summer CORE campaign against the all-White building trade unions. Building trades unions working on the project excluded Blacks.[123]

**Rutgers Houses, 65 Pike Street
(Google Maps, Street View)**

Seven were arrested while attempting to block concrete trucks from entering the work area. Bob Gore, from national CORE, was Black.[124]

**Bob Gore, National CORE
(CORE NYC, www. corenyc.org)**

All six of the remaining arrested were white: Lisa Henri, Walter Flesch, Harold Kerster, Mickey Schwerner and Rita Schwerner. Samuel H. Friedman, a 66-year-old former socialist candidate for Vice President, was also arrested.[125] While being carried during the arrest, demonstrators assumed their *most correct nonviolent, civil-disobedient, limp body position*.[126]

Participants who pled not guilty were given sentences of 60 days. Defendants who pled guilty, but refused to deny future participation, received 30-day sentences. Women were sent to the Women's House of Detention in Greenwich Village. Men were sent to Rikers Island. Mickey drew a sixty-day sentence. Rita was sentenced to 30 days in jail.[127] All arrested were released on appeal after about 3 days. About 2 years later, all sentences were overturned on appeal. Disorderly conduct convictions were not dismissed.[128] Ultimately, the case was continued indefinitely.[129]

The March on Washington, being led by Reverend Martin Luther King, Jr., was scheduled for August 28, 1963. Mickey Schwerner asked the Directors of Hamilton-Madison House to provide funds for transportation of a group of residents to participate in the March. The Directors denied the request, having decided that the Directors did not have the authority to spend funds on transportation. Mickey raised the money from an "unidentified source." This source was likely his parents. With this money, two buses were hired for the trip. Mickey Schwerner and 90 young Blacks from the Hamilton-Madison House participated in the March on Washington on August 28, 1963.[130]

On September 15, 1963, four very young Black girls were murdered in a bombing at the Sixteenth Street Baptist Church in Birmingham. These murders deeply affected Mickey Schwerner. Mickey decided that his work at the Hamilton-Madison House was too safe and easy. Nothing short of a complete commitment to the Movement would satisfy that inner need. He made the fatal decision that cost him his life -- to go South. Mickey wanted to be where the going was toughest. MS was the state with the most hard-core problems. Mickey and Rita would move to MS.[131]

Mickey and Rita needed some support, at least for travel expenses. SNCC, the Student Non-Violent Coordinating Committee, a new more aggressive organization, was selecting workers to send into Black communities in MS. Mickey and Rita applied for a position. Ed Pitt, Mickey's friend, was a member of SNCC. Ed wrote a recommendation for the pair. After careful consideration, SNCC rejected the application. SNCC members felt that a Black person would be a better selection. A white worker would be conspicuous in MS. Local Black residents would take longer to accept and to trust a white worker.[132]

Since Mickey and Rita were rejected by SNCC, the couple applied to CORE. In his application for the CORE position, Schwerner wrote *I have an emotional need to offer my services in the South.*[133]

Several people wrote letters of recommendation for Mickey and Rita. Mrs. Diane King, Junior-Tween Program Supervisor at the Hamilton-Madison House stated *I have been impressed with his sincere and responsible commitment to helping others.* A fellow worker at Downtown CORE explained *Mickey is very calm is his outlook and manner of action ... he is fully in command of himself at all times.* One professor from Queens College who had Rita as a student declared *Rita is a fine young woman, and should make an excellent worker for CORE's task force ... She is a lively, intelligent, energetic, dedicated, sensitive, and warm young woman.*[134]

Mickey and Rita Schwerner received notification of acceptance into the CORE Task Force on Thanksgiving, 1963. Their reporting date was January 17, 1964, at the CORE office in Jackson, MS. Upon arrival in Jackson, an assignment somewhere in MS would be given to the couple.[135]

In November, 1963, a meeting was held by members of SNCC and CORE to organize COFO. COFO was an up and coming civil rights organization formed to manage the Movement in MS. Bob Moses, from SNCC, was named to be Program Director for all COFO sponsored activities in MS. Activity directors from SNCC were assigned to manage projects in four out of five MS voting districts. CORE staff member Matteo Suarez was assigned as Activity Director for the 4th Voting District of MS. Suarez would direct activities from Canton, MS. Meridian would be within the sphere of control of COFO and Suarez.[136] Activities in MS would be managed from the COFO office at 1017 Lynch Street in Jackson.[137]

On January 15, 1964, Mickey and his wife Rita left New York in their VW Beetle for Mississippi.[138] Mickey drove all day and through the night. A little after dawn, the couple crossed into MS.[139] The couple arrived in Jackson on January 16, 1964.

As requested, the couple reported to the COFO offices in Jackson, on January 17, 1964. Over two days, discussions were conducted between COFO Project Director Bob Moses, Mickey, and Rita. After consultation with Matteo Suarez, Activity Director for the 4th Voting District of MS, Moses assigned Mickey and Rita to the Meridian office. The couple was to organize a Community Center, similar to a settlement house.[140] Mickey and Rita Schwerner were the first white civil rights workers to be based outside of the capitol of Jackson.[141]

Mickey and Rita Schwerner departed for Meridian on January 19, 1964.[142] Five months later, Mickey would enter the cold, empty space of death.

Activities by the Schwerners, Chaney Prior To Murders

Once in Meridian, Schwerner quickly began civil rights activities with the help of local Black residents and NAACP members.

Albert Jones was a wealthy, 60-year-old Black real estate developer in Meridian.[143] Alvin Fielder was a local Black pharmacist. Fielder owned the building in which office space was rented.[144] These two Black professionals were members of the NAACP and leaders in the civil rights movement in Meridian when the Schwerners arrived on January 19, 1964.

About 5 P.M. on Sunday, January 19, 1964, the couple arrived in Meridian. An office had been rented for COFO at 2505 1/2 Fifth Street. This location was in a building owned by Negro pharmacist Alfred Fiedler. The office space was five rooms on the second floor.[145]

**Fielder Pharmacy
2505 1/2 Fifth Street
(Larry Primeaux)**

Rita recalled the perceptions of the pair upon entering the office space.

Mickey unlocked the door and we walked through those five cold, empty, dirty, and decaying rooms... We only saw the rooms as we hoped to make them: colorful, filled with ... happy people working to become better and more useful citizens of MS and the US.[146]

Organizing activities by the Schwerners began immediately. On January 25, 1964, Rita Schwerner sent a written progress report to the national headquarters of CORE in New York City. Books were collected for the library. Voter registration classes were scheduled for Tuesday and Thursday evenings at 8:30 pm. An existing NAACP Youth Council meeting was held to solicit ideas for activities at a new community center being organized.[147]

Housing was a big problem for Mickey and Rita Schwerner from the beginning. At first, five homes of Black residents provided housing for the Schwerners. After a few days in a home, the pair was asked to move. Phone calls made threats. Neighbors applied pressure out of fear of retribution from violent whites. Some Blacks who helped were threatened with being fired. Many nights during January and February, 1964, the Schwerners slept in the community center. Mickey slept on the floor. Rita slept on a cot. The building did not have heat during the very cold winter months. Doors could not be locked so the safety of the couple was at risk.[148]

In early February, 1964, Mickey Schwerner attempted to recruit workers from a Black school in Meridian, the TJ Harris Senior High School and Junior College. Professor Walter Reed, Principal of the school, slammed the door in Mickey's face. Mickey and Rita attended the next game of the local basketball team. Flyers were handed out at the game by the Schwerners. Ultimately, 50 out of 650 students joined the Movement with the Schwerners and became active workers. One of those recruited was Sue Brown. Brown became the office manager of the COFO office.[149]

After one month in Meridian, around February 19, 1964, Schwerner reported his activities to CORE national headquarters. A 10,000-volume library was housed in the Community Center. Shelf space was lacking so all of the books could not be actually uncrated. Story hours, games, and music activities were being conducted to attract children from 5-6 years old. Every day, door to door canvassing was accomplished to solicit Black adults willing to try to register to vote. Twice weekly voter registration classes were being conducted. Employers were being solicited to hire Blacks for other than menial jobs.[150]

These activities were making Mickey Schwerner highly visible in the community after only a month. As Schwerner's activities became more known to the racist white community in Meridian, the number of abusive phone calls increased significantly.[151] Recruiting adult Blacks to register to vote brought notoriety to the Schwerners from racist local residents.

By March 1, 1964, Schwerner felt that activities in Meridian were up and running. Schwerner provided another status report to CORE headquarters in NYC. A house was rented for the Schwerners and others for $9 a week by Black real estate developer Albert Jones. This yellow house was located at 306 44th Avenue in Meridian.[152]

**306 44th Avenue
Meridian
(Google Maps Streetview)**

The priest of the Black Catholic Church in Meridian visited Mickey Schwerner. Mickey and Rita had attended services at the Church in mid-

February, 1964. This priest agreed to urge his parishioners to use the Community Center.[153]

In this same report, Schwerner described his relationship with various local communities. Influential local Blacks provided a mixed response to the efforts of Schwerner. A few locals were helpful. Other locals were hypocritical, appearing friendly but really not wanting the activities. Some influential local Black leaders, such as Professor Walter Reed, Principal of the TJ Harris School, were openly hostile. Other than the harassing phone calls, the white community remained quietly hostile. So far, arrests and picks by law enforcement were non-exist.[154] That situation was about to change.

Mickey and Rita attended their first service in a white church in Meridian on Sunday, March 10, 1964. The pair were actually invited by the white minister. Two Black girls attended the services with the Schwerners. This group was seated but were frequently subjected to blank and hostile stares by white congregants. In the days following the service, local residents reacted. Members threatened to leave the church. An effort was initiated to remove the minister. A vindictive editorial appeared in the Meridian newspaper.[155]

The Schwerners were attracting a lot of negative attention among white racists in MS. Conducting a door to door campaign to promote Black voter registration started the negative attention. Attending and integrating a white church significantly increased negative attention towards the Schwerners. These white racists began to act using local law enforcement officers as the tool. On Wednesday, March 13, 1964, Mickey Schwerner was picked up by the police for the first time in Meridian.

He was at the book counter of one of the chain stores when a plain clothes detective approached him and asked him to come to the police station. Mickey asked what he was charged with and the answer was: "Nothing now but I will charge you." At the station, Mickey was questioned for a few minutes, asked to show his identification, and was released without being charged.[156]

Harassment had now increased to include both abusive phone calls and arrest and questioning.

On March 15, 1964, a statewide meeting of the White Knights of the Ku Klux Klan was held in Brookhaven. At this meeting, 30 Klaverns were chartered by Sam Bowers, Imperial Wizard, of the White Knights.[157] Both the Neshoba County and Lauderdale County Klaverns were likely chartered. By June 21, 1964, the day of the murders, these Klaverns were well populated and organized in order to have committed the murders of Schwerner, Chaney, and Goodman.

As early as March 18, 1964, COFO publicly announced the upcoming Freedom Summer activities in MS. Plans for upcoming summer activities called for 2,000 full-time workers to come to MS. Over half of these workers were to be students. Workers would conduct Freedom Schools, establish community centers, register Blacks on a mock voter list, and conduct a mock election among the Black voters.[158]

With all of the negative publicity in Meridian, Mickey and Rita Schwerner were now in the sights of the state government. Andy Hopkins, an investigator for the MS Sovereignty Commission, contacted the Meridian Police Department. He established contact with a plainclothes detective in the Meridian PD named GL Butler. On March 19, 1964, Butler transmitted a copy of a report on Mickey Schwerner. This report is on a Meridian Police Department, Detective Division form.

Checked on Michael H. Schwerner at 306 44th Avenue and the house belongs to Roy Cunningham, wm, and he applied for water February 4, 1964, giving his previous address as New York City, also giving his occupation as Meridian Community Center. We checked and there is no place listed by that name.[159]

Plainclothes Detective GL Butler took Schwerner in for questioning on March 13, 1964. Butler made a copy of Schwerner's MS Driver's License. A street address was obtained from the MS Driver's License. Detective Butler then began checking municipal records for information about Schwerner. These checks required a couple of days. Records were not computerized back in those days. Immediate results were sent to MS Sovereign Commission investigator Andy Hopkins on March 19, 1964.

On March 19, 20, 1964, Butler continued his investigations into Schwerner. Investigation results were forwarded to Andy Hopkins. Hopkins may have also conducted his own investigation. Investigator Andy Hopkins issued his own report about Mickey and Rita Schwerner for the records of the Sovereignty Commission on March 23, 1964.

In this report, Hopkins described a lot of details about the Schwerners, including birthdates, physical characteristics, past addresses both in and out of MS, vehicles owned, and drivers' licenses. A lot of data involved out of state information, such as the NYC address of Mickey Schwerner. Hopkins and Butler must have interacted with out of state law enforcement agencies and possibly the FBI. Most importantly, Hopkins described the purpose of the Schwerners in Meridian.

Both Michael and Rita Schwerner are in Meridian working for CORE. Their purpose there is evidently to contact local Negroes [sic] for the purpose of encouraging them to register to vote and also how to pass the voter registration examination.[160]

This statement alone alerted the state of MS that the Schwerners were dangerous to the future of segregation in the state.

However, the last paragraph of the report was the most chilling part.

Chief O A Booker, Detective G L Butler [both from the Meridian PD] and the sheriff's office of Lauderdale County are cooperating in this matter by keeping these subjects under surveillance and are getting information from reliable informants.[161]

Local law enforcement in Meridian and Lauderdale County were keeping the Schwerners under constant surveillance. Since law enforcement proved to be members of the White Knights, this surveillance was the equivalent of being under surveillance by the White Knights. Any disruptive actions by the Schwerners would be immediately reported to the White Knights.

Some Meridian Police Officers were related to members of the Meridian White Knights. Meridian PD Officer Lee Roberts, was the brother of Alton Wayne Roberts.[162] Wayne Roberts was the Klan trigger man who actually shot Michael Schwerner and Andrew Goodman. Any information about the activities discovered by the Meridian PD surveillance would be transmitted from brother Lee to White Knights member Wayne.

Ultimately, this surveillance with reporting to the White Knights contributed to the murders of the Schwerner, Chaney, and Goodman.

Community Center activities were thriving. Library usage was increasing. Voter registration canvassing was moving full steam every day. Mickey and Rita decided to take the next step -- equal employment opportunities. A simple goal was defined. Find one Black who can and will take a job. Then, locate a job opportunity for that person. After success with one employer, then work could begin on two, then, three, and so on.[163] This effort was the first actual direct confrontation by the Schwerners with a segregationist.

Mickey and Rita identified a young Black woman who could work as a clerk in a variety store. For several weeks, the pair worked with the women, preparing her to take a clerk position. When the woman was ready, a variety store about a block from the Community Center was chosen as the target. This store was small. Most of its sales were to Blacks. Black employees were kept invisible, cleaning and working in the back of the store.[164]

In early April, 1964, Mickey and Rita approached the manager. *We wanted to persuade him to break the ice and hire our candidate for his first Black [sales]clerk ... he figured that if he did nothing, his troubles would go away. He made the usual excuses ... he'd have trouble with his white employees, he'd be boycotted by his white customers, and probably burned out or dynamited.*[165]

Mickey and Rita decided to stage a boycott. Starting around April 15, 1964, the Schwerners and James Chaney began to hold mass meetings every night.[166] These meetings were held either at the Community Center or some Black Church.[167] Lots of local Black residents showed up and got involved: Catherine Crowell, Agnes Smith, AC Henderson, Polly Heidelberg, George Smith, Jr., Sue Brown, Roscoe Jones, Louise Moore Smith, Isaiah Thigpen, Freddy Watson and Sam "Freedom" Brown participated. These participants were locals who had been involved in civil rights activism before the Schwerners arrived. Everyone was more than ready time to step up and fight for freedom.[168]

Mickey Schwerner felt that more needed to be done in outlying counties around Meridian. Blacks in Meridian were relatively well off. Police brutality was at a minimum. About 1700 Blacks were able to vote. Many Blacks lived comfortably. Adult Blacks in Meridian did not want to take risks. Most support for the activities of Schwerner and Chaney in Meridian came from teenagers. However, Blacks in rural counties, such as Neshoba County, lived a rougher life. Black adults in those areas were more willing to take risks to push for more immediate gains.[169]

Any Black person in Neshoba County was expected to stay in their place. Blacks had to *act like a n-**** and talk like a n-*****. All white men were called Mister. All white women were addressed as Ma'am. Blacks were only given menial jobs, such as sweeping, mopping, digging, and moving. If a Black had a menial job, that person was expected to show up on time and *work like a n-***** at the menial job. After work, Blacks were expected to disappear. Ghettos existed for Black residents. Blacks could not register to vote, use a public pool, or use a public golf course. A young Black male could not get educated and seek a job as a policeman or fireman. A young Black woman could not get educated and seek a job as teacher, a salesgirl, or a secretary at the courthouse.[170]

In April, 1964, Mickey Schwerner began to extend operations into nearby Neshoba County, a very rural county with suppressed Blacks. Schwerner and Chaney made trips into Neshoba County to meet with several Black leaders. These trips were considered dangerous, due to the reputation of Sheriff Lawrence Rainey. Rainey was elected *to handle the n-****s and the outsiders*. So, the pair made these trips at night and at extremely high speeds. Through these meetings, Schwerner and Chaney finally persuaded Black leaders in the Longdale Community to risk allowing a Freedom School at Mt Zion United Methodist Church.[171] This decision was the beginning of the end for Schwerner, Chaney, and Goodman.

Over the months since moving to Meridian, Mickey and Rita had been helped extensively by James Chaney, a local Black man from Meridian. On April 23, 1964, Mickey and Rita sent a letter to CORE HQ in NYC asking that James Chaney be added to the Meridian staff. In this letter, the Schwerners summarize all of the volunteer work performed by James Chaney. *We consider James part of the Meridian staff, and he is in on all major decisions which are made here . . . We believe that since he long ago accepted the responsibilities of a CORE staff person, he should be given now the rights and privileges which go along with the job.*[172] CORE HQ listened. James Chaney was hired as a member of the staff at the Meridian CORE office. Despite requests for additional staff at CORE offices in Jackson and Canton, Chaney was the only person added to the CORE staff during this period.[173]

For two solid weeks, the mass meetings continued every night. Speakers were Mickey, Preston Ponder (from Hattiesburg) and James Chaney. Emphasis was placed on discipline, good conduct, and non-violence.

Participants were taught not to lose their heads when cursed and tainted. If struck, a protestor should not fight back.[174] These principles were the foundation of non-violence, perfected by CORE over the years.

After two weeks of daily mass meetings, the group of CORE volunteers were ready to begin this first boycott. A group of 50 young Blacks, ages from 14 to 21, would be the troops in this first battle. Each participant received a new T-shirt with FREEDOM NOW emblazoned across the chest to wear. A Saturday was chosen as the day to begin the boycott. Saturdays were the traditional big-business day in the South. People who lived out in the country came into town to trade.[175]

On Saturday, April 25, 1964, the boycott began as scheduled. The "kids" in the T-shirts picketed the variety store about a block from the Community Center. Leaflets were passed out to Black residents across the city to urge all Blacks to join the boycott until the variety store agreed to hire its first visible Black salesclerk.[176]

On that Saturday, the picket/boycott was noisy. Drivers slowed to watch the excitement jamming the street. Police Officers whistled at these drivers, waving them to move on. Groups of white youths jostled the picketers. Taunts were thrown hot, heavy, and ugly by the white youths. *You know what the Governor said about'cha, don't-cha? NAACP-n-****, Apes, Alligators, Coons, and Possums!* These derogatory slang references to Blacks were repeated over and over by the whites.[177]

Police mostly observed, only stepping into the mix when physical altercations became imminent. Black shoppers supported the boycott by staying away from the store. As a result, the variety store sales were less than half the normal level for a Saturday. This first picket/boycott was highly successful.[178]

However, the aftermath was not so pretty. On Monday, April 27, 1964, the boycott continued with far less fanfare. Fewer people were around. Meridian Police arrested Mickey Schwerner, Lenora Thurmond, a young Black woman, and all of the Black protesters in front of the variety store. Schwerner was charged with blocking a crosswalk. Lenora Thurmond faced a charge of interfering with a man's business.[179]

Jails were dangerous places for any civil rights worker in MS. Prisoners were incarcerated by race. A Black person was likely to be beaten by the jailers. A white worker was likely to be beaten by other white prisoners. Mickey Schwerner requested to be placed with Black male prisoners to avoid being beaten by the other white prisoners. *You're in our house now, boy. We'll decide where to put you. Ya'll go in with the whites.*[180]

Mickey Schwerner entered that cell with fear and trepidation. This situation might be his first experience with MS justice. Schwerner was approached by the toughest looking white man. *Keep your mouth shut, boy. I know who you are and what you been doing. But the others don't know much. So, keep your mouth shut and I'll see you don't get hurt. I don't think you're a sonofabitch. [sic]. I just think you're a goddam [sic] fool. Lot of fools in the world.* This fellow prisoner was true to his word. Schwerner was not beaten by the other white prisoners.[181]

Stories abounded of white jailers using Black female prisoners for sex shows. A young Black girl was locked in a cell with an aggressive Black male. Jailers watched as the male raped the female. On Tuesday, April 27, 1964, Rita Schwerner paid a $50 fine to have Lenora Thurmond released from the jail. Release insured that Lenora would not be subjected to this kind of humiliation and physical danger.[182]

On Wednesday morning, April 28, 1964, Mickey Schwerner and the Black demonstrators were released from the jail. Schwerner was required to attend a hearing at the Lauderdale County Courthouse in Meridian on the afternoon of his release. Mickey Schwerner waited an hour for the charges against him to be heard. All charges would be dismissed.

While he waited for his hearing, Schwerner was observed by a muscular, hard eyed young man. This man made a statement to Mickey Schwerner. *In some way I'm gonna git my hands on the n-****-loving Jew sonofabitch. And when I do, he ain't never gonna see the sunrise again.*[183],[184]

Some uncertainty exists as to the identity of the young man who threatened Schwerner. Two sources claim to provide the information about the identify of the young man. Both sources provide essentially the same statement above.

One source fails to identify who repeated the quote to the author. This source also fails to identify the young man who made the threat. But, this source claims that this person was eventually indicted by the 1967 Federal Grand Jury for participating in the conspiracy.[185] Given the description of the man and the location in Meridian, this young man may have been Alton Wayne Roberts, the actual murderer of Mickey Schwerner and Andy Goodman.

Another source specifically identifies the threatening young man as Billy Birdsong. Sgt Wallace Miller, an FBI informant, is given as the source that identified Birdsong and who repeated the quote.[186] Birdsong was active in the White Knights and would participate in the burning of Mt Zion Church that led to the murders. However, he was not involved in the actual murders. He was also not indicted by the Federal Grand jury for participating in the murders, as claimed by the first source.

Both possible candidates for the delivering the physical threat to Schwerner were active and violent members of the Lauderdale County White Knights. Regardless of who made the threat, the delivery of a threat of physical violence by a member of the White Knights showed that Mickey Schwerner was on the radar of the Klan.

Mickey Schwerner was a marked man in MS!

Mickey Schwerner scored his first victory. He successfully used the CORE techniques of picketing and non-violence to establish a boycott. Blacks were sticking together, not making purchases at the targeted variety store. Shortly, the store manager capitulated. He hired the trained Black woman as a salesclerk. She worked out front, greeting other Black customers. And she was paid the same as a white salesclerk.[187]

By the winter of 1964, Sam Bowers was operating his pinball machine business in Laurel, MS. Bob Stringer was a teenager who worked for Bowers. His main job was to collect cash from pinball machines operated by Bowers. Stringer also typed Klan propaganda, distributed the propaganda, and attended Klan events. Despite his role as an assistant to Bowers, Stringer was never a member of the Klan and did not participate in any Klan violence.[188]

Bob Stringer
Assistant to Sam Bowers

On May 3, 1964, Bowers and Stringer attended a meeting of the White Knights inside the Boykin Methodist Church near Raleigh, MS.

Boykin Methodist Church
(Chuck McKinley)

Armed Klan guards were on the road leading up to the Church. More than 100 members of the White Knights sat on wooden pews as Bowers began to speak to the assembly.

*We are here to discuss what we are going to do about COFO's n-**** communist invasion, which will begin in a few days.*[189]

Bowers then read an Imperial Executive Order that he had written.

THIS ORDER WILL BE READ TO OR BY AND UNDERSTOOD BY EVERY MEMBER OF THE ORGANIZATION.

Our best students of enemy strategy and technique are in almost complete agreement that the events which will occur in MS this summer may well determine the fate of

Christian Civilization for centuries to come . . When the Black waves hit our communities, we must remain calm and think in terms of our INDIVIDUAL ENEMIES rather than our MASS ENEMY . . . Any personal attacks on the enemy should be carefully planned to include only the leaders and prime white collaborators of the enemy forces. These attacks against those selected individual targets should, of course, be as severe as circumstances and conditions will permit . . . We must use all of the time which is left to us in these next few days preparing to meet this attack. Weapons and ammunition must be accumulated and stored.[190]

Mickey Schwerner was one of the leaders and prime white collaborators that Sam Bowers had in mind. As a result of his organized boycott of the variety store which sold mostly to blacks beginning on April 25, 1964, Schwerner was well known to Bowers and the White Knights.

After the meeting, copies of this Imperial Order were distributed. These copies were recopied and distributed throughout the state of MS to White Knights not in attendance. Bowers was mobilizing his troops for the coming battle of Freedom Summer.

Earnest Kirkland was a primary contact between Mickey Schwerner and James Chaney and the Blacks in the Longdale area of Philadelphia. Kirkland lived with his father Frank in Longdale and was a member of COFO in Meridian, which was managed by Schwerner.[191]

In early May, 1964, Schwerner and Chaney went to the house of Cornelius Steele, a local Black resident of Longdale/Philadelphia. The two civil rights workers wanted to discuss the need for voter registration and Freedom Schools for local Blacks in the Longdale area around Mt. Zion Methodist Church.[192] Steele agreed to organize a meeting of many of the local Black leaders.

Later, in mid-May, Schwerner and Chaney this meeting of local Black leaders in the Longdale area near Mt. Zion Methodist Church. This meeting was held at the house Frank Kirkland. Again, the two civil rights workers wanted to discuss the need for voter registration and Freedom Schools for local Blacks in the Longdale area. About 10 local Black residents and leaders attended this meeting.[193] Attendees at this meeting included Frank Kirkland, Ernest Kirkland, Melvin Kirkland, Cornelius Steele, Buford Cole, and Ruben Green.[194]

Emboldened by this first success at a boycott on April 25, 1964, Mickey Schwerner chose to expand his boycotting efforts in Meridian. On May 22, 1964, picketing/boycotts were initiated against three 5 and 10 cent stores - Kress's, Newberry's, and Woolworth's. These stores refused to serve Black people at the lunch counters. Despite having a large number of Black customers, only white salesclerks were visible. Flyers were distributed telling Black people to boycott the stores.[195]

These direct-action tactics kept many black people from shopping in those stores.[196]

On May 23, 1964, Frank Calhoun, age 15, and Fred Watson, age 21, were arrested for distributing leaflets. These leaflets encouraged Blacks to boycott several city stores, probably Kress's, Newberry's. and Woolworth's. A municipal ordinance prohibited distributing of leaflets. This pair was held on $50 bond. Ultimately, CORE paid the bond.[197]

Schwerner and Chaney publicly spoke at the Mt Zion Methodist Church in Philadelphia on Memorial Day, May 25, 1964. Between 50 and 60 people attended this speech by Schwerner and Chaney.[198] Both speakers discussed setting up a school to train people who wanted to register to vote.[199] At that time, MS required that applicants pass a literacy test. Training in reading and writing and interpreting the Constitution was needed for many Blacks who had little or no education.

In late May, 1964, between May 22 and May 30, Sam Bowers and Bob Stringer, his teenage assistant, attended a small meeting of several White Knights at Boykin Methodist Church in Raleigh, MS. Bowers, Stringer, Edgar Ray Killen, and one other person who accompanied Killen were at this meeting. Schwerner's name monopolized the conversation.

Goatee is like the queen bee in the beehive. You eliminate the queen bee and all the workers go away.[200]

Sam Bowers had just authorized Edgar Ray Killen from Philadelphia to arrange for the murder of Mickey Schwerner.

After the meeting between Bowers and Killen, another small meeting of the White Knights was held in Laurel, MS, later in May, 1964.[201] Sam Bowers, Imperial Wizard attended. James Jordan, Pete Harris, and Earl Akin,[202] all members of the Meridian Klavern, were at this meeting with

Bowers. Bowers gave instructions to Jordan. *That savage Kike[203] Schwerner is a "thorn in the side of everyone living, especially the white people. He needs to be taken care of."[204]* Bowers was giving his permission as Imperial Wizard of the White Knights to "eliminate" Schwerner.

Arrests on May 23, 1964, were not the end of arrests meant to stop the boycotts by Schwerner and CORE in Meridian. Eleven more pickets were arrested on May 30, 1964. These picketers were charged with interfering with a man's business. This charge was the same charge that was previously used against Mickey Schwerner.[205]

After a few months in Meridian, Schwerner believed he had made the right decision in coming to Mississippi. *Mississippi is the decisive battleground for America. Nowhere in the world is the idea of white supremacy more firmly entrenched, or more cancerous, than in Mississippi.*[206]

Mickey Schwerner and Rita organized a Black community center, canvassed Blacks to register to vote, integrated a white church, and conducted extensive, costly and successful boycotts. Known to the White Knights of Lauderdale(Meridian) and Neshoba(Philadelphia) counties as "Goatee"[207], Micky Schwerner was the most despised civil rights worker in Mississippi.[208]

In accomplishing these tasks, Mickey Schwerner riled a nest of hornets in Lauderdale County - the newly formed White Knights of the Ku Klux Klan. At least one of those Klansman could identify Schwerner and had threatened his life. Schwerner was also starting to be known for his activities in Neshoba County A formal elimination order was issued by Sam Bowers, Imperial Wizard. This order was issued separately to Edgar Ray Killen from Philadelphia and James Jordan and others from Meridian. Schwerner was living on borrowed time.

Mickey Schwerner's days were numbered. With activities proceeding so well in Lauderdale County, Mickey made the fatal decision to further expand his activities in Neshoba County. By spending time in Neshoba County, Schwerner exposed himself in isolated areas where the White Knights could conduct his elimination.

Burning of The Mt. Zion Methodist Church

Since Bowers had given permission to "eliminate" Schwerner at several meetings in late May, 1964, Klansmen were looking for an opportunity to accomplish this "project". Mickey was expanding his activities into Neshoba County. Members of the White Knights hoped to perform the elimination in Neshoba County. Neshoba County was far more remote. A murder was more easily conducted in secrecy. Performing the murder in another County gave coverage to the Klan members in Meridian. Meridian Klan members could claim they were not involved.

On June 16, 1964, a rumor was being passed around that Mickey Schwerner was in Neshoba County and might be at Mt. Zion Methodist Church.[209] A meeting was to be held at an abandoned gym at the old Bloomo School[210] that was east on Highway 16 and a short distance south of the Highway.[211] The meeting was to start between 8pm and 9pm.[212] More than 75 people attended this meeting.[213]

**Bloomo School, Neshoba County
(Old Restored Postcard)**

Preacher Killen called the meeting to order. As Killen was making routine announcements, one of the attendees spoke out.[214] Ethal Glen "Hop" Barnette, former Neshoba County Sheriff, explained that he had passed

Mt Zion Church on his way to the meeting. He had noticed that the meeting was heavily guarded. Burnette suggested that the presence of guards indicated that the meeting was important. So, Hop wanted to know what the group wanted to do about this meeting.[215]

Another attendee suggested that the presence of guards suggested that civil rights workers must be at the meeting.[216] Everyone agreed that something must be done.[217]

Preacher Killen solicited volunteers.[218] Wayne Roberts and other attendees from Meridian agreed to go with the group.[219] Hop Barnette, Billy Wayne Posey and other volunteers from Philadelphia also left with the group.[220] All of the White Knights in the group going to take action were armed.[221]

When the group arrived at Mt. Zion Church, all of the Meridian Klansmen went to one exit of the Church.[222] Klansmen from Philadelphia went to the other exit of the Church.[223]

The meeting of Mt. Zion Methodist Church leaders and stewards had started about 8:30 pm and was disbursing at about 9:30 pm.[224] Five Black men and three Black women left the Church from the meeting. Black men attending included Bud Cole, Cornelius Steele, TJ Miller, Jim Cole, and John Thomas Rush. Attending Black females included Beatrice Cole, Mavis Steele, and Georgia Rush.[225]

Thirty or so masked white men, about half at each exit, were lined up with military fashion rifles and pistols blocking their path. These masked men told the Church members that they were searching for the "Jew Boy"[226]

All of the Blacks who chose the exit guarded by the Meridian White Knights were beaten.[227] None of the Blacks who chose the exit guarded by the Philadelphia White Knights were beaten.[228]

Georgia Rush and John Thomas (J.T.) Rush, her son, were driving away from the meeting in their truck. A short distance down the road,[229] armed Klansmen swarmed toward them, blocking the truck.

The Klansmen demanded to know where were the white men. **These masked Klansmen were specifically looking for the "Jew Boy",**

Mickey Schwerner.[230] J.T. explained that whites had not been at the church. The Klansmen were infuriated. "Shut up," one said. "Drive that damn truck into the ditch." J.T. did as he was told. The door was jerked open by the Klansmen. J.T. was hauled from the cab. He was beaten savagely in the face. Another man began cursing Georgia Rush. Georgia was beaten about her head with a pistol as she cringed in the cab of the truck. As she was beaten about the head, Georgia screamed loudly.[231] Finally, Georgia Rush and her son were allowed to leave.[232]

As Bud and Beatrice Cole drove down the road to leave the Church area, a group of white men waited. Three, four, or more of these white men were dressed in black hoods and robes.[233] Others were dressed in "short shirt sleeves", normal everyday clothes.[234] Among the waiting white men were at least two police officers in uniform.[235]

**White Knights Stop Bud and Beatrice Cole On Road Out
(Klansmen: Library of Congress, [LC-USZ62-49988])**

One of the white men standing in the road blocked their car.[236] This man instructed Bud to turn his car lights off. Then, the man shone a light in the Bud's face. Bud was asked about the location of any guards. Bud claimed that guards were not used for Church meetings. The white man accused Bud of being a liar. He pulled Bud from the car.[237] The white man started slugging Bud. He told Bud that Bud had better reveal the locations of the guards. Otherwise, the white man said he would kill Bud. Bud quietly accepted the beating.[238]

A different white man then turned his attention to Beatrice Cole. He pulled Beatrice out of the car.[239] This white man asked Beatrice what she had in her purse. Beatrice told the man that she had Sunday School literature. This man searched her purse. After finishing the search and finding nothing, this second white man threw her purse into the car.[240]

Then, a bunch of white men pushed Bud up against the car. Bud was forced to stretch his hands across the car. He was then searched.[241] As Bud was being searched, a policeman in uniform[242] called Beatrice to come a short distance from the car down the road. He then had Beatrice turn and face the direction of the car. Bud was still being beaten. A loud scream was heard coming from down the road.[243] This scream was emitted by Georgia Rush who was being beaten about the head. Beatrice asked if she could pray. Beatrice started praying.[244] "Lord have mercy, Lord have mercy. Don't let them kill my husband."[245]

A second uniformed[246] policeman came to the other side so that Beatrice was surrounded on both sides by police officers.[247] Beatrice kept praying. Then, a different white man came up to Beatrice with a club.[248] The white man with the club drew back to hit Beatrice with the club. Beatrice asked the policeman on the right if she could pray. This policeman told Beatrice that if she thought it would do any good, she should pray. In response, the policeman on the left told Beatrice that she was too late, that praying would not do any good.[249]

Beatrice fell on her knees and still kept praying. "Father, I stretch my hand to thee. I stretch my hand to thee. No other help I know."[250] One of the policemen finally told the man with the club to let Bud live.[251] Everyone stopped beating on Bud.[252]

Bud was laying on the ground. Beatrice went to her husband. She lifted him as best as she could. Bud fell to the ground. Beatrice lifted Bud to his knees. Again, Bud fell to the ground. One more time, Beatrice lifted Bud as best as she could.[253] She helped him stagger to the car. For a while, Bud just leaned against the car trying to recover himself after being savagely beaten. Then, the couple struggled into the car. Bud and Beatrice just drove away. The white men and the policemen just watched this happen.²⁵⁴

Back at the Church, one of the white men at the Church spread diesel fuel around the inside of the church then set the Church on fire. Mt Zion Methodist Church burned to the ground.²⁵⁵

Between 45 minutes and an hour later, the Klan group returned to the meeting at the Bloomo School.²⁵⁶ Members of the Meridian group complained that that the members of the Philadelphia group had not beaten any Blacks. Billy Wayne Posey, from Philadelphia explained that his group thought that the goal was to retrieve any white persons exiting from the Church. Obviously, the objective was to bring Mickey Schwerner to the Klan meeting to teach him a lesson.²⁵⁷

After this discussion, the meeting adjourned.

Although his life was spared, Bud Cole suffered permanent physical damage. In 2004, Lavada Cole, his daughter-in-law, described the long-term effects of the beating that Cole had received.

*Bud Cole suffered permanent nerve damage to his back. His leg was 75 percent paralyzed as a result of the brutal attack. He walked with a limp for the rest of his life. He died with that limp. He wore a brace constantly because of the injuries he received and used a cane until he died.*²⁵⁸

Georgia Rush had suffered a shattered collarbone as a result of the beating. Despite the shattered collarbone, Georgia returned to work the day after the incident. Her boss fired her that day! The boss may have been a member of the White Knights. Or, he simply may have been afraid that his business would be attacked. Either way, Georgia was unemployed.²⁵⁹

Freedom Summer Training in Ohio

Training for the upcoming Freedom Summer was being held at Western College for Women [now part of Miami University] in Oxford, Ohio.²⁶⁰ About 800 volunteers were trained during the period June 14, 1964 - June 27, 1964.²⁶¹

Orientation over the two-week period worked with two different groups of volunteers. Week one, June 14, 1964 - June 20, 1964, focused on conducting voter registration drives. During the second week, June 21, 1964 - June 27, 1964, emphasis was on establishing and operating Freedom Schools and Community Centers.

In the mornings, students attended general sessions in lecture halls at the University, like Leonard Theatre and Kelly Auditorium. Each afternoon, volunteers attended area meetings in classrooms or out on the lawn areas. At these area meetings, volunteers learned about a specific community in which they would live. Project skills to apply to their work were also taught in the afternoon sessions.[262]

Morning sessions during both weeks involved lectures by those with either special expertise or real experience in MS. On Monday, Robert Moses, SNCC Director for MS, and James Foreman, Executive Secretary of SNCC, introduced Mississippi conditions and gave an overview of the Project. Tuesday speakers focused on African American history and informed participants about white resistance in Mississippi. Speakers included Reverend Vincent Harding and the attorney Charles Morgan. Both speakers shared personal experiences in the South.

**Robert Moses Conducts A Freedom Summer Orientation Session
(Ted Polumbaum, The Newseum)**

Wednesday sessions explored nonviolence in a lecture by the Reverend James Lawson. During the second week, Bayard Rustin also lectured on nonviolence. Thursday morning covered legal issues and informed volunteers what to do if arrested and how to navigate the idiosyncrasies of the Mississippi justice system. Notable civil rights lawyers providing their expertise included Jess Brown, John Pratt and Jack Greenberg. Sessions on Friday examined the role of the federal government. John Doar, First Assistant AG from the US DOJ, provided this lecture on the role of the Federal government.[263]

Frequently, afternoon sessions utilized role-playing workshops on the lawn to practice nonviolent responses when attacked by local white residents or local white law enforcement. These sessions also explored situations that might be faced within the Black community ("Possible Role-Playing Situations"). Volunteers needed to learn how to respond when arrested by a Southern policeman, and the volunteers also had much to learn about communicating with the local black community.[264]

Practicing Nonviolent Reponses On The Lawn
(Ted Polumbaum, The Newseum)

Volunteers were regularly warned about the limited objectives that could be obtained through participation in MS. Robert Moses, SNCC Director for MS, described the frustrations and limited reception by local Blacks.

*We want to establish some very limited things. We want the Negro to have the right to have white people in his house, because the Negro community must be open if there is to be any progress in the state. If nothing else happens, we'll have established a breakthrough.*²⁶⁵ Barney Frank, a doctoral student in political science for Harvard, also explained the limited expectations of the program. *The movement is really one of chastened idealism. We're not really making a one hundred percent commitment to what is a very tough fight that lasts the year around.*²⁶⁶

A large part of the training was preparation for the violent resistance from whites expected in MS. On the first day of training, several SNCC leaders warned of the dangers that would be faced in MS during the summer.

James Foreman, Executive Secretary of SNCC, warned of the extreme nature of the conditions. *I may be killed. You may be killed. The whole staff may go.*²⁶⁷

Sandy Leigh, Field Secretary of SNCC and soon to be leader of the Hattiesburg Project, gave an ominous warning to the volunteers.

I'm just wondering if people in this room understand that people in this room should expect to get beaten, they should expect to spend time in jail and it may go beyond the summer when they are in jail depending on what the bond is. They should expect possibly somebody to get killed. I was just wondering if there was any reaction to it, or has that been discussed ... Newsreel video shows a pensive Andy Goodman listening to these warnings. Goodman swallowed nervously as he thought about these warnings that he may be killed.²⁶⁸

Robert Moses told the volunteers of violence directed specifically against him. Moses was beaten up with brass knuckles by a white man as he led a Black to register to vote. A car pulled up alongside a car in which Moses was riding. One of the passengers in the overtaking car opened fire on Moses with a submachine gun.²⁶⁹

Willie Peacock and some other SNCC members were driving to a meeting in MS. A cop pulled the group to the side of the road on a traffic violation. This group was arrested and taken to the local MS jail.

*When you go down those cold stairs at the police station, you don't know if you're going to come back or not. You don't know if you can take those licks without fighting back, because you might want to fight back. It all depends on how you want to die.*²⁷⁰

After arriving at the jail, Peacock [and presumably the others] were subjected to harsh physical treatment.

"N-****", the man told me, "do you believe I'd just as soon kill you as look at you?" ... "I'm going to erase every doubt from your mind ... Ain't the white people been good to you -- ain't they taken good care of you?"[271]

Classes were held that taught volunteers how avoid trouble and how to protect themselves from police batons and dog bites.[272]

Never drive anywhere at night with a Negro in your car -- you're likely to be stopped by a copy for questioning. Take a jacket with you when you go into a sullen crowd -- you can wrap it around your head if you are attacked. If you are struck down, lie in a kind of prenatal crouch, knees up to protect the belly and genitals, and arms wrapped around the head. If a police dog comes at you, try to stun it with a chop across the nose delivered with the side of your hand.[273]

Volunteers came to expect the absolute worst from MS.[274]

Schwerner and Chaney were attending a COFO training session that had begun on June 14, 1964.[275]

Mickey and Rita Schwerner Receive A Lecture On The Lawn Mickey Schwerner In Overalls, Upper Right, Rita At His Left (Steve Schapiro)

On the morning of June 19, 1964, the attendees were addressed by John Doar, Deputy Chief of the Civil Rights Division for the US DOJ. *There is no Federal police force -- the responsibility for protection is that of the local police.* Many of the attendees were hostile and booed Doar. Despite the negative response, Doar commended the attendees. *I admire what you intend to do. The real heroes in this country today are the students and particularly those students who have given their time, energy, and dedication to correct the very bad and evil problems in the South with respect to the way in which American Negro citizens are treated before the law.* Schwerner, Chaney, and Goodman were all in the audience at the time.[276]

After receiving news of the burning of the Mt. Zion Church, Schwerner and Chaney decided to immediately return to Meridian to investigate. Andy Goodman, a brand-new recruit, decided to join their effort in Meridian.[277]

Andy Goodman and Friends at the Ohio Training Session (The Andrew Goodman Foundation)

Schwerner, Chaney, and Goodman left Ohio early in the afternoon of June 19, 1964. After a short night's sleep and breakfast, Schwerner, Chaney, and Goodman continued to Meridian.[278] The group arrived in Meridian on the night of June 20, 1964.[279]

This arrival was the first time that Goodman had ever entered the state of MS. Andy Goodman was to die about 24 hours later.

The Murders On Rock Cut Road

Investigating The Burned Church

On June 21, 1964, Schwerner, Chaney, and Goodman decided to travel from Meridian to the burned down Mt. Zion Methodist Church and gather the facts about the burning. Around 11am, the trio departed the COFO headquarters in Meridian. Before heading for the church in Longdale outside Philadelphia, Andy Goodman sent a postcard from Meridian to his parents in NYC.

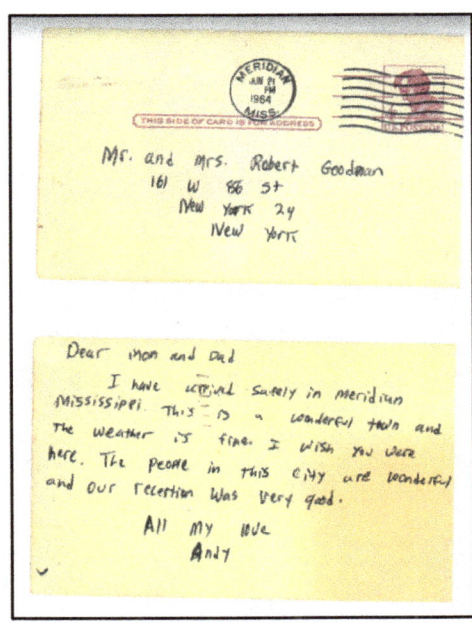

Last Postcard Sent By Andy Goodman From Meridian To Parents (Historical Archives, the Andrew Goodman Foundation)

After mailing the postcard, the trio then departed for the Church in Longdale, which was near Philadelphia in neighboring Neshoba County.

Schwerner, Chaney, and Goodman were traveling in a medium blue[280] metallic[281] 1963 Ford Fairlane Ranch Wagon[282]. This station wagon was owned by COFO in Meridian.[283] The Ranch Wagon model was a big vehicle. With a third seat in the rear, eight passengers could ride comfortably in the Ranch Wagon.

1963 Ford Fairlane Ranch Wagon In Victory Blue

The COFO office at 2505 1/2 5th Street in Meridian was 38.4 miles from the Mt. Zion Methodist Church in the Longdale Community of Philadelphia.[284] A most direct route follows Highway 19 north and then transitions to Highway 491 north. This Highway intersects Highway 16 west. After several miles, Road 747 is taken north to the Church. About one hour of driving is necessary. Schwerner, Chaney, and Goodman arrived at the ruins of the burned down Church at approximately noon (12 pm) on June 21, 1964.

**Burnt Ruins At Mt Zion United Methodist Church
(Jim Lucas Estate, ©2014)**

The group spent about 1 ½ hours examining the burnt remains of the Church. After examining the ruins, the group visited with several Black families who had been beaten by the Klan members as well as other members of the community.[285] Ernest Kirkland accompanied the trio on these visits.[286] Homes visited by the trio included the residences of Cornelius Steele, George Lewis, Georgia Rushing, and J.R "Bud" Cole.[287]

After visiting these homes, Schwerner, Chaney, and Goodman, and Ernest Kirkland, returned to the home of Earnest and Frank Kirkland. Each of the workers had a glass of water. Andy Goodman spent some time talking with Frank Kirkland. James Chaney chatted with the sister of Ernest Kirkland. After about thirty minutes,[288] the three civil rights workers and Ernest Kirkland entered the 1963 Ford Ranch Wagon.[289]

The trio along, with Kirkland, then headed south on County Road 747. Kirkland rode as far south as the home of General Wells. He exited the Ranch Wagon.[290] Schwerner, Chaney, and Goodman continued driving south on County Road 747. After several miles, the workers arrived at Highway 16. Their Ranch Wagon turned west onto Highway 16 towards Philadelphia, enroute to Meridian.[291]

The First Arrest

As the Ranch Wagon containing the workers proceeded west on Highway 16 towards Philadelphia, Neshoba County Deputy Sheriff Cecil Price was traveling east in his two-tone blue[292] 1956 Chevy cruiser[293] at about 65 miles per hour towards American Legion Lake Road (now County Road 539). Price was chasing a lead on George Raymond, head of the Council of Federated Organizations in Mississippi[294], who was rumored to be in the American Legion Lake area.[295] His intention was to turn south on American Legion Lake Road[296] (now County Road 539) [297].

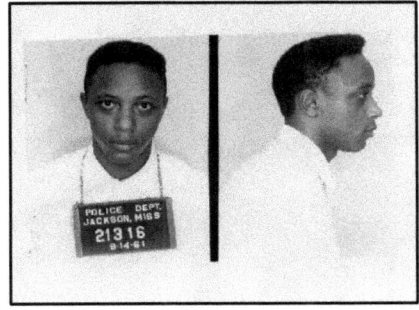

George Raymond
(Jackson PD Booking Photo)
(August 14, 1961)

As he drove east on Highway 16, Deputy Price saw a Mississippi Highway Patrol white 1962 Pontiac Catalina[298] parked in the shade on the south side of the Highway about 4 miles east of downtown Philadelphia[299]. A seldom used lane entered Highway 16 at this location. Immediately to the east of this location was a low hill or rise in Highway 16.[300] Shade on the south side of Highway 16 at this location was provided by a group of large trees.[301] **[C]** Sitting in this car were Highway Patrolmen Earl Poe and Harry Wiggs.[302]

Earl Poe

Patrol Officer

MS Highway Patrol

This vehicle was about 0.5 miles west of American Legion Lake Road.[303]

MS Highway Patrol Vehicle Parked (C)
(FBI-MBI, p. 45; FBI FOIA Image, 1-49 Photo 23-2)

About 0.15 miles (265 yards) west of County Road 539, Price saw a vehicle coming towards him. **[A]** Price recognized this vehicle as the 1962 Ford Fairlane Ranch Wagon registered to the Congress of Federated Organizations. He drove the short distance to County Road 539, then reversed his path, heading west on Highway 16. **[B]**

Price Recognizes Ranch Wagon (A)
Price Turns Around To Pursue Ranch Wagon (B)
(FBI-MBI, p. 45; FBI FOIA Image, 1-49 Photo 23-1)

After turning around and heading west, Deputy Price chased after the Ranch Wagon. Price overtook the Ranch Wagon about 1 mile west of County Road 539, just past Dogwood Lane. **[D]**

Price Overtakes Ranch Wagon (D)
(FBI-MBI, p. 46; FBI FOIA Image, 1-49 Photo 24-1)

After about 2.5 miles from County Road 539, Deputy Price began to clock the speed of the Ranch Wagon. **[E]**

Price Starts Clocking Ranch Wagon (E)
(FBI-MBI, p. 46; FBI FOIA Image, 1-49 Photo 24-2)

Price continued to clock the Ranch Wagon speed another 0.5 mile, where the vehicles crossed the city limit into Philadelphia. **[F]**

**Ranch Wagon Crosses Philadelphia City Limits (F)
(FBI-MBI, p. 47; FBI FOIA Image, 1-49 Photo 25-1)**

After clocking the Ranch Wagon for another 0.4 miles, Price turned on the emergency lights and sounded his siren. **[G]**[304]

**Price Activates Light, Siren On Police Cruiser (G)
(FBI-MBI, p. 47; FBI FOIA Image, 1-49 Photo 25-2)**

Despite the lights and siren, the Ranch Wagon continued traveling another 0.2 miles towards Philadelphia.[305] After passing the 1st United Methodist Church, the Ranch Wagon took the right fork of the intersection between Main Street and Beacon Street towards Beacon Street.[306] **[H]**

**Ranch Wagon Has Flat Tire, Price Arrests Trio(H)
(FBI-MBI, p. 48; FBI FOIA Image, 1-49 Photo 26)**

A homeowner living at the intersection of Main and Beacon Street heard a loud racket. Then, a hub cap came rolling down the street. After driving 50 yards to the west on Beacon Street[307], the Ranch Wagon pulled to the curb with a flat right-side rear tire.[308, 309]

Deputy Price in his 1956 Chevy cruiser pulled of the road and parked just behind the 1963 Ford Ranch Wagon.[310] Immediately after he stopped, at about 3:00 pm,[311] Deputy Price placed a radio call to Highway Patrolman Poe and Wiggs, asking them to come to his aid with a stopped speeder.[312] Price gave his location as the First United Methodist Church, at the intersection of Beacon and Main Streets.[313] James Chaney, who had been driving, began changing the tire.

Price had incorrectly reported his position. Both his 1956 Chevy cruiser and the 1963 Ford Ranch Wagon were 50 yards west of the intersection between Main Street and Beacon Street. This location was about 80 yards to the west of the First United Methodist Church. Despite this small difference in location accuracy, Poe and Wiggs did not have any problem locating the Ranch Wagon and the 1956 Chevy cruiser.

A few minutes later, the Highway Patrol cruiser with Patrolmen Poe and Wiggs pulled in behind Deputy Price's 1956 Chevy cruiser. Chaney completed changing the tire as Price, Poe, and Wiggs simply watched him do all the work.[314]

After the tire had been changed, Deputy Sheriff and Philadelphia Klan member[315] Cecil Price arrested Schwerner, Chaney, and Goodman. Price alleged that their vehicle was speeding inside the city limits. Highway Patrol Officer Wiggs entered the Ranch Wagon along with James Chaney.[316] Deputy Price entered his own Police cruiser. Schwerner and Goodman entered the back seat of the Patrol cruiser.[317] Highway Patrolman Poe sat in the driver's seat of the Patrol cruiser.[318]

A caravan was formed by the Ranch Wagon with Wiggs and Chaney, followed by Price in his 1956 Chevy cruiser, and then Poe, Schwerner and Goodman in the 1962 Pontiac Catalina bringing up the rear.[319] This order of vehicles was the result of the order in which the vehicles had arrived at the arrest location and had parked on the side of Beacon Street.

This caravan headed west towards the Neshoba County jail. Price along with MS Highway Patrolmen Harry Wiggs and Earl Poe transported the arrested workers to the Neshoba County jail in Philadelphia, Mississippi.

At the time, Beacon Street and Main Street were two parallel streets that traveled in an east-west direction through downtown Philadelphia. Driving towards the west from the Church, the caravan took the Beacon Street branch of the road into Philadelphia. Beacon Street is the street closest to the Neshoba County Jail. Eventually, the caravan encountered the intersection with Center Avenue. A right turn was taken onto Center Avenue. After a block, Price made a left turn onto Myrtle Street. He was followed by Patrolman Poe who was transporting Schwerner and Goodman. One half block further down Myrtle, Price parked his cruiser in front of the Neshoba County jail.

Highway Patrol Officer Wiggs, driving the Ranch Wagon, continued on about 1/2 block on Center Avenue. Wiggs then parked the Ranch Wagon in the parking lot of the Philadelphia City Hall and Police Department Building.[320] After parking the Ranch Wagon, Highway Patrolman Wiggs escorted Chaney across the street and down Myrtle Avenue to the Neshoba County Jail.

At approximately 3:30 pm,[321] the trio was booked into the Neshoba County Jail. Since Chaney was driving,[322] Chaney was charged with speeding. Goodman and Schwerner were charged *for investigations*.[323]

Mickey Schwerner

Booking Photograph

(MSC SCR ID

2-112-1-40-1-1-1)

After aiding Deputy Price to transport the three workers to Neshoba County Jail, Highway Patrolmen Poe and Wiggs, continued on their normal patrol routine. At first, the patrolmen parked at the Philadelphia City Square on the east side of the Courthouse.[324] While parked, Inspector R. Maynard King, their Commanding Officer, arrived for a conference.[325]

Maynard King

Inspector

MS Highway Patrol

During the conversation with Inspector King, Price arrived at the location. At this time, Price asked Poe to submit a request to the MS

Highway Patrol Dispatcher in Meridian. Price wanted a vehicle ownership inquiry performed on the Ranch Wagon in which Schwerner, Chaney, and Goodman had been arrested. Poe used his car radio to submit the inquiry. Price departed from the Courthouse area before the ownership information was received. He later received the ownership information by radio.[326]

After the conference with King had completed, Wiggs and Poe proceeded to travel south on Highway 19. This segment of their routine patrol was for the purpose of checking for dragsters south of the city prior to going off duty for the day.[327] Drag racing was a common problem on the streets of Philadelphia during that time period. Photostats of the Philadelphia Police Department Daily Operators Log for Unit 40 at about 10 pm on June 21, 1964, report drag racing observed on State Street.[328]

Mobilizing The White Knights

Immediately after incarceration, Price contacted Preacher Edgar Ray Killen, from Philadelphia.[329] Killen was a Kleagle or recruiter/organizer in the Philadelphia Klavern of the White Knights[330] and known to Deputy Price, also a member of the Philadelphia Klavern.

Preacher Killen immediately reached out and connected with Jerry Sharpe and Jimmy Townsend, two other members of the Philadelphia Klavern. Additionally, Killen contacted Olen Burrage to arrange a burial location for the bodies.[331] Killen, Sharpe, and Townsend entered a gray and white 1959 Chevy owned by Sharpe. In the 1959 Chevy, these White Knights proceeded to the Longhorn Drive-In on Tom Bailey Drive in Meridian.[332]

The Longhorn Drive-In restaurant served as a social gathering and Klavern meeting location for members of the Meridian Klavern of the White Knights.[333] Frank Herndon, James Jordan, and Pete Harris, members of the Meridian Klavern of the White Knights, were already gathered at this restaurant for social purposes. Operator of the Longhorn was Frank Herndon.[334]

**Longhorn Drive-In, Meridian, MS
(Darrel Wayne Thomas)**

Both Frank Herndon and Pete Harris were officers of the Meridian Klavern of the White Knights. Frank Herndon served as the Exalted Cyclops (President) of the Meridian Klavern of the White Knights. James "Pete" Harris was a Meridian Klavern Investigator.[335]

Killen, Sharpe, and Townsend arrived at the Longhorn Drive-In about 6:30 pm.[336] Killen called Frank Herndon out to the front porch of the restaurant. Killen engaged Herndon in short conversation. Then, Killen called Jordan over to the front porch for another short discussion. Killen asked Jordan to participate in a trip over to Philadelphia. Three civil rights workers were being held on a minor charge in the Neshoba County Jail. These workers needed to have their "asses tore up." Since the charges were minor, the workers had to be released shortly. So, the job had to be completed in a hurry. Jordan agreed to participate.[337]

Frank Herndon started calling other Klansmen. He contacted Travis Barnette and Jimmy Snowden[338], both fellow members of the Meridian Klavern. Travis Barnette and Snowden agreed to meet behind Akin's trailer at Akin's Mobile Homes, also on Tom Bailey Drive in Meridian. Bernard Akin, owner of the mobile home sales company, was an active member of the Meridian Klavern.[339]

Everyone present at Longhorns Drive-In agreed to reassemble behind Akin's trailer at Akin's Mobile Homes. Killen, Townsend, Herndon, and

Harris immediately departed for Akin's Mobile Homes in an unspecified automobile.[340]

**Akin Mobile Homes, Meridian, MS
(Postcard, Owned by Author)**

Sharpe and Jordan entered the 1959 Chevy owned by Sharpe. Sharpe and Jordan went to the home of Wayne Roberts in Mountain View Village of Meridian. Roberts was a member of the Meridian Klavern along with Jordan. Jordan asked Roberts to participate in the upcoming activity. Roberts agreed. Sharpe, Jordan, and Roberts proceeded to Akin's Mobile Homes to assemble with the other participants.[341]

About 8:00 pm, Travis Barnette arrived at Akins Mobile Homes. His immediate action was to call Jimmy Arledge. Arledge and Doyle Barnette were having dinner together at the home of Arledge. Travis invited Jimmy and Doyle to participate in the upcoming activities. Travis Barnette and Doyle Barnette were half-brothers. Both agreed. Travis instructed them to assemble immediately at Akins Mobile Homes.[342]

Doyle and Arledge drove to Akins Mobile Home in a 1957 Ford owned by Doyle Barnette. Barnette's 1957 Ford was a Ford Fairlane 500 Sedan. This four door[343] sedan was two tone blue, combining a dark blue and a light blue. The light blue areas were so light as to appear almost white to an observer.[344] Barnette removed the license plate on his 1957 Ford prior to leaving his home.[345]

**1957 Ford Fairlane Owned By Doyle Barnette
(FBI 1-49 Photo 27)**

By 9:00 pm, a large group of White Knights had gathered together at Akins Mobile Homes. Jordan, Herndon, Harris, Travis Barnette, Snowden, Doyle Barnette, Arledge, Roberts, and Akin from the Meridian Klavern were all present. Killen, Sharpe, and Townsend from the Philadelphia Klavern were also in attendance.

Pete Harris left the group. Since he was an officer of the White Knights (an Investigator), Pete was prohibited from participating in "projects". Frank Herndon also left the group. He was also an officer of the White Knights(the Exalted Cyclops) and was prohibited from participation.[346] Bernard Akin simply stated "I can't go, wish I could".[347]

These withdrawals left a group at Akins Mobile Homes consisting of Jordan, Travis Barnette, Snowden, Doyle Barnette, Arledge, and Roberts, from the Meridian Klavern. Killen, Sharpe, and Townsend from the Philadelphia Klavern were also present.

At the request of Killen, Roberts, Sharpe and Jordan went to purchase rubber surgical gloves. The Klansmen entered the 1959 Chevy owned by Sharpe. A short trip took place to Dick Warner's Grocery Store, on Grand Avenue in Meridian, a short distance from Akins Mobile Homes. Shortly, Sharpe and Jordan returned to Akins Mobile Homes with six pairs of brown cloth gloves (not rubber gloves).[348]

Killen then issued instructions to the assembled group. Doyle Barnette, in his 1957 Ford, would go to the west side of the Neshoba County Courthouse and wait for further instructions. Jordan, Travis Barnette, Snowden, and Aldredge would accompany Doyle Barnette. Killen, Sharpe, Roberts, and Townsend would proceed in the 1959 Chevy owned by Sharpe to the Neshoba County Jail. Their purpose was to see if "everything was OK." After checking, this group would meet with the Klansmen in the 1957 Ford on the west side of the Courthouse.[349]

Killen also explained that officers of the Highway Patrol would apprehend the civil rights workers upon release. Then, the two groups of Klansmen could take over from the Patrolmen.[350]

Doyle Barnette, James Jordan, Travis Barnette, Arledge, and Snowden (all from Meridian) drove to the west side of the Courthouse in the 1957 Ford, owned by Doyle Barnette. Upon arrival at the west side of the Courthouse, Barnette parked the 1957 Ford alongside a black pickup truck that contained Hop Barnett, former Neshoba County Sheriff, and another individual. Hop greeted this group. Passengers of the 1957 Ford and the black pickup waited for the arrival of Killen.[351]

Killen, Townsend, and Sharpe (all from Philadelphia) and Roberts (Meridian) drove to the Neshoba County Jail in the 1959 Chevy, owned by Sharpe. At the Jail, Killen confirmed that the civil rights workers were still incarcerated.[352]

After leaving the Jail, Killen, Sharpe, Townsend and Roberts proceeded in the 1959 Chevy to the west side of the Neshoba County Courthouse. At about 9:30 pm[353], at this location, Killen and company in the 1959 Chevy owned by Sharpe met with Doyle Barnette and his group waiting in the 1957 Ford owned by Doyle Barnette. Killen informed both groups of a location where the caravan could wait for notification that the civil rights workers had been released from Jail.[354] Killen also informed the group that "we have a place to bury them, and a man to run the dozer to cover them up."³⁵⁵

Jerry Sharpe with his passengers Roberts and Townsend in the 1959 Chevy proceeded immediately to the new location. Hop Barnette and his passenger in the black pickup truck departed and were not part of the subsequent activities.³⁵⁶

Since Killen was an officer (Kleagle), he could not participate in the "project". He had to provide himself with an alibi. Doyle Barnette, in his 1957 Ford, along with his passengers Jordan, Travis Barnette, Snowden, and Aldredge, dropped Killen at the McClain-Hayes Funeral Home.³⁵⁷ about 2 blocks from the Courthouse.³⁵⁸ His uncle, Alex Rich, was lying in state at the funeral home.³⁵⁹ Killen arrived just after 9:30 pm.³⁶⁰ Immediately upon his arrival, Killen signed the guest book at the funeral.³⁶¹ He claimed he did not depart until after 2:30 am on July 22, 1962.³⁶²

However, this claim turned out to be a lie. Carolyn Dearman was the former wife of Neshoba Democrat editor Stanley Dearman. Carolyn was living in Ohio with her new husband whose last name was Barret. Her youngest daughter Leslie was four, going on five years old. Leslie contracted a high fever and died on Friday, June 19, 1964. After the autopsy, the body of Leslie was flown to Neshoba County for interment. Carolyn drove to Neshoba County with her husband and their two other children. They arrived at McClain-Hayes Funeral Home on June 21, 1964. *We got to the funeral home by 10:00 pm and it was already closed down and shut, no lights or cars ... It was dark. He [Killen] was not there.* Carolyn and the family left the funeral home and drove to the family's house in Williamsville. Everybody was still awake, waiting for them to arrive.³⁶³

Edgar Ray Killen likely returned to his own home just a mile from Rock Cut Road where the murders would occur. He did not participate in the remaining events of the night. However, he had orchestrated those events and established his alibi by signing the book at the McClain-Hayes Funeral Home around 9:30 pm.

After dropping Killen at the funeral home, Barnette in his 1957 Ford along with his passengers Jordan, Travis Barnette, Snowden, and Arledge, proceeded to the new location waiting for notification of the release of the civil rights workers. Jerry Sharp and his group in the 1959 Chevy owned by Sharpe were already waiting.[364]

Both cars containing White Knights (1957 Ford, 1959 Chevy) waited near a warehouse[365] on a small, dark street a few blocks on the northwest side of the jail for the civil rights workers to be released.[366] Billy Wayne Posey (from the Philadelphia Klavern) drove up in his red and white[367] 1956 Chevy[368] where the other cars were waiting on the side street.[369]

Posey, Townsend, and Sharpe (from Philadelphia), joined Roberts (from Meridian) in the **1956 Chevy** owned by Posey. Doyle Barnette, Jordan, Travis Barnette, Arledge, and Snowden (all from Meridian) remained in the **1957 Ford** owned by Doyle Barnette.[370] Sharpe left his 1959 Chevy parked near the warehouse. He had entered the 1956 Chevy owned by Billy Wayne Posey.

Incarceration While Awaiting Bail

Horace Virgil Milton Herring and Minnie Lee Herring, his wife, were a middle aged couple serving as the jailers in the Neshoba County Jail. The married couple actually lived on the jail premises.[371] Since Virgil was not in good health, Minnie assisted Virgil in the handling of inmates and performing other duties at the jail.[372] Minnie had many relatives and friends in Neshoba County. Some of these friends and relatives were members of the White Knights. She had a formidable reputation. Minnie was known to call a man a *gawddamn sonofabitch* as fiercely as any man.[373]

When Price first brought the workers into the jail, he requested that all three be locked in the same cell. Horace, the jailer, informed Price that a Black prisoner could not be housed with white prisoners. Chaney was then locked into a different cell than Schwerner and Goodman. This cell contained another Black prisoner.

About 3:30 pm until 3:45 pm, Schwerner asked to make a telephone call to his wife in Meridian. Mickey explained to Horace, the jailer, that his wife would be *uneasy* if he did not return from Philadelphia.[374]

In response, Horace explained that he could not allow Mickey to leave his cell to make a phone call. The jailer did offer to make the call to Mickey's wife, if the call could be made collect. Schwerner declined the offer by the jailer.³⁷⁵ With this subterfuge, Horace was able to deny Mickey his right to make a phone call.

The volunteers were being held in the jail until Justice of the Peace Leonard Warren was available to set bail for Schwerner.³⁷⁶ Warren was Justice of the Peace for District 1 of Neshoba County.³⁷⁷

Justice of the Peace Leonard Warren was not available until 10 pm. When he arrived, JP Warren set bail for Chaney at $20. Chaney borrowed the $20 from Schwerner.³⁷⁸ After Chaney paid the $20 bail set by Warren, the civil rights workers were released at approximately 10:30 pm.³⁷⁹ The trio was escorted by Cecil Price to the Police Dept parking lot where their impounded Ranch Wagon was parked. As he released the three workers at the lot, Deputy Price told them to *see how quickly you can get out of Neshoba County*.³⁸⁰

After taking a left turn out of the parking lot onto Center Avenue, the workers drove several blocks to Main Street. As the trio traveled down Center Avenue towards Main Street, Deputy Sheriff Price, in his 1956 Chevy Cruiser, immediately began following the trio in the 1963 Ford Ranch Wagon.³⁸¹ Philadelphia Police Officer Richard Willis shortly joined and followed the trio and Price in his own Police Department vehicle.³⁸²

At the intersection of Center Avenue and Main Street, the trio took a left turn onto Main Street. Driving east on Main Street, the workers arrived at the intersection of Highway 19, towards Meridian. At this intersection, the trio made a right turn and proceeded south towards Meridian. Price and Willis followed the trio south on Highway 19 until reaching the Philadelphia city limits. At the time, the Philadelphia city boundary was at the intersection of Highway 19 south and St. Francis Drive.³⁸³ Price and Willis then turned back towards downtown Philadelphia.³⁸⁴

Apprehension and Second Arrest

Highway Patrolmen Harry Wiggs and Earl Poe were heading south on Highway 19 looking for dragsters. The Patrol officers pulled into a Standard Service Station on the east (left) side of Highway 19 just on the outskirts of Philadelphia.³⁸⁵ This service station was at the top of a hill where Pilgrim's Store³⁸⁶ was located.³⁸⁷ Pilgrim's Store was about 1 mile south of downtown Philadelphia.³⁸⁸ A curve in the road gave a warning sign at the location of the Service Station and Pilgrim's Store.³⁸⁹

A short time after the release, Richard Willis, the Philadelphia Police Officer, who was elderly and heavy set,[390] drove up to the Klansmen. waiting on Oak Street near the old warehouse. Willis told the Klansmen that the released civil rights workers were heading south on Highway 19.[391] Posey drove his car up to the Barnette vehicle. He told Barnette that the workers had been released. Posey took the lead and the two cars took off to locate the Ranch Wagon heading south on Highway 19.[392]

The two Klan vehicles pulled over to talk with the Highway Patrol Officers at the Standard Service Station on Highway 19.[393] The 1956 Chevy driven by Posey pulled just past the Highway Patrol cruiser. Doyle Barnette in his 1957 Ford pulled in just behind the 1956 Chevy. Billy Wayne Posey, the driver of the 1956 Chevy, exited his car and came to the driver side of the Highway Patrol cruiser. Posey said to Wiggs, the Patrol officer driving the cruiser, *Where is Price? Which way did he go?* In response, Wiggs told Posey that he had not seen Price.[394]

As Posey was talking with Wiggs, Deputy Sheriff Price arrived in his 1956 Chevy Cruiser. Price said that he would find the Ranch Wagon with the workers. Price headed south on Highway 19. The Klan vehicles followed Price with the Posey 1956 Chevy in the lead, followed by the Barnette in the 1957 Ford. After Price and the two Klan vehicles had departed, the Highway Patrol cruiser headed back towards Philadelphia.[395]

True to his word, Cecil Price was able to overtake the trio, despite their head start. Chaney had been driving the Ranch Wagon at a reasonable speed to avoid being arrested again for speeding. A short distance north of House, MS, Price in his 1956 Chevy Cruiser overtook the trio in the 1963 Ford Ranch Wagon. Posey and his fellow Klansmen in his 1956 Chevy were not far behind Price. Bringing up the rear was Doyle Barnette and his fellow Klansmen in his 1957 Ford.

When Price and the Klan vehicles came barreling down out of the dark, a high-speed chase began, continuing south on Highway 19.³⁹⁶ As Price gave chase, the Ranch Wagon and Price in his Cruiser passed the gas station operated by Billy Wayne Posey.

**Posey Gas Station Highway 19 ½ Mile North Highway 492
(FBI 1-58 Photo 14)**

(19 South To Left)

Price in his 1956 Chevy was bearing down on the Ranch Wagon. James Chaney driving the Ranch Wagon exited Highway 19 onto Highway 492, heading west, still at high speed.³⁹⁷

Intersection Highway 19 Highway 492
(FBI 1-58 Photo 05)

(19 South From Top, 492 West To Left)

Price was somewhat ahead of the other two Klan vehicles. However, Posey and Barnette were close enough to see Price chase the Ranch Wagon west onto Highway 492. Just north of Highway 492, the 1956 Chevy driven by Posey pulled to the right/west side of Highway 19. This location was within sight of Posey's Store located on the on the right/west side of Highway 19 as the group headed south. The 1956 Chevy had developed a carburetor problem.[398]

Doyle Barnette in his 1957 Ford pulled over to the side of the road to talk with Posey. Posey motioned Doyle Barnette to continue to follow Deputy Price in his Cruiser.[399] Posey and the passengers of his 1956 Chevy remained together at the side of the road on Highway 19 south.[400]

The workers' 1963 Ford Ranch Wagon continued to be chased by Price in his 1956 Chevy Cruiser until a location on Highway 492 west of Highway 19 between House, MS, and Union, MS.[401] Total distance from

Philadelphia was about 16 miles.⁴⁰² At this location, *the road went down a hill, had pasture land on each side, and just before a small bridge."*⁴⁰³ Just before the bridge is a dirt road on the left. After the bridge, Highway 492 continues onward and exhibits a gentle turn to the right.⁴⁰⁴

2nd Arrest Location Highway 492

(FBI 1-49 Photo 30)

A bridge appears on Highway 92 approximately 3.23 miles west of Highway 19. This bridge is about 16 miles (15.88 miles) from Philadelphia. Features around the bridge match the features above.⁴⁰⁵

At this location, Price in his 1956 Chevy Cruiser, passed in front of the 1963 Ford Ranch Wagon containing the trio.⁴⁰⁶ This action by Price forced the workers' vehicle over to the side of the road.⁴⁰⁷

Price went up to the driver's side of the Ranch Wagon being driven by Chaney. Price stated, *I thought you were going back to Meridian if we let you out of jail?* Chaney replied, *We were doing that.* Then, Price asked, *Why are you taking the long way around?*"[408] In their panic at being followed, the workers had turned west on Highway 492. Highway 492 east leads to Meridian. So, the workers had turned in the opposite direction. This fatal mistake was probably the result of their panicked mental state and their lack of knowledge regarding the Philadelphia area.

After a short period, Doyle Barnette and his fellow Klansmen, in the 1957 Ford, arrived and pulled in behind the 1963 Ford Ranch Wagon.

The Murders on Rock Cut Road

After this discussion, *Price ordered the workers to get out of the Ranch Wagon and into his Police cruiser.*[409] The three civil rights workers exited their Ranch Wagon and entered the rear of the Sheriff's cruiser. Price used his blackjack to strike Chaney on the back of the head.[410] Arledge and Snowden exited the 1957 Ford driven by Doyle Barnette. Arledge entered the Ranch Wagon that had been driven by the Civil Rights workers. Snowden sat in the front seat of the Price cruiser.[411]

Deputy Sheriff Price, Snowden, and the three civil rights workers were in the Price cruiser. Doyle Barnette, Jordan, and Travis Barnette were in the 1957 Ford owned by Doyle Barnette. Arledge drove the Ranch Wagon.

Deputy Sheriff Price turned around heading back eastward, followed by the Ranch Wagon, and then the 59 Ford. This caravan traveled eastward back to Highway 19. Upon reaching Highway 19, Price turned north and was followed by the Ranch Wagon and the 1957 Ford.[412]

A short distance after turning north on Highway 19, the caravan encountered Posey's 1956 Chevy which had experienced carburetor problems. Price pulled to the left side of the Highway, stopping in front of Posey's 1956 Chevy. Both the Ranch Wagon and the 1957 Ford pulled in behind the Price cruiser. Posey, Sharpe and Roberts entered the Ranch Wagon being driven by Arledge.[413] Townsend was left with the 1956 Chevy owned by Posey. He was supposed to fix the carburetor problem.[414]

Deputy Sheriff Price, Snowden, and the three civil rights workers were in the Price Cruiser. Doyle Barnette, Jordan, and Travis Barnette were in the 1957 Ford owned by Doyle Barnette. Arledge, Posey, Sharpe, and Roberts were in the Ranch Wagon belonging to the workers.

Price in his cruiser, the 1957 Ford, and the Ranch Wagon drove north in a caravan on Highway 19[415] until reaching an unpaved road that exited west from Highway 19.[416] This road was 3-4 miles north of the entry onto Highway 19 at Highway 492.[417] About 150 yards south of the intersection to the gravel road to the west is another gravel road heading east from Highway 19.[418]

**Rock Cut Road Entrance
(FBI 1-58 Photo 07)**

(19 North At Top, Gravel Road 1st Right, Rock Cut Road 1st Left)

At this intersection between Highway 19 and the gravel road heading west, a red brick house was on the east side of the Highway. Immediately after turning onto the gravel road heading west was a wood frame house on the left side of the road.[419]

Road 515 is a gravel road heading west off Highway 19 that is 3.41 miles north of the intersection with Highway 492. This state road is also 9.5 miles south of the city of Philadelphia, MS.[420] A local name for this road was the Rock Cut Road. About 150 yards south of Road 515 (Rock Cut Road[421]) is a gravel road that heads east from Highway 19.

Rock Cut Road Entrance From Highway 19

(FBI 1-49 Photo 34)

Price in his cruiser led the 1957 Ford and the Ranch Wagon to the west down Road 515, at the time an unpaved road.[422]

The gravel road leads from Highway 19 in a westerly direction **bending slightly to the left** *and then* **curving to the right** **in a gradual upgrade**. *Just prior to the crest of this hill, there is a band along the south side of the road approximately 5 and 1/2 feet in height which consists of rock and clay and has* **a deep ditch running along the edge of the road**. *On the north side of the road is a shallow ditch, no bank and the trees grow near the edge of the road.*[423]

**Rock Cut Road Entrance From Above
(FBI 1-58 Photo 10)**

(Bends Slightly Left, Then Curving To Right)

Furthermore, the murder location was at least 300 yards past the intersection of Road 515 and Highway 19.[424]

Some distance after the murder location, Road 515 made a sharp curve to the south (left) as the vehicles faced westward. [425]

When heading west on Road 515, Road 515 makes a slight bend to the left, then curves to the right as the Road travels uphill.[426] About 175 yards past the gradual right turn and uphill peak, a fairly deep ditch appears on the south (left) side of the road.[427] At some distance past the area of the ditch on the left side, the road curves sharply to the left.[428]

The actual murders were accomplished in the area of the ditch at the south (left) side of the road at some distance before the sharp curve to the left.[429] This location is on Road 515 is about 350 yards west of the intersection of Road 515 and Highway 19.[430]

**Rock Cut Road Murder Location
(FBI 1-49 Photo 36)**

Deputy Sheriff Price parked his car on the right side of the road.[431] Doyle Barnette parked the 1957 Ford behind the Price cruiser on the right side of the road. About one car length separated the Price cruiser form the Barnette 1957 Ford.[432] Arledge parked the Ranch Wagon on the left side of the road about two car lengths in front of the Price Cruiser.[433] A ditch was on the left side of the road.[434]

Immediately after stopping, Wayne Roberts jumped out of the Ranch Wagon on the left side of the road. Roberts ran back to the Deputy Sheriff's cruiser. Opening the left rear door of the cruiser, Roberts pulled Schwerner from the vehicle. Roberts took Schwerner over to the left side of the road across from and between the Price cruiser and the Barnette 1957 Ford.[435]

Then, Roberts asked Schwerner, "Are you that n-**** lover?". Schwerner replied, "Sir, I know just how you feel." Wayne Roberts then shot Mickey Schwerner[436] directly in the chest[437], killing him. Even with his obviously impending death, Mickey Schwerner expressed empathy for his murderer.

Schwerner's body lay in the ditch on the left side of the road, across from and between the Price 1956 Chevy cruiser and the Barnette 1957 Ford. His body was face down, headed west, and parallel to the road.[438]

Wayne Roberts then returned to the Sheriff's cruiser. He retrieved Goodman from the vehicle. Goodman also was taken by Roberts to the left side of the road, across from and between the Price cruiser and the Barnette 1957 Ford. Wayne Roberts then shot Andy Goodman[439] directly in the chest,[440] killing him.

After being shot, Goodman's body was in the ditch on the left side of the road, across from and between the Price 1956 Chevy cruiser and the Barnette 1957 Ford. His body lay crumpled in the ditch, face down, headed south, and perpendicular to the direction of the road.[441]

James Chaney was still alive. James Jordan exclaimed *Save one for me!* Jordan exited the 1957 Ford owned by Doyle Barnette. He went over to the Sheriff's cruiser. Jordan extracted James Chaney from the back seat of the cruiser.[442] Chaney was taken by Jordan to a position at the edge of the ditch on the left side of the road and about one car length behind the Ranch Wagon and one car length in front of the Price cruiser.[443]

James Jordan turned James Chaney to face the ditch by the side of the road. Jordan placed the muzzle of his 38 Smith and Wesson pistol very close to the back of the head, just behind and near the middle of the auricle of the right ear. Jordan pulled the trigger.[444] Chaney died instantly.[445] James Chaney tumbled into the ditch, laying face up.[446]

After shooting Chaney in the head, Jordan declared, *You didn't leave me anything but a n-****, but at least I killed me a n-****!*[447]

Chaney's body lay in the ditch on the left side of the road, one car length behind the Ranch Wagon and one car length in front of the Price cruiser. His body lay face up,[448] headed west and more or less parallel to the road.[449]

After Chaney landed on his back face up in the ditch, Roberts and Posey moved to the edge of the ditch. Roberts and Posey were filled with blood lust at this *n-***** who dared to interfere with white control of Neshoba County. In a blood lust frenzy, this pair began pumping lead at the body of James Chaney. Roberts shot into the left chest of the body. A bullet from Posey entered the right lower abdomen of the body. Two more bullets were shot into the body of James Chaney. One shot was into the right forearm. Another shot was into the left shoulder.[450] Other shots fired in the frenzy missed and plugged into the dirt on the other side of the ditch.

These bullets to the arms were seen in x-rays but have never been recovered.[451] Posey and Roberts each took a second shot. Given the position of the body and entry of the first shot by Roberts, a second, wild shot by Roberts entered into the left shoulder. The bullet in the right forearm was a second, wild shot by Posey.[452]

Multiple residents in the area reported hearing gunshot discharges around 11 pm on June 21, 1964.[453] However, a careful timeline analysis reveals that the shooting actually occurred around midnight on June 22, 1964.

Wayne Roberts (Schwerner and Goodman) and James Jordan (Chaney). were the actual killers. Roberts and James Jordan were members of the Meridian Klavern of the White Knights in Lauderdale County. Billy Wayne Posey was a member of the Philadelphia Klavern of the White Knights but did not actually participate in the murder. Chaney died instantly when Jordan discharged the bullet into Chaney's head.

Burying The Bodies on Old Jolly Farm

Schwerner was lying face down in the ditch on the left side of the road, body oriented in a westerly direction parallel to the road. Goodman was also lying face down in a crumpled position on the left side of the road. However, his body was positioned in a southerly direction, perpendicular to the road and about the same location as Schwerner. Both Schwerner and Goodman were located midway between Price's 1956 Chevy cruiser and Doyle Barnett's 1957 Ford Fairlane.[454]

Chaney was lying face down in the ditch on the left side of the road, body oriented in a westerly direction parallel to the road. Chaney was about one car length behind the Ranch Wagon and one car length in front of Price's cruiser.[455]

Deputy Price entered his police cruiser. He left the scene, returning to Philadelphia via Highway 19 north.[456]

Someone said, *Help us get these empty shells. I've already got mine.*" All of the expended shells were retrieved.[457]

Posey said, *Let's load these guys in their wagon and take them to the spot.*[458] The *spot* referenced by Posey was a dam under construction located on the Old Jolly Farm, owned by Olen Burrage.[459]

The victims were loaded into the Ranch Wagon. Schwerner and Goodman were loaded first. Then, Chaney was thrown on top of Schwerner and Goodman.[460]

Posey said, *Everyone follow me. We'll go the back way.* Posey, Sharpe[461] and Roberts[462] entered the 1963 Ford Ranch Wagon that contained the bodies. Snowden, Jordan, Arledge, Travis Barnette, and Doyle Barnette entered into the 1957 Ford owned by Doyle Barnette. Doyle Barnette was the driver of his 1957 Ford.[463]

The Ranch Wagon, followed by the 1957 Ford, traveled northward towards the outskirts of Philadelphia and westward on gravel roads.[464]

After a lot of turns, while traveling north on Road 365, the vehicles encountered Highway 21, a paved road. The caravan turned to the right.

About 3/4 of a mile north on Highway 21,[465] the vehicles turned left onto a dirt road. This dirt road was the equipment access road for the dam being constructed on the Old Jolly Farm[466]. The caravan encountered a fence that had been constructed from light posts and barbed wire. A gap in the fence allowed the caravan to proceed down the dirt road.[467] After following the dirt road, the vehicles arrived at the dam.[468]

**Dam At Old Jolly Farm
(FBI 1-58 Photo 18)**

(Parking Area At Lower Right, Burial At Middle, Top Of Dam)

Posey parked the 1963 Ford Ranch Wagon perpendicular to a mound of dirt about 3 feet high. Barnette parked his 1957 Ford a short distance from the dam. Everyone exited the vehicles.[469]

**Parking Locations
(FBI 1-49 Photo 47)
(Lower Half)**

Posey, Sharpe, Roberts, Snowden, Jordan, Arledge, Travis Barnette, and Doyle Barnette were now all at the dam.

Someone suggested that a lookout would be a good idea. So, Jordan and Snowden proceeded down the dirt equipment access road, taking a position near a gap in a row of trees.[470]

A bulldozer operator was needed to bury the bodies. These bulldozers were likely the Caterpillar Bulldozer Model D6B with a 10-foot blade. This bulldozer was the most popular bulldozer at the time. A Caterpillar Bulldozer Model D6B with a 10-foot blade was later brought to the dam when the FBI came to dig up the bodies.[471]

During the planning activities, Edgar Ray Killen contacted Olen Burrage and arranged for Burrage to provide a bulldozer operator. That operator was Herman Tucker, a contractor working for Olen Burrage, who was operating the bulldozers during the day at the dam under construction.[472]

A location was determined where Burrage and Tucker were to be available.[473] This location was about 1 mile from the equipment access road to the dam and 1 mile from Burrage Trucking Company and Garage.[474] In other words, the 1955 Chevy owned by Tucker was halfway between the entrance to the dam and the garage.

Posey asked, *I wonder where our operator is? Someone go and get the operator.*[475]

Doyle Barnette, Arledge, and Roberts entered Barnette's 1957 Ford.[476] Barnette drove off down the dirt equipment access road to find Tucker, the bulldozer operator. Posey, Sharpe, and Travis Barnette waited at the dam for the arrival of Tucker, the bulldozer operator.

Barnette and his 1957 Ford returned down the equipment access road to the paved road, Highway 21. Turning north, the 1957 Ford proceeded about a mile down the highway. A green and white 1955 Chevy was parked on the left side of the road. Olen Burrage, Herman Tucker, and one other unidentified person were waiting in the 1955 Chevy.[477]

Tucker owned and was driving the 1955 Chevy. Burrage, a passenger in the 1955 Chevy, told Doyle Barnette, the driver of the 1957 Ford, to follow Tucker.[478] Tucker drove south on Highway 21 about 120 yards to a dirt road, currently paved and known today as Bureau of Indian Affairs O228.[479] After driving down this road for 0.789 miles, the caravan came to a location that was mostly undeveloped fields between road O228 and the north end of the dam.[480]

Roberts exited the 1957 Ford. Tucker exited the 1955 Chevy. Roberts and Tucker walked about 1/2 mile south across fields to the north end of the dam.[481] Burrage in the 1955 Chevy and Doyle and Arledge in the 1957 Ford then drove to Burrage's auto repair garage.[482] Upon arrival at the garage, Doyle Barnette attached the license plate which had been removed back onto his 1957 Ford Fairlane.[483]

The Burrage Truck Company and auto repair garage was located on Highway 21, 1 1/2 miles west of the Williamsville area.[484] Olen Burrage lived in a house directly across Highway 21 from the Burrage Truck Company and auto repair garage.[485] This location was on Highway 21 approximately 2 miles north of the equipment access road to the dam area on the Old Jolly Farm.[486]

Posey, Sharpe, and Travis Barnette were waiting at the dam. Roberts and Tucker had walked about 1/2 mile (0.473 miles)[487] across the fields to the dam. Snowden and Jordan were waiting down the equipment access road to the south of the dam, acting as lookouts.

The 1963 Ford Ranch Wagon driven by the victims was still at the dam. Both the 1957 Ford, owned by Doyle Barnette and the 1955 Chevy owned by Tucker were now parked at the Burrage auto repair garage.

Once Herman Tucker, the bulldozer operator, returned to the dam from the north across the fields, a signal was given to Snowden and Jordan serving as lookouts down the equipment access road south of the dam. After about 20 - 30 minutes standing guard[488], Snowden and Jordan heard a whistle. Jordan asked, *What is it?* Snowden responded, *Nothing. The operator is there and taking care of things.*[489]

An excavation for the dam had been formed as part of the normal ongoing construction activity. This excavation was in an east - west direction and 547 feet in width. Filling of the excavation to construct the dam had begun on the east side of the dam. The excavation had been filled up to about 191 feet from the west end of the excavation.[490]

All three bodies were dumped onto the ground into the unfilled excavation area close its easternmost edge, 191 feet from the west end of the dam.[491]

**Burial Location
(FBI 1-49 Photo 43)**

Using the Caterpillar Bulldozer, Tucker covered the bodies in the unfilled area with dirt. He used the blade of the bulldozer to level the dirt over the top of the covered bodies. He then drove over and over the now buried bodies with the Bulldozer to compact the dirt over and around the bodies. Compaction ensured that the bodies would not be accidentally found.

While standing guard down the equipment access road, Jordan and Snowden, had heard a noise similar to a tractor. This sound was caused by Tucker performing the burial operations. After about 15 minutes, the tractor sound stopped. The bodies had been successfully buried.[492]

When the bodies were buried, the dam had been extended at least another 7 feet, 6 inches towards the west end. Thus, the bodies were buried between 183 and 191 feet[493] from the west end of the dam. Dumping the bodies, covering the bodies, and packing the dirt over the bodies took about 15 minutes.[494]

The bodies were buried in a section of dirt that was 6 feet, 9 inches across the top from north to south, 7 feet, 6 inches wide from east to west, and 14 feet, 11 inches below the top of the dam.[495]

After the burial was completed, Posey, Sharpe, Travis Barnette, Roberts and Tucker entered the 1963 Ford Ranch Wagon that had belonged to the victims. Posey drove the wagon down the equipment access road to the dam where Jordan and Snowden were serving as lookouts. Jordan and Snowden entered the vehicle. Seven passengers were not a problem for the Ranch Wagon. This vehicle had a comfortable passenger limit of eight persons. Posey than drove the Ranch Wagon north on Highway 21 to the Burrage Truck Company and auto repair garage.[496] The Ranch Wagon arrived at the Burrage Truck Company and auto repair garage around 2:00 am, now June 22, 1964.[497]

The Ranch Wagon had arrived at the garage 30 minutes after Doyle Barnette in his 1957 Ford.[498] Subtracting the 15 minutes utilized to bury the bodies, an additional 15 minutes had been needed to gather Jordan and Snowden and drive to the garage.

Burial of the bodies took about an hour. Retrieving Tucker, the bulldozer operator, took 30 minutes.[499] Burying the bodies consumed another 15 minutes.[500] Then, an additional 15 minutes were required to gather Jordan and Snowden and drive to the garage.[501]

Posey, Sharpe, Travis Barnette, Roberts, Tucker, Snowden, Jordan, Doyle Barnette, Arledge, Burrage, and an unidentified person were all assembled at the Burrage Truck Company and auto repair garage.

The 1963 Ford Ranch Wagon driven by the victims, the 1957 Ford, owned by Doyle Barnette ,and the 1955 Chevy owned by Burrage were now all assembled at the Burrage Truck Company.

Disposing of the Vehicle

One final problem had to be solved. The 1963 Ford Ranch Wagon driven by the victims had to be eliminated. Herman Tucker was going to drive the vehicle into Alabama. Once a suitable disposal location was identified, the vehicle would be burned.[502] Distance from Philadelphia to the Alabama border is about 37 miles.

Herman Tucker needed someone to follow him. Otherwise, he would not be able to return. Burrage told Tucker, *I will use a diesel truck to pick you up. No one will suspect a truck on the road at this time of night.* Olen Burrage took one of the diesel trucks from under a trailer parked at his Garage.[503] He then retrieved a glass gallon jug, filling this jug with gasoline. This gasoline would be used to burn the Ranch Wagon after being abandoned.[504]

Tucker, in the 1963 Ford Ranch Wagon of the victims, and Burrage, in the diesel truck, exited the garage and started north on Highway 21. After passing through Philadelphia, the two vehicles continued traveling north east on Highway 21.

Approximately 1.1 miles past the intersection of Highway 21 and Highway 491, Tucker pulled the Ranch Wagon off to the left or north side of Highway 21.[505] This location was 112 feet east of the east end of a concrete bridge over Bogue Chitto Creek.[506]

This location was well inside the borders of MS. For reasons never disclosed, Tucker chose to abandon and burn the vehicle inside the border of MS rather than continuing on to Alabama, as originally instructed.

Tucker drove the Ranch Wagon headfirst off the road, so that the rear of the vehicle was facing Highway 21. He encountered a barbed wire fence at a distance of 43 feet from the north edge of Highway 21.[507] Tucker simply drove the Ranch Wagon through the wire. This action deposited paint smears from the body of the Ranch Wagon onto the broken wire.[508] He drove the Ranch Wagon until the rear of the car was 78 feet from the north edge of Highway 21.[509]

Using the gasoline in the glass gallon jug, Tucker and Burrage set the Ranch Wagon on fire.

Burrage and Tucker then entered the diesel truck that had been driven to the location by Burrage as a follow up vehicle. Burrage drove back towards his Truck Company and auto repair garage on Highway 21 south of Philadelphia. This garage was located on Highway 21, 1 1/2 miles west of the Williamsville area.[510]

Burrage parked the diesel truck in his auto repair garage about 3:00 am.

Burrage had driven Herman Tucker's green and white 1955 Chevy to the garage after leaving Tucker to walk into the burial site. Tucker entered his own car, then drove home.

**Burrage Trucking Co
(FBI 1-58 Photo 01)**

Olen Burrage walked across Highway 21 to his home and went to sleep.

Several witnesses passed by the burning vehicle.

Just after 2:30 am on June 22, 1964,[511] T. Hudson was driving south west[512] on Highway 21 towards Philadelphia.[513] Just before the Bogue Chitto Bridge, Hudson saw the burning car off to the right.[514]

Rodney Harrison was a passenger in another car[515] driving north east along Highway 21 away from Philadelphia.[516] Also in the car were Raymond Dallas and another Black person.[517] This car passed the burning Ranch Wagon[518] early that morning. Harrison saw the Ranch Wagon burning off to the left.[519] As the car containing Harrison approached the burning car, another car was just departing from the area of the burning car heading south east towards Philadelphia.[520] Given the remote location, the passing car moving in a south west direction was likely the car driven by T. Hudson.

The Perpetrators Disperse

As Posey had initially driven into the Burrage Truck Company and garage, the unidentified man was driving away from the Garage.[521]

After Tucker and Burrage departed the garage to dispose the Ranch Wagon of the victims, Doyle Barnette, Posey, Sharpe, Travis Barnette, Roberts, Snowden, Jordan, and Arledge climbed into the 1957 Ford owned by Doyle Barnette. Exiting the garage, Doyle Barnette drove his 1957 Ford north along Highway 21 into Philadelphia.[522]

Highway 21 enters Philadelphia on Main Street. Barnette drove the car east on Main Street towards Highway 19 to Meridian.[523] At around 2:00 am, as he was driving the car down Main Street, a Philadelphia Police Cruiser pulled behind the 1957 Ford and blinked his lights. Posey told Doyle Barnette, who was driving, to pull over to the side of the road. Barnette pulled over as he was told.[524] When pulled over, the 1957 Ford was near the parking lot of an A&P Grocery store.[525] Everyone exited the 1957 Ford.[526]

Sheriff Lawrence Rainey, Deputy Sheriff Cecil Price and Philadelphia Police Officer Richard Willis emerged from the Patrol Car.[527] Willis was the same Philadelphia Police Officer who had told the waiting Klansmen that the released civil rights workers were driving down Highway 19 south.[528]

Willis had originally informed the waiting Klansmen about 10:30 pm. The time was now about 2 am on June 22, 1964.

The group talked for about two or three minutes. Then, Sheriff Rainey said, "I'll kill anyone who talks, even if it was my own brother."[529]

All of the Klansmen climbed back into the 1957 Ford, with Doyle Barnette driving. The vehicle headed south towards Meridian on Highway 19. Eventually, the vehicle came to the location where Posey had abandoned his car due to carburetor problems. Townsend was still guarding the car. Posey and Sharpe, both from Philadelphia, exited the 1957 Ford.[530] Eventually, Posey, Sharpe, and Townsend returned to their homes in Philadelphia. Presumably, Posey was driving his repaired vehicle and gave Sharpe and Townsend rides home.

After dropping Posey and Sharpe, Doyle Barnette continued driving south on Highway 19 towards Meridian. Upon reaching Meridian, Barnette dropped Roberts at home. He then dropped Travis Barnette at home. Jordan and Snowden were left at Akins Mobile Homes. Arledge was then given a ride home by Barnette. Finally, Doyle Barnette went to his own home.[531]

At 2:00 am, Doyle Barnette driving his 1957 Ford had met Price, Rainey, and Willis, on Main Street in Philadelphia. Meridian is 45 minutes from Philadelphia. Another hour was likely consumed with taking the participants to their homes. So, Doyle Barnette finally parked his 1957 Ford in his garage about 3:30 am on June 22, 1964.

Jordan and Snowden departed Akins Mobile Homes. Jordan was driving. He first gave Snowden a ride home. After leaving Snowden, Jordan drove to his own home in Meridian.[532]

Schwerner, Chaney, and Goodman were dead, buried, and forgotten.

Reporting Back to Sam Bowers, Imperial Wizard

"Everything was well done. It was a job to be proud of."[533] said Sam Bowers to Pete Harris and to James Jordan.

This statement was made in mid-July, 1964, about a month after the murders. Pete Harris, an investigator for the Meridian Klavern, and James Jordan, a member of the Meridian Klavern who had shot James Chaney, were in a meeting with Sam Bowers. This meeting was in Laurel,[534] the location of the national headquarters of the White Knights. Laurel was also the hometown of Bowers.

Sam was congratulating Harris and Jordan for the successful murders. Bowers also told them, "The best thing to do is not to talk about it. If there were any instruments involved, they should be gotten rid of."[535]

The Search, The Autopsies, And The Funerals

Finding The Ranch Wagon

Everyone working in the COFO office in Meridian had a communications protocol when leaving the office to go out into the field. Once in the field, the rights worker would check into the office via phone at regular intervals to report his whereabouts. Mickey Schwerner was almost religious about this protocol. He felt so strongly about this protocol, that Mickey often reprimanded others who failed to call in as required.[536]

Mickey had not called in his location since he left for Mt. Zion Methodist Church.[537] People working in the COFO office in Meridian were becoming more and more worried as time passed. Action had to be taken to locate Schwerner, Chaney, and Goodman. Workers in the office started reaching out to contacts all over the US.

June 21, 1964

One person contacted was Sherwin Kaplan, a law student. At 10:00 pm, June 21, 1964, Kaplan contacted H. F. Helgesen, a Jackson FBI Agent. Kaplan told Helgeson that Schwerner, Chaney, and Goodman were missing. He requested an investigation. Helgeson was noncommittal, simply requesting that Kaplan keep him informed about anything that happened.[538]

Frank Schwelb[539], a Justice Department attorney, was in Meridian at this time. At 10:30 pm, June 21, 1964, a member of the Meridian COFO officer called Schwelb. Schwelb was informed of the disappearance of the 3 workers. A member of the Jackson COFO office called Schwelb at 11:00 pm. At this time, Schwelb did not indicate that any action had been taken.[540]

Robert Weil from the Jackson COFO office called Scwhelb at 12:00 am on June 21, 1964. Weil provided Schwelb with the license plate of the COFO vehicle that had been driven by Schwerner and company. Schwelb was also given the home addresses of the 3 workers in Meridian. Weil then requested that the FBI investigate. Schwelb refused to investigate. He claimed that the FBI was not a police force. He was not sure that a

Federal offense had been committed. As a result, Schwelb felt that he could not act. Weil countered by citing the provision in the US Code that authorized FBI arrests. Despite this citation, Schwelb still felt that he did not have authority to act.[541]

After completing the call to Schwelb, Weil from the Jackson COFO called H. F. Helgesen, the Jackson FBI Agent. Helgeson curtly accepted the license plate and home address information. He then terminated the conversation. Weil then called the MS Highway Patrol. Again, the license plate and home address information was accepted without result.[542]

Tick tock, tick tock. As the clock ticked without any communications from Mickey Schwerner, members of both the Meridian and Jackson COFO offices became more and more concerned about the safety of Schwerner and his companions.[543]

June 22, 1964

Rita Schwerner, Mickey's wife, was still in Oxford, Ohio, attending the class on civil rights protest strategies that Schwerner and Goodman had abandoned. She was asleep in the dormitory. At 1am, on June 22, 1964, she was awakened. Rita was asked to come to the office of the Western College for Women, where the class was being hosted. Upon arrival, she received a phone call from the Jackson COFO office. In this call, Rita was informed that the trio, including her husband, were missing and presumed to be in jail somewhere in MS. After daylight, she learned that the trio had been released from the Philadelphia jail around 10:30 the previous night. Her husband and his companions were definitely missing.[544]

Starting at 1:00 am on June 22, 1964, Ron Carver from the Atlanta SNCC office made multiple calls to John Doar, Asst AG of the Justice Department in Washington, DC. Carver pressured Doar to act and to get the FBI involved. Finally, at 6:00 am, Doar stated, *I have invested the FBI with the power to look into this matter.*[545]

Attempting to confirm search activity, Weil of the Jackson COFO office called the MS Highway Patrol at 7:00 am on the same morning. Despite having been called at least 4 times during the previous night, no one at the MS Highway Patrol seemed to know anything about the case.[546]

Once the FBI received the authorization from John Doar, Asst AG of the US DOJ, 4 FBI agents were dispatched to Philadelphia. By 11:30 am on June 22, 1964, these 4 FBI agents had arrived in Philadelphia to begin investigating.[547]

Throughout the day, June 22, 1964, extensive effort was made to motivate Federal agencies to swing into action. Repeated calls to the FBI offices in Jackson and New Orleans did not yield any response. Calls to the DOJ attorneys, including John Doar, were unanswered.[548]

Lawrence Rainey, Sheriff of Neshoba County, expressed cynicism over the disappearance of Schwerner, Chaney, and Goodman. On Monday, June 22, 1964, Rainey was interviewed by newsmen. *I feel that the disappearance is probably nothing more than a publicity stunt in connection with a desegregation drive in the Philadelphia area.*[549]

Upon hearing of the disappearance of Schwerner, Chaney, and Goodman, MS Gov Paul Johnson became worried. Murder, violence, and disappearing civil rights workers were not good for the reputation of MS. Herman Glazier, Admin Asst to Gov Paul Johnson, gave another reason. Johnson was *determined to keep the peace in the state of MS. Gov Johnson had his hand on everything.*[550]

Midday on June 22, 1964, Gov Johnson notified T B Birdsong, MS Commissioner of Public Safety, to activate all 200, all-white MS Highway Patrol Officers. These officers were given several missions. Search for the 3 missing men. Cooperate with Federal investigators. Watch and record all movements by the FBI. Commissioner Birdsong was ordered to present updated briefings to Gov Johnson every day at 9 am, 1:30 pm, and 5 pm.[551] MS Highway Patrol Officers were to spy on the FBI investigators, recording all of their movements.[552]

FBI Agents knew that the MS Highway Patrol officers were stalking and reporting as the Agents investigated. FBI Agent Roy Moore was dispatched to the Philadelphia area to help with the search. *We quickly realized that we were both the hunters and the hunted. All I had to do was look into the rear-view mirror.*[553]

Due to the absence of FBI responses, several Black leaders decided to elevate concern upward in the FBI hierarchy. Marvin Rich, Public Relations Director of CORE and James Farmer, Executive Director of

CORE, called Cartha "Deke" DeLoach, Deputy Associate Director of the FBI. DeLoach was the third highest person in the FBI after J Edgar Hoover and Clyde Tolson. Also called were Burke Marshall, Head of the Civil Rights Division of the Justice Department and Lee White, Presidential Assistant.[554] During the day, James Farmer also publicly demanded that an air and ground search be conducted by the Meridian Naval Air Station.[555]

At 5:20 pm on June 22, 1964, John Doar called the Atlanta SNCC office. Doar stated that the MS Highway Patrol had issued an All-Points Bulletin. Doar also informed that both the FBI and the Sheriff of Neshoba County, Lawrence Rainey, were conducting searches. Rainey claimed that Schwerner, Chaney, and Goodman had last been seen heading south on Highway 19 for Meridian.[556]

At 9:30 pm on June 22, 1964, reporters in the Philadelphia area contacted the Meridian COFO office. Four agents from the FBI New Orleans office were reported to be in Philadelphia. These agents claimed that a road search would be conducted starting in the morning. Edmond Guthman in the Justice Department in Washington officially announced around 10:00 pm that the FBI was ordered to investigate the case. Goals of the investigation were to determine if the trio were being held against their will or if their civil rights had been violated. Clearly, the assumption was that Schwerner, Chaney and Goodman were still alive.[557]

The first call was on June 21, 1964 at 10:00 pm. By 5:20 pm on June 22, 1964, the FBI was finally deployed into the area and actively searching. After about 20 hours, the Department of Justice and the FBI finally acted. This long delay was unacceptable to many people, given that the lives of 3 young civil rights workers were at risk.

June 23, 1964

In late 1964, Rita told author William Bradford Huie, *I knew that they were dead*.[558] That realization must have been horribly painful.

Meridian FBI Resident Agent John Proctor and FBI Special Agent Harry Saizan were at the Meridian COFO office at 10:10 am on June 23, 1964. These agents were collecting information about the case and obtaining photos of Mickey Schwerner[559]

Proctor and Saizan immediately departed for Philadelphia. These agents began interviewing Blacks, community leaders, Sheriff Rainey, and Deputy Price. Ten additional FBI agents from various other FBI Field Offices joined Proctor and Saizan in Philadelphia later that morning.[560]

Rita Schwerner spent all day Monday, June 22, 1964, in Oxford, OH, waiting for any further word about Mickey and the group. Having heard nothing further, she decided to return to Meridian. Late in the morning on June 23, 1964, several students drove her the sixty miles to Cincinnati airport. While waiting for her plane, she learned that the burned car had been found. Rita had to go to Atlanta to connect to the plane to Meridian. She spent the night in a motel in Atlanta to catch the connecting flight to Meridian.[561]

At 12:35 pm on June 23, 1964, President Lyndon Johnson received a call from Lee White. White was a holdover from the Kennedy administration who served as the chief aide to Johnson on Civil Rights. That public demand by James Farmer, Executive Director of CORE, for a search had to be answered. Farmer also requested a meeting with President Johnson.

In the phone conversation, Johnson summarized for Lee White all of his actions to date.

Johnson: I asked Hoover two weeks ago and I've told the Attorney General to fill up MS with FBI men and infiltrate everything he could ... I've asked him to put 4 men after these three kids ... I'm shoving it as much as I know how ... I can't control the actions of MS people. The only weapon I have to locate them is the FBI ... I've got all I've got looking after them ... I've given them already standing orders to stay on it day and night ... We don't see people who get in the newspaper [Farmer] before they get an appointment ...

Lee White: Helicopters at the naval base at Meridian are being made available to the FBI to scour the countryside.

Johnson: Inform Farmer of what we've done and make a list for me.[562]

In the early afternoon of June 23, 1964, Joe Sullivan, FBI Major Case Inspector, arrived in Philadelphia.[563]

Joe Sullivan

Major Case Inspector

At about the same time as Sullivan's arrival, FBI Agent John Proctor, of the FBI Office in Jackson, was contacted by Lonnie Hardin. Lonnie was Superintendent of the Choctaw Indian Agency in Philadelphia, MS. Lonnie provided Proctor with a tip regarding a burnt-out Ranch Wagon east of the intersection between Highway 21 and Highway 491.[564] Upon receiving this tip, Agent Proctor went to the identified location. He was accompanied by Meridian Special Agent Henry McConnell.[565]

John Proctor

FBI Special Agent

At approximately 1:32 pm on June 23, 1964, FBI agents Proctor and McConnell reported that a 1963 Ford Ranch Wagon had been found. License plate number on this vehicle was H25503. This number matched the number of the COFO owned vehicle that had been driven by the missing trio. This vehicle was found off Highway 21, 1.1 miles east of the intersection between Highway 21 and Highway 491.[566]

The wagon was located 112 feet east of the east end of a concrete bridge over Bogue Chitto Creek. This vehicle was parked facing north with the rear of the vehicle facing Highway 21. Vehicle rear was 48 feet north of the north edge of Highway 21.[567]

Rear Of Ranch Wagon Well Hidden

(FBI 1-50 Photo 57)

(48 Feet From Hwy 21 North

As the FBI reported, the Ranch Wagon exterior was extensively damaged and severely burned.[568]

Debris from the burned interior had fallen to the floor. All tires and wheels, except the left front, were burned and charred. Paint on the exterior was scorched and burned off with a few exceptions.[569]

Front
Scorched
Exterior
Of
Ranch
Wagon

(FBI 1-50
Photo 55)

Side
Scorched
Exterior
Of
Ranch
Wagon

(FBI 1-50
Photo 54)

Rear
Scorched
Exterior
Of
Ranch
Wagon

(FBI 1-50
Photo 52)

Interior of the vehicle was burned to bare metal.⁵⁷⁰

Burned Interior Of Ranch Wagon

(FBI 1-50 Photo 59)

Most importantly, *"no human remains were found."*⁵⁷¹

President Johnson received a message from Attorney General Robert Kennedy. Johnson was in a television studio making a public statement on Laos. At 3:35 pm on June 23, 1964, Johnson tried to return Kennedy's call. Kennedy was unavailable, also having gone to a television studio. Johnson was informed that Kennedy would not return for another hour. Johnson spoke instead to Deputy Attorney General Nicholas Katzenbach.

Johnson: ... I ought to consider seeing their [Schwerner, Chaney, and Goodman] parents. I've been considering it all day ... I'm afraid that if I start house mothering each kid that's gone down there and that doesn't show up, I'll have a White House full of people every day asking for sympathy and Congressman too ... I've told them what we've done ... there's not anything new I can tell them ... the FBI has substantially augmented their personnel in the last few hours ... what do you think happened to them ...

Katzenbach: I think they've been picked up by some of those Klan people.

Johnson: and murdered?

Katzenbach: Yes ... I would not be surprised if they'd been murdered.[572]

President Lyndon Johnson had spent 8 years in the US Senate, from 1952 until 1960, when he became the Vice President for John Kennedy. During both his Vice Presidency and his Presidency, Johnson maintained close contacts with his former Senate colleagues. On June 23, 1964, at 3:59 pm, Johnson contacted MS Senator James Eastland. Eastland was a virulent opponent of the Civil Rights Movement. Eastland downplayed the disappearance.

Eastland: I don't believe there's three missing ... I believe it's a publicity stunt ... I'm on tell ya why I don't think there's a damn thing to it. They were put in jail in Philadelphia ... and they were going to Meridian. There's not a Ku Klux Klan in that area. There's not a Citizen's Council in that area. There's no organized white man in that area. So, that's why I think it's a publicity stunt ... I don't think there's anything to it.

Johnson: I made a statement ... I'm going to try to get them [the parents] to see an assistant of mine [Lee White, for Civil Rights] so I don't add to the fuel ... Burke Marshall [Asst AG US DOJ] called Attorney General Patterson [MS AG]. They will do everything they could to help. Would you advise I call MS Gov Johnson?

Eastland: No, I'm not gonna advise it. I don't think it would mean anything either way. He's gone do everything he can. I can call him.

Johnson: Let's do that and I'll say I've communicated with the proper people and I'm doing everything I can with everybody I know ... You tell him I want to see him any time he wants to ... I'm ready ... We got to appoint a conciliator under this law [Civil Rights Act of 1964[573]*]. I've got to have some Southerner who knows something about the South and that the Negroes will have confidence in and won't say that I've fixed 'em. If you've got any ideas, anybody that's worth a damn, I wish you'd let me know ...*

Eastland: I'll do it.[574]

Title I of the Civil Rights Act of 1964 specifically enforced the Constitutional right to vote. These provisions prohibited discriminatory practices for depriving the right to vote. Practices such as a literacy test had long been used by Southern state District Court Clerks to prevent Blacks from registering to vote. ... *informal methods of conference, conciliation, and persuasion* needed to be initially employed to resolve issues under the Act.575

Technically speaking, Johnson was not legally obligated to appoint a conciliator at this time. On June 19, 1964, the US Senate passed the Act in a 73 to 27 vote. However, the US House would not pass the Act until July 2, 1964, by a vote of 289 to 126.576 Since the Act would not become law until July 2, 1964, Johnson did not have to appoint a conciliator. However, Johnson was confident that the Act would pass. So, appointing a conciliator would put President Johnson ahead politically.

Literally within a minute of completing the call with Senator Eastland, President Johnson received a call from J Edgar Hoover, Director of the FBI. At 4:05 pm on June 23, 1964, Hoover informed President Johnson that the Ford station wagon of Schwerner, Chaney, and Goodman had been found.577

Hoover: I wanted to let you know we found the car ... This is not known. Nobody knows this at all, but the car was burned. We do not know yet whether any bodies are inside of the car because of the intense heat that is still in the area of the car ... It wasn't going towards Meridian, but it was going in the opposite direction ... Apparently what's happened, these men have been killed.

Johnson: what would make you think that they have been killed?

Hoover: because it is the same car that they were in Philadelphia ... the same license number is on the outside of the car ...

Johnson: or, maybe kidnapped and locked up ...

Hoover: I would doubt that those people down there would give them that much of a break ... An Indian agent saw the car and notified us ... the car is still burning ...

Parents of Andy Goodman and Nathan Schwerner, the father of Mickey Schwerner, had traveled to Washington DC. Henry Wolf, attorney for the Goodmans, had accompanied them to the capital city. During the afternoon of June 23, 1964, this group first met with Robert Kennedy, Attorney General, and a few other high-ranking members of the Justice Department.578

Kennedy explained to the parents the limitations that were faced by the US DOJ and its Department heads. According to Kennedy, the FBI was assuming that the trio had been kidnapped. This assumption allowed the FBI to participate under Federal law, which made kidnapping a Federal crime. After defining the legal limits of the Justice Department in detail, Kennedy realized how hollow these technicalities must seem. Parents of Schwerner and Goodman were on the verge of open grief. Kennedy apologized to the parents, thanking them for their patience in listening. Parents told the Attorney General that every effort must be made to find the missing trio and to protect the rest of the civil rights workers in the area.[579]

Also, during the afternoon of June 23, 1964, MS Gov Paul Johnson convened a news conference to discuss the efforts to find the missing civil rights workers.[580]

State units are working with local and Federal officers on the case. I sent investigators into the area on Monday morning [June 22, 1964] without the request of County officials. State investigators are empowered to do any and all things. I'm in touch with the Highway Patrol at all times. They will keep me abreast of happenings in the area ... Two investigators and 8 to 10 units of two-man Highway Patrol units are now in the area ... I have talked with FBI agents for the past 24 hours ... Several government helicopters and planes are being used in the search for the missing trio. We will press the search unrelentingly ...

Throughout the day, reports from MS Highway Patrol officers in the field flowed in from Neshoba County. These reports went first to A D Morgan, Chief of the MS Highway Patrol. Morgan summarized these handwritten reports into short typed documents. These typed summaries were forwarded from Chief Morgan to MS Public Safety Commissioner T B Birdsong. Commissioner Birdsong reviewed the report. After his review, Birdsong initialed the report *TBB*. Initialed summaries were forwarded directly to MS Gov Paul Johnson.[581] As requested, these summaries arrived for Johnson 3 times daily: 9 am, 1:30 pm, and 5 pm.

In his 5 pm report, on June 23, 1964,[582] Commissioner T B Birdsong forwarded a one-page report that Birdsong received from Chief A D Morgan.

*Car was found 12 miles northeast of Philadelphia on Highway 21 ... approximately 100 feet off the highway. Fifteen to 20 FBI men and one deputy sheriff and the sheriff [Price and Rainey] are on the scene ... The FBI is taking pictures and they had the scene roped off. Footprints were being taken around the scene. No bodies were found in the car. The car had been burned sometime before and was now cold.*583

Despite his earlier reluctance to meet with the parents, President Johnson changed his mind after learning about finding the station wagon. Johnson now had some positive news for the parents. About 5:15 pm on June 23, 1964, parents of Andy Goodman and Nathan Schwerner, the father of Mickey Schwerner, met with President Johnson for 21 minutes. During that visit, the group learned the news from Johnson that the car had been found. At 5:44 pm on June 23, 1964, Johnson called Secretary of Defense Robert McNamara with the parents present in the office. McNamara assured the group that the Federal government was doing everything possible to find Schwerner, Chaney, and Goodman.584

Around 6 pm on June 23, 1964, US Attorney General Robert Kennedy had arrived at the White House. AG Kennedy worked with President Johnson to plan the US DOJ involvement in the investigation to find the trio and to potentially prosecute the perpetrators. Kennedy also proposed that Johnson appoint former CIA Director Allen Dulles to become an impartial observer of the situation in MS. Dulles was not to investigate or to conciliate, only to observe.585

AG Robert Kennedy felt that the situation in MS was dangerous. MS segregationists had threatened to resist the alleged invasion of MS that was about to be conducted by students from the North and East with force. The objective of this invasion was to aid Blacks in their struggle for equality in MS. Anyone associated with the US DOJ would only tend to inflame an already impassioned populace.

Allen Dulles was recommended by AG Kennedy for several reasons. Dulles was above politics, had a reputation for integrity, and had qualities of prudence and caution. His CIA background would serve well in making an objective analysis of the situation. Most importantly, Dulles was an outsider, not a member of the US DOJ.586

After Kennedy and Johnson agreed to appoint Dulles, President Johnson and AG Robert Kennedy phoned former CIA Director Allen Dulles. This 9:27 minute call was between 6:30 and 7:00 pm on June 23, 1964.[587]

Johnson: The Attorney General and I are sitting here talking. The Governor of MS this afternoon sent me word this afternoon that he would like for me to pick some impartial, objective observer that would represent the President and come down and talk to him and let him show my representative what he was doing to try to prevent violence ... and review what his problem was. We wanted to get someone we thought all the country would respect ... We concluded that you were about the best, the only fella that could get that job done for me and we wanted to talk to you about it ...

Dulles: ... whether I'm the best man for this or not, I don't know.

Johnson: Oh, yes, you are. I know you are.

Kennedy: The situation is extremely explosive in MS. There is very little contact and has been for the last few years between the authorities down there and the Federal authorities. And the fact that the Governor said that this was a possibility he'd accept ... I think could be a big help and give us some breathing space ... I think it would be a question of going down there, talking to him, talking to some of these students, talking to some of the Negro people down there, talking to some of the FBI, and then coming in and talking quite frankly with the Governor, then talking quite frankly with President Johnson about what you think needs to be done.

Dulles: I'm not a great expert on this subject really.

Kennedy: I thinks it's just a question of decency, really, and just looking at the facts ... The fact that you have no communication in such an explosive situation is very, very dangerous for the country ... This is not a question of needing a great deal of expertise on civil rights or the problems of Negroes ...

Dulles: My job is purely advisory.

Kennedy: That's right. I think you go down and report on what the facts are and make suggestions ...

Dulles: What is the timing on this. I'm on this other commission you know and we're trying to finish up our work. I don't want the Chief Justice to think I'd run out on him.

Kennedy: What I think is if you could go down there for a day or so or a couple of days, and then come back up here ... but, I think just to get it started would be helpful! ... Even if you found out he [the Governor] wasn't [in good faith] ... even that's helpful to the country ... The fact that he's opened this door is very important ... If President Johnson has to take some steps later on and these things have such an effect across the country ...

Johnson: I'll talk to the Governor and then I'll give you a ring back. Perhaps we can get together in the morning.

Dulles: ... if you think I can do it. I'm not so sure. This is a field I'm no expert in ...

Johnson: You're the man for it ...

Dulles: You remember that you put me on this commission with the Chief Justice and the others. That is now reaching a point where I wouldn't want to neglect that ...

Johnson: No, I understand that ... but I'll put a plane at your disposal. You can come back in the evening after a couple of days there.

Allen Dulles did not want this job. Dulles gave several excuses. He was not qualified in the area of civil rights. He was involved in the Warren Commission with Chief Justice Earl Warren to investigate the assassination of President John Kennedy.[588] This commission was at a critical point. Dulles expressed self-doubt in his own abilities several times, to both AG Robert Kennedy and President Johnson.

But President Johnson always got what he wanted, always. Johnson brushed aside the objections offered by Dulles. Then, Johnson assumed that Dulles was appointed to the position. Johnson gave Dulles instructions. Ignoring objections and proceeding was classic Lyndon Johnson behavior.

At 7:15 pm on June 23, 1964, FBI Director J Edgar Hoover called with additional information about the burned car that was found. Informally, agents concluded that the bodies were not in the car.

Hoover: The Governor [Johnson] has issued the statement that he will give every assistance, even to the extent of calling out the National Guard to aid in any search that you might desire ... we have moved all the inside of the car from the place the car was found to Meridian ... the impression of the agents who have removed the material, most of which is ashes and all kinds of debris. There was no bones that could be found, although bones would burn in a fire as hot as that ... the offhand assumption is that the bodies were not in the car ... we will not know that definitely until the laboratory men ... will make the determination ...

Johnson: Any information they get if they call you tonight or during the morning, you call me.[589]

President Johnson needed to discuss the appointment of Dulles with MS Governor Paul Johnson. Gov Johnson had to agree to receive Dulles. At 8:25 pm on June 23, 1964, President Johnson placed a call to MS Governor Paul Johnson to discuss the appointment of Dulles.[590]

Pres Johnson: I was talking to [Senator] Jim Eastland ... and he said that you were deeply concerned about this situation as I was ... he said that you had suggested that you'd be glad if I sent an impartial objective observer down to talk to you so you could tell 'em what you were doing and see themselves what all was happening ... I think that's a good idea and I asked Allen Dulles ... to fly down there and told him that you'd ask us to do that and I'm going to ask him to go down there tomorrow or the next day ... I want him to talk to you and any people that you suggest ... send him to anyone that you think he ought to see, send him to any local officials or state officials ... I think he ought to before he comes back to see some of the Negro groups, so he can hear anything they've got to say, I think he ought to talk to the FBI people that are in there ... I'm deeply concerned about this situation as I know you are.

Gov Johnson: The real danger in it ... is these youngsters who come into a situation where you already have a hard-core group of people with long police records that are professional agitators. These youngsters don't realize what they are getting into. They've been in here a good while and they've stirred up a great deal of tension and now these youngsters come in where the tensions are gettin' near the boiling point ...

Pres Johnson: ... I appreciate your invitation to have this objective observer. I'm going to send Mr. Dulles ... I want him to come back and give me some information because they are picketing us tomorrow and say that we're not taking steps, so we want to be sure we do everything we possibly can consistent with getting results.

After talking with MS Gov Johnson, President Johnson called the parents of Mickey Schwerner at 8:35 pm on June 23, 1964. Anne Schwerner answered the call from the President.

Johnson: We have received word from Mr. Hoover that the investigation of the car and the kids, that there were no people in the car, and it's very likely that none of them were burned ... I have talked to the Governor there and he is making all of the facilities of the state available for the search ... He has seen some tracks leaving the car ... We are flying some people in from the FBI tonight ... I just wanted you to know that and that was a little hope we didn't have earlier ...

*Anne Schwerner [with obvious tears in her voice]: Thank you so much, President Johnson. I appreciate this. Thank you very much.*⁵⁹¹

Robert Goodman, Goodman father of Andy Goodman, received a call at his home in New York at 8:50 pm on June 23, 1964. This call was from President Johnson. Johnson had ordered more FBI and Department of Defense personnel to comb the countryside to find Schwerner, Chaney, and Goodman.⁵⁹²

Johnson: The FBI got into the car and think there are reasons to believe that no people were in the car, because we are unable to find any evidence of that. And, there are indications that there were tracks leading back from the car to the highway and we don't know where we'll go from there but I thought you should have that information as soon as we had it. We've talked to the Governor and he's agreed to make available all of the facilities at his command ... We are making arrangements to send additional people in tonight and tomorrow.

*Goodman: I can't express the words to thank you for what you are doing for these boys and for us ...*⁵⁹³

Once President Johnson had the agreement with MS Gov Johnson to send Allen Dulles, the White House released a statement on the evening of Tuesday, June 23, 1964. *Dulles will confer with MS officials in an effort to improve the state's racial climate.* After the public announcement by the White House, MS Gov Paul Johnson provided a public acknowledgement.

Allen Dulles has a reputation for a spirit of cooperation and fairness. I shall be glad to meet with him and discuss with him whatever he may wish to discuss. I shall be pleased to give him any information he wishes relative to Civil Rights activities and the failing efforts of hard-nosed professional agitators.

So long as Mr. Dulles is objective, I have no doubt he will find law and order prevail, and will be maintained by state and local authorities; that harmony and great progress follow in the wake of close cooperation among our citizens, and that any incident of strife or disorder comes from professional visiting trouble makers.[594]

Allen Dulles expressed his personal commitment to the trip to MS. *I view the job as a call to public service in a pretty difficult situation.*[595]

Tuesday night, June 23, 1964, saw the arrival in Meridian of James Farmer, Executive Director of CORE. Farmer was met at the Meridian airport by a police escort. A news conference was held by Farmer shortly after deplaning. During the news conference, Farmer announced that he would go to Philadelphia. However, he refused to give any definite details about when. Then, Farmer was escorted to his motel in Meridian by a police cruiser.[596] Comedian Dick Gregory joined Farmer in Meridian.[597]

Search for the Missing Workers Begins

Tremendous national publicity and pressure was now focused on finding the missing workers.

Based on the order from Johnson, on June 23, 1964, a huge Federal manhunt began in the Philadelphia area.

June 23, 1964

Late in the afternoon on June 23, 1964, law enforcement officers and volunteers gathered to organize searching for the missing trio. FBI Major Case Inspector Joe Sullivan, Meridian Resident Agent John Proctor, and Special Agent Don Cesare were all at this meeting. Sullivan was the lead agent on the investigation.[598] Inspector Sullivan and Agent Proctor met for the first time at this initial meeting.[599]

Maynard King, a MS Highway Patrol officer from Philadelphia, also attended this meeting. Inspector Joe Sullivan established a friendly relationship with King starting at this first meeting. King would be known as Mr. X. As Mr. X, King would serve as a conduit between a Neshoba County resident who became a paid informant and the FBI during the search. Sullivan himself left many clues that clearly pointed to Maynard King as Mr. X. Over the years, multiple FBI agents have confirmed that Maynard King was Mr. X.[600]

At this organization meeting on June 23, 1964, the FBI, the MS Highway Patrol, and the Neshoba County Sheriff's Dept each contributed 20 men to this first search posse. These searchers formed groups of 3. Each group combed the lonely area of overhanging trees and dark bayous around the location of the burned vehicle.[601]

Once faced with the burned car, confidence of the local residents began to slip. The burned car opened the possibility that the trio had come to real harm and maybe were even dead. Now, members of the community started to express excuses based on racist concepts. Some residents felt that the trio had no business coming to Philadelphia. Other residents expressed doubt that anything had happened to the workers, but . . . if the trio had been subjected to violence, that violence was well deserved. Local residents sometimes claimed that the trio would have not experienced any violence if they had stayed home where they belonged.[602]

Almost immediately, extensive efforts by local community members were devoted to making the whole disappearance look like a hoax by COFO to gain attention. Local residents believed that the burned car did not prove anything. COFO must have burned their own car. Burning the car was necessary to make the hoax look convincing. Many residents believed that the trio were far out of Neshoba County having a good laugh at the expense of the uneducated local residents.[603]

A few honest residents, such as Florence Mars, *knew that when the Ranch Wagon was found, the trio was dead.*[604]

June 24, 1964

On the morning of Wednesday, June 24, 1964, an intense, house-to-house investigation was begun in Neshoba County. About 200 combined[605] FBI Agents and plainclothes MS Highway Patrolmen were conducting the search.[606] This search continued throughout the day. An area stretching from 18 miles south of Philadelphia and 17 miles to the north of Philadelphia was to be covered by the search.[607]

That same morning of June 24, 1964, Philadelphia turned into an armed camp. MS Highway Patrolmen wearing blue helmets formed into a cordon around the Neshoba County Courthouse. These Patrolmen were armed with shotguns. Neshoba County Deputy Sheriffs were staged at strategic locations downtown and in the Courthouse area. These Sheriffs were armed with carbines and pistols. FBI Agents mingled with the crowd to aid the officers. Newsmen were required to receive a special pass from the MS Highway Patrol in order to enter the town.[608]

Curious whites were not allowed to congregate in the Courthouse square in downtown Philadelphia.[609] Tensions mounted over fear of the possibilities of a serious public disturbance.[610]

Controversy over the civil rights movement and the missing workers erupted in the US Senate on June 24, 1964. On that day, the Senate convened at 12 o'clock noon.[611] MS Senator John Stennis asked that President Johnson intervene to prevent the invasion of MS by civil rights workers.[612]

Mr. President, since the Mississippi invasion was first announced many weeks ago, I have repeatedly and consistently called on those planning the project to abandon it. I have pointed out repeatedly that their drive could only succeed if they could provoke incidents, strife, and violence to get the Federal Government to intervene—that this was the real purpose of those organizations sponsoring this summer project. It was also clear, as I pointed out, that Mississippi had been selected by them as the whipping boy.

... I am also deeply concerned about the safety and welfare of the people of Mississippi ... If violence and bloodshed do erupt as a result of the invasion of my State by these freedom riders, demonstrators, and agitators, the blood will be on the hands of those who planned this drive and who are determined to carry it through regardless of everything else.

... What is really needed, however, is to get to the root of the trouble. This invasion of Mississippi must be stopped ... I again urge the President and the Attorney General to use his influence and his power of persuasion to stop this invasion immediately. This is the only effective answer.

... I believe that virtually every Member of the Senate knows in his heart that this invasion can only be highly provocative and make the situation even worse.

Apparently, all members of the Senate did not agree. NY Senator Jacob Javits immediately responded to the speech by Stennis.[613]

Mr. President, I should like to be recognized at this time for 3 minutes because I could not disagree more with the Senator from Mississippi, and I should like to utilize that time now.

Senator Javits then exhorted President Johnson to act in MS.

Mr. President, the tragedy which may have happened to the young boys in Mississippi can neither be ignored nor begged.

... The Federal authority is being directly challenged. The United States cannot tolerate interposition, secession, or nullification of the Constitution.

... It is a fundamental proposition that the privileges and immunities of every citizen of the United States—including ... the right to assist others in the attaining of their constitutional rights, including the right to vote—extends to every State of the United States, notwithstanding the opposition of local officialdom or the local population.

As a necessary corollary to this proposition, it is the responsibility of the Government of the United States to safeguard the enjoyment of these privileges and immunities where they are jeopardized or denied.

Under these statutes [1957 and 1969 civil rights laws], the Department of Justice has the power to provide Federal presence, through use of U.S. marshals and agents of the Federal Bureau Of Investigation, to attempt to avoid, in advance, the violence and intimidation.

The law of the United States must be enforced ... The presence of U.S. marshals and agents of the FBI in Mississippi, wherever these groups of young college people are in operation, is clearly necessary.

These two Senators were exactly opposite in terms of Federal involvement in MS. Stennis was attempting to shift blame for any violence in MS from the violent racists to the organizers of the upcoming summer program. He wanted to blame the victims rather than the perpetrators. Stennis wanted the President to exert his influence to stop MS Freedom Summer.

Senator Javits turned the disappearance and ultimate murders of Schwerner, Chaney, and Goodman into the Pearl Harbor of the Civil Rights Movement. Pearl Harbor ushered the US into WWII. MS

Freedom Summer was the WWII of the Civil Rights Movement. Disappearance and death of the trio should usher the US into the Civil Rights Movement. The weight and might of the people of the US, should be brought to the front lines of the battle over Civil Rights about to take place in the state of MS.

President Lyndon Johnson assigned 200 sailors[614] from the Meridian Naval Air Station to join the search party. These sailors arrived in Philadelphia at about 1 pm on June 24, 1964.[615]

Around 1:30 pm on June 24, 1964, a 7 car[616] motorcade approached the city of Philadelphia. One car in this motorcade contained James Farmer, Executive Director of CORE, Dick Gregory, the comedian, George Raymond, MS Field Secretary of CORE, and John Lewis, representative of SNCC. MS Highway Patrolmen halted the motorcade on the outskirts of Philadelphia. A single car containing the 4 Civil Rights leaders and Rita was escorted into the city.[617]

This quartet was hustled through the cordon of law enforcement officers into the Neshoba County Courthouse. In the Courthouse, the group was met by Herman Alford, Neshoba County Attorney, Gwin Cole, head of the MS Highway Patrol investigation team, and Charlie Snodgrass, assistant head of the MS Highway Patrol investigation team.[618]

James Farmer asked permission to visit the location where the burnt station wagon was found. Authorities were willing to escort the 4 leaders to the location. Farmer demanded that the whole motorcade, still waiting on the outskirts of Philadelphia, be allowed to visit the location. Investigators refused the motorcade access request. Farmer and the others were asked to rejoin the motorcade and return to Meridian. *You will be kept advised of the results from the search [for the missing trio].*[619]

After the half hour[620] meeting concluded, MS Highway Patrol officers escorted the group of 4 leaders back to the motorcade detained on the outskirts of town. The motorcade was then ordered to turn around and head back to Meridian. Cars in the motorcade complied. MS Highway Patrol officers escorted the motorcade all the way back to Meridian.[621]

At 3:10 pm, on Wednesday afternoon, June 24, 1964, Allen Dulles arrived by US Air Force C-140 Executive Jet (Lockheed JetStar VC-140B[622]) in

Jackson, MS.[623] Burke Marshall, Asst US AG for Civil Rights, was on the plane. Burke did not deplane. He returned to Washington, DC, with the government jet. US DOJ Civil Rights Attorney John Doar was also on the plane. Doar waited until Dulles and newsman departed before deplaning.[624]

Allen Dulles exited the plane wearing a double-breasted grey suit and sporting a close-cropped white mustache. Dulles was met by Capt Tom Turner, manager of the Jackson Airport, Gen T B Birdsong, Director of the MS Highway Patrol, and MS Highway Patrolman Billy Harper. More than two dozen newsman were awaiting the arrival of Dulles. Dulles answered questions by the newsmen patiently and politely.[625]

The purpose of my visit has been misunderstood. I am here to discuss various problems arising out of law enforcement with Gov Johnson. I will bring back to President Johnson a personal report on this situation, which he is deeply interested in. I am not here to participate in any investigation.[626]

Before being whisked away from the airport, Dulles looked around at the Jackson air terminal. He commented to Capt Turner, the airport manager: *A lovely airport you have here, very lovely.* Allen Dulles entered the private automobile of Governor Johnson. Dulles was driven to the MS Governor's Mansion in Jackson.[627]

Mrs. Paul Johnson met Allen Dulles at the front door of the Mansion and immediately walked upstairs to meet with the Gov Johnson.[628] Dulles met with MS Gov Paul Johnson for a 90-minute closed session. A brief press conference was held by the Dulles and Johnson after this meeting.[629]

Johnson: I have told Mr. Dulles more or less all I know about my own state. I explained the tranquility existing between our races. I outlined the steps taken to beef up state law enforcement ... The people of MS are happy to have men [Dulles] of this type in our state who are here for the purpose of doing good. Mr. Dulles has a carte blanche to go anywhere in MS as far as I am concerned. I'm sure anywhere he goes, he will be welcome.

Dulles: I will take no part in the investigation of the trio's disappearance. I conferred with FBI Director J Edgar Hoover yesterday before leaving Washington. The investigation is in the good hands of the FBI ... Gov Johnson and I discussed law enforcement as respects this type of situation ... Mississippi's racial problems are not unique. My native NY state has problems of its own ... I intend to meet with a number of people, possibly including representatives of COFO and Jackson businessmen before returning to Jackson.

Johnson: We are determined to maintain peace and order in this state, and we are going to cooperate with all proper authorities in order that our laws are obeyed, and that peace and tranquility may prevail.[630]

Following the press conference, Dulles met with Erle Johnston, Director of the MS State Sovereignty Commission. Dulles told a reporter that the meeting with Erle Johnston *was amicable.*[631] Gov Johnson and Dulles had dinner together at the MS Governor's Mansion.[632] Attending the dinner along with Johnson and Dulles were Lt Gov Carroll Gartin, Jackson Mayor Allen Thompson, and MS State Sovereignty Commission Director Erle Johnston, Jr. Discussions with this group lasted far into the night on that Wednesday, June 24, 1964.[633] Dulles was then taken to a local hotel to spend the evening.[634]

After returning to Meridian, on the night of Wednesday, June 24, 1964, comedian Dick Gregory attended a combined news conference and civil rights rally. This combined event was at a Black church in Meridian. At the event, Gregory offered a $25,000 reward for information on the location of the bodies of Schwerner, Chaney, and Goodman.[635] Reward money was provided by Playboy Magazine owned by Hugh Hefner.[636] In 1961, Dick Gregory was performed at the Black owned Roberts Show Bar in Chicago. Hefner hired Gregory as the regular comedian at the Playboy Club in Chicago.[637]

US AG Robert Kennedy made a public statement on the night of June 24, 1964, about participation during the upcoming Freedom Summer activities in MS. *Even under the proposed Civil Rights Bill [of 1964], the Justice Dept would have only limited authority to step into a racial crisis such as the one in MS. It won't give us authority because we have no national police force.*[638]

June 25, 1964

MS Highway Patrol officers escorted Dulles throughout his visit. These escort duties led to the inevitable reports through the Highway Patrol hierarchy, finally arriving to MS Gov Johnson. In his 9 am report on June 25, 1964, Johnson received a description of the movements of Dulles after the meeting ended on the previous evening. This 3-page memo was prepared by Highway Patrol investigator Al Richburg, one of the officers in the Dulles escort.

We left the Capital enroute to the Sun-N-Sand [Motel, in Jackson]. Mr. Dulles advised Mr. [Sam] Finney, [his assistant]. 'We have a little problem and we had better advise our friends.' Mr. Finney advised, 'I think we do and believe you are right ... Dulles checked into room 415. Finney checked into room 416. Suite 404 was between the two rooms.'[639]

After a single day of discussions and meetings, Dulles already determined that a problem existed in MS. President Johnson and AG Kennedy, his 'friends', needed to be informed. Astoundingly, this memo contained confidential discussions between Dulles and Finney.

Sailors deployed by President Johnson from the Meridian Naval Air Station began participating in the search early in the morning of June 25, 1964. A first contingent of about 60 sailors from the 200 assigned by Pres Johnson arrived at the location of the burned car in 3 gray buses. These sailors gathered around Lt Commander James Wassell, the officer in charge for instructions. Wassell advised the sailors to use caution. *If you find anything, don't pick it up.*[640]

These sailors re-boarded the buses. Buses then traveled to a spot about a half mile south of the location where the burnt station wagon was found. Small search parties of about 10 men each were dropped off at various locations. Searchers began beating their way into the dense Bogue Chitto Swamp. A big orange Navy helicopter whirled about 200 feet over the sailors during the search through the dense undergrowth.[641]

This search of the Bogue Chitto Swamp was incredibly dangerous. Sailors were ill-dressed for the terrain. Most of the sailors were wearing bell-bottom trousers tucked into their socks and old shoes.[642] Swamps in MS are heavily populated by cotton mouth water moccasins. These snakes are extremely poisonous. A bite can be serious with an occasional death. Bites can lead to temporary and/or permanent tissue and muscle damage; loss of an extremity, depending on the location of the bite; internal bleeding; and extreme pain around the injection area.[643]

Water moccasins tend to hide curled up under brush. Sailors pushing and disturbing the brush make these snakes think that an attack is underway. As a result, the snake strikes and bites the cause of the disturbance. Special thick, usually leather, leggings are best worn when creating disturbances in heavy water swamp areas where these snakes reside. If the leggings are thick enough, a snake bite strike does not penetrate.[644] Sailors searching the swamp beginning on June 25, 1964, did not have the protection of these leggings.

Also starting early in the morning on Thursday, June 25, 1964, the 200-man force of FBI agents and MS Highway Patrol officers continued the door-to-door canvas started on the previous day. Plans were being developed to drag farm ponds and the deeper swamp sloughs in the area around the location of the burnt ranch wagon.[645]

At midmorning of June 25, 1964, former CIA Director Allen Dulles met with a bi-racial group of ministers at the local Catholic Chancery.[646]

Comedian Dick Gregory returned to Chicago late in the morning of June 25, 1964. *There is a long shot that they might be alive. Because of this, in association with Playboy, I offered a $25,000 reward for information leading to the location of the trio.*[647]

Also, late in the morning of June 25, 1964, Robert and Carolyn Goodman and Nathan and Anne Schwerner met with reporters in NYC.[648] Carolyn Goodman spoke for the group.

As a mother, and as a parent of one of the 3 boys who are missing, I am making this plea to all parents everywhere. Particularly to the parents of MS, who like myself have experienced the softness, the warmth, and the beauty of a child whom they cherish and love and want to protect. I want to beg them to cooperate in every way possible for the search for these three boys and to come forward with any information of any kind which will help in the search. I want them to do everything in their power as parents, as people, as human beings to protect all the young people in their state. I cannot but feel that parents, no matter what their beliefs, no matter what their views, value their children above all else. And, therefore, will understand and share our concern. At this moment, there is nothing more urgent than finding the 3 young men who have been missing since Sunday. For our sons, all of them, I beseech your help and cooperation.[649]

At a lunch meeting on June 25, 1964, Allen Dulles met with business leaders from Jackson.[650] One of the attendees at this meeting was Robert Ezelle. Ezelle was past President of the Jackson Chamber of Commerce.[651]

Members of the US Congress addressed the issues and racial problems in MS on Thursday, June 25, 1964. At 12 noon, the US House of Representatives convened for the day.[652] MS Representative Arthur Winstead, from Philadelphia, MS, placed blame on the government and churches outside the state of MS.

... It is the belief of many prominent citizens that this incident is part of a plan to bring discredit to the State of Mississippi ... Even the church-burning, some people believe, may be a hoax. At this time, however, no one actually knows whether there has been violence in this case ... it is indeed unfortunate that high officials of our government and so-called church leaders have been instrumental in creating situations of this kind by encouraging activities which could lead to nothing short of violence ...

I submit, Mr Speaker, that the fate of any troublemakers ... can be laid at the door of high Government officials who cater to pressure groups and who so enthusiastically offer "protection" at any time they decide to invade MS and interfere in State and local affairs.[653]

A short time later on June 25, 1964, John Bell Williams, another MS Congressman, spoke to the US House. Williams complained that President Johnson exceeded his authority sending sailors into MS.

It should be pointed out that Mississippi's Governor Johnson had offered the facilities of the National Guard to assist in the Search as long as 2 days ago, only to be turned down. Further, it should be noted that Governor Johnson was neither consulted about sending Marines into Our State, nor was he informed of plans to do so ...

Mr. Speaker, in my opinion, this action is a calculated and deliberate insult to the State of Mississippi, the Governor of Mississippi, and every member of the Mississippi National Guard. It may mollify the radical elements who have demanded a military occupation of our State, but will be resented, I am sure, by the great majority of our people when they learn the facts.[654]

Williams was followed by another MS Congressman, William Colmer. Colmer claimed that the people of MS wanted to be left alone to enforce their own laws. President Johnson sent the 100 sailors into the state without being requested by the Governor.

... every thinking, every intelligent, every knowledgeable person knows that this crusade was organized to go into my great State to create trouble, and they will not be satisfied until they get it ... These agitators are not going to stop there until they bring about some bloodshed. The whole thing is a part of a planned conspiracy to bring down upon the white people of the South the castigations of these misguided people, do gooders, and politicians, who are trying to reform and to remake this great country of America.

The people of Mississippi do not want these people in there. They do not want any bloodshed. They do not want any trouble. All they want is to be let alone so that their laws can be observed; and they resent this intrusion from outside ...

I do not think the President should send Marines into New York any more than he should send them to Mississippi. In fact, there is no authority therefore. These are matters for the States to handle. As a matter of fact, the Constitution only gives the President such authority when requested by the legislature or the Governor of the State. The President had no such request.[655]

During that same afternoon, members of the US Senate also spoke on issues currently facing MS. At 12 noon, on June 25, 1964, the US Senate convened for the day.[656]

Senator Jacob Javits demanded that Federal marshals be dispatched to MS to enforce law and order and to protect citizens of the US in MS.

... This new barbarism in Mississippi must face Federal superior authority to enforce the laws of the United States, everywhere in the United States—including Mississippi ... This is no longer a racial matter; this is a matter of law and order in the United States, the authority of the U.S. Government to enforce its laws and to protect its citizens wherever they may go in the United States on legitimate business ...

It is nothing less than a confrontation between the lawless element in Mississippi and the Government of the United States. There is no alternative but to assert the power of the United States with all its majesty and authority, to enforce the laws, and to see that every citizen, wherever he may be, is safe guarded. ...

Mr. President, I ask that Federal marshals be dispatched so that the presence of the authority of the United States in this situation may be unmistakable, and so that no one will get the idea that this will be overlooked. It is necessary for our country to maintain its dignity as the enforcer of the law.[657]

After his lunch meeting, Allen Dulles continued with his meetings in Jackson. Dulles met with a large group of local leaders of Black groups. This meeting was followed by a meeting with local business leaders from various outlying areas of the state.[658]

Rita Schwerner was frustrated that the body of her husband had not been found. She decided to go to Jackson to meet with Governor Paul Johnson. Her goal was to plead with him to ask Johnson to devote more MS resources for the search.

On Thursday, June 25, 1964, at about 3 p.m., Rita went to the MS State Capitol building in Jackson. Rita was accompanied by Robert (Bob) Zellner, a SNCC Field Secretary, and Reverend Edwin King, the Tougaloo College Chaplain. She attempted to see the Governor to ask for his promise of help in the search for Schwerner, Chaney, and Goodman. She was told by Senator Frank Barbour, executive assistant to Governor Johnson, that the governor was out for the afternoon and could not be contacted. Barbour was extremely rude to Rita Schwerner.[659]

Rita, Bob, and Ed then walked over to the Governor's Mansion, arriving just as Governor Johnson walked up the steps with Governor George Wallace of Alabama. Johnson and Wallace were returning from a Wallace Presidential Rally at the State Coliseum in Jackson.[660] The group followed the Governors up the steps. Bob Zellner introduced himself by name to Governor Johnson. Zellner and Johnson shook hands. Zellner then turned towards Rita. He introduced Rita as the wife of Michael Schwerner, one of the three missing men. Bob said that Rita would like to speak for a moment with the Mississippi Governor.[661]

At the moment Johnson heard the identity of Rita, he turned and bolted for the door of the Mansion. Johnson locked the door. A group of Mississippi highway patrolmen surrounded Rita, Bob, and Ed. An officer with the name plate "Harper" refused to allow the trio to request an appointment with the Governor. Harper said that he would not convey the appointment request to Johnson.[662]

Before his departure to the Jackson airport, in the evening of June 25, 1964, Allen Dulles had one final meeting with MS Gov Paul Johnson. From the Governor's mansion, Dulles proceeded directly to the Jackson Airport.[663]

Three times a day, reports were still arriving from MS Highway Patrol officers to MS Gov Johnson. In his 5 pm report from Highway Patrol inspector Al Richburg on June 25, 1964, Johnson received details of the activities of Allen Dulles during the day.

At 10 am, Mr Dulles and Mr Finney came out of the room and asked me to take them to the Catholic Bishop's. Arriving there, I noticed one Protestant preacher, two Negro preachers, and several Catholic priests going into the building. I found out later, the two Negro ministers were Hawkins and a subject by the name of Whitney. They were driving cars with tag numbers H 28603 and HB 533. Also, in the parking lot were cars with these tag numbers V 1972, T 9254, H 18954, and H 39889 ...

At 14:15, an NBC camera crew came on the scene. Mr Dulles came out, made a talk similar to the rest of his talks to newsmen, then went back into the motel. I inquired as to what the NBC men were doing. They advised that they were making a one-hour long program for NBC which would be broadcast or televised this Saturday night.[664]

Two pages clipped to this memo listed the names of the tag owners identified in the report. This list proved that MS Highway Patrol officers actually ran checks on the tags. As ordered by MS Gov Johnson, MS Highway Patrol officers were spying on Federal officials and local citizens. Tracking the movements of both groups was using law enforcement to act as spies on citizens of the US. This usage was highly illegal and questionable. Yet, MS Gov Paul Johnson appeared not to have any qualms about using MS Highway Patrol officers for spying.

On Thursday evening, June 25, 1964, around 10 pm,[665] Allen Dulles met with newsmen at the Jackson airport just prior to boarding the plane for Washington, DC.

There is a real and serious problem in the racially tense states ... The civil rights situation in MS presents a very real and very difficult problem which will take many months to solve ... However, the situation is not explosive. I found great willingness among white leaders to face racial problems frankly.

I will present to President Johnson practical recommendations for meeting the situation at the President's convenience. I expect to report to the President on Friday [6/26/1964] ...

I have nothing to do with the search for the 3 young civil rights workers missing since Sunday. The massive hunt is in very competent hands.[666]

After the conference was completed, Dulles flew back to Washington, DC on a US Air Force C-140 Executive Jet (Lockheed JetStar VC-140B[667]).

On Thursday, June 25, 1964, the *Meridian Star* ran a front-page story: MAY BE A PUBLICITY HOAX, WINSTEAD TELLS HOUSE. This article described the speech by US Representative Arthur Winstead. Winstead, who lived in Philadelphia, told the House of Representatives that no evidence exists to prove that the workers had been harmed. He went further to say that some people think that the disappearance was a hoax for publicity purposes.[668]

On that same day, an editorial appeared in the *Meridian Star.* The writer bemoaned that the nation and the world was being given an entirely confused picture of Neshoba County. Black integrationist leaders were admonished to remain elsewhere until the integration was completed and all the facts were known. He expressed complete confidence in the ability of local law enforcement to investigate and find the answers.[669]

June 25, 1964, The CBS Special News Report

A CBS Special News Report about the ongoing search for Schwerner, Chaney, and Goodman, was broadcast in the evening of June 25, 1964. These broadcasts were typically in prime time, around 8 pm or 9 pm EST. This report was anchored by Walter Cronkite, later identified as *the most trusted man in America.* Cronkite was given that epithet by a 1972 Oliver Quayle and Company poll of 8,780 respondents in 18 states.[670]

Sandy Leigh, Field Secretary of SNCC, gave an ominous warning to the volunteers attending the Miami University Freedom Summer training. *They should expect possibly somebody to get killed.*[671] A close up appears of a worried Andy Goodman listening to this and other warnings.

That dark haired boy sitting in the middle of a group of civil rights workers was Andrew Goodman as he listened to a lecture at a civil rights seminar in Ohio last week. Tonight Andrew Goodman and two companions, Mickey Schwerner [sic] and James Chaney, are the focus of the whole country's concern. They have been missing since Sunday where they had gone as part of the MS Freedom Summer Project, a project designed to draw national attention to the problem of Negro rights in that state.[672]

This opening of the CBS News Special Report initiated the massive flood of national resources dedicated to controlling the violence and asserting the rights of Blacks in MS. For the state of MS, the opening segment was the beginning of the end for racist violence in the state of MS.

First, assurances of peace by MS Congressional members and Governor Paul Johnson were shown to be hypocritical and dishonest. MS Representative William Colmer: *The people of Mississippi ... do not want any bloodshed. The do not want any trouble.*[673] Gov Paul Johnson: *We are determined to maintain peace and order in this state, and we are going to cooperate with all proper authorities in order that our laws are obeyed and that peace and tranquility may prevail.*[674]

Despite these public assurances, something was wrong in MS. *They should expect possibly somebody to get killed.* Three young civil rights workers were missing since Sunday. Viewers were inescapably drawn to the conclusion that the trio was murdered.

Second, national attention was now placed directly on MS and its abhorrent behavior towards Black Americans. National public pressure would begin to mount to dedicate resources to managing the violence and resistance in MS.

A large portion of this News Special extensively covered the upcoming Freedom Summer activities. An overview of the training sessions was provided. A number of the volunteers were introduced and interviewed.[675]

An interview with MS Senator James Eastland described his white view of MS seen with rose-colored glasses.

We have more peace and harmony in MS than any state in the Union ... Industry is coming in from the North. People are employed and are prosperous. We don't have any racial friction. A Negro in MS is employed, makes good wages, is prosperous, he has the finest school system in the US for his children to attend, they're doing alright ... They have hospitals ... There is nothing closed about the society.[676]

Throughout his interview, Senator Stennis repeatedly used the word n-**ra, a colloquial shorthand for n-****. By using this word, Stennis was demonstrating his belief in the inferiority of Blacks. Hearing this word created disgust in the minds of the large number of national viewers.

In contrast, the interview with white Senator Stennis was followed by an interview with Aaron Henry, a Black businessman from Clarksdale. Henry owned a drugstore.

In our state, 30% of the people all over earn less than $3,000 a year ... In the MS Delta where we are now, 51% of us earn less than $1,000 a year. We have a question of educational attainment that places MS at the bottom of the ladder of the 50 states ... It's this kind of affinity for the bottom that present politicians are not willing to tout. We have a question, the real essence of the problem, the right to vote. In the last 4 years, some 69,000 Negroes have gone to the registration offices asking for the right to vote. And around 6,000 have gotten by. The question of justice in the courts is a real issue with us. We don't feel as Negroes that we have any opportunity of successfully defending ourselves. When we are charged of a crime by any white man, by any member of the police department, we are always automatically convicted. There is never enough evidence to convict a white man of a crime against a Negro. There is always enough evidence to convict a Negro against a white man.[677]

This contrast between the views of the white Senator James Stennis and the black business owner Aaron Henry was startling to viewers. Stennis gave condescending generalizations. Henry provided issues and facts. Aaron Henry was also calm, poised, and educated. Henry himself was the perfect counterexample of the inferior, lazy, illiterate Black implied by the use of the word n-***ra by Stennis.

Blacks who wanted to vote in MS were afraid to try to register. These Blacks said that attempts to register resulted in being beaten, bombed out, fired from their jobs, or even lynched. MS Gov Paul Johnson denied these fears.

I don't find that there is any great deal of intimidation. I'm sure that there is some intimidation, and I'm sure that that intimidation does exist, in every state of the American union. There has always been some intimidation on the part of one race against another race ... but I don't find the intimidation to be prevalent in this state.[678]

This statement by Johnson was a complete lie. Gov Paul Johnson was born and grew up in Hattiesburg, MS. He personally knew Luther Cox and Theron Lynd, the Forrest County Circuit Court clerks. Johnson knew all about the Federal lawsuits starting in 1955 against Cox and Lynd for preventing Blacks from registering to vote. Johnson was well connected with the White Citizens Council in Hattiesburg. He regularly attended their meetings and obtained their support for his election to MS Governor. Cox, Lynd, and the White Citizens Council were well connected to the White Knights of the Ku Klux Klan. Many Blacks in Forrest County who tried to register to vote were beaten and fired from their jobs. Paul Johnson knew all about these activities.

Nationwide viewers who heard Johnson make this statement were shocked by the boldness of his lies in this interview. His dishonesty further heightened the distrust in the nation for the leaders of MS. Throughout his interview, Gov Johnson also regularly used the word n-***ra when referring to Blacks. This continued condescension by a MS state official was upsetting to viewers.

James Silver, a prominent historian from the University of MS, gave a final warning to the state officials of MS. Inevitably, the Civil Rights movement will be successful in MS.

The only choice that the white MS leadership has now is to bring this inevitable result here as a result of bargaining, of negotiating, of dealing with these representatives of the Negro race. The Negroes in Jackson and the Negroes in Canton say that they can't even talk with the mayors of those towns on the telephone. This leaves them only one recourse, and that is demonstration. And the demonstration may lead to violence. So, I say, not because of the resources of Mississippians, but because the rest of the country demands it, that MS must conform. It can no longer subvert the Constitution of the US.[679]

Silver correctly identified the mood of the rest of the country. This CBS News Special Report both identified the position of the majority and created additional supporters for civil rights in MS.

In his closing remarks, Walter Cronkite placed the search for Schwerner, Chaney, and Goodman into historical perspective.

The search in MS is twofold. Tonight, it centers on 3 young men whose convictions about civil rights led them into what they knew was a dangerous situation. But long after their fate is determined, the search for peace, tranquility and equality will continue in MS, the Magnolia state.[680]

This CBS Special News Report was about far more than the disappearance and search for Schwerner, Chaney, and Goodman. After summarizing the disappearance and the search, the bulk of the Report was far more reaching. Schwerner, Chaney, and Goodman were the vanguard of the coming MS Freedom Summer Project involving thousands of students and ministers. An overview of the Project was given, including the objectives, volunteer training, and introduction to some of the volunteers. White MS and Black MS were sharply contrasted.

Extensive coverage of the racial problems in MS was provided. White MS was shown to the nation in all its ugliness and meanness while hiding behind a mask of supposed civility. MS Governor Paul Johnson, MS Senator James Stennis, and local white businessmen represented MS in their own damning words. Segregation and racist violence were incorporated into the state government and white society in MS. Despite its structure for resistance, MS had no choice. Obvious violence against Schwerner, Chaney, and Goodman was the beginning of the end for white racists and segregationists. The nation required that civil rights guaranteed by the Constitution be extended to Blacks in MS.

Public concern and interest in the disappearance and fate of Schwerner, Chaney, and Goodman was the Pearl Harbor of the Civil Rights movement. White Knights had perpetrated the murders as a warning to stop the MS Freedom Summer project and to warn the nation to stay out of MS. These heinous murders had the opposite effect. Thanks in large part to this CBS Special News Report, the disappearance of the trio increased national pressure for civil rights for Blacks in MS.

June 26, 1964

Allen Dulles in his US Air Force C-140 Executive Jet (Lockheed JetStar VC-140B[681]) arrived in Washington, DC, sometime after midnight[682] on June 26, 1964. News reporters were actually waiting for Dulles as he deplaned down the exit stairway at the Washington airport.

During this news conference, Dulles summarized his mission and his general findings. Dulles refused to state any recommendations without first discussing those recommendations with President Lyndon Johnson.

... there is a real problem there, there is no question about that. There is a very difficult problem. I don't see any likely explosion or anything of that kind. But you have a situation that requires careful handling ... [683]

... [my specific mission] was fact finding and to talk with, as we have done, with all of the interested groups, the government, the business men, the church people, the Negro leaders and to see what their attitude was, what the problems were, and what could be done to further the coordination of local and government actions in the civil rights issue.[684]

... there will be continuing problems. This is not something that can be settled overnight, over a weekend, or over a month end. It's a problem that will require working on for many months, for a long while.[685]

... we did accomplish what we are trying to do in the sense of talking with a wide group of people ... .[686]

... I had no intention of getting into that [the search for the trio], that was not part of the mission, I did not get into that.[687]

We have here in MS, a very real, a very difficult problem. It's one on which everyone has to work. I found a great willingness to take a very frank view of the situation.[688]

These views by Allen Dulles were extremely naive, to say the least. Three young civil rights workers were missing and likely dead. Racial tensions were extremely high throughout MS and especially in Neshoba County. Concluding that the situation was not explosive was thoroughly misguided and a complete misrepresentation of the situation. MS people, including government officials, that talked with Dulles were performing the typical MS shuffle. Appear reasonable on the surface, while directing the racists violence behind the scenes.

During the late morning on June 26, 1964, Allen Dulles gave his informal report to President Lyndon Johnson. This meeting lasted for almost 2 hours.[689] Dulles and President Johnson then discussed the report with MS Gov Paul Johnson in a phone call. Dulles summarized 3 specific recommendations to MS Gov Johnson.

Contact should be maintained between President Johnson you [the MS Governor] to facilitate state and appropriate Federal action to control and, when necessary, punish terroristic activities, particularly the activities of clandestine groups.[690]

Review the role of the FBI in the state and its staff to see whether the security situation could be improved by any beefing up of the staff of the FBI.[691]

[Conduct] quiet and informal discussions with the National Council of Churches pointing out to them the security problems which have been created by these groups going in and to make sure that they understand the nature of their responsibility in connection with that.[692]

President Johnson then began to discuss the recommendations made by Allen Dulles with MS Gov Paul Johnson.

The only real help [to avoid acts of terror] we can be at the moment is providing all the FBI people that we can there to work closely with your people ... I think that we ought to do everything we can ... to prevent them, but where they are committed, we ought to see what we can to do to get them convicted.[693]

MS Governor Johnson gave a different explanation to President Johnson.

These acts we have had, every one of 'em has been immediately investigated by the state. And, they have been investigated by the FBI ... these kinds of matters are the very devil to try to solve. An activity on the part of the Klan, they don't use local people. They'll use somebody from outside to come in and administer a whippin' to someone, and that's what throw ya' off, and makes it very, very difficult to ever run down. That's one reason that these people have not been brought to trial.[694]

Paul Johnson was dishonest here. Outsiders from another County did generally perpetrate the violence. But the real reason that perpetrators were never caught was that many local law enforcement officers were members of the Klan. These law enforcement Klan members escorted the perpetrators into the local area to the scene of violence. After the violence was perpetrated, the same law enforcement Klan members escorted the violators from the scene of violence. Even if not involved in the violence, local law enforcement officers in the Klan would not investigate to find the perpetrators. Worse yet, Paul Johnson knew all that local law enforcement throughout the state was heavily involved in Klan activities.

President Johnson simply said: *Uh, huh.*[695] Allen Dulles would be meeting with FBI Director Hoover to see if more FBI agents could be assigned.[696]

MS Gov Johnson gave a final warning to President Johnson.

I'd like to get this across to you. If they continue to send these youngsters in, without them properly being oriented, and realizing what they are gettin' into with a nucleus of your hard core communist leaning type people with police records, unless that comes about and the Council of Churches keeps these youngsters out of here, the best that they possibly can, we gonna' have lots of acts of violence. I wanted you to know that. Those are things you couldn't prevent if you had a thousand FBI in each county in the state.[697]

This statement by Paul Johnson is astounding. Johnson claimed that he cannot control violence in his own state. Law and order did not prevail in the state of MS. A sufficient number of residents of the state would be participating and supporting the violence. Worse yet, Paul Johnson is attempting to place fault on the Council of Churches. He is avoiding that fact that is own state government was implicit in the violence by failing to enforce the law and order.

A short time later, Allen Dulles and President Lyndon Johnson called FBI Director J Edgar Hoover. Dulles relayed his recommendations about increasing the FBI presence in MS. However, Dulles warned Hoover about the role of the agents deployed to MS. *The number of agents you have in that state, they're not really going to enforce this business.*[698]

On the afternoon of June 26, 1964, MS Gov Paul Johnson travelled from Jackson to the city of Philadelphia. Johnson's car was escorted into Philadelphia by several MS Highway Patrol cruisers. Upon arrival, Johnson exited his car and was standing on the side of the street on downtown Philadelphia. He was dressed in shirtsleeves and wearing a straw hat. Gov Johnson first conferred with Col T B Birdsong, head of the MS Highway Patrol.⁶⁹⁹

Newsmen then gathered around Johnson for a question and answer session right there on the street in the sweltering heat.

*I am going to try to locate those people [the trio] if they are in this area ... I wanted to make a personal check to be sure everything possible is being done ... I plan to cooperate in the search in every way ... The search will continue until all agencies in the investigation felt that further efforts would be futile.*⁷⁰⁰

Just to make his public position on the missing civil rights workers clear, on June 26, 1964, Governor Johnson published a statement. This statement was published by United Press International (UPI) out of Jackson. A copy of this statement appeared that day in the *Meridian Star* with the headline: COULD HAPPEN ANYWHERE, GOVERNOR SAYS.⁷⁰¹

> *... Johnson told newsmen the disappearance of the three that "could happen anytime" in any part of the country. "It happens in New York every night" ... "I'm satisfied that everything is being done that could be done to find them"*

During the day on Friday, June 26, 1964, Robert Shelton, Imperial Wizard of the United Klans Of America, also made a public statement about the missing civil rights workers. Shelton had arrived in Philadelphia on the previous evening, Thursday.

*My purpose in visiting Philadelphia is not to add to the violence or tension, but merely to make a quiet investigation of my own. The disappearance of the three civil rights workers is a hoax intended to raise more money for the civil rights movement. The national Council of churches pledge $250,000 to finance the civil rights invasion of MS. they are in financial difficulty.*⁷⁰²

These things follow a pattern. This is the same story that we had in Birmingham and in Albany, GA. These people [integrationists] like to dramatize situations in order to milk the public of more money for their causes. So, they create a hoax like this, put weeping mothers and wives on national television and try to touch the hearts of the nation. Their whole purpose is just to get more money. I understand that these funds are slowly coming in.

No KKK demonstrations or acts are planned during my 24-hour visit. I will confer with members of the Klan in this area. They will continue the investigation. We are convinced that these three young men who are missing will turn up somewhere else and the whole plot will be exposed. [703]

During the next 24 hours, nothing further was heard from Robert Shelton. Shelton departed on Saturday, June 27, 1964, for a Klan meeting in Tuscaloosa, AL.[704]

On that evening of June 26, 1964, MS Gov Paul Johnson made an appeal to local farmers on a local radio station. *If anything had happened to the civil rights workers, the persons responsible would have dumped the bodies on farms other than their own ... I urge you local farmers to search your own premises ... Take a few hours and look for clues in the strange disappearance of three civil rights workers.*[705]

J E Crawford was a farmer who lived about two miles from the burned Mt Zion Methodist Church in Longdale. Crawford disagreed with Gov Johnson about searching the farms.

Everybody knows that they [the trio] are alive. Anybody guilty of harming the workers would have driven the car much deeper into the swamp, rather than leaving it in full view of anyone travelling along Hwy 21 ... I don't believe that the church was set afire, since Negroes in the area told me that the fire could have been caused by faulty electrical wiring. Negroes frequently attended civil rights meetings at the church but no one ever bothered them. [706]

Initially, FBI agents had focused the search for the workers on the area surrounding the charred Ranch Wagon. This very swampy area was heavily searched with the assistance of a large number of Navy personnel from the Meridian Naval Air Station. When this effort failed, the FBI widened its search area. An extensive number of other searches were conducted in locations throughout Neshoba County. All of these searches failed to locate Schwerner, Chaney, and Goodman.[707]

June 27, 1964

President Lyndon Johnson asked former CIA Director Allen Dulles to meet with the Council Of Churches on behalf of the President. On Saturday, June 27, 1964, Dulles met for more than 2 hours with civil rights leaders from the national Council of Churches. Burke Marshall, head of the USDOJ Civil Rights Division and John Doar, assistant to

Marshall, also attended the meeting. These representatives of the USDOJ did not actively participate in the discussion.[708]

National Council of Churches representatives at the meeting were Dr. Robert Spike, Executive Director of the Committee on Religion and Race, and John Pratt, attorney for the Council.

After the meeting, Dulles and Spike gave comments to news reporters.

Dulles: *We discussed students going into danger areas. I thought perhaps they could go into areas not so dangerous ... I won't specify the areas I consider dangerous, but they are known ... I don't think the government should tell Americans where they should go or where they shouldn't go ... Everything should be done that could be done to assure the visits of the students did not lead to violent incidents ... I want to stress the importance of civil rights workers keeping local law enforcement advised of their whereabouts and the location of their activities ...*

Spike: *I will recommend to my Committee on Monday [June 29, 1964] that more adults be sent with the students into MS. We understand fully the danger that confronts these students. If I were a parent, or even one of them [the students], I would be very concerned. The danger is grave.*

Again, Allen Dulles showed the extent of his naivety. Informing local law enforcement of the location of a student would be placing a target on the back of the student. Local law enforcement would be able to easily notify and direct fellow Klan members where to take care of these agitators.

President Johnson talked with FBI Director J Edgar Hoover by telephone again on Saturday, June 27, 1964. After this conversation, Johnson flew to Detroit then to Minneapolis to attend a political dinner. After arriving in Minneapolis, Presidential Press Secretary George Reedy held a press conference.

Former CIA Director Allen Dulles recommended to President Johnson an increase in FBI agents in MS to help further deter violence ... Mr. Hoover will augment FBI personnel in the state of MS. They will be there as long as necessary in whatever areas they are needed to investigate violations of Federal laws.[709]

Late in the afternoon of Saturday, June 27, 1964, search efforts were concentrated on the nearby Pearl River near Highway 19 south of Philadelphia. FBI Agents, Pearl River was the river where the body of accused Black rapist Mack Charles Parker was found 5 years earlier.[710] Game Wardens, and MS Highway Patrolmen entered small boats. These boats were then used to roam all over the River, hoping to find bodies that had floated to the surface.[711]

Re-Opening The FBI Field Office[712]

Initially, the FBI opened the Jackson Division in May 1941. Percy Wyly was the first Special Agent in Charge. Wyly had served as the first Special Agent in Charge of the FBI San Diego Field Office, serving from 1939 to 1941. After leaving the Jackson Field Office, he later served as head of the Jackson and Albuquerque Field Offices.

During its early years, FBI Jackson searched for fugitives and investigated crimes such as motor vehicle theft and violations of the White Slave (interstate prostitution) and Selective Service Acts. After World War II, Jackson caseload diminished significantly. When the Bureau's staffing budget was cut the FBI decided to close the Jackson Division in 1946. Jackson Division cases were divided between the New Orleans and Memphis Divisions.

Then, in the early 1960s, Mississippi exploded with violence.

Twenty bombing and arson incidents occurred in MS prior to July 10, 1964. On June 12, 1963, Medgar Evers, Mississippi Field Secretary of NAACP, was shot in the back by a high-powered sniper rifle. Almost exactly one year later, Schwerner, Chaney, and Goodman were murdered on June 21, 1964.

The charred Ranch Wagon discovered by FBI agents on June 23, 1964, led to the FBI case name "MIBURN," for Mississippi Burning.

With the growing presence of the FBI searching for the missing civil rights workers, President Lyndon Johnson told Director J. Edgar Hoover that the FBI should have a stronger official presence in Mississippi.

Memphis SAC Karl Dissly
(FBI Web Site)

At that time, Memphis Special Agent in Charge (SAC) Karl Dissly was responsible for investigations in the northern part of Mississippi.
Around June 28, 1964, Dissly was sent to Jackson by Hoover to hunt for office space. He faced some challenges. Suitable space was needed quickly. Local prejudices meant that finding a landlord willing to rent to an integrated agency would be difficult. Black support staff and Black agents were employed by the FBI.[713]

June 29, 1964 -- July 2, 1964

After a fruitless week of searching for the missing trio, the FBI decided on Monday, June 29, 1964, to expand the search outside of Neshoba County. All of MS and LA, AR, TN, and AL became part of the search area. These 4 additional states all bordered and surrounded MS. Beginning on that day, thousands of posters with pictures of the three workers were mailed to post offices motels, and law enforcement agencies.[714]

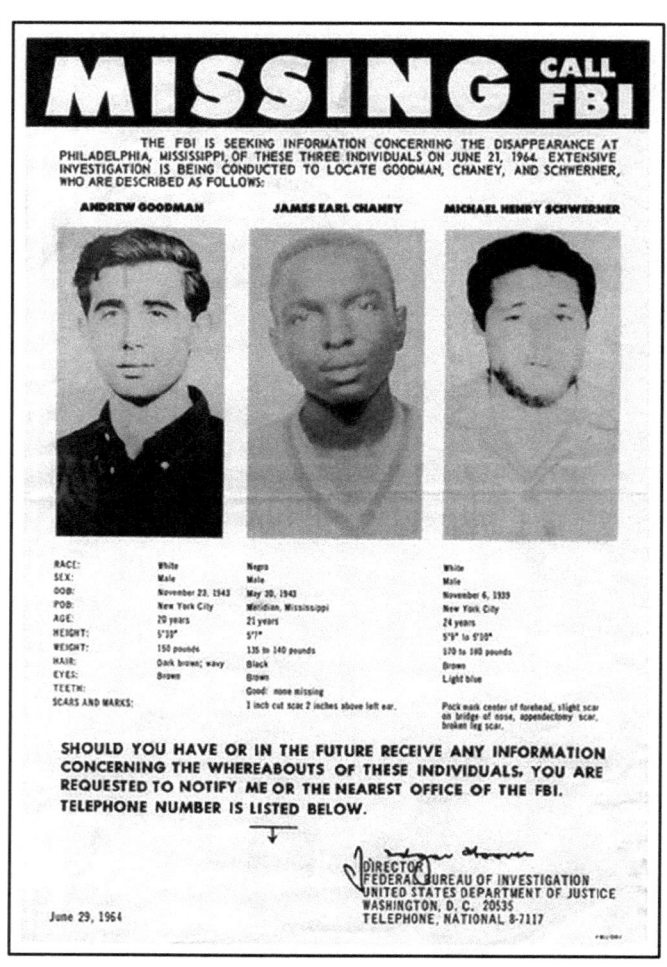

FBI Poster, June 29, 1964

Pearl River search activities that started on Saturday, June 27, 1964, failed to uncover the bodies of Schwerner, Chaney, and Goodman.[715] Dewitt Hutton of the MS Game and Fish Commission described the search efforts. *We've covered 55 miles of the Pearl itself and haven't even found a net.*[716] On Sunday, June 28, 1964, dragging operations were conducted on the Pearl River. Bodies of the trio were still missing. As a result, on Monday, June 29, 1964, dragging operations turned to private small lakes and ponds that dotted the search area. A few landowners were reluctant to allow the dragging teams on their lakes and ponds. However, most of the landowners cooperated.⁷¹⁷

Rita Schwerner, the wife of Mickey Schwerner, met with President Lyndon Johnson for about 10 minutes in the late morning of Monday, June 29, 1964. President Johnson was attending a White House reception for his Commission on Stroke, Cancer, and Heart Disease. Johnson left the event to meet with Rita Schwerner in the nearby Green Room of the White House.⁷¹⁸ During this meeting with President Johnson, Schwerner asked the President to send 5,000 men into MS to join the search efforts. Johnson advised Schwerner that so many searchers could not be sent.⁷¹⁹

Shortly after the meeting between President Johnson and Rita Schwerner, White House Press Secretary George Reedy met with reporters.

The President saw Mrs. Michael Schwerner. She told him about her trip to MS and expressed hope that there would be adequate manpower supplied in the search for the three missing civil rights workers. The President told Mrs. Schwerner that he had been in touch with both FBI Director J Edgar Hoover and Defense Secretary Robert McNamara, while the White House staff also was keeping in touch with Justice and Defense Department officials about the search effort. The President assured Mrs. Schwerner that he would put into MS as much manpower as they could effectively use and competently direct in the search.

*This does not indicate any present plans to expand the force of FBI agents, sailors, and others who are helping state officials.*⁷²⁰

After leaving the President, Rita Schwerner spent some time during the afternoon with Lee White. White was Associate White House Counsel for Civil Rights.⁷²¹

President Johnson was trying to walk a fine line here. Johnson assured Rita Schwerner that he would devote sufficient resources to search. At the same time, he was assuring MS Gov Johnson and MS US Senator James Stennis that more FBI Agents would not enter the state as yet.

At that same White House briefing on Monday, June 29, 1964, White House Press Secretary George Reedy announced the FBI distribution of the missing posters throughout the surrounding states. Media representatives asked Reedy if the broadened hunt meant that the FBI now believed that the civil rights workers left the MS. *No, the FBI acted solely on the assumption that nothing should be left undone.*[722]

On June 29, 1964, FBI Director J Edgar Hoover reported to Johnson. *I am opening a main office at Jackson, Mississippi ... [but] it won't be able to be effective for three or four days.*[723]

MS Gov Johnson applied continued pressure to MS Highway Patrol investigators involved in the search for the bodies. On Tuesday, June 30, 1964, Patrol Chief A D Morgan issued a memo to Highway Patrol investigators in Philadelphia.

The Governor is vitally interested in finding the subjects involved. He is also interested in being informed of any incident in the state of MS that may be connected with the incident at hand at any time of day or night ... You establish liaison with the [Neshoba County] Sheriff's Department, [Philadelphia] police, the FBI and the Navy[Meridian Naval Air Station] if necessary so that you may keep informed and, in turn, keeps us informed ... Restrict news releases to just routine facts of the investigation. New leads or developments are to be forwarded immediately to Patrol headquarters in Jackson and then to the Governor's office.[724]

Gov Johnson wanted to hear about new leads before the general public. Johnson also wanted to control the public announcements about new leads that might be issued by any MS officers and authorities.

False sightings of Mickey Schwerner popped up all over during the next month. On Tuesday, June 30, 1964, Corinth Police Chief Art Murphy claimed he saw Schwerner at a bus station a few days earlier.[725] An unidentified white victim of a hit and run accident in Batesville was at first reported as possibly being either Schwerner or Goodman.[726]

Ground searchers were moved to the east towards the Alabama state line on Thursday, July 2, 1964. Search parties were composed of FBI Agents, Highway Patrolmen, and the 400 sailors from the Meridian Naval Air Station. These search parties began a foot by foot search in the snake infested woods area of rural Kemper County.[727]

Another false alarm was generated on July 2, 1964. Two white men accompanied by a Black man sped away from a Kosciusko service station early in the day without paying for gas. One of the white men was reported to have a beard. Mickey Schwerner had a beard. A statewide alert was issued by the MS Highway Patrol.[728]

July 2, 1964 -- Civil Rights Law of 1964 Signed

Extensive civil rights legislation was initially proposed during the term of President John F. Kennedy. On June 19, 1963, Pres Kennedy transmitted to Congress a proposed Civil Rights Act of 1963. This proposed bill was introduced into the House of Representatives as HR 7152 and into the Senate as S 1731. Of course, both bodies immediately referred the legislation to various committees.[729]

This legislation contained protections for voting rights, equal access to public accommodations, desegregation of public schools, and methods for protecting those rights.[730] On February 10, 1964, the House of Representatives voted in favor of HR 7152.[731] A modified Senate version was finally approved on June 19, 1967, in a 73 to 27 vote. This Senate version was approved by the House on July 2, 1964, by a vote of 289 to 126.[732]

Pres Lyndon Johnson signed the legislation in a nationally televised broadcast on that same day.[733] Johnson commented on the significance of this new law.

... We believe that all men are created equal. Yet many are denied equal treatment. We believe that all men have certain unalienable rights. Yet many Americans do not enjoy those rights. We believe that all men are entitled to the blessings of liberty. Yet millions are being deprived of those blessings—not because of their own failures, but because of the color of their skin ...

The purpose of the law is simple. It does not restrict the freedom of any American, so long as he respects the rights of others. It does not give special treatment to any citizen. It does say the only limit to a man's hope for happiness, and for the future of his children, shall be his own ability. It does say that there are those who are equal before God shall now also be equal in the polling booths, in the classrooms, in the factories, and in hotels, restaurants, movie theaters, and other places that provide service to the public ...

Let us close the springs of racial poison. Let us pray for wise and understanding hearts. Let us lay aside irrelevant differences and make our Nation whole ...[734]

Despite this significant new law, the bodies of Schwerner, Chaney, and Goodman were still missing.

Government leaders were bracing for the invasion of MS during the Freedom Summer activities. All eyes were focused on locations in MS during the remainder of the summer. Even greater attention would be paid to Philadelphia since the bodies still had not been discovered.

On July 2, 1964, Mayor Ab Davis Harbour issued a public statement. This statement was posted in the Philadelphia City Hall and throughout the city of Philadelphia.

We may be visited by people from other areas of the United States to engage in "civil rights" activities. They can do irreparable damage to the friendly relations that exist among all of our people, and regardless of how well-meaning their intentions might be, such activities tend to create tension among the citizens of our city and state.

It is the earnest desire that no harm should come to these young people, and your city officials urge that these young people who have come into Mississippi on the summer project, sponsored by the National Council of Churches and others, go immediately to the Chief of Police and register with him, in order that precautions may be taken by local officials in their behalf.[735]

Local residents, including law enforcement officers. generally ignored these posted warnings. Joseph Llelyveld, a reporter for the *New York Times*, was in Philadelphia on the day that the statement was issued. Llelyveld was the son of Rabbi Arthur Llelyveld. Rabbi Llelyveld was savagely beaten with a tire iron in Hattiesburg about a week later on July 10, 1964. Joseph Llelyveld and his photographer were in downtown Philadelphia. A gang of livid townsmen surrounded Llelyveld and his photographer. These townsmen told the pair that their lives would be worth nothing if the pair remained in town.

The photographer had a copy of the statement by Mayor Harbour. He pointed to the statement. Clyde Parker, a Philadelphia jeweler, was the leader of the gang. Parker expressed the opinion of most of the townspeople. *I didn't like the damned Mayor's statement. And I know a lot of other people who didn't like it either. No Mayor is going to tell us what to do.* Llelyveld and the photographer departed for the office of Neshoba County Sheriff Lawrence Rainey. Upon arriving at the office of the Sheriff, the pair asked for protection while doing their jobs. Asking for protection was the approach requested by Major Harbour in his statement. Joseph Llelyveld and the photographer were told to leave town.[736]

July 3, 1964 -- July 9, 1964

After a day in Kemper County east of Neshoba County, searchers were moved from Kemper County on Friday, July 3, 1964. Assigned sailors were divided into four groups of 100 sailors each. Two groups were assigned to Newton County on the south side of Neshoba County. Remaining two groups went to Winston County on the north side of Neshoba County.[737]

On Saturday, July 4, 1964, the searchers moved into the hot, damp, and muddy woodlands and swamps of Leake County. This County was west of Neshoba County. Everyone started search activities late on the morning of Independence Day. Heavy rain began pouring down on the previous day. Searching on July 4 was delayed until the rain ceased.[738]

Rumors and reports of sightings from widely scattered areas complicated the search for the missing workers. On Sunday, July 5, 1964, a spokesman for the FBI complained about this problem. *Each such report has to be carefully checked out by FBI Agents. We have over 55 Field Offices throughout the country manned by 6,000 special agents. We can get one of our men to any point in the US within an hour.*[739]

A group composed of 8 members of the Board of Directors of the NAACP arrived in Philadelphia on Monday, July 6, 1964. Appearance of these Black leaders attracted over 200 townspeople, who gathered in the Neshoba County Courthouse square. This group requested permission to visit the location where the burned station wagon was found. Local authorities denied the group permission to visit the location.[740]

After being denied, the group went to Meridian and registered quietly at an all-white[741] motel. This registration was the first desegregation of public accommodations in Meridian. A press conference was held in Meridian. NAACP Director Dr Claude Hudson, expressed dissatisfaction that the Board was denied access to the location of the burned ranch wagon.[742]

Another false alarm occurred on Wednesday night, July 8, 1964. A freshly dug grave was found on the banks of the Chunky River. This fresh grave on the Chunky River was in Newton County, west of Neshoba County.[743]

Of course, Sam Bowers could not resist chiming into the mix. Bowers occasionally published bulletins under the name WASP, Inc. In early July, 1964, Bowers published WASP Inc. Bulletin #64-641. This bulletin was circulated on the streets of Philadelphia. Among the statements made by Bowers in the Bulletin are the following:

> *The new technique is the well-known persecution hoax. That is, to kill one of their own members, bomb one of their own installations, or arrange a "disappearance" of some of their own agitators...*
>
> *5. Civil Rights Agitators "disappear" in Philadelphia. Cheap car burned. No evidence of foul play. Massive propaganda campaign...*
>
> *WASP, INC, urges all citizens to refuse to answer any question on any subject whatsoever which is asked by a Federal Police Agent.*[744]

MS Highway Patrol officers continued forwarding reports to Chief Morgan and to Commissioner Birdsong. In the 5 pm report on July 9, 1964, absence of progress in the search for the bodies was discussed.

> *Inspector Glenn, Gwin Cole, Charlie Snodgrass, and Jack Smith were in the office this morning to discuss the investigation and to try to decide what we should do now. They advise that we have no additional leads, neither does the FBI have any leads which they have any confidence in.*[745]

July 10, 1964, Jackson FBI Field Office Reopens

FBI Memphis SAC Karl Dissly rented two full floors in the First Federal Savings and Loan Building in Jackson.[746] On July 2, 1964 FBI Director J. Edgar Hoover called FBI Special Agent Roy Moore[747] in Little Rock, AK.[748] Hoover ordered Moore to go Jackson to begin putting everything together to open the office in the space rented by Dissly. On the morning of Sunday, July 5, 1964, Moore reported to Jackson.[749] Preparations were completed and the office opening planned for Friday, July 10, 1964.[750]

J Edgar Hoover travelled to Jackson to attend the opening of the new Jackson Division office on Friday, July 10, 1964. Upon arriving at the

Jackson airport in the morning, Hoover was met by Jackson Mayor Allen Thompson, Jackson Police Chief W D Rayfield, Public Safety Commissioner T B Birdsong, and newsmen. J Edgar Hoover greeted Commissioner Birdsong. *Good to see you Colonel. You and I have been more or less partners in crime for a long time.*[751] Thompson was complementary in his initial introduction to Hoover. *I don't know of anybody I would rather see here than you.*[752]

From the airport, Hoover, Thompson, Rayfield, and Birdsong went to the MS Governor's Mansion to meet with MS Gov Paul Johnson. MS AG Joe Patterson[753] was waiting with Gov Johnson. Birdsong called Highway Patrol Chief A D Morgan to join the meeting. *All Hoover wanted was to be convinced that we intended to enforce the law. Paul [Johnson] was trying to tell him that. I [Morgan] came in and told Hoover that we would enforce the law. We all shook hands.* Hoover seemed satisfied. *I'm well pleased with this trip.*[754]

After the meeting with MS Gov Johnson and the others,[755] Director Hoover attended the re-opening of the Jackson Division office. His attendance demonstrated the Bureau's commitment to its civil rights and other investigative work in the state.

275

Hoover Opens Jackson Office
(FBI Web Site)
(Left to Right:
Roy Moore, New SAC, Deke DeLoach, FBI Asst Director,
J Edgar Hoover, FBI Director)

Gov Paul Johnson, Jackson Mayor Allen C. Thompson and Rayfield, Patterson, Birdsong, and Morgan also attended the opening ceremony at the new field office.[756]

**Hoover And Locals At Jackson Office Opening
(FBI Web Site)**

**(Left to Right:
WD Rayfield, Chief, Jackson PD, J Edgar Hoover, FBI Director,
Allen Thompson, Jackson Mayor)**

Roy Moore, Director of the MS Field Office, was personally introduced by FBI Director Hoover.

In my 27 years with the FBI, I have never questioned where J Edgar Hoover has sent me ... I am looking forward to an enjoyable stay in Jackson, just as in Little Rock.[757]

At a news conference immediately following the ceremony on Friday, July 10, 1964, Hoover announced that 153 agents were assigned to the new FBI Jackson Division Office.[758]

After this announcement, Hoover answered various questions posed by the newsmen at the conference.

The FBI most certainly does not and will not give protection to civil rights workers in Mississippi this summer. The Bureau is not a police organization, but our business is investigation. Requests by integration groups for Federal protection while they are in Mississippi on the so-called "Summer Project" are turned down. Protection is in the hands of local authorities ...

My decision to open the Jackson office followed conversations with troubleshooter Allen Dulles who made a brief fact-finding trip to Mississippi last month on behalf of Pres. Johnson. The Jackson office is not the result of any recommendation of Mr. Dulles, but does follow conversations in which he [Dulles] stressed that there should be closer liaison between our agency and local and state officials ...

It is my personal belief that the three civil rights workers missing since June 21 when they disappeared in the Philadelphia area are dead. I am optimistic about this case being solved, although there is, at the present time, no positive indication that there is an imminent break in the investigation. The investigation is intensely being carried on. This may be a prolonged effort. But it will be continued until it is solved, until we find the bodies of those three men that have disappeared and the persons who may be responsible for their disappearance. The possibility of an elaborate hoax being staged by civil rights workers in the did in the disappearance is far removed from my thinking.[759]

After the news conference, Director Hoover spent the night in Jackson. Hoover departed Jackson to return to FBI HQ in Washington, DC, on the morning of Saturday, July 11, 1964.[760]

Roy Moore was assigned as the Special Agent in Charge (SAC) of the Jackson Field Office.[761] James Ingram was appointed to be Deputy SAC of the Jackson Field Office.[762]

Roy Moore

SAC, Jackson

Among its first acts, Jackson FBI opened 100 cases on individuals associated with the KKK and additional white supremacist organizations. Soon 1,540 total cases were being handled by the Division office. Dozens of agents worked exclusively on MIBURN. Another 33 agents handled special assignments pursuing numerous other civil rights investigations. Finally, 60 agents handled a range of other cases.

Between July 11, 1964 and December 31, 1964, 45 additional bombing and arson incidents occurred. Murders, church burnings, bombings, shootings, and attacks on buildings holding classes for blacks continued for years after the opening of the Field Office.

On January 10, 1966, members of the Laurel Klavern of the White Knights of the KKK firebombed the home of Vernon Dahmer. Dahmer died as a result of smoke inhalation burns on his lungs. He lived in Kelly Settlement just outside Hattiesburg. Dahmer was former President of the Forrest County NAACP. He had been an outspoken supporter of the need for local Blacks to register to vote. Agents from FBI Jackson Division were heavily involved in the investigation of his murder.

The Field Office also investigated riots, beatings, and threats made by the KKK and other extremist groups and the intimidation of voters and registration workers during elections. The Jackson Division lent its support to federal peacekeeping efforts at civil demonstrations as well, including when 16,000 individuals rallied at the state capitol in 1966 to protest the shooting of James H. Meredith, the first African-American to enter the University of Mississippi.

July 12, 1964 - July 20, 1964: Searching Continues

A sluggish offshoot of the MS River, the Old River, moved through Tallulah, LA. Tallulah is about 50 miles west of Jackson and 18 miles west of Vicksburg, just across the Louisiana border. On Sunday, July 12, 1964, the lower half of a Black male body was found in this river. The feet of the body were tied together. Local officials ordered a further search of the Old River on the possibility that this body was that of James Chaney. [763]

On Monday, July 13, 1964, Tensas Parish Sheriff W M Seaman spotted a second body bobbing near the surface about 5 miles downstream from the location of the first body. This second body was also a half body and fully clothed. Using keys and a belt buckle found on the first body, officials were able to identify the first body as that of Charles Moore, 20, of Meadville, MS. Moore's family reported that Moore had left home *to go to LA to work.*[764]

Six Navy divers joined the Old River search for both upper bodies on Tuesday, July 14, 1964. About 35 searchers, mostly from the LA Wildlife and Fisheries Commission and the MS Game and Fish Commission also continued the search for additional portions of the bodies. Henry Dees, also age 20, was identified as the second half body found. Moore and Dees were seen together in Meadeville, MS, in early May, 1964.[765]

These bodies were another false alarm in the search for Schwerner, Chaney, and Goodman.

By Friday, July 17, 1964, Freedom Summer had arrived in MS. Several volunteers were assigned to Philadelphia. Dan Pearlman, 23, a Columbia University law student was assigned to Philadelphia. David Welsh, 28, a freelance writer for Jet Magazine from Detroit, was also assigned to Philadelphia. On this date, these two volunteers were attacked by 3 white men on Main Street in Philadelphia. Pearlman was hit on the head with a chain. Welsh was kicked and beaten. Deputy Sheriff Cecil Price was vague in his assessment. *The two workers were roughed up by three unknown persons.*[766]

As long as the search continued, MS Highway Patrol officers forwarded field reports to Chief Morgan and Commissioner Birdsong. After review, Birdsong still provided the reports to MS Gov Paul Johnson. On Saturday, July 18, 1964, a report to Gov Johnson indicated again the absence of progress by all parties involved in the search for the bodies.

I checked with the FBI [Agent] Mr Phillips and inquired as to what they had pertaining to finding a grave. He advised that they had nothing whatsoever. However, that they had heard some rumors and said they thought they [the bodies] could have been ... by a wooded area near Sebastopol where a small mound was found. Patrolmen, FBI Agents were with the searching party. The patrolmen and agents viewed the mound and said that it was where a tree had fallen down about 30 years ago and left a mound of dirt. The leaves and grass were undisturbed but they decided that it might cause a rumor and took a shovel and dug into the mound.[767]

Digging into the mound failed to expose any bodies, as suggested by the undisturbed leaves and grass on the mound.

Throughout the remainder of July, 1964, FBI agents daily searched the homes of Black residents of Neshoba County. Many of the FBI agents felt that Schwerner, Chaney, and Goodman were hiding in a Black residence. One FBI agent was sympathetic to Jewel McDonald, daughter of Georgia Rush, who had been beaten at Mt Zion Methodist Church on June 16, 1964. This agent gave Jewel a dime and a list of sympathetic FBI agents. He told Jewel to call one of the sympathetic agents in any emergency. The Rush residence did not have a phone, so the dime was necessary to use a public pay phone. Emergency was code for an attack by White Knights.[768]

As time passed, more and more FBI agents and volunteers were involved in searching for the three civil rights workers. Every attempt to search an area failed to locate the bodies. When each search failed, Sullivan turned to Maynard King/Mr. X for help. "I'd touch base with him, or he'd touch base with me," Sullivan said. "I'd give him questions and if he had answers, we'd meet. "We often met in a remote location, Sullivan said. "We'd meet out in the open, or we'd meet on the street corner or somewhere where we weren't under observation." King/Mr. X would share information about the Klan or information such as "whose neighbors were friendly with who."[769]

July 22, 1964 - July 31, 1964

MS Senator James Eastland published a statement in the *Meridian Star* on July 22, 1964. In this statement, Eastland demanded that if some evidence of a crime is not produced soon, other alternative, more valid solutions needed to be considered. Then, the people of America would have to reject the accusation of the agitators that a heinous crime had been committed.[770]

On July 22, 1964, a search was conducted of an area called "The Junius and O. A. Fox Farms." On this farm was a small pump house over a well. This farm was thoroughly searched. Bodies of Schwerner, Chaney, and Goodman were not found at this location.[771]

During the period, July 21, 1964 to July 24, 1964, Dr. Martin Luther King, Jr., made a four-city tour of MS. This tour included Greenwood, Jackson, Vicksburg, and Meridian. His objective during this tour was to encourage Blacks to join a new political party being formed: the MS

Freedom Democratic Party. Black members of this new party would be elected to represent the state of MS at the upcoming Democratic Nominating Convention. These elected representatives would then try to unseat the White MS Delegation to the Convention.[772]

King was warned of a planned assassination attempt. Despite this warning, King chose to make the trip anyhow. He felt an imperative to help boost this new party. During the whole trip, Reverend King moved through the state in the center of tight security by Federal, state, and local law enforcement officers.[773]

On July 24, 1964,[774] Dr. King made a side trip to Philadelphia. His trip consisted first of visiting the newly opened COFO office in Independence Quarters. Then, King was driven through downtown Philadelphia. He and his escort drove east on Highway 16 to visit the Longdale community and the ruins at the Mt. Zion Church.[775] At the charred ruins of the Church, King spoke of the symbolism of the charred ruins of the Church.

The ruins speak of the element of lawlessness symbolic of too many in the deep South, yet the Church is also symbolic of the Blacks' civil rights struggle.[776]

Dr. King's trip to Philadelphia was quiet and uneventful, completely without violence. After all, he was accompanied by a large security force of Federal, state, and local law enforcement officers.

After visiting Philadelphia, King moved on to Meridian. His visit to Meridian consisted of visiting the COFO office where Schwerner, Chaney, and Goodman had worked before their disappearance. He spent the night in Meridian at a small hotel that catered to Blacks a few doors down from the COFO office. He departed MS on Saturday, July 25, 1964, by airplane.[777]

A more extensive property owned by O. A. Fox was searched on July 29, 1964. This property was located six miles southwest of Philadelphia, midway between State Highway 488 and State Highway 21. A search party was formed that included 100 naval officers and enlisted men, two MS Highway Patrolmen, and four FBI agents. Over 300 acres and 12 wells were thoroughly searched by this party. Bodies of Schwerner, Chaney, and Goodman were not found at this location either.[778]

Maynard King/Mr. X finally informed Sullivan that he was ready to meet and to reveal the location of the bodies. On July 31, 1964,[779] Sullivan and King/Mr. X met over dinner at the restaurant in the Holiday Inn North in Meridian. Inspector Sullivan was staying at this Holiday Inn while working on the investigation. Apparently, King/Mr. X was a "steak man". This restaurant had the best steaks, according to King/Mr. X.[780]

At this meeting, King/Mr. X told Sullivan that the bodies of the trio were buried deep under a dam on the Old Jolly Farm.[781] While this information provided a general location, a more accurate location was needed. Sullivan sent out agents that morning to interview key suspects in the case, floating the idea of a reward for identification of the exact location of the bodies.[782]

One key suspect was Sheriff Lawrence Rainey. On July 31, 1964, Rainey was contacted at his office by FBI Agents Art Murtaugh and John C. Gordon. These Agents informed Rainey that he was a suspect. In an effort to intimidate Rainey, Murtaugh and Gordon explained that the FBI had enough evidence on Rainey to have Rainey kicked out of office. Rainey was offered protection and twenty-five or thirty thousand dollars if he would give the Agents information about the disappearance of the three civil rights workers that would break the case open. Rainey was further told that if he did not cooperate, he would owe several thousand dollars in income tax. Rainey did not accept the offer.[783]

A short time later, Deputy Sheriff Cecil Price, another suspect of the FBI, was also approached by FBI Agents Murtaugh and Gordon. At the time of the approach, Neshoba County Attorney Rayford Jones was in Price's office. The Agents informed Price that the government had spent three million dollars on the case. Therefore, if Price would give the FBI information about the disappearance of the three civil rights workers that would break the case open, Price could receive a million dollars. As an enticement, the Agents suggested that Price could buy a cattle ranch in Wyoming with that kind of money and never have to work again. Price did not accept the offer.[784]

President Johnson had ordered 400 US Navy sailors to help search for the bodies. These sailors worked with state officers, such as Game Wardens. With this search force, ten counties in East MS were scoured for the bodies of Schwerner, Chaney, and Goodman. This search force spent forty-four days covering these ten counties. Search activities failed to uncover the bodies, despite the size of the force and the wide geographic area that had been covered.[785]

August 3, 1964 - August 4, 1964

An unidentified local Neshoba resident approached King/Mr. X. This resident offered to provide an exact location in exchange for the $30,000 fee. Working through Maynard King/Mr. X, Sullivan arranged to pay the unidentified local Neshoba resident $30,000 for the accurate location of the bodies. Multiple FBI agents over the years have confirmed that the money was actually paid. Two FBI agents brought the money in cash. This cash was turned over to King/Mr. X, who paid the unidentified Neshoba resident.[786] King/Mr. X immediately relayed to Sullivan the accurate location of the bodies that were provided by the unidentified local Neshoba resident.

Armed with this accurate location of the bodies from an informant, the FBI filed for a search warrant. This warrant was filed with the Southern District of MS, Biloxi Division, on August 3, 1964. In the court record, this filing is listed as Commissioner's Docket #1, Case #70. Plaintiff in the filing was United States of America. "Unknown Occupants of the Old Jolly Farm" were identified as the defendants. Verta Lee Swetman, US Commissioner, signed the search warrant on that day.[787]

Heavy earth moving equipment had been brought from Jackson and staged outside Old Jolly Farm. Hyde Construction Company[788] provided two pieces of heavy equipment for use during the excavation for the bodies. A bulldozer and a dragline were provided by Hyde.

Fine grading dirt over a rough surface could be performed with a Caterpillar Bulldozer Model D6B with a 10-foot blade.[789] Using the Bulldozer, the top of the dam could be graded to increase the width of the top of the dam to 12 feet. With this greater width, the Drag Line could be positioned on top of the dam for easy movement to additional digging locations.[790] A Link-Belt Drag-Line Crane/Excavator, Model LS68 with a 36-foot boom was available to scoop and to lift dirt when excavating.[791]

Special Agent John Proctor, Jr., had positioned the dragline and the bulldozer nearby the entrance to Old Jolly Farm, just off Highway 21.[792]

At 8:12 am CST on August 4, 1964, FBI Special Agent Henry McConnell[793] served the search warrant on Olen Burrage at his place of business, The Olen Burrage Truck Company. This company was located on MS State Highway 21, about 1 1/2 miles east of the Williamsville community. Burrage advised that he was the owner and had control of the area called Old Jolly Farm.[794] Burrage was compliant, insisting that he wished to cooperate fully.[795]

Agent McConnell then notified FBI Inspector Joe Sullivan, his supervisor, by radio. Inspector Sullivan sent a radio message to Special Agent John Proctor, Jr., to move the equipment onto Old Jolly Farm at 8:15 am CST on August 4, 1964, just 3 minutes later.[796]

Digging Up the Bodies

Once notification was received by Agent John Proctor, the dragline and the bulldozer were moved down a small dirt access road winding west from Highway 21. A dam was under construction at the end of this access road.[797]

Prior to excavation, measurements were taken of the various dimensions of the dam. Length from West to East was 547 feet. At its highest point, width of the dam at the top was 11 feet. At this same point, dam height was 20 feet. The dam was wider at the bottom with a width at the base of 83 feet, 6 inches at this same location.[798]

At 9:00 am CST on August 4, 1964, the Bulldozer operator was instructed to blade off the top of the dam to a uniform 12 feet width.[799]

Bulldozer Blades Top Of Dam To Uniform 12' Width

A point approximately 150 feet from the west end of the dam was selected as the initial digging location. The Drag Line Crane/Excavator operator positioned the Drag Line at the digging location. location. Digging was initiated with the Drag Line.[800]

Dragline Digs Up Bodies Starting At 150' From West End of Dam

Around 11 am CST on August 4, 1964, after approximately two hours of excavation using the Drag Line Crane/Excavator, faint traces of the peculiar pungent odor of decaying human flesh were noticeable. FBI agents warned the Drag Line operator to proceed with extreme caution, to avoid any damage to bodies that might be uncovered.[801]

At approximately 2:50 pm CST on August 4, 1964, the stench of decaying flesh was clearly discernible.[802] By this time, the excavation had proceeded from the start location 150 feet from the west end of the dam to the location of the bodies which were 191 feet from the west end of the dam.[803]

Agents instructed the Bulldozer operator to make several light passes over the bottom of the pit. After each pass, agents inspected the area at the bottom of the pit. At 3 pm, after the third pass, heels and back portions of a pair of man's boots had been exposed. Careful removal of the dirt around the area of the boots exposed the outline of a human body around 3:18 pm CST on August 4, 1964.

**First Body Naked From Waist Up
(FBI 2 Photo 09)**

Removal of the impacted clay-like earth continued.

Almost two hours later, around 4:45 pm CST on August 4, 1964, Body #1 was completely exposed. This body was lying face down with the head pointed in an easterly direction towards the side of the dam. Arms of the body were extended over the head.[804] This body was naked from the waist up.[805] A small wound was found under the left armpit, suggesting a bullet wound to the chest.[806]

**Body #1 Fully Exposed
(FBI 2 Photo 03)**

(Body On Right, Arms Extended Over Head)

A wallet was found in the left hip pocket of the blue jeans on the body. In this wallet was a Selective Service card that identified the holder as Michael Henry Schwerner. Other items on the body further indicated that **Body #1** was the body of Mickey Schwerner.[807]

Careful removal of dirt in the pit was continued. At 5:07 pm CST on August 4, 1964, a second body was found. This body was lying face down and partially under Body #1. As with Body #1, **Body #2** was found with the head pointing in an easterly direction. A wallet was found in the right hip pocket of the trousers on the body In this wallet was a Selective Service card that identified the holder as Andy Goodman.[808]

**Body #2 Fully Exposed
(FBI 2 Photo 12)**

(Clenched Left Hand In Bag)

Body #2 was found with its left hand clenched. Inside the clenched fist was a rock like object.[809] Finding the rock like object in the clenched fist would lead to speculation by some individuals that Goodman was still alive when buried.

At 5:14 pm CST on August 4, 1964, **Body #3** was found. This body was laying on its back with the head pointed toward the west. Its left arm and shoulder were drawn up across the body. Its right arm was lying along the side of the body.[810] Body #3 was James Chaney.

Exhuming operations were continued. Further dirt was removed around the bodies in the pit. However, the bodies were left unmoved as exposed. This approach was utilized to insure that the examination by the Coroner would not be compromised or effected in any way.[811]

By about 5:45 pm CST on August 4, 1964, the 3rd body had been completely exposed. In Washington, DC, the time was now 6:45 EST. President Johnson had to be informed.

Assistant FBI Director Cartha "Deke" DeLoach called President Johnson at 8:01 pm EST (7:01 CST) on August 4, 1964. DeLoach informed the President that the bodies of Schwerner, Chaney, and Goodman had been found.[812]

DeLoach: Mr. Hoover wanted me to call you and let you know that the FBI has found 3 bodies 6 miles southwest of Philadelphia, MS. A search party of agents turned up the bodies just about 15 minutes ago while they were digging in the woods and underbrush several hundred yards off route 21 in that area. We are going to get a coroner there right away, sir, and we are going to move these bodies into Jackson, MS, where we can hope they can be identified. We have not identified them as yet. But we have every reason to believe they are the 3 missing men. They were at the sight of a dam that had been constructed near Philadelphia, MS.

Johnson: When are you going to make the announcement?

DeLoach: Within 10 minutes, sir ... From Washington, here, sir.

Johnson: If you can hold it for 15 minutes, I think we have to notify these families ... I think that we can tell them we don't know [haven't identified the bodies] but we found them and I think that will kind of ease it a little bit ... Wait, I'll get right back to you.

Almost immediately after this conversation with Deloach, about 8:05 pm EST (7:05 CST) on August 4, 1964, President Johnson called Lee White, his key advisor on Civil Rights.[813]

Johnson: They found those 3 bodies 6 miles southwest of Philadelphia. They don't know that these are the bodies. They are moving them into Jackson to identify them ... They have every reason to believe they are the bodies. So, call the families and tell them there will be an announcement in the next 10-15 minutes. As soon as we get proper identification, we'll let them know further.

White: All right, I'll call all 3 of them right now.

Shortly after 8 pm CST on August 4, 1964, Fulton Jackson, Neshoba County Coroner, appeared at the scene. An examination was performed on the bodies by the Coroner as they lay exposed and unmoved in the pit.[814]

After completing his examination, Jackson placed the bodies in large plastic body bags. These bags were sealed. After the body bags were loaded into the Coroner's hearse, Jackson departed the grave site at about 11:14 pm CST on August 4, 1964. His hearse was led by a MS Highway Safety Patrol vehicle and followed by a vehicle containing FBI Special Agents.[815]

Jackson drove his hearse containing the bodies to the University of MS Medical Center in Jackson. Autopsies were to be performed by pathologists at the Medical Center.[816]

An inventory of items removed from the grave site was prepared by Special Agents of the FBI. Three bodies were included in the inventory. A copy of this inventory was provided to Olen Burrage at Burrage Truck Company. Burrage accepted the copy of the inventory. He signed a carbon copy of the receipt for the inventory report, acknowledging that his receipt of a copy of the inventory.[817]

After the bodies were removed, the dimensions of the pit containing the bodies were measured. Length of the grave site pit from east to west was 7 feet, 6 inches. Pit width from north to south was measured to be 6 feet, 9 inches. From the top of the dam to the bottom of the pit was 14 feet, 11 inches.[818]

Excavation to uncover the bodies began at a location 150 feet from the west end of the dam. The bodies were found 191 feet from the west end of the dam. Therefore, 41 feet of the dam was uncovered from west to east. The dam was 11 feet across at the top of the dam in this area. At the base in this area, the dam was 83 feet, 6 inches across.[819] Average width of the dam was 47 feet based on the width at the top and the bottom of the dam. From the top of the dam to the bottom of the pit was 14 feet, 11 inches.[820]

A dirt volume 41 feet by 11 feet x 14 feet, 11 inches was excavated to find the bodies. This volume consists of approximately 33,358 cubic feet of dirt. At the time of the excavation, the FBI reported that about 27,000 cubic feet of dirt had been removed.[821]

Only one excavation had been required to find the bodies. This fact clearly indicates that the approximate location of the bodies was known to the informant.

Martin Luther King Speaks Out

Despite the desire by President Johnson to keep the news about the bodies under wraps, this news was released. Late in the afternoon of August 4, 1964, around 6 pm CST (7 pm EST), the FBI released a statement about the finding of the bodies.

Atty. Gen. Robert F Kennedy announced that FBI agents today located three bodies in graves at the sight of a dam near Philadelphia, Mississippi ... The bodies are being removed to Jackson, Mississippi, where an effort will be made to identify them and determine the cause of death ...[822]

Regular television programming was interrupted at 6:45 pm CST (7:45 pm EST) to reveal the news that the bodies had been found.[823]

Once he was informed that the bodies had been found, Martin Luther King scheduled a news conference. This conference was held at Ebenezer Baptist Church in Atlanta, GA, later in the evening of Tuesday, April 4, 1954. Beginning January 24, 1960, Martin Luther King, Jr, was serving as co-pastor with his father Martin Luther King, Sr, at this church.[824] King sat at a table surrounded in front by an array of microphones.

As I stand here tonight, thinking about the discovery of these three young men, I think about the fact that it is urgent and it is important for the federal government through the FBI to use all of its resources to discover who killed those men. They have the technical know-how, they have the machinery, and it is my faith that somehow, they will discover who committed that dastardly act.

But tonight, I'm concerned about the deeper question. It's a haunting poignant question, a question facing everybody under the sound of my voice tonight, and every person who lives in this nation. It's not so much who kill those young men, but what kill them. And, when we move from the who to the what. In a strange sense, their death involves all of us, those of us who have been negligent about trying to register and vote participated in that act. Those men who have been silent when they should have been speaking participated in that act. Those who have allowed a system of segregation to thrive and grow and develop participated in that act.[825]

King made two important points. Blacks needed to actively pursue and to participate in the right to vote. Whites who were silent and who allowed segregation to thrive and grow were just as responsible for the murders as the murderers themselves.

COFO Volunteers Receive The News[826]

COFO was hosting a statewide Convention in Meridian for volunteers who were working throughout the state in Freedom Schools. This event began in the evening on August 4, 1964, the day that the bodies were found. Folk singer Pete Seeger came to start the event with a kick-off concert.

As he was singing, someone approached Seeger from off to the side. This person whispered into the ear of Seeger – the bodies of Schwerner, Chaney and Goodman had been found. Seeger made an announcement to the attendees at the concert. He informed the group that the bodies had been found.

Pete Seeger Leads Freedom School Convention In Song
(Mark Levy Collection, Queens College/CUNY Archives)

Pete Seeger asked the group to join hands and to sing *We Shall Overcome*.

Performing The Autopsies

Once discovery of the bodies was known to law enforcement, officials moved into action. William Waller, District Attorney for Hinds County, filed a motion with the Hinds County Circuit Court, MS 1st Judicial District.[827] This motion was to allow a community pathologist to perform the autopsies.[828] Using a community pathologist rather than a pathologist from the University of MS Medical School was expected to insure objective autopsies. A fear was that a university pathologist might be subject to pressure from local law enforcement.

A judge from the Hinds County Circuit Court, 1st Judicial District, did sign the motion.[829] Dr. William Featherston, a private practicing pathologist and partner in the Bratley Medical Laboratory in Jackson, was the community pathologist appointed to perform the autopsies.[830]

Nathan and Ann Schwerner, parents of Mickey Schwerner, also were worried about integrity of the autopsies. The Schwerners requested that Dr. Charles Goodrich and Dr. Alfred Kogan be allowed to observe the autopsies. Goodrich and Kogan were in Jackson already working with the Medical Committee for Human Rights.[831] Between 10 pm and 12 pm, Goodrich called Dr. Featherston. He asked that he be allowed to observe the autopsies on behalf of the families of victims. Featherston refused permission.[832]

Featherston provided Goodrich several reasons for denial of permission Currently, a large number of persons had been approved for observation Insufficient space was available for additional observers. Other physicians who had requested access to observe had also been denied, for the same reason.[833]

By 1 am on August 5, 1964, the bodies had been delivered to the University of MS Medical School in Jackson. Dr. William Featherston was present to perform the autopsy on the three bodies.[834] Dr. Reuel May, a dentist from Jackson, was on hand to capture any remaining dental structure of the bodies.[835]

Thirteen witnesses were also present throughout the whole autopsy.[836]

FBI Special Agent Jay Cochran from the FBI Laboratory in Washington, DC, accompanied the bodies and was part of the witness group.[837]

Jay Cochran

FBI Laboratory

Four more FBI Special Agents were also observing. Dr. Joel Brunsun, Dr. John Grondille, and Dr. Roger Arhelger[838] were all present as witnesses. These physicians were faculty members from the Department of Pathology of the University of MS Medical School. Photographers from the MS Highway Patrol and the FBI were on hand to take photographs. Neshoba County was represented in the witness group by Coroner Fulton Jackson, Sheriff Lawrence Rainey, and Deputy Sheriff Cecil Price.[839]

Body #1 was the body of Mickey Schwerner.[840] Dr. Featherston began an autopsy of Body #1 at 1:35 am August 5, 1964 by taking a total body x-ray.[841] Then, Dr. May recorded the dental structure in the skull and the lower jaw. The tips of each finger were removed for potential fingerprint ridge identification.[842] An 8 mm (0.31 in) entry wound was located in the chest to the right the centerline near the 4th rib. Featherston removed the bullet **(#1)** about 120 mm (4.7 in) to the left of the centerline near the 9th rib.[843]

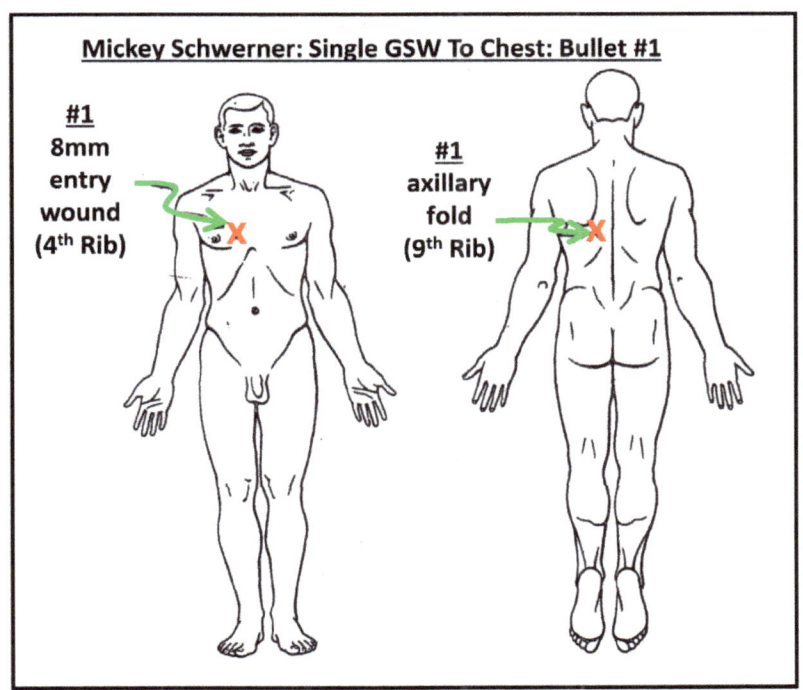

Body #1
Mickey Schwerner Autopsy

(Annotations By Orrin Terry, MD)

Detailed examination of the body and the x-rays did not reveal any other bullets in the body.

Featherston stated that the death of Body #1 was the result of the bullet wound.[844] By 2:30 am, the autopsy of Body #1 was completed.[845] All during the autopsy, photographs were taken by one of the FBI Special Agents and the MS Highway Safety Patrol photographer.[846]

Body #2 was the body of Andy Goodman.[847] While Body #1 was undergoing an autopsy examination, Body #2 had been subjected to x-ray examination. Dr. May began the autopsy of Body #2 at 2:40 am August 5, 1964. He recorded the dental structure in the skull and the lower jaw. Dr. Featherston then removed the tips of each finger for potential fingerprint ridge identification.[848] A 14 mm (0.55 in) entry wound was located in the chest to the right of the centerline around the 4th rib. Featherston removed a bullet **(#2)** lodged in the spine in the 6th thoracic interspace.[849]

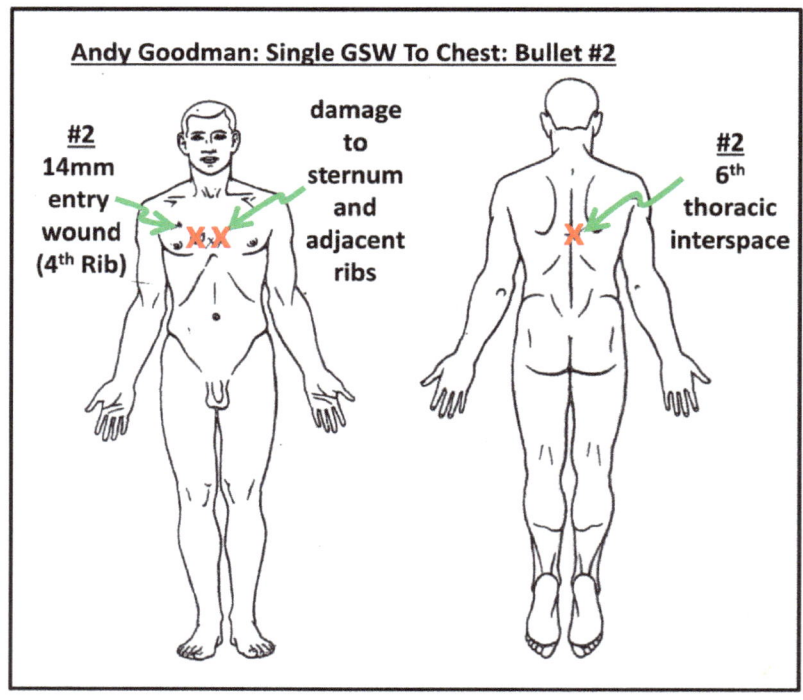

Body #2
Andy Goodman Autopsy

(Annotations By Orrin Terry, MD)

Detailed examination of the body and the x-rays did not reveal any other bullets in the body.

Featherston stated that the death of Body #2 was the result of the bullet wound.[850] By 3:26 am August 5, 1964, the autopsy of Body #2 was completed.[851] All during the autopsy, photographs were taken by one of the FBI Special Agents and the MS Highway Safety Patrol photographer.[852]

Body #3 was the body of James Chaney. While Body #2 was undergoing an autopsy examination, Body #3 had been subjected to x-ray examination. Dr. May began the dental examination of Body #3 at 3:27 am August 5, 1964. He recorded the dental structure in the skull and the lower jaw. Dr. Featherston then removed the tips of each finger for potential fingerprint ridge identification.[853] Three bullets were removed from Body #3 by Featherston.

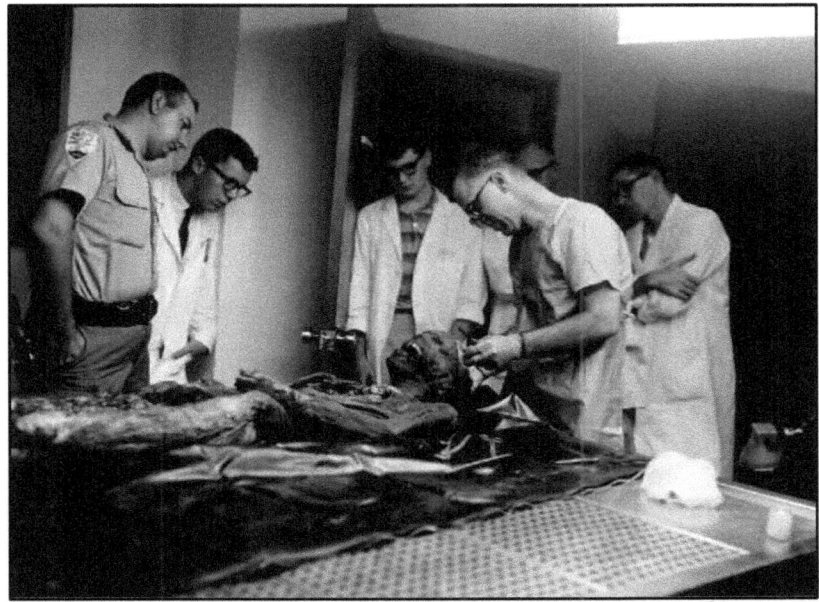

Dr. William Featherston Performs Autopsy On James Chaney (MS Highway Patrol)

(Dep Sheriff Cecil Price on left, Dr. William Featherston over Chaney)

One bullet **(#3)** entered in the center of the chest, just to the left of the centerline/sternum. This bullet was removed from a small incision into the back to right of centerline/spine Another bullet **(#4)** was found in the front, lower abdomen about 50 mm (2 in) to the right of the centerline/sternum. An entry point for this bullet was not found.[854]

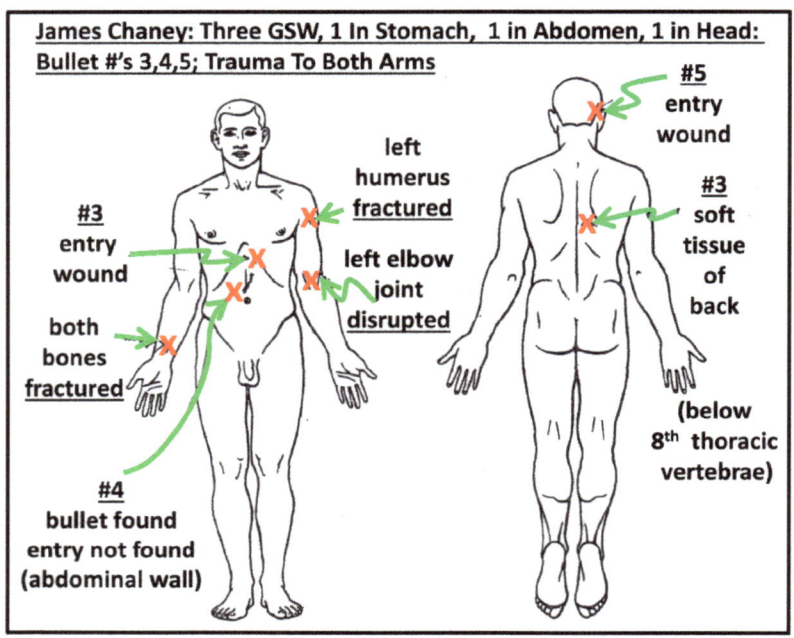

**Body #3
James Chaney Autopsy
(Annotations By Orrin Terry, MD)**

A large explosive fracture was located on the right side of the skull in the back of the head near the middle of the right ear lobe. Fracture lines extended downwards towards the base of skull.[855]

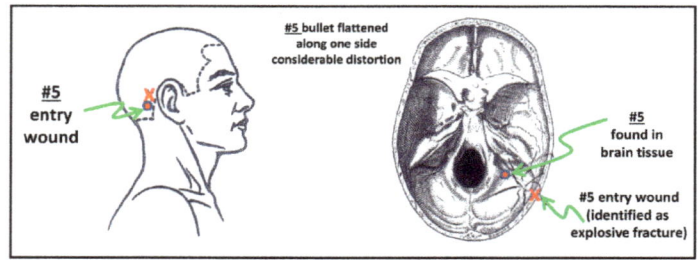

**James Chaney Head Shot
(Annotations By Orrin Terry, MD)**

Another bullet **(#5)** was found in the brain matter near this fracture.[856]

The explosive fracture with the radiating fracture lines was the entry wound of the head shot. After traveling a short distance, the bullet stopped in the nearby brain matter. This head shot immediately terminated the life of James Chaney.

Featherston claimed that the entry wound was not found. But then he stated that Chaney died from the bullet wound to the head. This explosive fracture had to be the entry wound of the bullet. This mistake would be the cause of some controversy over the years as to the source of the head wound.

Additional body damage was identified by Featherston in Body #3. This damage was to the bones in the left arm, and bones in the right arm.

A fracture of the left humerus was found about 45 mm (1.8 in) below the shoulder. Marked disruption of the left elbow joint was seen. Both the radius and ulna of the right forearm exhibited transverse fractures about 90 mm (3 in) above the wrist.[857]

Featherston declared that death was most likely the result of the bullet to the head.[858] By 4:15 am August 5, 1964, the autopsy of Body #3 was completed.[859] All during the autopsy, photographs were taken by one of the FBI Special Agents and the MS Highway Safety Patrol photographer.[860]

Body #1 (Mickey Schwerner) was killed by a bullet **(#1)** to the right side of the chest. Body #2 (Andy Goodman) was killed by a bullet **(#2)** to the right side of the chest. Body #3 (James Chaney) was killed by a bullet **(#5)** to the head. Two other bullets were found in Body #3. One bullet **(#3)** entered in the left, center chest. Another bullet **(#4)** was found in the front, lower abdomen. These bullets were not lethal.

At the time of his autopsy, Dr. Featherston did not find any bullets in the left arm or the right arm of the body of James Chaney. This absence of bullets in the arms would lead to extensive controversy over the manner in which Chaney was murdered.

Reactions By The Families

During the early morning hours of August 5, 1964, relatives of the victims were informed that the bodies had been found.

When told that the body of her son James Chaney was found, Mrs. Fannie Lee Chaney, his mother made a public statement.

My boy died a martyr for something he believed in-I believe in-and as soon as his little brother Ben gets old enough, he'll take James' place as a civil rights worker.[861]

A pre-dawn call from the White House had informed Mr. and Mrs. Robert Goodman that one of the bodies was their son. A public statement by Mr. Goodman at his home in New York described the feelings of the Goodmans.

Our grief, though personal, belongs to our nation. This tragedy is not private. It is a part of the public conscience of our country.[862]

Rita Schwerner, widow of Mickey Schwerner, also made a public comment about the death of her husband.

I feel pity for anyone so frightened, so afraid, so full of hatred themselves, that the only action they can take is to lash out. I vow to continue in civil rights work as long as I live.[863]

Representative Arthur Winstead, from Philadelphia, who had publicly stated that the disappearance was a publicity hoax, also spoke publicly on August 5, 1964.

No one can condone murder and violence, but folks have been killed in other sections of the country in racial outbreaks. When people form one section of the country go into another section looking for trouble, they usually find it.[864]

This statement by Winstead is hypocritical. He condones murder and violence, then justifies that behavior against Schwerner, Chaney, and Goodman. Worse yet, the meanness of this statement is apparent and directly in contrast to the responses of the parents and the widow. Fanny Chaney, Robert Goodman, and Rita Schwerner spoke eloquently, with empathy, and looked to the future. Their inherent dignity shines through. These grieving people resisted a call for violence in response to the cruel deaths of their loved ones.

A stark contrast exists between their statements and that of Winstead. Winstead justified the murders despite the first sentence. By the second sentence in his statement, Winstead clearly demonstrates all that was wrong with Mississippi.

The Independent Autopsy

Dr. David Spain started his career as a Medical Examiner for Westchester, NY. When the bodies were found, he was Chief of the Pathology Department at the Brookdale Medical Center in Brooklyn, NY. Spain was also a teacher, serving as the Clinical Professor of Pathology at the State University of New York.[865]

On August 5, 1964, Spain was vacationing at his summer home on Martha's Vinyard. At 1:30 am, his phone rang. The operator told Spain that Jackson, MS, was calling. Dr. Charles Goodrich, a New York physician, was the caller. Goodrich had been spending his vacation in MS giving medical aid to civil rights workers as a volunteer for the Medical Committee for Human Rights.[866]

Goodrich wanted Spain to come to MS to observe the autopsies of Schwerner, Chaney, and Goodman that were to occur later that day. Spain told Goodrich that if Goodrich could arrange transportation, he would come to MS. Goodrich called Spain again at 3:00 am. Goodrich had arranged for a 7:00 am special flight from the small airport at Martha's Vinyard to Kennedy Airport in NY. Spain could then take the 9:15 am flight from Kennedy to Jackson, MS.[867]

Unfortunately, the plane for the special flight had engine trouble. Spain hopped a 10 am flight from Martha's Vinyard into Kennedy. At Kennedy, he grabbed a helicopter to Newark. From Newark, Spain was able to take the 4 pm flight into Jackson. On the flight to Jackson, Spain met Dr. Aaron Wells, Chairman of the Medical Committee for Human Rights. Wells was also traveling to Jackson.[868] When the plane made a stop in Birmingham, the plane had engine trouble. After a time, the plane continued to Jackson. Spain and Wells landed in Jackson after dark on August 5, 1964.[869]

After Dr. Spain had checked into Room 119 of the Sun and Sands Hotel[870] in Jackson, Dr. Goodrich called the room. He asked Spain and Wells to come down to the room of John Pratt. Pratt was from upstate NY. He represented the Lawyers Constitutional Defense Committee in

Jackson. Pratt was handling the arrangements for access to the autopsies.[871]

MS officials were playing a game in the criminal legal world called "hide the ball." Officials were asserting one legal roadblock after another to prevent Spain from obtaining access to the autopsies.[872] Of course, the autopsies had started about 1:35 am at about the same time that Spain had received the first call from Goodrich. Furthermore, the autopsies had been completed by 4:15 am, before Dr. Spain had even left Martha's Vinyard. Observing of the autopsies was out of the picture.

Since the autopsies had been completed, Pratt was trying to obtain permission for Spain to examine the bodies and possibly perform his own autopsies. Pratt and his staff spent all day, August 6, 1964, gathering all the affidavits and notarized documents required by the authorities for permission for Spain to examine the bodies. Every time Pratt satisfied one legal roadblock, MS authorities created another roadblock. In order to stop this nonsense, Pratt asked Mrs. Fannie Lee Chaney, mother of James Chaney, who lived in Philadelphia, to give written permission to have her son's body examined by Dr. Spain. Mrs. Chaney agreed without hesitation.[873]

Finally, at 1 am on August 7, 1964, all of the necessary legal papers were gathered together. Pratt called the home phone of Raiford Jones, the Neshoba County District Attorney in Philadelphia, to have him authorize the Director of the University of MS Medical Center to release the bodies for examination by Dr. Spain. Pratt was told that DA Jones' phone was out of order. According to the operator, Jones' phone would be out of order for twenty-four hours.[874]

After breakfast, the next morning on August 7, 1964, Spain went out to the pool. Pratt was sitting by the pool relaxing. All that Pratt and Spain could do was wait until DA Jones finally authorized release of the body.[875]

About 1:00 pm, Pratt was paged on the public address system. He went to answer the page. When Pratt returned, he told Spain that the wait was over. Pratt and Spain headed for the morgue at the Medical Center. Official reception at the morgue was cool but courteous.[876]

Goodman's corpse had been sent out the night before on August 6, 1964, and buried. MS authorities refused to allow Schwerner's parents to give telephone permission for Spain to examine the body. Mrs. Chaney had provided a written, notarized authorization that could not be refused by the authorities. Dr. Spain was limited to examination of the body of James Chaney.[877]

At 2:30 pm, August 7, 1964, Spain began his examination of the body of James Chaney.[878] Dr. William Featherston had departed the autopsy location. However, Dr. Joel Brunson, Dr. John Gronvoll, Dr. Roger Arhelger, who had witnessed the Featherston autopsy, were still present.[879]

During the examination, Spain was careful to conduct only a visual examination. He did not make any incisions into the body. Spain had the normal paranoia of most northerners regarding the state of affairs in MS. He was worried that any incisions made would lead to legal action by MS officials. His greatest fear was that he *would be charged with performance of an autopsy in a state where he was not licensed to practice medicine.*[880]

In lay terminology – the jaw was shattered, the left shoulder and upper arm were reduced to a pulp; the right forearm was broken completely across at several points, and the school bones were broken and pushed in towards the brain.

Under the circumstances, these injuries could only be the result of an extremely severe beating with either a blunt instrument or chain. The other fractures of the skull and ribs were the result of bullet wounds. It is impossible to determine whether the deceased died from the beating before the bullet wounds were inflicted.[881]

Spain was very careful in one important regard in his dictated autopsy report [see actual Spain Autopsy in the Appendices]. He carefully stated that a determination could not be made as to whether the beating had occurred before the bullet wounds were inflicted.

After completing the examination, Dr. Spain returned to the hotel. He immediately dictated a report. Then, Spain left for the airport. *It was obvious to any first-year medical student that this boy had been beaten to a pulp.* His anger at the MS pathologists for failing to report the injuries overwhelmed him. Dr. Spain could not wait to leave MS.[882]

Once he returned to NYC, Spain conducted a complete autopsy of the body of Michael Schwerner. The body was shipped to the I J Morris Funeral Home in Brooklyn. On August 10, 1964, Dr. Spain conducted an autopsy of the body of Mickey Schwerner at the Funeral Home. Four witnesses attended during the autopsy at the Funeral Home.[883] Presumably, Spain did not find anything remarkable during this autopsy. A copy of the autopsy report has not survived. Furthermore, Spain did not make any public comments regarding the results of the Schwerner autopsy. If the autopsy results were remarkable or controversial, Dr. Spain would have publicly spoken out.

On August 12, 1964,[884] the FBI Laboratory issued its forensic toolmark analysis (*ballistics report*) of the bullets found in the bodies of Schwerner, Chaney, and Goodman. Five bullets were examined in the FBI Lab Report. Each bullet was characterized. Bullets were then compared to determine which bullets were discharged from the same firearm.

LabID	Bullet:Body	Entry Location	Caliber	Lands,Grooves
Q64	1: Schwerner	Chest	38 S&W	5, Right Twist
Q76	2: Goodman	Chest	38 S&W	5, Right Twist
Q86	3: Chaney	Center Chest	38 S&W	5, Right Twist
Q87	4: Chaney	Lower Abdomen	38 S&W	7, Right Twist
Q88	5: Chaney	Back Of Head	38 S&W	5, Right Twist

The bullet taken from Schwerner (Q64), the bullet taken from Goodman (Q76), and the bullet that entered the chest taken from Chaney(Q86) were discharged from the same firearm.[885]

Bullet Q88 found in the back of the head near the middle of the auricle of the right ear of Chaney was discharged by Jordan.

Since the bullet from the lower abdomen (Q87) had 7 lands and grooves, this bullet was definitely discharged from a different firearm.[886]

In addition to having 7 lands and grooves, the FBI Crime Lab also claimed that the bullet in Chaney's lower abdomen (Q87) was discharged by a 38 Smith and Wesson.[887]

News of Dr. Spain's findings had quickly spread far and wide, even before he returned to his home. Civil rights activists hailed Spain as a minor hero. Spain did not feel that he was a hero. He simply went to MS for one day to perform a job for which he had been trained.[888]

Some people were not happy with the findings published by Dr. David Spain, the independent pathologist recruited by the Chaney family.

J. Edgar Hoover, Director of the FBI, was one of those people. On August 13, 1964, Hoover wrote personal letters to the faculty and staff of the University of MS Medical Center. These letters were dated 8 days after the official autopsy by Featherston. Hoover sent these letters to Medical Center pathologists who participated in the autopsy. In these letters, Hoover *expressed sincere thanks for the outstanding cooperation and skillful assistance which the doctors had rendered* during the autopsy conducted by Featherston.[889]

Dr. William Featherston was another one of those people. During the last week of August, 1964, Featherston went across Jackson from Bratley Medical Center, where he was a partner, to the offices of the MS Sovereignty Commission at the New Capital Building. When Featherston arrived at the Commission, he met with Earle Johnston, Director of the Commission.[890]

Featherston was incensed that Dr. Spain would make accusations about omissions from the autopsy report. Spain had not seen an autopsy report.[891] In fact, all reports that Spain had seen were summaries that were published in newspapers.[892] Since Spain had not seen an autopsy report, Featherston was totally surprised when he saw a paper in the local press on August 8, 1964, where Spain heavily criticized inaccuracies in the official autopsy reports.[893]

Dr. Featherston and Dr. Spain were both members of the College of American Pathologists. This College had a strict rule about second autopsy reports. A pathologist was not allowed to conduct a second autopsy or issue a report on a second autopsy without the consultation with the first pathologist. Featherston was upset. Concluding that a "crushed skull" or "beating by chains or iron bar" were the cause of death could not be substantiated.[894]

An official breach of ethics complaint was filed by Featherston with the College. This complaint was scheduled to be heard at the annual meeting in Miami, FL, on October 16, 1964.[895]

Featherston was meeting with Johnston to make a request. He asked the Commission to perform an investigation to determine who had authorized Spain to perform his autopsy. He also asked that the Commission determine any relationship between Dr. Goodrich who called him originally to request access to observe the autopsy and Dr. Spain. Featherston did not give any recorded reasons for requesting the investigation.[896]

Dr. Spain was not investigated further by the Sovereignty Commission. However, the Sovereignty Commission already had Dr. Goodrich in its sights. Goodrich was helping as a volunteer to provide medical care to civil rights workers through the Medical Committee for Human Rights. Earle Johnston agreed that the Sovereignty Commission would continue to investigate Dr. Goodrich.[897]

The Funerals Of Schwerner, Chaney, and Goodman

Three services were held for James Chaney. A burial, a funeral, and a memorial were conducted at different times and different locations.

On August 7, 1964, James Chaney was buried in Meridian, MS. Chaney was a native of Meridian. His family lived in Meridian. James Chaney was buried on the grounds of the newly opened Memorial Park (Okatibbee) Cemetery atop Mount Barton. This cemetery is located a few miles outside of Meridian. Chaney was the second person to be buried at the Cemetery. A short, private burial was witnessed by approximately fifteen family members and close friends."[898]

Later that evening, hundreds of local blacks and a smaller number of white activists marched through Meridian to gather for a public funeral service for Chaney.[899] This public service was held at 7 pm at Meridian's First Union Missionary Baptist Church.[900]

Memorial Service Announcement

James Chaney

August 7, 1964

Ben Chaney, little brother of James Chaney, was at both the funeral and the memorial service. Ben was only 12 years old at the time. He was then known as "Little Ben Chaney." His resemblance to his brother was uncanny, Ben had the same almond-shaped eyes, high forehead and oval-shaped lips.[901]

At the memorial service, eulogies were to be given by Dave Dennis and Rev. Ed King, the current Chaplain at Tougalou College, in Jackson, MS.

Dave Dennis was one of the co-leaders of CORE activities in MS.[902]

Reverend Edwin King had been born in Vicksburg, MS[903] in 1936.[904] He left MS and became an ordained Methodist minister. In January of 1963, Rev. Edwin "Ed" King returned to his home state of Mississippi and became the Chaplain at Tougaloo College. On June 18, 1963, white civil rights fighters Ed King and John Salter both lay unconscious in Salter's blue 1961 Rambler on Hanging Moss Road—victims of an official police traffic accident. This accident was very suspicious. This wreck disfigured the right side of King's face. Despite the disfigurement and pain from regular medical treatment, King continued to visibly participate in various civil rights activities.[905]

In November, 1963, the NAACP sponsored an independent, mock election Freedom Vote among Blacks in MS. Aaron Henry, a Black man and President of the MS Branch of the NAACP, ran for Governor. Ed King, a white man and ordained Methodist minister, was his running mate as Lt. Governor.[906]

Dave Dennis gave his Eulogy to James Chaney first. Some implored Dennis to make his speech quiet, low-key. But Dennis recalls looking at those gathered in the church and seeing Ben Chaney, James' little brother.[907] As Dennis was starting to speak, Ben was slumped over crying so hard that his thin body shuddered.[908]

"I lost it. I totally just lost it," Dennis said. Instead of a low-key eulogy, he pleaded with those gathered.

> *Don't bow down anymore! Hold your heads up! We want our freedom now! I don't want to have to go to another memorial. I'm tired of funerals, tired of 'em! We've got to stand up.*[909]

Dennis was so emotionally drained that he was unable to finish his eulogy. He collapsed into the arms of Reverend Ed King.[910]

Reverend Edwin King was next to address the funeral service of Chaney. King spoke as a white minister addressing both Blacks and whites in MS.

> *The greatest tragedy that has occurred here is not just these deaths, but the failure in the white community that brought this about; that has brought this about, that has tolerated it.*[911] *. . . The only hoax is that these people think they have found the prize, the Christian way. That these people think that their religion, which is a religion based on white supremacy's southern way of life first, and Americanism and Christianity second. This is the hoax.*[912] *. . . When freedom comes to one half of Mississippi it will bring freedom to the other half.*[913]

King, a white Methodist minister, was admonishing whites. He stated that their Christian way was being used as an excuse to hide from responsibility for mistreatment of Blacks in the South.

After King's speech, the members of the Meridian COFO staff were called to the front to lead in the singing of "We Shall Overcome". After the singing of the hymn, Rev Ed King delivered a final benediction.[914]

The grave of James Chaney has a headstone and a gravestone flat on the ground. Inscribed in large letters on the gravestone appears the following:

"THERE ARE THOSE WHO ARE ALIVE YET WILL NEVER LIVE, THERE ARE THOSE WHO ARE DEAD YET WILL

LIVE FOREVER, GREAT DEEDS INSPIRE AND ENCOURAGE THE LIVING."

Rita Schwerner, the widow of Mickey Schwerner, requested that her husband be buried next to James Chaney at the black cemetery in Meridian. After all, Chaney was his friend in the struggle. Her request was denied. James E. Bishop, the Black funeral director handling Chaney's remains, refused to accept Schwerner's body. Bishop owned Enterprise Funeral Home in Meridian. He told Rita that "he feared Mississippi authorities would revoke his license-or worse-if he did."[915]

Then Rita Schwerner contacted several white undertakers. She requested transportation of Schwerner's remains to the black cemetery. All of white undertakers refused. In the end, the Schwerner family arranged to have Mickey's remains cremated and transported back to New York. This thwarted effort to integrate one Mississippi cemetery revealed that racial segregation was fully entrenched even in death on both sides of the racial divide.[916]

Mickey Schwerner had his cremated body flown from MS to New York on August 9, 1964. During the evening of that same day, a Memorial Service was held for Michael "Mickey" Schwerner. This service was held at the Community Church, 40 East 35th Street, in New York City. Around 2,000 attendees assembled for the service. Some of the overflow listened at a basement loudspeaker and others waited on the sidewalks.[917]

Speakers at the service included James Farmer, National Director of the Congress of Racial Equality, William M. Kunstler, a lawyer and family friend; John Lewis, chairman of the Student Nonviolent Coordinating Committee; David Dennis, an assistant program director for the Mississippi Summer Project; and Edward Pitt and John Garment, two friends of Schwerner.[918]

At the service, James Farmer, declared, "Evil societies always try to kill their consciences."

John Garment recalled his first acquaintance with Mickey Schwerner when both were students at Cornell. Both had worked together in a campaign to bring racial integration to their fraternity.

Dave Dennis voiced doubt that the deaths of the three young men would have attracted so much attention if all had been Negroes. Dennis also stated that "They were not the first to be killed in Mississippi. I feel they are not going to be the last. Tomorrow it might be your son or daughter, or you yourself."

Bill Kunstler concluded the service by saying:

"I urge you to walk out into the night on 35th Street with something more than pity and regret. We can look to tomorrow with brighter, clearer eyes because our three friends laid down their lives in the dark of a Mississippi night."

As the crowd moved somberly out of the building, the strains of "We Shall Overcome" rose from the crowd.

Bill Kunstler said that Mickey Schwerner's. body had been cremated.[919]

Andy Goodman's family had requested that his remains be transported back to New York. Immediately after the official autopsy by Dr. Featherston during the early hours of August 5, 1964, Andrew's body was shipped back to New York.

A funeral was held for Andy Goodman on August 10, 1964. This funeral was held at the Ethical Culture Society's meeting house, 64th Street and Central Park West, in New York City.[920]

Around 1700 attendees were at the service. Over 1,200 people filled the seats in the auditorium In addition, 150 persons in the basement listened to the service over a loudspeaker. More than 500 potential attendees were turned away. Those attendees waited patiently on the sidewalk outside. Many of the attendees were the same as those attendees for the Schwerner service on the previous night.

Goodman lay in state in a mahogany coffin. This coffin rested on a pedestal beneath the lectern. A single yellow rose lying on its closed lid.

Robert and Carolyn Goodman, Andrew's parents, were seated in the second pew and facing the coffin. His younger brothers, Jonathan and David, were seated with the parents.

Mrs. Fannie Lee Chaney, mother of James, sat in the front row, to the right of the Goodman family. Michael Schwerner's parents, Nathan and Anne Schwerner, and his widow, Rita Schwerner were sitting with Fannie Chaney.

Carolyn Goodman sobbed quietly several times during the service. Her husband Robert clasped her hand, with tears welling in his own eyes.

During the service, an anonymous telephone caller warned NY Police Headquarters that a bomb had been placed in the building. Policemen moved quietly into the filled 1,200-seat auditorium. A quick low-key search by the policemen scrutinized the crowd. Two large vases of flowers were removed from the podium. Searching and removal were completed without interruption of the service. Few attendees even realized the reason for the police intrusion. The bomb scare proved a hoax.

Eulogies were first given by Ralph Engelman and Barbara Jones. Ralph and Barbara were friends of Andrew.

"In going to Mississippi," said Ralph Engelman, "Andy risked not only death but dying in vain." Only the future could tell whether the death of Andrew and his companions had achieved anything.

Martin Popper, a lawyer and friend of the Goodman family, spoke after Engleman and Jones. Popper asserted that the sacrifice of the three young men had indeed served a great purpose. "Their deeds and their sacrifice will become an integral part of the culture of our nation," he said.

Main eulogist for the service was Rabbi Arthur J. Lelyveld of Cleveland. Llelyveld was a friend of the slain youth's parents, Robert and Carolyn. Goodman. Rabbi Lelyveld, was 51 years old. Llelyveld was himself beaten by a mob in Hattiesburg, MS., on July 10, 1964. In his eulogy, Lelyveld stated:

> *There are two levels to our grief today and paradoxically the two are one. First and foremost, we grieve for a precious individual. A rare blend of tenderness and manliness marked his unfolding years. But the tragedy of Andy Goodman cannot be separated from the tragedy of mankind.*

> *Along with James Chaney and Michael Schwerner he has become the eternal evocation of all the host of beautiful young men and women who are carrying forward the struggle for which they gave their lives. None of these civil rights workers—certainly not Andy or Michael or James—would have us in resentment and vindictiveness add to the store of hatred in the world.*[921]

Algernon D. Black, a leader of the Ethical movement, closed the service. In his closing, Black stated the following.

> *Wherever Negro and white stand up together, there will be the spirit of these three young men... and it's got to happen to every one of us personally."*

As her son's coffin was borne up the aisle, Carolyn Goodman reached out for the hand of Fannie Lee Chaney. Anne Schwerner joined hands with the other two mothers. All three mothers walked out of the building with arms linked.

Hundreds who had waited on the sidewalk began quietly singing "We Shall Overcome." Those mourners who emerged from the meeting house joined the singing. Soon, the civil rights song filled the block of 64th Street west of Central Park.

Andrew was buried in Mount Judah Cemetery at Cypress Hills in Brooklyn. Traditional Jewish graveside services were held.[922]

The grave of Andy Goodman has a headstone. Inscribed in large letters on the headstone appears the following:

"HE TRAVELED A SHORT WHILE TOWARDS THE SUN AND LEFT THE VIVID AIR SIGNED WITH HIS HONOR"

A Memorial Service Is Held at Mt Zion Methodist Church

On August 16, 1964, a Memorial Service was held for Schwerner, Chaney, and Goodman at the burned ruins of Mt. Zion Methodist Church in Philadelphia, MS.[923]

The most important speaker at this Memorial Service was Fannie Lee Chaney, the mother of James Chaney. Fannie Chaney made as short but very emotional plea.

But, right here at home. That's where I need help. And I'm lookin' for you all to help me. Don't let those children's life go in vain. They dead. Don't let their work die. That's when freedom started. When they beat, destroyed and 'buked my child and those other boys. That's when freedom started.[924]

As history would show, the plea by Fanny Chaney did not go unheeded.

A Post Autopsy Radiology Report

After the published allegations by Dr. David Spain, Dr. William Featherston decided to obtain a post autopsy radiology report.

Dr. James Packer was a practicing radiologist in Jackson. Radiologists are medical doctors that specialize in diagnosing and treating injuries and diseases using medical imaging (radiology) procedures (exams/tests) that employ X-rays, computed tomography (CT), magnetic resonance imaging (MRI), nuclear medicine, positron emission tomography (PET) and ultrasound. With his experience as a radiologist and reading x-rays, Dr. Packer was considered a reasonable choice for a second opinion.[925]

At the time of these autopsies in 1964, x-rays were the only imaging technologies available to pathologists. CT scans, MRI scans, PET scans and nuclear medicine were not invented for medical use until after 1964.

On August 28, 1964, a post autopsy radiology report based on the x-rays was provided to Dr. Featherston by Dr Packer. This report was delivered a short 23 days (slightly more than 3 weeks) after the official autopsy by Featherston. A signed copy of this report appears in an Appendix.[926]

Dr. Packer may not have known the identities of the victims in the autopsy. When the x-rays were created, the identification that had been assigned by Featherston were maintained. X-ray Set 1 was Body 1. This body had been identified as Mickey Schwerner. X-ray Set 2 was Body 2. Featherston had identified this body as that of Andy Goodman. Body 3 was X-ray Set 3. Body 3 was identified as James Chaney. However, in his report, Packer makes a point of indicating that he is using the x-ray numbers to identify the autopsy results. This insistence on using the x-ray numbers strongly suggests that Dr. Packer was not informed that he was reviewing the x-rays of Schwerner, Chaney and Goodman.

Using the x-ray/body numbers to identify the results was an excellent decision by Featherston. In this way, Packer was able to perform an objective autopsy without the fear of political harassment

Victim [Shooter]	Bullet	Fracture Observed	Bullet/Fragment Locations
Mickey Schwerner [Roberts]	#1	fractured right rib adjacent to fragments	fragments right upper chest fragments right scapula
Andy Goodman [Roberts]	#2	fractured 3rd right rib mid-axillary area	bullet, midline, upper dorsal
James Chaney [Roberts]	#3	left 4th rib	fragments in area
James Chaney [Posey]	#4	not found	not found
James Chaney [Jordan]	#5	temporo-parietal area of skull	bullet left of midline
		lower right radius	bullet superimposed
		upper left humerus	multiple adjacent fragments
		upper left ulna	multiple fragments in area

Packer Radiology Report Summary

X-ray technology at the time was not the greatest. X-rays were not particularly clear. Edges of objects may have been indistinct. Also, the forensic experience level of Dr. James Packer is not known. While he may have had extensive experience reading x-rays, Packer may have had little or no experience reading x rays from a forensic perspective. Nonetheless, useful results can be extracted from his report through careful interpretation.

Packer identifies a fractured rib adjacent to some bullet fragments in the right upper chest and near the right scapula in x-ray 1 (Schwerner). He also clearly states that the left chest is obscured by grumous material representing soil or rocks. Therefore this fractured rib must be on the right side of the chest.

The fractured right rib with bullet fragments near the right scapula indicates that the bullet entry into the body was into an upper right rib of Mickey Schwerner.

In his analysis of x-ray2 (Goodman), Dr. Packer provides more precise information about the bullet entry location. A fractured 3rd right rib in the mid-axillary area is noted by Packer. This fractured rib is the entry point of the bullet into body #2 (Goodman).

Using x-ray3 (Chaney), Packer analyzes 2 bullet effects that he finds in the x-rays. A fracture of the left 4th rib is noted. This fracture indicates the location of bullet #3 entry into the body of James Chaney. Additionally, Dr. Packer identifies a bullet fragment in the temporo-parietal area of the skull. This location is the resting location of the bullet first fired into the head of Chaney.

Dr. Packer also identified additional fractures in x-ray3 (Chaney). Locations of these fractures were the lower right radius, the upper left humorous, and the upper left ulna. Bone fractures at these locations were surrounded by bullet fragments or a bullet. The additional fragment information confirms that bullets actually entered the body of James Chaney at these locations.

Effects of the Murders on Freedom Summer

In the poorly educated minds of the White Knights, the murders of Mickey Schwerner, James Chaney, and Andy Goodman had a single purpose. These murders served as a notice to the civil rights workers who planned to invade MS for Freedom Summer. *Stay out of the state. You are placing your life on the line if you show up in MS.* This strategy backfired. If anything, volunteers became more resolute. The nation and national news media were focused on MS throughout the summer.

During June 20-21, 1964, the first 250 voter registration volunteers spread throughout the state of MS. Beginning June 27, 1964, an additional 300 Freedom School and community center workers arrived.[927] Friday, September 4, 1964, was the recognized end of Freedom Summer.[928] By this date, most of the volunteers had left MS to return to their homes.

Nearly 1500 volunteers worked in 32 project offices[929] scattered across the state of MS. In addition to the volunteers, 122 paid workers from SNCC and CORE worked alongside the volunteers. Volunteers came from several sources: 1027 white students from northern colleges; 254 clergy sponsored by the National Council of Churches; 169 attorneys recruited by the National Lawyers Guild and the Lawyers Constitutional Defense Committee; and, 50 medical professionals from the Medical Committee for Human Rights.[930] This group was a veritable army.

From June 16, 1964 – August 26, 1964, 417 incidents against MS Freedom Summer volunteers were recorded. About 213 of these incidents were violent. Violence included 80 beatings and burning or bombing of 67 churches, homes, and businesses. Over 1000 volunteers were arrested.[931] Despite the murders and the ongoing violence campaign conducted by the White Knights and the United Klans of America, the volunteers continued undeterred.

Only a few hundred new black voters were able to register with MS county officials. Over 40 Freedom Schools opened in 20 communities. More than 2,000 students enrolled in classes led by 175 teachers.[932] Harassment and reprisals against the volunteers were widely covered in the national media. Public outrage helped swell support for new laws and federal intervention.

A part of the Freedom Summer activities was to *register* Black voters in MS into the MS Freedom Democratic Party. An unofficial mock election with all Black candidates was conducted to demonstrate that Blacks would vote when registered. This Freedom Vote was held October 31-November 2, 1964. Approximately 70,000 Blacks from MS cast ballots in this mock election, despite shootings, beatings, intimidation, and arrests. In most counties, Freedom Voters outnumbered regular Democratic Party voters.[933]

During much of Freedom Summer, the search for the bodies of Schwerner, Chaney, and Goodman was conducted in the presence of the Freedom Summer volunteers. When the bodies were found, Freedom Summer volunteers were inspired by the bravery and sacrifice of Schwerner, Chaney, and Goodman.

In reality, the murders backfired on the White Knights. National attention was drawn to the search for the bodies. This attention focused the national media on the ongoing work by the Freedom Summer volunteers. As a result, the public became informed and aware of the plight of Blacks in MS and in the South. Public pressure grew significantly to apply the resources of the US government to resolving the plight of Blacks in MS and the South. This kind of public attention and dedication of resources was not what the White Knights wanted.

However, thanks to the sacrifices of Schwerner, Chaney, and Goodman, and the Freedom Summer volunteers, the White Knights received what they deserved. The ire of the American public and the resources of a powerful federal government were focused on breaking the violent stranglehold of the White Knights on the state of MS.

The murders of Schwerner, Chaney, and Goodman, Freedom Summer and Bloody Sunday in Selma (March 7, 1965) had an important affect. Lyndon Johnson was facing an uphill battle with Dixiecrats to obtain passage of the Voting Rights Act of 1965. These three events combined gave significant momentum to Johnson in his uphill battle against the Dixiecrats. On August 6, 1965, Johnson signed the Voting Rights Act into law. This Act banned literacy tests, authorized US DOJ to investigate the use of poll taxes in state and local elections and provided conditions for federal oversight of voter registration.

Part 4: Forensic Evidence Analysis

5 bullets were recovered from the bodies during the Featherston autopsy.
2 additional bullets were discovered in Chaney in a later review of x-rays.

Wayne Roberts shot bullet #1 into the chest of Mickey Schwerner.
Wayne Roberts shot bullet #2 into the chest of Andy Goodman.
Wayne Roberts shot bullet #3 into the chest of James Chaney.
Billy Posey shot bullet #4 that ended in the abdomen of James Chaney.
James Jordan shot bullet #5 into the brain of James Chaney.

Bullet #1 into Mickey Schwerner went front to back, right to left, downwards.
Bullet #2 into Andy Goodman went front to back, right to left, downwards.
Bullet #3 into James Chaney went front to back, left to right, upwards.
Bullet #4 into James Chaney took an unknown path through the body.
Bullet #5 into James Chaney went back to front, right to left, upwards.

Wayne Roberts shot an additional bullet into the left arm of James Chaney.
Billy Posey shot an additional bullet into the right forearm of James Chaney.

Andy Goodman was not buried alive.
James Chaney was not shot while running away.
James Chaney was not castrated.
James Chaney was not beaten.

James Jordan took James Chaney to the side of Rock Cut Road.
James Jordan faced James Chaney towards the ditch on the side of the road.
James Jordan (#5) shot James Chaney in the back of the head.
James Chaney fell into the ditch face up.
Wayne Roberts (#3) shot James Chaney in the left chest.
Wayne Roberts took a second shot into the left arm of James Chaney.
Billy Posey (#4) shot James Chaney in the right lower abdomen.
Billy Posey took a second shot into the right forearm of James Chaney.
Roberts and Posey pumped 4 bullets into James Chaney after he was dead.

Dr. William Featherston performed a thorough, accurate autopsy.
Dr. William Featherston did not hide evidence that James Chaney was beaten.
Dr. William Featherston did not control the distribution of his autopsy report.
Dr. David Spain made accusations based on invalid assumptions.
Dr. David Spain made accusations without seeing the autopsy report or x-rays.

Dr James Packer, radiologist, confirmed the Featherston autopsy results.

A Word Of Caution

This section begins construction and development of the evidence created by a shooting incident reconstruction expert that would be used in a trial. A forensic analysis is performed using the autopsy reports and firearms toolmark analysis (*ballistics report*) created by the FBI Lab. Clues and indicators from the FBI investigations are used to determine the locations involved on the day of the murders. A detailed step-by-step visual reconstruction is generated. This reconstruction uses the forensic analysis results, the locations involved, and the confessions by James Jordan and Doyle Barnette.

A few words of caution are appropriate here. General readers, and even experts, need to use caution in reading these sections.

Every claim must be derived from a foundation of evidence.

Analyses and reconstructions depend on specific claims regarding who, what, when, where, and how. Every claim must be based upon a foundation of evidence. These foundations can be drawn from autopsy reports, toolmark analyses, confessions, investigation results and reports, physics, science, experiments and personal experiences. Use of personal experiences should be based on specific foundations. A claim should not be justified based solely on *my personal experience*. Specific aspects of the personal experience should lay the foundation for the claim.

Avoid the anything can happen trap.

Many readers, and even experts, fall into the *anything can happen* trap. Just because an alternate claim or interpretation can be formulated doesn't mean that the claim makes sense in a specific situation. An alternate claim must be founded on specific evidence in the situation. Given the conditions and evidence of the situation, anything cannot happen. Only alternate claims or justifications that can be derived based on evidence can be used.

Criticize the foundation or the application of the foundation to the claim.

During the trial, cross examination is conducted. Criticism during cross-examination should be dependent on shortcomings in the foundation or flaws in the conclusion derived from the foundations. Criticisms may be based on additional foundation or reasonable but different conclusions that may be derived from the same foundation.

Reasonable interpretations based on the foundational data are acceptable. Formulating a simple counterexample does not invalidate a reasonable interpretation. Anyone can formulate a counterexample in any situation, especially if the existing facts or foundation are ignored.

When reading the forensic analysis, the location determinations, and shooting reconstruction, review carefully the foundation used to justify results. If a claim is based on a logical and careful application of all the foundational material presented, first accept that claim as valid. Then, determine if the application of the foundational material logically leads to the claim being offered.

Alternate claims/interpretations must be based on an additional foundation or a different reasonable interpretation of the same foundational material.

Forensic Evidence Analysis

During the actual shootings on Rock Cut Road, only three of the Klansman performed the shooting. Alton Wayne Roberts, James Jordan, and Billy Wayne Posey, all from the Meridian Klavern, were the shooters. The Autopsy Report by Dr. William Featherston and the FBI Lab Firearms Toolmark Report (ballistics report) are used as the foundation to determine more details. Bullet entries and final locations in the bodies are determined from the Autopsy Report. Data provided in the FBI Lab Firearms Toolmark Report link shooters to the bullet entries. A comprehensive bullet path analysis correlates the shooters, bullet entries, and bullet directions of travel in the bodies.

Forensic analysis data, as detailed above, other research results, and personal firearms technology and operations knowledge are used to evaluate some of the myths surrounding the murders. Four alternate theories are presented of the shooting details on Rock Cut Road. Forensic analysis data is used to evaluate the alternate theories. This same information is used to reconstruct what really happened on Rock Cut Road when James Chaney was murdered.

Throughout these evaluations, visual representations are used to explain and to justify the conclusions. Photos taken by the author at the actual murder location on Rock Cut Road are often used.

All the analyses and shooting theory evaluations are based on foundations of modern medical forensic techniques and modern ballistic forensic techniques. Even when personal experience is used, specific details of experience are provided. ***These analyses and shooting theory evaluations have never been previously accomplished.***

Autopsy Summary

Dr William Featherston performed autopsies on the bodies of Schwerner, Chaney, and Goodman on August 5, 1964, at the University of Mississippi (Univ of MS) Medical Center, in Jackson, MS. A copy of the autopsy report by Dr. Featherston appears in the Appendices.

Body #1 was the body of Mickey Schwerner.[20] An 8 mm (0.31 in) entry wound was located in the chest to the right of the centerline near the 4th rib. Featherston removed the bullet **(#1)** about 120 mm (4.7 in) to the left of the centerline near the 9th rib.[21]

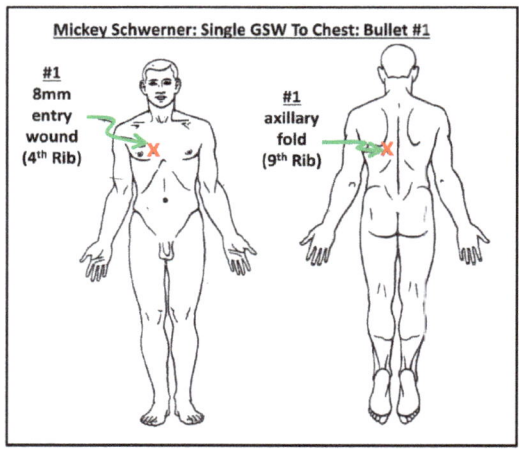

Body #1
Mickey Schwerner

(Annotations:
Orrin Terry, MD)

Featherston stated that the death of Body #1 was the result of the bullet wound.[22]

Body #2 was the body of Andy Goodman.[23] A 14 mm (0.55 in) entry wound was located in the chest to the right of the centerline around the 4th rib. Featherston removed a bullet **(#2)** lodged in the spine in the 6th thoracic interspace.[24]

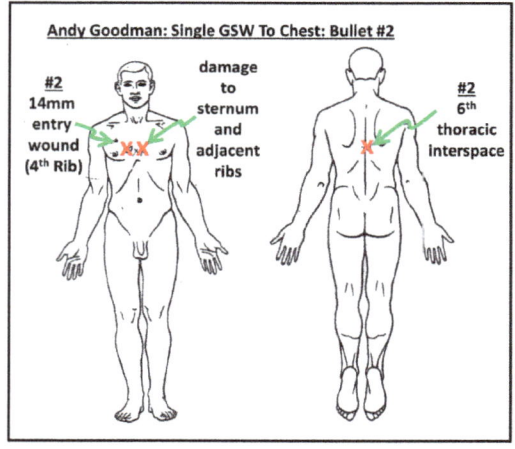

Body #2
Andy Goodman

(Annotations:
Orrin Terry, MD)

Featherston stated that the death of Body #2 was the result of the bullet wound.[25]

Body #3 was the body of James Chaney. Three bullets were removed from Body #3 by Featherston. One bullet **(#3)** entered in the center of the chest, just to the left of the centerline/sternum. This bullet was removed from a small incision into the back to the right of the centerline/spine Another bullet **(#4)** was found in the front, lower abdomen about 50 mm (2 in) to the right of the centerline/sternum. An entry point for this bullet was not found.[26]

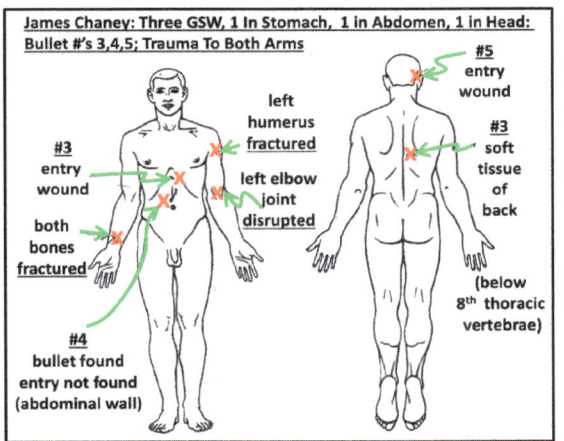

Body #3
James Chaney

(Annotations: Orrin Terry, MD)

A large explosive fracture was located on the right side of the skull in the back of the head near the middle of the right ear lobe. Fracture lines extended downwards towards the base of skull.[27]

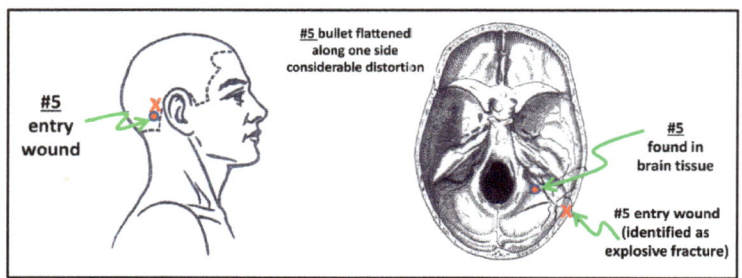

James Chaney Head Shot
(Armed Forces Medical Examiner, Annotations: Orrin Terry, MD)

Another bullet **(#5)** was found in the brain matter near this fracture.[28]

The explosive fracture with the radiating fracture lines was the entry wound of the head shot. After traveling a short distance, the bullet stopped in the nearby brain matter. This head shot immediately terminated the life of James Chaney.

Featherston claimed that the entry wound was not found. But then he stated that Chaney died from the bullet wound to the head. This explosive fracture had to be the entry wound of the bullet. This mistake would be the cause of some controversy over the years as to the source of the head wound.

Additional body damage was identified by Featherston in Body #3. This damage was to the bones in the left arm, and bones in the right arm.

A fracture of the left humerus was found about 45 mm (1.8 in) below the shoulder. Marked disruption of the left elbow joint was seen. Both the radius and ulna of the right forearm exhibited transverse fractures about 90 mm (3 in) above the wrist.[29]

This additional damage to the skull and arms of the body of Chaney was omitted from the FBI summary, not the Featherston autopsy.[30] The original autopsy by Dr. Featherston clearly and concisely identified this additional damage.

Featherston declared that death was most likely the result of the bullet to the head.[31]

Body #1 (Mickey Schwerner) was killed by a bullet **(#1)** to the right side of the chest. Body #2 (Andy Goodman) was killed by a bullet **(#2)** to the right side of the chest. Body #3 (James Chaney) was killed by a bullet **(#5)** to the head. Two other bullets were found in Body #3. One bullet **(#3)** entered in the left, center chest. Another bullet **(#4)** was found in the front, lower abdomen. These bullets were not lethal.

At the time of his autopsy, Dr. Featherston did not find any of the bullets in the left arm or the right forearm of the body of James Chaney. This failure to find the bullets in the arms lead to extensive controversy over the manner in which Chaney was murdered.

Ballistics Summary and Analysis

On August 12, 1964,[32] the FBI Laboratory issued its forensic toolmark analysis (*ballistics report*) of the bullets found in the bodies of Schwerner, Chaney, and Goodman. Five bullets were examined in the FBI Lab Report. Each bullet was characterized. Bullets were then compared to determine which bullets were discharged from the same firearm.

LabID	Bullet:Body	Entry Location	Caliber	Lands,Grooves
Q64	1: Schwerner	Chest	38 S&W	5, Right Twist
Q76	2: Goodman	Chest	38 S&W	5, Right Twist
Q86	3: Chaney	Center Chest	38 S&W	5, Right Twist
Q87	4: Chaney	Lower Abdomen	38 S&W	7, Right Twist
Q88	5: Chaney	Back Of Head	38 S&W	5, Right Twist

The bullet taken from Schwerner (#1, Q64), the bullet taken from Goodman (#2, Q76), and the bullet that entered the chest taken from Chaney(#3, Q86) were discharged from the same firearm.[33] This conclusion is consistent with the confession of Doyle Barnette that Wayne Roberts shot both Schwerner and Goodman. Furthermore, Roberts had *a snub nose gun, probably a revolver, in caliber .38 Smith and Wesson, of English origin similar to a Police Special.*[34]

According to the confession by Doyle Barnette, James Jordon killed James Chaney. Bullet (#5, Q88) found in the back of the head near the middle of the auricle of the right ear of Chaney was discharged by Jordan.

The bullet that entered Chaney's chest (#3, Q86) was discharged from the same firearm that shot Schwerner (#1, Q64) and Goodman (#2, Q76).[35] Assuming that this finding by the Laboratory is correct, then the shot to the chest of Chaney was delivered by Wayne Roberts.

Since the bullet from the lower abdomen (#4, Q87) had 7 lands and grooves, this bullet was definitely discharged from a different firearm.[36]

In addition to having 7 lands and grooves, the FBI Crime Lab also claimed that the bullet in Chaney's lower abdomen (#4, Q87) was discharged by a .38 Smith and Wesson.[37] Billy Wayne Posey *had a pistol, make and model unknown.* Jimmy Arledge had *a long-barreled pistol similar to the type referred to as an "Old Horse Pistol". This weapon had a ring in the butt and the barrel is either hexagon or octagon.*[38]

Arledge could not have discharged the bullet into Chaney's lower abdomen. His *Old Horse Pistol* was actually a percussion black powder pistol. These pistols were in caliber .58 to .75, not in caliber .38 as the lower abdomen bullet. Furthermore, these pistols were generally smooth bore -- meaning, no lands and grooves. Therefore, a bullet discharged from an Old Horse pistol could not have exhibited 7 lands and grooves.

Therefore, the *unknown make and model pistol* possessed by Billy Wayne Posey discharged the bullet into lower abdomen of James Chaney. Assuming that the FBI Crime Lab was correct, this bullet to the lower abdomen was also a .38 Smith and Wesson.

Wayne Roberts shot Mickey Schwerner (#1, Q64) and Andy Goodman (#2, Q76) in the chest. Wayne Roberts also shot Chaney in the chest (#3, Q86). Billy Wayne Posey shot Chaney with a bullet that landed in the lower abdomen (#4, Q87). James Jordan shot James Chaney in the back of the head (#5, Q88). (# is Featherston autopsy identifier, Q is FBI Lab identifier).

Bullet Path Specification

When a bullet enters a body that consists of living tissue, the bullet crushes the tissue in front of its path through the body.[39] Eventually, the bullet either comes to a stop in the body or completely exits the body. By connecting the entry location and the final location in the body (or the exit location), a bullet path can be constructed. Using the bullet path, a reverse trajectory potentially enables the location of the shooter to be determined.

A human body is a 3-dimensional object. Once the elements that determine the path of the bullet are identified, that path can be characterized in all 3 dimensions: depth direction, vertical direction, and horizontal direction.

These bullet travel directions are described relative to a set of anatomical body planes. Since 3 dimensions need to be described, 3 anatomical body planes are identified.

Depth directions are defined relative to a frontal plane. A vertical direction is described relative to a transverse plane. The sagittal plane is the basis for indicating a horizontal direction.

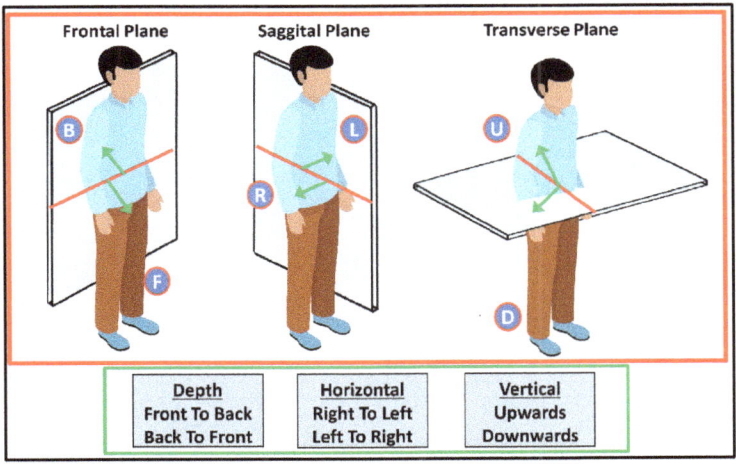

Anatomical Body Planes
(Figures: N Kuvshinov, All Annotations: Bruce Krell, PhD)

The frontal body plane divides the body into a front portion and a back portion. A depth bullet path direction can be front to back or back to front relative to the frontal plane. The sagittal body plane divides the body into a right portion and left portion. A horizontal bullet path direction can be right to left or left to right relative to the sagittal plane

The transverse body plane divides the body into an upper portion and a lower portion. A vertical bullet path direction can be upwards or downwards relative to the transverse plane.

When using these planes to specify the direction of a bullet, the desired plane is assumed to be centered at the bullet entry location. For instance, if a bullet enters the chest, the transverse plane is assumed to pass through that entry location in the chest. A bullet that stops in the body below that plane travels in a downward direction relative to the transverse plane. In common practice, reference to the body plane is omitted. A medical examiner simply declares that the bullet path travels in a downward vertical direction.

Graphic visual presentations are the simplest approach to characterize bullet path inside the body. Only two graphics are necessary to represent all 3 directions of the bullet path.

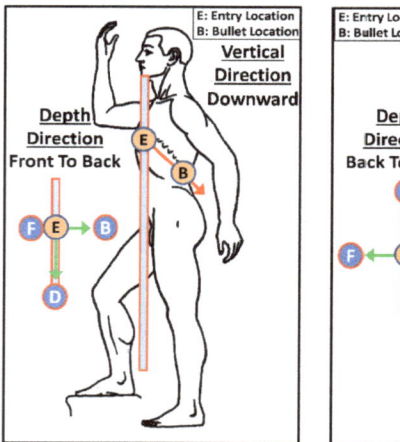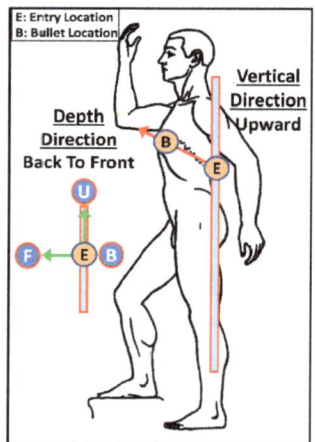

Bullet Path Directions
(Armed Forces Medical Examiner, Annotations: Bruce Krell, PhD)

A standard lateral/sideways autopsy diagram is used to represent both depth and vertical directions of a bullet path. Bullet entry location **(E)** and bullet resting/exit location **(B)** are placed on the diagram. An imaginary vertical anatomical plane is drawn through the bullet entry. A line is drawn between the bullet entry and the resting/exit location.

This line represents the bullet path. A bullet path line represents two directions (depth, vertical). The depth direction/component is described as either front to back or back to front. Bullet path vertical direction/component can clearly be seen as upwards or downwards. An annotation is used to simultaneously display both directions of the bullet path from the plane. Depth and vertical components of direction are marked on the annotation using arrows, as shown in the example above.

In practice, the imaginary vertical anatomical plane is often omitted. Arrowheads are also generally omitted when drawing the bullet path.

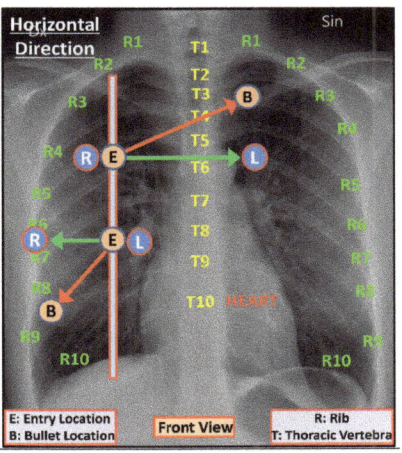

Horizontal Direction of Bullet Path
(X-Ray: Steve Cohen, MD, Annotations: Bruce Krell, PhD)

Horizontal bullet path in the chest is demonstrated using a front view x-ray of the ribs (R1 - R10), thoracic vertebrae (T1-T10), and the heart. Bullet entry location **(E)** and bullet resting/exit location **(B)** are placed on the diagram. An imaginary vertical anatomical plane is drawn through the bullet entry. A line is drawn between the bullet entry and the bullet exit/resting location. Horizontal direction of the bullet path is either left to right or right to left. An annotation is used to display the horizontal direction of the bullet path from the plane. Horizontal direction from the plane is then marked on the annotation using an arrow, as shown in the example above.

In practice, the imaginary vertical anatomical plane is often omitted. Arrowheads are also generally omitted when drawing the bullet path.

Only horizontal bullet path should be informed with this front x-ray. This front x-ray of the body components is a mathematical projection of a 3-dimensional body onto a 2-dimensional surface. As a result of the flat surface projection, only left and right directions can be determined from this x-ray.

Bullet Path Analysis

All of the 5 bullets discharged into Schwerner, Chaney, and Goodman stayed in the bodies. An entry location and a final location for each bullet were identified in the autopsy by performed by Dr. William Featherston.

Victim [Shooter]	Bullet	Entry	Location
Mickey Schwerner [Roberts]	#1	right of midline 4th rib	4.7" left of midline 9th rib, rear axillary fold
Andy Goodman [Roberts]	#2	right of midline 4th rib	midline 6th thoracic interspace
James Chaney [Roberts]	#3	left of midline upper epigastric region	slightly right of midline back, below vertebra T8
James Chaney [Posey]	#4	not found	2" right of midline front abdominal wall
James Chaney [Jordan]	#5	right occupito-temporal area	inside the brain mass

These locations were identified with reasonable accuracy by Dr. Featherston. Bullet paths are constructed using these locations.

Wayne Roberts discharged bullet #1 into the chest of Mickey Schwerner.

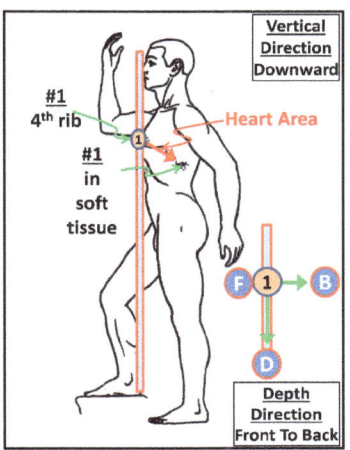

Depth, Vertical Bullet Path for Bullet #1 into Mickey Schwerner

Bullet #1 traveled through the body of Mickey Schwerner from front to back and downward.

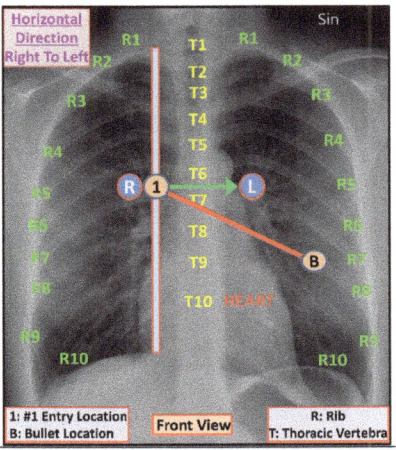

Horizontal Bullet Path for Bullet #1 into Mickey Schwerner

As the bullet was moving front to back and downward, bullet #1 also travelled from right to left through the body. This bullet passed through the top of the heart. As a result, Mickey Schwerner died lying face down in the ditch from loss of blood about 10 seconds to 16 seconds later.[40]

Wayne Roberts discharged bullet #2 into the chest of Andy Goodman.

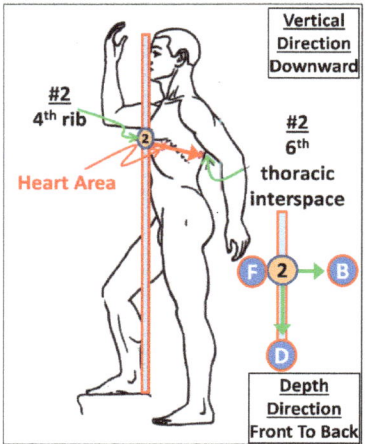

Depth, Vertical Bullet Path for Bullet #2 into Andy Goodman

Bullet #2 traveled through the body of Andy Goodman from front to back and downward.

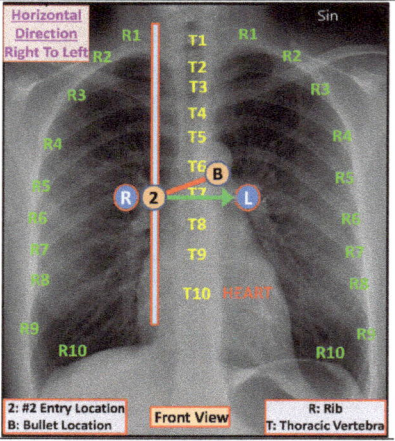

Horizontal Bullet Path for Bullet #2 into Andy Goodman

As the bullet was moving front to back and downward, bullet #2 also travelled from right to left through the body. This bullet passed through the top of the heart. As a result, Andy Goodman died lying face down in the ditch from loss of blood about 10 seconds to 16 seconds later.[41]

James Jordan discharged bullet #5 into the head of James Chaney.

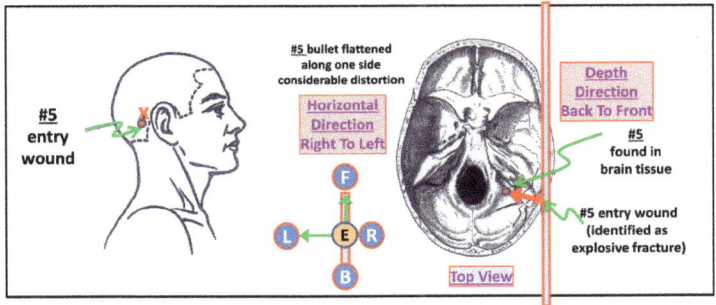

Depth, Horizontal Bullet Path for Bullet #5 into James Chaney

Bullet #5 traveled through the head of James Chaney from back to front and slightly upward.

As the bullet was moving back to front and slightly upward, bullet #5 also travelled from right to left through the brain. This bullet passed through the center of the brain mass. As a result, James Chaney instantaneously died from penetration of the Central Nervous System (CNS).[42]

Wayne Roberts discharged bullet #3 into the chest of James Chaney.

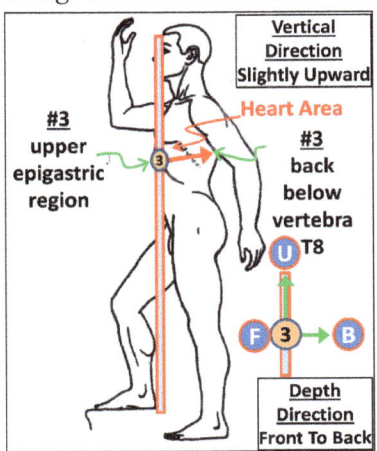

Depth, Vertical Bullet Path for Bullet #3 into James Chaney

Bullet #3 traveled through the body of James Chaney from front to back and slightly upward.

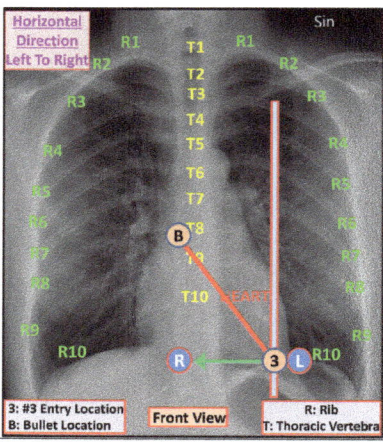

Horizontal Bullet Path for Bullet #3 into James Chaney

As the bullet was moving front to back and upward, bullet #3 also travelled from left to right through the body. This bullet passed through the middle of the heart. However, James Chaney was already dead from bullet #5 to the back of the head discharged by James Jordan.

Billy Wayne Posey discharged bullet #4 into the body of James Chaney.

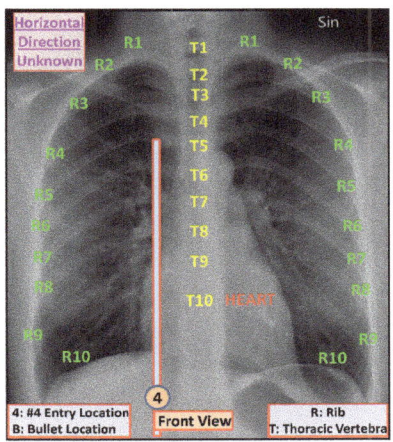

Resting Location of Bullet #4 in James Chaney

Bullet #4 was found in the front abdominal wall body of James Chaney. Dr. Featherston failed to determine an entry location for the bullet. Without an entry location, a bullet path cannot be determined based on the autopsy report. However, James Chaney was already dead from the head shot (#5) by James Jordan at the time this bullet was discharged into the body.

Close scrutiny of the bullet paths reveals some important features that are helpful in a determination of the shooting activity on Rock Cut Road.

Victim	Bullet	Depth	Vertical	Horizontal
Mickey Schwerner [Roberts]	#1	F => B	Downward	R => L
Andy Goodman [Roberts]	#2	F => B	Level	R => L
James Chaney [Roberts]	#3	F => B	Slightly Upward	L => R
James Chaney [Posey]	#4	unknown	unknown	unknown
James Chaney [Jordan]	#5	B => F	Upward	R => L

Mickey Schwerner was shot in the chest through the heart. Schwerner bled to death. The bullet path of bullet #1 confirms this conclusion.

Andy Goodman was also shot in the chest through the heart. Goodman also bled to death. The bullet path of bullet #2 confirms this conclusion.

Several aspects of the shooting of James Chaney are important. Bullet paths for bullet #5 and bullet #3 provide this important information. Chaney was shot by James Jordan first, according to the confession of Doyle Barnette. James Chaney died immediately from bullet #5 through the brain mass. Jordan was behind Chaney in order to shoot Chaney in the back of the head with bullet #5. However, bullet #3 entered the body of James Chaney from the chest, demonstrated by the bullet #3 path. Shots were discharged into James Chaney from both the back and the front of his body.

Another important aspect of the shooting of James Chaney is revealed by the path of bullet #3. This bullet path went from left to right and slightly upwards. This path has important implications to the location at which the shooter was positioned during the discharge of bullet #3.

Any theory of the way James Chaney was murdered has to satisfy two conditions. Bullets entered James Chaney from opposite sides, back (#5) and front (#3). Bullet #3 travelled left to right and slightly upward through the body of James Chaney.

Bullet Penetration Depth Analysis

A total of 5 bullets were removed from the bodies of Schwerner, Chaney, and Goodman during the Featherston Autopsy. According to the FBI Lab Report, these bullets were all caliber .38 Smith and Wesson. This bullet is light (146 grains/0.33 ounces) and slow moving (muzzle velocity 680 ft/sec).[43]

Every bullet has a maximum penetration depth. A maximum penetration depth is necessary to ensure that the bullet hits a vital organ. Penetration depth is determined by the weight, muzzle velocity, design (shape, distribution of mass, and type) of the bullet, the entry location, and the entry angle. A .38 Smith and Wesson bullet moving through human tissue has a somewhat short penetration depth.

Mechanics of bullet penetration into human tissue are well understood. A bullet causes tissue disruption. This concept of tissue disruption was identified through the works of Theodor Kocher from 1875-1885.[44] Tissue disruption is the destruction of the normal anatomical structures of the tissue. The operative word here is destruction. Tissue disruption means that the bullet destroys the tissue.

Kocher also defined the cavitation mechanics of bullet penetration into human tissue. A bullet that penetrates human tissue causes two cavities. As the bullet moves through the tissue, the tissue in front of the bullet is crushed by the force of the moving bullet. Crushed tissue leaves an open cavity where the crushed tissue has been broken. This cavity is permanent and is roughly the diameter of the bullet unless the bullet is yawing or tumbling.[45]

As the bullet passes through an area, the tissue to the sides stretches outward. Tissue stretching results in a large cavity. However, the force to the sides is generally not enough to break or to crush the tissue. So, this stretched tissue tends to retract to its original position. This larger cavity is called the temporary cavity and does not cause any wounding damage.[46]

In 1984, Dr. Martin Fackler published an article entitled, *Bullet Fragmentation: A Major Cause Of Tissue Disruption.*" In this article, Dr. Fackler accomplished two important tasks. As part of the research for this article, Dr. Fackler developed a gelatin for wound profile testing that simulates human tissue response to bullet penetration. This gel composition was validated against swine (pig) tissue. A second accomplishment was to evaluate the effect of bullet design on bullet impact mechanics. Fackler determined that full metal jacket bullets penetrate deeper than soft point bullets. He also discovered that soft point bullets fragment, causing greater disruption/tissue damage.[47]

Penetration depth testing using tissue simulant ballistic gelatin has become standard in the ammunitions manufacturing industry. Law enforcement agencies use these penetration depth test results to select ammo for use by their agencies.

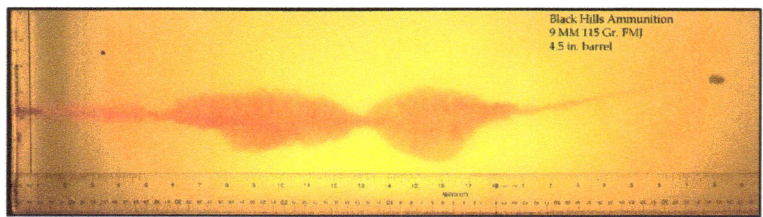

9 mm Discharged into Ballistic Gel Simulant (Martin Fackler, MD)

In 1985, Dr. Fackler published an article entitled *The Wound Profile: A Visual Method For Quantifying Gunshot Wound Components*.[48] A live fire test is performed using the tissue simulant ballistic gelatin. Test results are depicted using this visual technique.

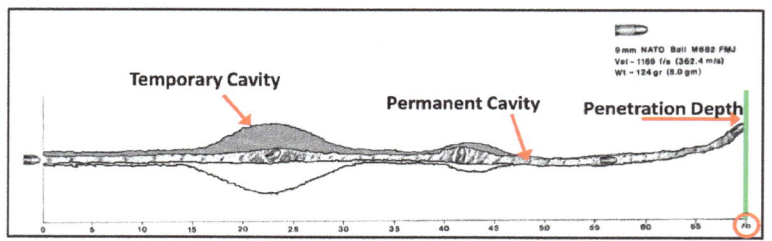

Ballistic Wound Profile for 9 mm Gel Test (Martin Fackler, MD)

This diagramming technique displays the features of the temporary cavity and the permanent cavity. Actual measurements of temporary cavity size, permanent cavity/wound path diameter, and penetration depth are provided for any cartridge.

In 1987, the FBI conducted the *Wound Ballistic Workshop*. Dr. Martin Fackler, Dr. Vince DiMaio, and others participated in this workshop. Several factors were identified that serve as aids in causing maximum tissue disruption. (1) In order to cause immediate death (called instant incapacitation), a handgun bullet must penetrate the central nervous system, such as the brain. (2) A handgun bullet must be capable of penetrating the chest at least 12" to guarantee impact with a vital organ. (3) A handgun bullet that penetrates a vital organ can only cause death from a sustained blood loss. (4) A sustained blood loss for 10-16 seconds is necessary to cause death. (5) A bigger bullet disrupts more tissue and causes greater blood loss. (6) Penetration depth is a function of design (soft point, full metal jacket, and hollow point). (7) Penetration depth is also a function of combined bullet mass and velocity (momentum and the force at impact).[49]

A minimum penetration depth of 12" is meant to be a guarantee of hitting a vital organ with a chest shot for all body types. An impact through the chest may certainly hit a vital organ in less than 12" for a fairly thin body. But, if the target is a 400-pound person, a much greater penetration depth is necessary to guarantee hitting a vital organ through the chest. As with most engineering disciplines, a worst-case scenario is adopted. Use a cartridge capable of greater penetration depth into a large, heavy, fat covered body. With a fat covered body, vital organs are deeply hidden. Use a cartridge capable of penetrating in the worst case of a large body. In the best case when the body type is thin, the more capable bullet successfully penetrates, hitting vital organs.

After the bullet enters the body, the bullet may come to a resting location in the body or may exit the body. Final bullet location (resting or exit) is dependent on the potential penetration depth, the angle of penetration into body, body characteristics such as height and weight, and type of tissue penetrated.

Front to back penetration of a bullet controls whether a bullet rests in the body or exits the body. A bullet that penetrates less deeply front to back has a greater chance of remaining in the body.

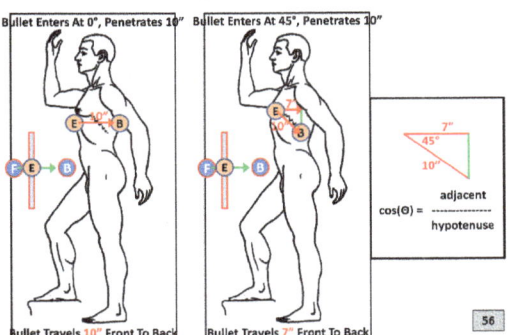

Effect of Impact Angle on Front to Back Depth

These examples demonstrate the effect of impact angle on front to back depth. Both examples employ a bullet that has a penetration depth of 10". In the example on the left, a bullet enters the chest with a 0° impact

343

angle. This bullet travels straight towards the back and obtains a front to back depth of 10". The bullet may stay in the body or exit the body. A bullet enters the chest on the right at a downward angle of 45°. Using trigonometry (cosine), this bullet can only travel front to back (straight towards the back) for a depth of 7". This bullet will stay in the body if the person is an adult. Both bullets can still cause significant damage because a 10" actual penetration depth has a likelihood of hitting a vital organ.

Body type is another factor that determines the final location of a bullet that enters a body. Front to back penetration of a bullet controls whether a bullet rests in the body or exits the body.

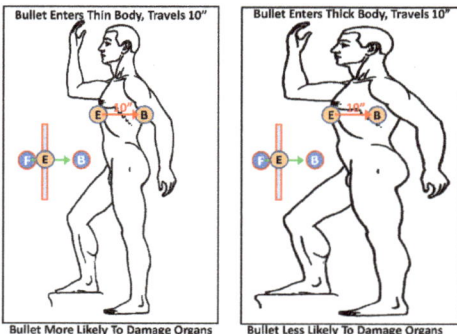

Effect of Body Type on Front to Back Depth

These examples demonstrate the effect of body type on front to back depth. Both examples employ a bullet that has a penetration depth of 10". In the example on the left, a bullet enters the chest of a thin body. This bullet travels straight towards the back and obtains a front to back depth of 10". The bullet may stay in the body or exit the body. A bullet enters the chest of a thick body on the right. This bullet travels straight towards the back and obtains a front to back depth of 10". This bullet will stay in the body.

A bullet entering a thin body with a penetration depth of 10" can cause significant damage to a thin body. An adult thin body is typically 10" deep so that the bullet has a likelihood of hitting a vital organ. A bullet entering a thick body with a penetration depth of 10" may not cause significant damage to a thick body. An adult thick body is typically 12" deep so that the bullet has less likelihood of hitting a vital organ.

All of the bullets fired into Schwerner, Chaney, Goodman were identified by the FBI laboratory as caliber .38 Smith and Wesson. This cartridge was originally designed in 1877, when revolvers were the only type of handgun available. Early penetration depth tests on cadavers and live animals demonstrated that this light weight, slow velocity, lead bullet did not penetrate deeply.[50]

At the time of the shooting in 1964, the most common form of .38 Smith and Wesson cartridge fully loaded used a lead bullet with a round nose.

38 Smith & Wesson
Bullet Type: lead round nose
Weight: 146 grain
Muzzle Velocity: 680 ft/sec

**38 Smith and Wesson Cartridge With Lead Round Nose
(Photo: Aaron Brudenell, Forensic Scientist)**

This bullet weighed 146 grains (0.33 ounces). Muzzle velocity for this cartridge was 680 ft/sec.

Modern penetration depth testing using tissue stimulant gelatin confirms the short penetration depth of the .38 Smith and Wesson cartridge.

A penetration depth test was performed with two different .38 Smith and Wesson cartridges. Both bullets were hand loaded by the tester, not commercially manufactured. Each cartridge was loaded with the same amount of powder, 2.8 grains of smokeless AA#2 smokeless powder. After the powder was loaded, a bullet was then inserted into the cartridge. A 2.25" short barrel Colt Pocket Positive was used to discharge the bullet from the cartridge into the ballistic material.[51] Tissue simulant used for these tests was ballistic soap. Soap is a bit more dense than 10% ballistic gelatin. Penetration depth is around 2/3 the depth determined with ballistic gel.[52] Measured penetration depths have to be increased by 1/3.

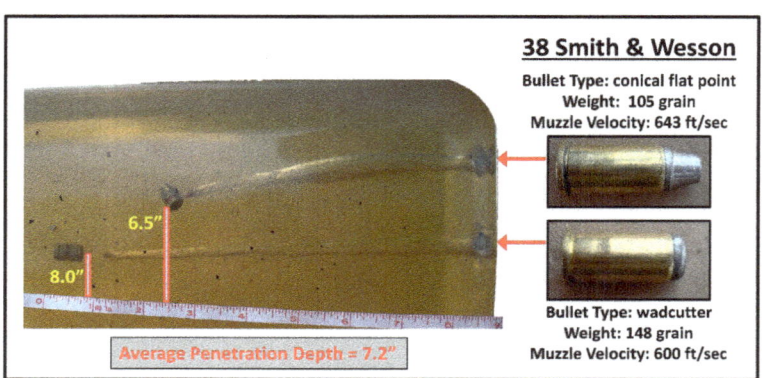

38 Smith and Wesson Ballistic Soap Penetration Depth Testing
(Aaron Brudenell, Forensic Scientist)

Neither bullet exactly matches commercially sold .38 Smith and Wesson bullets. Commercial bullets are light (146 grains/0.33 ounces) and slow moving (muzzle velocity 680 ft/sec). However, this test is close enough to understand the behavior of the bullets discharged into Schwerner, Chaney, and Goodman.

A 105-grain conical flat bound bullet only penetrated 6.5". This bullet had a muzzle velocity that closely compares to the commercially available cartridges. The 148 grain wadcutter bullet penetrates about 8" into the test material. This bullet weights about the same as a commercially available bullet and has a muzzle velocity well below the velocity of a commercial bullet. One test bullet was closer in weight. The other test bullet was closer in muzzle velocity. Using the average of a sample is a standard statistical technique. So, the average penetration depth of the caliber .38 Smith and Wesson bullet is 7.2 inches.

Since ballistic soap was used as the test medium, this depth needs to be adjusted by 1/3. After this adjustment, the average penetration depth is 9.5 inches. A typical male human body is 10 inches (thin body) to 12 inches (thick body) deep. Therefore, a .38 Smith and Wesson bullet will likely stop at a location inside the body.

In order to evaluate the bullet depths from the autopsy reports, the body types of Schwerner and Goodman need to be determined. Data is available about their body types.

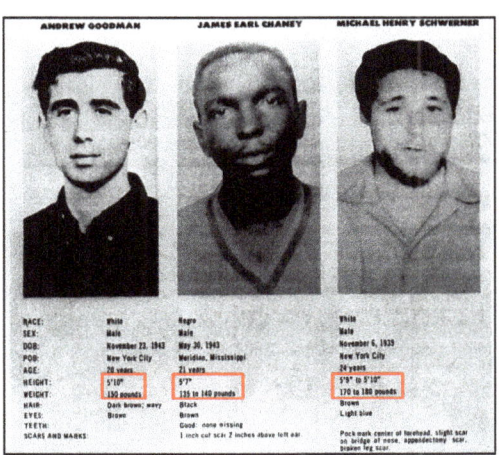

**Height and Weight of Schwerner, Chaney, and Goodman
(FBI Missing Poster, June 29, 1964)**

Mickey Schwerner was 5"10" tall and weighed 180 pounds. With this height and weight, Schwerner was certainly thick-bodied. Front to back depth at his chest was about 12". Andy Goodman was also 5'10" tall. However, Andy only weighed 150 pounds. Goodman was thin-bodied. Front to back depth at his chest was about 10". With a front to back penetration depth of 9.5", a .38 Smith and Wesson bullet would likely have stayed within each body.

A comparison of the autopsy diagrams demonstrates that the .38 Smith and Wesson bullets did stay within the bodies of Schwerner and Chaney. Furthermore, the effects of impact angle and body thinness/thickness are also demonstrated by this side by side comparison of the diagrams.

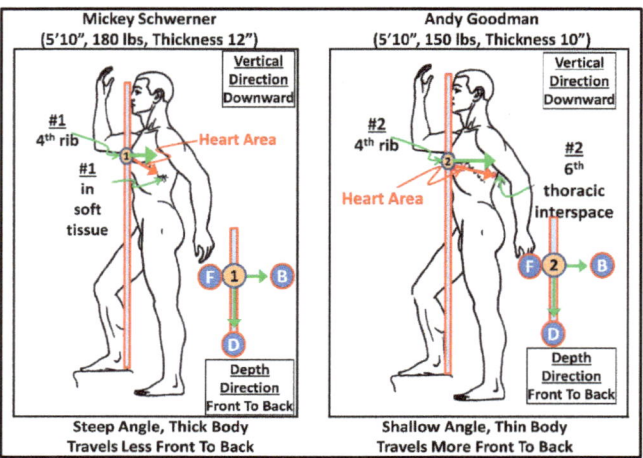

Autopsy Diagram Comparison Of Schwerner and Goodman

Featherston failed to provide bullet front to back depth information. However, the autopsy diagrams provide a means to obtain some relative comparisons. In this figure, the heavy red arrow represents the bullet path. The heavy green arrow represents the front to back penetration depth in each body.

A bullet entered the chest of Andy Goodman at a very slight downward angle. After entering at the chest, the .38 Smith and Wesson bullet travelled 9.5" (penetration depth) along the bullet path (red arrow). Front to back depth (green arrow) is almost 9.5" (red arrow). Goodman had a thin body with a front to back depth of 10". As expected, the slightly angled bullet shot into the thin body of Andy Goodman stopped just short of the back of the body.

A bullet entered the chest of Mickey Schwerner at a fairly steep downward angle. After entering at the chest, the .38 Smith and Wesson bullet travelled 9.5" (penetration depth) along the bullet (red arrow). Front to back depth (green arrow), maybe 7", is far less than 9.5" (red arrow). Schwerner had a thick body with a front to back depth of 12". As expected, the steeply angled bullet shot into the thick body of Mickey Schwerner stopped far short of the back of the body.

Both bullets were found inside the bodies at the expected locations based on .38 Smith and Wesson penetration depth, impact angle, and body type.

Despite the failures to exit the bodies, these bullets were fatal. Both bullets pierced the heart of the victim. Each victim bled to death in 10-16 seconds due to extensive loss of blood.

Comparison of the Featherston and Spain Autopsies

On August 7, 1964, Dr. David Spain performed a second autopsy on the body of James Chaney. This autopsy was also conducted at the Univ of MS Medical Center. A copy of the autopsy report by Dr. Spain is contained in the Appendices.

Spain was publicly critical of the autopsy performed by Dr. Featherston.

It was obvious to any first-year medical student that this boy had been beaten to a pulp.[53]

Anger at Dr William Featherston for failing to report the injuries overwhelmed Spain.[54] Spain publicly declared this anger in an article entitled "Mississippi Autopsy" in *Ramparts* magazine on Monday, October 25, 1964.[55]

Dr Louis Lasagna on the faculty of the Johns Hopkins School of Medicine was also publicly critical of the autopsy by Featherston.

... the wire services of our country carried a report that a private pathologist ... had examined the three bodies and reported that all three of the boys had been shot, but that there was no other evidence of mutilation or bodily injury.[56]

Dr David Spain and Dr Louis Lasagna were wrong in their accusations of Dr. Featherston. A review of the original Chaney autopsy by Featherston reveals that Featherston did describe the additional damage that might have indicated a beating. **This additional damage to the skull and arms of the body of Chaney was omitted from the FBI summary, not the Featherston autopsy.**[57] At the time of his criticisms, Dr. Spain had not seen the Featherston autopsy, the X-rays, or the FBI summary.

A comparison of the original autopsy by Dr. Featherston with the later autopsy by Dr Spain clearly demonstrates that Featherston described the same additional damage.

Featherston Autopsy	Spain Autopsy
right occupito-temporal fracture	left fronto-parietal fracture
fracture lines towards base	fracture extending through base
left humerus fracture	left humerus fracture
left elbow joint disruption	not mentioned at all
right radius transverse fracture	right radius fracture across
right ulna transverse fracture	right ulna fracture across

The fracture in the first row is the entry of the bullet into the skull. Additional fracture lines described in the second row were created by the bullet passing through the skull.

Some differences do appear in the autopsies by Featherston and Spain. Featherston described the location of a depressed fracture to the head of Chaney in the **right** occupito-temporal area of the skull. Spain described that same fracture in **left** fronto-parietal area. These descriptions characterize radically different locations in the skull.

In those days, medical terminology was not standardized. One pathologist might describe a location relative to the body looking at the observer. Another pathologist might describe a location relative to the observer looking at the body. So, the same relative location could be on the left side for one pathologist and the right side for the other pathologist. This dilemma was ultimately resolved using autopsy diagrams and standardization of autopsy specification methods. Both Featherston and Spain were describing the same side of the skull but from different frames of reference.

However, Featherston was actually correct. James Jordan turned James Chaney to face the ditch by the side of the road. Jordan placed the muzzle of his .38 Smith and Wesson pistol less than an inch (contact distance) from the skull. The muzzle was at the back of the right side near the middle of the ear lobe, as indicated by Featherston. Bullet entry was to the right side of the body of Chaney.

This discrepancy between the two locations may have occurred for several possible reasons.

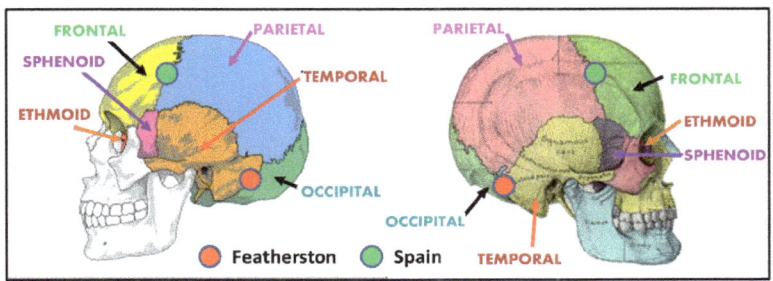

**Elements of the Calvarium of the Skull
(Left: Edoarado, Wikipedia, Right: Liberal Dictionary)**

Using areas to describe the location rather than actual measurements is inherently inaccurate. These areas of the skull are imprecise and subjective. During the autopsy, the calvarium of the skull was removed by Featherston. Spain could easily have been confused about the orientation of the calvarium when this portion of the skull was sitting to the side on a table top. All the colored skull sections on the left of the skull in the figure above are the calvarium of the skull.

The Featherston location was determined with the calvarium of the skull intact. When Spain performed his autopsy, the calvarium of the skull [colored skull sections] had been removed. Spain confused the correct orientation of the separated skull piece when locating the hole described as the bullet entry.

Additional information in the autopsy by Featherston provides corroboration that his location for the bullet entry location is correct. Bullet #5 was found in the mushy mass of the brain. In order to be in the mushy mass of the brain, this bullet location was near the skull fracture location identified by Featherston. Featherston also described the condition of the bullet found. *It is flattened along one surface and shows considerable distortion.*

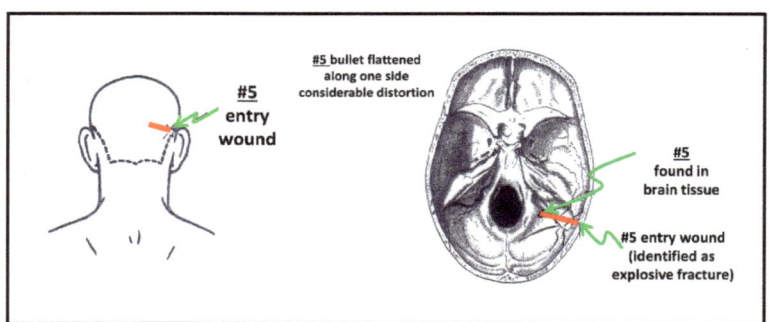

James Chaney, Head Shot, Bullet Path

A bullet path was formed between the entry point of the bullet and the final resting location of the bullet in the brain. For this bullet path to have formed, James Jordan stood behind and to the right of James Chaney. Jordan turned James Chaney to face the ditch by the side of the road. He took a position behind and to the right of James Chaney. Jordan placed the muzzle of his .38 Smith and Wesson pistol close to the skull (contact distance). The muzzle of the revolver was on the right side of the skull in the back of the head near the middle of the right ear lobe. Jordan pulled the trigger.

This bullet is light (158 grains/0.36 ounces) and slow moving (689 ft/sec).[58] As the bullet impacted the skull, the heavier bone in this area of the skull forced the bullet sideways to angle a bit from its trajectory. As a result, the bullet entry hole was widened. The bullet itself was flattened along the side that pushed against the heavier skull.

This distorted and angled bullet entered the brain matter. Essentially, the bullet was moving through the brain angled slightly off center from the direction of movement. As the bullet moved through the brain, stiff resistance was encountered. The slightly off center, distorted, and flattened bullet presented a greater cross-sectional area to the brain matter. Greater resistance was the result. This damaged bullet could not go very far under these conditions. Such a damaged bullet would end up at a final resting place near the location of entry -- the entry location indicated by Featherston.

Dr. Spain actually contributed one piece of additional corroborating evidence for the Featherston location. Spain recorded that the entry hole was 3 cm (1.2 inches) wide. Bullet diameter for the .38 Smith and Wesson bullet is 0.361 inches.[59] As the bullet deflected somewhat to the side due to the thickness of the skull, a wider entry hole was created. A 1.2-inch entry hole for an angled 0.361 diameter bullet is very reasonable.

A bullet that entered from the top of the head as claimed by Spain would have ended up near the top of the head. The final resting place of the bullet reported by Featherston was nowhere near the top of the head.

Inaccuracies in locating wounds and body damage were resolved in later years. Body locations, both in the skull area and elsewhere in the body, are indicated using a standard frame of reference. Typically, this frame of reference includes an offset from the top of the head and an offset from the vertical centerline of the body. These precise locations are given along with autopsy diagrams, removing any confusion about body locations.

Featherston and Spain disagreed on the significance of the skull fracture and the fracture lines.

Featherston: *The fracture of the skull was definitely related to the gunshot wound.*

Spain: ... *these injuries could only be the result of an extremely severe beating with either a blunt instrument or chain.*[60]

All of the evidence appears to support the conclusion stated by Featherston. Worse yet, Spain completely missed the significance of the size of the fracture that he correctly recorded. A hole that size is caused by a bullet entering the skull.

Another difference exists between the two autopsies. Dr. Spain describes a badly shattered jawbone. *A complete through and through comminuted fracture was present in the center of the mandible.*[61] In his subsequent publications, Spain elaborated on the extent of damage to the jaw. *I noticed Chaney's jaw. It was broken: the lower jaw was completely shattered, split vertically, from some tremendous force. I moved the shattered pieces of his jaw in vertical directions for the three doctors to see.*[62] Spain failed to identify which jawbone, left or right, in all his writings. Featherston did not mention a fractured jawbone.

This conclusion by David Spain assumes that the jawbone was broken before the autopsy was initiated. No proof exists that the jawbone was badly broken and smashed at the beginning of the autopsy by

Featherston. The body of James Chaney had been clearly torn apart during the autopsy.

Damage to the jawbone could have happened during the highly destructive autopsy. Dr. Reuel May, a dentist from Jackson, recorded the dental structure in the skull and the lower jaw of each body. A mostly decomposed jawbone might have been broken trying to open the mouth to get dental impressions. Dr May might even have purposely torn the jawbone apart in order to make his dental impressions.

Many of the conclusions in the autopsy by David Spain are questionable.

In his published writings, Spain clearly states that the fractures to the skull, the damage to the jaw, and the damage to the left and right arms were caused by a beating.

... these injuries could only be the result of an extremely severe beating with either a blunt instrument or chain.[63]

But one thing was certain: this frail boy had beaten in an inhuman fashion. The blows that had so terribly shattered his bones - I surmised he must have been beaten with chains or a pipe - were in themselves sufficient to have caused death.[64]

These conclusions are completely unfounded. The skull fracture is the bullet wound from the head shot by James Jordan. Damage to the arms turned out to be caused by other bullets! Jawbone damage could have been caused during the autopsy or during the burial process.

Spain described damages to a body that had undergone an extensive autopsy. At the heart of his criticism was an assumption that he was observing the original damage to the body of Chaney caused by the 3 bullets. But, Featherston had extensively cut the body apart.

The peritoneal cavity is opened and the chest cage is dissected away anteriorly. On reflecting the heart and lung toward the right and medially, a bullet exit is noted in the posterior rib cage ... Two ribs are dissected free and a tract is found to extend into the subcutaneous tissue space... The anterior abdominal wall is dissected laterally ... The skull is denuded of soft tissue ... The calvarium is removed with slight difficulty ...

These actions described a body that had been cut apart.

In his autopsy, David Spain further characterized the devastation to the body of James Chaney as a result of the autopsy.

The body was ... opened from the neck to the pubis anteriorly ... The organs had been removed ... The top of the calvarium had been sawed and was independent of the base of the skull. The organs had been removed ... On the left of the sternum the ribs were shattered into many fragments ... On the left of the sternum the ribs were shattered as were the ribs directly posteriorly just next to the vertebral bodies.

David Spain assumed that the damage he observed was created during the murders. This assumption appears to be totally unfounded. Much of the damage that Spain claimed was the result of a beating was the result of taking the body apart for the autopsy.

Bodies of Schwerner, Chaney and Goodman were dropped onto an empty area at the west end of the dam. An area 14', 11" x 7', 6" x 6',9" was filled with dirt. Filling this area required 27 cubic yards of dirt. Fill dirt containing gravel, stone, and sand was used to fill the area. This kind of dirt averages about 2000 pounds per cubic yard.[65] After all the dirt was filled, 27 tons of dirt had been dropped on the bodies.

This dirt had to be compacted to be stable, otherwise the bodies would be accidentally uncovered when the dirt came apart. Compacting a pond dam is a well-known process.

COMPACTED FILL. As the dam is built, including filling back the core trench, the soil should be added in no more than 6-inch layers and compacted by driving back and forth over fill.[66]

Compaction of the dirt over the bodies was accomplished using a Caterpillar Bulldozer Model D6B. This bulldozer weighs about 25 tons.[67] As the bulldozer moved back and forth over the surface, this 25 tons was added to the 27 tons of weight from the dirt itself. Conceivably, some damage could have been done to the bodies from all this weight. All three bodies were roughly stacked, but portions of bodies were exposed and subjected to all of that weight. Since Schwerner and Chaney were on top, these bodies should have experienced some damage. However, no such damage was exhibited. If the head of Chaney were exposed and subjected to all that weight, this situation could have caused the damage to the jawbone of James Chaney. Jawbones are tubular and break very easily.

After 46 days, the bodies were badly decomposed, as both Featherston and Spain described. Decomposition during this long a period certainly weakened the bone structure, making the tubular jawbone even more easily broken. Removing the bodies from the dam could have caused damage to the significantly decomposed jawbone of Chaney.

The autopsy by Featherston was far more detailed than the autopsy by Spain. Featherston wrote 5 pages with fairly detailed medical descriptions. Spain wrote a single page with minimal details.

Featherston's autopsy was inadequate by current standards. Any damages to the body should be precisely located using a standard frame of reference. A common definition of left and right side of the body is important. Autopsy diagrams should be labeled with measurements. Every bullet entry and exit or final resting location should be precisely located and shown on an autopsy diagram. Visual lines on the diagram should be used to show bullet path.

But, the autopsy by Spain was hugely flawed. Spain only performed a visual evaluation of a previously dissected body. Then, Spain incorrectly assumed that the damage he found was the result of violence instead of the destruction caused by the autopsy performed by Featherston or even by other bullets -- which turned out to be the situation!

In his article and his book about his autopsy, Dr. David Spain admits that he never saw an official autopsy report. *I did not base my conclusions on the official autopsy report, because there was none.*[68]

Dr David Spain was irresponsible in his criticisms of Featherston. Spain claimed that Featherston omitted important details from his autopsy report of James Chaney. But David Spain had not seen the Featherston autopsy at all, by his own admission. Furthermore, Spain assumed that the damage he saw to the body of James Chaney was created by the murderers. Yet, David Spain was looking at the damage that resulted from the extensive autopsy conducted by Featherston and by other bullets on the body of James Chaney.

A Post Autopsy Radiology Report By James Packer, MD

On August 28, 1964, a post autopsy radiology report was provided to Dr. Featherston by Jackson radiologiest Dr James Packer.

Original Autopsy Protocols

Prior to each autopsy, the body was x-rayed. Taking an x-ray preserves the state of the body **BEFORE** the autopsy. Autopsies are destructive. In order to determine bullet entries and bullet paths, the body is often cut apart. Additionally, these bodies had been buried for about 44 days. Significant decomposition occurred during this period of time, especially in the hot muggy summer weather of southeast Mississippi. Large areas of each body were covered with grumous material representing soil and rocks. X-rays also preserve the location and the initial condition of metal objects, such as bullets and fragments, inside the body.

Additional analyses can be accomplished using the x-rays and can be expected to be reasonably accurate, subject to some limitations.

For the bodies of Schwerner, Chaney and Goodman, Featherston had an additional goal. He had *x-rays taken of the severely decomposed bodies documenting every fracture . . .*[69] Any alleged fracture that did not appear on an x-ray did not exist when the autopsy began.

Radiology Report Results

Dr. Packer may not have known the identities of the victims in the autopsy. When the x-rays were created, the identification that had been assigned by Featherston were maintained. Xray Set 1 was Body 1. This body had been identified as Mickey Schwerner. Xray Set 2 was Body 2. Featherston had identified this body as that of Andy Goodman. Body 3 was Xray Set 3. Body 3 was identified as James Chaney. However, in his autopsy, Packer makes a point of indicating that he was using the Xray numbers to identify the autopsy results. This insistence on using the x-ray numbers strongly suggests that Dr. Packer was not informed that he was reviewing the x-rays of Schwerner, Chaney and Goodman.

Using the x-ray/body numbers to identify the results was an excellent decision by Featherston. In this way, Packer was able to perform an objective radiology report without the fear of political harassment.

Victim [Shooter]	Bullet	Fracture Observed	Bullet/Fragment Locations
Mickey Schwerner [Roberts]	#1	fractured right rib adjacent to fragments	fragments right upper chest fragments right scapula
Andy Goodman [Roberts]	#2	fractured 3rd right rib mid-axillary area	bullet, midline, upper dorsal
James Chaney [Roberts]	#3	left 4th rib	fragments in area
James Chaney [Posey]	#4	not found	not found
James Chaney [Jordan]	#5	temporo-parietal area of skull	bullet left of midline
		lower right radius	bullet superimposed
		upper left humerus	multiple adjacent fragments
		upper left ulna	multiple fragments in area

Packer Radiology Report Summary

Xray technology at the time was not the greatest. X-rays were not particularly clear. Edges of objects may have been indistinct. Also, the forensic experience level of Dr. James Packer is not known. While he may have had extensive experience reading x-rays, Packer may have had little or no experience reading x rays from a forensic perspective. Nonetheless, useful results can be extracted from his report through careful interpretation.

Packer identified a fractured rib adjacent to some bullet fragments in the right upper chest and near the right scapula in x-ray 1 (Schwerner). He also clearly states that the left chest is obscured by grumous material representing soil or rocks. Therefore this fractured rib must be on the right side of the chest.

The fractured right rib with bullet fragments near the right scapula indicates that the bullet entry into the body was into an upper right rib of Mickey Schwerner.

In his analysis of x-ray2 (Goodman), Dr. Packer provides more precise information about the bullet entry location. A fractured 3rd right rib in the mid-axillary area is noted by Packer. This fractured rib is the entry point of the bullet into body #2 (Goodman).

Using x-ray3 (Chaney), Packer analyzes 2 bullet effects that he finds in the x-rays. A fracture of the left 4th rib is noted. This fracture indicates the location of bullet #3 entry into the body of James Chaney. Additionally, Dr. Packer identifies a bullet fragment in the temporo-parietal area of the skull. This location is the resting location of the bullet first fired into the head of Chaney.

Dr. Packer also identified additional fractures in x-ray3 (Chaney) Locations of these fractures were the lower right radius, the upper left humorous, and the upper left ulna. Bone fractures at these locations were surrounded by bullet fragments or a bullet. The additional fragment information confirms that bullets actually entered the body of James Chaney at these locations.

Autopsy and Radiology Report Comparison

Bullet entries identified in the Packer radiology report can be compared with bullet entries identified in. the original Featherston autopsy.

Victim	Bullet	Bullet Entry (Featherston)	Bullet Entry (Packer)
Mickey Schwerner [Roberts]	#1	right of midline 4th rib	fractured right rib adjacent to fragments
Andy Goodman [Roberts]	#2	right of midline 4th rib	fractured 3rd right rib mid-axillary area
James Chaney [Roberts]	#3	left of midline upper epigastric region	left 4th rib
James Chaney [Posey]	#4	not found	not found
James Chaney [Jordan]	#5	right occupito-temporal area	temporo-parietal area of skull
		lower right radius	bullet superimposed
		upper left humerus	multiple adjacent fragments
		upper left ulna	multiple fragments in area

Featherston/Packer Bullet Entry Comparison

While some information is available describing final bullet locations, this information is insufficient for determining any of the bullet paths from any of the x-rays. Packer seems to give final bullet and fragment locations in very broad areas, such as the mid-axillary area and the upper dorsal area. These areas cover large sections of the human body. Therefore, this information simply is not specific enough to plot bullet paths.

Bullet fragment locations generated do not indicate the final location of a bullet. Fragments are caused when a bullet impacts a hard object – the bone inside a body. These fragments are generally deflected into a path that differs significantly from the original bullet path. Therefore, the fragments can not really be used as the final resting location to generate a bullet path.

Both Featherston and Packer agree that bullet # 1 into Mickey Schwerner entered at a rib on the right side of the chest. Featherston provides a specific rib number on the right side. Packer does not provide the same specific detail as provided by Featherston. Featherston had access to the actual body so his greater detail should not be surprising.

According to both Featherston and Packer, bullet #2 entered into Andy Goodman at a right side rib. However, the pair differ as to the rib number. Featherston claims the entry was at the 4th right rib. Packer claims that the entry was at the 3rd right rib. Featherston was likely correct since he examined the actual body. X-ray technology at the time may have created an image in which some of the ribs appeared vague or ghostlike. As a result, the two doctors counted slightly different rib numbers. But both agreed that the bullet entry was on the upper right side of the chest.

Bullet #3 entered James Chaney at the left of the midline in the upper epigastric region according to Featherston. Packer was more precise than Featherston. According to Packer, this bullet entered Chaney around the 4th left rib, as indicated by a broken rib at that location.

Both Featherston and Packer fail to provide any information about the entry or path of bullet #4 into James Chaney. Bill Featherston identifies the bullet in the body. Jim Packer does not reference bullet #4 at all.

Bullet #5 is identified as a head shot by both Featherston and Packer. Featherston identifies the location of a bullet fragment in the occipito-temporal area of the skull. In apparent contrast, Packer locates the bullet fragment in the temporo-parietal area of the skull. At first glance, these two locations appear to contradict each other.

However, a closer look reveals that the two locations are approximately the same locations.

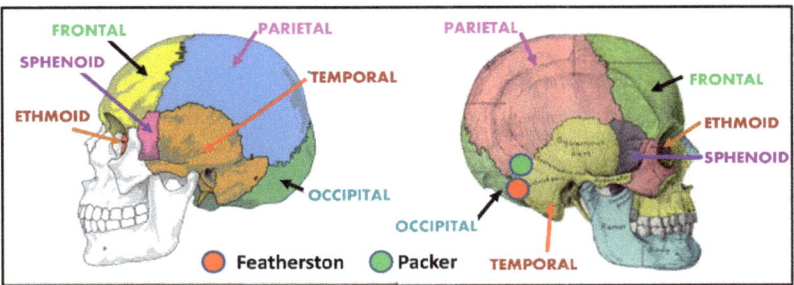

Featherston/Packer Skull Bullet Location Comparison
Source: Annotated By Author

Both of these locations are on the edges of two very large areas. Boundaries of these areas are pretty vague. Given the vagueness of these areas, each location is correct. One pathologist might easily call the location in occipito-temporal area while the other physician might denote the area as the temporo-parietal area. As the figure demonstrates, both pathologists are talking about the same location in the skull.

These minor differences in location are also a result of the x-ray equipment. Locations on an x-ray are affected by several equipment factors. One factor is the exact angle between the x-ray source and the x-ray film behind the body part. Another factor is the distance between the object and the x-ray film.[70]

A simple experiment demonstrates these factors. Hold your left hand a foot above a table. Place a flashlight in your right hand. Then, hold the flashlight in your right hand, about another foot above your left hand. Your left hand forms a shadow on the top of the table. Move your right hand closer or further from the left hand, changing the distance. The shadow below your left hand changes. Return your right hand to its original position a foot above your left hand. Then, move your right hand holding the light forwards, backwards, left and right. Again, the shadow below your left hand changes.

Your right hand represents the source of the x-rays. Your left hand represents the object being x-rayed. The table top is the x-ray film behind the object. As the x-ray source location is moved closer or nearer, or at an angle forward, backward, left or right, the image of the object appears to change its location on the x-ray film.

Radiology Report Analysis

Dr. James Packer emphasized the disruption of anatomy and physiology. His autopsy provided sufficient information to confirm the important elements of the autopsy originally conducted by Dr. Featherston. Bullet entry locations of bullet #1 into Mickey Schwerner, bullet #2 into Andy Goodman and bullet #3 into James Chaney match with the corresponding locations identified by Featherston. Bullet #5 into the head of James Chaney is identified as coming to rest in the same approximate location by both Featherston and Packer.

Packer did find some bullet wounds that had been missed by Featherston. Fractures, bullets and fragments were found by Packer in locations not recorded in the Featherston autopsy. A fracture and bullet fragments were found in the upper left humerus. Additionally, a fracture and bullet fragments were observed in the upper left ulna. Packer described an actual bullet found in the lower right radius. All of these fractures and fragments were caused by separate bullets fired into the left and right arms of James Chaney.

Arm wounds to Chaney identified by Packer were caused by multiple independent bullets discharged while Chaney was lying dead in the ditch.

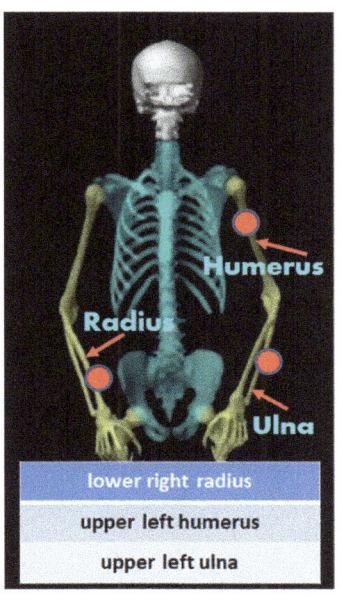

Arm Wound Locations to Chaney Identified By Dr. James Packer

Source: Radiation Oncology Annotated By Author

Bone fractures were observed by Packer at all of these locations. A bullet was identified at the lower right radius. Fragments were located at the remaining two (2) locations in the left arms. Fractures at these locations were caused by impact of a bullet at each location. Two of these bullets were soft and fragmented after impact. Lead core bullets are soft and generally will fragment upon impact.

A single bullet could not have caused these fractures. These locations are widely spread apart, on both sides of the body and at the upper and lower areas of the left arm. The fracture at the lower right radius was clearly caused by the bullet found at that location. The left side fractures were caused by separate bullets at the two locations. One location was at the top of the left arm. The other location was towards the bottom of the left arm. Fragments from a single bullet could not have travelled that distance, up or down, inside the arm. Separate, soft bullets caused the high and low fractures in the left arm.

A bullet from inside the body could not have caused the left arm fractures. This assassination was accomplished by aiming the gun straight at the body of James Chaney while standing in front. Discharged bullets would enter the body and generally follow a path from front to back.

According to Newton's laws of motion, these bullets stay on the same path unless a force has been applied to change the path. In order for a bullet traveling straight through the body to deflect towards the left arm, the bullet would have to impact a bone. After impact, the bullet would have to turn 90 degrees towards the left arm and additionally be deflected either upward or downward. The bullet could not travel both upward and downward to hit both locations in the left arm. This combination of events is pretty much impossible.

Another possible explanation is that a bullet fragmented upon impact with the bone. Then, these fragments turned 90 degrees and travelled upwards and downwards to fracture the locations in the left arm. This explanation also seems highly unlikely. Fragments moving through tissue are generally slowed by the density and tensile strength of the tissue. If the fragments had exited the body, then the left side of the body would have exhibited a large gaping hole wound. As the fragments exited the left side of the body, extensive tissue would have been shredded, ripped and torn. This gaping wound on the left side would have been clearly visible on the x-rays and reported by Dr. Packer. A gaping wound was not reported.

Dr. David Spain conducted a very short autopsy of the body of James Chaney after the autopsy had been completed by Dr. Featherston. This autopsy occurred several days after the Featherston autopsy. Spain conducted a visual inspection that lasted about 10 minutes.[71] Spain saw a body that was severely decomposed and cut apart by Dr. Featherston. Spain did not see any of the x-rays. And, yet Dr. Spain claimed that the arm fractures were the result of an extensive beating. But, Dr. Packer saw the bullet and the bullet fragments in the right and left arms. These arm fractures were caused by three separate bullets. Spain did not see the bullets or the x-rays. Any claim that the arm fractures in James Chaney were caused by a beating is unfounded and is spurious.

In addition to the fractured arms, Dr. Spain reported that the jaw bone of James Chaney was completely shattered. Autopsies are destructive. The bodies were in a state of significant decay. The jaw bone of Chaney was likely shattered during the autopsy by Featherston. Significantly, the autopsy by Dr. Packer did not mention any fracture of the jawbone.

Packer was very alert to the fractures exposed in the x-rays of James Chaney. A fractured jawbone would have been significantly revealed in the x-rays. **These x-rays were taken before the autopsy to preserve the exact state of the body and specifically to record the fractures**, since autopsies are so destructive. If the jawbone had been fractured prior to the autopsy, as alleged by David Spain,

(1) Featherston would have taken an x-ray of the fracture;

(2) Packer would have seen this fracture in the x-rays; and,

(3) Packer would have identified the fractured jawbone.

Packer was highly sensitive to bone fractures in the x-rays. He identified all of the fractures that were shown in the x-rays.

Since Packer did not report a fractured jawbone in the x-rays, the fracture of the jawbone did not occur prior to the autopsy. The jawbone fracture was a result of the destruction of the highly decomposed body of James Chaney during the Featherston autopsy.

Summary and Conclusions

Dr. William Featherston was concerned that his autopsies of Schwerner, Chaney and Goodman would be widely criticized. Before he began each autopsy, Featherston ordered that each body be extensively x-rayed. X-rays preserved the exact state of the body because autopsies are destructive. Furthermore, x-rays preserve the extent of damage from the bullets and the locations of any bullets and fragments. By this time, taking x-rays may have been standard practice. But, given the widespread search for the bodies, Featherston had to suspect that his work would be heavily criticized. So, taking x-rays of each and every fracture was important.

Several days after performing his autopsies, Dr William Featherston forwarded the x-rays to Dr. James Packer of The Radiological Group in Jackson. Packer used the x rays to conduct an independent post autopsy radiology analysis based on the x rays. Post autopsy radiology analysis may have been a common medical practice. On August 28, 1964, Dr. Packer returned the x-rays to Featherston along with a written report.

Dr. James Packer provided sufficient information to confirm the important elements of the autopsy originally conducted by Dr. Featherston. Fractures, bullets and fragments observed by Packer confirmed the entry points of bullets into all 3 civil rights workers. Packer also confirmed the resting place of the bullet in the brain of James Chaney. Packer emphasized the disruption of anatomy and physiology, not wounds and bullet paths. While he does record the existence of obvious bullets and fragments, Packer did not provide sufficient information for the construction of bullet paths.

Fractures, bullets and fragments found by Packer within the x-rays identify bullet impacts in both the left and right arms of James Chaney. These identifications confirm that the wounds to the arms of James Chaney were caused by bullet impacts, not a beating. Dr.. Packer did not indicate any fracture of the jaw bone, confirming that the jawbone of James Chaney was also intact prior to the Featherston autopsies. Therefore, the jawbone fracture was also not the result of a beating.

Dr. David Spain conducted a 10 minute visual inspection of the body of James Chaney several days after the Featherston autopsy. Spain concluded that Chaney had been beaten based on the arm and jawbone fractures. However, using x-rays of the bodies before the autopsy, Dr. James Packer clearly proved that the arm fractures were caused by bullets. Packer also showed that the jaw fracture was caused by the autopsy and the decomposition of the body. David Spain was just plain wrong.

Claims About The Murders Over The Years

In June, 1962, *Ramparts* magazine was established by Edward Keating in Menlo Park, CA. Originally, the Magazine was designed *to publish fiction, poetry, art, criticism and essays of distinction, reflecting those positive principles of the Hellenic-Christian tradition which have shaped and sustained our civilization for the past two thousand years, and which are needed still to guide us in an age grown increasingly secular, bewildered, and afraid.*[72]

In short order, this magazine gravitated towards grappling with substantial issues. On Monday, October 25, 1964,[73] a special issue of *Ramparts* magazine was published that was entitled *Mississippi Eyewitness*.

Louis Lomax, author of *The Negro Revolt*, and 9 other researchers went into MS. These researchers conducted interviews throughout the Neshoba County area. After the trip, the collected information was used to construct an alleged eyewitness account of the murders. "The Road To Mississippi", the first article in this special edition, described the murders.

The frogs and the varmints are moaning in the bayous. By now the moon is midnight high. Chaney, the Negro of the three, is tied to a tree and beaten with chains. His bones snap and his screams pierce the still midnight air. But the screams are soon ended. There is no noise now except for the thud of chains crushing flesh -- and the crack of ribs and bones. Andrew Goodman and Michael Schwerner look on in horror. Then they break into tears over their Black brother.

*"You goddam n-**** lovers!" shouts one of the mob. "What do you think now?" Only God knows what Andrew Goodman and Michael Schwerner think. Martin Luther King and James Farmer and nonviolence are integral parts of their being. But all of the things they have been taught suddenly became foreign, of no effect.*

Schwerner cracks; he breaks from the men who are holding them and rushes toward the tree to aid Chaney. Michael Schwerner takes no more than 10 steps before he is subdued and falls to the ground. Then Goodman breaks and lunges toward the fallen Schwerner. He too is wrestled into submission.

The three civil rights workers are loaded into a car and the five-car caravan makes its way toward the predetermined burial ground. Even the men who committed the crimes are not certain whether Chaney is dead when they take him down from the tree. But to make sure they stop about a mile from the burial place and fire three shots into him, and one shot each into the chests of Goodman and Schwerner.[74]

Murder is appalling. This description of the murders was even more horrifying. Visual and audio cues such as screams, crushing, cracking of ribs and bones are included for sensationalism. Their use is intended to make the reader both sick and angry.

The problem with this alleged eyewitness account is that almost all of these details are fictional exaggeration. Very few of these details coincide with the details of the confessions provided by Doyle Barnette and James Jordan. Only the autopsy by Dr. David Spain seems to corroborate these alleged details of the murders. As explained, this autopsy is based on several key assumptions that were questionable.

Unfortunately, this mostly fictitious description has been relayed as fact and distorted as the passage of time shrouded the details of the murders.

In the environment of anger, fear and inaccuracy, distortions these and other extensive distortions have been claimed over the years. Most of these distortions are easily disproved.

Remember that a reconstruction is the putting together the physical evidence and eyewitness accounts into a meaningful scenario that best explains a crime scene. There is always uncertainty, where new or missed evidence might significantly alter that scenario. Joseph Orantes, former head of the San Diego Police Crime Laboratory (ca. 1996).

Claim: Andrew Goodman Was Buried Alive

The autopsy revealed red clay in Goodman's lungs and clenched in his fist. Almost certainly, he was buried alive.[75]

Significant evidence exists to prove that Andy Goodman died on Rock Cut Road. James Jordan shot Goodman in the chest. [Confession by Doyle Barnette]. The bullet passed through the heart of Goodman [Bullet Path Analysis]. Within 10 – 16 seconds, Goodman bled to death. [Medical Literature]. Chaney was murdered (10 minutes). The bodies were transported across back roads to the dam (45 minutes). A short drive was necessary to retrieve Tucker to operate the bulldozer. (15 minutes).

Townsend walked ½ mile cross country through a forested area to reach the burial location (15 minutes). Using the bulldozer, Townsend buried the bodies. (15 minutes) [Timing estimates measured by author at locations]. With a bullet passing through the heart, Andy Goodman was dead within 16 seconds after being shot on Rock Cut Road. Goodman did not survive the 100-minute delay to be buried alive.

These facts clearly show that Andy Goodman died within 16 seconds in the ditch on the left side of Rock Cut Road where he was murdered. He could not possibly have lived to be buried alive when buried 100 minutes after being shot through the heart.

Forensic medical doctors have long known that only hits to the central nervous system can cause instant death with a handgun. During September 15-17, 1987, the FBI conducted a Wound Ballistics Workshop at the FBI Academy. Seven forensic doctors discussed the factors in handgun wounding.

Except for hits to the central nervous system (CNS), reliable and reproducible instant incapacitation is not possible with any handgun bullet ... a bigger bullet will disrupt more tissue and hopefully cause greater bleeding. Barring a CNS hit, incapacitation can only be forced by blood loss and that takes time as well as sufficient penetration to hit major blood vessels through intervening musculature, fat, clothing, arms, etc. Any bullet that will not reliably penetrate a minimum of 10 to 12 inches of soft tissue is inadequate.[76]

Even the most disruptive heart wound cannot be relied upon to prevent aggression before 10 to 15 seconds has elapsed.[77]

Andy Goodman did not show any signs of being buried alive. Extensive published anecdotal and scientific publications exist that describe the physical manifestations of being buried alive.

At autopsy, facial congestion; petechial hemorrhages in the conjunctivae and the oral mucosa; skin petechiae at the face, neck and upper chest; congestion and hemorrhages in the cervical lymph nodes; and some minor hemorrhages in the cervical muscles were found in both victims. Little sand was evident in the airway, while sand debris was found in the oral cavity.[78]

Examining the interior of the lungs, the larynx and the trachea was necessary to determine if red clay was inhaled while the victim was still alive.

Absolutely no one involved in the autopsy mentioned any red clay in the lungs! Featherston did not even dissect the lungs of Andrew Goodman during the autopsy!

The chest cage is exposed ... The internal organs show marked decomposition and they are dissected away free from the vertebral column.[79]

Featherston removed the lungs from the body as part of the internal organs. He did not cut open the lungs and then examine the interior of the lungs. Due to the advanced state of decomposition, dissecting into the lungs would have been futile if looking for the presence of dirt or even tissue damage from a bullet.[80]

Examinations of the lung interior, the larynx, and the trachea were not performed by Featherston. After 46 days of decomposition, the delicate lungs had significantly decomposed into a wad of goop. Cutting open this mass of decomposed tissue would hardly have revealed anything about the nature of death. During burial and subsequent decomposition, surrounding clay and sand could have mixed into the mouth and trachea, and wound up in the lungs. So, the presence of any clay and dirt in the interior of the lungs would not have been very revealing.[81]

Featherston did not bother to dissect the lungs, the larynx, or the trachea because dissection would have been a waste of time. Instead, he just removed the mass of the heart and lungs out of the body to get to the buried bullet found in the subcutaneous tissue of the back.

Dr. William Featherston, Dr. David Spain. the thirteen witnesses in attendance, the MS Highway Patrol and FBI Crime Lab photographers did not mention red clay in the lungs. If Goodman did have red clay in the lungs, that fact would have been recorded, reported, and trumpeted by national news agencies. Everyone would have known at the time.

An Evaluation of the FBI Lab Report

This rumor about the death of Goodman is founded upon an inaccurate and flawed report by the FBI in its Lab Report on August 13, 1964.[82]

In its investigation reports, the FBI described the body of Andy Goodman when the body was unearthed in the dam at Old Jolly Farm.

> ... *the body of a second individual lying in a face down position ... was located ... The head ... was likewise pointed in an easterly direction with arms generally extended over its head. The left hand of this body was clenched in a tight fist. Opening of this fist disclosed a rock-like object.*[83]

This object was sent to the FBI Lab in Washington, DC, along with all of the other evidence. In its Lab Report on the examination of the evidence, the FBI did make specific conclusions about the object found in the hand of Andrew Goodman. Several evidence items were identified.

Q111   Object found in Goodman's hand

K27 – K50   Twenty-four soil samples from the crime scene.[84]

After identifying the evidence, the FBI Lab Report summarized comparisons made between the object (Q111) and the soil samples.

> *The Q111 object, thought to be a rock, is a lump of red-streaked gray clay coated with reddish yellow sandy soil. This material **is similar to** the K27 clay and soil taken from near the left hand of body #2 [Goodman]. The Q111 clay and soil **could have come from** the area represented by K27 ... No indication was found that the clay and soil of Q111 was acquired outside of the grave and the dike area.*[85]

On the surface, an uninformed reader would likely conclude that this report says that Goodman grabbed the clay while being buried alive.

That interpretation is ill-founded and incorrect for a number of reasons.

In the Report, the FBI Lab used the phrase **this material is similar to**. This conclusion in the Lab Report is stated without any foundation. The method of comparison is not identified. A visual comparison of the samples was likely used to compare the samples. An examiner looks at both samples side by side, perhaps under a microscope. This examiner concludes that the samples are similar because he **_sees_** that they are similar. These subjective visual comparisons are not scientific.

An underlying scientific method includes describing the comparison method, testing, data collection and analysis, statistical hypothesis testing, and probability of error. Criteria for similarity must be explicitly stated. Examination data must be presented that clearly shows how the criteria were met in order to conclude that the material in the hand was similar to the material at K27. Furthermore, data must also be provided that supports the conclusions that all the other material samples were dissimilar. The FBI Lab failed to accomplish any of these steps to make the decision that K27 was similar to the material in the hand. No steps were taken that justified concluding that all of the other material samples were dissimilar from the material in the hand.

The statement by the FBI Lab is vague and misleading. Notice the careful use of the term **_could have come from_**. That statement is not a 100% absolute conclusion. Using the term *could have* leaves open the distinct possibility that the clay and soil *could not have* come from the area near the left hand of Goodman. A clear, correct, and precise statement by the FBI Lab should have been made. For example, the FBI Lab should have made the following statement:

The Q111 clay and soil could have come from or could not have come from the area represented by K27! Either possibility is equally likely based on the evidence that we examined.

This revised statement admits to both possibilities which are implied by the statement in the Lab Report if correctly read by an informed reader. Another feature of this revised statement is that the probability associated with each outcome is clearly stated. Each outcome has a 50% probability of being true. Instead, the FBI Lab chose to make a biased and misleading statement.

Another very suspicious aspect of this conclusion is that only the soil sample next to the left hand matched. All of the dirt used to bury the victims came from the local area around the dam where the bodies were buried. Multiple matches should have been observed.

Perhaps the most objectionable statement was that *no indication was found that the material in the hand of Goodman was acquired outside the grave.* This statement exhibits a major flaw in the investigation into the material found in the hand of Andy Goodman. Red-streaked, gray clay coated with reddish, yellow sandy soil is a predominant soil mixture throughout Neshoba County.

Soil at the murder location on Rock Cut Road and side ditches is composed of red-streaked, gray clay coated with reddish, yellow sandy soil. Soil, dirt, and clay samples were not taken by the FBI on Rock Cut Road in the area of the murders. This failure to take soil samples or even consider soil from the murder location brings the conclusion by the FBI Lab into serious doubt.

Conclusions regarding the soil lump found in the hand of Andy Goodman should have been based the techniques of road building, on soil science, and a deeper and wider investigation into the source of the lump of soil found in the hand of Goodman.

Road Building Techniques

Rock Cut Road was originally named after the technique used to create the road. Literally, the road was cut out of the underlying bedrock. Bedrock is the main mass of rock that forms the Earth. This rock is everywhere below all soils. In many locations, bedrock is below the soil materials on the surface. In some locations, bedrock is exposed. Exposed bedrock is called an outcropping.[86]

A cut road is constructed using a multistep process. Initially, soil above the bedrock is removed, exposing the bedrock. After being exposed, the bedrock is leveled to the width of the desired roadbed. Multiple layers of material are then added, ultimately leading to a drivable road surface. This road surface may be either gravel or paved. Most often, city and country roads are paved with asphalt.

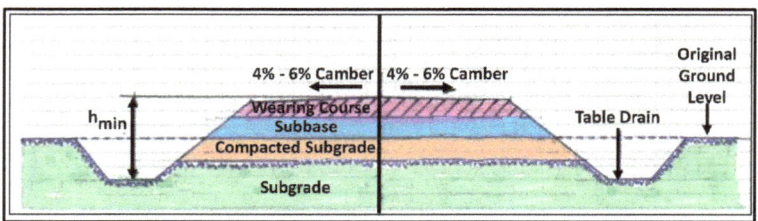

Layers Above Bedrock Of A Cut Road
(Food and Agricultural Organization of the UN)

A subgrade is the first road layer above bedrock. Subgrade materials are gathered from the side of the roadbed. Materials such as clay, silt, or sand are generally used. Another layer of these same local materials is added above the subgrade. These materials are then compacted to provide strong support for the upper layers. An 18-24-inch-deep subbase is created using nearby gravel or crushed stone. Using nearby soils helps to keep the cost down and the construction time short. At the top of these layers, the wearing course is created. This final layer is usually 18-inches-deep and composed of graded gravel or crushed stone. This material is also usually drawn from the local area.[87]

During the cut road building process, ditches are created on both sides of the road. A large amount of bedrock and other soil materials remain in these ditches at the sides of the roadway. This bedrock material remains intact in the ditches for a long time after the road has been built. Erosion of rock takes a long time.

Murder Location On Rock Cut Road At Time Of Murders (FBI As Indicated)

A thorough investigation into the source of the soil material found in the hand of Andy Goodman should have considered ALL of the possible sources. Since Goodman was murdered and died on Rock Cut Road, the murder location was also a possible source for the material.

Samples of the bedrock, the bedrock debris and other materials in the ditches should have been collected by the investigators and evaluated by the FBI Lab. Andy Goodman died in the ditch on the left side of the road within 16 seconds after being shot through the heart. This bedrock debris might be the soil material found clenched in the hand of Andy Goodman.

Soil Science Principles

Soil at any location is composed of horizons of soil material. These horizons consist of vertically stacked layers of soil material. A horizon profile presents a side view of the horizons at a specific location.[88]

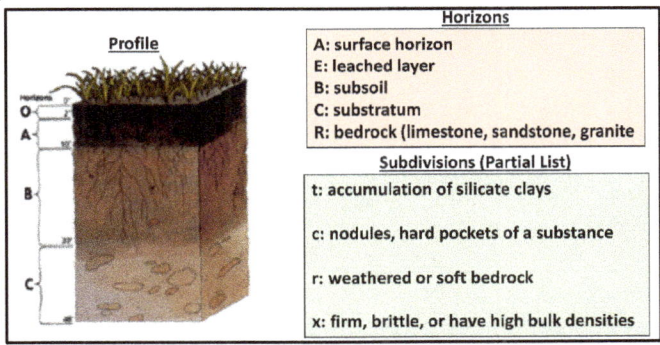

**Horizon Profile of Soil At A Location
(Natural Resources Conservation Service, USDA)**

Five standard horizons/layers are defined, labelled A, E, B, C, and R. At any given location, all or some of these horizons will be present. Soil horizons may be further classified according to subdivisions. For instance, Bt indicates the presence of a subsoil layer that is enriched by silicate clays. Every horizon is characterized by depth below the surface, its texture, and its color.

Soil texture describes the proportionate distribution of different sizes of mineral particles in the soil. Mineral particles are divided into groups based on the size of the mineral particle.[89]

Group	Crystal Size (mm)	Minerals
Clay	< 0.002	aluminum, iron, magnesium
Silt	0.002 – 0.05	quartz, feldspars, chlorites, micas
Sand	> 0.05	quartz

Soil Textures Divided Into Groups By Particle Size
(*Agronomy Fact Sheet Series: Fact Sheet SL-29*)

When describing soil texture, the term loam is used to indicate a soil mixture of minerals that are equal parts clay, silt, and sand. However, some soils exhibit textures that consist of unequal parts from each of the three groups. These textures are described by the dominating unequal part. For instance, sandy loam contains a larger percentage of sand than the percentages of silt and clay.

Mineral content in a soil is identified by assigning a color to the soil. In 1905, Albert Munsell designed a precise system for indicating a color. Munsell was an art professor. He designed this color specification system for communicating colors to his art students. Every color can be described by three specific features. Hue is a basic color. Value is the lightness of the color along a range from black to white. Chroma is the intensity of the color.[90]

Extensive color charts have been scientifically developed over the years to provide a visual picture a specific combination of hue/value/intensity.

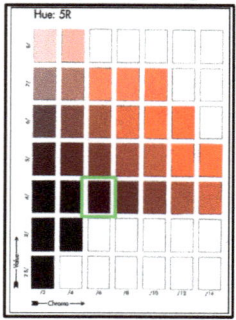

Color Chart for Hue 5R
(Lynn and Pearson)[91]

This approach to soil color specification has been adopted by soil scientists. For example, the mineral hematite often appears in soil. This mineral contains iron which is red in color. Using the Munsell color system, the color of hematite is characterized as 5R 4/6. A green box has been placed around this hue/value/chroma combination in the figure above.

Soil Comparison Between The Murder And Burial Locations

According to the FBI Lab report, *a lump of red-streaked gray clay coated with reddish yellow sandy soil* was found clenched in the hand of Andy Goodman. An evaluation of the soil at both burial and murder locations reveals that the lump of soil most likely came from the murder location. FBI investigators and the FBI Lab completely failed to consider this possibility.

A satellite photo from 1996 clearly shows the reddish clay nature of the soils in the area of the burial location.

Burial Location Showing Reddish Clay Soils

Exact features of the soil around the area of the burial location are revealed by a Soil Map.

Soil Identification At Burial Location (Soil Web) (UC Davis)

According to this Soil Map, the predominant soil in the upper half of the area surrounding the dam is identified as Smithdale. A profile of this type of soil identifies the horizons, their depth, colors, and textures.

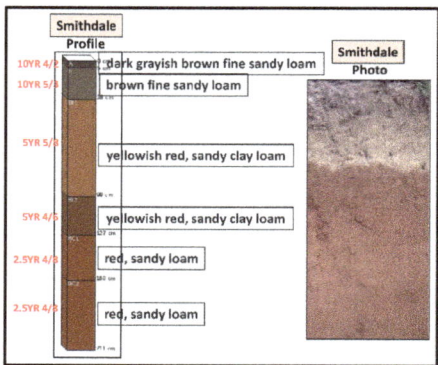

Smithdale Soil Horizon Profile[92]
(US Dept of Agriculture)

Colors red and yellow certainly appear in the profile. Textures clay and sand also appear in the profile. A *lump of red-streaked gray clay coated with reddish yellow sandy soil* as found clenched in the hand of Goodman could have come from this soil.

This analysis seems to confirm the FBI Lab finding that the lump of material found in the hand of Andy Goodman came from the burial location. However, this conclusion fails to consider the soil material at the murder location.

A similar analysis also can be performed for the soil at the murder location on Rock Cut Road.

Murder Location Showing Reddish Clay Soils

This satellite photo clearly reveals the reddish clay nature of the soils in the area of the murder location.

Exact features of the soil around the area of the murder location are revealed by a Soil Map.

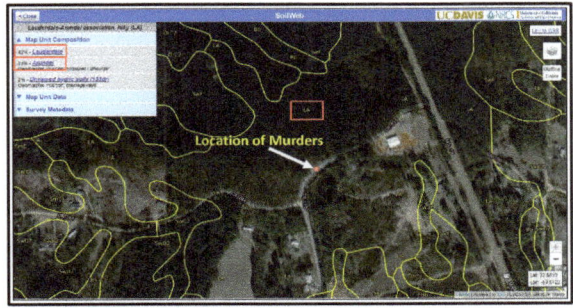

**Soil Identification
At
Murder Location
(Soil Web)
(UC Davis)**

Two soils are revealed at the murder location: Lauderdale (42%) and Arundel (38%).[93] Both soils are similar so that only one of these soils needs to be considered.

A profile of the Lauderdale type of soil at the murder location also identifies the horizons, their depth, colors, and textures.

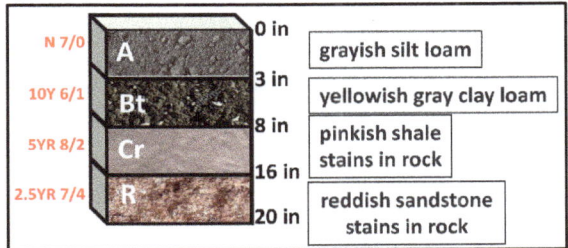

**Lauderdale Soil Horizon Profile[94]
(US Dept of Agriculture)**

Colors red and yellow certainly appear in the profile. Textures clay and sand (in both loam horizons) also appear in the profile. A *lump of red-streaked gray clay coated with reddish yellow sandy soil* as found clenched in the hand of Goodman could definitely have come from this soil.

379

Corroboration From Rock Cut Road Today

As late as 1988, a newspaper reporter commented on the nature of Rock Cut Road at the site of the murders. *[Ben] Chaney and I walked warily through the streets. We traveled up Rock Cut Road, a desolate strip of red clay outside town* ...[95] Unfortunately, Rock Cut Road [County Road 515] has been paved with asphalt. However, additional evidence exists as to the nature of the soil and bedrock in that area. This evidence demonstrates that the bedrock is composed of red-streaked, gray clay coated with reddish, yellow sandy soil.

Examples east of, at, and west of the location of the murders demonstrate the existence of *red-streaked, gray clay coated with reddish, yellow sandy soil*. An outcropping of bedrock is 350 yards to the east of the murder location. Crushed bedrock is exposed at the actual location of the murders. An unpaved road is 125 yards to the west to the murder location

Adjacent to the south side of Road 515 at the intersection with Hwy 19 is an outcropping of bedrock that demonstrates the soil composition in the area. This location is 350 yards to the east of the location of the murders.

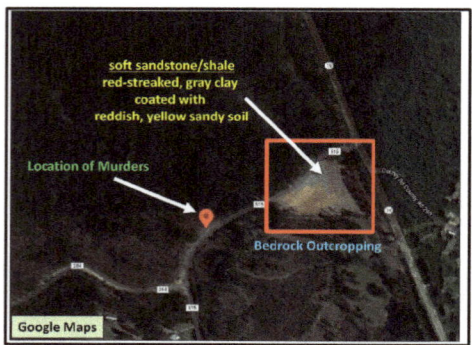

Exposed Area On Rock Cut Road At Hwy 19

Gray clay is exhibited in the upper half of the exposed area. Reddish sandstone and shale compose the exposed bedrock. Yellow sandy soil mixed with and covering the gray clay appears in the lower half of the exposed area. At the time of the murders, mixed bedrock and clay from cutting the road had settled in the bottom of the ditches to either side of the road. These colors and materials match the description of the soil material found clenched in the hand of Goodman.

Crushed bedrock materials and soil are exposed on the side of the road at the location of the murders.

Exposed Bedrock At The Location Of The Murders

Reddish sandstone and shale compose the exposed bedrock. Yellow sandy soil appears to be mixed with the reddish sandstone and shale. These colors and materials also match the description of the soil material found clenched in the hand of Goodman.

An example of the bedrock sandstone and shale mixed with reddish yellow sand material exists just 125 yards to the west of the murder location. This location is at the intersection of Road 515 and Road 284.

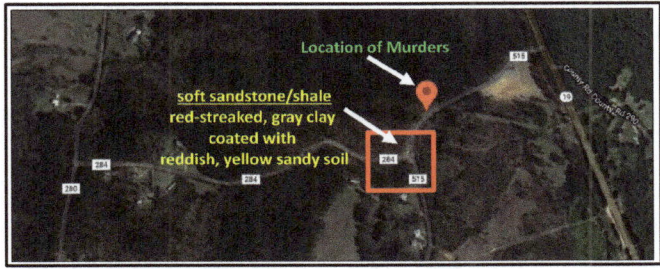

Intersection At Road 515 And Road 284

While Road 515 (Rock Cut Road) was paved with asphalt, Road 284 remains unpaved.

Bedrock Sandstone/Shale Used at Road 284

Reddish sandstone and shale from bedrock was used to create the wearing course of Road 284. Yellow sandy soil appears to be mixed with the reddish sandstone and shale. These colors and materials also match the description of the soil material found clenched in the hand of Goodman.

A visual of inspection of the exposed bedrock and road materials east of, at, and west of the murder location were demonstrated above. This inspection reveals that these materials along Road 515/Rock Cut Road match the FBI Lab description.

Reviewing the photo of the murder location at the time of the murders shows that both ditches are filled with rocks and gravel.

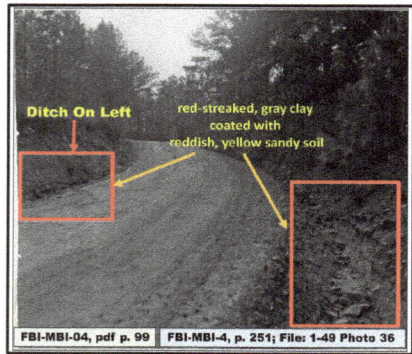

Location of Murders Taken By FBI, June 1964

Large and small rocks and chunks of clay are clearly visible in the ditch on both sides of the road. These materials were the reddish sandstone and shale from bedrock that was spilled into the ditches as the road was cut. Gray clay and yellow sandy soil mixed with the reddish sandstone and shale used from the surrounding area was used for the upper layers of the road. This material also spilled into the ditches at the side of the road.

Goodman fell into the ditch on the left side of the road after being shot. This ditch was filled with large and small chunks of red streaked sandstone and shale and gray clay coated with reddish yellow sandy soil. The material found in the hand of Andy Goodman matches this material in the ditch on Rock Cut Road.

How Andy Goodman Had the Soil In His Hand

Andy Goodman was shot in the chest. The bullet traveled almost straight through from the front to the back of his body. During its movement through the body, the bullet penetrated through the heart. Even with a heart pierced by the bullet, Goodman still took 10 to 16 seconds to die, since the heart is not part of the CNS.

Goodman fell over into the ditch, taking those additional 10 to 16 seconds to die. He was in tremendous physical pain. In response to that pain, Goodman clenched his fists. As he clenched in pain, Goodman unconsciously grabbed in his hand a *lump of red-streaked gray clay coated with reddish yellow sandy soil* from the ditch. He died with the lump from the ditch clenched in his hand. When the body was recovered, hat lump of soil was still clenched in the hand of Andy Goodman.

Andy Goodman was not buried alive. Clay was not found in his lungs or his clenched fist. A rock like object was found clenched in his fist. That chunk of material was later identified with features that matched the soil and bedrock materials in the ditch on Rock Cut Road.

Claim: James Chaney Was Castrated

... he [Chaney] fell to the ground, and then they castrated him as Goodman and Schwerner watched.[96]

Dr. William Featherston did not mention castration. Dr. David Spain did not mention castration. Thirteen witness attended the autopsy conducted by Featherston. None of the thirteen witnesses mentioned castration. A

MS Highway Patrol photographer and an FBI Crime Lab photographer took extensive photographs at every step of autopsy process. Neither of these photographers mentioned anything about castration.

If James Chaney were castrated, that fact would have been recorded, reported, and trumpeted by national news agencies. Everyone would have known at the time. Press reports on the day after the autopsy make absolute clear that the bodies did not exhibit any mutilation. *There was no Indication they had been mutilated, all bodies having been found intact.*[97]

This rumor is an example of how historians distort facts as each new writer summarizes and interprets historical facts from previous writers. The actual truth degrades. History is distorted.

A real castration of a Black man did occur -- in 1957, 7 years before the death of James Chaney, and in AL, not MS!

The Original Ku Klux Klan of the Confederacy was a violent, paramilitary Ku Klux Klan offshoot founded by Asa "Ace" Carter. Despite its name, this organization was incorporated almost 100 years after the Civil War in Birmingham, AL, on November 20, 1956.[98] Its founder Ace Carter was a filling station operator and former newscaster.[99] Secrecy was the watchword of the group. Violence was one of its core principles. All members openly carried guns during meetings.[100] Meetings were conducted in a ritualistic manner. Every member was required to take a blood oath. His wrist was slashed with a knife. An oath was signed using blood from the wrist slash.[101]

On September 2, 1957, six members of the group formulated a test to determine if Bart Floyd was qualified to be the captain of their group. That test was to *grab a Black and scare hell out of him.* Joe Pritchett, James Griffin, Bart Floyd, William Miller, Jesse Mabry and Grover McCullogh randomly abducted Judge Aaron, a Black mechanic. Aaron and a friend, Cora Parker, were walking along Tarrant Huffman Road near Airport Road, north of the Birmingham Airport. Aaron was driven to the lair[102], a cinder-block shack,[103] in Chalkville, AL, [104] about 7 miles northeast.[105]

Exalted Cyclops Joe Pritchett supervised the activities at the shack wearing a red-trimmed Klan robe.[106] Aaron was tortured. He was kicked in the face, struck in the head by a pistol, and hit on the head with a tire tool. Then, Bart Floyd castrated Aaron with a razor blade, excising the entire scrotum and contents in the process. Kerosene and turpentine were poured on his wounds. His severed testicles were passed around in a paper cup for inspection. Aaron was dumped on Springdale Road, about 2 miles outside Tarrant, AL,[107] 7.5 miles southwest of Chalkville and the lair.[108] Aaron was found about 11 pm by Tarrant City Policeman R. R. Johnson and a fellow officer who answered an anonymous call.[109] These officers called an ambulance that took Aaron to Veterans Hospital.[110] Judge Aaron was treated and eventually released.

On September 7, 1957, William Miller and James Griffin were arrested for the castration. Griffin and Miller gave statements describing the events in detail. Joe Pritchett was immediately arrested.[111] Jesse Mabry was arrested later that day.[112] Bart Floyd himself was arrested on September 8, 1957.[113] On September 9, 1957, Grover McCullough, the last participant, was arrested.[114]

Miller and Griffin testified in trials during October 1957, through February 1958, leading to the conviction of the four others on charges of mayhem. Each of the others were sentenced by Judge Alta King to 20 years in prison.[115] Griffin and Miller plea bargained for five-year sentences and served those sentences in full. Their mayhem felonies were kept on their records. All four of the convicted Klansmen were paroled in 1964 and 1965. These paroles were granted by a parole board after the first appointment to the board by AL Gov George Wallace.[116] During 1965, Asa Carter worked as a special assistant and speech writer for AL Gov George Wallace.[117]

William Bradford "Bill" Huie was one of the most successful American journalists and authors of the 20th century. Huie was a prolific writer, investigative reporter, editor, national lecturer, television host, and masterful storyteller. After the murders of Schwerner, Chaney, and Goodman, Huie wrote a book about the murders. *Three Lives For Mississippi* was published by Huie in 1965. Huie spent a lot of time in Neshoba County and conducted a lot of investigative research.

In his book, Huie wanted to show the violent nature of race relations in the South. A detailed history of the castration of Judge Edward Aaron in Birmingham in 1967 was the demonstration vehicle. Bill Huie even interviewed Judge Aaron himself.[118]

Many authors have written about the history of Schwerner, Chaney, and Goodman. *Three Lives For Mississippi* was a main source for many of the writers. These writers inaccurately combined the castration of Aaron with the murders of Schwerner, Chaney, and Goodman. Over the years, this distortion was taken as fact and repeated by many writers.

James Chaney was not castrated before he was murdered. Judge Aaron was castrated many years before Chaney was murdered.

Claim: James Chaney Was Beaten

But one thing was certain: this frail boy had beaten in an inhuman fashion. The blows that had so terribly shattered his bones - I surmised he must have been beaten with chains or a pipe - were in themselves sufficient to have caused death.[119]

Dr. David Spain made this conclusion based on the skull fracture, the broken ribs, the fractured jaw, and the damage to the left and right arms.

Spain incorrectly concluded that the skull fracture was the result of being hit with a pipe. The skull fracture was created by a bullet shot to the head, which was the cause of death.

Ribs were broken by a shot to the chest that was delivered to James Chaney. Dr. Featherston created more rib damage during the autopsy ... *the chest cage is dissected away anteriorly* ... *Two ribs are dissected free* ... In order to locate the bullet in the chest, Featherston had to break open the ribs. Dr. Spain was not justified in concluding that the rib damage was caused by the blunt force trauma of a beating with a pipe.

No evidence exists indicating that the jawbone was broken before the shooting. The autopsy performed by Dr. James Packer using the x-rays after the Featherston autopsy does not indicate any jawbone fractures. Featherston was careful to capture all of the fractures in the x-rays taken before the autopsies. Packer was sensitive to and documented all of the fractures that he saw in the x-rays. If the jawbone had been fractured prior to the autopsy, Packer would have indicated this in his report. Since Packer did not indicate any jawbone fracture, the jawbone of Chaney was most likely broken during the highly destructive autopsy of the decomposed body.

Medical evidence exists that describes the type of fracture that results from blunt force trauma of a pipe or chain.

.. tubular bones are subject to compressive (impact site) and tensile (opposite impact site) forces; this causes bones to break in tension before compression, producing Y-shaped fracture patterns with breakaway (butterfly) fragments. ... Fracture production and patterning of blunt impacts to 255 sheep femora were analyzed ... the results suggest that the impact site is located on one of the Y-fracture's arms ...[120]

In his autopsy, Dr. Spain carefully described the fracture to the jawbone *A complete through and through comminuted fracture was present in the center of the mandible.*[121] The mandible (jawbone) is a tubular bone bent into a horse-shoe shape. This bone is prone to fracture without particularly excessive force.[122]

A comminuted fracture is a break or splinter of the bone into more than two fragments.[123] A through and through break or splinter means that the jawbone broke into two or more separate pieces. This type of fracture is different from a Y-fracture which leaves the tubular bone intact. Dr. David Spain did not identify a fracture that showed the physical characteristics of blunt force trauma to the jawbone of James Chaney.

Dr. Featherston recorded the damage to the left arm and to the right forearm. His conclusion about this damage was non-committal. *When and how this was sustained could not be determined.* When he reviewed the damage to the bones of the arms, Dr. Spain explicitly stated that *There was no evidence of a bullet wound at this site.* Featherston did not make any conclusions. Spain categorically denied that the damage to the left arm and to the right forearm were caused by a bullet.

Dr. Spain was completely wrong in his conclusion.

During preparation for the 2005 trial of Edgar Ray Killen, MS AG Jim Hood hired world renowned pathologist Dr. Michael Baden as an outside pathologist. Dr. Baden worked with MS state forensic pathologist Dr. Steven Hayne to perform a forensic pathology analysis for the prosecution. Baden and Hayne studied autopsy reports, testimony, photographs, FBI reports, X-rays, and other documents in the killings of the trio.

There are still bullets in the body of James Chaney ... x-rays show that two other bullets struck Chaney and are still there ... two other shots struck Chaney in the arms ... the fracture to Chaney's right wrist suggests either a bullet that passed through or possible blows ... but the deformed left upper arm is due to shooting.[124]

Fractures in the right wrist were described by Featherston. *Also, there is a transverse fracture of both bones of the right forearm about 90 mm above the wrist joint.*

Blunt force trauma causes Y/butterfly fractures.[125]

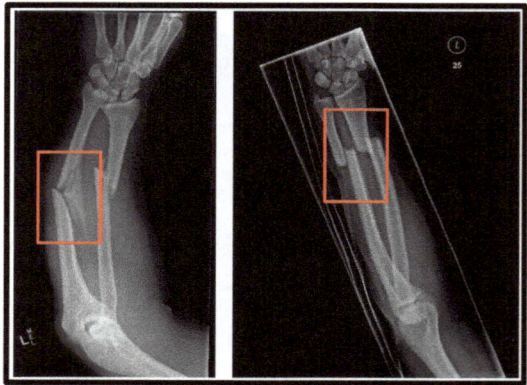

**Bone Fractures (Y/Butterfly on Left, Lateral on Right)
(Radiopaedia, https://radiopaedia.org/)**

Dr Featherston characterized the fractures to the right arm radius and ulna bones as lateral fractures. These right forearm fractures are either bullet fractures or blunt force trauma created fractures (*blows*) according to Dr Baden. *Baden found bullets in both arms, including the right arm.* Since a lateral fracture is not a butterfly fracture, the lateral fractures in the right forearm must have been caused by that bullet to the right forearm seen in the x-ray.

Chaney's skull fracture was caused by a head shot. His broken ribs were caused by a bullet to the chest and further broken during the autopsy. Both left and right arms were broken by bullets. The fractured jaw could have been caused at any time, during the shooting, during the burial, during the excavation, or during the autopsy.

This beating claim is another instance of inaccurate history along with exaggeration. Other Blacks in the area were beaten then murdered, just not James Chaney. Perhaps the most well-known example of the beating and the murder of a Black in MS is the case of Mack Charles Parker in Poplarville. Poplarville is about 150 miles due south of Philadelphia, MS.

On February 23, 1959, Jimmy Walters, his pregnant wife June, and their 4-year-old daughter Debbie Carol, were driving north on Highway 11 towards Hattiesburg. The Walters lived in Petal, a small suburb of Hattiesburg just across the Leaf River.[126] About 11:30 pm, 7 miles south of Lumberton, their 1949 Dodge gave a loud metal on metal clank. Walters pulled the car to the side of the road. This battered, old car had thrown a main bearing. As a result, the engine had locked up. Jimmy Walters began walking to Lumberton to get a tow truck, leaving his wife June and daughter Debbie Carol in the car.[127]

Mack Charles Parker, Curt Underwood, his brother in law, and Tommy Lee Grant, David Alfred, and Norman *Rainbow* Malachy, three of his friends, spent the evening drinking and gambling at a bar named Bojack's in the Black section of Poplarville. After a night of partying, the group was heading back along Highway 11 from Poplarville to Lumberton. The group spotted the Dodge sitting helplessly next to the road. Parker stopped and jumped out of the car. He wanted to see if the tires were worth stealing. Parker shined his light into the car. Seeing the wife and daughter, Parker chose to leave right away. As the group drove away, Parker jokingly suggested, *Why don't we stop and get some o' that white stuff.* Curt Underwood, brother in law of Parker, responded. *Man, you talkin' crazy.* Tommy Lee Grant commanded, *Take us home, crazy man.*[128]

Parker and his friends passed Jimmy Walters with his thumb out, trying to hitch a ride. Parker simply drove past Walters.[129] Parker drove into Lumberton with his friends. He dropped Curt, Tommy Lee, and Rainbow at their homes in the Black district of Lumberton. Parker stopped by his own home first. At his home, Parker retrieved a toy cap pistol. The group had been out drinking. Parker drunkenly fell on a porch railing, cutting his hand. He wrapped an old washrag around his hand. Then, he dropped David Alfred at his home. Alfred told his parents that Parker was planning to go back to the stranded vehicle and take advantage of the white woman.[130]

An hour and a half after Jimmy Walters left his wife and daughter, a middle-aged Black man drove up behind the stranded car. Allegedly, the man had a cloth wrapped around his left hand and a pistol in his right hand. This man used the pistol to break the vent window and to enter the car. Threatening June and Debbie at gunpoint, this Black man kidnapped the pair. The kidnapper drove the prisoners in his car to an isolated location. He raped the wife, June. After raping June, the middle-aged Black man immediately released June and Debbie. The pair were picked up by a MAC tractor-trailer driver on the way walking into Lumberton.[131]

June Walters immediately reported her rape to local authorities. Walters described her rapist in detail. Her assailant was a middle-aged Black man, about 39 to 40 years old, weighing 160-170 pounds, and approximately 5 feet, 10 inches tall. Walters also described the car of her assailant in detail. This car was dark, had a torn seat, a broken down light, a broken horn ring, and a broken door on the passenger side.[132] Notably, June Walters said that her assailant admitted that he had escaped from prison and that he had killed 5 other people.[133]

A wide dragnet was established. Roadblocks were established on all roads around Lumberton and Poplarville. This dragnet led to the apprehension of about 30 blacks. All these suspects were herded into Lumberton for a possible police lineup.[134]

During the next morning, Rev Alfred, father of David Alfred came to the office of Lamar County Sheriff C H Hickman. *M C Parker is your man. The other boys got in about 12:30. My boy told us then he was afraid of it. I should've come to you then, but I didn't think he'd do it. MC got in after three.*[135]

About 9:45 AM on February 24, 1959, Lumberton City Marshal Hamond Slade and several deputies[136] arrested Mack Charles Parker at his home. Parker was hauled out of the house and across the road into the woods. Once out of sight, deputies began to beat Parker heavily to force Parker to confess. Parker's screams could be heard several homes away. Parker did not confess despite the beating.*[137]*

Several hours later, Jimmy and June Walters arrived at the jail in Lumberton. A lineup was held with 5 Black men. Each man was required to say the same threatening sentence. Under threats, Parker shouted the threatening statement loudly. June Walters identified Parker as the assailant based on hearing his shouted threatening statement. However, she could not make a positive physical identification. June Walters was just not completely sure. Another issue for Walters was that the normal voice of Parker was different from the loud voice in which Parker had yelled the threatening statement.[138]

When she saw the car driven by Parker, June Walters could not be sure that this car was the same car driven by her assailant. A thorough search of the Parker home discovered a cap pistol. Authorities agreed that this toy pistol was too fragile to break a car window.[139]

Everyone also seemed to forget that Parker did not match the original description of the assailant given by Walters. Her assailant was a middle-aged Black man, about 39 to 40 years old, weighing 160-170 pounds. Mack Charles Parker was 23 years old. Parker weighed about 200 pounds. All of the evidence against Parker was weak.

Once the community found out about the arrest of Parker, the mood in the Lumberton grew quickly ugly. A Black man raping a white woman was a cardinal sin in MS. Officers of the MS Highway Patrol transferred Parker to the Hinds County Jail in Jackson. Mack Charles Parker denied outright that he had anything to do with the rape of June Walters. Parker consistently adhered to that position throughout all the events that followed.[140] While in the Hinds County Jail in Jackson, Parker submitted to several lie detector tests. These tests either exonerated Parker or were inconclusive about guilt.[141]

Those friends that accompanied Mack Charles Parker on the night of the incident were subjected to harsh interrogation. After 3 grueling and threatening interrogations, Curt Underwood, the brother in law, admitted to many of the details of the first encounter. Underwood also described the suggestion Parker made to return to the stranded car for sex with a white woman. Tommy Lee Grant and David Alfred corroborated the details about the initial meeting and the joking statements by Parker under prodding by the police. Rainbow Malachy never provided any incriminating evidence.[142]

An all-white Pearl River County grand jury indicted Parker for rape and two counts of kidnapping on April 13, 1959. Testimony by Underwood,

Grant, and Alfred helped to secure the indictments. Two days later, on April 15, 1959, Parker was transferred to the Pearl River County Jail. The Jail was housed on the second floor of the Pearl River County Courthouse in Poplarville. This transfer was in preparation for an upcoming appearance before Judge Sebe Dale.[143] In a hearing on April 17, 1959, Judge Dale scheduled a trial for April 27, 1959.[144]

Mack Charles Parker was awaiting trial in the Pearl River County Jail. From 8 to 10 men entered the Jail between 11:30 PM, April 24, 1959, and 12:15 AM, April 25, 1959. One man wore a mask, the rest covered their faces with bandanas.[145] *Boy, where is MC Parker at? We want him.*[146] Three members of the group chased Mack Charles Parker into the toilet area. These men jumped Parker and began beating him with their clubs.[147]

Parker was viciously beaten by the three mob members with fists and clubs. Parker resisted being tied up, fighting wildly. At one point, a broom handle was used to beat Parker viciously over the head. This beating continued until the broom handle broke. A garbage can was emptied and smashed over the head of Parker.[148]

After the beating, Parker was dragged by his heels down a dozen steps to the first floor of the Courthouse. His head was hitting each of the steps. These steps were covered with blood. Mack Charles Parker was dragged out of the courthouse and down the courthouse steps still by the heels. As he was dragged outside of the Courthouse, Parker continued screaming. Parker's screams loudly pierced the night air. In response to the screams, cars were backed up in front of the Courthouse a long distance. Blood stains from his badly beaten body were all along the path from his cell, down the stairs, across the courthouse, and down the courthouse steps.[149]

Outside the jail, Parker was thrown into a car. Just before Parker was thrown into the back seat, one of the mob clubbed Parker two more times.[150] Kidnappers drove to a remote spot where the Bogalusa Bridge crossed the Pearl River into LA, approximately 20 miles west of Poplarville.[151]

Parker was then pulled from the car. Despite being bound and badly beaten, Parker tried to run away but was captured in the center of the bridge. One of the kidnappers shot Parker twice in the chest with a .38 caliber revolver, a handgun, from a range of approximately six inches. One shot pierced the heart of Mack Charles Parker.[152] Parker died within 10-16 seconds.[153] Logging chains were produced from the trunk of one of the cars. These chains were used to weight the body down. Once the chains were secured, the weighted body was tossed over the concrete railings of the bridge into the rain-swollen waters of the Pearl River below.[154]

On May 4, 1959, the bloated and decomposing body of Mack Charles Parker was found floating in the waters of the Pearl River. The body was found 2.5 miles south of the Bogalusa Bridge.[155] Almost immediately, the FBI extended its investigative force. A total of 60 agents of the FBI descended upon the town of Poplarville.[156]

Hundreds of potential witnesses and suspects were interrogated. In a series of interview from May 9, 1959, until May 13, 1959, Arthur Smith, who participated in the murder, identified the participants and confirmed the role of each participant. FBI agents took the Smith confession to Jewel Alford, County Jailer, who had also participated on May 14, 1959. Alford had been increasingly troubled by his participation. In the face of the Smith confession, Alford broke. He confessed his participation and identified some of the other participants, confirming and expanding the details of the Smith confession.[157]

FBI agents pursued other remaining participants. Eventually, the FBI agents solved the case, firmly established motive, modus operandi, secured the corpse, and connected the criminals to the corpse. However, agents were unable to prove violations of the Lindbergh kidnapping law (across state lines) or violation of Federal civil rights statutes.[158]

Efforts to convict the murders in a MS criminal court failed. On November 2, 1959, Judge Sebe Dale impaneled an all-white, all male Grand Jury.[159] The Pearl River County DA refused to submit the FBI evidence to the Grand Jury.[160] At 2 pm on November 3, 1959, the Pearl River County Grand Jury announced its results. Not surprisingly, this Grand Jury failed to return any indictments against any of the mob members.[161]

Acting US AG Lawrence Walsh ordered US Attorney Robert Hauberg in Jackson to bring civil rights charges against the mob members. This order was issued less than 3 hours after the Grand Jury results were announced.[162] Mob members were charged under Title 18, Section 241, conspiracy to deprive civil rights, and Section 242 of the US Code - depriving civil rights under color of law. Hauberg brought charges in the Southern District of MS of the US 5th Circuit.

Judge Sydney Mize presided over the District Court. Judge Mize convened a Federal Grand Jury on January 4, 1960, in the Biloxi Division of the Southern District of MS.[163] In Federal courts, the judge selects the Grand Jury members. Mize, an ardent segregationist, selected 1 male Black member.[164] Remaining members were all-white and all-male. At 10:35 am on Thursday, January 14, 1960, foreman Charles Long announced that the Grand Jury failed to arrive at any true bill -- no indictments.[165]

None of the murderers of Mack Charles Parker were ever convicted.

Mack Charles Parker was badly beaten several times - once when he was arrested, again when he was kidnapped from the jail. In both instances, his screams were loud, piercing, and traveled long distances. Parker was beaten so badly during the kidnapping that he left an extensive blood trail throughout and outside the Pearl River County Jail and Courthouse. He was then murdered.

James Chaney was shot 5 times: in the head, in the chest, in the lower abdomen, in the left arm, and in the right forearm. However, Chaney was not beaten with a pipe or chain.

James Chaney -- What Really Happened

An analysis of what really happened to James Chaney begins with some basic facts, some of which were discovered above. James Jordan shot James Chaney in the back of the head (#5, Q88). Wayne Roberts shot Chaney in the chest (#3, Q86). Billy Wayne Posey shot Chaney in the lower abdomen (#4, Q87). Chaney was shot in both the left shoulder (Dr Baden) and in the right arm (fracture analysis).

At the time of discharge to the head, James Jordan was positioned behind and slightly off to the right of Chaney.

Bullet #4 was found in the lower abdomen of Chaney. An entry point was not located by Dr. Featherston during his autopsy. One of the key factors in determining possible theories of the shooting of James Chaney includes varying the entry point of Bullet #4 between the front and the rear of the body.

Doyle Barnette stated in his confession that Chaney was standing in front of the ditch on the left side of the road when shot by Jordan.[166] In his confession, James Jordan stated that the body of Chaney ended up in the ditch on the left side of the road.[167]

This situation is complicated. Bullet (#5, Q88) was to the back of the head. Bullet (#3, Q86) was into the chest with an entry point in the front chest. This chest entry was on the opposite side of the body from the head shot. Bullet (#4, Q87) found in the lower abdomen entered the body either from the front or from the back. Bullet entries on opposite sides of the body creates the complications.

Bullet (#3, Q86) passed through the body, front to back, slightly upward, and left to right.

An objective, scientific approach requires that multiple theories be formulated and evaluated. These evaluations must be objective, based on a foundation. This foundation can come from physical evidence, science, physics, experiments, published research and literature by experts, and sometimes personal experience.

Theory 1:

Jordan (#5) shot Chaney in the back of the head while he was running away. At the same time, Posey (#4) also shot Chaney in the back near the lower abdomen as he was running away. Jordan and Posey shot Chaney in the arms as he was running. After Chaney fell, Roberts (#3) turned Chaney over and shot Chaney in the chest. Chaney was then dragged to the ditch.

This theory assumes that bullet #4 entered Chaney from the rear.

Theory 2:

Posey (#4) shot Chaney in the back near the lower abdomen as he was running away. Jordan and Posey also shot Chaney in the arms as he was running. After he fell down, Jordan (#5) shot Chaney in the back of the head. Roberts (#3) turned Chaney over and shot Chaney in the chest. after Jordan shot Chaney. Chaney was then dragged to the ditch.

This theory also assumes that bullet #4 entered Chaney from the rear.

Theory 3:

Jordan (#5) shot Chaney in the back of the head. At the same time, Posey (#4) shot Chaney in the lower abdomen from the front. Roberts (#3) shot Chaney in the chest from the front at the same time as Posey. While standing in the front of Chaney, Posey and Roberts continued to shoot Chaney in the arms at the same time as Jordan was shooting from the back. Chaney was then dragged to the ditch.

This theory assumes that bullet #4 entered Chaney from the front.

Theory 4:

Jordan (#5) shot Chaney in the back of the head. Chaney fell into the ditch face up and dead. After Chaney fell into the ditch, Posey (#4) shot Chaney in the lower abdomen from the front. At the same time as Posey, Roberts (#3) also shot Chaney in the chest. Both Roberts and Posey took a second shot at the dead body of Chaney laying in the ditch. A second shot by Posey impacted the right forearm. With his second shot, Roberts hit Chaney in the left shoulder.

This theory also assumes that bullet #4 entered Chaney from the front.

All these theories incorporate several same important facts that are undeniable. At the time of discharge to the head, James Jordan was positioned behind and slightly off to the right of James Chaney. His Bullet #5 entered the back of the head. Bullet (#3) discharged by Wayne Roberts into the chest entered the front of the body of James Chaney.

A lot of other theories can be formulated. However, these theories represent a reasonable and broad range of possibilities. Two of the theories assume that Bullet #4 into the lower abdomen entered from the rear of the body. Remaining theories assume that Bullet #4 into the lower abdomen entered from the front of the body.

Setup For Evaluation Of Theories

Visualization is an important aspect for evaluating theories related to shooting incidents. A standard visual frame of reference is used when evaluating the above theories about the shooting of James Chaney.

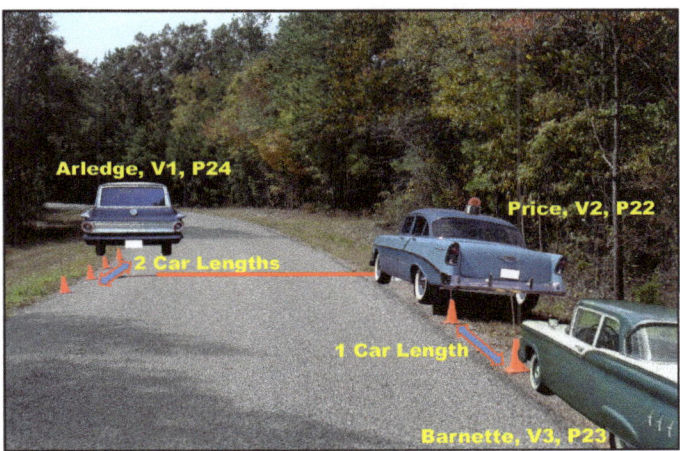

Standard Visual Frame of Reference

This photo was taken by the author at the actual location of the murders in Philadelphia, MS. Photos of the exact vehicles, by make, model, year, and coloring have been placed on top of the background photo. Each vehicle is labeled by the driver, a vehicle identifier, and a passenger list identifier. At the location, orange traffic cones were placed at separation distances indicated in the confessions by James Jordan and Doyle Barnette.

This standard visual frame of reference based on actual evidence enables demonstration of the location of the participants and their actions. Using visualization at the actual location helps the reader understand the validity of the evaluations being described.

Lighting conditions at the time of the incident can also be demonstrated. Powerpoint was used to reduce the light levels in the standard visual frame of reference. Overgrown, remote country roads can be really dark at night, especially on the side of the road below the overgrowth. Overgrowth really blocks even a full moon. Brightness was reduced by 50% in the standard visual frame of reference. This value is midway between pitch black and daylight. Using this brightness reduction gives a fair representation on the effects of lighting conditions on Rock Cut Road at the murder location at the time of the murders.

Theories 1,2: Chaney Running Away

Both theories assume that Chaney was running away when shot from behind. Under the conditions at the time of the shooting. these hits from behind Chaney were extremely unlikely.

In 1964, revolvers chambered in .38 Smith and Wesson were extremely inaccurate. Effective usage was only at very short distances, within a foot or so from the target. This light, slow moving bullet did not have the accuracy for shooting at long distances.

James Jordan, Wayne Roberts, and Doyle Barnette were not accurate shooters. These shooters were poorly educated and were untrained shooters. Dozens of hours of training are required to become an accurate shooter.[168] Accuracy requires recoil control, learned in training. Jordan, Roberts, and Barnette were not the type who would be interested in training. Like most violent racists, these shooters were not interested in education and literacy. These racists were employed in jobs that required little or no formal education, demonstrating their lack of interest in education.

Hitting a moving target is extremely difficult. Dozens of hours of advanced training by an accurate shooter are needed to hit a moving target. Hitting a target in the dark is even more difficult if not impossible without a light to aim and special training by an accurate shooter.

Rock Cut Road was heavily overgrown at the time of the murders.

**Rock Cut Road
(FBI FOIA, 1-49-36)**

This picture was taken by the FBI during the investigation in the days after the murders. Both the remoteness and the overgrowth on either side of the road can be seen.

A full moon would not have helped with the brightness on this remote road. The road was very, very dark with this overgrowth to the left side and to the right side of the road. Even if the shooters had flashlights, these shooters did not have the training to use flashlights properly to simultaneously light up the target and aim and shoot 1 handed.

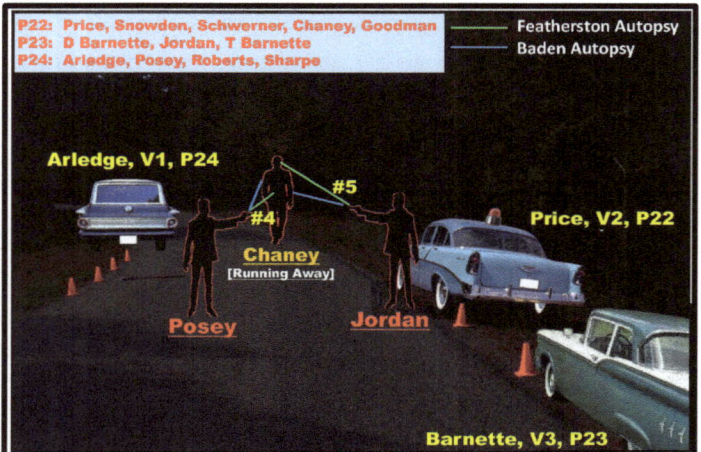

**Shooting At Chaney As He Ran Away In The Dark
(Figures: N Kuvshinov, fotosearch)**

The combined conditions were terrible: inaccurate firearm, small caliber ammunition, untrained shooters, a very dark environment, a moving target that was getting smaller as the target moved away, and a thin Black person as target.

The back of a human head is about an 8-inch oval target. This target was way too small to be hit under these conditions. This small target of the back of the head of a Black person was not clearly visible in the darkness. While the back is a much larger target, a moving target with such poor lighting is also a difficult, if not impossible, shot for an untrained shooter.

If he was running, James Chaney most certainly was running away from the shooters, not towards the shooters.

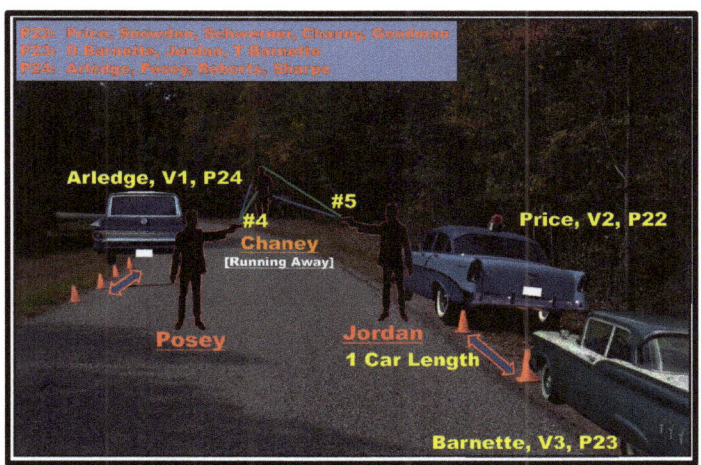

**Shooting At Smaller Chaney Running Away In The Dark
(Figures: N Kuvshinov, fotosearch)**

As Chaney ran away, both the back of his head, an 8-inch oval, and his back, became smaller and smaller. When combined with the really poor lighting conditions, hits from the rear were just not possible. For James Jordan to shoot Chaney in the back of the head, Jordan was up close and personal -- at contact distance less than a foot.

Several other problems exist with these two theories of the murder of James Chaney. If Chaney were running away, James Jordan could not have shot Chaney standing next to the ditch on the left. The group would not have wasted the time to dump Chaney in the ditch, then throw Chaney into the back of the station wagon. Chaney was shot last. His body would have been just thrown into the back of the station wagon.

Other evidence exists that further argues against Chaney being shot while he was running away. In his confession, Doyle Barnette described how Jordan shot Chaney.

I remember Chaney backing up, facing the road, and standing on the other side of the ditch and Jordan stood in the middle of the road and shot him.[169]

Barnette appears to have made an error in claiming that Chaney was *facing the road*. Chaney could not have been facing the road and have been shot

401

in the back of the head by Jordan. James Chaney had his back to Jordan in order for Jordan to shoot Chaney in the back of the head.

Another more important reason exists to rebut the argument that Chaney was shot in the back (head or body) while running away. Chaney could not possibly have run away under the conditions.

Twelve Klansmen were in the arrest party. Schwerner and Goodman were dead. James Chaney was outnumbered and outgunned. Deputy Sheriff Price arrested the trio. Price ordered the arrested trio into his Cruiser. Chaney was under arrest. Running away guaranteed Chaney would be shot for resisting arrest. Chaney sat quietly in the Sheriff's Cruiser, awaiting his fate.

One of the original charges against Deputy Sheriff Price and the group was using color of law to deprive Schwerner, Chaney, and Goodman of life without due process. In US vs Price, the Supreme Court ruled that the Klansmen who were not law enforcement officers could be charged as working under color of law. Their reasoning was that the trio could not escape because the Deputy Sheriff had arrested them. Klansmen were using the restraint on escape to ensure that the trio would not run away. This reasoning by the Supreme Court confirms that Chaney would be in fear of trying to run away. When a person is arrested, his freedom of action is completely taken away.

Theories 1 and 2 that involve Chaney being shot while running away don't stand up to criticism. Chaney was not shot while running away.

Theory 3: Simultaneous Shooters Front And Back

Under this theory, shooters were discharging simultaneously from the front and from the rear of Chaney. James Jordan discharged bullet #5 into the back of the head. At the same time, Billy Posey discharged bullet #4 into the front of Chaney so that the bullet rested in the lower abdomen. Roberts also was positioned in front of Chaney, shooting bullet #3 into the chest at the same time as Jordan and Posey.

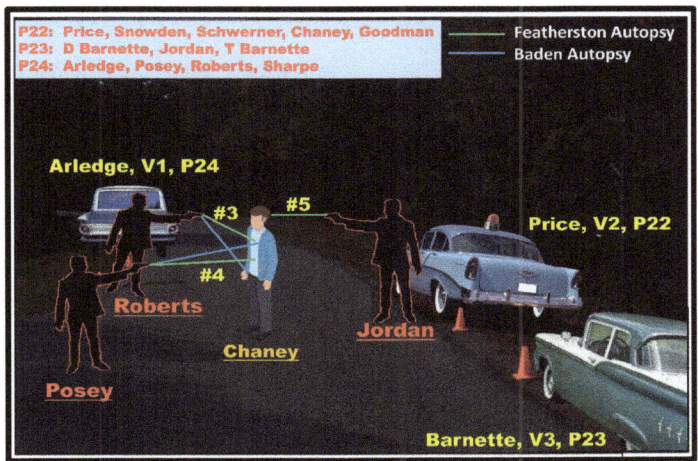

**Chaney Being Shot Front And Back
(Figures: N Kuvshinov, fotosearch)**

An immediate problem with this theory is clear. Roberts and Posey are shooting in the direction of Jordan. Jordan is shooting in the direction of Roberts and Posey. All three shooters were untrained. Given the lack of training and the really poor lighting conditions, all three shooters likely discharged multiple rounds that missed Chaney. In this situation, the shooters are just as likely to hit each other as James Chaney.

This theory also suffers from the same shortcoming as the theories that involve Chaney running away. If Chaney was standing in the middle among Roberts, Jordan, and Posey, Chaney was in the middle of the road. James Jordan could not have shot Chaney standing next to the ditch on the left. The group would not have wasted the time to dump Chaney in the ditch, then throw Chaney into the back of the station wagon. Chaney was shot last. His body would have been just thrown into the back of the station wagon.

This theory assumed that Posey was standing next to Roberts in the front of James Chaney when Posey delivered his shot to the lower abdomen of James Chaney. If Posey is assumed to be standing next to Jordan and both are simultaneously shooting from the rear of James Chaney, these same flaws appear in this theory.

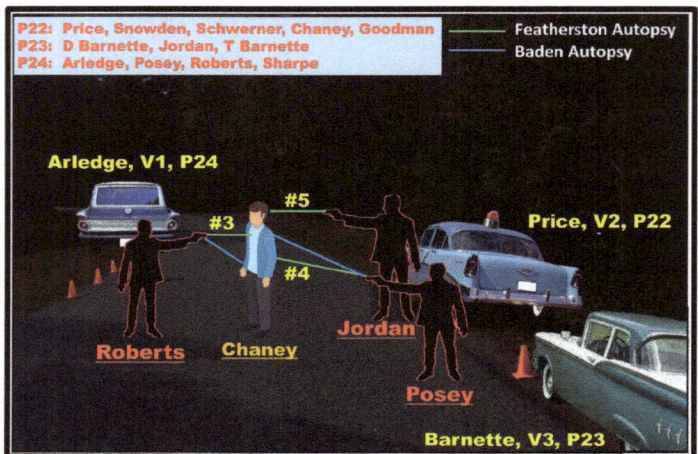

**Posey Shooting From The Rear Instead Of From The Front
(Figures: N Kuvshinov, fotosearch)**

Two groups of shooters are simultaneously shooting at each other. These shooters are just as likely to hit each as James Chaney, as rounds are rapidly discharged without aiming. Chaney still must be in the middle of the shooters for wounds on both sides of his body. Since Chaney was the last to be shot, dragging Chaney to the ditch then to the wagon just does not make sense.

James Chaney was not murdered by simultaneous shooters to the front and to the rear. This conclusion remains the same regardless of whether Billy Posey shot into the abdomen from the front or from the rear of James Chaney.

Theory 4: Shots To Body After Falling In Ditch

A theory about the shooting of James Chaney must explain the way in which shots can occur on both sides of the body. Additionally, this theory must also explain the front to back, slightly upward, and left to right bullet path of one of the bullets.

In his confession, Doyle Barnette explained the murder of James Chaney by James Jordan. James Jordan took James Chaney from the Sheriff's cruiser and walked him to the opposite side of the road from the cruiser.

Jordan himself identified the location of the body of James Chaney.

The Negro was lying in the ditch on the left side of the road face down, headed West and body more or less parallel to the road and about a car length behind the station wagon and a car length in front of Price's car.[170]

Based on this description, Jordan took Chaney to a position about a car length behind the station wagon and a car length in front of Price's car.

**James Jordan Shooting James Chaney on the Opposite Side of Road
(Figures: N Kuvshinov, fotosearch)**

James Chaney was facing away from James Jordan for Jordan to shoot Chaney in the back of the head.

Jordan (bullet #5) then shot James Chaney in the back of the head. After being shot, James Chaney fell straight down into the ditch on the side of the road, next to where he was standing when shot by Jordan. James Chaney landed face up in the ditch.

At this time, only James Jordan had shot James Chaney. Any other shots were made after Chaney fell dead into the ditch. All remaining hits were on the same side of the body. Dr. Featherston identified the entry point of bullet #3 in the chest to the left of the midline in the upper epigastric region. Analysis of the FBI Lab Report determined that Wayne Roberts shot James Chaney in the chest.

Using the bullet path analysis results, a reverse trajectory shows the position of Wayne Roberts at the time James Chaney was struck in the chest by bullet #3.

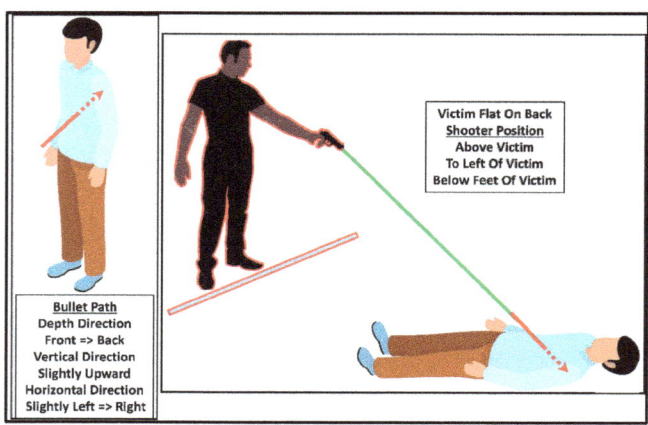

**Bullet Path Analysis To Determine Position Of Shooter Of Chaney
(Figures: N Kuvshinov, fotosearch)**

Bullet #3 entered to the left of the midline of the body of James Chaney. This bullet travelled front to back, slightly upwards, and left to right. This path for bullet #3 is shown above on the left. Chaney fell into the ditch face up after being shot in the head by Jordan. A face up landing is the explanation that allows for a chest entry with a front to back bullet path.

Horizontally rotating the body image 90° while maintaining the bullet path enables identification of the location of Wayne Roberts, the shooter.[171] A reverse trajectory is created from the bullet path in the body laying horizontally in the ditch.[172] A shooter is on that reverse trajectory if the shooter is above the victim, to the left of the victim, and below the feet of the victim. This bullet path could only have been obtained if Wayne Roberts were standing at the top of the ditch, shooting down at the dead body of James Chaney.

With Chaney face up in the ditch, bullet #4 discharged by Billy Posey also entered in the front of the body. Bullets into the left shoulder and into the right forearm also entered from the front.

All of these front entries could only happen if Chaney fell into the ditch and landed face up. Then, all of the other wounds (chest, lower abdomen, left shoulder, right forearm) entered from the front. The shot to the back of the head (#5) and the shot to the chest (#3) were on opposite sides of the body. The bullet path of the shot to the chest (#3) was front to back, slightly upwards, and left to right. This explanation satisfies the two conditions identified from the bullet path analysis.

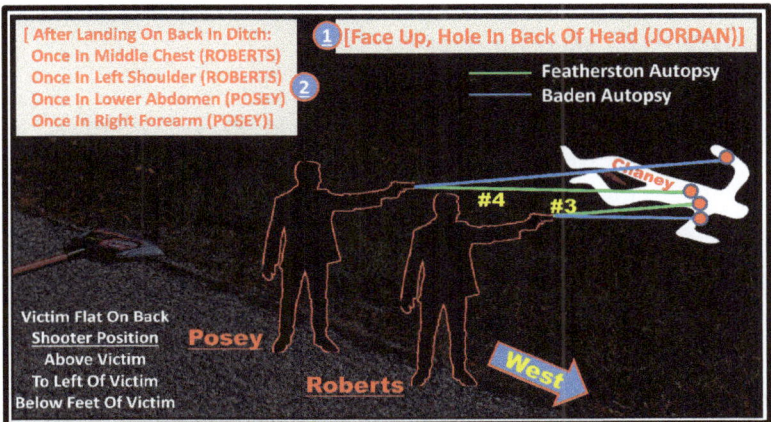

Posey and Roberts Shooting into Chaney Lying in the Ditch (Figures: N Kuvshinov, fotosearch)

Once he fell dead on his back in the ditch, Chaney was an easy target Wayne Roberts was closest to the chest. Roberts (#3) shot James Chaney in the chest. Roberts then quickly discharged a second shot, hitting Chaney in the closest body part, the left shoulder. At the same time, Billy Posey was closest to the lower abdomen. Posey (#4) shot James Chaney in the lower abdomen. In his state of elevated adrenaline, Posey quickly discharged a second shot himself. This discharge hit the closest body part to the lower abdomen, the right forearm. All four shots entered from the front of the body.

This version of the shooting best satisfies the evidence. James Jordan took James Chaney to the opposite side of the road. Jordan shot James Chaney in the back of the head. Chaney fell into the ditch just below where he was shot. Chaney landed face up in the ditch. Wayne Roberts discharged a shot into the chest. Billy Posey shot Chaney in the lower abdomen. This theory is the only theory that adequately explains shots on opposite sides of the body: a shot into the back of the head and 4 shots into the front of the body.

Involvement of Wayne Roberts in the shooting of James Chaney should not be a surprise. Roberts was filled with blood lust. He had just executed Schwerner and Goodman. Roberts also had a need to express his anger and hatred at Black James Chaney for his participation in civil rights activities. Out of control due to his blood lust, Wayne Roberts just jumped into the fray, letting loose a spray of bullets into the dead body of James Chaney. Other bullets were likely shot by Roberts and Posey that missed and were buried in the ground around the bodies.

Firearm accuracy, shooter ability, and lighting conditions were not an issue with this theory. An unmoving target lay a very short distance from the shooters.

Distance from Shooters on Side of Road to Body in Ditch

When the background photograph was taken at the location of the murders, the distance from the side of the road to the bottom of the ditch was measured. This distance was measured to be 6 feet or 2 yards. Handgun training classes generally start at 3 yards. A large, human body size target at 2 yards is fairly easy to hit. With the overgrowth at the time of the murders, only the outline was visible in the darkness at the bottom of the ditch. But this outline was quite large and an easy target.

Such a large, unmoving target in low light is easy to hit at 2 yards, even with a low accuracy revolver and poorly trained shooting skills. This situation is comparatively a far cry from shooting at the 8 inch back of a skull of a running Black man in dark conditions.

One discrepancy does exist between this theory of the shooting of James Chaney and the description of the body location by James Jordan. This theory requires that James Chaney landed face up in the bottom of the ditch by the side of the road. In his confession, James Jordan claimed that the body lay face down in the ditch.

Sometimes witnesses make mistakes. Adrenaline level was high. The body was shrouded in darkness in the ditch. Most importantly, if the body had fallen face down in the ditch after being shot by Jordan, Wayne Roberts could never have shot James Chaney in the chest.

This theory of the shooting of James Chaney best fits all of the evidence, despite the inaccuracy of the body position described by James Jordan.

Using the dead body of James Chaney laying in a ditch for target practice is far more degrading than being beaten.

Forensic Analysis Conclusions

Mickey Schwerner (#1, Q64) was shot in the chest by Wayne Roberts. Andy Goodman (#2, Q76) was also shot in the chest by Wayne Roberts.

James Chaney was shot 5 times: in the head, in the chest, in the lower abdomen, in the left arm, and in the right arm.

James Jordan (#5, Q88) shot James Chaney in the back of the head.

Chaney fell face up, on his back into the ditch on the left side of the road. Wayne Roberts shot Chaney in the left chest (#3, Q86) after Chaney was lying face up in the ditch. Roberts shot one additional bullet into the left shoulder of Chaney. Billy Wayne Posey shot Chaney in the lower right abdomen (#4, Q87) after Chaney was lying face up in the ditch. An additional bullet was discharged by Posey into the right forearm.

Andy Goodman was not buried alive. James Chaney was not shot while running away. James Chaney was not castrated. James Chaney was not beaten. The truth is much worse. James Jordan executed James Chaney by a shot to the back of the head. Wayne Roberts and Billy Posey indiscriminately discharged 4 bullets into the body of James Chaney after Chaney lay dead in the ditch by the side of the road.

Dr William Featherston provided sufficient detail in his autopsy to enable reconstruction of the actual shooting activities on Rock Cut Road. Reasonable details were provided by Featherston in his autopsy. Using the anatomical and physiological descriptions provided by Featherston, bullet paths were reconstructed for each bullet. Using these details, greater insight into the death of James Chaney was provided.

Accusations by Dr David Spain were **unfounded**. Dr Spain did not see a copy of the autopsy or the x-rays by his own admission. Yet, Spain claimed that important information was not included in the autopsy. Dr Spain made extensive assumptions about the state of the body before the autopsy without considering the destructiveness of the autopsy.

Autopsy Claims and Findings

An extensive forensic analysis has been performed on the Featherston Spain autopsy and the Packer radiology report. Additional medical evidence was introduced. Additional evidence included the time to bleed out after being shot and the determination of shooter position from bullet path in the body. The combination of forensic analysis and additional medical information have been used to evaluate the murders of Schwerner, Chaney, and Goodman. Additionally, an extensive soils survey and analysis enabled evaluation of the claim that Andrew Goodman was buried alive.

A summary of the various claims about the murders and the findings appears in the table below. Detailed analyses performed to evaluate the claims appear in previous sections.

Claim	Finding
Featherston Suppressed Autopsy	AG Johnson, MS 8th Circuit, Controlled Release
Featherston Autopsy Inaccurate	2nd Autopsy By Packer Confirmed Featherston
James Chaney Beaten	Body Significantly Decomposed After 60 Days Fell Apart At Touch
Chaney Broken Jaw Caused By Beating	Destructive Autopsy, Decomposed Body
Chaney Broken Arms Caused By Beating	Rain Of Bullets From Multiple Shooters
Spain Performed Independent Autopsy	Looked At Body For 10 Min After Destructive Autopsy
Spain Was Accurate	No Physical Autopsy No Review of Written Featherston Autopsy No Review Of X-rays
Goodman Was Buried Alive	Bled Out in 16 Sec, Buried At Least 45 Min Later
Goodman Clutched Red Soil From Burial Site	Clutched Red Soil From Murder Site

.**Autopsy Claims and The Findings**

James Chaney was not beaten. James Chaney died immediately from a discharge to the head. He was then used as a target in a volley of discharges by multiple shooters. Andrew Goodman was not buried alive. Andrew Goodman bled to death in about 16 seconds and in great pain. He was transported to the burial location after he died. This trip took at least 45 minutes. David Spain did not conduct an autopsy. He did conduct a short, 10 minute visual inspection. Spain made unfounded conclusions based on a decomposed body that had been physically destroyed by the real autopsy.

Impacts from the Spain Autopsy

Dr. David Spain cast nationwide doubt on the reputation of Dr. William Featherston based on a 10 minute visual inspection of the autopsy destroyed body. Spain did not see the x-rays or the body before the autopsy. His conclusions were totally unfounded, based on a preconceived stereotype of all doctors in MS. Spain should have been held accountable for his unscientific and inaccurate conclusions that destroyed the career of Dr. William Featherston.

However, Featherston maintained the confidence and the respect of the MS Attorney General and the University of MS Medical School. He continued to conduct autopsies for the Medical School after the autopsy of Schwerner, Chaney and Goodman, despite the allegations by Spain.

My father and his partner, Dr. Forrest Bratley, performed hundreds of medical-legal autopsies in Miss. before the Office of the State Medical Examiner was created by the legislature. My father was instrumental in getting the legislature to pass the medical examiner bill because he and Dr. Bratley were performing numerous autopsies at the request of law enforcement for minimal pay set by statute, which took too much time away from their clinical practice.[173]

Unfortunately, the unfounded accusations by David Spain did have a major impact on the University of MS Medical Center. The whole affair *cast a shadow over the Medical Center which loomed there for a long time.*[174]

One problem that seemed to stimulate the accusations was the refusal to release the autopsy to the public. A number of vocal, published critics felt that this suppression of the autopsy was an attempt to hide something in the autopsy. However, neither Featherston nor the Medical Center had control over the release of the autopsy. The autopsy had been forwarded to W H Johnson, District Attorney of the 8th District Court of MS, serving Neshoba County and several other counties. AG Johnson had complete control over release of the autopsy.

Johnson refused to release the autopsy. His justification was that the autopsy was evidence in an ongoing investigation. On June 1, 1965, Featherston wrote directly to Johnson, requesting that he be allowed to release the autopsy to the Ethics Committee of the College of American Pathologists. Featherston wanted to use the autopsy as support against an ethics complaint he had filed against David Spain.

Johnson responded to the request on June 9, 1965. *We do not wish to have any public release of the autopsy involved in this case. However, I can see no harm in giving you the authority to release the autopsy to members of the proper committee, of your national organization, provided that you will impress upon them the necessity for holding the information confidential.*[175]

Without release of the autopsy to the public, critics continued to hold the Medical Center responsible for hiding the autopsy to avoid criticism. As a result of these criticisms, the Medical Center came under national scrutiny.

The Medical Center had been formed in 1955 and was heavily dependent on Federal grants. A financial statement for the Medical Center for 1963 - 1964, shows that the school had received $2,192,299 in federal funds during the period, with an additional $334,323 due. Those funds were essential to survival.[176] Losing these funds would have likely caused the closure of the Medical Center and the Medical School.

As a result of the additional scrutiny, specific actions were taken against the Medical Center. Submission of a Federal Compliance Questionnaire was required to ensure that the Medical Center was not enforcing segregation. If an inspection found any segregation after submission of the Questionnaire, the Medical Center would lose these pending and future Federal Funds.[177]

Additionally, the NAACP Legal Fund targeted the Medical Center. On March 6, 1965, the Associated Press ran a story that the NAACP had filed civil rights complaints against 29 hospitals in southern states. These complaints were filed with the US Dept of Health and Human Services. The University of MS Medical Center and its University Hospital was one of the 29 hospitals that received a civil rights complaint claiming enforcement of segregation. All pending and future grants were suspended until the Medical Center and the University Hospital were inspected.[178]

Local administrators of the Medical School were able to correct all issues with the aid of the attorneys of the Medical Center. Local civil rights groups, such as the MS Field Office of the NAACP, were invited to participate and to address any segregation related issues.[179]

Further Impacts On Dr. Featherston

After the FBI investigation and the confessions by Klansmen James Jordan and Doyle Barnett , civil rights charges were brought against the Klansmen for the murders. The participating White Knights were charged under USC 18 Section 241 with depriving Schwerner, Chaney and Goodman of their lives without due process of the law. A trial was held from October 9 – 20, 1967, in the Southern District of MS, of the US 5th Circuit. Dr. William Featherston testified in that case.

When the witness list was released by the prosecution as required by law, Dr. Featherston was listed as a witness for the prosecution. Prosecutor John Doar planned to call Featherston to testify on his autopsies. His goal was to have Featherston verify that Schwerner, Chaney and Goodman were murdered by gunshot. This testimony would establish that the trio had been deprived of life and without due process (by murder). Remaining witnesses would prove the who, when, and where the deprivation of life had been accomplished.

Not surprisingly, the witness list of the prosecution was leaked to the Klan community in Neshoba County. Local Klan members were angry after learning that Featherston planned to testify. Direct threats were delivered in order to intimidate Featherston against serving as a witness for the prosecution. As Becky Featherston recalled, *The KKK called my father and threatened to firebomb our house if he got on that stand in 1967 and testified. My very brave ethical father sent my siblings and I to Mobile, Al and he testified.*[180]

Dr Featherston served as a witness for the prosecution in that case. On October 11, 1967, Prosecutor John Doar called Dr. William Featherston to the witness stand. Under direct examination, Featherston accurately described the wounds, the bullets found, and reviewed the x-rays. He clearly stated that Schwerner, Chaney and Goodman had each died from the gunshot wounds received.[181] Despite the threats, Featherston delivered clear and convincing medical evidence that the trio had been deprived of life and without due process (by murder).

During his time on the witness stand, Featherston was questioned extensively in a lengthy direct examination by Prosecutors John Doar, Robert Hauberg, and Robert Owen. Then, he was subjected to several cross examinations by defense attorneys. One cross was by Travis Buckley, another by Howard Pigford, and yet another cross by Laurel Wier. Prosecutors conducted a redirect to clarify issues identified by the defense attorneys. Defense Attorney Travis Buckley then conducted a final recross examination. **Dr. William Featherston did not waiver in his conclusions.** Schwerner, Chaney and Goodman were murdered by the gunshot wounds as he identified in his autopsy report.[182]

Harassment by the White Knights did not end after the trial.

He received so many death threats over the years from the Klan...he held his breath every time he cranked his car.[183]

In the face of threats that persisted throughout his life, Dr. William Featherston showed extensive courage by telling the truth.

Part 5: Foundations Of Visual Reconstruction

35 locations were involved in the murders on June 21, 1964.

Some of these locations have been lost over time.

Using evidence clues and FBI photos, all locations have been found.

An appendix contains a precise latitude and longitude for each location.

Each murder can be characterized as a series of step-by-step actions.

Every action involves shooters and/or victims.

Actions also involve movements from one location to another.

Mickey Schwerner was murdered first by Wayne Roberts.

Andy Goodman was murdered second by Wayne Roberts.

James Chaney was murdered last by Jim Jordan.

Posey and Roberts discharged bullets into the dead body of Chaney.

Location Analysis and Identification

Extensive analysis of the historical description reveals that 35 locations were involved on June 21, 1964, the day of the murders. While these locations were identified by name, many of the exact geographical locations have been lost. A geographical location is specified by latitude and longitude. Using clues from the historical description, exact geographical locations have been found.

Clues from the historical description are repeated without footnotes. These clues were extensively footnoted during the historical description. Repeating the footnotes for the clues again is unnecessary.

FBI Map Corrections

Events leading up to the first arrest of Schwerner, Chaney and Goodman all took place on Highway 16 heading West into downtown Philadelphia. A map of these locations was created by the FBI.

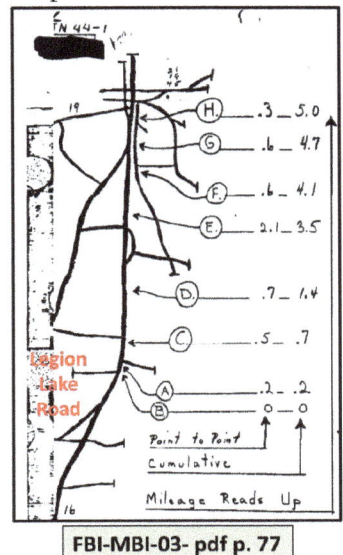

FBI Map of Locations to First Arrest

This map accurately depicts the locations. However, the mileages indicated on the map are incorrect. These inaccuracies were the result of the type of speedometers in automobiles at the time. Distances were determined by using the speedometer of a 1963 Chevrolet owned by the

Bureau. Older speedometers only measured distances in 0.10 (tenths) of a mile. This level of measurement was acceptable for longer distances However, for shorter distances, these old analog speedometers were notoriously inaccurate.

Google Earth was used to reconstruct the diagram with the correct locations and distances.

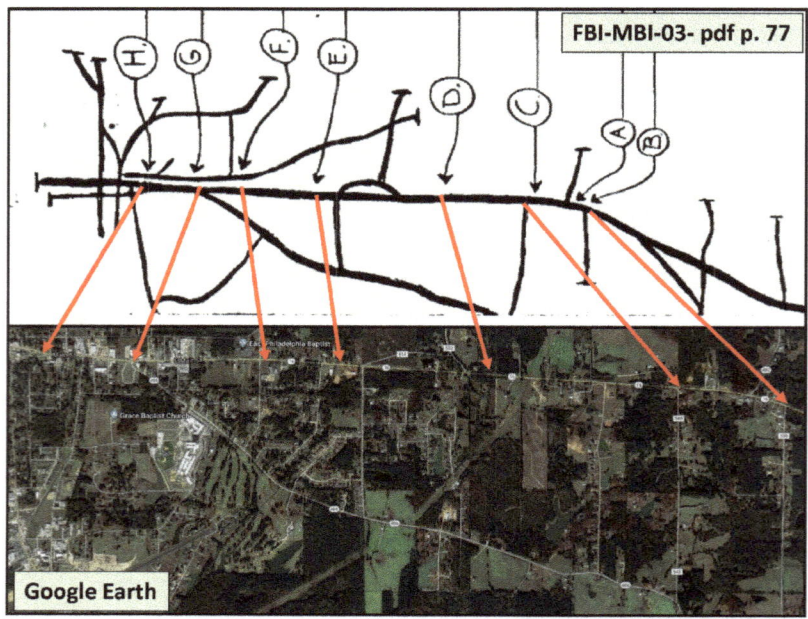

Reconstructed Chase, Arrest Locations Using Google Earth

Locations are easily identified using the geometric layout of the original map created by the FBI. For instance, consider location G. This location is at a point where two roads meet. One road is Highway 16 heading westward towards Philadelphia. Another road is Highway 486 heading northwest and merging with Highway 16. All of the other locations are similarly identified using geometric cues from the map.

Once each of the locations is identified, Google Earth provides an accurate latitude and longitude for each location. An accurate distance between each location is also determined using Google Earth.

Updated, accurate distances from Google Earth are provided below.

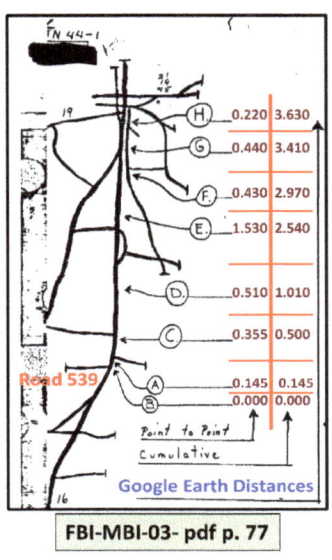

Corrected FBI Map

Locations to First Arrest

FBI-MBI-03- pdf p. 77

Legion Lake Road, the location where Price turned around, is now Road 539. Differences in the distances are significant. According to the FBI map, Price chased Schwerner, Chaney and Goodman for a distance of 5 miles between road 539 and the first arrest location (B – H). Yet, the actual distance is only 3.63 miles. All of the other distances also vary.

All of the distances are off by the same percentage: 72%. Actual total chase distance relative to FBI total chase distance (B – H) is 72% (3.6/5.). Actual distance from Road 539 to location E (B – E) is 72% of that same distance as measured by the FBI. (2.54/3.5). This consistent difference demonstrates that the measurements recorded by the FBI were accurate at the time using the speedometer technology available.

First Arrest Location

Deputy Sheriff Cecil Price arrested the trio at location H on the map. This location was 3.63 miles west of Road 539, as indicated in the corrected FBI map. In addition to the map, a clear visual clue is available in the form of a photograph. This photograph was annotated by the FBI in preparing a report about the murders.

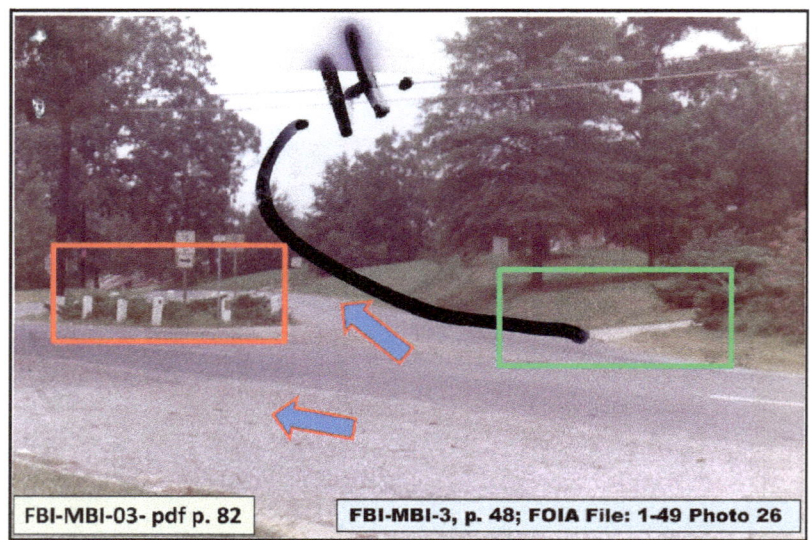

Location At Which Trio Was First Arrested (FBI)

A landscaped area (red box) appears at the center between Beacon Street and Main Street, the two streets that split from Highway 16. Across from and further east from the landscaped area is a driveway where Schwerner, Chaney and Goodman were arrested (green box).

This location was further described as being along the right fork of Highway 16 towards Beacon Street, 50 yards west of the intersection.

Using these clues, Google Maps was employed to find the exact location.

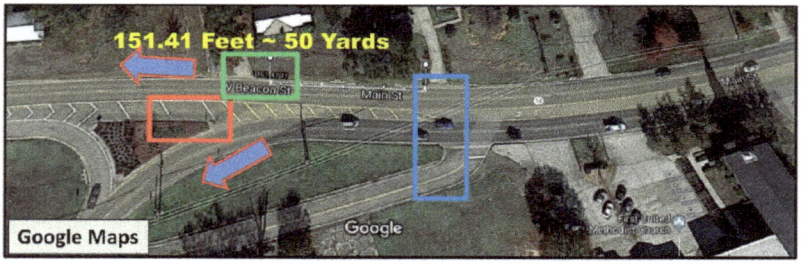

50 Yards Past Highway 16 Intersection With Beacon Street

A blue box indicates the location of the split from Highway 16 onto Beacon Street. This location was chosen because the road at the bottom of the blue box is the current merger of Main Street with Highway 16 The landscaped area identified in the FBI photo is indicated using a red box. The green box shows the location that is 50 yards from the intersection located by the blue box. This location is across from and to the east of the landscaped area, just as indicated in the FBI photo.

This location is further verified by using Google Maps and the corrected data in the FBI map.

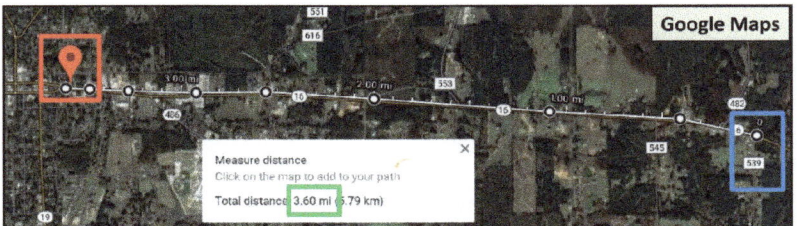

Distance From Road 593 to the First Arrest Location

According to Google Maps, the distance between Road 539 and the location selected is 3.60 miles. This distance is close enough to the 3.63 miles in the corrected FBI map to be accepted.

Now that this location has been identified and validated, Google Maps provides an accurate latitude and longitude.

First Arrest Location: 32.771459, -89.1034082

Location of Old City Hall

Highway Patrol Officer Wiggs drove the Ranch Wagon into Philadelphia with James Chaney as his prisoner. Wiggs parked the Ranch Wagon in the parking lot in front of Philadelphia City Hall. At the time, City Hall was at a different location from the location today.

A Philadelphia city map of locations in the city was included in the FBI report generated at the time.

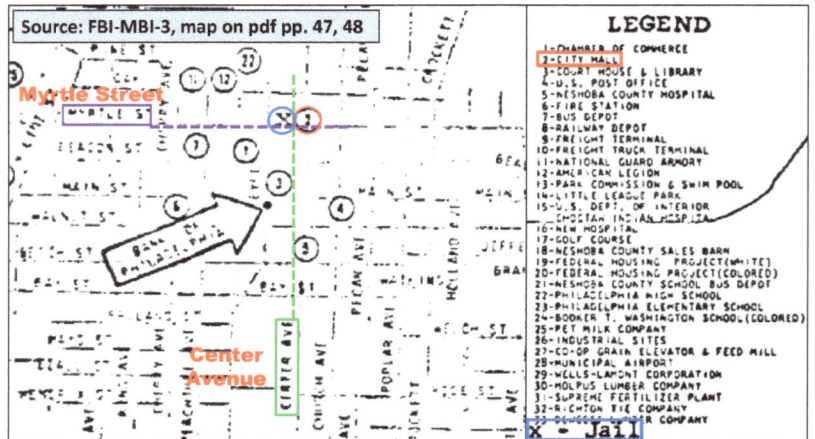

Philadelphia City Map on June 21, 1964

Both Philadelphia City Hall and the Philadelphia Jail are located on this map. The old City Hall was on the northeast corner of the intersection of Myrtle Street and Center Avenue.

A building still exists at the location of the old City Hall.

Philadelphia City Hall on June 21, 1964

This Google Earth view shows the location of the old City Hall on the northeast corner of Myrtle Street and Center Avenue. A parking lot is just above the City Hall building in the Google Earth view. This parking lot is the location where Patrol officer Wiggs parked the Ranch Wagon prior to escorting Chaney into the Jail.

Old City Hall Location: northeast corner, Myrtle St, Center Ave

Klan Staging Location

Doyle Barnett and some of the White nights were waiting on the west side of the Neshoba County Courthouse. Edgar Ray Killen arrived and directed these waiting Klansmen to a staging location. Someone would come to the staging location and inform the waiting Klansmen when the trio was released.

This staging location was near an *old warehouse down a small, dark street a few blocks from the northwest side of the jail.* An old satellite photo from 1996 helps to find this location.

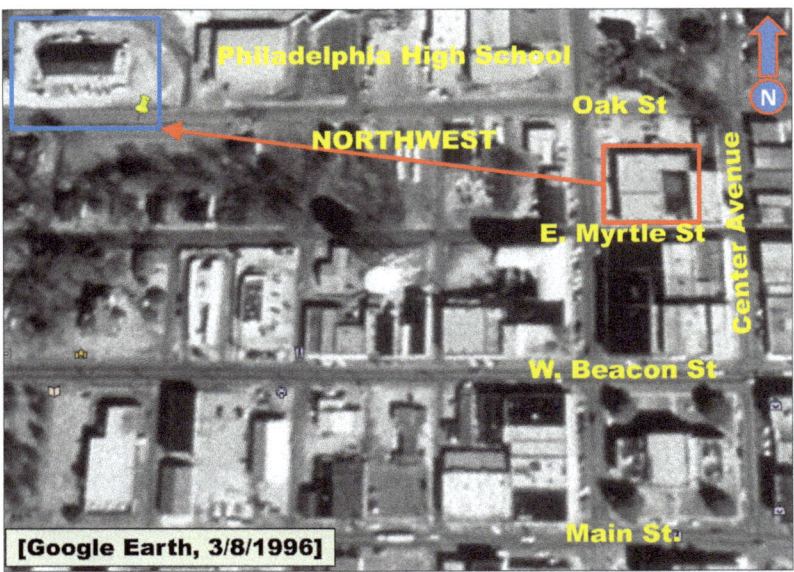

Satellite Photo from 1996 Showing Klansmen Staging Location

A red box indicates the location of the Neshoba County Jail. The northwest corner of the Jail is fairly close to Oak Street. Heading west on Oak Street, just past the Philadelphia High School, is an old building on the right. This building is a few blocks down Oak Street from the northwest corner of the Jail.

During his testimony in the civil rights case in 1967, Jim Jordan described this old building as an *old warehouse*. However, historical records show that at the time, this building was the National Guard Armory. Jim Jordan likely misclassified the old building as a *warehouse*.

Jordan was from Meridian. He was not familiar with this area of Neshoba County and of Philadelphia. Jordan admitted that this location was down a small, dark street. In the darkness, Jordan only saw a general outline of a building. Jim Jordan did not identify the location in his earlier confession in 1964. His identification of the building was 3 years later at the civil rights trial in 1967. Details fade after 3 years. He knew that murder was about to be committed. His heart was likely racing. With his heart racing, identification of details was almost impossible Jordan incorrectly identified an *old building*, the National Guard Armory, as an *old warehouse*.

The building on Oak Street is an old building. The old brick material used to construct the building indicates that this building is an older building. This *old building* is the *old warehouse* described by Jordan in the 1967 civil rights trial.

Old Brick Materials In Old Building On Oak Street In 1964

This building is the only *old building* in this area on Oak Street or even in that general area of downtown Philadelphia. Therefore, the term *old building* is used rather than the term *old warehouse*.

Oak Street itself is a small street. At the end of Oak Street, in the area of the old building, the street is overgrown by trees. Back in 1964, this area of Oak Street near the old building was very dark.

Oak Street in the Area of the Warehouse

This location on Oak Street is the only location in the area that is *a small dark street with an old building*.

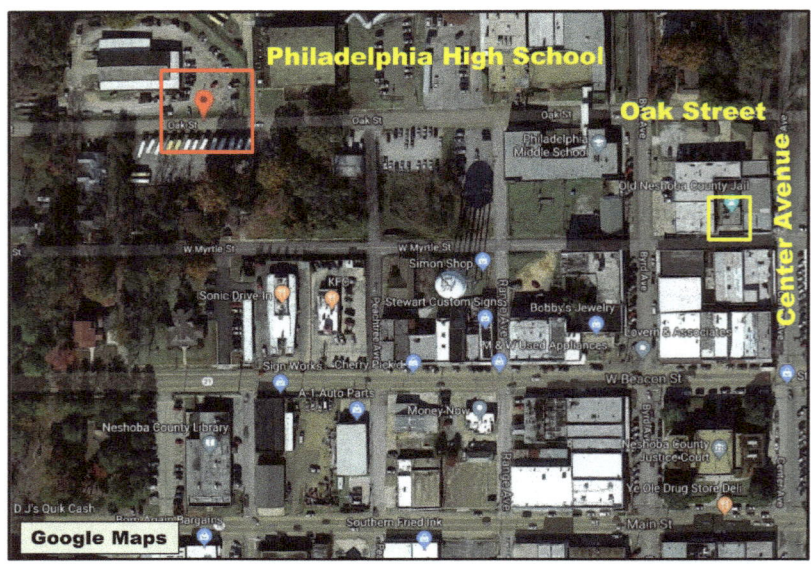

Oak Street in the Area of the Warehouse Viewed From Above

Philadelphia High School fills the area from the intersection of Center Avenue and Oak Street all the way down to the warehouse. Therefore, this old building on Oak Street is the only possible candidate that meets all the criteria for the staging location of the White Knights.

White Knights Staging Location: 32.77297, -89.11342

Price Takes The Lead

After the release of Schwerner, Chaney and Goodman, the White Knights were informed of both the release and their path towards Meridian. The waiting Klansmen then drove south on Highway 19 towards Meridian. Eventually, the Klan vehicles encountered Highway Patrol Officers Poe and Wiggs. At this location, the Klansmen waited for Deputy Sheriff Cecil Price to take the lead.

This location is described as being on the outskirts of town, about 1 mile south on Highway 19. A curve in the road provided a warning just before the location. A Standard Service Station on the east side of the highway was the location where the White Knights met Highway Patrol Officers Poe and Wiggs and waited for Deputy Sheriff Price to take the lead.

A map of that area of Philadelphia at the time of the murders was included in an FBI report. Using this map, the meeting location is identified.

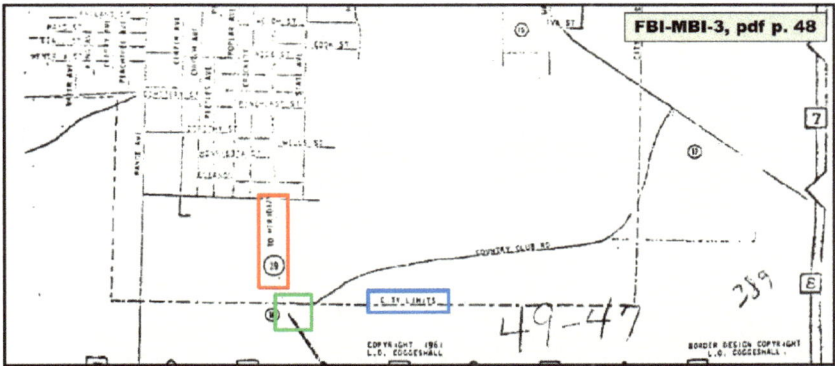

Southern City Limit of Philadelphia in Summer, 1964

A blue box indicates the actual southern city limit of Philadelphia. Highway 19 South is identified using a red box. This Highway makes a left curve at the city limit and is located using a green box.

Google Earth satellite imagery clearly shows that this curve in Highway 19 South is approximately 1 mile south of the city. A measurement tool is provided by Google Earth. This tool is extremely accurate, being based on the latitude and longitude data from Earth maintained databases.

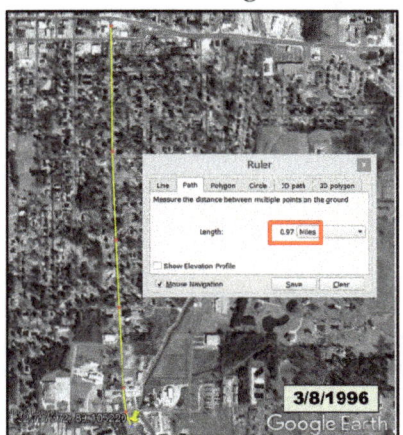 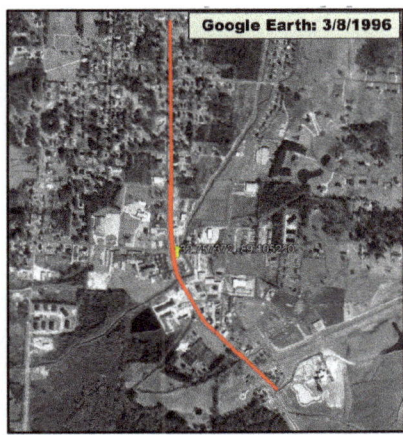

Earlier Satellite Imagery of South Philadelphia City Limits

This same imagery also demonstrates that Highway 19 South makes a curve at that location. A search of the remainder of Highway 19 South towards Highway 492 reveals that this location is the only curve before Highway 492.

Zooming into the image reveals a structure that was standing at that location, at least in 1996.

Structure Just Outside City Limit At Turn in Highway 19

This structure is surrounded by a red box. A blue box indicates the parking lot where the Klansmen met the Highway Patrol Officers and waited for Deputy Sheriff Price.

O'Neal's Gas Station is currently housed on the location where the Standard Service Station used to exist. A nice big parking lot appears just past the pumps, at the same location where the Klansmen waited for Deputy Sheriff Cecil Price.

O'Neil's Gas Station Just Past The Curve In Highway 19 South

The parking lot that was the meeting location where Price took the lead in the chase of the trio is identified using a blue rectangle.

Price Takes Lead Location: 32.757372, -89.105220

Chevy Has Carburetor Problem

As Deputy Sheriff Price led the two cars filled with Klansmen south on Highway 19 to recapture the trio, the 1956 Chevy Bel Air driven by Billy Wayne Posey began to develop carburetor problems. Posey pulled the car to the side of the road. Price and Doyle Barnette continued with the chase of Schwerner, Chaney and Goodman.

This location was described as being on the right side of Highway 19 as the group headed south. More precisely, Posey in his 1956 Chevy pulled over just north of Highway 492, north of House, MS. The location was within sight of Posey's Store. This store was actually a combined gas station and convenience mart.

A Google Earth satellite photo from 1997 clearly reveals the location.

A red rectangle identifies the location of Posey's Gas Station/Store.

Location Of Posey's Gas Station and Convenience Mart

This location is on the right headed south on Highway 19, north of Highway 492 and north of House, MS. A bypass road on the east side of Highway 19 across from the location allows a driver to bypass the intersection with Highway 492 and enter House directly.

During the investigation after the recovery of the bodies, the FBI took an aerial photo of the location of Posey's Gas Station/Store.

Aerial Photo Of Location Of Posey's Gas Station

A number of additional identifying features are seen in this photo. Entrance/exit aprons appear on the south side and the north side of the store. Set back behind the store is a house. The entrance to the shortcut road to House, MS, appears right across Highway 19 from the store.

After all these years, the store itself does not exist. However, this area is easily identified from a Google Maps aerial view using all of the features that have been identified.

Google Maps Aerial View Of Location Of Posey's Gas Station

House, MS, is at the upper right of the view. Highway 19 South intersects Highway 492 at the lower right of the view. A red rectangle identifies the location of the original Posey's Gas Station/Store. Across Highway 19 appears the bypass road that leads directly to House, MS.

Zooming into the aerial view reveals the extent of area where the Gas Station used to exist.

Zoomed Aerial View Of Location Of Posey's Gas Station

Many of the features of the original FBI aerial view appear in this Google Maps aerial view. The house is set back from the road. A large apron area stretches from north to south. This area is indicated by a red rectangle. Entrance to the bypass road to House is just across the street from the apron area.

Additional corroborating features appear in a Google Maps Street View.

Street View Of Location Of Posey's Gas Station

North and south side aprons can be seen. The house is located far back from Highway 19. Entrance to the shortcut road is across the street.

This location is confirmed. Posey, Roberts, Sharpe and Townsend waited in the 1956 Chevy Bel Air while Schwerner, Chaney and Goodman were captured on Highway 492.

1956 Chevy Has Carburetor Problem Location: 32.628662,-89.005824

Price Overtakes Ranch Wagon

Deputy Sheriff Cecil Price took the lead to locate and to arrest the trio in the Ranch Wagon. Price overtook the Ranch Wagon a short distance north of Highway 492. An exact location has never been identified.

When Price overtook the Ranch Wagon a short distance north of Highway 492, James Chaney sped up the Ranch Wagon to evade capture. After a short distance, Chaney turned the Ranch Wagon west on Highway 492, continuing at high speed.

Price followed the Ranch Wagon west on Highway 492, continuing the high-speed chase. Posey and Barnette were not far behind Price. Posey and Barnette were close enough to see Price go west on 492. Then, Posey's 1956 Chevy developed carburetor problems.

The carburetor problems developed on Highway 19 north of Posey's station. Posey was able to drive his 1956 Chevy into his own station. He had to be close to his own station when the carburetor problem began. Posey told Barnette to continue to follow Price west on Highway 492.

Several criteria for the overtake location can be determined from these facts. This location must be north of Posey's station but close enough for Chaney to escape to Highway 492 without being forced to the side of the road. Additionally, the overtake location must be close enough to Posey's station for Posey to pull into the station with the carburetor problem.

Analysis to Determine Overtake Location

Posey's station is 0.51 miles (2693 feet) north of Highway 492. After another 0.164 miles (866 feet) north from Posey's station, the location found is 2/3 mile north of Highway 492.

Using 2/3 mile north of Highway 492 as the overtake location is a practical choice. This location gives Chaney 2/3 of a mile to speed up and to turn west on Highway 492 without getting caught by Cecil Price. When Posey's 1956 Chevy exhibits a carburetor problem, Posey has at least 866 feet to turn into his station.

Price Overtakes Ranch Wagon Location: 32.629788, -89.007777

Deputy Sheriff Cecil Price travels from the location at which he takes the lead to this location at which he overtakes the Ranch Wagon. Distance between these two locations is an important factor in determining the timeline associated with the events.

Using Google Maps, the distance between these two locations is easily determined.

**Distance Between
Takes The Lead Location To The Overtake Location**

The location at which Price takes the lead is in the upper left corner of the map. This location is identified by a blue rectangle. At the lower right corner is the location at which Price overtakes the Ranch Wagon. A red rectangle is used to identify this location. After taking the lead, Deputy Sheriff Price travels 10.6 miles to the location at which he overtakes the Ranch Wagon.

Second Arrest Location

Deputy Sheriff Price continued the ongoing pursuit of Schwerner, Chaney and Goodman. The trio headed west on Highway 492 towards Union, MS, hoping to outrun the pursuing Price in his 1956 Chevy Cruiser. Eventually, Price was able to pass the Ranch Wagon containing the trio, forcing the Ranch Wagon to the side of the road. At this location on Highway 492, Schwerner, Chaney and Goodman were arrested again. Barnette arrived at the arrest location some minutes later.

A number of clues characterize the location of this second arrest. This location was about 16 miles from Philadelphia on Highway 492, west of Highway 19. Just before the arrest location, the road went down a little hill. Pastureland was on each side of the road. The vehicle stop by Price occurred just before a small bridge. A fairly sharp right turn in Highway 492 followed just after the bridge.

During the investigation after the bodies were found, the FBI took a photograph of the 2nd arrest location. This photograph demonstrates the features near the arrest location.

Annotated Photograph of Second Arrest Location Taken by FBI

Older satellite imagery from 1996 locates a reasonable candidate for the second arrest location. A red box in the lower right corner identifies the intersection between Highway 19 South and Highway 492 West. Starting from this location, curves in the road are identified in order to find a location consistent with the remainder of the clues.

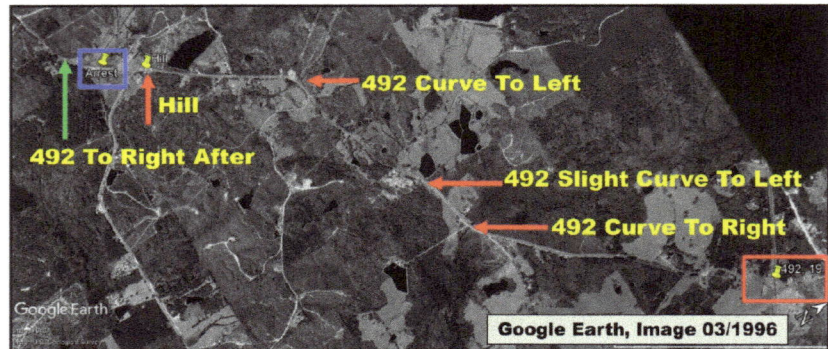

Satellite Imagery Identifying Highway 492 Road Features

After a short distance, Highway 492 curves to the right. A long straight stretch of road follows the curve to the right. After the straight stretch of road, Highway 492 curves to the left. Another straight stretch of road follows this left curve. A hill at the end of the straight stretch of road is identified by a yellow pin. Just past the hill is a road off to the left. A blue box marks the location of a bridge. Highway 492 then curves to the right after the bridge. This location is the only point in this area at which Highway 492 has a small hill, a bridge, and then curves to the right.

Zooming into the satellite imagery in the area of the slight hill followed by the right curve reveals further details regarding this location.

Satellite Imagery Showing Area On Highway 492 West

An area just past the slight hill on Highway 492 West is indicated using a red rectangle. This area is the pastureland on each side of the road before the location of the second arrest. A blue rectangle identifies the bridge just past the arrest location. This bridge enables the highway to cross Nelson Creek. After the bridge, Highway 492 curves to the right.

The exact location at which Deputy Sheriff Price forced the Ranch wagon of the trio to the side of the road is located using Google Maps.

Google Maps View of Bridge over Nelson Creek

A green rectangle verifies that this view contains the section of Highway 492 that crosses Nelson Creek. In this view, the bridge, indicated by a red rectangle, is clearly visible. Deputy Sheriff Price forced the trio off the road just before the bridge. Price, his vehicle, the trio, and their Ranch Wagon were all positioned in the area indicated by the blue rectangle.

In the previous images, a small hill on Highway 492 was identified Verification that this location is the top of a small hill is accomplished using the Google Earth elevation tool.

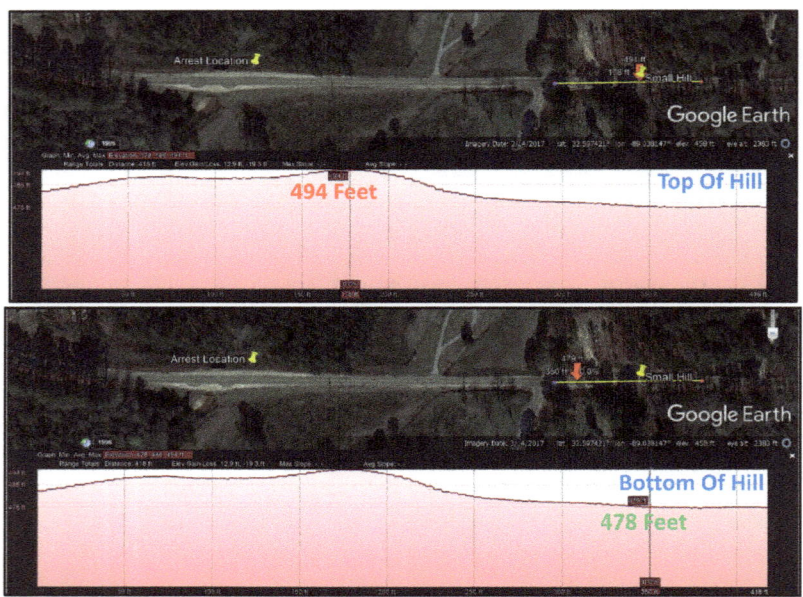

Elevation Evaluation at the Location of the Small Hill

A red pin indicates the location at which Google Earth specifies the elevation above sea level. In the top frame, this red pin is placed at the top of the hill, revealing an elevation of 478 feet. This pin is moved further west to the bottom of the hill in the bottom frame. At this location, an elevation of 449 feet is revealed. This difference of 16 feet in elevation qualifies as a small hill.

Using Google Maps, the distance from Philadelphia to just before the bridge on Highway 492 West can be determined.

The distance from Philadelphia along Highway 19 South to Highway 492 West is determined first.

Distance from Philadelphia to Highway 492

Philadelphia is in the upper left corner of this map (red box). In the lower right corner is the intersection of Highway 19 South with Highway 492 West (blue box). This distance is 12.65 miles. From this intersection, the distance to the area just before the bridge is measured.

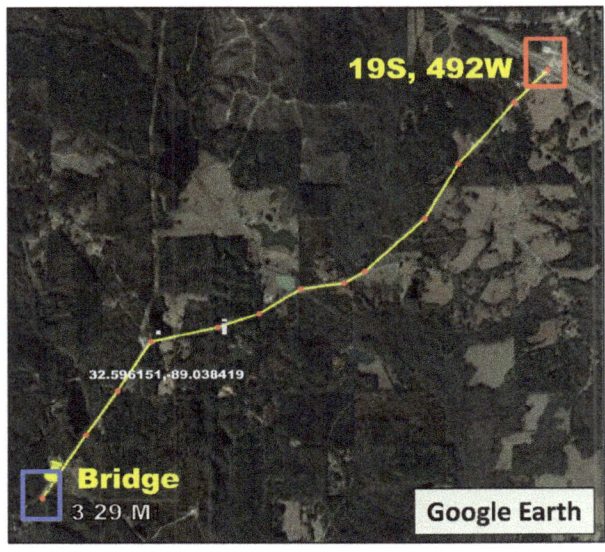

Distance from Highway 19 to Bridge

This distance is 3.29 miles. When combined, the total distance from Philadelphia to the area just before the bridge over Nelson Creek is 15.94 miles. Given the inherent inaccuracy of analog vehicle speedometers in 1964, this very slight difference from 16 miles is forgivable.

Clues to identify the arrest location were provided in the confession by White Knight Jim Jordan.

Clues By Jordan Identifying The Second Arrest Location

Highway 492 went down a small hill. Pastureland was on either side of the road. Price forced the Ranch Wagon to the right side of the road just before the bridge. This picture shows the approach to the bridge over Nelson Creek on Highway 492. All of these features described by Jordan appear in this location.

Three important clues were derived from the original FBI photo taken at the time of the investigation in Fall, 1964.

Evaluation Of Clues At Location From Original FBI Image

A side road appeared on the left before the bridge. After this side road, a bridge crossed a creek. Just past the bridge, the Highway 492 curves to the right. An actual photo of the location identified through the analyses is shown. As the annotations indicate, this location satisfies all of the clues that identify the original location.

The location just before the bridge across Nelson Creek on Highway 492 West satisfies all of the clues. This location is the second arrest location.

Second Arrest Location: 32.596151,-89.038419

Location Of The Murders

After the second arrest of Schwerner, Chaney and Goodman, the caravan of three vehicles returned to Highway 19. Posey, Roberts, and Sharpe were retrieved from the location of the stalled 1956 Chevy owned by Posey. Townsend remained with the stalled 1956 Chevy. The caravan of three vehicles then continued to Rock Cut Road, now Road 515, to commit the murders.

Multiple clues are available to determine the murder location on Road 515. The caravan traveled along this road past a bend to the left, a curve to the right, and up a small hill. The vehicles stopped at least 300 yards west of the intersection of Road 515 and Highway 19.

A photo was taken by the FBI during the investigation that provides several other clues.

Murder Location on Rock Cut Road

Road 515 curves to the left after the murder location. This location is before the intersection with Road 284 since that intersection is not visible. All of the bodies fell into a ditch on the left side of the road. A ditch appears on the left side of the road at this location.

An older satellite image from 1997 (closer to the time of the murders) is used to determine the murder location based on these clues.

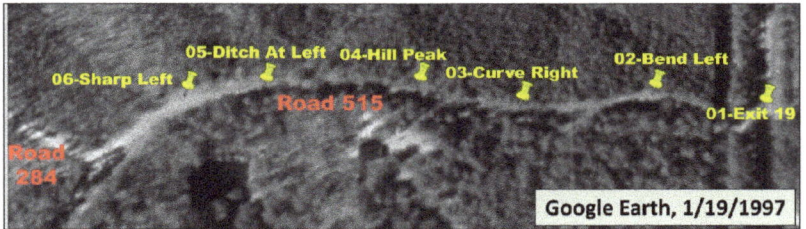

Rock Cut Road to the West of Highway 19

Yellow pins are used to identify the indicated clues. Location 2 is the bend to the left. A curve to the right is that location 3. At location 5, the road reaches the top of the hill. A sharp curve to the left is seen at location 6. Road 284 appears beyond these locations. Location 5 identifies the ditch at the left of the road in which the bodies initially fell.

Verification that location 4 is actually the top of the hill is accomplished using the Google Earth elevation tool.

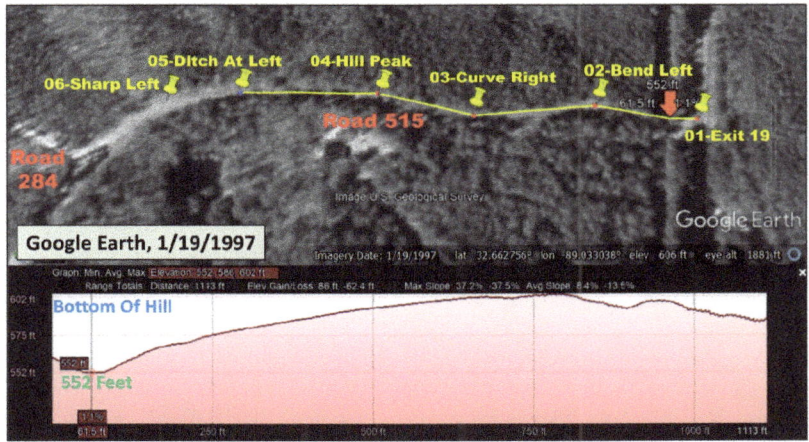

Elevation Evaluation at the Base of the Hill

A red arrow indicates the location at which the elevation above sea level is defined. This arrow is placed at the base of the hill just after the entrance from Road 515. At this location, the height is 552 feet.

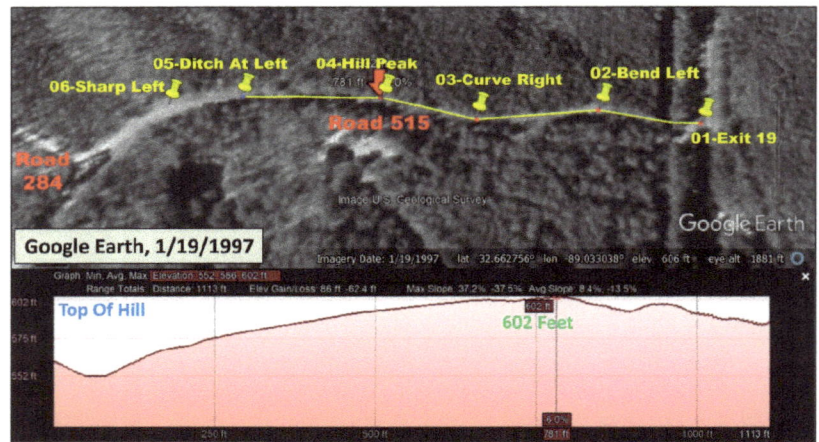

Elevation Evaluation at the Top of the Hill

Now, the red arrow has been moved to the top of the hill. At this location, the elevation is 602 feet. A difference of 50 feet indicates that a small hill is encountered at this location.

Using Google Maps, the distance from Highway 19 to the location of the ditch on the left side of the road can be determined.

Measured Distance from Highway 19 to the Murder Location

This distance is 350 yards, satisfying the clue that the murder location is at least 300 yards west of the intersection with Highway 19.

After each person was shot, the body fell into a ditch on the left side of the road. This location has a large ditch on the left side of the road.

Identifying Ditch On Left Side Of Road At Murder Location

A rod and plumb line were used to determine the depth of the ditch at the left side of the ditch. A rod is extended straight out, parallel to the road (left hand). A path is extended out visually from the rod where a plumb line was dropped vertically to the bottom of the ditch. The distance from the visual extension of the parallel rod down to the bottom of the ditch was measured to be 4 feet. A second measurement from the left shoulder to the top of the plumb line was measured to be 8.5 feet. Using these distances, the angle of the side of the ditch was computed to be 25°. [$\tan(\Theta) = 4/8.5$].

After the measurements were taken, a second rod was held in the right hand and positioned approximately parallel to the side of the ditch. This rod gives a visual impression of the depth of the ditch.

This murder location is before the intersection between Road 515 and Road 284, not at the intersection of the 2 roads.

Distance From Murder Location To Road 284

The murder location is 118 yards northeast from the intersection.

The location at which the ditch on the left side of the road is identified satisfies all of the criteria to be deemed the location of the murders.

Location Of Murders: 32.66214,-89.03410

Escape Route To The Burial Location

Once Schwerner, Chaney and Goodman had been murdered, the bodies were thrown into the Ranch Wagon. A caravan of vehicles then drove through back roads to the burial location on Old Jolly Farm. The escape route for the caravan began at the murder location. This route exited Road 365 on Highway 21 south of the entrance to the dam at Old Jolly Farm.

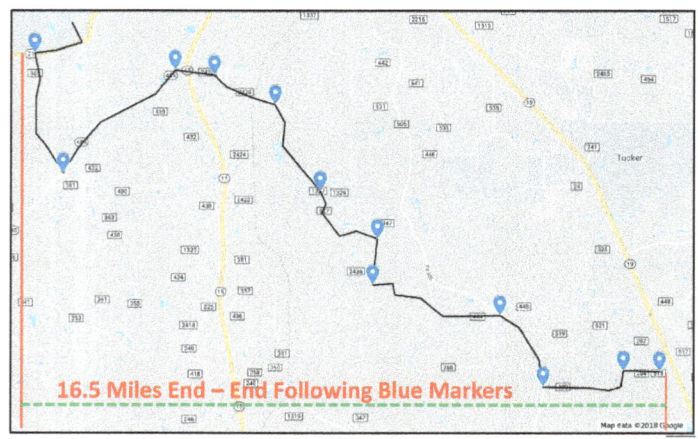

Most Likely Escape Route to the Burial Location

A number of possible cross-country escape routes exist between the start and end locations. This route appears to follow the shortest possible distance from Road 515 to the exit of Road 365 on the Highway 21. Each blue marker represents a location involving a left or right turn.

The perpetrators were in a hurry to dump the bodies and the Ranch Wagon. Participating members lived in the area and knew these back roads intimately. A route that minimized the amount of time to a burial location for the bodies was easily preplanned. While many of these roads are paved now, most were unpaved back in 1964. In order to navigate these roads in the dark and arrive at a desired location, the driver needed to know these roads well.

This map yields a series of left and right turns at various roads between the murder location on Road 515 and exiting Road 365 on Highway 21.

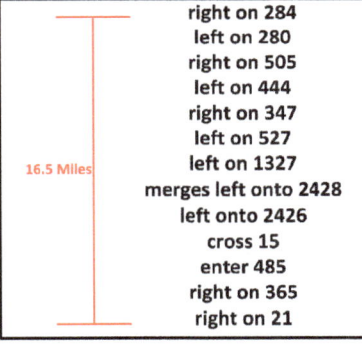

Shortest Cross-Country Route From Road 515 To Highway 21

This route is used for the visual reconstruction. However, one section of the roads no longer exists. A Google Maps satellite view identifies the section of the route that no longer exists.

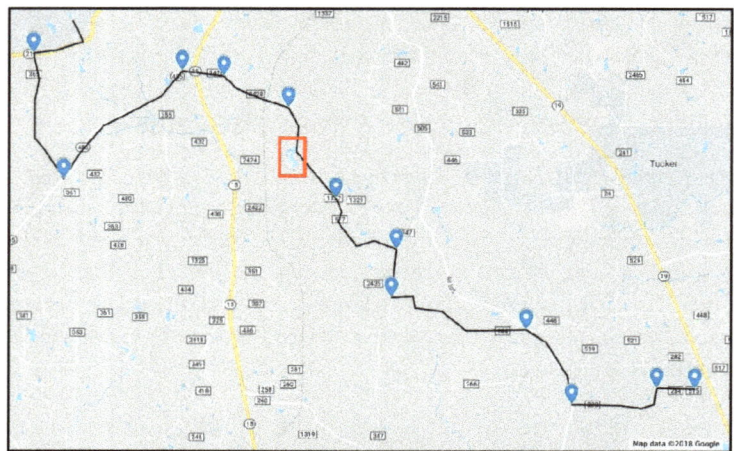
Section Of Escape Route That No Longer Exists

The road actually disappears when the section in the red box is approached. This missing portion of the road did not interfere with collecting photographs for the visual reconstruction of the escape route.

Enough portions of the route do exist that collecting photographs for the visual reconstruction was easily accomplished.

Entry Location To The Dam

The bodies of Schwerner, Chaney and Goodman were buried in a dam on Old Jolly Farm. Finding the entrance to the dam was a fairly simple task.

A right turn was taken as the caravan exited from Road 365 onto Highway 21. About 3/4 of a mile past Road 365, a dirt road on the left or west side of the Highway was the entrance into the area where the dam is located.

These conditions are located on a Google Maps satellite view. A red rectangle on the left indicates the exit location from Road 365 onto Highway 21. Another red rectangle on the right identifies the exit road on the left or west side of the Highway.

Route Along Highway 21 to Entrance to the Dam

Using the Google Maps measurement tool, the distance between these two locations is 0.73 miles.

A triangle characterizes the entry area to the dam. Using a satellite photo of this area from an earlier time, this area is confirmed as the entry location to the dam.

Entrance Area Leading to Dam

This image was taken before the area became so totally overgrown. At the lower right of this satellite image is the entrance location at the upper vertex of the triangle. A dirt road leads from this entrance location all the way to the middle of the dam.

Entrance To Burial Location: 32.734640, -89.183410

Bulldozer Operator Pickup Location

After the caravan of vehicles with the bodies arrived at the location of the dam, various people were dropped at locations in the area. A short drive was taken to retrieve the bulldozer operator.

Drive To Retrieve Bulldozer Operator

Bulldozer operator Herman Tucker was waiting 1 mile north of the entrance to the area of the dam along Highway 21. Both the entrance to the dam and the operator location are indicated on this Google Maps satellite view. A location 1 mile north along Highway 21 is determined using the Google Maps measurement tool.

Bulldozer Operator Pickup Location: 32.747558, -89.177210

Bulldozer Operator Dropoff Location

After the operator was retrieved on Highway 21, he was driven west on a dirt road. An undeveloped field allowed an easy walk from the dirt road down to the burial location at the partially completed dam.

During the investigation, an FBI map was drawn that shows this activity.

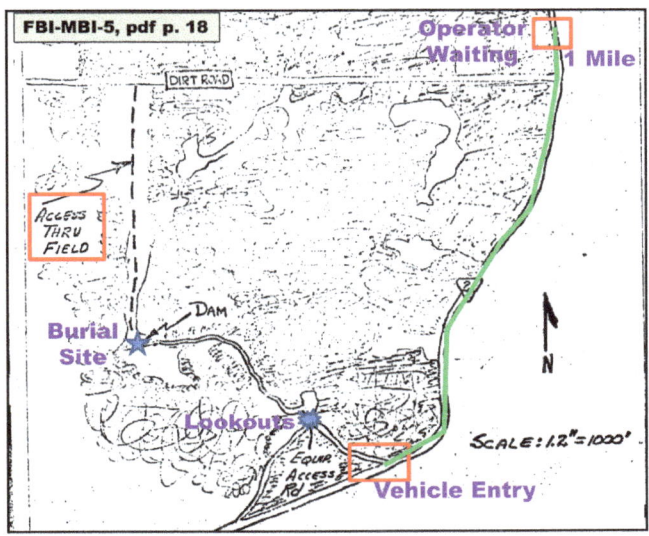

Delivery of Bulldozer Operator to Burial Site

The bulldozer operator was dropped approximately directly north of the burial site. An older Google Earth satellite image shows the drop-off location for the bulldozer operator.

Bulldozer Operator Drop-off Location and Path to Burial Site

Google Earth measurement tool was used to determine the distance from the drop-off location to the burial site. This distance was slightly less than half mile (0.473 miles).

Bulldozer Operator Dropoff Location: 32.746676, -89.192021

Burial Site Location

A simple diagram of the burial location was created by the FBI when the bodies were uncovered. This diagram clearly identifies the location of the bodies in the earthen dam.

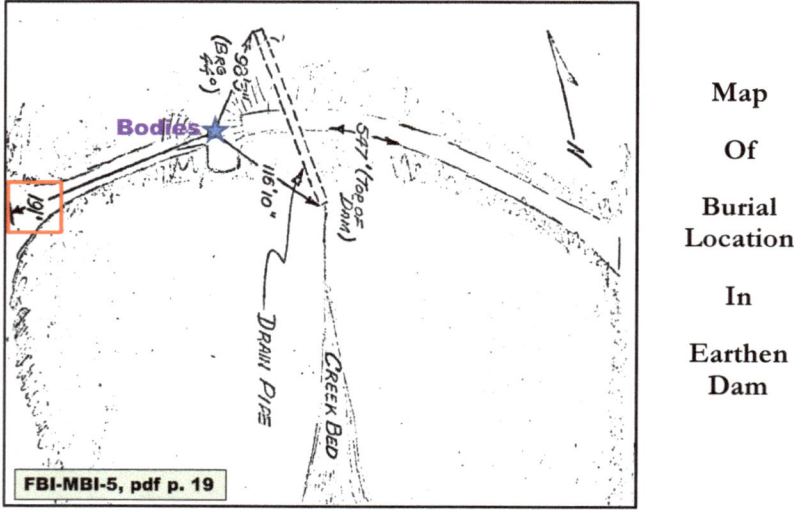

Map Of Burial Location In Earthen Dam

According to measurements taken by the FBI, the bodies were uncovered 191 feet from the west end of the dam.

An older satellite view from Google Earth is used to find this location.

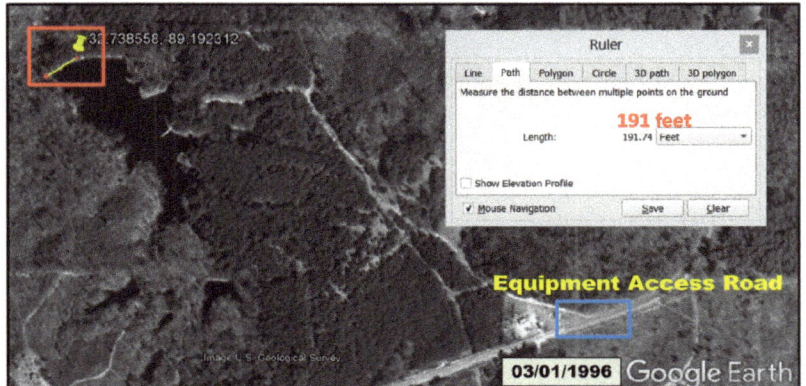

Burial Location at Time of Discovery of the Bodies

Unfortunately, this location was inaccessible. The dam and its pond are on private property. However, an excellent and clear photograph of the dam at the burial location was taken by the FBI at the time the bodies were discovered.

Burial Location 191 Feet from West End of Earthen Dam

This photograph has been annotated indicating approximately 191 feet from the west end of the earthen dam. This annotated photograph will be used for purposes of generating the visual reconstruction of events on the day of the murders.

Body Burial Location: 32.738558,-89.192312

Burrage Trucking Company Location

Now that the bodies were buried, the Klansmen had to dispose of the Ranch Wagon driven by the trio. Herman Tucker, who had operated the bulldozer, was to dispose of the Wagon across the border in AL. A second vehicle had to accompany the Ranch Wagon to return the driver after the Ranch Wagon was disposed.

An escort vehicle and driver were to be obtained from: Burrage at his Trucking Company. This company was located 1 ½ miles west of Williamsville, MS. Olen Burrage lived in a house across the street. Burrage was also a Deacon of the Fellowship Baptist Church, built near the Trucking Company.

Using Google Maps satellite view and the location information above, the location of the garage itself was found.

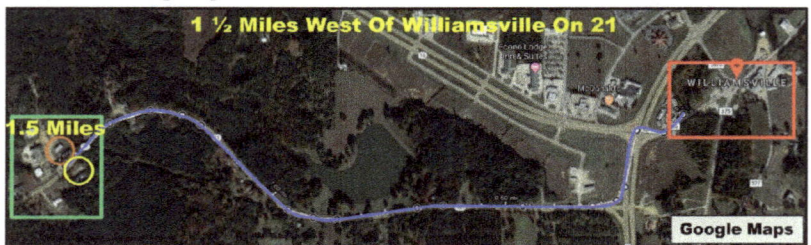

Location of Garage 1 ½ Miles West of Williamsville

Williamsville is identified by the red rectangle in the upper right corner of the satellite view. A green rectangle in the lower left corner indicates the location of the garage and the home of Olen Burrage in 1964. The orange circle is the location of the original garage operated by Burrage. Across Highway 21 is a yellow circle that locates his home at the time. A blue curve traces the path along Highway 21 between Williamsville and the Burrage property. This distance is 1 ½ miles according to the Google Maps measurement tool.

Zooming into the satellite view inside the green rectangle gives more insight into the layout of the buildings.

Layout Of Buildings In The Area Of Burrage Trucking Company

In 1964, the original Burrage trucking company was in the building area just behind the Heartfelt Hospice. Just across the street from the garage was the home of Olen Burrage. Burrage was able to grow his Trucking Company into one of the largest trucking companies in the area. As his business grew, Burrage grew the Trucking Company facilities to its current size. He also replaced the original home across the street with a modern, brick building commensurate with the wealth of the owner of a successful business Ultimately, Burrage sold the Trucking Company.

A caravan of three vehicles drove from the burial location to the Burrage Trucking Company. A single road was involved – – Highway 21.

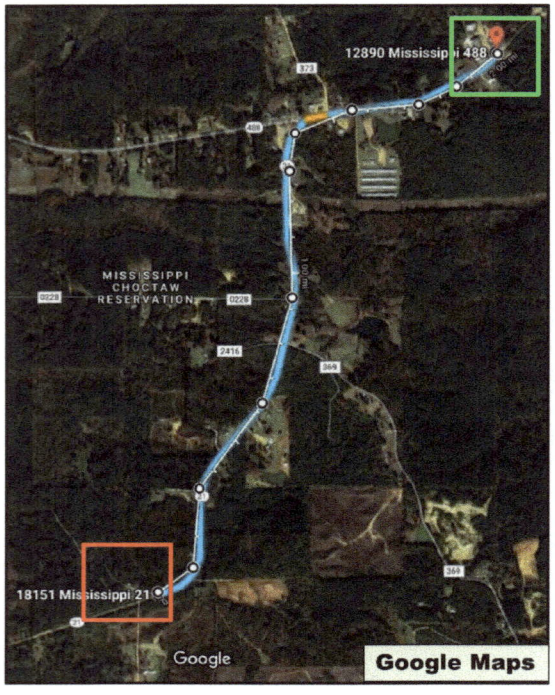

Route from Burial Location To Burrage Garage

Using the Google Maps measurement tool, the distance between the entry to the burial location and the Burrage Trucking Company is only 2 miles. This drive occurred early in the morning on Sunday, June 22, 1964. At this time, Highway 21 was totally deserted. A short drive along a deserted, well paved highway at that time did not take a long time.

Another interesting fact is revealed by this map. Herman Tucker, the bulldozer operator, was staged 1 mile from the entry to the burial site. This location was exactly ½ the distance between the burial site and the Burrage Trucking Company. Both the location of Tucker and his employment by Burrage clearly indicate that the kidnapping, murder, burial, and disposal of the vehicle were all premeditated. Once the Klansmen were activated, further phone conversation was not possible. Cell phones did not exist back in 1964. So, all of the locations and people involved had to be pre-determined.

Recruiting Herman Tucker and arrangement of the burial and meeting locations had been preplanned. Moreover, the common element between the burial location, the meeting location for Tucker, the Trucking Company for retrieving the escort vehicle was Olen Burrage. Furthermore, Burrage himself drove the escort vehicle. Despite his denials, Burrage was a key planner in the murders, the burial, and the disposal of the vehicle on the other side of Neshoba County.

Burrage Trucking Company Location: 32.756556,-89.167893

Ranch Wagon Disposal Location

A smaller caravan departed the Burrage Trucking Company to a disposal location for the Ranch Wagon on the other side of Neshoba County. This smaller caravan consisted of the Ranch Wagon and a truck escort to return the driver of the Ranch Wagon to Philadelphia after disposal.

Originally, the plan was for Herman Tucker, who had operated the bulldozer, to dispose of the Wagon across the border in AL. However, Tucker decided to dispose the Wagon on the opposite side of Neshoba County, for some unknown reason.

The burned-up Ranch Wagon was found just off Highway 21 about 1.1 miles past the intersection of Highway 21 North and Road 491. This location is easily found using Google Maps satellite views.

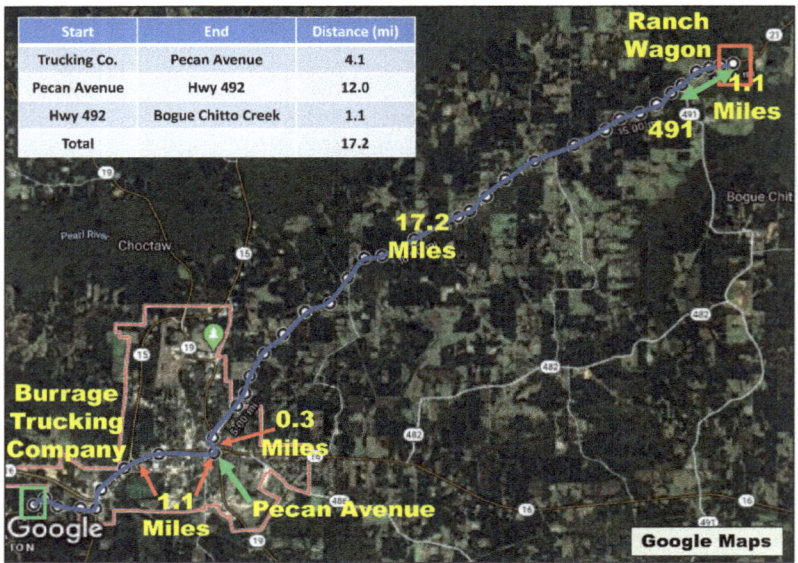

Route from Trucking Company to Vehicle Location

The intersection of Highway 21 and Road 491 is indicated in the upper right corner of this satellite view. A green, double-headed arrow shows the location 1.1 miles from the intersection. At the upper end of the arrow is a red rectangle. This rectangle identifies the location at which the burned – up Ranch Wagon was found.

A green rectangle in the lower left corner shows the location of Burrage Trucking Company. Using a blue line, a path of roads is drawn that connects the Trucking Company with the location of the burned-up vehicle. According to the Google Maps measurement tool, the distance between the Trucking Company and the vehicle location is 17.2 miles. All of the roads between the two locations were nicely paved. This route was traveled early in the morning on Sunday, June 22, 1964. All of the roads were empty at the time.

Several important sections of this route are shown on the map. One section shows the distance between the merge into Main Street and the turn onto Pecan Avenue. This distance is 1.1 miles. Another section is the distance between the turn onto Pecan Avenue and the merge onto Highway 21 north. This shorter distance is only 0.3 miles. These two sections totaling 1.4 miles are within the settled area of Philadelphia. Within these sections, the Ranch Wagon might have been spotted by residents. The combined sections represented the greatest risk to the perpetrators on that night. Since this route was traveled early in the morning, risk of exposure was exceptionally low.

Zooming into the upper right corner of the satellite view verifies the distance between the intersection of Highway 21 and Road 491 and the burned vehicle location.

Route Between The Intersection Of Road 491, Wagon Location

The actual intersection is located in the lower left corner and identified using a green rectangle. Ranch Wagon location is in the upper right corner, surrounded by a red rectangle. Using the Google Maps measurement tool, the distance between the two locations is determined to be 1.1 miles.

Additional details are available from the FBI files that more precisely identify the location of the burned-up vehicle. The vehicle was found off the road beyond the bridge that crossed Bogue Chitto Creek.

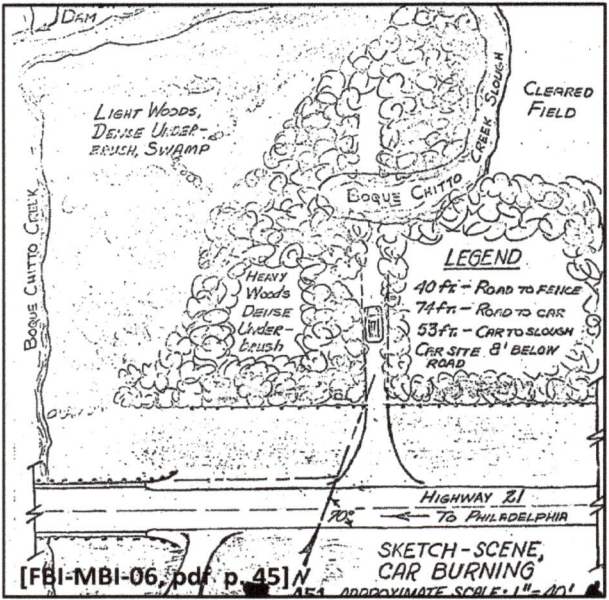

Vehicle Location Past the Bridge over Bogue Chitto Creek

Bogue Chitto Creek is on the left side of the diagram. The bridge is represented in the lower left corner of the diagram.

As this diagram shows, the burned-up Ranch Wagon was found 74 feet from the edge of the road inside the wooded area. Additionally, the vehicle was found 112 feet from the front edge of the bridge.

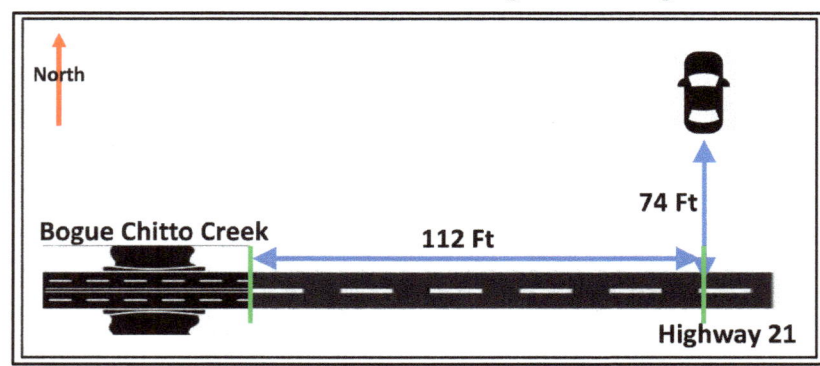

Location of Burned up Vehicle from Bogue Chitto Creek Bridge

Another Google Maps satellite view is used to find this actual location relative to the bridge across the Creek.

Location from Bridge to Burned-Up Vehicle Location

A green line marks the edge of the bridge on the north side of Highway 21. Moving 112 feet to the east shows where the Ranch Wagon was driven off Highway 21. At the time the vehicle was abandoned, the area off the Highway at this location was densely overgrown. Now, however, this area is cleared from the road out to 190 feet from the road.

A close-up view of this location 112 feet from the bridge reveals an interesting feature.

Ranch Wagon Exit Location from Highway 21 Today

An exit to nowhere has been paved. Perhaps this exit was paved to preserve the location for Civil Rights history tours that have been conducted from time to time.

Ranch Wagon Disposal Location: 32.881639,-88.938096

Conclusions

A total of 35 locations were involved in the murders of Schwerner, Chaney and Goodman on June 21, 1964. Some of these locations have been lost over the years. Using clues from the confessions, FBI photos taken during the investigation, trial testimonies, Google Maps and Google Earth, exact latitudes and longitudes have been determined for these lost locations.

An appendix contains all 35 locations, including those locations in this section, and a precise latitude and longitude for each location.

Murder Sequence Specification

Confessions by White Knight Klansmen Doyle Barnette and Jim Jordan provide extensive details into the murders of Schwerner, Chaney and Goodman. An extensive forensic analysis provided additional details. Using all of this information enables generation of a specific step-by-step sequence of activities involved in each murder on Rock Cut Road.

Each murder can be characterized as a series of step-by-step actions. Every action involves shooters and/or victims. Actions also involve exiting from vehicles and movements from one location to another.

Vehicle Placement Locations

Actions at the murder site on Rock Cut Road (Road 515) involved removing victims from vehicles. Location of the vehicles was well described in the confessions by Jim Jordan and Doyle Barnette.

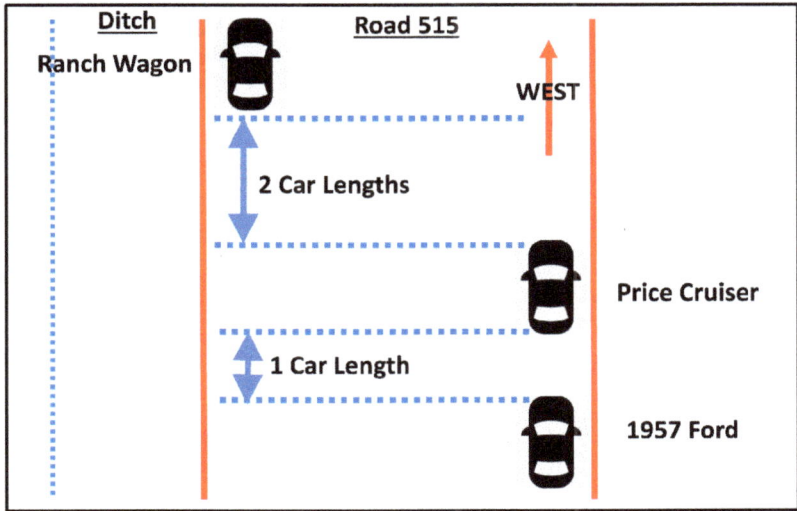

Location and Separation of Vehicles at Murder Location

Deputy Sheriff Cecil Price parked his Cruiser on the right side of Rock Cut Road. Jimmy Arledge drove past the Cruiser. Arledge parked the Ranch Wagon on the left side of the road, 2 car lengths in front of the

Price Cruiser. Doyle Barnette parked the 1957 Ford 1 car length behind the Price Cruiser. A ditch was on the left side of the road.

Murder of Mickey Schwerner

The first murder performed on Rock cut Road was the murder of Mickey Schwerner. Wayne Roberts committed this murder.

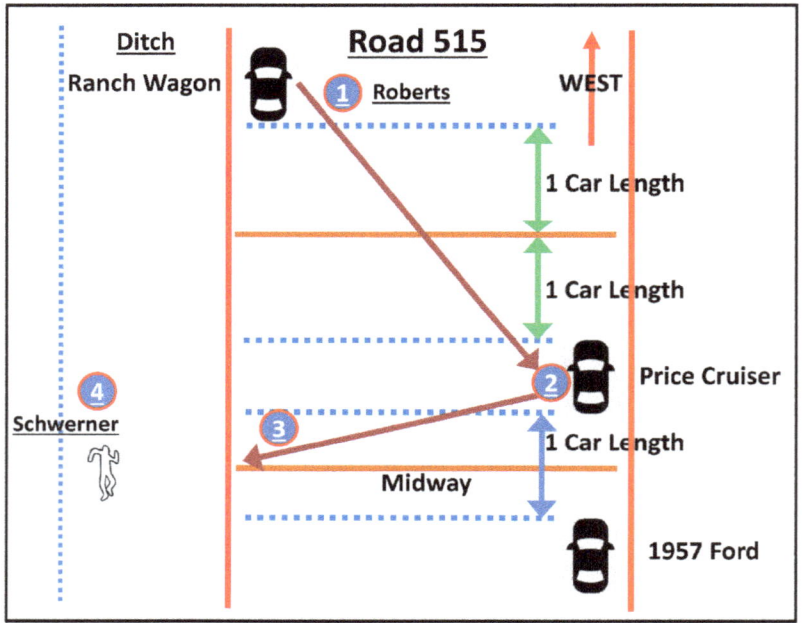

Actions in the Murder of Mickey Schwerner

Numbers in the diagram indicate the sequence in which the actions occurred in the murder of Mickey Schwerner.

1. Wayne Roberts exited the Ranch Wagon.
2. Roberts retrieved Mickey Schwerner from the Price Cruiser.
3. Roberts escorted Schwerner to the other side of the road, midway between the Price Cruiser and the 1957 Ford.
   Roberts shot Mickey Schwerner in the chest.
4. Schwerner fell into the ditch face down, headed west, parallel to the road.

While lying in the ditch, Mickey Schwerner bled to death. Bleeding to death took from 10 to 16 seconds.

Murder of Andy Goodman

After murdering Mickey Schwerner, Wayne Roberts proceeded to murder Andy Goodman.

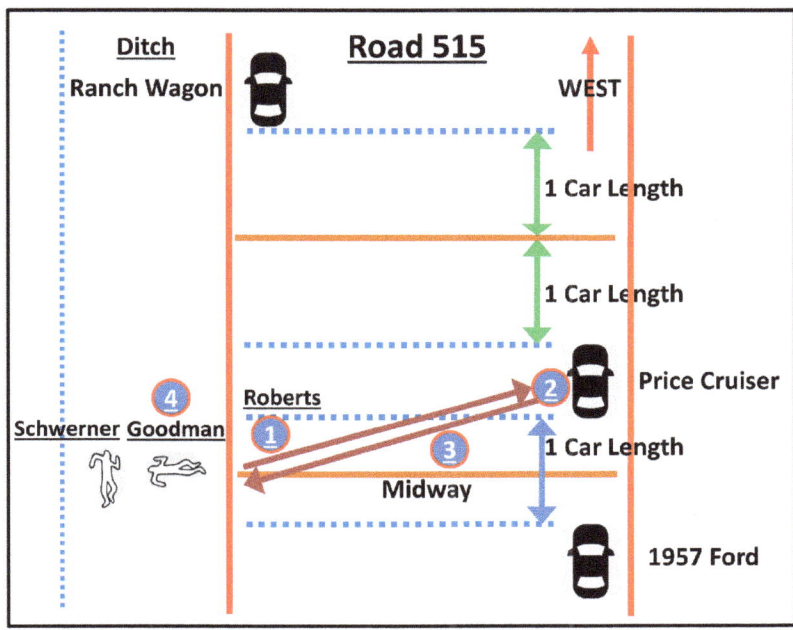

Actions in the Murder of Andy Goodman

Numbers in the diagram indicate the sequence in which the actions occurred in the murder of Andy Goodman.

1. Wayne Roberts crossed back over to the Price Cruiser.
2. Roberts retrieved Andy Goodman from the Price Cruiser.
3. Roberts escorted Goodman to the other side of the road, also midway between the Price Cruiser and the 1957 Ford.
   Roberts shot Andy Goodman in the chest.
4. Goodman fell into the ditch face down in a crumpled position, headed south, perpendicular to the road.

While lying in the ditch, Andy Goodman bled to death. Bleeding to death took from 10 to 16 seconds.

Murder of James Chaney

James Chaney watched his friends being murdered from inside the Price Cruiser. His turn to die was next.

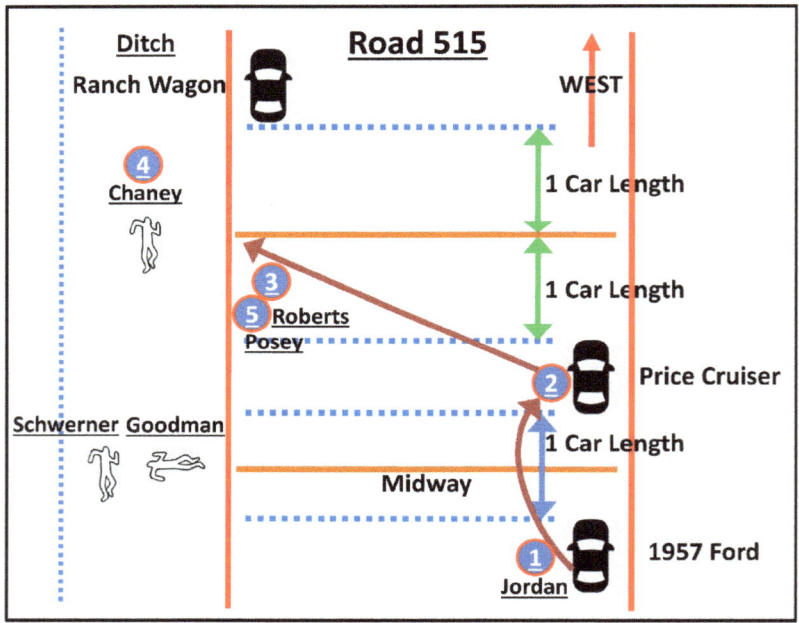

Actions in the Murder of Jim Chaney

Numbers in the diagram indicate the sequence in which the actions occurred in the murder of James Chaney.

1. James Jordan exited the 1957 Ford.
2. Jordan retrieved James Chaney from the Price Cruiser.
3. Jordan escorted Chaney to the other side of the road, one car length behind the Ranch Wagon.
   Jordan shot James Chaney in the back of the head.
4. Chaney fell into the ditch face up, headed west, parallel to the road.

5. In a frenzy of racist hatred, Wayne Roberts and Billy Posey moved to the edge of the ditch. Each of the Klansmen shot several rounds into James Chaney.

James Chaney died instantly from the shot to the back of the head. Additional shots into the body by Roberts and Posey were unnecessary and especially vicious.

Conclusions

Mickey Schwerner was murdered first by Wayne Roberts. Andy Goodman was murdered second by Wayne Roberts. James Chaney was murdered last by Jim Jordan. Posey and Roberts discharged additional bullets into the dead body of James Chaney.

Part 6: Detailed Shooting Incident Reconstruction

Perform A Forensic Reconstruction Of The Day

Answer Who, What, When, Where, How, Why

Take A Visual Tour Of 35 Locations Involved

See The Activities That Occurred At Each Location

Review Exact Exhibits Used By An Expert In A Trial

Visual Reconstruction Prerequisites

A visual reconstruction consists of a series of images or frames that explain an incident over a period of time Each image combines places, people, objects, actions and times in the order of occurrence. This reconstruction forms a movie on the written page.

This specific reconstruction is organized around a set of 35 locations that were involved in the murders of Schwerner, Chaney and Goodman on June 21, 1964. Each image in the reconstruction involves a specific location. At each location, the image shows people who were involved, vehicles used to move between locations, and the actions performed.

These images are exactly the images that would be used by the author, a reconstruction expert, in a trial involving murder. Every element must be based on actual evidence: science, math, physical evidence, witness testimony and experiments. Much of the information used in these images appears in the historical sections or previous forensic sections. Therefore, footnotes are not repeated again. Additional details, such as a detailed timeline and medical information about the body responses to fear from threats of violence, are introduced where needed.

This section does more than simply repeat the basic facts shown in the historical and forensic sections. Extensive additional insight is provided when various activities are discussed. An important objective is to put you in the moment, both visually and psychologically. Most of these activities took place late at night in the deep, dark roads of rural MS. A gang of thugs bearing down on the trio under cover of darkness is horrific. A sworn law enforcement officer using his legal authority to kidnap and to drive the trio to their deaths adds significantly to the horror.

In the end, extensive evidence, some factual, some circumstantial, leads to an inevitable conclusion. These murders were planned in great detail. Intent to commit murder was always part of that plan.

Murder convictions were never obtained for the cruel deaths!

In 2005, a Neshoba County Jury failed miserably to do its job. Members of the jury returned manslaughter convictions, claiming that intent was not provable. Given the complexity of these murders, intent was obvious.

Data Collection Notes

Each image in a reconstruction must realistically represent the situation. An image in a visual reconstruction has a background. Figures for people and objects are placed on the background. Sequences of actions are labelled. Realism is best obtained if the background is a photograph of the actual location.

On October 31, 2018, the author spent the day in Philadelphia, MS. He was accompanied by Matt Krell, his nephew. During the day, 33 of the identified 35 locations were visited. Since the burial location was on private land, this location was not visited. A visit was also not made to the location of the COFO HQ in Meridian. A total of 403 photographs were taken at these 33 locations. Arrival and departure times were recorded at every location for use in timeline reconstruction.

At least one photograph by the author is used as a background at each of the 33 visited locations. 60% of the photographs used in the visual reconstruction were actually taken by the author at these locations. Sometimes additional photographs were needed to establish a particular perspective at a location. Additional photographs were used from Google Maps, Street views. These additional photographs comprise about 40% of the backgrounds in the visual reconstruction.

Any photograph taken by the author is presented without a source annotation. These photographs belong to the author. All photographs used from Google Maps, Street views are clearly annotated, generally inside the photograph.

Vehicle and Passenger Lists

From a reconstruction perspective, the murders of Schwerner, Chaney and Goodman are complicated. On the day of the murders, 19 people, 8 vehicles and 35 locations were involved. Participants changed vehicles at various times depending upon who was doing what, where, and when.

Effectively tracking all of this activity requires a certain amount of organization. Two lists were created, one for vehicles and another for passengers. Each entry in the list was given an identifier for use as a reference to the list entry during the visual reconstruction.

A vehicle list contains all of the information regarding each of the vehicles involved on the day of the murders.

	ID	Year	Make	Model	Color	Owner
	V1	1963	Ford	Fairlane Ranch Wagon	Medium Blue Metallic	CORE
	V2	1956	Chevy	Bel Air	Two Tone Blue	Price/NCSD
	V3	1957	Ford	Fairlane 500 Sedan	Two Tone Blue	Barnette
	V4	1956	Chevy	Bel Air	Red and White	Posey
	V5	1955	Chevy	Bel Air	Green and White	Tucker
	V6	1962	Pontiac	Catalina (NBC Video)	White (6/28/1964)	Poe, Wiggs
	V7	?	Diesel	Escort Truck	? (Used 10' Freight)	Burrage
	V8	1959	Chevy	Bel Air	Gray and White	Sharpe
	V9	1957	Chevy	Bel Air	Black and White	Willis/PPD

Vehicle List Used During Visual Reconstruction

Appearing in the first column is a picture of the vehicle that is used in the visual reconstruction. These pictures exactly match the descriptive information in the remainder of the list. Each vehicle is characterized by an ID, year, make, model, color, and owner. When a picture of a vehicle is used in the visual reconstruction, the ID is given to link the picture to the descriptive information in this list.

These descriptions were collected from the history of the events on the day of the murders. For the most part, pictures of the actual vehicles do not exist. Black-and-white photos of the burned-out Ranch Wagon are in black and white. An actual black and white NBC video on June 28, 1964, shows the Pontiac Catalinas driven by the Mississippi Highway Patrol at the time. Google web searches were conducted to find images of vehicles that match the descriptions. Images found in the Google search appear in the list and are used in the visual reconstruction.

As the murder activities moved from place to place, the Klan perpetrators moved among the vehicles. A master passenger list was created to easily track the passengers in any vehicle at any time.

Location	PID	Vehicle	VID	Passengers				
Several Locations	P01	1963 Ford Ranch Wagon	V1	Schwerner	Chaney	Goodman		
To Jail	P02	1963 Ford Ranch Wagon	V1	Wiggs	Chaney			
	P03	1956 Chevy Cruiser	V2	Price				
	P04	1962 Pontiac Catalina	V6	Poe	Schwerner	Goodman		
To Longhorn Drive-In	P05	1959 Chevy Bel Air	V8	Killen	Sharpe	Townsend		
To Akins	P06	Unknown	?	Killen	Townsend	Herndon	Harris	
	P07	1957 Ford Fairlane	V3	D Barnette	Arledge			
To Roberts/To Akins	P08	1959 Chevy Bel Air	V8	Sharpe	Jordan	Roberts		
To Jail, West Side Of CH	P09	1959 Chevy Bel Air	V8	Sharpe	Killen	Roberts	Townsend	
To West Side Of CH	P10	1957 Ford Fairlane	V3	D Barnette	Jordan	T Barnette	Arledge	Snowden

Portion Of Passenger List Used During Visual Reconstruction

A portion of the passenger list appears above. The complete list is contained in the appendices.

Each entry in the list begins with the location at which the passengers enter a specific vehicle. An ID is associated with the passenger list entry for reference within the visual reconstruction. A cross-link to the vehicle list appears next. Finally, the list of passengers is provided.

Entry one (P01) states that Schwerner, Chaney and Goodman entered the Ranch Wagon (V1) at multiple locations. Any location at which Schwerner, Chaney and Goodman enter V1 will be identified as containing passenger list P01.

Annotation And Interpretation

Almost all of the frames in the visual reconstruction include pictures of vehicles. An important aspect of the reconstruction is identification of which persons were in which vehicles at the time of the frame. Annotating a frame with multiple vehicles to indicate the specific vehicle and passengers can very quickly clutter the frame. Too much clutter reduces understanding.

An annotation scheme that minimizes clutter was created to enable identification of a vehicles and its passengers within a frame.

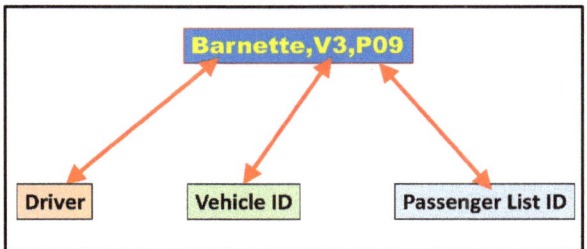

Vehicle Annotation Scheme Used To Minimize Clutter

Each annotation contains 3 entries. A Driver is identified. An identifier provides a link into the Vehicle List. Another identifier gives a link into the Passenger List. These identifiers can be used to consult the two lists to determine the vehicle and the passenger details.

Additional annotations can be seen in some of the frames. When a set of passengers enters a vehicle for the first time, the passenger list for that vehicle is repeated in the frame, generally at the top of the frame. Absence of a passenger list in a frame indicates that the driver and the passenger have not changed. This repeated passenger list annotation saves the effort of continually having to flip back to the Appendix to see the identities of the passengers.

Some frames include annotations that give the date and time of a specific activity.

Annotations labeled A – H appear in some frames. These letters refer to locations identified in the corrected FBI Map in the section on Location Identification.

Other annotations appear as the number 1 – 35. These numbers refer to the total List of Locations Identified that appears in the Appendix. After each number, the latitude and longitude are provided. Therefore, referring to the Appendix may be unnecessary.

Difference Between Night And Day

A large percentage of events on the day of the murders were at night. In the interest of clarity, these events are presented as if during daylight.

Several of the events were already shown under night conditions in the forensic analysis. Those events dealt with specific issues around lighting conditions during the actual murders on Rock Cut Road. In those events, the amount of light was an important issue. Therefore, showing darkened frames made sense in order to clarify the effect of the amount of light.

When a short sequence of events in the reconstruction begins, a time is always given. A sense of the amount of darkness can be based on the time and the location. For instance, the cross-country travel from the murder location to the burial location was between 11:45 pm – 12:45 am. This travel was through remote country roads completely without light. Based on that information, a reader can imagine how frightening that situation must have been.

Just to be sure, lighting conditions are described when appropriate, despite showing the frames as if during full daylight. In 1 situation, both the night and the daylight version of the situation are presented. During this activity, light conditions were an issue.

On the night of June 21, 1964, the moon was quite bright. On that night, the moon was in a waxing gibbous phase. In that phase, 89% of the surface of the moon is visible.[1] Often, that percentage can mean that night appears almost as bright as daylight.

But the bright moon did not have such an effect on Highway 19 south at the time and location where Cecil Price overtook the trio before the 2nd arrest.

According to a satellite image taken on January 1, 1997, that area was hugely overgrown with dense forest.

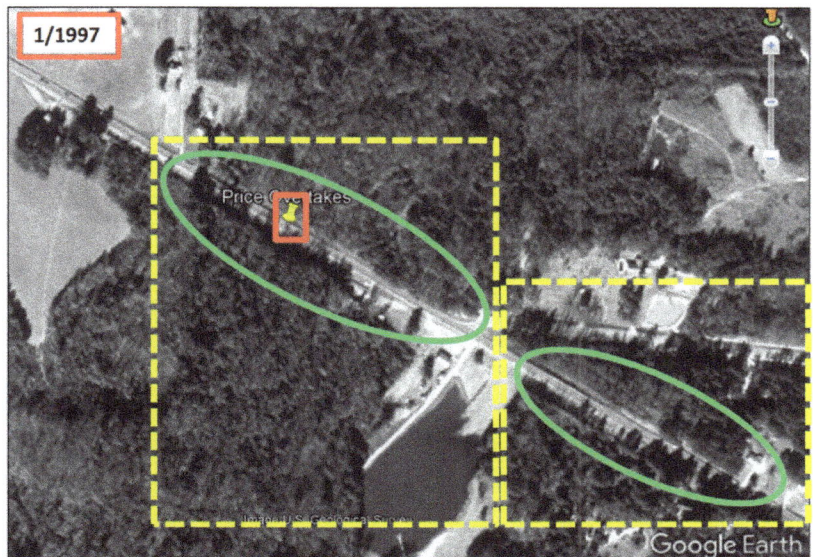

Forest Growth In Overtake Area of Highway 19 In 1997

A red box identifies the location ½ mile north of House, MS, where Price overtook the trio on Highway 19 south before the high-speed chase. Dashed yellow rectangles indicate the overgrown forest areas in 1997. Overgrowth inside the green ovals shows that the dense forest actually extends over and above the road. In 1964, this dense overgrowth was even worse. This dense overgrowth above the road combined with the complete absence of ambient background light (as seen in big cities) has an effect. These road sections are almost completely dark, even in full moonlight. So, the waxing gibbous phase moon did not brighten the very dark rural road on June 21, 1964.

Anyone who has experienced being chased knows the response to unknown threats. A significant increase in heart rate results from the increase in adrenaline levels in the body. Tunnel vision narrows your visual field of view and focus, increasing the apparent darkness level of the surrounding environment. These physiological effects of being chased (or of being subjected to any threat) have been medically well documented.[2] Deputy Sheriff Cecil Price appeared out of nowhere in the very dark night conditions on Highway 19 south. These physiological responses were experienced by Schwerner, Chaney and Goodman.

Already dark conditions became even more dark due to tunnel vision induced by the threat of being arrested again.

On a personal note, this author spent 18 years in MS, 6 years in LA, and 3 1/2 years in Texas. During that time, I traveled down many very remote country roads. Those 18 years in MS were at the time in which the murders of Schwerner, Chaney and Goodman took place. Dark, remote country roads are fearful, especially when you know the White Knights can emerge from any corner.

Role Of Radio Communications

At various times within the visual reconstruction, radio communications are discussed. These communications are among the Neshoba County Sheriff's Cruisers, the MS Highway Patrol Cruisers, and the Philadelphia Police Department Cruisers. Claiming that these communications did occur by radio is very reasonable for a number of reasons.

Evidence exists that at least one of these conversations did happen. At the first arrest of Schwerner, Chaney and Goodman, Deputy Sheriff Cecil Price transmitted a radio request to MS Highway Patrol Officers Harry Wiggs and Earl Poe. This request was for the Patrol officers to escort the trio to the Neshoba County Jail.

Law enforcement agencies then and now share common radio frequencies. Certain frequencies are allocated and restricted for use by public safety agencies by the Federal Communications Commission.

These frequencies are as follows:

Low VHF	25 – 50 MHz
High VHF	150 – 174 MHz
Low UHF	450 – 470 MHz
UHF TV Sharing	470 – 512 MHz
800 MHz	806 – 869 MHz.[3]

All federal, state, county, city agencies share these frequencies. Any agency is free to talk or to listen to other agencies on these frequencies.

Then and now, mobile radios are essential equipment for field units. Communications between command stations and patrol officers could only be accomplished by mobile radios in cruisers at the time of the murders. These radios accessed the frequencies above for all agencies.

An example of the type of radio in a law enforcement cruiser back in 1964 is the Motorola MOTRAC mobile radio.

Motorola Motrac Mobile Radio Mounted In A Police Cruiser

In 1958, Motorola introduced the Motrac radio. This radio was the first vehicular two-way radio with a fully transistorized power supply and receiver in the world. Use of transistors allowed the radio to operate at very low power levels. Its low power use enabled the radio to transmit without running the engine of the vehicle. As a result of this feature, the radio was extremely popular with law enforcement agencies.[4]

During specific events of this reconstruction, some radio communications are indicated. When radio communications are indicated, these events could only have happened if radio communications took place. Times between events were just too short to have happened without radio communications between officers of the 3 law enforcement agencies involved.

Philadelphia Police Cruiser Representation

Philadelphia Police Officer Richard Willis played a small but important role in the murders. Officer Willis in his police cruiser accompanied Deputy Sheriff Price when Price escorted Schwerner, Chaney and Goodman to the Philadelphia city limit. Willis then drove to the staging location of the White Knights next to the manufacturing plant on Oak Street. He informed the Klansmen that the trio had been released and were headed south on Highway 19.

Records do not indicate the make, model, year, and coloring of the Philadelphia Police Department Cruiser in 1964. At the time, one of the most popular Police Department cruisers was the 1957 Chevrolet Bel Air Model 150 with a powerful 283 cubic inch V-8 engine.[5]

1957 Chevrolet Bel Air Model 150 Police Cruiser

In 1964, this vehicle was a good bet for being the cruiser utilized by the Philadelphia Police Department. Philadelphia PD was not a rich department. Extensive efforts to save money were necessary to operate the department. Purchasing a used 1957 police cruiser from another department made perfect fiscal sense in this fiscal environment.

So, a 1957 Chevrolet Bel Air police cruiser is used in the visual reconstruction to represent the Philadelphia PD Cruiser driven by Richard Willis during the murder events. This cruiser appears in the vehicle list above.

Humanization of The Reconstruction

This visual reconstruction is intended to provide the exact exhibits that would be used by a reconstruction expert in a real criminal trial. Reviewing these exhibits gives a feel for the activities that occurred on the night of June 21, 1964.

A primary goal of this visual reconstruction is to put you into the moment as much as possible. Narratives have been designed to help you to understand the motivations of a person taking a specific action. Hopefully, you will feel and experience what a person felt or experienced when violence was directed at the person.

Intent based on racial animus is indicated when appropriate. Fear resulting from threat of violence is clearly described.

I provide these additional insights based on my personal experience during my first 18 years living in southern MS. I was directly threatened by Klansmen at various levels due to widespread racial hatred of Jews.

One time, a loaded, cocked handgun was pointed directly in my face. I was also chased by redneck law enforcement officers many times in rural locations in MS. I know the fear of being chased by a local Sheriff in a rural community who would just as soon beat you up as have you pay a fine. I have been caught and incarcerated pending payment of tickets from speed traps in really remote locations. I was met by the football team after one Christmas break. I was seen walking down the street with a Black friend. Walking with a Black justified the racial animus towards Jews. I impart those experiences to you through my interpretations of motivations and reactions of various people in this reconstruction.

CA Penal Code 720(a) identifies the qualifications of a person as an expert witness in the state of CA.

720. (a) A person is qualified to testify as an expert if he has special knowledge, skill, experience, training, or education sufficient to qualify him as an expert on the subject to which his testimony relates.[6]

Those 18 years of experience in Hattiesburg, MS, qualify me to explain intent based on racist animus and fear from threat of violence. Hattiesburg was one of the most-deep South cities in the deep South.

That city was the center of an area that perpetrated some of the most violent reactions during Freedom Summer, 1964. Another murder by the White Knights took place in Hattiesburg in January, 1966. I personally experienced behavior based on racial animus and reactions based on fear.

Detailed Timeline Analysis

A detailed timeline was constructed around the 35 activities on the day of the murders of Schwerner, Chaney and Goodman. Timeline analysis is necessary to demonstrate that the events did occur within identified time limits. Investigation results, confessions, and witness testimony recorded the actual times of some of the activities. The reconstructed timeline must match the documented actual times of those activities.

Time	Action	Distance (mi)	Speed (mph)	Travel (min)	Activity (min)	Activity Description
3:00	Price stops trio, calls Poe, Wiggs				10	Respond To Call
3:10	Escort To Jail	0.44	25	1.056	20	Finish Tire, Wiggs@PD
3:30	1st Arrest Booking					Conspiracy Organized
10:30	Escort Trio To City Boundary	1.23	25	2.952	5	Escort To Lot
10:38	Willis To WK	1.4	30	2.8	1	Willis Informs
10:42	WK To City Boundary	1.4	30	2.8		
10:45	Delay For Price				4	Poe Calls
10:49	Price To Overtake	10.6	60	10.6		
11:00	Price Overtakes Trio	Total		20.2		
10:38	Trio Boundary To Overtake	10.6	30	21.2		Travel Slowly, Avoid Arrest
11:00	Price Overtakes Trio					
11:00	Overtake To Arrest	3.89	60	3.89		
11:05	Barnette To Arrest	3.73	60	3.73		Carb Trouble
11:10	Put In Cars, Organize			10		
11:20	Pick Up Posey	3.73	40	5.595	3	Transfer Passengers
11:30	Travel To Murder Loc	3.13	40	4.695		
11:35	Murders Start			10		
11:45	To Burial Location (16.5 + 3/4)	17.2	25	41.28	20	Getting Organized
12:45	Pickup Operator	1	40	1.5	20	Walked across field
1:05	Bury Bodies (30 min + 15 min)				45	Move Bodies, Pack Dirt
1:50	Posey/Klansman To Garage	2	50	2.4	7	Put Truck In Position
2:00	Barnette To Downtown	4	50	4.8		
2:05	Barnette Meets Rainey/Price					
2:00	Burrage/Tucker To Dump Site	17.4	50	20.88	10	Dump Car, Set On Fire
2:30	Burrage/Tucker To Garage	17.4	50	20.88		
3:00	Burrage Walks To Home					

Detailed Timeline Analysis Of Important Activities

Neshoba County Jail records collected during the FBI investigation state that Schwerner, Chaney and Goodman were released at 10:30 pm on Sunday, June 21, 1964. During the Federal Civil Rights trial in 1964, a witness testified that he had seen the burning car *around 2 am* the next morning, Monday, June 22, 1964. That time is somewhat imprecise. Around 2 am could mean anytime between 1:45 am and 2:30 am. These two numbers place a range limit upon all the other activities. All of the activities between the release of the trio and the burning of the Ranch Wagon had to be completed between 10:30 pm – 2:30 am.

These activities took place at spread out locations from the southeast to the southwest to the northeast sections of Neshoba County. A lot of driving was necessary to accomplish all of the spread-out activities within the time limits.

Driving speeds were limited by automobile technology and by lighting and road conditions. In 1964, driving a car at 60 mph was considered fast, unless somehow the vehicle was supercharged. FBI pictures collected during the investigations fail to reveal any supercharged vehicles.

Road condition and light conditions were the greatest impediment to high speed driving on the day of the murders. Almost all of the rural roads involved in the events on the day of the murders were dirt or clay. Driving on dirt and clay can be dangerous. These road surfaces do not create much friction with a tire. Driving these surfaces at high speed likely leads to slippage. A slipping car can impact a large tree on the side of the road. That car is badly wrecked when a high-speed impact happens. A wrecked car is undrivable.

As discussed above, overgrown rural roads were dark, despite the brightness of the moon. Under all of these conditions, high speed driving was unlikely on rural, dirt roads.

For these reasons, low average speeds were generally assumed for the timeline analysis. During high speed activities, all driving speeds are kept within the 60-mph limit of automobile technology at the time. With these average speeds, the incidents in the analysis barely fit within the time limits 10:30 pm – 2:30 am.

Distances were determined using Google Maps. An average vehicle speed was assigned depending on expected driving conditions. Conditions considered include darkness, road surfacing, vehicle technology limitations and any other situational factors. Using distance and average speed, an expected driving time between any two locations can be determined by dividing distance by average speed.

Automobile technology was limited in those days so that 60 mph was a fast speed for a car. None of the vehicles were assigned a speed greater than 60 mph. City speed limits within a city were generally 30 mph at the time. Travel through cities were assigned a speed of 30 mph. This speed was sometimes adjusted downward if travel was during the daytime. A lot of traffic and traffic lights slowed movement, yielding a lower average speed. If the travel was at night and the road was paved and the person was in a hurry, an average speed of 40 mph was assigned.

A 10' truck was used as a follow vehicle during the trip to dump the Ranch Wagon. These heavy, low power trucks had a max speed of 55 mph at the time. However, the trip was partially through downtown Philadelphia. Speed was adjusted to 50 mph for the trips by the truck.

Some special situations required other speeds. When Price had to catch up to the Ranch Wagon which had a head start, the maximum speed of 60 mph made sense. Similarly, this speed was used during the high-speed chase. After the murders, the bodies were escorted across country using back roads. These roads were mostly clay/dirt and extremely dark. A speed of 25 mph for a 2-car caravan seemed reasonable.

In addition to driving time, some activities include an activity time. Either before or after participants had to drive, some physical activity may have been necessary. Estimates for these activities were determined by considering the extent of physical work that was required. Burying bodies by moving tons of dirt takes a lot of time compared to locating a position a 10' truck in a parking lot at a garage.

Several portions of the timeline occur simultaneously. These parallel activities are indicated using rectangles. The most important activities deal with a specific time period: turnaround by Price and Willis and travel south on Highway 19 by Schwerner, Chaney and Goodman

One activity involved Schwerner, Chaney and Goodman traveling south on Highway 19 towards the overtake location. At the same time, a series of activities took place involving Deputy Sheriff Cecil Price, Philadelphia PD Patrolman Richard Willis, and two cars full of White Knights. These parallel activities had to occur within the same time period that the trio used to travel to the overtake location. If that happened, Price and the Ranch Wagon would arrive at the overtake location at the same time.

A lot of activities had to happen quickly. Price had to travel at a higher speed to cover the 10.6 miles between the location where he took the lead and the location at which he overtook the Ranch Wagon.

Assumed speeds of all involved vehicles during the simultaneous activities are shown. Assumed activity times are shown with a short explanation of the activity.

Highway 19 south was and is a 2-lane, very dark road at night. Under those conditions, a slower speed is justified for the Ranch Wagon. However, another more justification also exists. James Chaney drove the Ranch Wagon very slowly and very carefully, taking care to avoid speeding. This section of Highway 19 was MS Highway Patrol territory. Chaney already knew that the Highway Patrol was involved. After all, Schwerner and Goodman had been escorted to the Neshoba County Jail by HP Officer Earl Poe in the HP Cruiser. Chaney himself was escorted to the Jail in the Ranch Wagon driven by HP Officer Harry Wiggs. Chaney did not want to provoke any possibility of a 2nd arrest. So, Chaney drove at a reasonable slow speed, assumed to be 30 mph.

Another factor dictates that Chaney drove the Ranch Wagon at such a slow speed going south on Highway 19. Without the slower speed, Cecil Price would not have reached the overtake location. If Chaney had been driving at 60 mph, the Ranch Wagon would have traveled 22 miles by the time Price reached the overtake location.[7] The trio would have been 12 miles further down the road from the overtake location.

Since both would be driving about 60 mph, Schwerner, Chaney and Goodman would have arrived at Meridian long before Price could catch them. The trio would still be alive. In order for Price to catch the trio, the Ranch Wagon had to go slower than Price. At the same speed, the Ranch Wagon and Price would stay the same distance apart. Price could never have closed the distance to the Ranch Wagon. The decision by James Chaney was a tremendously bad decision that lead to the death of the trio. Yet, Chaney can not be blamed for this decision. He did not have any idea that Price would be chasing him down for a 2nd arrest.

Using all of these assumed values, Schwerner, Chaney and Goodman arrived at the overtake location at 11:00 pm. Despite the complex simultaneous activities, Price also arrived at the overtake location at 11:00 pm. Posey and Barnette were close behind Price.

Simultaneous arrival after independent parallel activities indicates that the assumptions about the overtake location, speeds and activity times are quite valid. Frames in the visual reconstruction are annotated using these estimated times.

One time is not indicated in the timeline. HP Patrolmen Earl Poe and Harry Wiggs arrived at the Standard Oil Station just across the city boundary. That arrival time is easily determined. Price and Willis turned around and headed back to Philadelphia at 10:38 pm. When the White Knights arrived at 10:45 pm, Poe and Wiggs were parked in the south parking lot of the gas station. So, the HP Officers arrived sometime between these two times. For simplicity purposes, the midway time of 10:41 pm is used for the arrival time of Poe and Wiggs at the gas station.

Visual Reconstruction Of Murders

A visual reconstruction of the activities involved in the murders at all 35 identified locations is presented. This section is more than just a set of 35 pictures. Step by step activities are presented at each location. Activities are expanded at each location describing motivations of individuals involved and giving insights not described in the original history. ***This section is more than the historical description with pictures.***

All photographic images and Google Maps Street View images used in this visual reconstruction were taken at precise locations. These locations were the latitudes and longitudes determined during the Location Identification process.

1: Depart COFO Office In Meridian

On the morning of June 21, 1964, Mickey Schwerner, James Chaney, and Andy Goodman assembled at COFO Headquarters in Meridian, MS.

COFO Headquarters, 2505 ½ Fifth Street, Meridian
(Larry Primeaux)

Schwerner, Chaney and Goodman had returned early from training in Ohio to investigate the burning of Mount Zion Methodist Church in the Longdale community outside Philadelphia. In his heart and mind, Mickey Schwerner knew that this trip would be risking their lives. Yet, Mickey, along with Jim and Andy, did not hesitate to begin the trip. Members of Mount Zion Methodist Church were willing to risk their lives to support Freedom Summer activities at the church. Mickey, Jim and Andy could do no less in support.

At about 11:00 am, Schwerner, Chaney and Goodman entered the 1963 Ford Fairlane Ranch Wagon (V1) owned by COFO.

1963 Ford Fairlane Ranch Wagon, Medium Metallic Blue

Chaney drove the vehicle. He was from Meridian and knew the roads involved. This departure was the last time anyone from Meridian COFO would speak to or see Schwerner, Chaney and Goodman.

2 Inspection of burnt ruins at Mt Zion Church

A direct route was available from the COFO office in Meridian to the Mt Zion Methodist Church in Longdale outside Philadelphia.

Route From COFO Meridian To Mt Zion Methodist

A short 1.5-mile drive to the West led the trio to Highway 19. Heading north for 36 miles brought the trio to Philadelphia. From this city, Chaney drove east on Highway 16 for 8 miles.

Upon reaching Road 747, a turn to the north was necessary.

Chaney Turns North From Hwy 16 Onto Road 747

Immediately after turning north onto Road 747, a sign informed the trio that Mount Zion Methodist Church was 2.2 miles away.

Road 747 Sign Showing Distance To Mount Zion Church

Afraid for what they would see at the church, Schwerner, Chaney and Goodman hurried up the road.

At about 12:00 pm (noon), the trio approached the church. Chaney turned the car into the circular drive at the entrance to the Mt Zion Church. At this location, Bud Cole, Georgia Rush and her brother J T Rush had been beaten by the White Knights just a week earlier.

Chaney Turns Ranch Wagon Into Circular Drive At Mt Zion

Chaney drove the Wagon to the edge of the circular drive nearest the original location of the church building. Schwerner, Chaney, and Goodman exited the vehicle. What the trio saw was both appalling and horrific.

Trio Views Burnt Ruins Of Mt Zion
(Actual Ruins, Jim Lucas, Courtesy Jane Hearn)

In 1964, Mt Zion Methodist Church was an old wooden structure, as were most rural Black churches at the time. When the Klan set fire to the structure a week earlier, all that remained was ash and some unburned bricks. This damage was a clear signal to the trio and to local Blacks that anyone in Neshoba County who worked with Schwerner, Chaney and Goodman would be dealt with harshly.

3: Trio heads west on Hwy 16

Schwerner, Chaney and Goodman spent about 1 ½ hours examining the burnt ruins. After the examination, the trio visited the Longdale homes of Mt Zion congregants Cornelius Steele, George Lewis, Georgia Rushing, and Bud Cole. These visits consumed anouther 50 minutes.

Following these visits, the trio returned to the home of Earnest and Frank Kirkland in Longdale. About 30 minutes later, Schewner, Chaney and Goodman departed for Meridian. The trio jumped into the Ranch Wagon and headed south on Road 747. Again, Chaney was driving the Ranch Wagon. Departure from the Kirkland home occurred at about 2:50 pm.

Schwerner, Chaney and Goodman Approaching Hwy 16

So began the fated journey of Schwerner, Chaney and Goodman towards their ultimate death.

Shortly, the trio reached the intersection of Road 747 and Highway 16. A simple matter of retracing their original route would enable the trio to safely return to the Meridian COFO office.

Schwerner, Chaney and Goodman At The Hwy 16 Intersection

A right turn at the intersection heads the trio west on Highway 16 towards downtown Philadelphia.

The Trio Turns West On Hwy 16 Towards Philadelphia

This stretch of Highway 16 West heading towards Philadelphia is where the trouble begins for Schwerner, Chaney and Goodman.

4: Price first sights station wagon

Neshoba County Deputy Sheriff Cecil Price received a tip, probably through a phone call or a radio message. George Raymond, a Project Director from COFO in Canton, had supposedly been sighted in the American Legion Lake area. This lake was south of Highway 16, east of downtown Philadelphia, down American Legion Lake Road (Road 539).

Being the hard core racist that he was, Cecil Price became angry about George Raymond being in his county. At least mentally and perhaps verbally, Price expressed his anger and his intent. *What the hell is that n-**** doing' in ma county.? I'm gonna' get that boy and teach him a lesson.* Price headed east out Highway 16 in his police cruiser. This action by Price was the beginning of the end for Schwerner, Chaney and Goodman.

Price Sees Patrolmen Poe And Wiggs As He Heads East

As he passed Road 545 heading east on Highway 16 towards Road 539, Price in his Cruiser saw MS Highway Patrol Officers Earl Poe and Harry Wiggs in their Cruiser. These officers were sitting in their Patrol vehicle among the trees near the southeast corner of the intersection.

Poe and Wiggs had established a speed trap. At the time in 1964, speed traps in MS were conducted in a questionable manner. A sign was posted with a large speed limit, like 75 mph. Another sign was posted a short distance from the first sign. This second sign had a lower speed limit, such as 50 mph. Locations were chosen so that a driver would not have enough time to slow down upon encountering the sign with the lower speed limit. Highway Patrol officers were parked off to the side in trees or high brush preventing detection. The Patrol cruiser was usually parked perpendicular to the road. That way, when an unsuspecting out of town driver sped by between the two signs, the cruiser could easily pull out in either direction to give chase.

Poe and Wiggs were parked off behind some trees waiting to catch speeders, either from a speed trap or a radar gun or just watching. Deputy Sheriff Price passed the Highway Patrol vehicle about ½ mile to the west of Road 539 (American Legion Lake Road). Price was still planning to head south of Road 539 looking to find and to arrest George Raymond.

Then, Price had a bit of luck. Simultaneously, Schwerner, Chaney, and Goodman had some really bad luck. Price passed the trio heading east on his way west towards Road 539.

Price Passes Schwerner, Chaney and Goodman Heading West

Price was 0.145 miles west of Road 539. Imperial Wizard Sam Bowers had issued the elimination order back in May, 1964. Price knew the make and model of the COFO car from the previous trip by the trio to Philadelphia. He immediately recognized this vehicle as the COFO Ranch Wagon. An obvious conclusion was that Mickey Schwerner was inside the vehicle. Cecil Price needed a very quick turn-around to head back west.

Schwerner, Chaney and Goodman must have recognized the Price Cruiser. Markings on the side doors surely identified the vehicle as belonging to the Neshoba County Sheriff's Department.

5: Price turns around at 539

Price did have a convenient location for quick turnaround. He was only 0.145 miles west of Road 539, his original destination. As he approached Road 539, Price realized that he could quickly turn around.

Price Heading East In His Cruiser Approaches Road 539

Cecil Price then made a quick right turn down Road 539.

Price Turns Right On Road 539

After driving a short distance down Road 539, Price identified a location to make a turnaround.

Price Drives Down Road 539 Looking To Turnaround

At the time, Road 539 was unpaved and predominantly unsettled. Cecil Price may have been needed to drive a short distance to find a turnaround location. Searching for a turnaround took a few minutes.

After turning around, Price then drove back to Highway 16. He turned left on Highway 16.

Price Turning Left On Highway 16 After Turnaround

Now, Deputy Sheriff Price was heading east on Highway 16. Schwerner, Chaney and Goodman were also heading east on Highway 16. With a bit of speed, Price could overcome the trio despite the time consumed to make the turnaround on Road 539.

6: Highway Patrol at parking spot at 545

Fear had to be building in the minds of Schwerner, Chaney and Goodman, as the trio proceeded along Highway 16 west. Some likelihood existed that the driver of the Sheriff's Cruiser had recognized their Ranch Wagon. Knowing that the Cruiser might be bearing down on them, Chaney was probably tempted to speed. On the other hand, Chaney knew that big trouble would happen if he was caught speeding.

So, Chaney took his time, carefully driving under the speed limit. That decision paid an immediate benefit. A surprise waited at Road 545.

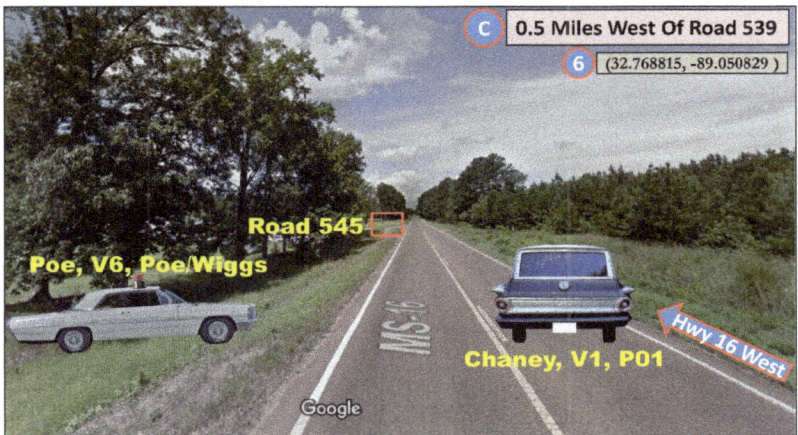

Trio Spots Poe And Wiggs Waiting In Speed Trap At Road 545

MS Highway Patrol Officers Earl Poe and Harry Wiggs were still parked in the speed trap near Road 545 where Cecil Price had seen them. By maintaining the speed limit, Chaney insured that an immediate arrest did not happen.

But this location was only ½ mile west of Road 539. By this time, Price had turned around and was on his way towards the Ranch Wagon.

7: *Price overtakes wagon again*

Chaney continued to drive within the speed limit west along Highway 16 heading into Philadelphia. About 0.510 miles past Road 545 and 1.01 miles past Road 539, the Ranch Wagon approached Dogwood Lane. Chaney looked into his rear-view mirror.

Approaching from the rear was the Neshoba County Sheriff's Department Cruiser driven by Deputy Sheriff Cecil Price.

Cecil Price Overtakes The Trio At Dogwood Lane

Chaney probably informed Schwerner and Goodman that a Neshoba County Sheriff's Cruiser had overtaken them. All 3 of the workers knew that being overtaken by a Neshoba County Sheriff's Cruiser was a problem, even if the identify of the driver was not known to them at the time.

However, the civil rights workers had a single choice of action. Chaney could calmly continue driving to the west towards Philadelphia. Accelerating beyond the speed limit would certainly result in an arrest.

So, Chaney kept driving west along Highway 16 towards Philadelphia.

Chaney Continues To Drive West On Highway 16 To Philadelphia

Unfortunately for the 3 workers, Deputy Sheriff Cecil Price continued to follow the civil rights workers. Price kept the Ranch Wagon in sight while continuing to follow the workers at the speed limit.

Schwerner, Chaney and Goodman knew that they were under surveillance by a law enforcement officer in Neshoba County. During the training in Ohio, the trio had been warned that local law enforcement was aligned with the Klan. This situation could not possibly lead to a pleasant ending for them. Anxiety started building in the minds of each worker.

8: *Price starts clocking wagon speed*

As he followed the trio, Cecil Price made an important decision. Price could see that Mickey Schwerner was in the Ranch Wagon. He decided to initiate action to enforce the *elimination* order that was issued by Sam Bowers.

However, Cecil Price needed an excuse for stopping the trio in the Ranch Wagon. Once the trio disappeared, outsiders might start asking questions.

So, Cecil Price needed to justify his actions. As his excuse, Price could easily use speeding.

While he was formulating his plan, the trio kept driving east on Highway 16. Cecil Price continued following the trio. Both vehicles were traveling at the speed limit. Schwerner, Chaney and Goodman were becoming increasingly more anxious at being followed. Their immediate future was uncertain as long as a law enforcement vehicle was following.

After another 1.53 miles from Dogwood Lane, the vehicles were approaching the intersection of Williamson Avenue and Highway 16.

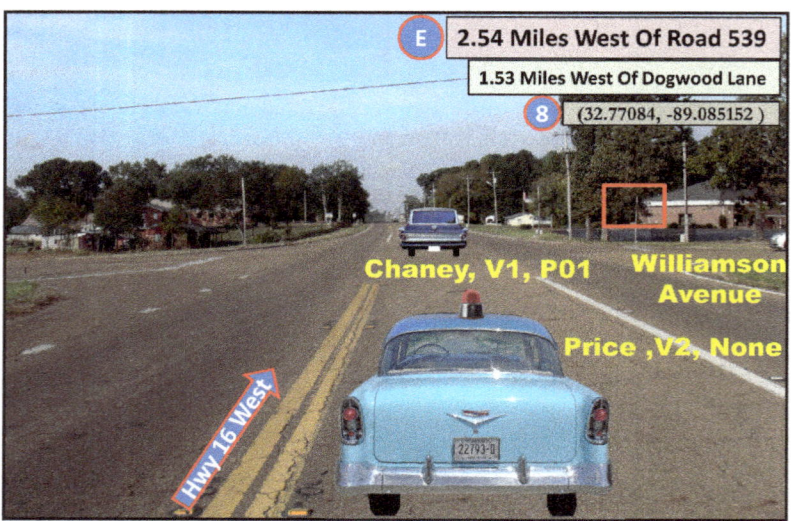

Trio Approaches Williamson Avenue With Price Following

Price now began to clock the speed of the Ranch Wagon. Most likely, he just watched his speedometer. Cecil Price needed to be able to say under oath that he had clocked the trio. Price also needed to be able to say that he had clocked their speed above the speed limit. However, during the ensuing investigation, Cecil Price never presented any written records that indicated the alleged speed at which the trio was traveling.

If asked to testify as to his reasons for stopping Schwerner, Chaney and Goodman, Cecil Price could say that he had clocked the trio. Price could declare that he started clocking them at Williamson Avenue.

9: Wagon passes city limit

At the time, the Philadelphia eastern city limit along Highway 16 was at Alexander Street.

Another 0.43 miles and now almost 2.97 miles past Road 539, the caravan of the Ranch Wagon and Price in his Cruiser crossed the city limits.

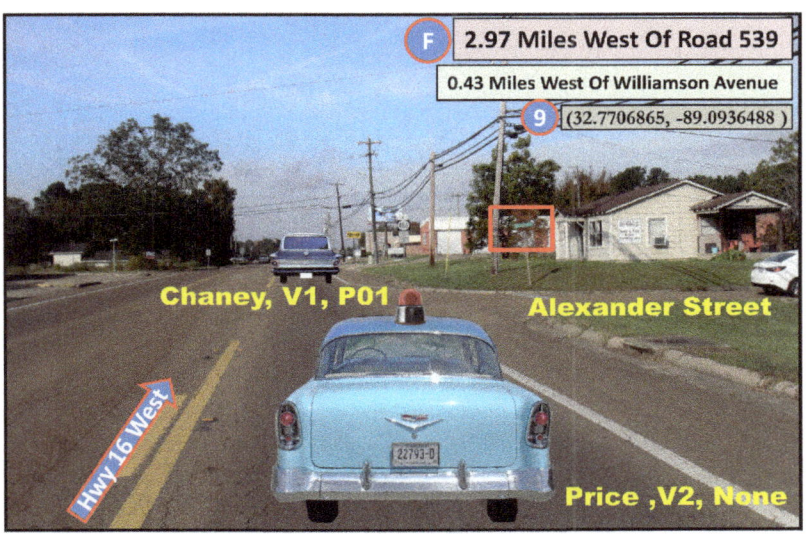

Trio And Price Crossing City Limit At Alexander Street

Cecil Price was patient. He wanted to spend enough time clocking so that he could say that he clocked the speed for sufficient time.

In the Ranch Wagon, Schwerner, Chaney and Goodman were feeling even greater pressure from being constantly followed by Price. This game of cat and mouse was hugely unsettling. Fear of the unknown is really upsetting. Cecil Price probably enjoying creating this kind of anxiety in the minds of his victims. In 1964, local MS law enforcement officers did not require intelligence or education. A desire to inflict harm to Blacks to keep them under control was the primary requirement to be hired.

10: Price turns on lights and siren

Chaney kept driving east on Highway 16 towards Philadelphia. Price continued to follow in the Cruiser. Anxiety from fear kept building in the minds Schwerner, Chaney and Goodman.

After another 0.44 miles (3.41 miles from Road 592), Deputy Sheriff Cecil Price had enough.

When the Ranch Wagon passed Valley View Drive, Price hit the light and siren on his Cruiser.

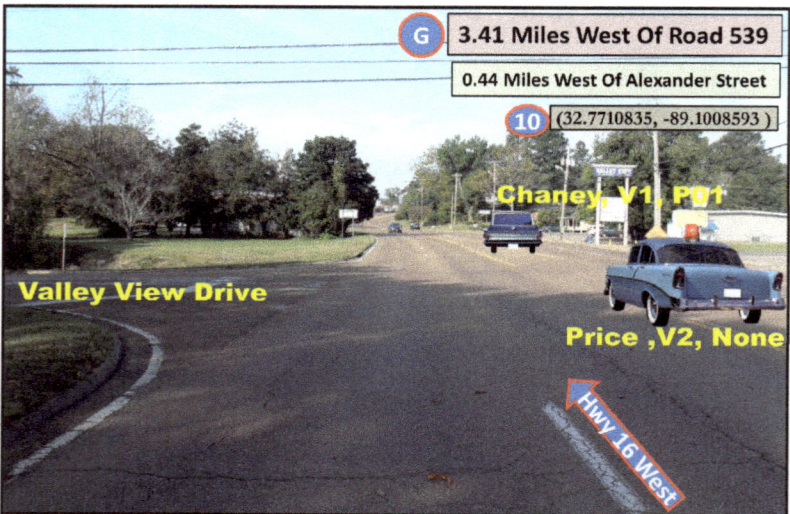

Price Initiates Chase With Light And Siren At Valley View Drive

In a startle response to the built-up anxiety, the light, and the siren, Chaney hit the gas pedal, now exceeding the speed limit. Being arrested by Price was clearly a situation that held great risk for the trio.

Unfortunately, Chaney had played right into the hands of Cecil Price. Chaney was speeding within the city limits of Philadelphia.

Chaney continued to speed while heading east on Highway 16 towards Philadelphia. Price was in pursuit with the light flashing and the siren blaring.

Chaney Continues West Towards Philadelphia While Price Chases

In the distance, the trio could see the edge of downtown Philadelphia. First Methodist Church was on the left side of Highway 16. Straight ahead was the intersection between Main Street and West Beacon Street. Perhaps Schwerner, Chaney and Goodman felt that entry into the city would provide some protection against abuse by Price after an arrest.

More than likely, Schwerner, Chaney and Goodman were just simply afraid of the consequences if stopped and arrested by Price.

11: Wagon tire changed, trio arrested

As the Ranch Wagon sped westward hoping to evade arrest by Price, the First United Methodist Church appeared on the left.

Ranch Wagon Passes Church With Price Chasing

Very shortly, the trio experienced a significant piece of bad luck.

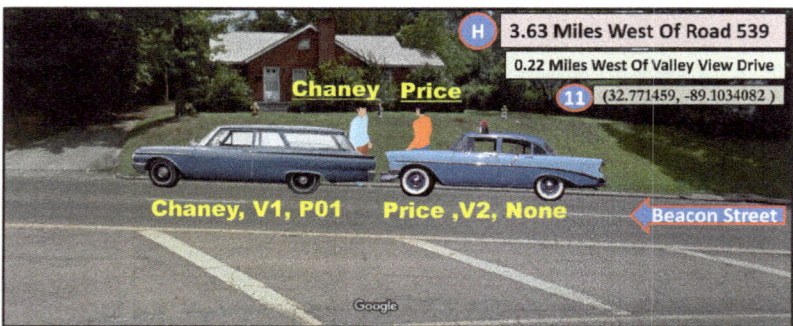

Chaney And Price Park On West Beacon Road After Time Blows

The right, rear tire on the Ranch Wagon blew out. Chaney pulled to the right side of West Beacon Road just after the intersection with Main Street. Both vehicles were now 3.63 miles west of Road 539, where Cecil Price had turned around. The chase had progressed for 0.22 miles since Valley View Drive where the chase had begun.

Price ordered Chaney to fix the flat tire so that the vehicle could be taken to the Neshoba County Jail on Myrtle Street downtown.

However, Price had an immediate problem. Price could not drive both vehicles downtown. He could not trust Chaney to voluntary drive the Ranch Wagon to the Jail. However, a solution was easily found. Price recalled that MS Highway Patrol Officers Earl Poe and Harry Wiggs were staged at a speed trap just past Road 545. This location was only 3.13 miles east of the current location. At 3:00 pm, Price contacted Poe and Wiggs on the radio, asking them to help. Using light and siren to clear traffic, the Highway Patrol vehicle arrived within 5 minutes.

HP Officers Poe And Wiggs Arrive At The Arrest Location

Chaney completed changing the blown-out right rear tire. Price, Poe, and Wiggs watched calmly as Chaney replaced the right rear tire. Deputy Sheriff Cecil Price then placed Schwerner, Chaney and Goodman under arrest. Chaney was arrested for speeding. Schwerner and Goodman were arrested *for investigations*.

After all, Chaney had been speeding once Price hit the light and the siren. However, Price overlooked the fact that he had been the cause of the speeding. He followed the trio for 2.41 miles (3.41 – 1.01) before acting.

Deputy Sheriff Price knew that following the trio created fear in the persons being followed. His action placed the trio in a position that resulted in a panicked reaction when the light and siren were activated.

Another aspect of the arrest signaled that the trio was in a difficult situation. When a vehicle is stopped for speeding, normally the driver is arrested. If the driver was from out of town, then the driver had to be arrested to ensure that bail was paid. **In this situation, Schwerner, Chaney and Goodman were all arrested.** Simultaneously arresting all 3 workers signaled that something was afoot.

12: Trio locked in Courthouse jail

Officers and prisoners were divided among the vehicles for the drive downtown to Neshoba County Jail on Myrtle Street. The vehicles were driven to Jail in the same order in which the vehicles had arrived at the arrest location.

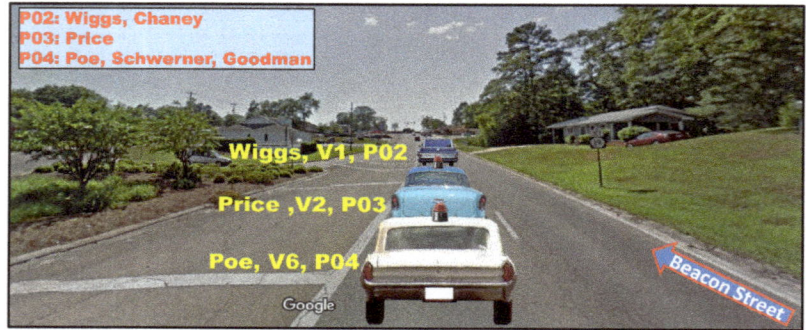

Vehicles Driving West On Beacon Street Towards Neshoba Jail

This caravan of vehicles headed west along Beacon Street towards downtown Philadelphia. MS Highway Patrol Officer Harry Wiggs drove the Ranch Wagon with James Chaney as a prisoner in the back seat. Deputy Sheriff Cecil Price drove his Sheriff's Department Cruiser without any passengers. MS Highway Patrol Officer Earl Poe was in the rear of the caravan driving his MS Highway Patrol Cruiser. Schwerner and Goodman were prisoners in the rear seat of this vehicle.

This ride must have given Schwerner, Chaney and Goodman a sinking feeling in the pit of their stomachs. Being trapped in the control of rural MS law enforcement officers was one of the situations that the training at Ohio had warned against. Fear for their personal safety was foremost in their minds. Maybe, the law enforcement officers were going to beat them senseless. Or, maybe, a lynching for each of the workers was in the immediate future.

All 3 vehicles drove west along Beacon Street towards downtown Philadelphia, staying together in a caravan.

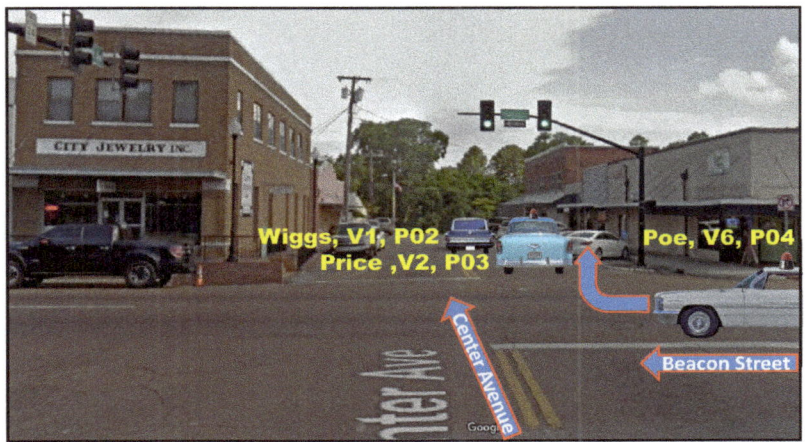

Caravan Escorting Trio Turns North On Center Avenue

At Center Avenue, in the middle of downtown, Patrol Officer Harry Wiggs leading the caravan in the Ranch Wagon took a right (north). Both of the remaining vehicles followed onto northbound Center Avenue.

As the caravan approached the cross-street Myrtle Avenue, each vehicle went in different directions. Patrol Officer Wiggs continued the Ranch Wagon north on Center Avenue towards the Philadelphia Police Dept parking lot.

Patrol Officer Wiggs Continues On Central To Police Parking Lot

Price in his Cruiser and Patrol Officer Poe with arrestees Schwerner and Goodman turned left onto Myrtle Avenue heading west.

Price And Poe Turn West On Myrtle Avenue Towards Neshoba Jail

Deputy Sheriff Cecil Prices arrived first at the Neshoba County Jail which was a short ½ block after turning onto Myrtle Avenue.

Deputy Sheriff Price Parks Cruiser In Front Of Neshoba Jail

After parking his Cruiser, Price exited the vehicle. He walked to the entrance on the left side of the Jail and entered, waiting for the others.

A very short time later Patrol Officer Earl Poe pulled into the parking lot of the Jail just to the side of the park Sheriff's cruiser.

Patrol Officer Poe Parks Highway Patrol Cruiser In Front Of Jail

Poe exited the vehicle and opened the rear door. Schwerner and Goodman exited the vehicle. Poe accompanied the two workers to the entrance of the Jail on the left side of the building. Cecil Price was waiting inside for the arrested workers.

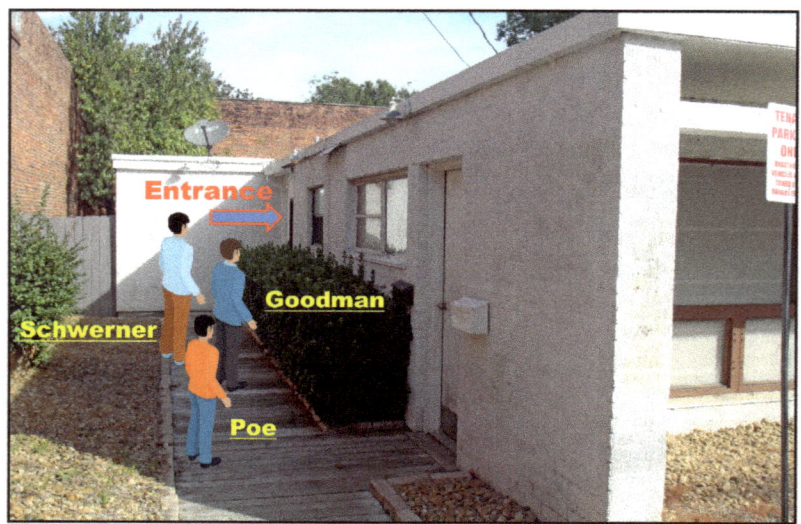

Patrol Officer Poe Escorts Schwerner And Goodman Into The Jail

Deputy Sheriff Price booked Schwerner and Goodman into the Jail. Schwerner and Goodman were booked *for investigations*. This charge was total nonsense. A person must be charged with a specific crime that violates the law. That specific violation must be explicitly stated. Using a vague term was a signal that the Price had some other objective in mind.

Over in the Philadelphia Police Department parking lot, Patrol Officer Harry Wiggs had parked the Ranch Wagon. Wiggs opened the rear passenger door of the Ranch Wagon. James Chaney exited the vehicle. Wiggs escorted Chaney across Center Avenue towards Myrtle Street.

Patrol Officer Wiggs Escorts Chaney Across Center Avenue

Wiggs and Chaney entered Myrtle Street and walked towards the Neshoba County Jail. After crossing the intersection, the pair headed down Myrtle Street towards the Neshoba County Jail.

Patrol Officer Wiggs Escorts Chaney West Down Myrtle Street

After that short 1/2 block walk, Wiggs and Chaney arrived at the Neshoba County Jail. Wiggs escorted Chaney to the entrance on the left side of the building.

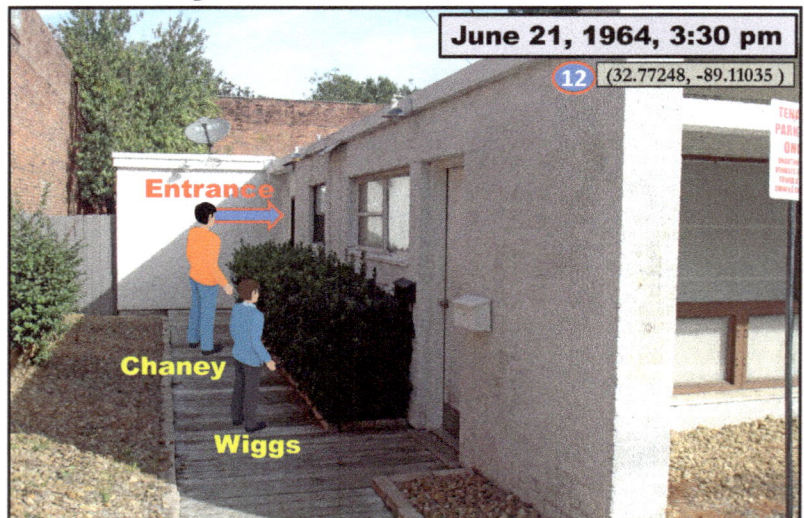

Patrol Officer Wiggs Escorts Chaney Into The Neshoba County Jail

Deputy Sheriff Cecil Price had completed booking Schwerner and Goodman into the Jail. Now, Price booked James Chaney into the Jail on a charge of speeding. All bookings were completed by 3:30 pm.

HP Officers Poe and Wiggs exited the Jail since their job was done.

Patrol Officers Poe And Wiggs Enter The Highway Patrol Cruiser

Parked in front of the building was the MS Highway Patrol Cruiser. Officer Earl Poe took the driver's seat. Harry Wiggs entered the front passenger's seat. Poe drove the Highway Patrol cruiser away from the Jail. Earl Poe drove the Cruiser over to the east side of the Neshoba County Courthouse. After a short period, Highway Patrol Inspector Maynard King arrived at the Courthouse.

Poe, Wiggs and King Meet On The East Side Of The Courthouse

Inspector King was the Commanding Officer of Earl Poe and Harry Wiggs. King had heard about the radio call to Poe and Wiggs by Price for escort assistance. Now, King wanted to confer with his subordinate officers to understand what had happened.

13: Local White Knights staged

Schwerner, Chaney and Goodman were now housed in the Neshoba County Jail. These three civil rights workers could not leave the jail until Deputy Sheriff Cecil Price decided to release them.

Since the trio was restrained, Price was free to activate the Klan. He could hold the trio in the Jail until his fellow Klansmen were in place. With this restraint on the trio at his discretion, Price was assured that sufficient time would be available to activate his fellow Klansmen. Sufficient time to position the Klansmen ensured the success of their actions against Schwerner, Chaney and Goodman.

Price next took a single action that resulted in the deaths of Schwerner, Chaney and Goodman. Cecil Price made a telephone call to Edgar Ray Killen, the Klan Kleagle/recruiter/organizer in the area.

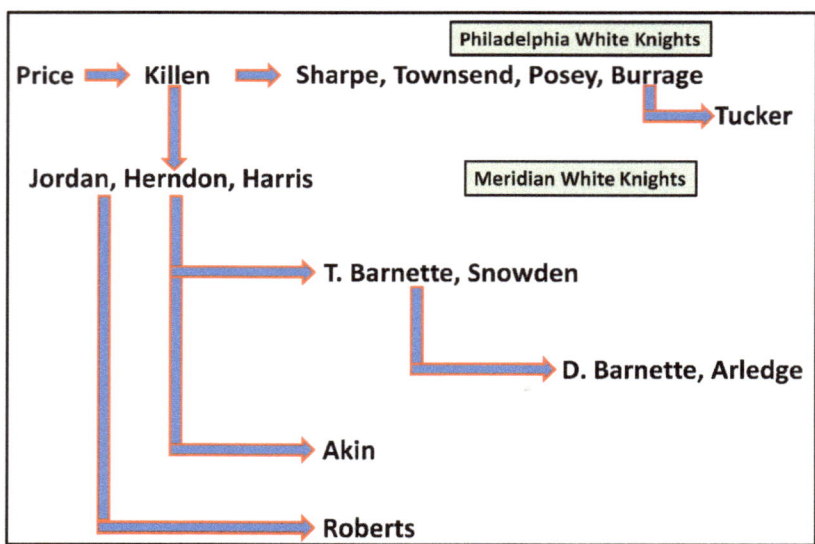

Price Initiates Activation Of Klan Members By Call To Killen

Edgar Ray Killen made phone calls to Klansmen Sharpe and Townsend in the Philadelphia White Knights. He then made a call to Frank Herndon of the Meridian White Knights at the Longhorn Drive-In in Meridian. Herndon and fellow Klansmen Jordan and Harris were already at the Longhorn Drive-In for a social meeting. Killen, Sharpe and Townsend then drove together to the Longhorn Drive-In. With these 3 phone calls (Sharpe, Townsend and Herndon), Edgar Ray Killen sealed the fate of Schwerner, Chaney and Goodman.

While Killen was activating the White Knights, Deputy Sheriff Cecil Price wanted additional information that only the Highway Patrol officers could provide. With a radio call, Price determined that Poe, Wiggs and King were on the east side of the Neshoba County Courthouse. Price asked the Highway Patrol officers to wait until he could meet with them. He assured the officers that he would arrive shortly.

Cecil Price exited the Neshoba County Jail. Price entered his Cruiser that had been parked out front when Schwerner, Chaney and Goodman were escorted to the Jail. In short order, he drove to the east side of the Courthouse. This drive was only a few blocks.

Price Meets Highway Patrol Officers On East Side Of Courthouse

Price asked the Patrol officers to submit a request to the MS Highway Patrol Dispatcher in Meridian. Price requested a vehicle ownership inquiry be performed on the Ranch Wagon. Poe submitted the query to the Dispatcher using his car radio. Price departed from the Courthouse. He later received the ownership information by radio.

Price returned to the Neshoba County Jail to monitor the imprisonment of Schwerner, Chaney and Goodman. He needed to ensure that the trio was not released until the White Knights had sufficient time to mobilize and to get into position.

After additional phone calls, the Meridian and Philadelphia White Knights moved to Akins Mobile Homes in Philadelphia. Those Klansmen who had been called from the Longhorn also arrived at Akins Mobile Homes. From Akins Mobile Home, the group split in 2 and drove off to 2 different locations.

One group drove to the Neshoba County Jail to verify that Schwerner, Chaney and Goodman were still in custody.

Sharpe Drives One Group Of Klansmen To Neshoba County Jail

Edgar Ray Killen, who was in charge of the group of Klansmen, was in the vehicle that went to the Neshoba County Courthouse. Price had returned to the Jail to ensure that the trio was not prematurely released. Killen entered the Jail. He told Price exactly where the White Knights would be staged down near the old building on Oak Street.

Another group drove to the west side of the Neshoba County Courthouse to await further directions from Edgar Ray Killen.

Barnette Drives Another Group Of Klansmen To Courthouse

After confirming that Schwerner, Chaney and Goodman were still in custody, the first group drove from the Jail to the Courthouse.

Sharpe Arrives At Courthouse With Killen As Passenger

Upon arrival at the west side of the Courthouse, Killen confirmed that the trio was still in custody. Killen directed Barnette to the staging location at the old building on Oak Street. This old building was several blocks to the northwest of the Jail, about a 4-block drive.

Sharpe dropped Edgar Ray Killen at McClain-Hayes Funeral Home about 2 blocks west of the Courthouse. Sharpe then drove to the old building on Oak Street where Barnette and his group were waiting.

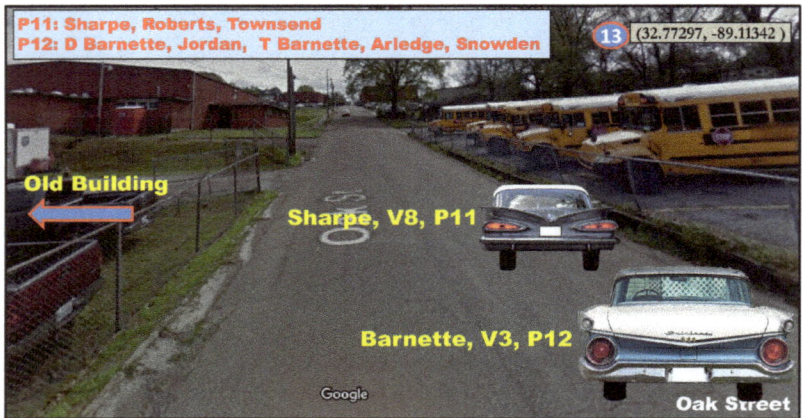

Klansmen Wait At Old Building For Notification Of Release

After a short period of time, Billy Wayne Posey arrived at the old building on Oak Street, where he had been directed by Edgar Ray Killen.

Posey Arrives At Old Building Where The Klansmen Are Waiting

Sharpe and his passengers exited from Sharpe's vehicle. This group joined Billy Wayne Posey in his car. Sharpe's car was abandoned, left parked on Oak Street near the old building. Posey took the lead in his vehicle.

Posey, Barnette and the 7 remaining Klansmen were staged, waiting for notification that Schwerner, Chaney and Goodman have been released.

14: Trio released from Courthouse jail

Deputy Sheriff Cecil Price felt that sufficient time had elapsed to enable Edgar Ray Killen to mobilize the White Knights. Price may have even received a confirmation phone call from Killen who was now at McClain-Hayes Funeral Home.

Allegedly, Justice of the Peace Leonard Warren was unavailable until 10 pm. Deputy Sheriff Price likely had control over when he was willing to let Schwerner, Chaney and Goodman meet with the JP. Price held the trio in the Jail until the White Knights had time to organize and stage.

Chaney paid bail of $20 that JP Warren had established. He borrowed the $20 from Mickey Schwerner. After Chaney paid the $20 bail, the civil rights workers were released.

Deputy Sheriff Cecil Price escorted Schwerner, Chaney and Goodman from the Neshoba County Jail just after 10:30 pm.

Price Escorts Schwerner, Chaney and Goodman From The Jail

Price was not going to allow the trio to delay the planned murder proceedings by a single second. Schwerner, Chaney and Goodman walked across the parking lot of the Jail escorted by the intimidating presence of Cecil Price.

At the edge of the parking lot, the trio turned left, heading east along Myrtle Street toward Center Avenue.

Price Accompanies The Trio As They Turn East Onto Myrtle Street

A half block later, the group arrived at the intersection between Myrtle Street and Center Avenue.

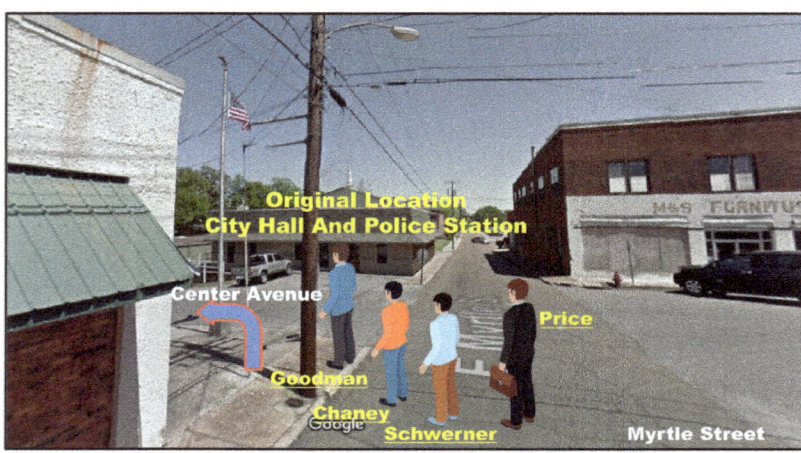

The Group Turns Left From Myrtle Street Onto Center Avenue

At this intersection, a left turn took the group onto Center Avenue. Crossing the street positioned Schwerner, Chaney and Goodman at the entrance to the Police Parking lot where the Ranch Wagon was parked.

Deputy Sheriff Cecil Price then gave a very clear instruction to the workers in the form of a thinly veiled threat.

Price Threatens The Trio As They Are Released To Their Vehicle

In his most threatening manner, Cecil Price spoke directly to Schwerner, Chaney and Goodman. *See how quickly you can get out of Neshoba County!* Deputy Sheriff Price then turned his back on the trio.

Cecil Price walked the ½ block west on Myrtle Street back to the Jail. Price entered his Cruiser which was parked out front. Once he was in the Cruiser, Price contacted Philadelphia Police Officer Richard Willis by radio. Willis was out on patrol in this police department cruiser. Price told Willis that the trio had been released. He asked Willis to join him to follow the trio south on Highway 19 to the city boundary. Price then took off after the Ranch Wagon.

15: *Released trio heads towards Meridian*

With this threat from Price hanging over their heads, Schwerner, Chaney and Goodman did not waste any time. Chaney got behind the wheel of the Ranch Wagon. Schwerner and Goodman entered the front seat passenger side door.

Chaney turned on the motor of the Ranch Wagon. He backed up, turned, and headed towards the parking lot exit on Center Avenue.

Chaney Turns Left From The Parking Lot Onto Center Avenue

After turning left onto Center Ave., James Chaney drove the Ranch Wagon heading south as quickly as the speed limit would allow. Their priority was to get out of Neshoba County as quickly as possible without breaking any laws and getting arrested again.

As he drove the Ranch Wagon south on Center Ave., Chaney approached Beacon Street. Chaney could take either Beacon Street or Main Street to Highway 19 south to Meridian. Chaney chose to drive along Main Street. Main Street was 1 long block further south past Beacon Street.

With a start and probably gasps, Chaney, Schwerner and Goodman all noticed that Cecil Price has pulled up behind them.

Ranch Wagon Heading South Approaches Beacon Street

Seeing Price in his Sheriff's Department Cruiser behind them gave the trio great concern. Price simply might be escorting the trio out of town. Or something more nefarious might be planned. This uncertainty about their safety certainly caused a knot in each of their stomachs.

Cecil Price contacted Richard Willis again by radio. He informed Willis as to his location and direction of travel.

Both Chaney in the Ranch Wagon and Price in his Cruiser crossed Beacon Street. This small caravan continued heading south on Center Avenue towards Main Street.

As the caravan approached Main Street, Richard Willis in his Philadelphia PD Cruiser pulled behind Price in his Cruiser. Now, the Ranch Wagon was being escorted by two local law enforcement officers, one from a County jurisdiction and the other from a city jurisdiction.

Willis Enters Behind Price Between Beacon St and Main St

Downtown Philadelphia is a small town, about 1 ½ miles from east to west. Willis easily came from wherever he was patrolling in the downtown area after he had been notified of the current location by Price. Arrival of Willis in his Philadelphia PD Cruiser further increased the anxiety felt by Schwerner, Chaney and Goodman. This situation was that worst situation that had been described in Ohio. The trio was under surveillance of multiple rural MS law enforcement officers.

Schwerner, Chaney and Goodman needed to go east to Highway 19. This Highway was the direct route to Meridian where the COFO office was located.

Main Street was the route Chaney had chosen to approach Highway 19 south. Main Street is 1 large city block south past Beacon Street.

James Chaney turned the Ranch Wagon left on Main Street.

Trio In Ranch Wagon And Escort Turn East Onto Main Street

After turning left on Main Street, the Ranch Wagon, Price and Willis traveled due east towards Highway 19 south.

Ranch Wagon And Escort Travel East Towards Highway 19

This stretch of Main Street between Center Avenue and Highway 19 south is only about 0.23 mile. All the while, Chaney drove under the speed limit. Anxiety about the future intent of Price and Willis was increasing as the trio travelled towards Highway 19 south. After all, Price had already demonstrated his willingness to follow for them for a short distance, then arrest them.

Finally, the caravan reached the intersection of Main Street and Highway 19 south which was the direct route to Meridian.

Ranch Wagon, Price, and Willis Arrive At Highway 19 Intersection
Chaney made a right turn at the intersection, heading south on Highway 19. Perhaps Schwerner, Chaney and Goodman felt some relief. Safety was only 37 miles away in Meridian. When Price and Willis also turned south on Highway 19, Schwerner, Chaney and Goodman were dismayed. Their ordeal was not yet over.

Price and Willis Follow Ranch Wagon South On Highway 19

Anxiety levels of Schwerner, Chaney, and Goodman increased.

After about a mile, the Ranch Wagon, Price and Willis approached the southern boundary of the city of Philadelphia. This boundary was at the intersection of Highway 19 and St Francis Drive.

Ranch Wagon, Price and Willis Approach City Boundary

If Price and Willis were going to take some action, now would be the best time. Chaney brought the Ranch Wagon to a full stop to avoid giving Price and Willis an excuse for another arrest.

After the full-stop, Chaney drove the Ranch Wagon across the city boundary into the jurisdiction of rural Neshoba County. As Neshoba County Deputy Sheriff, Cecil Price still had legal enforcement authority over Schwerner, Chaney and Goodman.

To the complete surprise of Schwerner, Chaney and Goodman, both Price and Willis made a 180-degree turn!

This turn-around was at 10:38 pm.

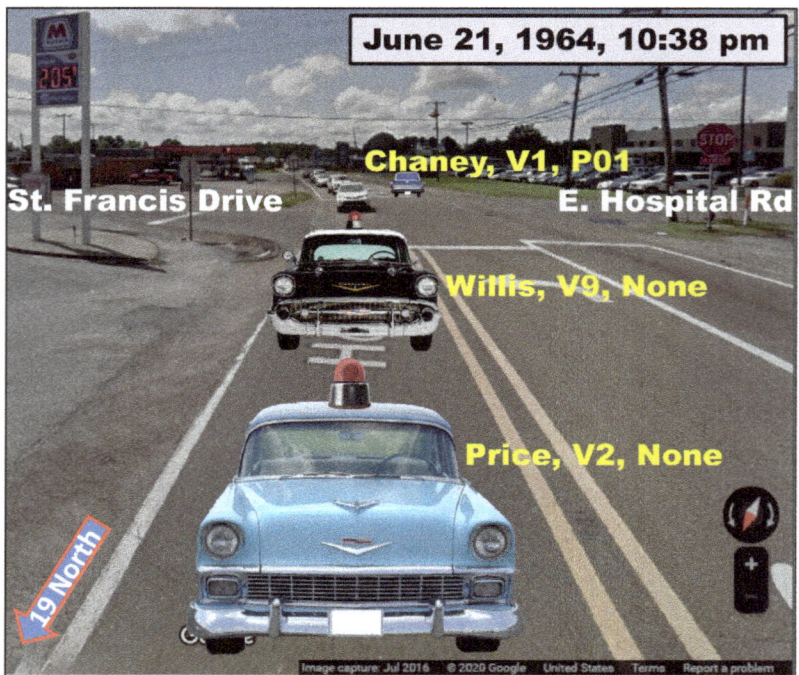

Price And Willis Drive Back Towards Downtown

As Schwerner, Chaney and Goodman continued south on Highway 19, the sight of Price and Willis disappearing into the distance was surely a relief. Safety in Meridian was just 37 miles away.

Unbeknownst to the trio, Price had not followed the trio to ensure they immediately left Philadelphia. His goal was for more nefarious. Price wanted to specifically confirm that Schwerner, Chaney and Goodman were taking Highway 19 south. With this information, Price could let the staged White Knights know where to find the trio.

As he and Willis headed north the short mile into Philadelphia, Price contacted Willis on the radio. Price gave Willis the location of the White Knights staged next to the old building on Oak Street. Price asked Willis to drive to the old building. Willis was to inform the staged Klansmen that the trio was headed south on Highway 19.

Willis agreed to inform the staged Klansmen. Richard Willis drove his Police Cruiser at a normal speed of 30 mph. At 10:38 pm on a hot summer Sunday night, downtown Philadelphia was not exactly crowded with traffic.

Turning around like this was an extremely cruel hoax. This action gave Schwerner, Chaney and Goodman a false sense of security that safety was at hand. Price had two motives. Sadistically, Price wanted to give the trio that sense of security. If the trio felt safe, Chaney would not be in a hurry to get to Meridian. Traveling at a relatively slow speed gave the staged White Knights time to catch the trio. Price also wanted to ensure that the trio was in fact traveling south on Highway 19. The waiting Klansmen would be assured of catching the trio without having to drive all over the County and possibly failing to find them. However, once Price confirmed that the trio was headed south on Highway 19, their doom was sealed!

Within minutes, at 10:41 pm, Richard Willis arrived at the old building on Oak Street where the staged Klansmen were parked and waiting.

Willis Meets Staged Klansmen At The Old Building On Oak Street

Richard Willis informed the waiting Klansmen that Schwerner, Chaney and Goodman were heading south on Highway 19. He told the Klansmen that the trio had just passed the city boundary a few minutes ago.

After a minute of discussion, the Klan occupied vehicles departed for Highway 19 south at 10:42 pm. Billy Posey in this 1956 Chevy along with several other Klansmen took the lead. Doyle Barnette in his 1957 Ford also along with several Klansmen followed. Both drivers traveled at a normal speed of 30 mph. Without any traffic in the city, the Klansman could travel across town without interference.

16: Price takes lead in chase

Philadelphia is a small town in a very remote section of MS. In 1964, the town pretty much closed down after dark. Teenagers did not have many avenues of entertainment. One favorite past time was building souped-up cars. Car designs were not that complicated. Modifications could be easily made by uneducated teenagers without special training. Many local teenagers installed high-powered, superchargers into engines of their vehicles. Adding huge amounts of horsepower to a car using a supercharger led to a second favorite past time. Later in the evening after the local movie theater was closed, local teenagers met and participated in drag races with these supercharged vehicles.

Drag races were not practical in downtown Philadelphia due to streetlights and roving police officers. However, just 1 mile south of Philadelphia on Highway 19 was a perfect location to conduct drag races.

At this location began a long two-lane highway without any lights. Long stretches of empty road without streetlights were ideal for drag racing – – as long as no law enforcement officers were around.

Since Highway 19 is a MS State Highway, the Highway Patrol had law enforcement jurisdiction. HP Officers Harry Wiggs and Earl Poe knew that this location was a favorite spot to start drag races. About 10:35 pm, Wiggs and Poe headed for the Standard Oil Station that was 1 mile south of downtown Philadelphia, just outside the city boundary.

HP Officers Poe And Wiggs Enter The Standard Station

HP Officer Earl Poe was driving the HP Cruiser. Officer. At 10:41 pm, HP Officer Earl Poe drove his Cruiser over to a parking area on the south side of the station.

Poe and Wiggs Park At The South Side Of The Standard Station

Poe and Wiggs sat waiting patiently, hoping that dragsters would arrive on Highway 19 south near the location where the pair was parked.

At 10:45 pm, two vehicles filled with White Knights drove up on the passenger side of the HP Cruiser.

Vehicles Containing Klansmen Drive Up Next To The HP Cruiser

Billy Posey drove his car just past the front of the HP Cruiser. Doyle Barnett pulled in behind Posey. Posey exited the car. He walked over to the driver's side of the HP Cruiser and began talking with Earl Poe, who was driving the HP Cruiser.

Posey and the Klansmen had been told previously by Price that HP Officers would inform the Klansmen as to the location of the trio. Earl Poe did not know anything about this situation. Officer Harry Wiggs contacted Price on the radio. Price told Wiggs to tell the Klansmen to sit tight. Price would be over very shortly.

At 10:48 pm, Cecil Price arrived at the Standard Station where the HP Officers and the two cars full of Klansmen were waiting.

Price Arrives At The Standard Station After Called By Poe

About 10 minutes had passed since Price had seen Schwerner, Chaney and Goodman depart from this location heading south on Highway 19.

After the release at 10:30 pm, the Ranch Wagon, Price and Willis traveled about 2.95 miles from the Neshoba Jail to this Standard Station. Willis traveled another 1.4 miles from the Standard Station to the old building on Oak Street. Two cars of Klansmen then travelled about 1.4 miles to return to the Standard Station. Right now, the time was about 10:48 pm.

Billy Posey walked from the driver's side of the HP Cruiser to the driver's side of the Neshoba County Sheriff's Cruiser. Posey asked Price about the location of the trio. Price stated that the trio had left from this location about 10 minutes previously.

Cecil Price was confident that he could catch the Ranch Wagon containing Schwerner, Chaney and Goodman. Price told Posey to follow him south on Highway 19. After a minute informing Posey, at 10:49 pm Price hit the light, turned on the siren, and charged down Highway 19 south at a speed of 60 mph. Billy Posey signaled Doyle Barnette to follow. Posey jumped in his car. Posey and Barnette then began driving at 60mph to keep Price in sight.

Price Leads Posey And Barnette South On Highway 19

As he took off in pursuit of the trio in the Ranch Wagon, Cecil Price had a bit of a head start over Posey and Barnette. However, the Klansmen were going to keep Price in sight. These Klansmen were out for blood, that of Schwerner, Chaney and Goodman. Keeping Price in his Sheriff's Cruiser in sight would ensure that outcome was obtained.

17: Price overtakes the ranch wagon

After being detained for 7 hours, Mickey Schwerner, James Chaney and Andy Goodman were released from the Neshoba County Jail. Deputy Sheriff Cecil Price and Philadelphia PD Patrolman Richard Willis followed the trio after their release. Chaney drove the Ranch Wagon with the trio past the Philadelphia city boundary at 10:38 pm. In response, Price and Willis reversed direction, heading back towards Philadelphia.

Schwerner, Chaney and Goodman breathed a sigh of relief. A weight had been lifted from their shoulders. Their futures were no longer at risk. James Chaney made the conscious decision to drive south on Highway 19 at a reasonable speed of 30 mph. This section of Highway 19 was Highway Patrol territory. Earlier, HP Officers Harry Wiggs and Earl Poe had escorted the trio to the Jail at the request of Cecil Price. Chaney did not want to give HP officers a reason to arrest the trio again.

This rural MS highway was 2 lanes wide. With the overgrowth of surrounding forest, this remote highway was very dark, despite the bright moon that night. This stretch of road was and still is highly isolated. Extreme silence surrounded the trio while driving south on the highway. Sounds carried for long distances on this remote, dark MS Highway.

The remoteness, the extreme silence, and the deep darkness were all unnerving. A person could disappear and never be heard from again.

After driving about 9 miles south on Highway 19, one of the trio heard something. A low hum could be heard in the silent, still, dark night air. As James Chaney continued driving calmly southward at 30 mph, the noise grew louder and louder. Now, several pinpoints of light were beginning to grow in the dark night. As the unsuspecting trio drove slowly onward, the sounds grew louder, the lights grew brighter.

Suddenly, Schwerner, Chaney and Goodman were able to see the cause of the lights and the sounds. The trio reacted in extreme horror.

Cecil Price Overtakes the Ranch Wagon on Highway 19 South

With the surprise, speed, and ferocity of an attack by a pack of wild rabid dogs, Deputy Sheriff Cecil Price and his fellow Klansmen came barreling down on the Ranch Wagon out of the deep, dark, silent night. Price had his light flashing and siren howling. A short distance behind Price were two other vehicles also barreling down out of the dark with bright front lights blazing.

Schwerner, Chaney and Goodman each experienced the same response. A sudden huge surge of adrenaline caused their hearts to pound. Each heart was pounding so hard that the person felt his heart would burst. Breathing became difficult and rapid. Panic set in among the trio in the Ranch Wagon.

Fear and stress from the violence of this attack bearing down on the trio out of the darkness caused tunnel vision. The night appeared even darker due to the tunnel vision, further raising the level of fear felt by each member of the trio.

At 11:00 pm, when Price caught up with the Ranch Wagon, Highway 492 was only 2/3 of a mile away. Chaney thought that taking this Highway might be an opportunity to escape arrest again. James Chaney reacted. He shoved the gas pedal to the floor. Fairly quickly, the Ranch Wagon was speeding south towards Highway 492 at 60 mph. Cecil Price in his Sheriff's Department 1956 Chevy Cruiser continued chasing the Ranch Wagon, also speeding at 60 mph. Two vehicles containing Klansmen followed at the same speed several hundred yards behind Price.

Schwerner, Chaney and Goodman were sick to their stomachs. As the vehicles bore down on them, each member of the trio knew that Cecil Price had cruelly duped and misled them. With a sinking feeling in their stomachs, Mickey Schwerner, James Chaney, and Andy Goodman knew with certainty that their lives would shortly come to a violent end.

This hunting down of Schwerner, Chaney and Goodman led by Cecil Price was the epitome of sadistic cruelty. Price released the trio at 10:30 pm. This release gave hope to the trio of returning alive to Meridian. By turning around at the Philadelphia border at 10:38 pm, Price further reinforced this hope of freedom and safety. Then, only 22 minutes later, Price and his fellow Klansmen suddenly came barreling down on the trio out of the darkness and silence. This surprise attack barreling down on the trio out of nowhere in the dark remote night with siren blasting and lights blazing cruelly eliminated all hope.

The trio was being hunted like animals. Yet, the hunters were the real animals. A violent gang of 9 thugs attacked a non-violent group of 3 innocent individuals. Striking under cover of darkness is an act of cowardice.

This sadistic cruelty by Neshoba County Deputy Sheriff Cecil Price is not surprising. During the 1950s and the 1960s, a person could obtain a position as a Sheriff, a Deputy Sheriff or a police officer without any kind of degree. However, sadistic cruelty towards Blacks and Jews was an important job qualification. Cruelty and violence were tools used by the white power structures in MS to control Blacks and Jews. Law enforcement officers were ordered by white state, county and municipal leaders to perform specific acts of sadistic cruelty as a tool of control. Many law enforcement officers were ignorant and obtained pleasure from applying the tools of cruelty. Only a true sadist could obtain pleasure in treating others with cruelty.

For comparison purposes, the same scene is presented under daylight conditions. Darkness certainly increases the level of fear felt by the object of a chase.

Cecil Price Overtakes the Ranch Wagon on Highway 19 South

Billy Posey, Doyle Barnette and fellow White Knights from Philadelphia and Meridian were a few hundred yards behind Price. Posey was driving his 1956 Chevy. Barnette was driving his 1957 Ford. These two vehicles were the sources of the additional blazing bright lights seen by the trio as Price was overtaking the Ranch Wagon.

18: Trio turns west on 492

James Chaney was speeding the Ranch Wagon towards Highway 492. As he approached, Chaney diverted the Ranch Wagon to the west. Price followed not far behind. Both vehicles were traveling at 60 mph.

Chaney Drives Ranch Wagon Towards The West On Hwy 492

Since both vehicles were now traveling at the same speed, Price was unable at this time to actually stop the Ranch Wagon.

Chaney turned on the straightaway and went speeding off into the night west along Highway 492. Price completed his turn onto the straightaway. He continued the high-speed pursuit of the trio in the Ranch Wagon.

Price Continues Chasing The Ranch Wagon West Along Hwy 492

Chaney had already made one fateful decision by driving south on Highway 19 at the reasonable speed of 30 mph. This slow speed enabled Price and the Klansmen sufficient time to overtake the trio, despite their head start. Now, the decision to turn to the west would remove any chance that the trio had to escape their deaths. Chaney headed the Ranch Wagon deeper into Neshoba County and away from Meridian rather moving closer towards Meridian.

19: WK 1956 Chevy has problem

Posey and his Klansmen passengers were also speeding at 60 mph south on Highway 19 towards Highway 492. Barnette and his Klansmen passengers were right behind Posey.

Posey and Barnette arrived north of Posey's station just in time to see Cecil Price head west on Highway 492. With this information, the pair knew that turning west on Highway 492 was necessary to overtake the evading trio in the Ranch Wagon.

Posey, Barnette Arrive To See Price Head West On Hwy 492

At this time, the 1956 Chevy Bel Air being driven by Billy Wayne Posey developed a carburetor problem. Thick, dark smoke started broiling out of the rear exhaust. Traveling at such a high speed for 10.6 miles had caused some part in the carburetor to break.

Posey Pulls To Apron In Front Of His Station, Waves Barnette On

Fortunately, Posey was a short distance (at most a hundred yards) north of the gas station which he managed. Posey pulled his 1956 Chevy out of the highway onto the apron of the gas station.

Barnette in his 1957 Ford pulled in next to the 1956 Chevy to talk with Posey. Posey waived Barnette onwards to continue to follow Price after the trio. Since he had seen Price turning to the west on Highway 492, Barnette did not need to be told anything by Posey.

Barnette continued traveling south on Highway 19 for that last ½ mile towards Highway 492. As he approached Highway 492, Barnette entered the right turn access lane for Highway 492.

Barnette Enters Access Lane For Hwy 492 West

Barnette exited the turn onto the straightaway of Highway 492. By this time, Price in his Cruiser and the trio in the Ranch Wagon were far out of sight further west on Highway 492.

Barnette Heads West On Hwy 492 After Price, The Ranch Wagon

Barnette again began speeding at 60 mph. He was not worried. Barnette had seen Price head west so knew that Price and the Ranch Wagon would be found up ahead somewhere.

20: Trio arrested on 492

James Chaney continued driving the Ranch Wagon west on Highway 492 at 60 mph. Cecil Price is his Chevy Cruiser was closing the distance between the two vehicles. Doyle Barnette and some fellow Klansmen were several miles behind the Ranch Wagon and the Cruiser.

As the chase continued to the west, Deputy Sheriff Price was about to encounter a problem. As Chaney continued westward, the Ranch Wagon got closer and closer to the southern boundary of Neshoba County. If the trio successfully passed across that boundary, Price no longer had arrest jurisdiction. Price had to make a move quickly.

After driving 3.2 miles west from Highway 19, Chaney drove the Ranch Wagon down a small hill. Pastureland was on both the left and the right sides of the Highway. Ahead was a small bridge spanning Nelson Creek. Just in front of that bridge was a small cleared area to the right side of the road. Highway 492 curved to the right after the bridge across Nelson Creek.

Ranch Wagon Goes Down A Small Hill On Hwy 492 West

This location would make a good place to stop the trio.

Unfortunately for the trio, Cecil Price also saw this bridge with the cleared area in front and just to the right. Price had been unable to find a suitable location to stop the Ranch Wagon up until now. However, this location was a mere 3.21 miles from the southern boundary of Neshoba County. If he did not act soon, the trio would be out of his jurisdiction. Cecil Price made his move.

Deputy Sheriff Price increased his speed significantly past the 60 mph that he had been maintaining. Unconcerned about or oblivious to the possibility of oncoming traffic coming around the curve, Price pulled into the left lane. Price passed the Ranch Wagon. He forced the Ranch Wagon to pull over into the cleared area on the right side of the road, just in front of the bridge over Nelson Creek.

At 11:05 pm on June 21, 1964, Cecil Price placed Schwerner, Chaney and Goodman under arrest for the second time that day. Once Price was able to place the trio under arrest, the trio did not have much longer to live.

Price Forces Ranch Wagon Into Clear Area On The Right

Price and the trio were midway between Highway 19 and the southern boundary of Neshoba County. Highway 19 was 3.22 miles to the east. The southern boundary of the County was 3.21 miles to the southwest.

After coming to a stop, Price turned off the motor, the light, and the siren. The Ranch Wagon was blocked by the Cruiser. Price exited his Cruiser. He walked calmly over to the driver's side of the Ranch Wagon.

Price Walks To The Driver Side Of The Ranch Wagon

Schwerner, Chaney and Goodman were not sure about what would happen during the next few minutes. Perhaps, Price would draw his firearm and shoot them on the spot. Instead, Price seemed almost cordial.

I thought you were going back to Meridian if we let you out of jail? quipped Price. Unsure, Chaney replied. *We were doing that!.* Again, Price seemed to make light of the situation. *Why are you taking the long way around?* After this comment, Chaney, Schwerner and Goodman were further sickened. Selected in panic, a route away from Meridian had been taken.

This attempt at humor by Cecil Price was abominable. Price knew exactly what destiny was planned for the trio. Here again Price was demonstrating his proclivity for sadistic cruelty.

As Price and Chaney were talking, Doyle Barnette finally arrived on the scene in his 1957 Ford Fairlane.

Barnette And Fellow Klansman Arrive At 2nd Arrest Location

Four other Klansmen were in the Ford along with Doyle Barnette. Schwerner, Chaney and Goodman could hardly have missed the implication of the arrival of this group. Something bad was about to happen to them. Something that involved significant amounts of violence in one way or another was going to happen.

21: Caravan returns to and turns north on 19

With the arrival of Barnette in his 1957 Ford, Deputy Sheriff Price now had the manpower to transport the prisoners and all of the vehicles.

Price ordered Schwerner, Chaney and Goodman into to the back seat of the Neshoba County Sheriff's Dept Cruiser.

Price Orders The Trio Into The Back Seat Of His Cruiser

By arresting the trio and ordering them into the back seat, Cecil Price was acting under his authority as a sworn law enforcement officer. Schwerner, Chaney and Goodman did not have any option but to obey. Refusal would have simply resulted in the trio being handcuffed and thrown into the back seat. By using his legal power to "arrest" the trio, Deputy Sheriff removed the freedom of movement to escape death. Price essentially was ordering the trio to their deaths without any ability to resist or escape because he was acting as a Deputy Sheriff!

This arrest was a kidnapping, pure and simple, disguised as an arrest.

Jimmy Snowden entered the front passenger door of the Cruiser, making himself comfortable on the front seat. Jimmy Arledge took the driver's seat of the 1963 Ford Ranch Wagon that had been driven by Chaney. Jim Jordan and Travis Barnette joined Doyle Barnette as front seat passengers of the 1957 Ford Fairlane.

All 3 vehicles were already in a caravan with the vehicles in the order of arrival at the arrest location. Price lead the caravan in a U turn back towards Highway 19.

Caravan With Arrested/Kidnapped Trio Heads East After U Turn

As the caravan headed east back towards Highway 19, the small hill in Highway 492 was encountered.

Caravan Containing Arrested Trio Drives Over Small Hill

While the caravan moved eastward, high speed was unnecessary. In fact, the caravan did not want to draw attention to itself. After driving 3.22 miles at 40 mph, the caravan approached the intersection of Highway 492 and Highway 19.

Caravan Transporting Arrested Trio Approaches Hwy 19

Edgar Ray Killen had given Deputy Sheriff Price the exact location for the murders. This location was on Rock Cut Road. Price knew that this location was a short distance north of this intersection.

Price took a left turn from Highway 492 east onto Highway 19 north.

Caravan With Captured Trio Turns North On Highway 19

Both Arledge in the 1963 Ranch Wagon and Barnette in his 1957 Ford blindly followed Price without question. All of the Klansmen knew that Schwerner, Chaney and Goodman were being led to their deaths. Mickey, Jim and Andy were also now absolutely certain that something really, really bad was going to happen to them.

22: WK picked up at 1956 Chevy

As the caravan containing the trio drove towards the north, the stranded 1956 Chevrolet driven by Billy Wayne Posey came into view. This location was ½ mile to the north of the intersection with Highway 492.

Escort Caravan Approaches Stranded 1956 Chevy At Posey's Station

Wayne Roberts, Jerry Sharpe, and Jimmy Townsend were waiting patiently with Posey for the caravan with the captured trio to arrive.

Price pulled his Cruiser over to the left side of Highway 19, almost in front of Posey's 1956 Chevy.

Arledge and Barnette followed Price to the left side of Highway 19, parking behind Price and in front of Posey's 1956 Chevy.

Escort Caravan Stops To Pick Up Waiting Klansmen

Posey, Roberts, Sharpe and Townsend wanted to be part of the bloodletting that was planned. Posey, Roberts and Sharpe joined Arledge in the Ranch Wagon. Townsend remained with Posey's 1956 Chevy at Posey's station. Townsend was to repair the 1956 Chevy.

23: Caravan turns west on Rock Cut Rd

Cecil Price was now leading a caravan including 2 other vehicles, 8 other White Knights and the 3 victims. Price knew exactly the destination.

Wayne Roberts, Jim Jordan, and Doyle Barnette knew exactly what was going to happen when the caravan arrived at that destination.

Price lead the caravan an additional 3.13 miles north on Highway 19 at a leisurely speed of 40 mph. As the caravan approached Rock Cut Road (now Road 515), Price signaled that a left turn onto Rock Cut Road was imminent. This Road was a remote road paved with dirt and red clay.

Caravan With Captured Trio Approaches Rock Cut Road On Left

Turning off a major road, such as Highway 19, onto a remote country road, such as Rock Cut Road, alerted the trio. Schwerner, Chaney and Goodman knew that the violence that would be directed towards them was about to happen. Their hearts pounded in their chests. Their breathing became more difficult as a result of the fear.

Price turned left onto Rock Cut Road/Road 515, leading the caravan in a westerly direction.

Price Leads Caravan West On Rock Cut Road (Road 515)

Price, Arledge, Barnette, the Klansmen and the trio continued to drive west at 40 mph on Road 515 (Rock Cut Road).

Caravan Continues Driving West On Road 515 (Rock Cut Road)

Now, Schwerner, Chaney and Goodman were horrified. This stretch of road was almost completely overgrown with trees on both sides of the road. A deep, silent darkness engulfed the caravan. Any violence perpetrated by Price and the White Knights would be completely hidden. The overgrowth of trees blocked the moonlight out and prevented sound from traveling. By now, the trio was sure that death was their destination.

24: Murder trio at murder site

Deputy Sheriff Cecil Price drove his Sheriff's Cruiser to the west along Road 515 (Rock Cut Road). Behind the Cruiser followed the 1963 Ranch Wagon driven by Jimmy Arnette and the 1957 Ford driven by Doyle Barnette.

Price drove 350 yards to the west after turning onto Road 515/Rock Cut Road from Highway 19 north.

The home of Edgar Ray Killen was 1 mile further down Rock Cut Road. Killen could drive past the location every time he drove into Philadelphia on business and pleasure. This drive gave Killen satisfaction knowing his part in the murders. Killen selected this location specifically for that continuing satisfaction.

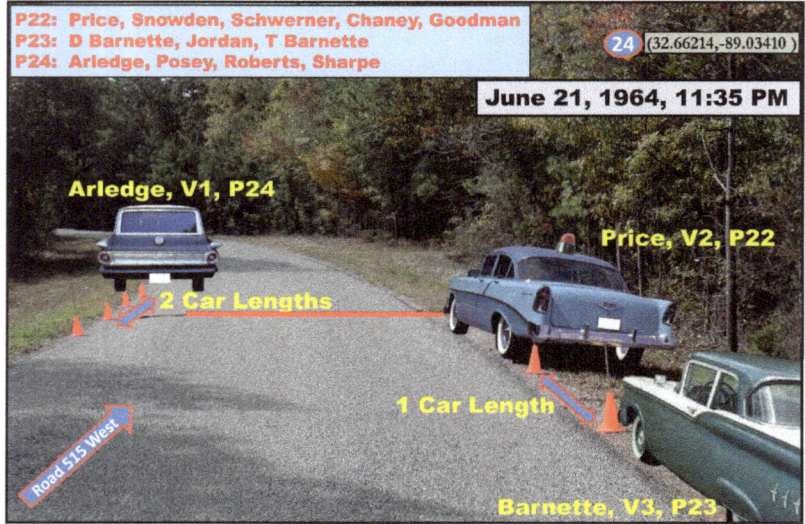

Caravan Parks On Rock Cut Road (Road 515) To Commit Murders

At 11:35 pm on June 21, 1964, Price pulled to the right side of the road. Arledge drove past the Sheriff's Cruiser. He parked the Ranch Wagon on the left side of the road, 2 car lengths in front of the Cruiser. Barnette parked his 1957 Ford on the right side of the road, 1 car length behind the Cruiser. A deep ditch existed on the left side of the road.

Immediately, the bloodbath began. Everything was pre-planned.

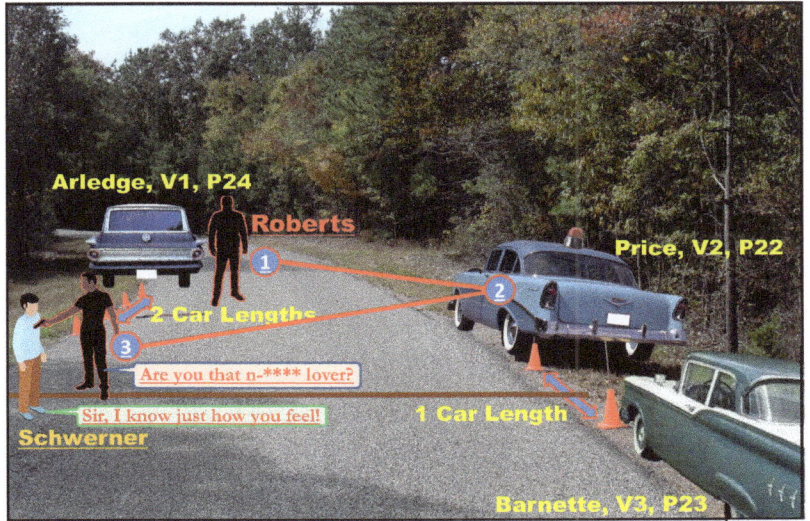

Wayne Roberts Murders Mickey Schwerner

Wayne Roberts quickly exited the Ranch Wagon. Roberts walked over to the Sheriff's Cruiser. **(1)** He opened the rear passenger door. After extracting Mickey Schwerner from the back seat, **(2)** Roberts escorted Schwerner to the left side of the road next to the ditch. Schwerner and Roberts were at a location that was midway between the Price Cruiser and the Barnette 1957 Ford. **(3)**

Are you that n-**** lover? snarled Wayne Roberts in a frenzy of hatred. Mickey Schwerner responded with dignity and with empathy. *Sir, I know just how you feel!* Wayne Roberts shot Mickey Schwerner in the chest.

Mickey Schwerner Falls Face Down Into Ditch After Being Shot

Mickey Schwerner fell into the ditch face down. His head was facing in a westerly direction. Schwerner experienced a painful death while he bled out for the next 10 – 16 seconds.

Schwerner was cruelly and brutally murdered. Yet, he died with dignity. – no screaming, no crying, no begging, just quiet dignity. Mickey Schwerner even expressed empathy for the White Knights Klansman who was about to murder him: *Sir, I know just how you feel.*

Wayne Roberts was not finished with his blood spilling. Roberts proceeded to murder Andy Goodman. Roberts walked back over to the Sheriff's Cruiser. **(1)**

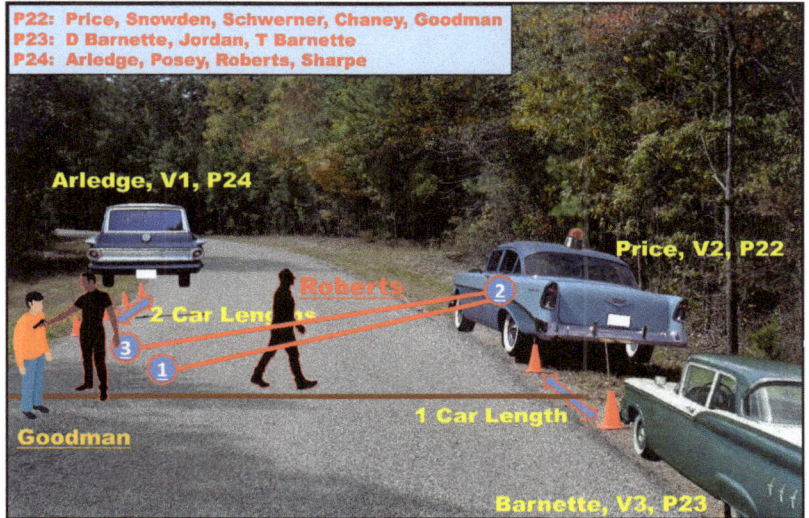

Wayne Roberts Murders Andy Goodman

Roberts reached into the open rear door of the Sheriff's Cruiser. **(2)** He dragged Andy Goodman out of the rear seat. Roberts pulled Goodman over to the ditch on the left side of the road. **(3)** This location was the same location where Mickey Schwerner was shot. Without a word, Wayne Roberts shot Goodman in the chest.

Andy Goodman fell into the ditch at the left side of the road.

Andy Goodman Falls Face Down Into Ditch After Being Shot

Goodman fell into the ditch on top of the body of Mickey Schwerner. His body was face down in a crumpled position, headed south, perpendicular to the road. Schwerner experienced a painful death while he bled out for the next 10 – 16 seconds. During his death throes, Goodman clenched his fists. During the clenching, Andy Goodman grabbed a loose piece of rock and clay. After he died, his clenched fist still held the piece of rock and clay.

Andy Goodman was also cruelly and brutally murdered. Goodman also died with dignity. – no screaming, no crying, no begging, just quiet dignity.

James Chaney was the last to be murdered on that day on Rock Cut Road. His murder was committed by Jim Jordan.

Jim Jordan Murders James Chaney

Jordan was sitting in the 1957 Ford that was driven by Doyle Barnette. He watched while the murders of Schwerner and Goodman were committed by Wayne Roberts. Then, from inside the 1957 Ford, Jordan suddenly exclaimed *Save one for me!* Jim Jordan did not want to be left out of the blood spilling.

Jim Jordan exited the 1957 Ford. (1) He walked over to the open rear door of the Sheriff's Cruiser. Reaching into the rear seat, Jordan pulled James Chaney from the back seat. (2) With Chaney in tow, Jordan walked over to the left side of the road. The pair was located midway between the Ranch Wagon and the Price Cruiser, 1 car length from each vehicle. (3) This location was several yards north of the location where Schwerner and Goodman were shot by Roberts.

Jim Jordan turned James Chaney with his face towards the ditch on the left side of the road. Jordan pointed his pistol very close to the back of the head, just behind and near the middle of the auricle of the right ear. Jordan pulled the trigger. Chaney died instantly.

James Chaney tumbled into the ditch, laying face up.

This murder made Jim Jordan ecstatic. *You didn't leave me anything but a n-****, but at least I killed me a n-****!* he proclaimed with great excitement.

Despite his death, the Klansmen were not finished with James Chaney.

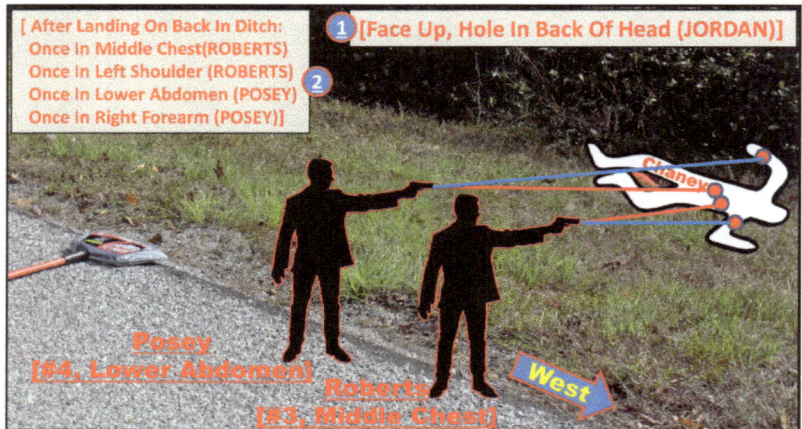

Posey, Roberts Shoot Into The Face Up Body Of James Chaney

In a frenzy of racist hatred, Wayne Roberts and Billy Posey moved to the edge of the ditch. Each of the Klansmen shot several rounds into the now dead body of James Chaney. Roberts shot into the middle chest and into the left shoulder. Bullets were discharged by Posey into the lower abdomen and the right forearm of the now dead body.

By 11:45 pm, the murders of Schwerner, Chaney and Goodman were completed. All that remained was to dispose of the bodies in a location far enough away to divert attention from the actual murderers.

James Chaney was even more cruelly and brutally murdered. Chaney died instantly from the shot to the head. His body was used for target practice after his death. Yet, Chaney also died with dignity. – no screaming, no crying, no begging, just quiet dignity.

Deputy Sheriff Cecil Price watched calmy while each of the trio was murdered. When he was sworn into office, Price took an oath and an obligation to protect the innocent and the weak. By the oath, Cecil Price had an obligation to protect Schwerner, Chaney and Goodman. In his fanatic racism and his sociopathic mental state, Price ignored those duties of his office.

Worse yet, Price actually did exactly the opposite. He conspired in the commission of the murders. Price arrested/kidnapped the trio. He led the killers to the murder location. And he simply stood by and watched while these cruel murders were committed. His crimes were even more heinous because he abused his law enforcement powers to conduct the commission of the murders.

Local residents also have culpability (guilt) in the commission of these murders. A popular vote at the time elected Lawrence Rainey to be Sheriff specifically for his use of cruelty to control Blacks. Rainey appointed Price specifically for his use of cruelty to control Blacks. Until 2004, residents of Neshoba County refused to have anything to do with holding Rainey and Price in any way culpable.

Murder convictions were never obtained for the cruel deaths!

25: *Caravan travels cross country to Hwy 21*

Deputy Sheriff Cecil Price was done. Price detained the trio while the murder plan was initiated and created. He illegally arrested/kidnapped Schwerner, Chaney and Goodman. Price then drove the trio to the murder location, leading the murderers. He idly watched Schwerner, Chaney and Goodman be brutally murdered by Roberts and Jordan. Since he had completed his part in the murders, Cecil Price entered his Sheriff's Cruiser. He drove east on Road 215, turned north on Highway 19, and drove back to Philadelphia.

Roberts, Jordan, and Posey had discharged firearms. Some of these firearms were semi-automatic handguns. These handguns ejected casings while cycling a new cartridge into the chamber. Someone said, *Help us get these empty shells. I've already got mine."* All of the casings were found and packed away. These casings were disposed and never found during the subsequent FBI investigations.

Now, the bodies had to be disposed. Billy Wayne Posey took control. *Let's load these guys in their wagon and take them to the spot.* The *spot* referenced by Posey was a dam under construction located on the Old Jolly Farm, owned by Olen Burrage. Edgar Ray Killen had arranged with Burrage to bury the bodies in the uncompleted dam. Burrage would have a bulldozer operator waiting to bury the bodies.

The victims were retrieved from their locations in the ditch on the left side of the road. Schwerner and Goodman were loaded first into the Ranch Wagon. Then, Chaney was thrown on top of Schwerner and Goodman.

Posey said, *Everyone follow me. We'll go the back way.*

Posey, Sharpe and Roberts entered the 1963 Ford Ranch Wagon that contained the bodies. Snowden, Jordan, Arledge, Travis Barnette, and Doyle Barnette entered into the 1957 Ford owned by Doyle Barnette. Doyle Barnette was the driver of his 1957 Ford.

Caravan Starts Cross Country Route To Preplanned Burial Location

The back way used 13 remote, mostly dark, unpaved gravel and raw dirt roads. These roads did not have any streetlights. In those days, many of these roads did not have any street signs to mark the way. Despite all of these limitations, Billy Wayne Posey was able to successfully navigate and lead Barnette through this maze of country roads.

Old Jolly Farm was located on Highway 21, southwest of Philadelphia. Posey and Barnette formed a caravan. Posey led Barnette as a caravan from Rock Cut Road/Road 515 to Highway 21. This route was 16.5 miles long. With the poor quality of the roads and the almost complete absence of lighting, average speed for the caravan was about 25 mph.

A person had to know the exact roads and turn locations to cover this remote area in the pitch-black night. Getting lost with 3 dead bodies on these remote roads would lead to the group being caught. These bodies had to be buried long before dawn. The Ranch Wagon also had to be disposed long before dawn.

Posey and Barnette just started straight west from the murder location on Rock Cut Road. Road 284 intersected Road 515 a short 118 yards to the west of the murder location after the Road 515 curved to the left.

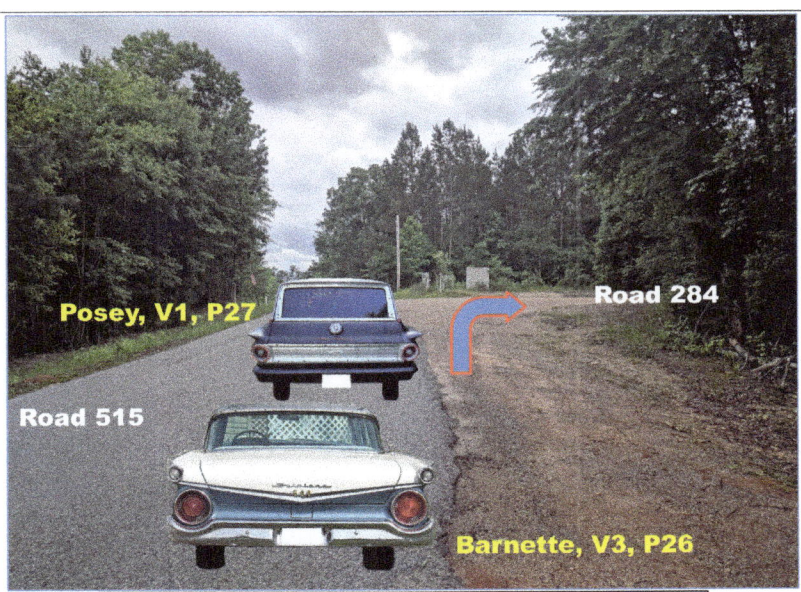

Caravan With Bodies Turns Right/West On Road 284

After this turn, a series of turns were necessary. Posey knew the exact route to follow without wasting any time at all.

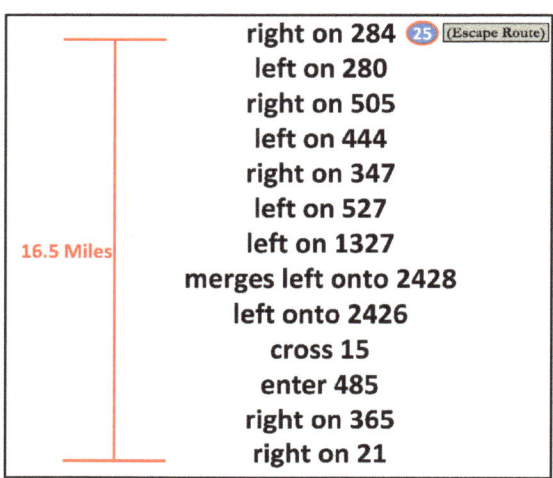

Cross Country Route From Murder Location To Hwy 21

Road 1327 even today is typical of the condition of the backroads that were followed by Posey and Barnette.

Caravan Turns Onto Road 1327 On Its Way To Hwy 21

Travel on this road took place about 12:15 am on the morning of June 22, 1964. The murders were completed about 30 minutes earlier. At that time, this road was pitch black due to heavily overgrown trees to either side of the road. Red gravel/clay formed the surface of the road.

Caravan Turns Onto Road 1327 In Pitch Blackness

Posey knew to take this road on the route to Highway 21. He also knew that the road merged left onto Road 2428. That merger location was not marked in those days. But, even if a sign identified the location, reading the sign was impossible in the pitch black.

Without any difficulty, Posey lead Barnette through the complicated series of 13 turns to the intersection of Road 365 and Highway 21.

Posey, Barnette, and Bodies Successfully Arrive At Hwy 21

By taking the leadership in transporting the bodies to the burial location, Billy Wayne Posey ensured the temporary success of the murders. This cross-country route using these remote, pitch black, gravel/clay roads was extremely complicated. Only a person who knew the area well or had practiced the route could have successfully navigated through the almost pitch-black dark.

Immediately after the murders, Posey ordered the others to follow him to *the place* to bury the bodies. Posey knew the cross-country route to follow through the pitch-black countryside roads. Planning a murder location, a burial location, and a cross-country route between the two locations proves intent to commit murder.

26: Caravan exits right from cross country route

Posey and Barnette were almost at the burial location when the caravan arrived at the intersection of Road 365 and Highway 21. A right turn was necessary to merge onto Highway 21.

Caravan Turns North From Road 365 Onto Hwy 21

After turning right onto Highway 21, the entrance to Old Jolley Farm was 3/4 of a mile further north.

This short distance was traveled in 1 ¼ minute at 40 mph.

Caravan With Bodies Travels North On Hwy 21 Towards Farm

Navigating through the complex web of pitch-black, gravel/clay country roads was the most difficult part of the whole arrest/murder/burial activities. Successful navigation of this route with the bodies ensured success of the activities of the night. Once the bodies were buried in the dam, Schwerner, Chaney and Goodman would never be found. This disappearance further enabled the local MS residents to continue that claim that the trio was somewhere else.

At least permanent disappearance of the bodies was the plan. In the end, Olen Burrage himself informed the FBI of the location of the bodies in exchange for a $30,000 fee.

27: Turn onto access road to dam

A dam was under construction at Old Jolly Farm owned by Olen Burrage. Surrounding areas were all dug up, graded flat, mostly shorn of vegetation. Piles of dirt were everywhere. Bulldozers were on site to move and to pack dirt into the dam. A temporary, dirt equipment access road was built. This access road enabled movement of bulldozers and other heavy equipment into the area where the dam was under construction.

At 12:45 am on Sunday, June 22, 1964, the caravan with the bodies encountered the equipment access road.

Caravan With Bodies Enters Equipment Access Road To Dam

Billy Wayne Posey, in the lead, took a left turn from Highway 21, onto the equipment access road. Doyle Barnette in his 1957 Ford followed Posey onto the access road. After driving 447 feet, the caravan encountered a fence that had been constructed from light posts and barbed wire. A gap in the fence allowed the caravan to continue down the access road.

About ½ mile from the entrance, the caravan encountered the end of the equipment access road.

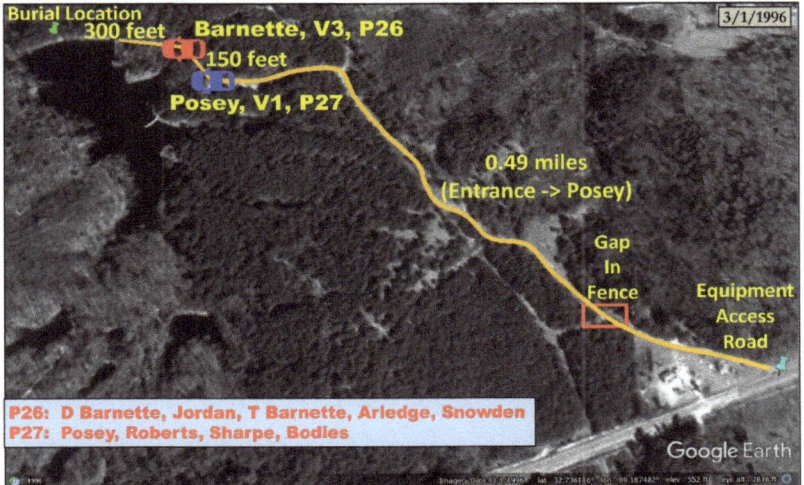

Caravan Travels Down Access Road, Parks At End

Posey parked the 1963 Ford Ranch Wagon right at the end of the road, perpendicular to a mound of dirt about 3 feet high. Barnette pulled his 1957 Ford off to the right 150 feet. He was able to drive off the road because the area was graded flat and clear for the construction of the dam. Doyle Barnett parked his 1957 Ford about 300 feet from the dam. Everyone exited the vehicles. Posey, Sharpe, Roberts, Snowden, Jordan, Arledge, Travis Barnette, and Doyle Barnette were now all at the dam.

Someone recognized that posting a lookout might be a good idea. Jim Jordan and Jimmy Snowden volunteered to serve as lookouts. Jordan and Snowden began walking back up the equipment access road towards the entrance.

After walking to the area near the opening in the fence, the pair found a gap in a row of trees. This gap was off to the side of the road.

Jordan And Snowden Position As Lookouts In A Gap In Trees

Jordan and Snowden positioned themselves within the gap in the trees. This position allowed the pair to have a clear view of the road while remaining hidden. If anyone unwanted approached the dam during the next few hours, one of the pair could run back to the dam and give warning to the others.

28: Locate bulldozer operator

A bulldozer operator was needed to bury the bodies. Operation a bulldozer required training and experience. Edgar Ray Killen arranged with Olen Burrage to have Herman Tucker, his regular construction operator, ready and available to bury the bodies.

Still acting in charge of the group, Billy Wayne Posey issued an order to go find the bulldozer operator. *I wonder where our operator is? Someone go and get the operator.* Posey told Barnette where the bulldozer operator was staged, waiting to be retrieved for the burial of the bodies. Doyle Barnette, Arledge, and Roberts entered Barnette's 1957 Ford.

Barnette and his 1957 Ford returned down the equipment access road to the paved road, Highway 21.

Barnette And Fellow White Knights Depart For Bulldozer Operator

Billy Wayne Posey, Jerry Sharpe, and Travis Barnette remained at the dam while Herman Tucker, the bulldozer operator was retrieved. Those remaining had the grisly task to watch over the bodies. Jordan and Snowden remained in their lookout position in the gap in the woods near the opening in the fence. If someone unwanted tried to enter the dam, the pair would run to warn Posey and the others. Presumably, if warned, Posey would jump in the Ranch Wagon and drive away, removing the bodies from the area until all was clear.

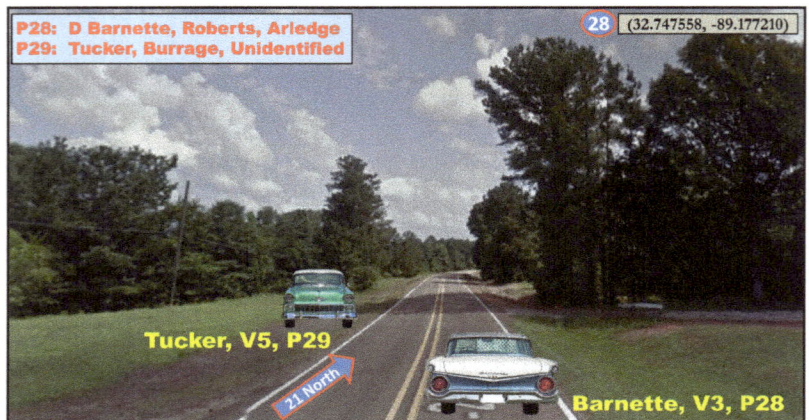

Barnette Encounters Tucker Waiting 1 Mile North On Hwy 21

Turning north on Highway 21, Barnette drove the 1957 Ford 1 mile north on Highway 21 at 40 mph. At this speed, this short drive consumed 1.5 minutes. A green and white 1955 Chevy was parked on the left side of the road. Olen Burrage, Herman Tucker, and one other unidentified person were waiting in the 1955 Chevy.

29: Deliver bulldozer operator

Doyle Barnette made a U turn and pulled up next to the passenger side of the 1955 Chevy. Olen Burrage, a passenger in the 1955 Chevy, told Doyle Barnette, the driver of the 1957 Ford, to follow Tucker.

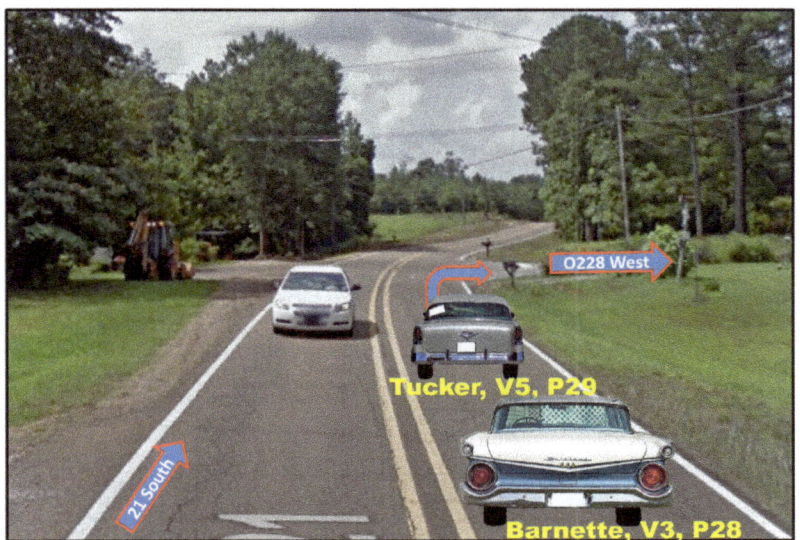

Tucker Takes Lead To The Drop Off Location

Tucker drove south on Highway 21 at 40 mph for about 120 yards to a dirt road. Currently this road is paved and known today as Bureau of Indian Affairs O228.

After driving down this road for 0.789 miles at a speed of 40 mph, the caravan came to a location with mostly undeveloped fields between Road O228 and the north end of the dam.

A walk to the dam was fairly easy across these undeveloped fields. Extensive vegetation and overgrowth was not around to slow progress across the fields.

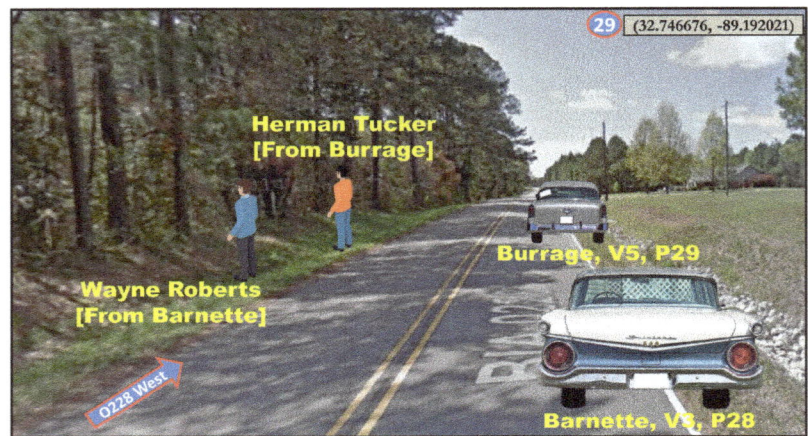

Herman Tucker, Wayne Roberts Exit Vehicles Due North Of Dam

Herman Tucker exited his own 1955 Chevy. Olen Burrage moved from the front passenger seat to the driver's seat. Wayne Roberts exited from the 1957 Ford driven by Doyle Barnette. Tucker and Roberts crossed O228 to other side. Together, the pair entered the pastureland and proceeded to walk ½ mile to the south towards the dam.

Burrage in the 1955 Chevy owned by Tucker and Barnette in his 1957 Ford made a U-turn on O228, heading east back towards Highway 21.

Burrage, Barnette Approach Hwy 21 After Dropoff

Burrage and the original unidentified passenger were in the 1955 Chevy owned by Herman Tucker. Within the 1957 Ford were Doyle Barnette and Jimmy Arledge. All 4 of these Klansmen were done for the night.

Burrage, Barnette Turn Vehicles North On Hwy 21

Burrage and Burnette drove 2 miles at 40 mph to the Burrage Trucking Company garage. After this short 3-minute drive, the two vehicles arrived at the garage. At the garage, Doyle Barnette attached back onto his 1957 Ford Fairlane the license plate which had been removed. Barnette, Arledge, and Burrage all waited at the Garage for Posey and the burial team to arrive with the Ranch Wagon.

Pickup and drop-off of Tucker and Roberts took about 5 minutes.[8] Tucker and Roberts were able to walk the 0.473 miles across the undeveloped fields north of the dam in about 15 minutes. Retrieving Herman Tucker to operate the bulldozer took a total of 20 minutes.

At 1:05 am on Sunday, July 22, 1964, Tucker and Roberts appeared at the top of the dam. Posey, Sharpe, and Travis Barnette were waiting at the dam. Snowden and Jordan were waiting down the equipment access road to the south of the dam, still acting as lookouts.

Jordan and Snowden had been standing as lookouts for about 20 minutes now. A whistle sound penetrated the dark night. Jordan asked, *What is it?*. Snowden responded, *Nothing. The operator is there and taking care of things.*

Tucker, Roberts Arrive At Top Of Dam After ½ Mile Walk

Construction of the dam had proceeded from east to west. A large completed section began on the east side of the dam. An area of unfilled excavation began at the end of the completed section. This unfilled excavation extended all the way to the western edge of the dam.

30: Bodies buried in unfilled excavation

The Klansmen chose to bury the bodies just at the edge of the completed area of the dam. Burying the bodies at this edge made the burial site look like part of the work completed on the previous day. That disguise prevented workers arriving at the start of the next workday from asking too many questions.

This burial location was 356 feet from the eastern edge of the dam.[9] The bodies were in the Ranch Wagon at the end of the equipment access road. This location was on the eastern edge of the dam and 450 feet further away.[10] Combined, the bodies had to be transported 806 feet or 269 yards. Dead bodies are more difficult to transport. Moving the bodies took 30 minutes because of the dead weight and the distance.

Posey, Roberts, Sharpe, Travis Barnette, and Tucker carried the bodies 269 yards from the Ranch Wagon to the edge of the completed area of the dam. These 5 Klansmen did not appear to have any guilt or empathy for carrying the bodies across the side area and the top of the dam.

Bodies Are Buried At The Edge Of The Unfilled Excavation

All three bodies were dumped onto the ground into the unfilled excavation area close its easternmost edge, 191 feet from the west end of the dam. Using the Caterpillar Bulldozer, Herman Tucker covered the bodies in the unfilled area with dirt. He used the blade of the bulldozer to level the dirt over the top of the covered bodies. He then drove over and over the now buried bodies with the Bulldozer to compact the dirt over and around the bodies. Compaction ensured that the bodies would not be accidentally found.

The bodies were buried in a section of dirt that was 6 feet, 9 inches across the top from north to south, 7 feet, 6 inches wide from east to west, and

14 feet, 11 inches below the top of the dam. A total of 758 cubic feet of dirt was moved and packed.

A cubic foot of dirt weighs 74 pounds.[11] In the process of burying the bodies, Herman Tucker moved and packed 56,193 pounds (28 tons!) of dirt. This process consumed 15 minutes. These bodies were well hidden.

At 1:50 am on Sunday, June 22, 1964, the bodies had been moved (30 minutes) and the dirt covered and packed (15 minutes). All of the White Knights involved in the murders could now breathe a sigh of relief. These bodies were well hidden. Finding the bodies was unlikely, ... unless someone talked.

Cowards like the White Knights are not loyal to each other. Sooner or later, someone would reveal the location in their own self-interest. That person was Olen Burrage, who had participated in a big way. Burrage took a $30,000 payoff as a secret informant to reveal the burial location.

Now, disposal of the Ranch Wagon as quickly as possible was paramount.

31: Wagon driven to garage

Time was running out for the murderers. Dawn was on the way. Disposal of the Ranch Wagon was now extremely high priority. Putting significant distance between the bodies in the dam and a disposed Ranch Wagon was important to hiding the murders.

After the burial was completed, Posey, Sharpe, Travis Barnette, Roberts and Tucker entered the 1963 Ford Ranch Wagon that had belonged to the victims.

Posey Drives Ranch Wagon Away From Burial Location

Posey drove the wagon down the equipment access road to the dam where Jordan and Snowden were serving as lookouts. Jordan and Snowden entered the Ranch Wagon. Seven passengers were not a problem for the Ranch Wagon. This vehicle had a comfortable passenger limit of eight persons.

Posey than drove the Ranch Wagon headed north on Highway 21 towards the Burrage Truck Company and auto repair garage.

Ranch Wagon Approaches 488, 21 North Intersection

With time slipping away, Posey felt a need for speed. He drove at a speed of 50 mph. After 1 ½ miles, Posey and the Ranch Wagon arrived at the intersection of Highway 488 and Highway 21.

After bearing to the right at the intersection, Posey entered the last ½ mile stretch before the Burrage Truck Company and Garage.

Posey Enters The Last ½ Mile Stretch Before The Garage

Still traveling at 50 mph, the Ranch Wagon passes the Fellowship Baptist Church on the left 85 yards before the Garage.

Fellowship Baptist Church On Highway 21

In the future, Olen Burrage became a Deacon (community leader) of this Church. This Church was within walking distance of both the Garage and the home of Olen Burrage.

Driving another 85 yards north on Highway 21 led Posey and the Ranch Wagon to the entrance of the Burrage Truck Company facility.

Ranch Wagon Approaches Burrage Trucking Company On Left

Posey rapidly made a left turn into the Garage entrance area at high speed. He hit the brakes and came to a screeching halt

Posey Brakes To A Screeching Halt At Garage Entrance

The Ranch Wagon arrived at the Burrage Truck Company Garage around 2:00 am, now June 22, 1964.

Billy Wayne Posey, Wayne Roberts, Jim Jordan, Doyle Barnette, Travis Barnette, Jimmy Arledge, and Jerry Sharpe, Jimmy Snowden, Herman Tucker, and Olen Burrage were now assembled at the Burrage Trucking Company. All 3 vehicles were also assembled at the Garage: the Ranch Wagon, the 1957 Ford owned by Doyle Barnette, and the 1955 Chevy owned by Herman Tucker.

32: Wagon, truck escort travel north on 21

A simple plan was determined for disposal of the Ranch Wagon. Herman Tucker would drive the Ranch Wagon into AL. The AL border was only 37 miles from Philadelphia. Olen Burrage would follow Tucker in a 10' diesel truck to return Tucker to the Garage. *No one will suspect a truck on the road at this time of night.*

Olen Burrage retrieved one of the diesel trucks from under a trailer parked at his Garage. Burrage retrieved a glass gallon jug, filling this jug with gasoline. This gasoline would be used to burn the Ranch Wagon after being abandoned.

Tucker, in the 1963 Ford Ranch Wagon of the victims, and Burrage, in the diesel truck, exited the garage and started north on Highway 21.

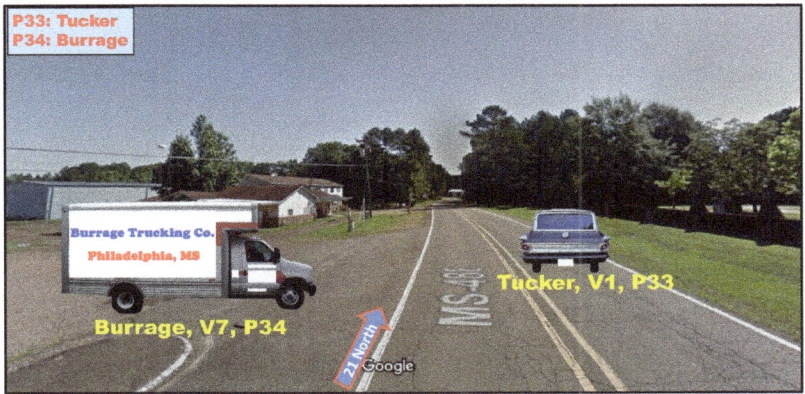

Tucker, Burrage Leave Garage For Disposal Location

This truck could not move that fast. Tucker, leading the way in the Ranch Wagon, had to accommodate the speed limit of the diesel truck. Based on the limited speed of the truck, the caravan only moved at 50 mph.

Driving for 1.3 miles at 50 mph took the caravan to the intersection of Highway 21 North and 21, 15, 16 north. This intersection is on the western edge of downtown Philadelphia.

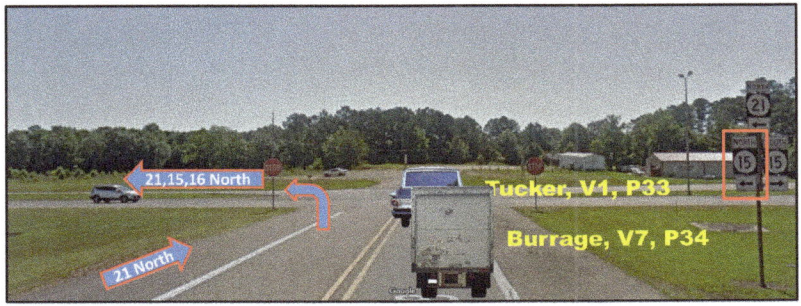

Caravan Arrives At Intersection of Hwy 21 and Hwys 21, 15, 16

As the caravan moved closer and closer to downtown Philadelphia, the risk of discovery increased. Even the possibility of having the Ranch Wagon sighted inside the city limits could lead to exposure of all the killers in a later investigation.

A left turn onto this spur road resulted in the caravan driving in a northerly direction along the spur road. Another 0.85 miles at 50 mph led to a split in the spur. Bearing to the right at the split in the spur road led the caravan into a 0.65-mile city access road. At the end of this section, the caravan arrived at the entrance to Main Street.

Caravan With Ranch Wagon Approaches Main Street Downtown

For the next 1.1 miles, the caravan drove down Main Street to Pecan Avenue. Risk of exposure was extremely high along this section. This section was the western edge of downtown Philadelphia. Getting stopped was not very likely. Sheriff Lawrence Rainey, Deputy Sheriff Cecil Price and Philadelphia Patrolman Richard Willis were the only law enforcement officers on duty with any jurisdiction. These officers were all part of the conspiracy to murder Schwerner, Chaney and Goodman. If the caravan were discovered by any of these officers, a safe escort across town would be the response.

However, if an uninvolved resident, and especially a Black resident, saw the Ranch Wagon, a hue and cry would result. Independence Quarters, the Black Section of downtown, was only ½ mile north of this section of Main Street. Every Black resident knew that the trio was missing. If the Ranch Wagon was seen, an extensive investigation would be directed at Philadelphia and Neshoba County.

This drive down the 1.1-mile section of Main Street to Pecan Avenue was driven at normal traffic speed of 30 mph so as not to raise attention.

Perhaps the likelihood of being sighted was small. Although the drive was through downtown Philadelphia for 1.1 miles, this was rural Philadelphia a few minutes after 2:00 am on a Sunday morning. Streets were deserted at that time.

At 2:05 am, the caravan took a left turn to the north on Pecan Avenue.

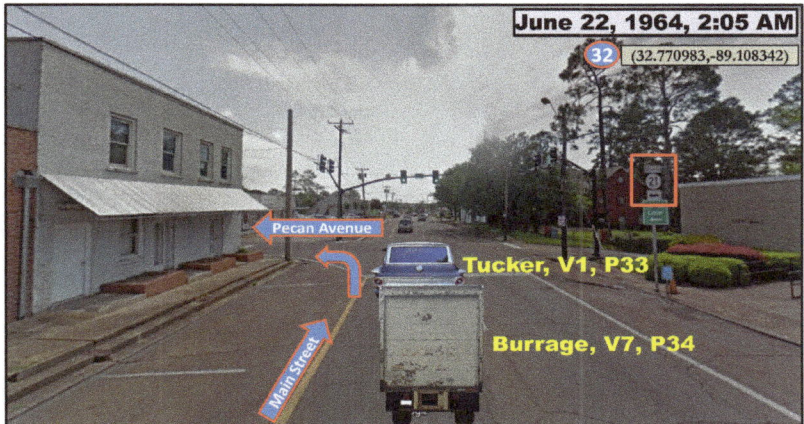

Caravan Turns North On Pecan Avenue In Downtown

Another 0.3 miles north on Pecan Avenue led to a split in the road. Taking the split to the right in the road merged into Highway 21 north.

Caravan Travels North On Pecan Avenue Towards Hwy 21 North

Driving along this short 0.3-mile section was an even greater risk than driving along the section of Main Street. Pecan Avenue north of Main Street is a residential street, not a business street like Main Street. Residents were at home at 2:05 am on a Sunday. Driving the Ranch Wagon along a residential street increased the risk of being seen precisely because residents were at home at that time.

As the caravan merged right onto Highway 21, speed was again increased to 50 mph.

Caravan Passes Intersection Hwy 21 North With Highway 491

Another 12 miles north on Highway 21 led to the intersection with Highway 491. At 50 mph, the caravan took 15 minutes to cover this distance.[12] At 2:20 am, Sunday, June 22, 1964, the caravan passed the intersection with Highway 491.

Originally, Herman Tucker was to drive the Ranch Wagon across the AL border. From the intersection of Highway 21 and Highway 491, the shortest route to the AL border was 41.2 miles.

Shortest Route From Hwy 491 To AL Border

At 50 mph, traveling all the way into AL would take another 50 minutes.[13] Right now, the time was 2:20 am. Driving another 50 minutes was dangerous. The chances of identification or even being stopped were extremely high now.

Worse yet, Herman Tucker probably did not know the route to the AL border. Following Highway 21 to Shuqualak, a very small rural town, was easily accomplished. However, after this town, navigating a series of remote country roads was necessary. Discovering this route on the fly was not likely. Herman Tucker and Olen Burrage, in the diesel truck, would get lost. The risk of discovery was just too great.

Herman Tucker panicked. A convenient location to dispose the Ranch Wagon needed to be found now!! Any location clear enough to drive the Ranch Wagon out among the trees would do. In a matter of minutes, the Ranch Wagon could be consumed in flames using the gasoline that Olen Burrage had procured prior to departure.

Tucker led the caravan along for another mile at 50 mph. After this short, 1-minute drive,[14] the caravan encountered the bridge over the Bogue Chitto Creek.

Caravan Crosses The Bridge Over Bogue Chitto Creek On Hwy 21

As he exited the east end of the bridge, Tucker grew excited. His prayers for a near-by disposal location had been answered.

33: Wagon diverted into swamp past 491

Just up ahead past the east exit of the Bogue Chitto Creek Bridge, Herman Tucker saw the solution to the disposal problem. Tucker drove 112 feet past the edge of the bridge.

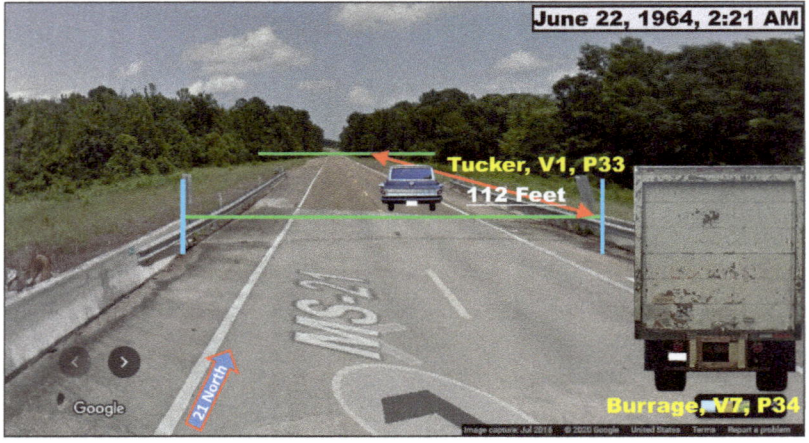

Tucker Drives Ranch Wagon 112 Feet Past East Exit Of Bridge

At 2:21 am, on Sunday, June 22, 1964, Herman Tucker in the Ranch Wagon made a hard left at 112 feet past the east edge of the Bridge.

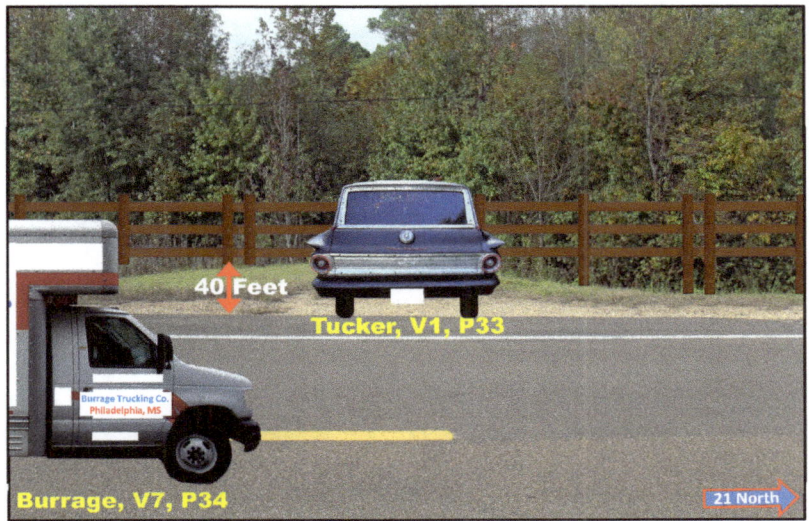

Tucker Faces Country Fence After Turning Left From Hwy 21

After turning left, Tucker encountered a wooden country fence. This fence was 40 feet from the edge of Highway 21. Country wooden fences tend to be cheaply built (to save money) and rickety and degraded from long exposure to weather. Tucker knew that such a flimsy wooden structure would not be an impediment.

Herman Tucker slammed the gas pedal to the floor. The Ranch Wagon jerked forward, slamming into the fence. As expected, the flimsy wooden fence collapsed under the force of the heavy, moving Ranch Wagon.

Tucker, Burrage Watch As Ranch Wagon Engulfed In Flames

Olen Burrage parked the diesel truck facing north at the side of Highway 21. Burrage rushed through the fence opening to stand behind and off to the side of the Ranch Wagon.

Immediately after the crash through the fence, Herman Tucker jumped out of the Ranch Wagon. Tucker grabbed the gasoline bottle. He proceeded to douse the Ranch Wagon in flames. Tucker threw a lit match into the Ranch Wagon. Burrage and Tucker watched as the gas exploded into giant flames engulfing the Ranch Wagon. These flames could be seen for miles in the deep, dark, rural MS night. Fortunately, no one was around to see them.

Burrage and Tucker watched the growing flames long enough to ensure that the Ranch Wagon was totally engulfed and would be destroyed. Just before 2:30 am on Sunday, June 22, 1964, disposing of the Ranch Wagon was completed.

The pair then turned back towards Highway 21 to leave for the Garage.

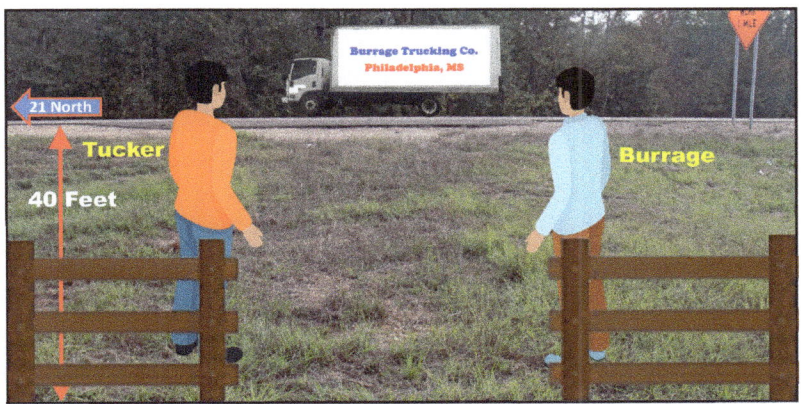

Burrage, Tucker Run Back To The Waiting Diesel Truck

Passing through the opening in the fence, Burrage and Tucker ran the 40 feet back up the hillside to the waiting diesel truck that Burrage had parked on Highway 21. Immediately, Burrage started the truck. He made a U-turn on Highway 21, speeding back south towards his Trucking Co. Garage at 50 mph.

Just in time, ...

Tucker had been correct in his fears of discovery. Just after 2:30 am, two cars had passed the burning Ranch Wagon. T. Hudson was driving south west on Highway 21 towards Philadelphia. Just before the Bogue Chitto Bridge, Hudson saw the burning car off to the right.

Rodney Harrison was a passenger in another car driving north east along Highway 21 away from Philadelphia. Also in the car were Raymond Dallas and another Black person. Harrison saw the Ranch Wagon burning off to the left. As the car containing Harrison approached the burning car, another car was just departing from the area of the burning car heading south east towards Philadelphia. The passing car moving in a south west direction was the car driven by T. Hudson.

Burrage and Tucker completed the burning and departed just minutes before these two cars saw the burning Ranch Wagon! The pair just barely missed being caught in the act of destroying the Ranch Wagon.

34: Truck returns to garage on 21

Burrage simply followed a reverse path from the disposal location back to his Garage. This disposal location was on Highway 21 north east of Philadelphia. His home was situated on Highway 21 southwest of Philadelphia. Only 17.2 miles to cover before Burrage and Tucker were free and clear.

As he drove the diesel truck southwest on Highway 21, Burrage passed Highway 491 on his left. This intersection was the location where Tucker decided to find an immediate disposal location for the Ranch Wagon

Burrage, Tucker Pass Intersection With Highway 491

Upon reaching downtown Philadelphia, Olen Burrage took a slightly different route through the city. In the trip out to the disposal location, Main Street was the first cross town street that Tucker had encountered. Tucker drove on Main Street to Pecan Avenue For the return trip, Burrage turned right from Pecan Avenue on to Beacon Street. Coming from the north, Beacon Street was the first cross town street that Burrage encountered.

Burrage, Tucker Turn Right From Pecan Avenue To Beacon Street

Burrage correctly anticipated the risk of exposure for the murders during the return trip when the truck was driven by itself. Risk of exposure was non-existent through the Pecan Avenue residential district and through downtown on Beacon Street.

After passing through the highway spur roads at the west end of downtown, Burrage headed west on Highway 21 towards his Garage.

Burrage, Tucker Arrive At The Burrage Trucking Co. Garage

At 3:00 am on Sunday, June 22, 1964, Olen Burrage and Herman Tucker arrived at the Garage. Burrage drove the diesel truck deep into the parking apron back to its original location under the trailer. He turned off the motor. Everyone would think that the truck had never moved from its parked location on the previous day.

Burrage and Tucker felt that a weight was lifted from their shoulders. The Ranch Wagon was on the other side of the County and severely burned. Association with the White Knights or any individuals was not really possible, even if the burnt Ranch Wagon was found.

35: Burrage returns to home

After Tucker and Burrage departed the garage to dispose of the Ranch Wagon of the victims, Doyle Barnette, Posey, Sharpe, Travis Barnette, Roberts, Snowden, Jordan, and Arledge climbed into the 1957 Ford owned by Doyle Barnette. Exiting the garage, Doyle Barnette drove his 1957 Ford north along Highway 21 into Philadelphia. Sheriff Lawrence Rainey, Deputy Sheriff Cecil Price, and Philadelphia PD Officer Richard Willis overtook the 1957 Ford. Klansmen and law enforcement officers had a short discussion. After the discussion, the Klansmen entered the 1957 Ford. Eventually, everyone returned to their homes.

Burrage and Tucker were the only remaining Klansmen out and about.

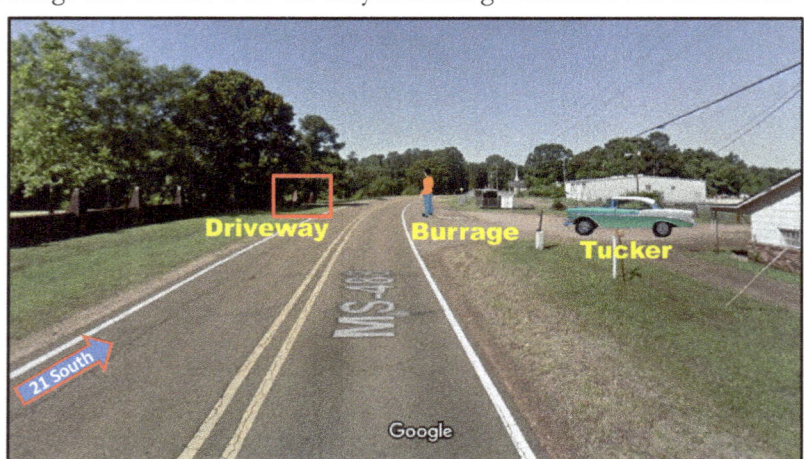

Burrage, Tucker Depart For Their Respective Homes

Herman Tucker's 1955 Chevy was parked at the Trucking Co. Olen Burrage drove the Chevy to the Garage after dropping Tucker on O228 to bury the bodies. Herman Tucker retrieved his car. Tucker bid goodnight to Burrage. He departed for his home.

Burrage simply walked across Highway 21 to his driveway entrance. Olen Burrage was pleased with the work of the Klansmen that night. Two n-****-loving Jews and their n-**** friend who were troublemakers were gone, never to return. Their bodies were buried in an unmarked grave that was difficult to find. Their Ranch Wagon was disposed on the other side of Neshoba County, making association with the Klansman difficult, if not impossible. A problem was solved. A lesson was delivered to these trouble-making civil rights agitators and local Black residents.

Many Southerners who believed in the white Southern tradition sang the Confederate anthem *Dixie* at times when white racism triumphed. Olen Burrage was probably humming the words to himself as he crossed Highway 21 and walked down the driveway to his home.

I wish I was in the land of cotton, old times there are not forgotten,
Look away, look away, look away, Dixie Land.
In Dixie Land where I was born in, early on a frosty mornin',
Look away, look away, look away, Dixie Land.

Then I wish I was in Dixie, hooray! hooray!
In Dixie Land I'll take my stand to live and die in Dixie,
Away, away, away down South in Dixie,
Away, away, away down South in Dixie.

In Dixie Land, I'll take my stand, and live and die in Dixie. Indeed!!

Olen Burrage continued to walk down the driveway towards his house after crossing Highway 21.

Burrage Walks Down Driveway And Enters House

Burrage entered his home. He prepared for bed. By 3:15 am, on Sunday, June 22, 1964, Olen Burrage was sleeping soundly, without a second thought or any feeling of remorse.

Olen Burrage, like the other participating Klansmen, did not have any empathy for the pain these deaths would cause to a wife, parents, brothers and sisters, and other relatives.

These White Knights were also totally unprepared for the reaction to the murders by US citizens outside of MS. A massive onslaught of Federal resources would be directed at solving these murders.

These ignorant, arrogant, racist thugs knew that a MS jury would never convict them for the murders. And, in the end, their assumptions were correct. Convictions delivered by juries were for violation of the civil right of due process and for manslaughter

Ill-Fated Decisions By Chaney

James Chaney was driving the Ranch Wagon on that fateful day, June 21, 1964. Chaney made two decisions that cost the lives of the trio. After the trio passed the Philadelphia city border driving south, Chaney chose to drive at the normal city speed of 30 mph. In panic after being overtaken by Deputy Sheriff Price and the cars full of Klansmen, Chaney turned west onto Highway 492.

If these decisions had been made differently, Schwerner, Chaney and Goodman would have survived the night.

This evaluation is not meant to be any kind of indictment of Chaney. His decision to drive at the city speed limit was reasonably justified under the conditions. Turning west onto Highway 492 was a decision made in panic in response to a mob of racist madmen bearing down on the trio out of the deep, dark silent night. However, both of these decisions were ill-fated, contributing to the death of Schwerner, Chaney and Goodman.

Geographic Characterization of the Area

Objectively evaluating these decisions requires an understanding of the geographic layout at the time of the decisions.

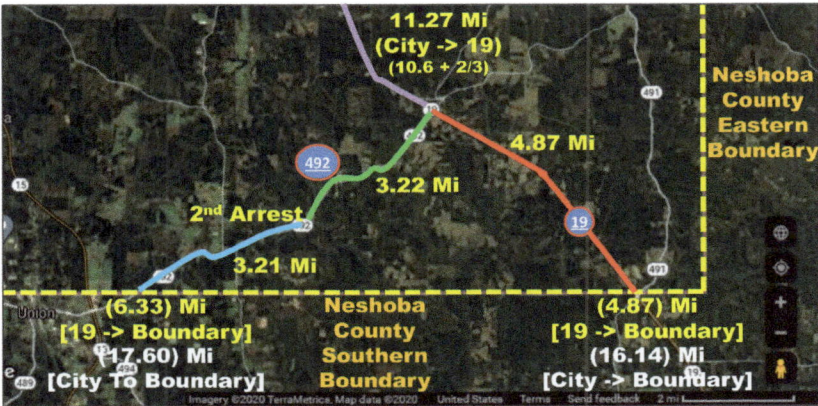

Geographic Layout Where Trio Was Overtaken, Arrested

Deputy Sheriff Cecil Price only had arrest jurisdiction up to the Neshoba County boundaries. In order to be totally safe from further harassment or even worse from Price, the trio had to travel beyond Neshoba County boundaries.

Deputy Sheriff Price and Philadelphia PD Willis reversed direction at the southern city boundary of Philadelphia. At this location, the Ranch Wagon was 16.14 miles from the Neshoba County boundary directly along Highway 19. When the Ranch Wagon turned west on Highway 492, the distance from the southern city boundary of Philadelphia to the Neshoba County boundary was 17.60 miles.

At the intersection of Highway 19 and Highway 492, two routes were available to the Neshoba County southern boundary. Continuing south on Highway 19, the Neshoba County Boundary was 4.87 miles away. Turning west on Highway 492 from this intersection, the distance to the Neshoba County boundary was 6.33 miles.

Driving At Normal City Speed

James Chaney made a conscious decision to proceed at a normal city speed of 30 mph when driving south from the southern boundary of Philadelphia. Under the conditions, that decision made some logical sense. As with all MS highways, this section of Highway 19 was under the jurisdiction of the MS Highway Patrol.

At the first arrest, MS HP Officers Harry Wiggs and Earl Poe escorted the trio and their Ranch Wagon to the Neshoba County Jail. This escort was accomplished at the request of Deputy Sheriff Cecil Price. However, Chaney could not have known that the escort was in response to a radio request by Price. For all that Chaney knew, these MS HP Officers might have been involved. So, Chaney drove at 30 mph in order to avoid giving the HP Officers a chance for a second arrest.

At 10:38 pm, Chaney, Schwerner and Goodman departed the southern city boundary of Philadelphia. At 11:00 pm, Deputy Sheriff Price, followed by Klansmen, overtook the trio at a location 10.6 miles from the boundary. Price and the Klansmen took 11 minutes to coordinate and get organized and 11 minutes to overtake the Ranch Wagon. Price and the Klansmen were able to overtake the Ranch Wagon in 22 minutes precisely because Chaney drove south on Highway 19 at a city speed of 30 mph, to be safe.

If Chaney had driven the Ranch Wagon at 60 mph, a different outcome would have resulted. Driving for 22 minutes at 60 mph would have enabled the Ranch Wagon to travel 22 miles.[15]

On Highway 19, the distance between the southern boundary of Philadelphia and the boundary of Neshoba County is 16.14 miles. If Chaney had driven straight down Highway 19 at 60 mph, the Ranch Wagon would have been 5.86 miles into Lauderdale County.[16] This location is 2 miles short of Collinsville, MS. The trio would have been completely out of the jurisdiction of Deputy Sheriff Price!

Of course, Price could have waved the Klansmen on to capture the trio. Some of the Klansmen were from Meridian. However, the Klansmen in an unmarked car did not have arrest jurisdiction. So, the trio did not have to pull the Ranch Wagon if ordered by the Klansmen.

Furthermore, the Klansmen were 11.4 miles behind the Ranch Wagon. In order to overtake the Ranch Wagon, the Klansmen had to travel at a speed greater than 60 mph to close down the distance between the vehicles. The Ranch Wagon would only have been 15 miles from COFO HQ in Meridian. At 60 mph, the Ranch Wagon would reach the COFO HQ in another 15 minutes.[17]

In order to catch the Ranch Wagon, the Klansmen would have to make up the 11.4 miles and cover an additional 15 miles, all in that same 15 minutes. Covering 26.4 miles in 15 minutes required that the Klansmen travel at a speed of 105 mph.[18] That 1957 Ford Fairlane driven by Doyle Barnette was really only capable of sustained speed of 60 mph.

James Chaney should have increased his speed to 60 mph once out of sight of Deputy Sheriff Price and Philadelphia PD Officer Richard Willis. Chaney also should have proceeded straight south on Highway 19 without any detours. At this speed, Price could not have overtaken the Ranch Wagon before crossing the Neshoba County boundary. Barnette in his 1957 Ford Fairlane could not have overtaken the Ranch Wagon before safely reaching Meridian.

Schwerner, Chaney and Goodman could have avoided being murdered.

Turning West on Highway 492

When Deputy Sheriff Cecil Price overtook the Ranch Wagon ¾ mile north of Highway 492, Chaney, Schwerner and Goodman all panicked. Chaney then made a panicked decision to lead the high-speed chase onto Highway 492 west.

This decision was wrong for a number of reasons. As Price joked, the Ranch Wagon was headed away from Meridian instead of towards Meridian. By going the wrong way, Chaney increased the distance to safety as opposed to getting closer to safety.

The Neshoba County border is 4.87 miles southeast from the intersection between Highway 19 and Highway 492. Once Chaney turned onto Highway 492 west, the Neshoba County border was 6.33 miles southwest of the intersection. Besides being in the wrong direction away from Meridian, this added 1 ½ miles to the distance to safety for the trio.[19] On this remote country road, opportunities to force the Ranch Wagon to the side of the road were limited due to the heavy forest overgrowth. This seemingly short added distance gave Price a greater opportunity to find a place where he could force the trio to the side of the road.

This decision was only a bad decision because of the first bad decision by Chaney. Chaney drove at a speed that allowed Price to overtake the Ranch Wagon while still on Highway 19.

This situation would not have even been a problem if Chaney had simply driven at 60 mph straight south on Highway 19 towards Meridian. That speed and route would have enabled Chaney to take advantage of that 11-minute head start while Price and the Klansmen consolidated at the southern city border of Philadelphia.

Summary and Conclusions

In May, 1964, White Knight Imperial Wizard Sam Bowers ordered the *elimination* of Mickey Schwerner, Goatee, *the Jew Boy*. White Knight Kleagle Edgar Ray Killen began planning the murders. At some time, Schwerner would come back into Neshoba County. A plan was needed.

On June 21, 1964, at 3:30 pm, Deputy Sheriff Cecil Price notified Killen that Schwerner and 2 others were in custody, including that n-**** James Chaney.

Killen activated the conspiracy to carry out the plan. Murder was the single intent of this conspiracy from the beginning.

- A known murder location was chosen. Deputy Sheriff Price led the murderers directly to the murder location.
- Designated executioners were chosen. Wayne Roberts and Jim Jordan carried loaded firearms to commit the actual murders.
- A known burial location was chosen. Billy Wayne Posey led the burial team directly to the burial location through a complicated route of dark country dirt roads.
- A bulldozer operator was staged near the burial location to bury the bodies in a secret grave.

All of these points prove that murder was the single intent of this conspiracy from the beginning.

A very complex set of activities with a large number of participants was accomplished within a short period of time (10:30 pm – 3:00 am). Detailed planning to accomplish the murders and the burials was necessary for success. These factors further corroborate that murder was the single intent of the conspiracy from the beginning.

Edgar Ray Killen was the chief conspirator.

- Killen activated the members of the conspiracy.
- Killen arranged for the Klansmen to stage at the old building.
- Killen selected the murder location within a mile of his home.
- Killen arranged for the body to be buried on Old Jolly Farm.

Deputy Sheriff Cecil Price was the chief enabler.

- Price arrested and held the trio to enable activation.
- Price notified Killen that the trio had been arrested.
- Price arrested the trio again using his law enforcement arrest powers to transport the trio to their deaths.
- Price watched the murders being committed without arresting the murderers as required by his job.

Olen Burrage was the chief cleanup organizer.

- Burrage allowed the bodies to be buried on his farm.
- Burrage arranged for the bulldozer operator to be staged near the dam.
- Burrage drove the escort/recovery vehicle during the disposal of the Ranch Wagon.

Wayne Roberts and Jim Jordan were the executioners.

Herman Tucker buried the bodies and drove the Ranch Wagon to the disposal location.

These murders were an act of cowardice. Eight violent, racist Klansmen overwhelmed 3 innocent victims in the darkest of night. Even with the overwhelming force in their favor, the White Knights still hid behind the law enforcement arrest powers of Deputy Sheriff Cecil Price.

In 2005, a Neshoba County jury had the opportunity to set justice right. Edgar Ray Killen was charged with 3 counts of conspiracy to commit murder. Despite the above overwhelming evidence, this jury convicted Edgar Killen of 3 counts of the lesser charge of manslaughter.

Jury members claimed that intent to commit murder was not proven by the prosecution. During the trial, the prosecution presented all of the above facts. Edgar Ray Killen was the chief conspirator. Murder was the single intent of the conspiracy from the beginning.

<u>Murder convictions were never obtained for the cruel deaths!</u>

Part 7: The Past Is Never Dead

The Author Pays A Scary Visit To Philadelphia

The FBI Refuses To Release Unredacted Records

A Dark Cloud Over Neshoba County

In 2016, an FBI report informed the MS AG about the possible future of any prosecution. Almost everyone involved was dead. Most witnesses were either dead or suffered from imperfect recollections due to the passage of time. A few witnesses who had clear recollection refused to be threatened into cooperating.

The dark cloud over Neshoba County should have disappeared. If only, ...

Neshoba County On October 31, 2018

As part of the research for this book, I identified 35 locations involved in the events on June 21, 1964. As a shooting reconstruction expert, I always take photos of every location involved. I use these photos as background to reconstruct the sequence of events. So, once I identified the 35 locations, I had to go to Philadelphia to photograph all of those locations for my reconstruction.

I asked my nephew Matt to go along with me. Matt is a member of the Bar in both MS and AL. With my history growing up Jewish in MS and my knowledge that I was going into the devil's den, I wanted company.

On Oct 31, 2018, I was in Philadelphia, MS, with my nephew Matt. We were retracing the 35 locations involved in the whole sequence of events. Of course, we started with Mt Zion United Methodist Church.

We had stopped at a location on Hwy 16 west heading towards Philadelphia to photo a specific location. While I was taking pictures, my nephew went across the street to a convenience store to get some water. The people in the store asked him what I was doing. He said nothing.

At this stop, an older lady came out of her home and talked to us. She introduced herself and asked what we were doing. I told her what we were doing. We chatted a bit. She told me that she had lived in Philadelphia at the time of the murders. After a few minutes, she went back into her home. Matt and I continued heading west towards Philadelphia on Hwy 16. [Yes, I have her name. No, I won't reveal her name, because of what happened next.]

About 10 minutes later, we are driving west on Hwy 16 between stops. I looked in the rear-view mirror. A Neshoba County Sheriff's cruiser was overtaking us at a high speed, with lights flashing and siren howling.

My heart began to race. My breathing rate jumped up from an adrenaline rush. This situation was exactly what Schwerner, Chaney, and Goodman faced on that dark night heading down Hwy 19 on June 21, 1964. All I could think was that history repeats itself. This situation was going to happen again. The Jew gets it again in Philadelphia!

Since the cruiser was displaying lights and siren, I pulled over to the side of the road to await the cruiser. Matt and I were not sure what would happen if the sheriff's cruiser actually pulled over behind us. The cruiser just passed us by at high speed.

My heart took several minutes to stop racing. My breathing finally calmed back to a normal rate after a few minutes.

This incident was a very short period after we had talked to the older lady a few stops back. This incident may have been a coincidence. The cruiser may have been on its way to handle another problem. Or, this incident may have been a nudge. After all, we had talked to the older lady a short time before the incident. She had plenty of time to call the Neshoba County Sheriff's Office and tell them about me and my investigation.

We know you are here. We are watching you. Don't go where you aren't wanted. Don't ask a lot of questions.

You can form your own opinion as to whether this incident was a coincidence or a nudge. Frankly, I don't believe in coincidences myself. However, my reaction clearly indicates that the dark cloud still hangs over Philadelphia, regardless of the 2005 conviction of Killen!

Eventually, we arrived at the location on Road 515 where the murders were performed. I started to position traffic cones and plungers to identify locations of vehicles and bodies during the night of the murders. After all was positioned, I started taking pictures. As I was taking pictures, a car drove up and stopped. I was here at the location where the murders took place. An older guy in a car drives up. Hmmm, . . . we started talking with the guy. He was very friendly. I did not ask his name.

He asked what we were doing. I explained about investigating the murders for my book. When he found out what we were doing, he said something that shook me to the core. *I lived down the road a bit. I was at home on the night of the murders. I heard gunshots that night.* At the time of the murders, houses a half mile on either side of the murder location on Road 515 were owned by relatives of Edgar Ray Killen. Maybe this person was one of the relatives of Killen. I excused myself and returned to taking pictures for my reconstruction. He watched for a few minutes, then drove away, waving as he went.

I tried to stay calm. I just continued my work. But I was nervous. After the incident with the Neshoba County Sheriff's cruiser, I was worried that the old guy would start making phone calls. As a result, a host of Neshoba County Sheriff's cruisers would converge on us out of nowhere. I kept working. Eventually, we left the site of the murders without incident.

After the White Knights killed the workers, the bodies were stuffed in the trunk of a car. This caravan traveled cross country using unpaved back country roads from the murder location to the planned burial location on Old Jolly Farm. We wanted to recreate the cross-county route, taking pictures at each intersection along the way.

On that route, we went deep into the countryside. We saw several homes flying the Confederate battle flag. Currently, the MS state flag has a Confederate battle flag in the upper left quadrant. A field of red covers the rest of the current flag. These homes were NOT flying the current flag of MS. A full Confederate battle flag was blowing in the wind.

I stopped at one of the houses to take a picture. As I was aiming my camera, a person from inside the house came running out towards me. I calmly entered the car. Then, we drove away at normal speed. I did not allow the White Knights to intimidate me when I grew up in Hattiesburg. So, I was not going to be intimidated now. But I was also not going to stay and get into a fight. I was not able to get a picture of the full Confederate battle flag blowing in the wind.

As a shooting reconstruction expert, I have been in some of the worst locations in Los Angeles and New Mexico. Many times, I went to South Central LA and to East LA in the dead of night to investigate lighting conditions during a shooting incident. These trips were not comfortable. You could hear gunfire popping all around in the dark black night. In Philadelphia, gunfire was not popping in the background. The weather was bright and sunny. Yet, these multiple coincidences of local contact in Philadelphia were far more unnerving to me than those rough conditions in South Central and East LA.

Maybe the ghosts of Mickey Schwerner, James Chaney, and Andy Goodman were talking to me. Certainly, looking at the plungers positioned in the gulley to represent the dead bodies sent shivers up and down my spine. Too many coincidences at too many locations involved in gruesome murders for me to be comfortable.

Frankly, I just don't see that the dark cloud over Philadelphia has disappeared. That dark cloud is psychological and leads to physical discomfort.

Questionable Secrecy Continues

Numerous references throughout the documented history state that the FBI files consist of 40,000 pages. *FBI Records: The Vault*[1] is an FBI web site for public dissemination of documents requested under the Freedom of Information Act (FOIA). This site provides 9 files from the FBI MIBURN case files. Yet, only about 1050 pages are contained in the MIBURN files available online at this web site. Many of these pages are nothing but cover sheets.

This few number of pages out of the total number of pages raises questions. Who chose these pages for release? Why are the remaining pages unreleased? Do these other pages have something to hide?

Worse yet, many of these pages are heavily redacted. Relevant and useful material is simply covered by thick black marks, completely hiding the real content in the page. Extensive public testimony was given in the 1967 and the 2005 trials. According to the 2016 DOJ Report, the case is long dead. All except two of the perpetrators are dead. Potential witnesses suffer from faded memories. Why is redaction of these details appropriate?

Ultimately, the US DOJ and the FBI never released complete and un-redacted copies of either confession by Jordan or Barnette. Versions of the confessions available on the FOIA web site of the FBI are heavily redacted.[2] Jerry Mitchell, an investigative reporter, made the full texts of both confessions available in 2010 on a web blog hosted by the *Clarion Ledger* of Jackson.[3]

These murders were accomplished 55 years ago. All except two of the perpetrators are dead. Potential witnesses suffer from faded memories. MS is a great place to live now (so many of the residents claim). Racial violence is no longer tolerated in Neshoba County and East Central MS.

I started filing FOIA requests with the FBI. On January 19, 2019, I filed a FOIA request for un-redacted and complete versions of 9 files available on the FBI web site. I also *asked please release any additional files that were created after the contents of these 9 files. Any additional files should be without redaction and should have all pages intact.* I wanted all 40,000 un-redacted pages. I provided 5 specific reasons that justified the release of the un-redacted files.

A reply from the FBI was fairly quick forthcoming. On February 21, 2019, I received a formal rejection from the FBI. *The records posted on the vault.fbi.gov website regarding Mississippi Burning do not warrant reprocessing. Therefore, your request is being closed.* I was also informed that I could file an appeal of the rejection of my request for releasing all files without redaction.

On April 25, 2019, I filed an appeal to the rejection for un-redacted records. Since the original request provided a detailed justification for the release of un-redacted records, I provided a short justification for the appeal.

In your own 2016 report to the MS Attorney General, you clearly state that the case is dead. After all these years, everyone involved is dead. The 1967 Federal trial and the 2005 Neshoba County trial exposed a lot of the details. But, as I explained, the transcripts fail to precisely relate specific activities to specific dates. A lot of the redacted versions clearly hide these details which would be very useful to historians like me.

As I was awaiting a response to the appeal, I became nervous. As an expert who has dealt with law enforcement, I came to feel that a more formal justification for release of the un-redacted files was needed. On August 29, 2019, I sent a formal letter to the Section Chief of the Record/Information

Dissemination Section of the FBI. I also sent the same letter to a reviewing attorney at the US DOJ who had written me on another request.

From both the Section Chief and the US DOJ attorney, I formally requested that I be sent all the un-redacted files. *I request that you send me a set of DVDs containing the* **unredacted 40,000** *pages of the FBI files on MIBURN.*

In these letters, I provided a more detailed justification for my release of the complete and un-redacted records.

1. The original incidents were in 1964. There was a Federal trial in 1967, and a local MS trial in 2005.

Much of the materials were released during the trials. Unfortunately, some of the details were lost during the trials. Releasing the unredacted materials will fill in a lot of important details for historians like me.

2. In 2016, the FBI sent a report to the MS AG indicating that everyone had been tried who could be tried. And, that everyone else was dead. The report clearly indicates that the case is dead.

3. In 2006, Sam Bowers, Imperial Wizard, died in Parchman Prison. In 2018, Edgar Ray Killen, Kleagle, died in Parchman Prison. Every involved is now dead.

4. Many of the identities of FBI Agents involved became public in the two trials. Jay Cochran, Jr, Roy Moore, and Henry Rask, for instance.

5. During the 1999-2000 era, MS AG Mike Moore indicated that they had received 40,000 pages of files from the FBI. The 2010 release on the FOIA website doesn't include near that many pages. So, a deep redaction was apparently performed by the FBI in 2010.

6. Many of the redacted items were partially released through testimony in the two trials but many critical details were lost. For instance, James Jordan talked to FBI agents on several days after his initial confession to FBI agents. Yet, the exact details on each day are redacted. For a serious historian, the contents of each day are important. They would likely show that a pattern of increasing details and guilt that would be important to capture in the history that I am writing.

7. I am a shooting reconstruction expert in both local and Federal criminal courts. I understand the reasons for redaction.

Any material that jeopardizes a future prosecution should be redacted. But, in this case, no more future prosecutions are possible. Everyone has been prosecuted or is dead.

Another reason for redaction is that to protect privacy. Again, everyone involved as a perpetrator or a witness has been publicly identified by now.

One final valid reason for redaction is the potential of a physical threat to someone who served as a witness. Everyone claims that the rogue violent element that was operation in east central MS (and all over MS) no longer exists. So, by using the potential of a threat as an excuse for redaction, the FBI is taking the public position that the rogue violent element is still operating in east central MS. I really don't think that is your intent or a message you want to give.

Read that last paragraph again. I don't understand the whole issue of potential violence. The year is now 2019. The murders were 55 years ago. Even privacy rights don't make sense. Pretty much everyone is dead.

Perhaps these letters to the FBI and the USDOJ Attorney helped. On September 25, 2019, I received a ruling on my appeal from the Chief of the Administrative Appeals of the Office of Information Policy of the Staff at the US DOJ.

I note that you requested reprocessing of the records posted publicly on the FBI's Vault website. After carefully considering your appeal, and as a result of discussions between FBI personnel and this Office, I am remanding your request to the FBI for reprocessing of the records available on the FBI's Vault. You may appeal any future adverse determination made by the FBI.

This statement appears does not really make a commitment as to whether the 40,000 pages of un-redacted documents will be released to me. The FBI is just being told to reconsider the decision about release of the completed and un-redacted records.

As of December 7, 2019, I do not have any notification on the reconsidered request. I do not have the 40,000 pages of un-redacted documents. I still don't understand the need to hide anything after all this time has passed.

A Final Warning

Sins of the fathers should not be visited on the sons and daughters. Current generations of leaders and residents should not be blindly held accountable for the bad behavior of past generations.

Steve Kilgore, current 8th Circuit Court District Attorney, expressed this opinion about the current generation in Neshoba County.

My generation (I'm 38) appreciates the gravity of these murders, but doesn't feel like it defines us.[4]

However, the White Knights were able to succeed because a silent majority allowed them to deliver violence and death with impunity.

Neshoba County and all of MS need to keep close watch to insure that racial violence and segregation do not occur and never gain control again. That danger still exists in the area. A Klavern of the Mississippi White Knights of the Ku Klux Klan is still active in Philadelphia. Some homes still fly the full Confederate battle flag. MS Legislators refused to remove the Confederate battle flag from the upper left quadrant of the current MS State flag until 2020.

Now, I don't mean to say that there is any kind of utopia now in Neshoba County; there is still anger, hate, and evil. I don't know that it will ever change . . .

Dick Molpus, "History Is Lunch", **June 18, 2014**[5]

The Past Is Never Dead, It's Not Even The Past

***Requiem For A Nun*, William Faulkner, Oxford, MS, 1951**

Introduction and Part 1 Endnotes

[1] *Docket*, Legal Information Institute, Cornell University Law School, retrieved 11/25/2019, https://www.law.cornell.edu/wex/docket.
[2] Molpus, Dick, "Philadelphia, MS: A Story of Racial Reconciliation", *Mississippi History Now*, Mississippi Historical Society, retrieved 6/17/2019, http://www.mshistorynow.mdah.ms.gov/articles/389/philadelphia-mississippi-a-story-of-racial-reconciliation.
[3] HUAC-2, pp. 293-294.
[4] FBI-MBT-2, part 5, p. 986, lines 20-22.
[5] FBI-MBT-2, part 5, p. 986, lines 8-10.
[6] FBI-MBT-2, part 5, p. 986, line 6..
[7] HUAC-2, pp. 293-294.
[8] FBI-MBT-1, part 14, p. 598, lines 10-17.
[9] "Nathan Schwerner, 80, Rights Worker's Father", *New York Times*, March 7, 1991.
[10] "Anne Schwerner, 80, Civil Rights Worker's Mother, 84", *New York Times*, December 4, 1996.
[11] HUIE, p. 48.
[12] "Mickey Schwerner Played Baseball, Was 1957 PMHS Grad", *The Pelhams-Plus*, 6/18/2014, retrieved 12/12/2019, http://www.pelhamplus.com/article_60d3beee-f6f1-11e3-8b2e-0017a43b2370.html.
[13] *The Pelhams-Plus*, 6/18/2014.
[14] *The Cornell Daily Sun*, September 23, 1964, p. 6.
[15] HUIE, p. 50.
[16] HUIE, p. 50-51.
[17] HUIE, p. 52-53.
[18] *The Cornell Daily Sun*, September 23, 1964, p. 6.
[19] HUIE, p. 55.
[20] HUIE, p. 56.
[21] HUIE, p. 56.
[22] HUIE, p. 56.
[23] HUIE, p. 60.
[24] HUIE, p. 70
[25] Congress of Racial Equality, "Michael Schwerner", *Chaney, Goodman, and Schwerner*, retrieved September 9, 2018,
 http://www.core-online.org/History/schwerner.htm.
[26] Congress of Racial Equality, "James Chaney", *Chaney, Goodman, and Schwerner*, retrieved September 14, 2018,
 http://www.core-online.org/History/chaney.htm.

[27] Congress of Racial Equality, "Andy Goodman", *Chaney, Goodman, and Schwerner*, retrieved September 14, 2018,
 http://www.core-online.org/History/goodman.htm.
[28] MSC, 10-60-0-21-1-1-1; DOJ p. 3.
[29] MSC, 10-60-0-21-1-1-1; DOJ p. 3.
[30] MSC, 10-60-0-21-1-1-1; DOJ p. 3.
[31] DOJ, p. 47.
[32] DOAR-W, p. 1.
[33] FBI-MBT, pdf pp. 46-47.
[34] DOJ, pp. 47-48.
[35] "Characteristics of the Population, Part 26, Chapter 3", *1960 Census: Population, Volume 1*, US Bureau of Census,
https://www.census.gov/library/publications/1961/dec/population-vol-01.html.
[36] FBI-MBI-3, pdf p. 3.
[37] FBI-MBT-1, section 9, page 475, line 25.
[38] FBI-MBI-3, pdf p. 4.
[39] DOJ, p. 6.
[40] MITCHJ, pdf p. 4.
[41] FBI-MBI-3, pdf. p. 4.
[42] MITCHJ, pdf. p. 4.
[43] MITCHJ, pdf. p. 5.
[44] FBI-MBI-3, pdf p. 7.
[45] MITCHB, pdf p. 12.
[46] MITCHJ, pdf p. 5, FBI-MBI-4, pdf p 102.
[47] MITCHJ, pdf p. 7.
[48] MITCHB, pdf p. 13
[49] FBI- MBI-5, pdf pp. 5-8.
[50] FBI- MBI-6, pdf pp. 21-27.
[51] DOAR-W, p. 1.
[52] LLC, 1/13/1965, p. 1.
[53] FBI-MBI-1, pdf p. 61.

Part 2 Endnotes

[1] NYT, 11/6/2006, https://www.nytimes.com/2006/11/06/us/06bowers.html.
[2] BOWERS-O, screen 9, p. 3.
[3] BOWERS-O, screen 7, p. 6.
[4] BOWERS-O, screen 9, p. 4.
[5] BOWERS-O, screen 15, p. 13.
[6] BOWERS-O, screen 15, p. 13.
[7] BOWERS-O, screen 13, p. 6.
[8] BOWERS-O, screen 14, pp. 1-2.
[9] BOWERS-O, screen 14, p. 5.
[10] BOWERS-O, screen 14, p. 6.
[11] BOWERS-O, screen 15, p. 5.
[12] BOWERS-O, screen 16, p. 6.
[13] BOWERS-O, screen 15, p. 6 and screen 17, p. 1.
[14] HUAC-H2, p. 2935.
[15] HUAC-1, p. 44.
[16] HUAC-H2, p. 2935.
[17] HUAC-H2, p. 2935.
[18] HUAC-1, p . 253.
[19] HUAC-2, pp. 288-289.
[20] White Knights, "Special Neshoba County Edition", *The Klan Ledger*, 1964.
[21] HUAC-2, pp. 293-294.
[22] HUAC-2, pp. 261-262.
[23] HUAC-2, p. 266.
[24] HUAC-2, pp. 266 - 267.
[25] FBI-WK3, pdf p. 140.
[26] BOWERS-T, p. 607.
[27] BOWERS-T, pp. 601, 608.
[28] FBI-WK3, pdf p. 140.
[29] Except as noted, adapted from *The Citizens Council Collection*, Archives and Special Collections, University of MS, retrieved 9/20/2020, https://egrove.olemiss.edu/citizens/.
[30] EJMSC, p. 12.
[31] MSC, p. 15.
[32] Adapted from "The MS State Sovereignty Commission: An Agency History", MS History Now, MS Historical Society, retrieved 9/20/2020, http://www.mshistorynow.mdah.ms.gov/articles/243/index.php?s=articles&id=243.

[33] MS Department of Archives and History, *Sovereignty Commission Online*, referenced 9/20/2020,
http://da.mdah.ms.gov/sovcom/scagencycasehistory.php.
[34] *American Civil Liberties Union v. Mabus*, 719 F. Supp. 1345 (S.D. Miss. 1989).
[35] *US Inflation Calculator*, https://www.usinflationcalculator.com/.
[36] EJMSC, multiple pages throughout the book.
[37] NAACP, "History of the NAACP", retrieved 9/23/2018,
https://naacp.3cdn.net/14a2d3f78c1910ac31_frm6bev0u.pdf.
[38] "Our History", *Mississippi NAACP*, retrieved 9/23/2018,
http://naacpms.org/mississippi-naacp/.
[39] Supreme Court, New York State, NAACP *Articles of Incorporation, June 9, 1911*,
http://credo.library.umass.edu/view/full/mums312-b007-i028.
[40] Supreme Court, New York State, NAACP *Articles of Incorporation, June 9, 1911*,
http://credo.library.umass.edu/view/full/mums312-b007-i028.
[41] Legal Defense Fund, *Thurgood Marshall*, retrieved 9/30/2018,
http://www.naacpldf.org/thurgood-marshall.
[42] National Archives, *Brown vs Board of Education Timeline*, Educator Resources, retrieved 9/30/2018, https://www.archives.gov/education/lessons/brown-v-board/timeline.html.
[43] National Archives, *Brown vs Board of Education Timeline*, Educator Resources, retrieved 9/30/2018, https://www.archives.gov/education/lessons/brown-v-board/timeline.html.
[44] Grossman, Ron, "The Birth of the Sit-In", *Chicago Tribune*, February 23, 2014, retrieved 10/4/2018, http://www.chicagotribune.com/news/ct-xpm-2014-02-23-ct-hyde-park-sit-in-0223-20140223-story.html.
[45] "Jack Spratt Coffee Shop Sit-In", *Chicago Time Machine*, WTTW Chicago, retrieved 10/4/2018.
[46] Farmer, James. *Lay Bare the Heart*. Texas Christian University Press, 1985, pp. 106-108.
[47] Rich, Marvin, "The Congress of Racial Equality and its Strategy", *The Annals of the American Academy of Political and Social Science, Vol. 357*, January, 1965, p. 114.
[48] Rich, Marvin, "The Congress of Racial Equality and its Strategy", *The Annals of the American Academy of Political and Social Science, Vol. 357*, January, 1965, p. 114.
[49] Meier, August and Rudwick, Elliott M., *CORE: A Study in the Civil Rights Movement, 1942-1968*. University of Illinois Press, 1975.
[50] "The History of CORE", *The Congress of Racial Equality*, retrieved 10/4/2018, http://www.core-online.org/History/history.htm.
[51] "The History of CORE", *The Congress of Racial Equality*, retrieved 10/4/2018, http://www.core-online.org/History/history.htm.

⁵² Rich, Marvin, "The Congress of Racial Equality and its Strategy", *The Annals of the American Academy of Political and Social Science, Vol. 357,* January, 1965, p. 114.
⁵³ "The History of CORE", *The Congress of Racial Equality,* retrieved 10/4/2018, http://www.core-online.org/History/history.htm.
⁵⁴ CORE, "Constitution of New Orleans CORE", *Southern Freedom Movement Documents, 1951 - 1968,* Congress of Racial Equality, Civil Rights Movement Veterans Web Site, retrieved 10/4/2018,
https://www.crmvet.org/docs/60_core_no-const.pdf.
⁵⁵ Laue, J. H., *Direct action and desegregation, 1969-1962.* Carlson Publishing, 1989.
⁵⁶ CORE, "Cracking the Color Line: CORE Actions 1943 - 1961", *Southern Freedom Movement Documents, 1951 - 1968,* Congress of Racial Equality, Civil Rights Movement Veterans Web Site, retrieved 10/4/2018,
https://www.crmvet.org/info/61_core.pdf.
⁵⁷ Hauser, George and Rustin, Bayard, *We Challenged Jim Crow,* Congress of Racial Equality and Fellowship of Reconciliation, 1947, p. 2, retrieved from UNC Greensboro Digital Collections,
http://libcdm1.uncg.edu/cdm/ref/collection/CivilRights/id/3675.
⁵⁸ Rustin, Bayard, Reminiscences of Bayard Rustin, An Oral History, Columbia Center for Oral History, Columbia University Libraries, 1987, retrieved 10/4/2018,
https://oralhistoryportal.library.columbia.edu/document.php?id=ldpd_4073467.
⁵⁹ Hauser and Rustin, *We Challenged Jim Crow,* p. 1.
⁶⁰ Hauser and Rustin, *We Challenged Jim Crow,* p. 3.
⁶¹ US Supreme Court, Boynton vs. Virginia, 364 U.S. 454 (1960).
⁶² US Supreme Court, Boynton vs. Virginia, 364 U.S. 454 (1960).
⁶³ CORE, "Cracking the Color Line: CORE Actions 1943 - 1961", p. 29.
⁶⁴ remainder of this section on Freedom Rides composed from multiple sources:
(1) "Freedom Rides of 1961", *Civil Rights Movement Veterans,* retrieved 10/5/2018, https://www.crmvet.org/riders/freedom_rides.pdf, and
(2) "Freedom Riders", Wikipedia, retrieved 10/5/2018, https://en.wikipedia.org/wiki/Freedom_Riders#CITEREFArsenault2006, and
(3) primary source: Arsenault, Raymond, *Freedom Riders: 1961 and the Struggle for Racial Justice.* Oxford University Press, 2006.
⁶⁵ CRMV, "Proposed Agenda", *Southern Negroes Leadership Conference,* retrieved 10/7/2018, https://www.crmvet.org/docs/5701_sclc_agnda.pdf.
⁶⁶ SCLCD, "SCLC History", retrieved 9/24/2018.
⁶⁷ CRMV, "A Statement to the South and Nation", *Southern Leaders Conference on Transportation and Non-Violent Integration,* retrieved 10/7/2018,
https://www.crmvet.org/docs/5701_statement.pdf.
⁶⁸ CRMV, "A Statement to the South and Nation", Title Page.

[69] CRMV, "A Statement to the South and Nation", *Southern Leaders Conference on Transportation and Non-Violent Integration*, retrieved 10/7/2018, https://www.crmvet.org/docs/5701_statement.pdf.
[70] Manis, Andrew M.,*A Fire You Can't Put Out: The Civil Rights Life of Birmingham's Reverend Fred Shuttlesworth*, University of Alabama Press, 1999.
[71] Padgett, Gregory B., *C. K. Steele, a biography* (Doctoral dissertation),Florida State University Digital Library, 1994, referenced: 10/7/2018, http://fsu.digital.flvc.org/islandora/object/fsu%3A108051#page/Page+i/mode/2up.
[72] CRMV, "A Statement to the South and Nation", pp. 3-4.
[73] FBI-SCLC-01, Anderson, Trezz, "New Rights Group Launched in Dixie", *Pittsburg Courier*, pdf pp. 3.
[74] Carson, Clayton, et al, The Papers of Martin Luther King, Jr., Volume IV, The Symbol of the Movement, University of CA Press, 2000, p. 23.
[75] BAKER, "Who Is Ella Baker", retrieved 9/24/2018.
[76] Carson, King Papers, Volume IV, p. 23.
[77] CRMV, "Crusade for Citizenship", *Southern Christian Leadership Conference*, retrieved 10/7/2018, https://www.crmvet.org/docs/sclc_crusade_58.pdf.
[78] CRMV, King, M.L, "Dear Brother and Coworker", January 20, 1958, *Southern Christian Leadership Conference*, retrieved 10/7/2018, https://www.crmvet.org/docs/5801_sclc_cfc.pdf.
[79] FBI-SCLC-01, pdf p. 6.
[80] CRMV, "SCLC Crusade for Citizenship", *1957*, retrieved 10/9/2018, https://www.crmvet.org/tim/timhis57.htm#1957sclccfc.
[81] CRMV, "Some Reasons Why The Churches Should Take The Lead In Registration and Voting", *Southern Christian Leadership Conference*, retrieved 10/7/2018, https://www.crmvet.org/docs/5805_sclc_churches.pdf.
[82] Adapted from "Birmingham Campaign", *Wikipedia*, retrieved 9/21/2020, https://en.wikipedia.org/wiki/Birmingham_campaign.
[83] Adapted from "Selma To Montgomery Marches", Wikipedia, retrieved 9/21/2020, https://en.wikipedia.org/wiki/Selma_to_Montgomery_marches.
[84] SNCCD, "Ella Baker", retrieved 9/24/2018.
[85] CRMV, "Youth Leadership Meeting", signed by MLK and EB, as Executive Director, SCLC, retrieved 9/24/2018, http://www.crmvet.org/docs/6004_sncc_call.pdf
[86] BAKER, "Who Is Ella Baker", retrieved 9/24/2018.
[87] SNCCD, "The Story of SNCC", retrieved 9/24/2018.
[88] SNCCD, "Establishing SNCC", retrieved 9/24/2018.

⁸⁹ "Student Nonviolent Coordinating Committee (SNCC) Founded", *Civil Rights Movement History 1960*, Civil Rights Movement Veterans, retrieved 9/22/1960, https://www.crmvet.org/tim/timhis60.htm#1960sncc.
⁹⁰ SNCCD, "Establishing SNCC", retrieved 9/24/2018.
⁹¹ Carson, Clayborne *In Struggle, SNCC and the Black Awakening of the 1960s*, Harvard University Press, 1981.
⁹² SVC, Vol 1, No 1, June 1960, p. 2.
⁹³ SNCCD, "Birth of SNCC", retrieved 9/24/2018.
⁹⁴ SNCCD, "Where Do We Go From Here", retrieved 9/24/2018.
⁹⁵ CRMV, "Staff Meeting -- October 8-10, 1961", retrieved 9/24/2018.
⁹⁶ SVC, Vol 1, No 2, August, 1960, p. 2.
⁹⁷ "Jail vs Bail", SVC, Vol 1, No 2, August, 1960, p. 7.
⁹⁸ "Nashville Students and SNCC Pick Up Freedom Rides", *Digital SNCC Gateway*, retrieved 9/22/2020, https://snccdigital.org/events/freedom-rides/, and "Freedom Riders", *American Experience, PBS*, 2011, retrieved 9/22/2020, https://web.archive.org/web/20170107073734/http://www.pbs.org/wgbh/americanexperience/freedomriders/people/roster/.
⁹⁹ "James Foreman", *SNCC Digital Gateway*, retrieved 9/22/2020, https://snccdigital.org/people/james-forman/.
¹⁰⁰ SNCCD, "Entering The Field", retrieved 9/24/2018.
¹⁰¹ "Into The Field", *Digital SNCC Gateway*, retrieved 9/22/2020, https://snccdigital.org/inside-sncc/the-story-of-sncc/into-the-field/.
¹⁰² SNCC: Structure and Leadership, SNCC, 1963, retrieved 9/22/2020, https://www.crmvet.org/docs/sncc63-1.pdf.
¹⁰³ SVC, Vol IV, No 2, August, 1963, p. 1.
¹⁰⁴ This section adapted from "March on Washington For Jobs and Freedom", *Civil Rights Movement History 1963 (July-December)*, Civil Rights Movement Veterans, retrieved 9/22/2020, https://www.crmvet.org/tim/tim63b.htm#1963mow, and "March on Washington for Jobs and Freedom", *Wikipedia*, retrieved 9/22/2020, https://en.wikipedia.org/wiki/March_on_Washington_for_Jobs_and_Freedom.
¹⁰⁵ SNCCD, "Council of Federated Organizations", retrieved 9/23/2018.
¹⁰⁶ SNCCD, "Council of Federated Organizations", retrieved 9/23/2018.
¹⁰⁷ SNCCD, "Challenging White Power", retrieved 9/24/2018.
¹⁰⁸ SNCCD, "Council of Federated Organizations", retrieved 9/23/2018.
¹⁰⁹ SNCCD, "Council of Federated Organizations", retrieved 9/23/2018.
¹¹⁰ WISC/BEECH, pdf p. 55, "How is COFO Financed", *What is COFO*, p. 1.
¹¹¹ "Mississippi NAACP History", *Mississippi NAACP*, retrieved 9/23/2018, http://naacpms.org/history/
¹¹² "Mississippi NAACP History", *Mississippi NAACP*, retrieved 9/23/2018, http://naacpms.org/history/

[113] Cortner, Richard, A "Scottsboro" Case in Mississippi, University Press of Mississippi, 1986, pp. 72-74.
[114] Evans, Adam, "Charles R. Darden", *Mississippi Encyclopedia*, retrieved 9/23/2018, https://mississippiencyclopedia.org/entries/charles-r-dowden/.
[115] Evans, Adam, "Charles R. Darden", *Mississippi Encyclopedia*, retrieved 9/23/2018, https://mississippiencyclopedia.org/entries/charles-r-dowden/.
[116] Evans, Adam, "Charles R. Darden", *Mississippi Encyclopedia*, retrieved 9/23/2018, https://mississippiencyclopedia.org/entries/charles-r-dowden/.
[117] Jones, Roscoe, Sr., *Roscoe Jones, Sr.*, retrieved 9/23/2018, https://cdn.ymaws.com/epfp.iel.org/resource/resmgr/wps/Roscoe_Bio.pdf.
[118] "Religion in Mississippi, by the numbers", CL, 4/28/2017, https://www.hattiesburgamerican.com/story/life/faith/2017/04/28/many-places-worship-mississippi/100997032/.
[119] "PCA Congregations in MS", *PCA Historical Center*, retrieved 12/22/2019, http://www.pcahistory.org/churches/mississippi.html.
[120] e-mail, Josh Parshall, PhD, Institute of Southern Jewish Life, 12/19/2019.
[121] *A Timeline of Gun and Firearm History*, American Firearms Institute, retrieved 1/27/2020, http://www.americanfirearms.org/gun-history/.
[122] "European exploration", *Encyclopedia Britannica*; "Colonialism and colonies", *Encarta 2004*.
[123] "European exploration", *Encyclopedia Britannica*.
[124] "Spain", *Columbia Encyclopedia*.
[125] Channing, William E., *Letter to the Honorable Henry Clay on the Annexation of Text to the United States*, dated 8/1/1837, Cambridge Press, 1837, from University of CA Libraries, https://archive.org/details/lettertohonhenry00chanrich/page/n6.
[126] O'Sullivan, John, "Annexation", *United States Magazine and Democratic Review*, Vol. 16, No 85, July and August 1845, p. 5.
[127] Heidler, Jeanne T, and David S. Heidler, "Manifest Destiny", *Encyclopedia Britannica*, retrieved 12/20/2019, https://www.britannica.com/event/Manifest-Destiny.
[128] "The saving of the soul; the deliverance from sin and its consequences", Oxford English Dictionary, 2nd ed. 1989.
[129] Scott, Donald, "Evangelicalism, Revivalism, and the Second Great Awakening", *The 19th Century*, National Humanities Center, retrieved 12/22/2019, http://nationalhumanitiescenter.org/tserve/nineteen/nkeyinfo/nevanrev.htm.
[130] Scott, Donald, "Evangelicalism, Revivalism, and the Second Great Awakening", *The 19th Century*, National Humanities Center, retrieved 12/22/2019, http://nationalhumanitiescenter.org/tserve/nineteen/nkeyinfo/nevanrev.htm.

[131] "The Second Great Awakening", Christianity.com, retrieved 12/21/2019, https://www.christianity.com/church/church-history/timeline/1701-1800/the-2nd-great-awakening-11630336.html.
[132] Delahunty, Andrew; Dignen, Sheila, *Oxford Dictionary of Reference and Allusion* (3rd ed.), Oxford University Press, 2010, p. 136.
[133] "The Second Great Awakening", Christianity.com, retrieved 12/21/2019, https://www.christianity.com/church/church-history/timeline/1701-1800/the-2nd-great-awakening-11630336.html.
[134] The following lists of descriptions extracted from SBC Staff, "The Sermon That Disappeared From Our Pulpits", *SBCLife*, 12/1/2002, retrieved 12/22/2019, http://www.sbclife.net/article/934/the-sermon-that-disappeared-from-our-pulpits.
[135] Quotes from this sermon extracted from Edwards, Jonathan, *Sinners in the Hands of an Angry God*, 7/8/1741, retrieved 12/22/2019, http://digitalcommons.unl.edu/cgi/viewcontent.cgi?article=1053&context=etas.
[136] *Triennial Convention*, Association of Religion Data Archives, retrieved 12/21/2019, http://www.thearda.com/timeline/events/event_15.asp.
[137] *Triennial Convention Formed For Missionary Support*, American Baptist Historical Society, retrieved 12/21/2019, https://abhsarchives.org/triennial-convention-formed-missionary-support/.
[138] "Infographic: United Methodist General Conference History and Highlights", *United Methodist Church*, retrieved 12/21/2019, https://www.umc.org/en/content/infographic-united-methodist-general-conference-history-and-highlights.
[139] Stone, Phillip, "How the Methodist Church split in the 1840s", *SC United Methodist Advocate*, 1/30/2013, published February, 2013, http://blogs.wofford.edu/from_the_archives/2013/01/30/how-the-methodist-church-split-in-the-1840s/.
[140] Furman, *Richard, Exposition of the Views of the Baptists Relative to the Coloured [sic] Population in the United States*, A E Miller, 1838.
[141] "Richard Furman", *Biographies*, Southern Baptist Historical Library and Archives, Southern Baptist Convention, retrieved 12/21/2019, http://www.sbhla.org/bio_furman.htm.
[142] All quotes demonstrating Biblical support of slavery extracted from Furman, *Richard, Exposition of the Views of the Baptists Relative to the Coloured [sic] Population in the United States*, A E Miller, 1838.
[143] Barrow, David, *Involuntary, Unmerited, Perpetual, Absolute, Hereditary Slavery Examined on the Principles of Nature, Reason, Justice, Policy, and Scripture*, D and E Bradford, 8/27/1807.

[144] *The Baptist Encyclopedia*, 1881, p. 83, from *Baptist History Homepage*, John Leland Baptist College, retrieved 12/21/2019, http://baptisthistoryhomepage.com/barrow.david.bio.tbe.html.
[145] Baker, Robert, "Southern Baptist Beginnings", *The Baptist History and Heritage Society*, retrieved 12/21/2019, http://www.baptisthistory.org/baptistorigins/southernbaptistbeginnings.html.
[146] Sobel, Mechal, "They Can Never Both Prosper Together: Black and White Baptists in Antebellum Nashville, TN", *Tennessee Historical Quarterly*, Tennessee Historical Society, Vol 38, No 3, Fall, 1979, pp. 296-307.
[147] All comments about slavery by Wesley extracted from Wesley, John, *Thoughts Upon Slavery*, Joseph Crukshank: Philadelphia, 1774, retrieved 12/21/2019, https://docsouth.unc.edu/church/wesley/wesley.html.
[148] Wolffe, John, and B Harrison, "Wilberforce, William (1759–1833)", *Oxford Dictionary of National Biography*, Oxford University Press, May 2006, doi:10.1093/ref:odnb/29386,
[149] Wesley, John, *Letter to William Wilberforce*, 2/24/1791, retrieved from Asbury Theological Seminary, https://place.asburyseminary.edu/engaginggovernmentpapers/10.
[150] Beck, Carolyn, Our Own Vine and Fig Tree: The Authority of History and Kinship in Mother Bethel, Review of Religious Research, Vol 29, No. 4, June, 1988, pp. 369-384.
[151] Stone, Phillip, "How the Methodist Church split in the 1840s", *SC United Methodist Advocate*, 1/30/2013, published February, 2013, http://blogs.wofford.edu/from_the_archives/2013/01/30/how-the-methodist-church-split-in-the-1840s/.
[152] "Abolition and the Splintering of the Church", *This Far by Faith: 1776-1865: From Bondage to Holy War*, PBS, retrieved 12/21/2019, https://www.pbs.org/thisfarbyfaith/journey_2/p_5.html.
[153] "Methodist Episcopal Church, South", *Prominent Religious Events and People in American History*, The Association of Religion Data Archives, retrieved 12/21/2019, http://www.thearda.com/timeline/events/event_186.asp.
[154] "Our History", *African Methodist Episcopal Church*, retrieved 12/21/2019, https://www.ame-church.com/our-church/our-history/.
[155] Maxwell, Joe, "Black Southern Baptists", *Christianity Today*, 1/15/1995, retrieved 12/21/2019, https://www.christianitytoday.com/ct/1995/may15/5t6026.html.
[156] *History of the National Baptist Convention*, The National Baptist Convention, USA, Inc., retrieved 12/21/2019, http://www.nationalbaptist.com/about-us/our-history/index.html.
[157] Broadus, John A, *A Treatise on the Preparation and Delivery of Sermons*, A C Armstrong and Sons, 1898, from "Founding: 1859-1878", The Southern Baptist

Theological Seminary, retrieved 12/23/2019, https://www.sbts.edu/about/history/founding-1859-1878/.
[158] *Report on Slavery and Racism in the History of the Southern Baptist Theological Seminary*, The Southern Baptist Theological Seminary, 12/12/2018, p. 5.
[159] *Report on Slavery and Racism in the History of the Southern Baptist Theological Seminary*, pp. 5-8.
[160] *Report on Slavery and Racism in the History of the Southern Baptist Theological Seminary*, p. 25.
[161] *Report on Slavery and Racism in the History of the Southern Baptist Theological Seminary*, p. 27.
[162] Pollard, Edward, , *The Lost Cause; A New Southern History of the War of the Confederates*, E. B. Treat and Company, 1866.
[163] *Report on Slavery and Racism in the History of the Southern Baptist Theological Seminary*, pp. 42-43; Gillespie, Michele and Randall Hall, eds, *Thomas Dixon Jr and The Birth of Modern America*, LSU Press, 2006..
[164] Rollin G. Osterweis, *The Myth of the Lost Cause, 1865–1900*, 1973, p. ix.
[165] Pollard, *The Lost Cause*, p. 752.
[166] *Report on Slavery and Racism in the History of the Southern Baptist Theological Seminary*, p. 32.
[167] Crowe, Karen, "Preface", Crowe, Karen (ed.), *Southern horizons : the autobiography of Thomas Dixon*, IWV Publishing, 1984, pp. xv–xxxiv; p. xvi.
[168] Crowe, Karen, "Preface", Crowe, Karen (ed.), *Southern horizons : the autobiography of Thomas Dixon*, IWV Publishing, 1984, pp. xv–xxxiv; p. xvi.
[169] Bloomfield, Maxwell, "Dixon's The Leopard's Spots: A Study in Popular Racism", *American Quarterly*, 16(3), 1964, pp. 387–401.
[170] "Rev Thomas Dixon Resigns", *New York Times*, 3/11/1895.
[171] "Rev Thomas Dixon Resigns", *New York Times*, 3/11/1895.
[172] Doc South Staff, "Controversial History: Thomas Dixon and the Klan Trilogy", *Documenting the American South*, Univ of NC, retrieved 12/23/2019, https://docsouth.unc.edu/highlights/dixon.html.
[173] All quotes by characters Rev John Durham and Col Charles Gaston and others extracted from Dixon, Thomas, Jr., *The Leopard's Spots: A Romance of the White Man's Burden--1865-1900*, Doubleday, Page, and Co, 1902.
[174] "The Baptist Argus", *Baptist Argus Two*, Baylor University Libraries Digital Collections, http://digitalcollections.baylor.edu/cdm/landingpage/collection/p17178coll1.
[175] Extract below from Robertson, Archibald, Prof, "The Problem of the Negro" [sic], *The Baptist Argus*, 4/10/1902, p. 5, retrieved 12/23/2019, http://digitalcollections.baylor.edu/cdm/compoundobject/collection/p17178coll1/id/13956/rec/15.

[176] *Report on Slavery and Racism in the History of the Southern Baptist Theological Seminary*, p. 43.
[177] *US Inflation Calculator*, retrieved 12/25/2019, usinflationcalculator.com.
[178] Franklin, John Hope ,"The Birth of a Nation: Propaganda as History", *Massachusetts Review*, 20 (3): 417–434, Autumn 1979.
[179] Lennig, Arthur, "Myth and fact: the reception of The Birth of a Nation", *Film History,* 16.2 (April 2004): 117.
[180] Stern, Seymour, ed by Ira H. Gallen, *The Birth of a Nation, D W Griffith's 100th Anniversary*, Friesen Press, 2014, p. 1.
[181] "The Birth of a Nation", NYT, 3/4/1915, p. 9.
[182] Drew, William, *D W Griffith (1875-1948)*, retrieved 12/25/2019, http://www.gildasattic.com/dwgriffith.html, excerpts from *D.W. Griffith's Greatest Films*, http://www.uno.edu/~drcom/Griffith/home.html.
[183] Stokes, Melvyn, D W, *Griffith's the Birth of a Nation: A History of "the Most Controversial Motion Picture of All Time"*, Oxford University Press. pp. 105, 122, 124, 178.
[184] *US Inflation Calculator*, retrieved 12/25/2019, usinflationcalculator.com.
[185] "The Various Shady Lives of the Ku Klux Klan", *Time Magazine*, April 9, 1965.
[186] Rawlings, William, "The Second Coming of the Invisible Empire", *Georgia Backroads*, Winter, 2012, p. 17.
[187] Rawlings, William, "The Second Coming of the Invisible Empire", *Georgia Backroads*, Winter, 2012, p. 16.
[188] *Book of Disciple*, United Methodist Church, Paragraphs 601-657.
[189] *Mississippi Conference of the United Methodist Church*, retrieved 12/26/2019, https://www.mississippi-umc.org/.
[190] "Annual Conferences", *Southeastern Jurisdiction, United Methodist Church*, retrieved 12/26/2019, http://www.sejumc.org/templates/System/details.asp?id=59478&PID=986509.
[191] *Book of Disciple*, United Methodist Church, Paragraphs 13-22, 501-511.
[192] *Book of Disciple*, United Methodist Church, Paragraph 511.
[193] *Book of Disciple*, United Methodist Church, Paragraph 509.
[194] "Gathered for Mission, Structured To Serve: A General Conference Primer", *The people of the United Methodist Church*, retrieved 12/26/2019, http://www.umcom.org/news/gathered-for-mission-structured-to-serve-a-general-conference-primer.
[195] "Why United Methodist General Conference?", *The people of the United Methodist Church*, retrieved 12/26/2019, https://www.umc.org/en/content/why-united-methodist-general-conference-history-and-highlights.
[196] Beck, Carolyn, Our Own Vine and Fig Tree: The Authority of History and Kinship in Mother Bethel, Review of Religious Research, Vol 29, No. 4, June, 1988, pp. 369-384.

[197] *Journal of the Uniting Conference*, The Methodist Publishing House, 1939.
[198] *Journal of the Uniting Conference*, The Methodist Publishing House, 1939, p. 431.
[199] *Journal of the Uniting Conference*, The Methodist Publishing House, 1939, p. 433.
[200] *Journal of the Uniting Conference*, The Methodist Publishing House, 1939, p. 434.
[201] *Journal of the Uniting Conference*, The Methodist Publishing House, 1939, p. 435.
[202] Murray, Peter, "The Racial Crisis in the Methodist Church", Methodist History, 26:1, October, 1987, p. 3.
[203] National Archives, *Brown vs Board of Education Timeline*, Educator Resources, retrieved 9/30/2018, https://www.archives.gov/education/lessons/brown-v-board/timeline.html.
[204] Murray, Peter, "The Racial Crisis in the Methodist Church", p. 3.
[205] Murray, Peter, *Methodists and the Crucible of Race, 1930-1975*, Univ of MO Press, 2004, p. 79, reviewed by Key, Barclay, Univ of FL, Nov, 2005, H-South.
[206] *Journal of the General Conference of the Methodist Church*, April 25-May 7, 1956, Minneapolis, MN, The Methodist Publishing House, p. 481.
[207] *Journal of the General Conference of the Methodist Church*, 1956, pp. 1403-1404.
[208] *Journal of the General Conference of the Methodist Church*, 1956, p. 1404.
[209] *Journal of the General Conference of the Methodist Church*, 1956, p. 1405.
[210] *Journal of the General Conference of the Methodist Church*, 1957, The Methodist Publishing House, p. 967-969, as cited in Collins, Donald, *When the Church Bell Rang Racist*, Merger University Press, 1998. [Google Books]
[211] Commission to Study and Recommend Action Concerning the Jurisdictional System [Commission of Seventy], "Report of the 1960 General Conference", Jan 6, 1960, n.p., 3-12, 20-24, as cited in Murray, Peter, "The Racial Crisis in the Methodist Church", p. 6.
[212] These efforts are extensively document in Murray, Peter, "The Racial Crisis in the Methodist Church", pp. 7-12.
[213] *Journal of the Last Session of the General Conference of the Methodist Church and the Uniting Conference of The United Methodist Church*, Dallas, TX, *April 21-May 4*, 1968, p. 360.
[214] "End of the Central Jurisdiction", *Archives and History*, The United Methodist Church, retrieved 12/28/2019, http://gcah.org/history/central-jurisdiction.
[215] *Journal of the Last Session of the General Conference of the Methodist Church and the Uniting Conference of The United Methodist Church*, 1968, pp. 1760-1762
[216] "End of the Central Jurisdiction", *Archives and History*, The United Methodist Church, retrieved 12/28/2019, http://gcah.org/history/central-jurisdiction.
[217] Ownby, Ted, "Americans for the Preservation of the White Race", *Mississippi Encyclopedia*, Mississippi Humanities Council, 2019, retrieved 12/30/2019, https://mississippiencyclopedia.org/entries/americans-for-the-preservation-of-the-white-race/.
[218] HA, 12/21/1963, p. 10.

[219] EJM, 8/19/1964, p. 4.
[220] Atwater, James, "If We Can Crack Mississippi", *Saturday Evening Post*, July 25, 1964, p. 18.
[221] This description of a Southern Baptist revival by a self-ordained preacher is from the actual experience of the author. At the time, the author was a 17 year old Jewish kid who attended the revival at the demand of his Southern Baptist girlfriend.
[222] Personally known by the author who lived in Hattiesburg.
[223] Daniel, Harrison, "Southern Presbyterians and the Negro in the Early National Period", *The Journal of Negro History*, Vol. 58, No. 3, July, 1973, pp. 291-312, page 312.
[224] *Minutes of the General Assembly, 1818*, p. 692, https://slavery.princeton.edu/uploads/Minute-on-Slavery-1818.pdf.
[225] *Minutes of the General Assembly, 1818*, p. 693.
[226] "Colonization", *The African-American Mosaic*, US Library of Congress, retrieved 12/26/2019, https://www.loc.gov/exhibits/african/afam002.html.
[227] *Minutes of the General Assembly, 1818*, p. 693.
[228] *Minutes of the Synod of Virginia, October 23, 1818*, Harrison, *The Journal of Negro History*, July, 1973, p. 311.
[229] "150 Try To Register", *The Student Voice*, Student Non Violent Coordinating Committee, 1/20/1964, p. 1.
[230] Lowrey, Leonard, "The Hattiesburg story is told at church meeting in Illinois", HA, 2/24/1964, p. 1.
[231] Lowrey, Leonard, "The Hattiesburg story is told at church meeting in Illinois", HA, 2/24/1964, p. 1.
[232] Lowrey, HA, 2/24/1964, p. 10.
[233] Lowrey, HA, 2/24/1964, p. 10.
[234] "Basic Beliefs", *Southern Baptist Convention*, retrieved 12/17/2019, http://www.sbc.net/aboutus/basicbeliefs.asp.
[235] "Begin Your Journey To Peace", Billy Graham Evangelistic Association, retrieved 12/27/2019, https://peacewithgod.net/.
[236] *Annual of the 2012 Southern Baptist Convention*, New Orleans, LA, June 19-20, 2012, Executive Committee, Southern Baptist Convention, p. 89.
[237] Phan, Katherine, "Sinner's Prayer Can Lead to Salvation, Say Southern Baptist Traditionalists", *The Christian Post*, retrieved 12/27/2019, https://www.christianpost.com/news/sinners-prayer-can-lead-to-salvation-say-southern-baptist-traditionalists.html.
[238] "Basic Beliefs", *Southern Baptist Convention*, retrieved 12/17/2019, http://www.sbc.net/aboutus/basicbeliefs.asp.

[239] "What is the procedure for ordination in the SBC", "Frequently Asked Questions", *Southern Baptist Convention*, retrieved 12/17/2019, http://www.sbc.net/faqs.asp.
[240] Bouie, Jamelle, "Christian Soldiers", *Slate*, 2/10/2015, retrieved 12/17/2019, https://slate.com/news-and-politics/2015/02/jim-crow-souths-lynching-of-blacks-and-christianity-the-terror-inflicted-by-whites-was-considered-a-religious-ritual.html.
[241] Marsh, Charles, *God's Long Summer: Stories of Faith and Civil Rights*, Princeton University Press, 1977, p. 51.
[242] 2005 trial testimony of Mike Winstead extracted from KILLEN-2, Disk 4, 6/17/2005.
[243] "Wesleys Take The Web: Three General Rules", *United Methodist Church*, retrieved 12/17/2019, https://www.umc.org/en/content/wesleys-take-the-web-three-general-rules.
[244] "Article XII -- The Judgment and the Future State", *Confession of Faith of the Evangelical United Brethren Church*, 8/13/2016, retrieved 12/17/2019, https://www.umc.org/en/content/confession-of-faith#judgment-future.
[245] "How the Process Works", *Appointments*, United Methodist Churches of Indiana, retrieved 12/17/2019, https://www.inumc.org/ministerial-services/appointments/how-the-process-works/.
[246] "Procedures for Referral and Investigation of a Judicial Complaint, *Book of Discipline*, United Methodist Church, The United Methodist Publishing House, 2016, paragraph 2704.3, p. 794, https://www.cokesbury.com/book-of-discipline-book-of-resolutions-free-versions.
[247] "Chargeable Offenses and The Statute of Limitations", *Book of Discipline*, paragraph 2702.1.c, p. 788.
[248] Bouie, Jamelle, "Christian Soldiers", *Slate*, 2/10/2015.
[249] Houston, Robert, et al, *American Identities: Contemporary Multicultural Voices*, Middlebury College Press, 1994, pp. 81-84.
[250] Pack, Robert, ed., Houston, Robert, et al, "Growing Up Southern", *Southern Exposure*, Volume VIII, no. 3, Fall,1980, pp. 94-95.
[251] Colloff, Pamela, "The Sins of the Father", *Texas Monthly*, April, 2000, retrieved 12/16/2019, https://www.texasmonthly.com/articles/the-sins-of-the-father-2/.

Part 3 Endnotes

[1] Federal Bureau of Investigation, "FBI Jackson Division Celebrates 50th Anniversary", *FBI Web Site*, retrieved 9/29/2018, https://www.fbi.gov/contact-us/field-offices/jackson/news/stories/fbi-jackson-division-celebrates-50th-anniversary.
[2] HUAC-H2, p. 2927.
[3] COFO-R.
[4] HEWITT, pp. 13-18.
[5] FBI, "FBI Jackson History", FBI > History > Field Office Histories, retrieved 10/11/2018, https://www.fbi.gov/history/field-office-histories/jackson.
[6] BON, p. 17.
[7] BON, p. xv.
[8] BON, p. 17.
[9] CL, 12/5/1964, p. 8.
[10] BON, p. xv.
[11] DDT, 12/6/1964, p. 20.
[12] BON, p. 18.
[13] BON, p. 17.
[14] BON, p. 208.
[15] CL, 12/5/1964, p. 8.
[16] DDT, 12/6/1964, p. 20.
[17] BON, p. 208.
[18] BON, p. 18.
[19] UA, 2/11/1954, p. 1.
[20] CL, 9/22/1954, p. 7; *Scott County Times*, 9/23/1954, p. 1.
[21] UA, 1/13/1955, p. 1.
[22] UA, 12/10/1959, p. 1.
[23] UA, 2/24/1955, p. 1; TNR, 10/18/1961, p. 4.
[24] HA, 3/26/1960, p. 6.
[25] UA, 6/8/1961, p. 1.
[26] CL, 11/28/1961, p. 8.
[27] *The Winston County Journal*, 4/19/1962, p. 5.
[28] US, 1/28/1960, p. 1; UA, 6/14/1962, p. 5.
[29] *MS Code Title 33, Military Affairs Section 33-3-5,. Military staff divided*, https://codes.findlaw.com/ms/title-33-military-affairs/ms-code-sect-33-3-5.html.
[30] CL, 1/17/1969, p. 49.
[31] BON, p. 208.
[32] STER, location 2949.
[33] STER, location 2987.

34 ELL, location 439.
35 ELL, location 4458.
36 ELL, location 4760.
37 CL, 12/5/1964, p. 8.
38 BON, p. 23.
39 "Lawrence Andrew Rainey", Find A Grave, retrieved 12/13/2019, https://www.findagrave.com/memorial/10320695.
40 "Lawrence A. Rainey", Wikipedia, retrieved 12/13/2019, https://en.wikipedia.org/wiki/Lawrence_A._Rainey.
41 Linder, Douglas, "Sheriff Lawrence Rainey", *Famous Trials*, University Of MO-Kansas City School of Law, retrieved 12/13/2019, https://famous-trials.com/mississippi-burningtrial/1973-rainey.
42 Linder, Douglas, "Sheriff Lawrence Rainey".
43 CL, 11/10/1959, p. 1.
44 HA, 10/27/1959, pp. 1-2.
45 CL, 11/10/1959, p. 1.
46 CL, 5/25/1962, p. 6.
47 CL, 5/25/1962, p. 6.
48 "Lawrence Rainey, 79, a Rights-Era Suspect", NYT, 11/13/2002, https://www.nytimes.com/2002/11/13/us/lawrence-rainey-79-a-rights-era-suspect.html.
49 Nevin, David, "A Strange, Tight Little Town, Loath To Admit Complicity", *Life*, 12/18/1964, https://books.google.com/books?id=kFEEAAAAMBAJ&pg=PA38&lpg=PA38&dq=Lawrence+Rainey+runs+for+Sheriff&source=bl&ots=x-MIz1rBem&sig=ACfU3U2Ddq9a1YkQwQ5uxYNbSjM4tkfkyg&hl=en&sa=X&ved=2ahUKEwjN69rX77PmAhWPnp4KHeY1CHEQ6AEwD3oECAoQAQ#v=onepage&q=Lawrence%20Rainey%20runs%20for%20Sheriff&f=false.
50 MITC, p. 115.
51 Nevin, David, "A Strange, Tight Little Town, Loath To Admit Complicity", *Life*, 12/18/1964.
52 Nevin, David, "A Strange, Tight Little Town, Loath To Admit Complicity", *Life*, 12/18/1964.
53 Nevin, David, "A Strange, Tight Little Town, Loath To Admit Complicity", *Life*, 12/18/1964.
54 Lawrence Rainey, 79, a Rights-Era Suspect", NYT, 11/13/2002.
55 CL, 8/29/1963, p. 4.
56 Kilgore, Steve, email correspondence with author, 12/15/2019.
57 CL, 12/10/1963, p. 4.
58 Linder, Douglas, "Sheriff Lawrence Rainey".
59 HUIE, p. 133.

60 "Cecil Ray Price", Find A Grave, retrieved 12/13/2019, https://www.findagrave.com/memorial/9901169.
61 Linder, Douglas, "Cecil Price", *Famous Trials*, University Of MO-Kansas City School of Law, retrieved 9/20/2018, https://famous-trials.com/mississippi-burningtrial/1971-price.
62 FBI-MBT-1, section 3, page 160, line 19; CL, 1/9/1964, p. 9.
63 DDT, 10/4/1964, p. 1.
64 DDT, 10/4/1964, p. 1.
65 HA, 10/3/1964, p. 1.
66 DDT, 10/4/1964, p. 1.
67 DDT, 10/4/1964, p. 1.
68 MITC, p. 116.
69 Linder, Douglas, "Cecil Price".
70 MITC, pp. 115-116.
71 WWTM, 5,00:15.
72 WWET, 2, 2:15.
73 WWTM, 6,01:30.
74 WWTM, 6,01:49.
75 WWHT, 13, 00:10
76 WWHT, 13, 00:28, CB phone interview.
77 CB phone interview.
78 WISN, Letter from Sandra Watts, COFO, to Tom Myers, President, 7/2/1965, pdf p. 15.
79 WWTM, 5,00:32.
80 *Inflation Calculator*, retrieved 7/16/2020, https://www.in2013dollars.com/.
81 WWHT, 1,00:36, 00:55, 01:11.
82 WWTM, 2,2:18.
83 WWTM, 2, 0:10.
84 WISN, Letter from J L Posey to Sandra Watts, COFO, to Tom Myers, President, 6/19/1965, pdf p. 38.
85 WWHT, 2, 00:20 - 01:10.
86 MSC, 2-112-1-2-1-1-1.
87 MSC, 2-112-1-20-1-1-1.
88 MSC, 2-112-1-35-1-1-1.
89 DDT, 4/26/1964, p. 1.
90 MARS, p. 80.
91 ND, 4/9/1964, in MARS, p. 80.
92 MARS, p. 81.
93 MARS, p. 81, downloaded from http://law2.umkc.edu/faculty/projects/ftrials/price&bowers/Klan.html.
94 MARS, p. 82.
95 ND, 5/14/1964, in MARS, pp. 82-83.

96 "Nathan Schwerner, 80, Rights Worker's Father", *New York Times*, March 7, 1991.
97 "Anne Schwerner, 80, Civil Rights Worker's Mother, 84", *New York Times*, December 4, 1996.
98 HUIE, p. 48.
99 Gavin, Patrick, "Answer This: Robert Reich", *Politico*, 7/30/2012, retrieved 5/8/2019, https://www.politico.com/story/2012/07/answer-this-robert-reich-079133.
100 HUIE, p. 48.
101 "Michael H. Schwerner '61' Possessed Strong Desire for Integrated Society", *The Cornell Daily Sun*, Volume LXXXI, Number 4, September 23, 1964, p. 6, https://cdsun.library.cornell.edu/cgi-bin/cornell?a=d&d=CDS19640923.2.21#
102 *The Cornell Daily Sun*, September 23, 1964, p. 6.
103 *The Cornell Daily Sun*, September 23, 1964, p. 6.
104 HUIE, p. 50.
105 Hannah-Jones-Nikole, A Brutal Loss But An Enduring Conviction, Pro Publica, *ProPublica*, July 22, 2014, retrieved May 10, 2019, https://www.propublica.org/article/a-brutal-loss-but-an-enduring-conviction.
106 Dewan, Shaila, "Widow Recalls Ghosts of '64 at Rights Trial", *The New York Times*, June 17, 2005. Retrieved May 10, 2019.
107 HUIE, p. 50-51.
108 Sitton, Claude, "3 In Rights Drive Reported Missing", *New York Times*, June 22, 1964.
109 HUIE, p. 51-52.
110 HUIE, p. 52-53.
111 HUIE, p. 53-54.
112 HUIE, p. 55.
113 Rachell, L.E.J., "Downtown CORE", *CORE NYC*, retrieved 5/11/2019, http://www.corenyc.org/downtowncore.htm.
114 *The Cornell Daily Sun*, September 23, 1964, p. 6.
115 Rachell, L.E.J., "Downtown CORE".
116 Rachell, L.E.J., "Downtown CORE".
117 HUIE, p. 55.
118 HUIE, p. 55.
119 Gilbert Sandler, "July 4, 1963, at Gwynn Oak Park Baltimore", *The Baltimore Sun*, February 17, 1998.
120 Gilbert Sandler, *The Baltimore Sun*, February 17, 1998.
121 Gilbert Sandler, *The Baltimore Sun*, February 17, 1998.
122 HUIE, p. 56.
123 Rachell, L.E.J., "Downtown CORE".
124 Rachell, L.E.J., "Downtown CORE".
125 Rachell, L.E.J., "Downtown CORE".

[126] HUIE, p. 56.
[127] HUIE, p. 56.
[128] Rachell, L.E.J., "Downtown CORE".
[129] HUIE, p. 56.
[130] HUIE, p. 56.
[131] HUIE, p. 57.
[132] HUIE, p. 58.
[133] Congress of Racial Equality, "Michael Schwerner", *Chaney, Goodman, and Schwerner*, retreived September 9, 2018,
 http://www.core-online.org/History/schwerner.htm.
[134] HUIE, p. 60.
[135] HUIE, p. 60.
[136] SNCC, *COFO: What It Is, What It Does*, 1964, retrieved from https://www.crmvet.org/docs/dochome.htm, May 10, 2019.
[137] HUIE, p. 69.
[138] Congress of Racial Equality, "Michael Schwerner", *Chaney, Goodman, and Schwerner*, retrieved September 9, 2018,
 http://www.core-online.org/History/schwerner.htm.
[139] HUIE, pp. 62,64.
[140] HUIE, p. 70
[141] Congress of Racial Equality, "Michael Schwerner", *Chaney, Goodman, and Schwerner*, retrieved September 9, 2018,
 http://www.core-online.org/History/schwerner.htm.
[142] HUIE, pp. 70-71.
[143] HUIE, p. 69.
[144] HUIE, p. 70.
[145] HUIE, pp. 70-71.
[146] HUIE, p. 71.
[147] HUIE, pp. 71-73.
[148] HUIE, pp. 73-74.
[149] HUIE, pp. 74-78.
[150] HUIE, pp. 78-80.
[151] HUIE, pp. 80-82.
[152] HUIE, pp. 86-87.
[153] HUIE, pp. 86-87.
[154] HUIE, pp. 87-88.
[155] HUIE, pp. 89-90.
[156] From report by Rita Bender to CORE HQ in NYC, in HUIE, p. 90.
[157] FBI-WK2, pdf p. 53.
[158] LLC, 3/18/1964, p. 5.
[159] SCR ID # 2-46-0-79-1-1-1, MS Sovereignty Commission, 3/19/1964, MS Dept of Archives and History,

http://www.mdah.ms.gov/arrec/digital_archives/sovcom/result.php?image=images/png/cd02/011154.png&otherstuff=2|46|0|79|1|1|1|10922|#.
[160] SCR ID # 2-46-0-77-1-1-1, p. 1. , MS Sovereignty Commission, 3/23/1964, MS Dept of Archives and History, http://www.mdah.ms.gov/arrec/digital_archives/sovcom/result.php?image=images/png/cd02/011145.png&otherstuff=2|46|0|77|1|1|1|10913|#.
[161] SCR ID # 2-46-0-77-1-1-1, p. 2. , MS Sovereignty Commission, 3/23/1964, MS Dept of Archives and History, http://www.mdah.ms.gov/arrec/digital_archives/sovcom/result.php?image=images/png/cd02/011145.png&otherstuff=2|46|0|77|1|1|1|10913|#.
[162] Smith, George, Jr, and Joe Morse, "Freedom is Not Free: The Meridian Civil Rights Movement of the Mid-Sixties", *Civil Rights Movement Archive*, retrieved 12/12/2010, https://www.crmvet.org/info/meridian.htm.
[163] HUIE, p. 97.
[164] HUIE, p. 97.
[165] HUIE, p. 97.
[166] HUIE, p. 98.
[167] HUIE, p. 99.
[168] Smith, George, Jr, and Joe Morse, "Freedom is Not Free: The Meridian Civil Rights Movement of the Mid-Sixties", *Civil Rights Movement Archive*, see above.
[169] HUIE, p. 117.
[170] HUIE, p. 129, and personal experience of author, Hattiesburg, 1949-1967.
[171] HUIE, p. 120.
[172] HUIE, pp. 94-95.
[173] HUIE, p. 110.
[174] HUIE, p. 99.
[175] HUIE, p. 98.
[176] HUIE, p. 98.
[177] HUIE, p. 99.
[178] HUIE, p. 99.
[179] HUIE, p. 100.
[180] HUIE, p. 100.
[181] HUIE, p. 100.
[182] HUIE, p. 101.
[183] HUIE, p. 102.
[184] WHIT, p. 176.
[185] HUIE, p. 102.
[186] WHIT, p. 176.
[187] HUIE, p. 102.
[188] CL, 5/14/2000, p. 12.
[189] CL, 5/14/2000, p. 12.
[190] "Imperial Executive Order", HUAC-6, pp. 169-170.

[191] FBI-MBI-3, pdf p. 64.
[192] FBI-MBT-1, section 3, page 131, lines 23-24.
[193] FBI-MBT-1, section 3, page 132, lines 6-19.
[194] FBI-MBT-1, section 3, page 132, lines 11-13.
[195] HUIE, p. 107.
[196] Smith, George, Jr, and Joe Morse, "Freedom is Not Free: The Meridian Civil Rights Movement of the Mid-Sixties", *Civil Rights Movement Archive*.
[197] DDT, 5/24/1964, p. 1.
[198] FBI-MBT-1, section 3, page 134, lines 13-14.
[199] SCHW, "The ND, On The Web"
[200] CL, 5/14/2000, p. 12.
[201] FBI-MBT-2, part 5, p. 986, lines 8-10.
[202] FBI-MBT-2, part 5, p. 986, line 6.
[203] HUAC-2, pp. 293-294.
[204] FBI-MBT-2, part 5, p. 986, lines 20-22.
[205] HUIE, pp. 107-108.
[206] Congress of Racial Equality, "Michael Schwerner", *Chaney, Goodman, and Schwerner*, retrievied September 9, 2018,
 http://www.core-online.org/History/schwerner.htm.
[207] FBI-MBT-1, part 14, p. 598, line 23.
[208] Congress of Racial Equality, "Michael Schwerner", *Chaney, Goodman, and Schwerner*, retrievied September 9, 2018,
 http://www.core-online.org/History/schwerner.htm.
[209] FBI-MBT-2, section 1, page 767, lines 24-25, page 768, lines 1-2.
[210] FBI-MBT-2, section 1, page 768, lines 6-7.
[211] FBI-MBT-2, section 1, page 769, lines 22-25.
[212] FBI-MBT-2, section 1, page 770, lines 10-11.
[213] FBI-MBT-2, section 1, page 770, line 15.
[214] FBI-MBT-2, section 1, page 771, lines 8-11.
[215] FBI-MBT-2, section 1, page 771, lines 15-20.
[216] FBI-MBT-2, section 1, page 771, lines 23-25.
[217] FBI-MBT-2, section 1, page 772, lines 1-2.
[218] FBI-MBT-2, section 1, page 772, line 25.
[219] FBI-MBT-2, section 1, page 774, line 4.
[220] FBI-MBT-2, section 1, page 774, lines 7-8.
[221] FBI-MBT-2, section 1, page 774, line 14.
[222] FBI-MBT-2, section 1, page 776, line 20.
[223] FBI-MBT-2, section 1, page 776, line 25.
[224] FBI-MBT-2, section 4, page 910, lines 9-12.
[225] FBI-MBT-2, section 4, page 910, lines 2-4.
[226] LINDER, p. 733.
[227] FBI-MBT-2, section 1, page 775, lines 21-23.

228 FBI-MBT-2, section 1, page 776, lines 11-13.
229 FBI-MBT-2, section 4, page 920, line 24.
230 LINDER, p. 733.
231 FBI-MBT-2, section 4, page 920, lines 23-24.
232 *MS Civil Rights Project*, "Rush, Georgia and Her Son Rush, Jr., John Thomas", https://mscivilrightsproject.org/neshoba/person-neshoba/georgia-rush-and-her-son-john-thomas-rush-jr/.
233 FBI-MBT-2, section 4, page 925, lines 10-11.
234 FBI-MBT-2, section 4, page 925, lines 14-15.
235 FBI-MBT-2, section 4, page 921, line 19.
236 FBI-MBT-2, section 4, page 911, lines 14-17.
237 FBI-MBT-2, section 4, page 914, lines 21-24.
238 FBI-MBT-2, section 4, page 915, lines 15-17.
239 FBI-MBT-2, section 4, page 916, lines 1-2.
240 FBI-MBT-2, section 4, page 916, lines 2-9.
241 FBI-MBT-2, section 4, page 916, lines 16-18.
242 FBI-MBT-2, section 4, page 921, line 19.
243 FBI-MBT-2, section 4, page 920, lines 23-24.
244 FBI-MBT-2, section 4, page 920, lines 1-12.
245 FBI-MBT-2, section 4, page 920, lines 20-21.
246 FBI-MBT-2, section 4, page 921, line 19.
247 FBI-MBT-2, section 4, page 921, line 4.
248 FBI-MBT-2, section 4, page 920, line 25.
249 FBI-MBT-2, section 4, page 921, lines 2-7.
250 FBI-MBT-2, section 4, page 921, lines 20-23.
251 FBI-MBT-2, section 4, page 922, line 7.
252 FBI-MBT-2, section 4, page 924, line 20.
253 FBI-MBT-2, section 4, page 925, lines 1-3.
254 FBI-MBT-2, section 4, page 925, lines 20-25.
255 LINDER, p. 733.
256 FBI-MBT-2, section 1, page 774, line 17.
257 FBI-MBT-2, section 1, page 776, lines 18-22.
258 ND, 6/24/2004.
259 LLC, 6/19/2004, p. 2.
260 Congress of Racial Equality, "Andy Goodman", *Chaney, Goodman, and Schwerner*, retrieved September 14, 2018, http://www.core-online.org/History/goodman.htm.
261 Pitman, Michael, "5 things to know about Miami University's unique role in the Civil Rights movement, *Journal-News* (Butler County, Ohio), retrieved 12/29/2019, https://www.journal-news.com/news/local/things-know-about-miami-university-unique-role-civil-rights/pIdQCZAWCOZIf9cIBiHb7I/.

[262] For accounts of the first week of training consult Barnes, Ellen, Journal, Western College Memorial Archives; Sugarman, Tracy, Stranger at the Gates; Holt, Len, The Summer That Didn't End; Sellars, Cleveland, The River of No Return; Carmichael, Stokely, Ready for Revolution; and Sutherland-Martinez, Elizabeth, Letters from Mississippi. For the second week, see Belfrage, Sally, Freedom Summer; Adams, Jane, Journal, Western College Memorial Archives; and Sutherland-Martinez, Elizabeth, Letters from Mississippi. This reference list provided by Armstrong, Ann Elizabeth, *The Mississippi Summer Project*, Miami University Press, undated, https://miamioh.edu/student-life/_files/documents/orientation-and-transition/srp_armstrong_chapter_508.pdf.pdf.

[263] This discussion of Ohio training activities extracted from Armstrong, Ann Elizabeth, *The Mississippi Summer Project*, Miami University Press, undated, https://miamioh.edu/student-life/_files/documents/orientation-and-transition/srp_armstrong_chapter_508.pdf.pdf, p. 3.

[264] Armstrong, Ann Elizabeth, *The Mississippi Summer Project*, p. 3.

[265] Atwater, James, "If We Can Crack Mississippi", *Saturday Evening Post*, July 25, 1964, p. 18.

[266] Atwater, James, *Saturday Evening Post*, July 25, 1964, pp. 16-17.

[267] Atwater, James, *Saturday Evening Post*, July 25, 1964, p. 16.

[268] CBS, 00:00 - 00:37.

[269] Atwater, James, *Saturday Evening Post*, July 25, 1964, p. 16.

[270] Atwater, James, *Saturday Evening Post*, July 25, 1964, p. 17.

[271] Atwater, James, *Saturday Evening Post*, July 25, 1964, p. 17.

[272] Moye, J. Todd, *Let the People Decide: Black Freedom and White Resistant Movements in Sunflower County, MS, 1945-1968*, Univ of NC Press, 2004, p. 120.

[273] Atwater, James, *Saturday Evening Post*, July 25, 1964, p. 17.

[274] Moye, J. Todd, *Let the People Decide: Black Freedom and White Resistant Movements in Sunflower County, MS, 1945-1968*, Univ of NC Press, 2004, p. 120.

[275] Congress of Racial Equality, "Andy Goodman", *Chaney, Goodman, and Schwerner*, retrieved September 14, 2018, http://www.core-online.org/History/goodman.htm.

[276] LINDER, pp. 731-732.

[277] DOJ, p. 6.

[278] LINDER, p. 731-733.

[279] DOJ, p. 6.

[280] FBI-MBI-6, pdf. p.26.

[281] FBI-MBI-6, pdf. p.80.

[282] FBI-MBI-3, pdf. p. 5.

[283] FBI-MBI-1, pdf. p.25.

[284] Google Maps, retrieved 12/12/2018.

[285] DOJ, p. 6.

[286] FBI-MBT-1, part 3, p. 137, lines 19-24.
[287] FBI-MBT-1, part 3, p. 137, lines 19-24,
[288] FBI-MBT-1, part 3, p. 140, lines 22-25.
[289] FBI-MBT-1, part 3, p. 141, line 3.
[290] FBI-MBT-1, part 3, p. 141, lines 3-5.
[291] FBI-MBI-3, pdf p. 3.
[292] FBI-MBI-3, pdf p.110.
[293] FBI-MBI-4, pdf p. 1.
[294] FBI-MBI-3, pdf p. 102.
[295] FBI-MBT-1, part 9, p. 471, line 21, p 472, lines 13-15.
[296] FBI-MBI-3, pdf p. 77; FBI-MBT-1, section 10, page 504, line 15.
[297] Google Maps, retrieved 9/15/2018.
[298] FBI-MBT-1, section 9, page 474, lines 20-21; NBC Broadcast, 6/28/1964.
[299] FBI-MBT-1, section 10, page 504, line 5
[300] FBI-MBI-3, pdf. p. 99.
[301] FBI-MBI-3, pdf. p. 96.
[302] FBI-MBI-3, pdf. p. 77.
[303] FBI-MBT-1, section 10, page 504, line 17
[304] FBI-MBI-3, pdf. p. 77.
[305] FBI-MBI-3, pdf. p. 77.
[306] FBI-MBI-3, pdf. p. 75.
[307] FBI-MBI-4, pdf. p. 2.
[308] FBI-MBI-3, pdf. pp. 113, 116.
[309] FBI-MBT-1, section 2, page 120, lines 1-3.
[310] FBI-MBT-1, section 2, page 120, lines 1-3.
[311] FBI-MBI-3, pdf p. 92.
[312] FBI-MBT-1, section 9, page 477, lines 18-19.
[313] FBI-MBI-3, pdf p. 92.
[314] FBI-MBT-1, section 2, page 121, lines 1-3.
[315] DOJ, p. 6.
[316] FBI-MBT-1, part 9, p. 479, lines 5.
[317] FBI-MBT-1, part 2, p. 121, lines 8-10.
[318] FBI-MBT-1, part 2, p. 121, lines 7-8.
[319] FBI-MBI-3, pdf. p. 93.
[320] HUIE, p. 177.
[321] FBI-MBT-1, part 9, p. 479, line 14.
[322] FBI-MBT-1, part 9, p. 478, lines 7-8.
[323] FBI-MBI-3, pdf p. 4.
[324] FBI-MBT-1, part 10, p 514, line 20.
[325] FBI-MBI-3, pdf. p. 103.
[326] FBI-MBI-3, pdf. p. 103.

327 FBI-MBI-3, pdf. p. 104.
328 FBI-MBI-6, pdf. p. 88.
329 DOJ, p. 6.
330 FBI-MBT-2, part 1, p 765, line 3.
331 MITCHB, pdf. p. 11.
332 MITCHJ, pdf p. 2.
333 DOJ, p. 7.
334 FBI-MBT-2, part 5, p. 959, line 15, MITCHJ, pdf p. 2.
335 FBI-MBT-2, part 5, p. 959, line 8.
336 MITCHJ, pdf p. 2.
337 MITCHJ, pdf p. 2.
338 MITCHB, pdf p. 11.
339 MITCHJ, pdf p. 2.
340 MITCHJ, pdf p. 2.
341 MITCHJ, pdf p. 2.
342 MITCHB, pdf p. 10.
343 FBI-MBI-4, pdf. p. 44.
344 FBI-MBI-4, pdf. p. 53.
345 MITCHB, pdf. p. 9.
346 MITCHJ, pdf p. 3.
347 MITCHJ, pdf p. 3.
348 MITCHJ, pdf p. 3.
349 MITCHJ, pdf p. 3.
350 MITCHJ, pdf p. 3.
351 MITCHJ, pdf p. 3.
352 MITCHJ, pdf p. 2.
353 MITCHB, pdf p. 11.
354 MITCHJ, pdf p. 4
355 MITCHB, pdf p. 11.
356 MITCHJ, pdf p. 4
357 FBI-MBT-3, part 6, p. 1573, line 23.
358 MITCHJ, pdf p. 4.
359 FBI-MBT-3, part 8, p. 1679, line 22.
360 FBI-MBT-3, part 8, p. 1680, line 23.
361 FBI-MBT-3, part 8, p. 1682, line 2.
362 FBI-MBT-3, part 8, p. 1680, line 23.
363 Campbell, James, Stanford University, *Interviews with Carolyn Dearman*, 6/22/2005. Amd 5/19/2022.
364 MITCHJ, pdf p. 4.
365 FBI-MBT-2, part 5, p. 968, line 16.
366 MITCHJ, pdf p. 4.
367 FBI-MBI-4, pdf pp. 77,84, FBI-MBT-2, part 5, p. 970, line 12, p. 971, line 10.

[368] MITCHJ, pdf p. 4.
[369] DOJ, p. 6-7.
[370] MITCHJ, pdf p. 4.
[371] FBI-MBI-4, pdf, p. 18.
[372] FBI-MBI-4, pdf, p. 16.
[373] HUIE, p. 164.
[374] FBI-MBI-4, pdf. p. 36.
[375] FBI-MBI-4, pdf. p. 37.
[376] FBI-MBI-3, pdf. p. 4.
[377] FBI-MBT-1, part 4, p 199, line 3.
[378] FBI-MBT-1, part 4, p. 193, line 16.
[379] FBI-MBI-6, pdf. p. 104.
[380] FBI-MBT-1, part 4, p. 193, line 25.
[381] FBI-MBI-3, pdf p. 4.
[382] FBI-MBI-3, pdf p. 4.
[383] FBI-MBI-3, map on pdf pp. 47, 48 and Google Maps.
[384] FBI-MBI-3, pdf p. 4.
[385] FBI-MBI-4, pdf p. 79.
[386] FBI-MBI-8, pdf p. 49.
[387] FBI-MBI-3, pdf p. 104.
[388] FBI-MBT-1, part 10, p 489, lines 3-4.
[389] FBI-MBT-1, part 10, p 491, lines 10-11.
[390] MITCHJ, p. 4.
[391] MITCHJ, p. 4; MITCH B, p. 11; DOJ, p. 18.
[392] MITCHJ, pdf p. 4.
[393] MITCHJ, pdf. p. 4.
[394] FBI-MBI-3, pdf p. 104.
[395] MITCHJ, pdf. p. 4.
[396] FBI-MBI-1, pdf p. 97.
[397] MITCHJ, pdf p. 5.
[398] MITCHJ, pdf. p. 5.
[399] MITCHB, pdf p. 11.
[400] MITCHJ, pdf. p. 5.
[401] MITCHJ, pdf p. 5.
[402] FBI-MBI-8, pdf p. 42.
[403] MITCHJ, pdf p. 5.
[404] FBI-MBI-4, pdf p. 93.
[405] Google Earth, Distance Measurement Tool, Historical Image March 1, 1996, retrieved 9/11/2018.
[406] FBI-MBI-1, pdf p. 98.
[407] MITCHJ, pdf p. 5.
[408] MITCHB, pdf pp. 11-12.

[409] MITCHB, pdf p. 12.
[410] MITCHB, pdf p. 12.
[411] MITCHJ, pdf p. 5.
[412] MITCHJ, pdf p. 5.
[413] MITCHB, pdf p. 12.
[414] MITCHJ, pdf. p. 5.
[415] MITCHJ, pdf p. 5.
[416] FBI-MBI-4, pdf pp. 89-103.
[417] FBI-MBT-2, part 5, p. 974, lines 11-13.
[418] FBI-MBI-4, pdf. p. 102.
[419] MITCHJ, pdf p. 5.
[420] Google Earth, Distance Measurement Tool, retrieved 9/11/2018.
[421] DOJ, p. 8.
[422] MITCHJ, pdf p. 5, FBI-MBI-4, pdf p 102.
[423] MITCHJ, pdf p. 7.
[424] MITCHJ, pdf p. 6.
[425] FBI-MBI-04, pdf p. 99.
[426] Google Earth, Imagery 1/19/1997, retrieved 9/11/2018.
[427] Author Site Visit, 10/31/2018.
[428] FBI-MBI-04, pdf p. 99.
[429] FBI-MBI-04, pdf p. 99.
[430] Google Maps, Distance Measurement Tool, 11/07/2018.
[431] MITCHJ, pdf p. 6.
[432] MITCHB, pdf p. 12.
[433] MITCHJ, pdf p. 6.
[434] MITCHB, pdf p. 12.
[435] MITCHJ, pdf. p 6.
[436] MITCHB, pdf p. 12.
[437] FBI-MBI-5, pdf p 94; Featherston Autopsy Report.
[438] MITCHJ, pdf. pp. 6-7.
[439] MITCHB, pdf p. 12.
[440] FBI-MBI-5, pdf p. 95; Featherston Autopsy Report.
[441] MITCHJ, pdf. pp 6-7.
[442] MITCHB, pdf p. 12.
[443] FBI-MBI-5, pdf p. 96.
[444] Featherston Autopsy Report.
[445] FBI-MBI-5, pdf p. 96.
[446] See "Forensic Evidence Analysis" in this book.
[447] MITCHB, pdf pp. 12-13.
[448] Featherston Autopsy Report.
[449] MITCHJ, pdf. p. 6.

[450] Forensic data from *Report of the Laboratory of the FBI*, FBI File No 44-25706, Lab No PC-81805 AR IZ HB, August 12, 1964, FBI-MBI-6, pdf p. 13-14 ; Featherston Autopsy Report; Dr. Michael Baden examination of x-rays, CL, 6/26/2005, p. 7.
[451] CL, 6/26/2005, p. 7.
[452] See "Forensic Evidence Analysis" in this book.
[453] FBI-MBI-4, pdf pp. 104, 106, 107,113, 114.
[454] MITCHJ, pdf. pp 6-7.
[455] MITCHJ, pdf. p 6.
[456] MITCHJ, pdf p. 7.
[457] MITCHJ, pdf. p 6.
[458] MITCHJ, pdf. p. 7.
[459] FBI-MBI-5, pdf p 8.
[460] MITCHJ, pdf. p. 7.
[461] MITCHJ, pdf p. 7.
[462] MITCHB, pdf p. 13.
[463] MITCHJ, pdf p. 7.
[464] MITCHJ, pdf p. 7.
[465] Google Earth, Distance Measurement Tool, retreived 9/13/2018.
[466] FBI-MBI-5, pdf p. 16, map notation.
[467] FBI-MBI-4, pdf p. 74.
[468] MITCHJ, pdf p. 7.
[469] MITCHJ, pdf p. 8.
[470] MITCHJ, pdf p. 8.
[471] FBI-MBI-5, pdf pp. 8-9.
[472] MITCHJ, pdf p. 8.
[473] MITCHB, pdf p. 11.
[474] Google Maps, Distance Measurement Tool, retrieved 12/27/2018.
[475] MITCHJ, pdf p. 8.
[476] MITCHB, pdf p. 13.
[477] MITCHB, pdf p. 13.
[478] MITCHB, pdf p. 13.
[479] MITCHB, pdf p. 13, FBI-MBI-5, pdf p. 16.
[480] FBI-MBI-5, pdf p. 16.
[481] FBI-MBI-5, pdf p. 16, map notations.
[482] MITCHB, pdf p. 13.
[483] MITCHJ, pdf p. 9.
[484] FBI-MBI-5, pdf p. 6.
[485] MITCHB, pdf p. 13.
[486] Google Maps, Distance Measurement Tool, 11/10/2018.
[487] Google Maps, Distance Measurement Tool, 12/21/2018.
[488] MITCHJ, pdf p. 8.

489 MITCHJ, pdf p. 8.
490 FBI-MBI-5, pdf pp. 17-18.
491 FBI-MBI-5, pdf p. 19.
492 MITCHJ, pdf p. 8.
493 FBI-MBI-5, pdf pp. 9,10, 17.
494 MITCHJ, pdf p. 8.
495 FBI-MBI-5, pdf p. 17.
496 MITCHB, pdf p. 9.
497 MITCHB, pdf p. 13.
498 MITCHB, pdf p. 13.
499 MITCHJ, pdf p. 8.
500 MITCHJ, pdf p. 8.
501 MITCHB, pdf p. 13.
502 MITCHJ, pdf p. 8.
503 MITCHB, pdf p. 13.
504 MITCHB, pdf p. 13.
505 FBI-MBI-6, pdf p. 22.
506 FBI-MBI-6, pdf p. 21.
507 FBI-MBI-6, pdf p. 75.
508 FBI-MBI-6, pdf p. 80.
509 FBI-MBI-6, pdf p. 45.
510 FBI-MBI-5, pdf p. 6.
511 FBI-MBI-4, pdf p. 52, FBI-MBT-1, part 5, p. 251, line 7.
512 FBI-MBT-1, part 5, p. 251, line 1.
513 FBI-MBT-1, part 5, p. 250, lines 12-13.
514 FBI-MBT-1, part 5, p. 253, lines 3-4.
515 FBI-MBT-1, part 13, p. 539, lines 11-12.
516 FBI-MBT-1, part 13, p. 540, lines 18-19.
517 FBI-MBT-1, part 13, p. 542, line 1.
518 FBI-MBT-1, part 13, p. 540, lines 20-21.
519 FBI-MBT-1, part 13, p. 540, lines 18-19.
520 FBI-MBT-1, part 13, p. 541, lines 20-25.
521 MITCHJ, pdf p. 9.
522 MITCHB, pdf p. 13.
523 MITCHJ, pdf p. 9.
524 MITCHJ, pdf p. 9.
525 MITCHJ, pdf p. 9.
526 MITCHB, pdf p. 13.
527 MITCHJ, pdf p. 9.
528 FBI-MBI-4, pdf p. 84.
529 MITCHB, pdf p. 14.
530 MITCHJ, pdf p. 9.

[531] MITCHB, pdf p. 14.
[532] FBI-MBI-8, pdf p. 12.
[533] FBI-MBT-2, part 5, p. 987, lines 9-10.
[534] FBI-MBT-2, part 5, p. 987, line 3.
[535] FBI-MBT-2, part 5, p. 987, lines 8-11.
[536] Schwerner, Rita L., "Testimony of Rita L. Schwerner", *Mississippi Black Paper: Fifty-Seven Negro and White Citizens' Testimony of Police Brutality, the Breakdown of Law and Order and the Corruption of Justice in Mississippi*, 1965, pp. 59-63, https://www.historyisaweapon.com/defcon1/schwernertestimony.html.
[537] Schwerner, "Testimony", pp. 59-63.
[538] CRMV, "Chronology of Contacts with Agents of the Federal Government" *Council of Federated Organizations, Meridian*, retrieved 10/10/2018, https://www.crmvet.org/docs/6406_cofo_csg-fedcontacts.pdf.
[539] Schudel, Matt, "Frank E. Schwelb, a civil rights lawyer who became a D.C. judge, dies at 82", *The Washington Post*, August 20, 2014, retrieved 10/11/2018, https://www.washingtonpost.com/local/obituaries/frank-e-schwelb-a-civil-rights-lawyer-who-became-a-dc-judge-dies-at-82/2014/08/20/da318932-2889-11e4-8593-da634b334390_story.html?noredirect=on&utm_term=.9bb99b5c2ede.
[540] CRMV, "Chronology of Contacts", retrieved 10/10/2018.
[541] CRMV, "Chronology of Contacts", retrieved 10/10/2018.
[542] CRMV, "Chronology of Contacts", retrieved 10/10/2018.
[543] CRMV, "Chronology of Contacts", retrieved 10/10/2018.
[544] HUIE, p. 201.
[545] CRMV, "Chronology of Contacts", retrieved 10/10/2018.
[546] CRMV, "Chronology of Contacts", retrieved 10/10/2018.
[547] JOHN-2, "Fill-up Mississippi with FBI Men", "Conversation with Lee White", June 23, 1964, Tape WH6406.13, 07:34.
[548] CRMV, "Chronology of Contacts", retrieved 10/10/2018.
[549] HA, 6/23/1964, p. 3.
[550] CL, 6/18/1989, p. 92.
[551] CL, 6/18/1989, p. 92.
[552] CL, 6/18/1989, p. 92.
[553] CL, 6/18/1989, p. 92.
[554] CRMV, "Chronology of Contacts", retrieved 10/10/2018.
[555] HA, 6/23/1964, p. 3.
[556] CRMV, "Chronology of Contacts", retrieved 10/10/2018.
[557] CRMV, "Chronology of Contacts", retrieved 10/10/2018.
[558] HUIE, p. 202.
[559] CRMV, "Chronology of Contacts", retrieved 10/10/2018.
[560] FBI-MBT-1, part 5, p. 243, line 1.
[561] HUIE, p. 202.

[562] JOHN-2, "Fill-up Mississippi with FBI Men", "Conversation with Lee White", June 23, 1964, Tape WH6406.13, Conversation 3818.
[563] FBI-MBT-1, part 5, p. 243, line 1.
[564] FBI-MBT-1, part 4, p. 225, lines 6-9.
[565] FBI-MBT-1, part 4, p. 228, line 5.
[566] FBI-MBI-6, pdf pp. 21-22.
[567] FBI-MBI-6, pdf pp. 21-22.
[568] FBI-MBI-6, pdf p. 26.
[569] FBI-MBI-6, pdf p. 26.
[570] FBI-MBI-6, pdf p. 26.
[571] FBI-MBI-6, pdf p. 41.
[572] JOHN-2, "What do you think happened to them", "Conversation with Nicholas Katzenbach", June 23, 1964, Tape WH6406.13, Conversation 3832.
[573] "Civil Rights Act of 1964", *Public Law 88-352 (78 Stat. 241)*, https://www.archives.gov/education/lessons/civil-rights-act.
[574] JOHN-2, "It's a publicity stunt", "Conversation with James Eastland", June 23, 1964, Tape WH6406.14, Conversation 3836.
[575] "Civil Rights Act of 1964", *An Act*, https://www.eeoc.gov/eeoc/history/35th/thelaw/civil_rights_act.html.
[576] *Roll Call Tally on Civil Rights Act 1964, June 19, 1964*, The Center For Legislative Archives, US National Archives, https://www.archives.gov/legislative/features/civil-rights-1964/senate-roll-call.html.
[577] JOHN-2, "we found the car", "Conversation with J Edgar Hoover", June 23, 1964, Tape WH6406.14, Conversation 3837.
[578] CRMV, "Chronology of Contacts", retrieved 10/10/2018.
[579] CRMV, "Chronology of Contacts", retrieved 10/10/2018; Lisagor, Peter, "Why Allen Dulles Was Chosen to Go Into Mississippi", *Chicago Daily News*, 6/25/1964, https://www.cia.gov/library/readingroom/docs/CIA-RDP70-00058R000300030080-7.pdf.
[580] Discussion of press conference by MS Gov Paul Johnson about search for missing trio conducted extracted from CL, 6/24/1964, pp. 1, 8.
[581] CL, 6/18/1989, p. 92.
[582] CL, 6/18/1989, p. 92. 1:30 pm report arrived before the finding of the vehicle at 1:32 pm. This report summarized efforts in the morning. Gov Johnson gave a news conference in the afternoon that described the search efforts. So, the report about the finding of the ranch wagon had to be in his 5 pm report.
[583] CL, 6/18/1989, p. 92.
[584] CRMV, "Chronology of Contacts", retrieved 10/10/2018; JOHN-2, "I'm here with the parents of the missing boys", "Conversation with Robert McNamera", June 23, 1964, Tape WH6406.14, Conversation 3855.

585 JOHN-2, "The bodies were not in the car", "Conversation with J Edgar Hoover", June 23, 1964, Tape WH6406.15, Conversation 3869.
586 Lisagor, Peter, "Why Allen Dulles Was Chosen to Go Into Mississippi", *Chicago Daily News*, 6/25/1964, https://www.cia.gov/library/readingroom/docs/CIA-RDP70-00058R000300030080-7.pdf.
587 JOHN-1, "Conversation with Allen Dulles and Robert Kennedy", Tape WH6406.15, Conversation 3868, https://millercenter.org/the-presidency/secret-white-house-tapes/conversation-allen-dulles-and-robert-kennedy-june-23-1964-0.
588 "Warren Commission -- Introduction", *JFK Assassination Records*, US National Archives, retrieved 1/3/2020, https://www.archives.gov/research/jfk/warren-commission-report/intro.
589 JOHN-2, "The bodies were not in the car", "Conversation with J Edgar Hoover", June 23, 1964, Tape WH6406.15, Conversation 3869.
590 JOHN-1, "Conversation with Paul Johnson", June 23, 1964, Tape WH6406.15, Conversation 3878, https://millercenter.org/the-presidency/secret-white-house-tapes/conversation-paul-johnson-june-24-1964-1.
591 JOHN-2, "Miss Schwerner", "Conversation with Nathan Schwerner", June 23, 1964, Tape WH6406.16, Conversation 3882.
592 CRMV, "Chronology of Contacts", retrieved 10/10/2018.
593 JOHN-2, "None of them were burned", "Conversation with Robert Goodman", June 23, 1964, Tape WH6406.16, Conversation 3884.
594 CL, 6/24/1964, p. 1.
595 HA, 6/24/1964, p. 1.
596 CL, 6/24/1964, p. 14.
597 HA, 6/24/1964, p. 2.
598 Mitchell, Jerry, "Mr. X, 'Unsung Hero' in Slaying of Three Men", *Clarion Ledger*, June 12, 2005, retrieved 10/12/2018, http://barrybradford.com/mississippi-burning-mr-x/.
599 FBI-MBT-1, part 5, p. 243, lines 11-14.
600 Mitchell, "Mr. X, 'Unsung Hero'.
601 HA, 6/24/1964, p. 1.
602 Mars, *Witness*, pp. 87-88.
603 Mars, Florence, *Witness in Philadelphia*, Louisiana State University Press, 1977, p. 87.
604 Mars, *Witness*, p. 88.
605 CL, 6/26/1964, p. 1.
606 DDT, 6/25/1964, p. 1.
607 CL, 6/26/1964, p. 20.
608 DDT, 6/25/1964, p. 1.
609 CL, 6/25/1964, p. 1.
610 DDT, 6/25/1964, p. 1.

[611] "Proceedings and Debates of the 88th Congress, Second Session", *Congressional Record*, Volume 110, Part 11, June 17, 1964 - June 26, 1964, p. 14809.
[612] Comments by Stennis extracted from *Congressional Record*, Volume 110, Part 11, pp. 14812-14813.
[613] Comments by Javits extracted from *Congressional Record*, Volume 110, Part 11, p. 14813.
[614] CL, 6/25/1964, p. 1.
[615] DDT, 6/25/1964, p. 1.
[616] *The Semi-Weekly Spokesman-Review* (Spokane, WA), 6/25/1964, p. 1.
[617] DDT, 6/25/1964, pp. 1-2.
[618] DDT, 6/25/1964, p. 2.
[619] DDT, 6/25/1964, p. 2.
[620] CL, 6/25/1964, p. 1.
[621] DDT, 6/25/1964, p. 2.
[622] "Lockheed JetStar", Wikipedia, retrieved 1/4/2020, https://en.wikipedia.org/wiki/Lockheed_JetStar.
[623] CL, 6/25/1964, p. 1.
[624] DDT, 6/25/1964, p. 1.
[625] CL, 6/25/1964, p. 1.
[626] CL, 6/25/1964, p. 14.
[627] CL, 6/25/1964, p. 14.
[628] CL, 6/25/1964, p. 14.
[629] DDT, 6/25/1964, p. 2.
[630] DDT, 6/25/1964, p. 2.
[631] CL, 6/25/1964, p. 14.
[632] CL, 6/25/1964, p. 14.
[633] CL, 6/26/1964, p. 1.
[634] DDT, 6/25/1964, p. 2.
[635] *The Semi-Weekly Spokesman-Review* (Spokane, WA), 6/25/1964, p. 1.
[636] CL, 6/26/1964, p. 20.
[637] Lutz, Phillip, "A Bit Slower, but Still Throwing Lethal Punch Lines", NYT, 2/19/2010.
[638] CL, 6/25/1965, p. 1.
[639] CL, 6/18/1989, p. 92.
[640] CL, 6/26/1964, p. 1.
[641] CL, 6/26/1964, p. 1.
[642] CL, 6/26/1964, p. 1.
[643] "Facts About Water Moccasin (Cottonmouth) Snakes", *Live Science*, retrieved 1/3/2020, https://www.livescience.com/43597-facts-about-water-moccasin-cottonmouth-snakes.html.
[644] Personal experience of author performing Search and Rescue missions in the South MS swamps with the Civil Air Patrol during 1965 - 1967.

645 CL, 6/26/1964, p. 20.
646 CL, 6/26/1964, p. 1; DULL, 01:21.
647 CL, 6/26/1964, p. 20.
648 CL, 6/26/1964, p. 20.
649 CBS, 04:30 - 05:49.
650 DULL, 01:30.
651 CL, 6/26/1964, p. 20.
652 Proceedings and Debates of the 88th Congress, Second Session", *Congressional Record*, Volume 110, Part 11, June 17, 1964 - June 26, 1964, p. 14962.
653 *Congressional Record*, Volume 110, Part 11, p. 14997.
654 *Congressional Record*, Volume 110, Part 11, p. 15005.
655 *Congressional Record*, Volume 110, Part 11, p. 15006.
656 *Congressional Record*, Volume 110, Part 11, p. 15062.
657 *Congressional Record*, Volume 110, Part 11, p. 15082.
658 DULL, 01:37, 02:05.
659 MBP, "Testimony of Rita Schwerner", pp. 59-63.
660 HUIE, "3 Lives", p. 203.
661 MBP, "Testimony of Rita Schwerner", pp. 59-63.
662 MBP, "Testimony of Rita Schwerner", pp. 59-63.
663 DULL, 01:53.
664 CL, 6/18/1989, p. 92.
665 "arrived after midnight", DULL, , 04:44 - 04:47; Jackson to Washington, DC is 980 miles, www.maps.google.com; maximum cruise speed of Lockheed C-140 Jetstar is 567 mph at 21,00 ft, https://en.wikipedia.org/wiki/Lockheed_JetStar; correcting for winds and lower flight altitude, air speed about 450 mph; approximately 2 hour flight time (980/450) and leaving 1/2 hour for news conference before departure gives an approximate time of 10 pm.
666 CL, 6/26/1964, p. 1.
667 "Lockheed JetStar", Wikipedia, retrieved 1/4/2020, https://en.wikipedia.org/wiki/Lockheed_JetStar.
668 Mars, *Witness*, p. 89.
669 Mars, *Witness*, p. 96.
670 "About Walter Cronkite", *American Masters*, Public Broadcasting System, retrieved 1/4/2000, http://www.pbs.org/wnet/americanmasters/walter-cronkite-about-walter-cronkite/561/; Campbell, Joseph, "Cronkite 'the most trusted? Where's the evidence", *Media Myth Alert*, retrieved 1/4/2020, https://mediamythalert.com/2012/06/09/cronkite-the-most-trusted-wheres-the-evidence/.
671 CBS, 00:00 - 00:37.
672 CBS, 00:37 - 01:08.
673 *Congressional Record*, Volume 110, Part 11, p. 15006.
674 CL, 6/26/1964, p. 1; CBS, 03:23 - 03:38.

675 CBS, 05:49 - 19:48.
676 CBS, 22:34 - 24:52.
677 CBS, 24:52 - 26:40.
678 CBS, 30:00 - 30:34.
679 CBS, 56:05 -- 57:05.
680 CBS, 57:05 -- 57:26.
681 "Lockheed JetStar", Wikipedia, retrieved 1/4/2020, https://en.wikipedia.org/wiki/Lockheed_JetStar.
682 DULL, 04:44 - 04:47.
683 DULL, 03:49 - 04:10.
684 DULL, 05:27 - 05:50.
685 DULL, 05:50 - 06:35.
686 DULL, 07:15 - 07:27.
687 DULL, 08:10 - 08:15.
688 DULL, 08:35 - 09:02.
689 CL, 6/27/1964, p. 1.
690 JOHN-1, "Conversation with Paul Johnson and Allen Dulles", Tape WH6406.17, Conversation 3919, June 26, 1964, https://millercenter.org/the-presidency/secret-white-house-tapes/conversation-paul-johnson-and-allen-dulles-june-26-1964, 01:05 - 01:25.
691 JOHN-1, Tape WH6406.17, Conversation 3919, June 26, 1964, 01:26 - 01:45.
692 JOHN-1, Tape WH6406.17, Conversation 3919, June 26, 1964, 01:46 - 02:14.
693 JOHN-1, Tape WH6406.17, Conversation 3919, June 26, 1964, 05:38 - 06:58.
694 JOHN-1, Tape WH6406.17, Conversation 3919, June 26, 1964, 06:58 - 08:00.
695 JOHN-1, Tape WH6406.17, Conversation 3919, June 26, 1964, 09:20.
696 JOHN-1, Tape WH6406.17, Conversation 3919, June 26, 1964, 09:45-10:13.
697 JOHN-1, Tape WH6406.17, Conversation 3919, June 26, 1964, 10:42-11:24.
698 JOHN-1, "Conversation with J Edgar Hoover and Allen Dulles", Tape WH6406.17, Conversation 3921, June 26, 1964, https://millercenter.org/the-presidency/secret-white-house-tapes/conversation-j-edgar-hoover-and-allen-dulles-june-26-1964-1, 00:40 - 00:50.
699 CL, 6/27/1964, p. 1.
700 CL, 6/27/1964, p. 1.
701 HUIE, p. 206.
702 CL, 6/27/1964, p. 13.
703 HA, 6/26/1964, p. 7.
704 CL, 6/27/1964, p. 13.
705 CL, 6/27/1964, p. 1.
706 CL, 6/27/1964, p. 8.
707 DOJ, Investigation, p. 10.
708 This discussion of the meeting between Allen Dulles and the representatives of the Council of Churches extracted from CL, 6/28/1964, p. 1.

[709] CL, 6/28/1964, p. 1.
[710] CL, 6/28/1964, p. 1.
[711] NBC Broadcast, 6/28/1964; CL, 6/28/1964, p. 1.
[712] Unless otherwise indicated, details of the Jackson Field Office extracted from FBI, "FBI Jackson History", FBI > History > Field Office Histories, retrieved 10/11/2018, https://www.fbi.gov/history/field-office-histories/jackson.
[713] FBI, "A Byte Out of History, 50th Anniversary of the FBI's Jackson Field Office", retrieved 12/8/2019, https://www.fbi.gov/news/stories/50th-anniversary-of-the-fbis-jackson-field-office.
[714] *Chicago Tribune* (Chicago, IL), 6/30/1964, pp. 1, 9.
[715] CL, 6/30/1964, p. 1.
[716] HA, 6/30/1964, p. 1.
[717] CL, 6/30/1964, p. 1.
[718] CL, 6/30/1964, p. 8.
[719] HA, 6/30/1964, p. 1.
[720] CL, 6/30/1964, p. 8.
[721] CL, 6/30/1964, p. 8.
[722] *Chicago Tribune* (Chicago, IL), 6/30/1964, p. 1.
[723] FBI, "A Byte Out of History, 50th Anniversary of the FBI's Jackson Field Office", retrieved 12/8/2019, https://www.fbi.gov/news/stories/50th-anniversary-of-the-fbis-jackson-field-office.
[724] CL, 6/18/1989, p. 92.
[725] HA, 6/30/1964, p. 1.
[726] EJM, 7/2/1964, p. 3.
[727] CL, 7/3/1964, p. 1.
[728] CL, 7/3/1964, p. 1.
[729] "Legislative History of HR 7152", *Reference Sources on the Civil Rights Act of 1964*, The Dirksen Congressional Center, retrieved 2/19/2020, https://www.dirksencenter.org/print_basics_histmats_civilrights64_doc7.htm#section1.
[730] "Legislative History of HR 7152", *Reference Sources on the Civil Rights Act of 1964*, The Dirksen Congressional Center, retrieved 2/19/2020, https://www.dirksencenter.org/print_basics_histmats_civilrights64_doc7.htm#section1.
[731] "Landmark Legislation: The Civil Rights Act of 1964", *US Senate*, retrieved 2/19/2020, https://www.senate.gov/artandhistory/history/common/generic/CivilRightsAct1964.htm.
[732] *Roll Call Tally on Civil Rights Act 1964, June 19, 1964*, The Center For Legislative Archives, US National Archives, https://www.archives.gov/legislative/features/civil-rights-1964/senate-roll-call.html.

[733] "Landmark Legislation: The Civil Rights Act of 1964", *US Senate*.
[734] "July 2, 1964: Remarks upon Signing the Civil Rights Bill", *Presidential Speeches*, Miller Center, University of Virginia, https://millercenter.org/the-presidency/presidential-speeches/july-2-1964-remarks-upon-signing-civil-rights-bill.
[735] ND, 7/2/1964.
[736] Llelyveld, Joseph, "A Stranger In Philadelphia, MS", NYT, 12/27/1964, p. 139.
[737] EJM, 7/3/1964, p. 3.
[738] CL, 7/5/1964, p. 12.
[739] CL, 7/6/1964, p. 6.
[740] EJM, 7/7/1964, p. 1.
[741] HA, 7/8/1964, p. 1.
[742] EJM, 7/7/1964, p. 1.
[743] CL, 7/9/1964, p. 1.
[744] Mars, *Witness*, pp. 90-91.
[745] CL, 6/18/1989, p. 92.
[746] NYT, "Mississippi Force Expanded by FBI", 7/11/1964, https://www.nytimes.com/1964/07/11/archives/mississippi-force-expanded-by-fbi-big-buildup-to-153-agents.html.
[747] FBI, "The FBI vs The Klan, Part 4: A Leader Emerges", retrieved 12/8/2019, https://archives.fbi.gov/archives/news/stories/2010/december/klan_121010.
[748] CL, 7/11/1964, p. 13.
[749] FBI, "The FBI vs The Klan, Part 4: A Leader Emerges", retrieved 12/8/2019, https://archives.fbi.gov/archives/news/stories/2010/december/klan_121010.
[750] FBI, "FBI Jackson Division Celebrates 50th Anniversary", *FBI > Field Offices*, retrieved 10/10/2018, https://www.fbi.gov/contact-us/field-offices/jackson/news/stories/fbi-jackson-division-celebrates-50th-anniversary.
[751] HA, 7/10/1964, p. 1.
[752] Original Caption, "Mayor Allen Thompson Meeting J Edgar Hoover At Airport", *Getty Images*, https://www.gettyimages.com/detail/news-photo/director-j-edgar-hoover-arrives-here-on-july-10th-to-confer-news-photo/515098376.
[753] NYT, "Mississippi Force Expanded by FBI", 7/11/1964, p. 1, https://timesmachine.nytimes.com/timesmachine/1964/07/11/118670312.html?pageNumber=1.
[754] CL, 6/18/1989, p. 92.
[755] Original Caption, "Mayor Allen Thompson Meeting J Edgar Hoover At Airport", *Getty Images*, https://www.gettyimages.com/detail/news-photo/director-j-edgar-hoover-arrives-here-on-july-10th-to-confer-news-photo/515098376.

756 NYT, "Mississippi Force Expanded by FBI", 7/11/1964, p. 1; CL, 7/11/1964, p. 1.
757 CL, 7/11/1964, p. 13.
758 NYT, "Mississippi Force Expanded by FBI", 7/11/1964, p. 1.
759 NYT, "Mississippi Force Expanded by FBI", 7/11/1964, p. 22. https://timesmachine.nytimes.com/timesmachine/1964/07/11/118670312.html?pageNumber=22; CL, 7/11/1964, p. 1.
760 CL, 7/12/1964, p. 1.
761 FBI, "The FBI vs The Klan, Part 4: A Leader Emerges", retrieved 12/8/2019, https://archives.fbi.gov/archives/news/stories/2010/december/klan_121010.
762 Case, Bert, "FBI Agent Roy Moore Laid To Rest", *WLBT TV*, 10/18/2008, retrieved 12/8/2019, https://www.wlbt.com/story/9198469/fbi-agent-roy-moore-laid-to-rest/.
763 EJM, 7/13/1964, p. 1.
764 EJM, 7/13/1964, p. 1.
765 CL, 7/15/1964, pp. 1, 14.
766 HA, 7/18/1964, pp. 1, 8.
767 CL, 6/18/1989, p. 92.
768 LLC, 6/19/2004, p. 2.
769 Mitchell, "Mr. X, 'Unsung Hero'"
770 Mars, *Witness*, p. 92.
771 FBI-MBI-8, pdf p. 102.
772 HA, 7/25/1964, p. 1.
773 HA, 7/25/1964, p. 1.
774 HA, 7/25/1964, p. 1.
775 "Downtown Philadelphia Historic District", National Register of Historic Places, NRIS Reference Number 05000280, April 14, 2005, p. 34, https://npgallery.nps.gov/pdfhost/docs/NRHP/Text/05000280.pdf, retrieved 2/1/2019.
776 HA, 7/25/1964, pp. 1,6.
777 HA, 7/25/1964, p. 6.
778 FBI-MBI-8, pdf p. 102.
779 Mitchell, Jerry, "New Details on the FBI paying $30K to solve the Mississippi Burning case", Journey To Justice Blog, Clarion Ledger, February 15, 2010, retrieved 10/12/2018, http://blogs.clarionledger.com/jmitchell/2010/02/15/did-the-fbi-pay-30k-to-locate-the-bodies-of-the-three-missing-civil-rights-workers/.
780 Mitchell, "Mr. X, 'Unsung Hero'"
781 Mitchell, "Mr. X, 'Unsung Hero'"
782 Mitchell, "New Details".
783 MSC, Hopkins, A. L., "Investigation of the finding of the bodies of the three civil rights workers who disappeared from Philadelphia, MS, on June 21, 1964",

August 6, 1964, p. 1, SCR ID # 2-112-1-49-5-1-1,
http://www.mdah.ms.gov/arrec/digital_archives/sovcom/result.php?image=images/png/cd05/038332.png&otherstuff=2|112|1|49|5|1|1|37738|#
[784] MSC, Hopkins, A. L., "Investigation of the finding of the bodies of the three civil rights workers who disappeared from Philadelphia, MS, on June 21, 1964", August 6, 1964, p. 1, SCR ID # 2-112-1-49-5-1-1,
http://www.mdah.ms.gov/arrec/digital_archives/sovcom/result.php?image=images/png/cd05/038332.png&otherstuff=2|112|1|49|5|1|1|37738|#
[785] HA, 10/11/1967, p. 4.
[786] Mitchell, "New Details".
[787] FBI-MBI-5, pdf p. 5.
[788] FBI-MBI-5, pdf p. 9.
[789] FBI-MBI-5, pdf pp. 8-9.
[790] FBI-MBI-5, pdf p. 9.
[791] FBI-MBI-5, pdf pp. 8-9.
[792] HA, 1/27/1965, p. 1.
[793] HA, 1/27/1965, p. 1.
[794] FBI-MBI-5, pdf p. 5.
[795] DOJ, p. 10.
[796] HA, 1/27/1965, p. 1.
[797] FBI-MBI-5, pdf p. 8.
[798] FBI-MBI-5, pdf pp. 10, 16.
[799] FBI-MBI-5, pdf p. 9.
[800] FBI-MBI-5, pdf p. 9.
[801] FBI-MBI-5, pdf p. 10.
[802] FBI-MBI-5, pdf p. 10.
[803] FBI-MBI-5, pdf pp. 16-19.
[804] FBI-MBI-5, pdf p. 11.
[805] FBI-MBI-5, pdf p. 11.
[806] FBI-MBI-5, pdf p. 12.
[807] FBI-MBI-5, pdf pp. 11-12.
[808] FBI-MBI-5, pdf p. 12.
[809] FBI-MBI-5, pdf p. 12.
[810] FBI-MBI-5, pdf p. 13.
[811] FBI-MBI-5, pdf p. 13.
[812] JOHN-2, "The FBI has found 3 bodies", "Conversation with Cartha Deloach", August 4, 1964, Tape WH6408.05, Conversation 4693.
[813] JOHN-2, "Call the families and tell them", "Conversation with Lee White", August 4, 1964, Tape WH6408.05, Conversation 4694.
[814] FBI-MBI-5, pdf p. 13.
[815] FBI-MBI-5, pdf p. 14.
[816] FBI-MBI-5, pdf p. 17.

817 FBI-MBI-5, pdf p. 6.
818 FBI-MBI-5, pdf p. 17.
819 FBI-MBI-5, pdf p. 18.
820 FBI-MBI-5, pdf p. 17.
821 FBI-MBI-5, pdf p. 13.
822 US Dept of Justice, *Press Releases, Speeches, Testimonies, and Other Records, 1933-1984*, Record Group 60, National Archives Identifier 5605357, https://catalog.archives.gov/id/5605357.
823 ND, 8/6/1964.
824 Rowley, Dean, *Chronology of Life of Dr. Martin Luther King, Jr*, NEH Civil Rights Institute, https://www.csub.edu/~gsantos/neh/materials/rowley3.html.
825 "Statement by Martin Luther King", transcribed from live video, https://www.youtube.com/watch?v=207Z5qVFJu0.
826 E-mail correspondence on 9/21/2020, with Mark Levy who was in attendance at this event.
827 FBI-MBT-01, Part 9, p. 451, lines 17-18.
828 DeShazo, Richard D., Smith, Robert, Skipworth Leigh, "A White Dean and Black Physicians at the Epicenter of the Civil Rights Movement", *The American Journal of Medicine*, Volume 127, No 6, June 2014, p. 473, https://www.amjmed.com/article/S0002-9343(14)00276-9/pdf.
829 FBI-MBT-01, Part 9, p. 451, lines 13-15.
830 MSC, Johnston, Earle, Jr., "Autopsy of Slain Civil Rights Workers", September 4, 1964, p. 1, SCR ID # 2-112-1-55-1-1-1, http://www.mdah.ms.gov/arrec/digital_archives/sovcom/result.php?image=images/png/cd05/038348.png&otherstuff=2|112|1|55|1|1|1|37754|#.
831 DeShazo, "White Dean", p. 473.
832 FBI-MBI-5, pdf p. 92.
832 MSC, "Autopsy", p. 1, SCR ID # 2-112-1-55-1-1-1, http://www.mdah.ms.gov/arrec/digital_archives/sovcom/result.php?image=images/png/cd05/038348.png&otherstuff=2|112|1|55|1|1|1|37754|#.
833 FBI-MBI-5, pdf p. 92.
833 MSC, "Autopsy", p. 1, SCR ID # 2-112-1-55-1-1-1, http://www.mdah.ms.gov/arrec/digital_archives/sovcom/result.php?image=images/png/cd05/038348.png&otherstuff=2|112|1|55|1|1|1|37754|#.
834 FEAT, p. 1.
835 FEAT, p. 2.
836 FBI-MBI-5, pdf p. 92.
837 FEAT, p. 1.
838 MSC, "Autopsy", p. 1, SCR ID # 2-112-1-55-1-1-1, http://www.mdah.ms.gov/arrec/digital_archives/sovcom/result.php?image=images/png/cd05/038348.png&otherstuff=2|112|1|55|1|1|1|37754|# and

Brunson, Joel G., "Letter to Dr. William Featherston", September 4, 1964, letter provided by the family of Dr. William Featherston.

[839] FBI-MBI-5, pdf p. 92.
[840] FBI-MBI-5, pdf pp. 11-12.
[841] FEAT, p. 1; FBI-MBI-5, pdf p. 92.
[842] FEAT, p. 2; FBI-MBI-5, pdf p. 93.
[843] FEAT, p. 2.; FBI-MBI-5, pdf p. 104.
[844] FEAT, p. 4; FBI-MBI-5, pdf p. 93.
[845] FBI-MBI-5, pdf p. 94.
[846] FBI-MBI-5, pdf p. 92.
[847] FBI-MBI-5, pdf p. 12.
[848] FBI-MBI-5, pdf p. 94.
[849] FEAT, p. 3; FBI-MBI-5, pdf p. 104.
[850] FEAT, p. 5; FBI-MBI-5, pdf p. 95.
[851] FBI-MBI-5, pdf p. 95.
[852] FBI-MBI-5, pdf p. 92.
[853] FBI-MBI-5, pdf p. 95.
[854] FEAT, pp. 3-4; FBI-MBI-5, pdf p. 104.
[855] FEAT, p. 4.
[856] FEAT, pp. 3-4; FBI-MBI-5, pdf p. 104.
[857] FEAT, p. 3.
[858] FEAT, p. 5.
[859] FBI-MBI-5, pdf p. 96.
[860] FBI-MBI-5, pdf p. 95.
[861] HA, 8/6/1964, p. 2.
[862] HA, 8/6/1964, p. 2.
[863] HA, 8/6/1964, p. 2.
[864] HA, 8/6/1964, p. 2.
[865] FBI-MBI-5, pdf p. 102.
[866] Spain, p. 23.
[867] Spain, *Post-Mortem,* p. 24.
[868] Spain, *Post-Mortem,* pp. 24-25.
[869] Spain, *Post-Mortem,* p. 26.
[870] MSC, "Autopsy of Slain Civil Rights Workers", SCR ID # 2-112-1-55-1-1-1, http://www.mdah.ms.gov/arrec/digital_archives/sovcom/result.php?image=images/png/cd05/038348.png&otherstuff=2|112|1|55|1|1|1|37754|#.
[871] Spain, *Post-Mortem,* p. 28.
[872] Spain, *Post-Mortem,* p. 28.
[873] Spain, *Post-Mortem,* p. 29.
[874] Spain, *Post-Mortem,* p. 30.
[875] Spain, *Post-Mortem,* p. 32.
[876] Spain, *Post-Mortem,* pp. 34-35.

877 Spain, *Post-Mortem*, p. 36.
878 FBI-MBI-5, pdf p. 102.
879 Brunson, Joel G., "Letter to Dr. William Featherston", September 4, 1964, letter provided by the family of Dr. William Featherston.
880 Spain, *Post-Mortem*, p. 39.
881 CRMV, Spain, Dr. David M., *Post Mortem Examination Report of the Body of James Chaney*, August 7, 1964, retrieved 10/14/2018, https://www.crmvet.org/docs/6408_chaney_spain.pdf.
882 Spain, *Post-Mortem*, pp. 37-38.
883 Spain, *Post-Mortem*, p. 39.
884 *Report of the Laboratory of the FBI*, FBI File No 44-25706, Lab No PC-81805 AR IZ HB, August 12, 1964, FBI-MBI-6, pdf p. 13-14.
885 FBI-MBI-6, pdf. p. 14.
886 FBI-MBI-6, pdf p. 11, p. 13, p. 14.
887 FBI-MBI-6, pdf. p. 14.
888 Spain, *Post-Mortem*, p. 38.
889 DeShazo, "White Dean", p. 476. Copy of confirmation letter from Hoover dated July 1, 1965, from Twiss Archives, University of Mississippi Medical Center Rowland Medical Library.
890 MSC., "Autopsy ", p. 1, http://www.mdah.ms.gov/arrec/digital_archives/sovcom/result.php?image=images/png/cd05/038348.png&otherstuff=2|112|1|55|1|1|1|37754|#.
891 MSC., "Autopsy ", p. 1, http://www.mdah.ms.gov/arrec/digital_archives/sovcom/result.php?image=images/png/cd05/038348.png&otherstuff=2|112|1|55|1|1|1|37754|#.
892 Spain, *Post-Mortem*, p. 30.
893 MSC., "Autopsy ", p. 1, http://www.mdah.ms.gov/arrec/digital_archives/sovcom/result.php?image=images/png/cd05/038348.png&otherstuff=2|112|1|55|1|1|1|37754|#.
894 MSC., "Autopsy ", p. 2, http://www.mdah.ms.gov/arrec/digital_archives/sovcom/result.php?image=images/png/cd05/038349.png&otherstuff=2|112|1|55|2|1|1|37755|#
895 MSC., "Autopsy ", p. 2, http://www.mdah.ms.gov/arrec/digital_archives/sovcom/result.php?image=images/png/cd05/038349.png&otherstuff=2|112|1|55|2|1|1|37755|#
896 MSC., "Autopsy ", p. 2, http://www.mdah.ms.gov/arrec/digital_archives/sovcom/result.php?image=images/png/cd05/038349.png&otherstuff=2|112|1|55|2|1|1|37755|#
897 MSC., "Autopsy ", p. 2, http://www.mdah.ms.gov/arrec/digital_archives/sovcom/result.php?image=images/png/cd05/038349.png&otherstuff=2|112|1|55|2|1|1|37755|#

[898] "Homecoming: A Time To Mourn", *Blvck Avrchives*, retrieved 10/17/2018, http://www.blvckvrchives.com/homegoing/, featuring extracts from Smith, Suzanne, *To Serve The Living: Funeral Directors and the African American Way of Life*, Belknap Press, 2010.
[899] "Homecoming: A Time To Mourn", *Blvck Avrchives*, retrieved 10/17/2018, http://www.blvckvrchives.com/homegoing/, featuring extracts from Smith, Suzanne, *To Serve The Living: Funeral Directors and the African American Way of Life*, Belknap Press, 2010.
[900] "In Memorium of James E. Chaney", *Patrick Quinn Papers, 1968-1974*, 2011; Z: Accessions, M82-409, http://server15932.contentdm.oclc.org/u?/p15932coll2,20400.
[901] Blake, John, "Mississippi Burning Murders Still Smolder for One Brother", *CNN US*, June 28, 2014, retrieved 10/16/2018, https://www.cnn.com/2014/06/28/us/mississippi-murders/index.html.
[902] "Dave Dennis, Freedom Summer of 1964, and the Eulogy For James Chaney", *Machine Mean*, retrieved 10/16/2018, https://machinemean.org/2014/02/04/dave-dennis-freedom-summer-of-1964-and-the-eulogy-for-james-chaney/.
[903] King, Rev . Ed, and Trent Watts, *Ed King's Mississippi: Behind the Scenes of Freedom Summer*, University Press of MS, 2014 , http://www.upress.state.ms.us/books/1693.
[904] "Ed King", *The Project on Lived Theology*, retrieved 10/16/2018, http://archives.livedtheology.org/node/764.
[905] Hanson, Lynette, "The Rev Ed King", *Jackson Free Press*, October 30, 2003, retrieved 10/16/2018, http://www.jacksonfreepress.com/news/2003/oct/30/the-rev-ed-king/.
[906] Hanson, "Rev Ed King".
[907] PBS, "The Eulogy", *American Experience*, retrieved 10/16/2018, http://www.pbs.org/wgbh/americanexperience/features/freedomsummer-eulogy/.
[908] Blake, "Murders Still Smolder"
[909] Lawson, William H., "A Righteous Anger In MS: Genre Constraints and Breaking Precedent", Florida State University Libraries, 2005, pp. 58-59.
[910] Machine Mean, Eulogy.
[911] Lawson, "Righteous Anger", p. 64.
[912] Lawson, "Righteous Anger", p. 65.
[913] Lawson, "Righteous Anger", p. 66.
[914] "Eulogies for James Chaney -- August 7, 1964", *The Project on Lived Theology*, retrieved 10/16/2018, http://archives.livedtheology.org/node/1396.
[915] "Homecoming", featuring extracts from "*To Serve The Living*".
[916] "Homecoming", featuring extracts from "*To Serve The Living*".

[917] "Slain Rights Workers Mourned By Thousands at Services Here," *NY Times*, August 10, 1964, retrieved 10/18/2018, https://www.nytimes.com/1964/08/10/archives/slain-rights-workers-mourned-by-thousands-at-services-here.html.
[918] "Workers Mourned," *NY Times*, retrieved 10/18/2018.
[919] "Workers Mourned," *NY Times*, retrieved 10/18/2018.
[920] "Workers Mourned," *NY Times*, retrieved 10/18/2018.
[921] "Workers Mourned," *NY Times*, retrieved 10/18/2018.
[922] "Workers Mourned," *NY Times*, retrieved 10/18/2018.
[923] Chaney, Fannie Lee, "Mrs. Chaney Speaking at the Schwerner-Chaney-Goodman Memorial Service", Philadelphia, MS, August 16, 1964, https://www.crmvet.org/info/6408_chaney_memorial.pdf
[924] Chaney, Fannie Lee, "Mrs. Chaney Speaking at the Schwerner-Chaney-Goodman Memorial Service", Philadelphia, MS, August 16, 1964, https://www.crmvet.org/info/6408_chaney_memorial.pdf
[925] American College of Radiology, "What is a Radiologist", retrieved 10/18/2022, https://www.acr.org/Practice-Management-Quality-Informatics/Practice-Toolkit/Patient-Resources/About-Radiology.
[926] This autopsy along with related correspondence was kindly provided to the author by the Featherston family, after reading the original Volume I.
[927] McAdam, Doug, *Freedom Summer*, Oxford University Press, 1988, p. 75.
[928] *Memphis World* (Memphis, TN), 9/5/1964, p. 6.
[929] McAdam, Freedom Summer, p. 75.
[930] "What Was the 1964 Freedom Summer Project", *Wisconsin History*, Wisconsin Historical Society, retrieved 4/9/2020, https://www.wisconsinhistory.org/Records/Article/CS3707.
[931] Tabulated from SNCCR, available at multiple sources.
[932] "What Was the 1964 Freedom Summer Project", *Wisconsin History*.
[933] *WISC-6*.

Part 4 Endnotes

[20] FBI-MBI-5, pdf pp. 11-12.
[21] FEAT, p. 2.; FBI-MBI-5, pdf p. 104.
[22] FEAT, p. 4; FBI-MBI-5, pdf p. 93.
[23] FBI-MBI-5, pdf p. 12.
[24] FEAT, p. 3; FBI-MBI-5, pdf p. 104.
[25] FEAT, p. 5; FBI-MBI-5, pdf p. 95.
[26] FEAT, pp. 3-4; FBI-MBI-5, pdf p. 104.
[27] FEAT, p. 4.
[28] FEAT, pp. 3-4; FBI-MBI-5, pdf p. 104.
[29] FEAT, p. 3.
[30] FBI-MBI-5, pdf p. 95.
[31] FEAT, p. 5.
[32] *Report of the Laboratory of the FBI*, FBI File No 44-25706, Lab No PC-81805 AR IZ HB, August 12, 1964, FBI-MBI-6, pdf p. 13-14.
[33] FBI-MBI-6, pdf. p. 14.
[34] MITCHJ, pdf p. 6.
[35] FBI-MBI-6, pdf. p. 14.
[36] FBI-MBI-6, pdf p. 11, p. 13, p. 14.
[37] FBI-MBI-6, pdf. p. 14.
[38] MITCHJ, pdf p. 6.
[39] Fackler, Martin, MD, "Bullet Fragmentation: A Major Cause of Tissue Disruption", *The Journal of Trauma*, Vol 24, No 1, January, 1984.
[40] FBI Academy,"9mm vs .45 Auto", September 15-17, 1987.
[41] FBI Academy,"9mm vs .45 Auto", September 15-17, 1987.
[42] FBI Academy,"9mm vs .45 Auto", September 15-17, 1987.
[43] .38 S&W / .38 Smith & Wesson High Power Loads", Load Data, retrieved 3/12/2020, https://loaddata.com/Cartridge/38-SW-38-Smith-Wesson-High-Power-Loads/1757; manufacturer data from Carter, Molly, "History of .38 S&W Ammo", *Ammoman*, retrieved 3/24/2020, https://ammo.com/handgun/38-s-w-ammo?bullet_type=870.
[44] Fackler, Martin, MD, and Dougherty, Paul, MD, "Theodor Kocher and the Scientific Foundation of Wound Ballistics", *Surgery, Gynecology and Obstetrics*, Vol 172, February, 1991, pp. 153 - 160.
[45] Fackler, Martin, MD, "Theodor Kocher and the Scientific Foundation of Wound Ballistics", pp. 153 - 160.
[46] Fackler, Martin, MD, "Theodor Kocher and the Scientific Foundation of Wound Ballistics", pp. 153 - 160.

[47] Fackler, Martin, MD, "Bullet Fragmentation: A Major Cause of Tissue Disruption", *The Journal of Trauma*, Vol 24, No 1, January, 1984.
[48] Fackler, Martin, MD and Malinowski, Jan, "The wound profile: a visual method for quantifying gunshot wound components", *The Journal of Trauma*, Vol 25, June, 1985, pp. 522-529.
[49] Summary conclusions extracted from FBI Academy, "9mm vs .45 Auto", *Wound Ballistics Workshop*, September 15-17, 1987.
[50] Barnes, Frank C, *Cartridges of the World: A Complete Illustrated Reference for More Than 1,500 Cartridges*, p. 349.
[51] Brudenell, Aaron, "38 S&W (The Other .38)", *Forgotten Weapons*, retrieved 3/24/2020, https://www.forgottenweapons.com/38-sw-the-other-38/.
[52] Brudenell, Aaron, e-mail correspondence, 3/24/2020.
[53] Spain, *Post-Mortem*, p. 37.
[54] Spain, *Post-Mortem*, pp. 37-38.
[55] Handler, MS, "Author Describes Slaying of 3 Rights Workers in Mississippi", NYT, 10/26/1964, p. 20; Spain, David, "Mississippi Autopsy", *Mississippi Eyewitness*, Ramparts Magazine, 10/25/1964, p. 57.
[56] Lasagna, Louis, "The mind and morality of the doctor. II. Physician and the macrocosm", *Yale Journal of Biological Medicine*, April, 1965, Vol 37, pp. 361-378, https://www.ncbi.nlm.nih.gov/pmc/articles/PMC2604730/.
[57] FBI-MBI-5, pdf p. 95.
[58] "38 S&W / .38 Smith & Wesson High Power Loads", Load Data, retrieved 3/12/2020, https://loaddata.com/Cartridge/38-SW-38-Smith-Wesson-High-Power-Loads/1757.
[59] Barnes, Frank C, *Cartridges of the World: A Complete Illustrated Reference for More Than 1,500 Cartridges*, p. 349.
[60] CRMV, Spain, Dr. David M., *Post Mortem Examination Report of the Body of James Chaney*, August 7, 1964.
[61] CRMV, Spain, Dr. David M., *Post Mortem Examination Report of the Body of James Chaney*, August 7, 1964.
[62] *Post-Mortem*, pp. 36-37.
[63] CRMV, Spain, Dr. David M., *Post Mortem Examination Report of the Body of James Chaney*, August 7, 1964.
[64] *Post-Mortem*, p. 37.
[65] "Buying Dirt: How Much Does a Cubic Yard of Dirt Weigh", *CreateItGo!*, updated 12/27/2019, retrieved 2/24/2020, https://www.createitgo.com/buying-dirt-how-much-does-a-cubic-yard-of-dirt-weigh/.
[66] *Basic Elements of a Pond Dam*, Shawnee County Conservation District, retrieved 2/24/2020, http://www.sccdistrict.com/pond-dams-build-right.html.
[67] "Dozers/D6", *Equipment/Dozers/Medium Dozers/D6*, CAT, retrieved 2/24/2020,

https://www.cat.com/en_US/products/new/equipment/dozers/medium-dozers/2145358496514125.html.

[68] *Post-Mortem*, p. 40.

[69] Becky Featherston, daughter of Dr. William Featherston, email correspondence, 9/13/2022, quoted by permission of author.

[70] This discussion regarding the effects of distance and angle on the x-ray image are courtesy of Dr. Orrin Terry, in an e-mail dated Nov 3, 2022.

[71] Brunson, Joel G, "Letter To Dr. William Featherston", Sept 4, 1964, Univ of MS Medical Center, letter provided by the family of Dr. William Featherston.

[72] "Editorial Policy," *Ramparts*, vol. 1, no. 1 (June 1962), p. 3.

[73] Handler, MS, "Author Describes Slaying of 3 Rights Workers in Mississippi", NYT, 10/26/1964, p. 20.

[74] RAMP, pp. 19-20.

[75] Gaillard, Frye, *A Hard Rain: America In The 1960s*, New South Books, 2018, "Chapter 21, Freedom Summer", p 11 of chapter.

[76] FBI Academy, "9mm vs .45 Auto", *Wound Ballistics Workshop*, September 15-17, 1987, p. 2.

[77] *Wound Ballistics Workshop*, p. 8.

[78] Kiryu, K, Takeichi, T, and Kitamura, O, "An Autopsy Report of Accidental Burial In A Beach Sand Hole", *Legal Medicine* (Tokyo, Japan), November 2018, Volume 35, pp. 88-90.

[79] FEAT, p. 3..

[80] Terry, Orrin, MD, e-mail exchange, 4/30/2020.

[81] Terry, Orrin, MD, e-mail exchange, 4/30/2020.

[82] FBI-MBI-6, pdf p. 17.

[83] FBI-MBI-5, pdf p. 12.

[84] FBI-MBI-6, pdf p. 17.

[85] FBI-MBI-6, pdf p. 18.

[86] British Geological Survey, "BGS Geology – Bedrock Theme", *BGS Web Site*, retrieved 6/8/2020, https://www.bgs.ac.uk/products/digitalmaps/digmapgb_solid.html.

[87] Food and Agricultural Organization of the UN, *Watershed Management Field Manual, FAO Conservation Guide 13/5*, 1998.

[88] Natural Resources Conservation Service, USDA, "A Soil Profile", *Soil Education*, retrieved 6/7/2020, https://www.nrcs.usda.gov/wps/portal/nrcs/detail/soils/edu/?cid=nrcs142p2_054308.

[89] Brown, R B, "Soil Texture", *Agronomy Fact Sheet Series: Fact Sheet SL-29*, Cornell University, Department of Crop and Soil Sciences, Sept, 2007. Retrieved 6/7/2020.

https://pdfs.semanticscholar.org/b275/a081bdcfa25258042d7c9b5f40cd1ccf5cf9.pdf
[90] Munsell, H A, *A Color Notation*; G H Ellis Co, 1905.
[91] Lynn, W.C. and Pearson, M.J., "The Color of Soil", *The Science Teacher*, May 2000.
[92] *Soil Data Explorer*, UC Davis, retrieved 6/8/2020, https://casoilresource.lawr.ucdavis.edu/sde/?series=smithdale.
[93] *SoilWeb*, UC Davis and NRCS, retrieved 6/8/2020, https://casoilresource.lawr.ucdavis.edu/gmap/.
[94] Standard horizon depths and textures from USDA adjusted for color based on actual colors at murder location, *Soil Data Explorer*, UC Davis, retrieved 6/8/2020, https://casoilresource.lawr.ucdavis.edu/sde/?series=lauderdale.
[95] Goldberg, Nicholas, *Where The Klan Once Ruled*, Los Angeles Times, 5/23/2009, retrieved 4/29/2009, https://www.latimes.com/archives/la-xpm-2009-may-23-ed-outhere23-story.html.
[96] Cass, Julia, "A Mississippi Freedom Summer Pilgrimage: An Atrocity We Must Never Forget", *The Huffington Post*, 7/25/2014, retrieved 2/25/2020, https://www.huffpost.com/entry/a-mississippi-freedom-sum_b_5622366.
[97] HA, 8/5/1964, p. 1.
[98] *Alabama Citizen* (Tuscaloosa, AL), 12/8/1956, p. 1.
[99] McMillen, Neil R., Citizens' Council, *Organized Resistance to the Second Reconstruction, 1954-1964*, Univ of IL Press, 1994, pp. 47-48.
[100] *The Birmingham News*(Birmingham, AL), 1/24/1957, p. 1.
[101] *The Birmingham News*(Birmingham, AL), 1/24/1957, p. 10.
[102] *The Birmingham News*(Birmingham, AL), 9/7/1957, p. 1.
[103] *The Birmingham News*(Birmingham, AL), 9/7/1957, p. 2.
[104] *Mabry vs State*, AL Court of Appeals, 110 So. 2d 250, 1/6/1959.
[105] Measured using maps.google.com.
[106] RKKK, p. 20.
[107] *The Birmingham News*(Birmingham, AL), 9/7/1957, p. 2.
[108] Measured using maps.google.com.
[109] *The Birmingham News*(Birmingham, AL), 10/30/1957, p. 4.
[110] *Mabry vs State*, AL Court of Appeals, 110 So. 2d 250, 1/6/1959; *Alabama Journal* (Montgomery, AL), 9/3/1957, p. 2.
[111] *The Birmingham News*(Birmingham, AL), 9/7/1957, p. 1.
[112] *The Birmingham News*(Birmingham, AL), 9/8/1957, p. 1.
[113] *The Birmingham News*(Birmingham, AL), 9/9/1957, p. 1.
[114] *The Montgomery Advisor* (Montgomery, AL), 9/10/1957, p. 13.
[115] Joe Pritchett, *The Huntsville Times*(Huntsville, AL), 11/1/1957, p. 7; Grover McCullough, The Anniston Star (Anniston, AL) 2/21/1958, p. 2.

[116] "Original Ku Klux Klan of the Confederacy", *Wikipedia*, retrieved 2/25/2020, https://en.wikipedia.org/w/index.php?title=Original_Ku_Klux_Klan_of_the_Confederacy&oldid=929964638.
[117] *The Montgomery Advisor* (Montgomery, AL), 10/17/1965, p. 1.
[118] HUIE, pp. 18-34.
[119] *Post-Mortem*, p. 37.
[120] Reber, SL, and Simmons, T, "Interpreting Injury Mechanisms of Blunt Force Trauma from Butterfly Fracture Formation", *Journal of Forensic Science*, Volume 60, Issue 6, pp. 1401-1411, November, 2015.
[121] CRMV, Spain, Dr. David M., *Post Mortem Examination Report of the Body of James Chaney*, August 7, 1964.
[122] Anyanechi, C E, and Saheeb, B D, Mandibular Sites Prone to Fracture", *Ghana Medical Journal*, Volume 45, Issue 3, September, 2011, pp. 111-114.
[123] "Communited Fracture Definition", *Spine-Health*, retreived 2/26/2020, https://www.spine-health.com/glossary/comminuted-fracture.
[124] CL, 6/26/2005, pp, 1, 7.
[125] Reber, SL, and Simmons, T, "Interpreting Injury Mechanisms of Blunt Force Trauma from Butterfly Fracture Formation", pp. 1401-1411, November, 2015.
[126] Smead, Howard, *Blood Justice: The Lynching of Mack Charles Parker*, Oxford University Press, 1986, p.3.
[127] Smead, 1986, p. 4.
[128] Smead, 1986, p. 5.
[129] Smead, 1986, p. 5.
[130] Smead, 1986, pp. 6-7.
[131] Smead, 1986, pp. 7-9.
[132] Smead, 1986, p. 10.
[133] Smead, 1986, p. 7.
[134] Smead, 1986, p. 11.
[135] Smead, 1986, p. 11.
[136] *Mack Charles Parker*, Federal Bureau of Investigation, Part 1a, pdf. p. 8.
[137] Smead, 1986, p. 12.
[138] Smead, 1986, p. 13.
[139] Smead, 1986, p. 14.
[140] Smead, 1986, p. 14.
[141] Smead, 1986, p. 16.
[142] Smead, 1986, p. 16.
[143] Smead, 1986, p. 21.
[144] Smead, 1986, pp. 21, 23.
[145] *Mack Charles Parker*, Federal Bureau of Investigation, Part 1a, pdf. p. 8.
[146] Smead, 1986, p. 50.
[147] Smead, 1986, p. 50.

[148] Smead, 1986, p. 51.
[149] CL, 4/26/2009, p. 8.
[150] Smead, 1986, p. 54.
[151] Smead, 1986, p. 55.
[152] Smead, 1986, p. 55.
[153] "9mm vs .45 Auto", *Wound Ballistics Workshop*, FBI Academy, September 15-17, 1987, p. 2.
[154] Smead, 1986, p. 56.
[155] Smead, 1986, p. 56.
[156] Smead, 1986, p. 75.
[157] Smead, 1986, pp. 131-132.
[158] Smead, 1986, p. 152.
[159] Smead, 1986, p. 174.
[160] Smead, 1986, p. 176.
[161] Smead, 1986, p. 175.
[162] Smead, 1986, p. 177.
[163] Smead, 1986, p. 180.
[164] Smead, 1986, p. 185.
[165] Smead, 1986, p. 196.
[166] MITCHB, p. 12.
[167] MITCHJ, p. 6
[168] All comments regarding accuracy and shooting conditions based on experience of author. For 22 years, author has taken and given shooting instruction on the various shooting conditions and situations. During that period, author trained several thousand shooters under the conditions described.
[169] MITCHB, p. 12.
[170] MITCHJ, p. 6.
[171] SPIT, p. 680.
[172] LATT, pp. 268-280.
[173] Bill Featherston, son of Dr. William Featherston, email correspondence, 11/23/2022, quoted by permission of author.
[174] DESH, p. 473.
[175] Johnson, W H, Jr, "Letter to Dr. William Featherston", June 9, 1965, letter provided by the family of Dr. William Featherston.
[176] DESH, p. 474.
[177] DESH, p. 475.
[178] DESH, p. 475.
[179] DESH, p. 476.
[180] Becky Featherston, daughter of Dr. William Featherston, email correspondence, 9/13/2022, quoted by permission of author.
[181] FBI-MBT-8, pdf pp. 21-50, FBI-MBT-9, pdf pp. 1-37.

[182] FBI-MBT-00_index, FBI-MBT-00-participants, FBI-MBT-8, pdf pp. 21-50, FBI-MBT-9, pdf pp. 1-37.
[183] Becky Featherston, daughter of Dr. William Featherston, email correspondence, 9/13/2022, quoted by permission of author.

Part 5 Endnotes

This part does not have any endnotes.

Part 6 Endnotes

[1] "Moon Phases June 1964", *Calendar-12*, retrieved 9/8/2020, https://www.calendar-12.com/moon_calendar/1964/june.

[2] Ledoux, Joseph and Pine, Daniel, "Using Neuroscience to Help Understand Fear and Anxiety: A Two-System Framework," *American Journal of Psychiatry*, 11/1/2016, Volume 173, Issue 11, pp. 1083-1093.

[3] Federal Communications Commission, *Public Safety Spectrum*, retrieved 9/11/2020, https://www.fcc.gov/public-safety/public-safety-and-homeland-security/policy-and-licensing-division/public-safety-spectrum.

[4] Motorola, *A Timeline Overview of Motorola History: 1928 – 2008*, retrieved 9/10/2020, https://www.landley.net/history/mirror/6800_MotDoc.pdf.

[5] Potrebic, Nikola, "Top 10 Best and Coolest American Police Cars, *Autowise*, 10/27/2019, retrieved 9/8/2020, https://autowise.com/best-american-police-cars/.

[6] *Evidence Code, Division 6. Witnesses, Chapter 3. Expert Witnesses, Article 1. Expert Witnesses Generally*, https://leginfo.legislature.ca.gov/.

[7] 22 minutes (10:38 – 11:00) / 60 minutes per hour * 60 miles per hour = 22 miles.

[8] 2 miles (1 mile + 120 yards/1763 + 0.789 miles) / 40 miles per hour * 60 minutes per hour = 3 minutes for travel time.

[9] 547 feet total width – 191 feet unfilled excavation = 356 feet completed dam.

[10] 300 feet to Barnette 1957 Ford + 150 feet to Posey Ranch Wagon = 450 feet.

[11] "How Much Does A Cubic Foot Of Dirt Weigh", *Dirt Connections*, 8/6/2019, retrieved 9/18/2020, https://www.dirtconnections.com/how-much-does-a-cubic-foot-of-dirt-weigh/.

[12] 12 miles / 50 miles per hour * 60 minutes / hour = 14.4 minutes.

[13] 41.2 miles / 50 miles per hour * 60 minutes / hour = 49.44 minutes.

[14] 1 mile / 50 miles per hour * 60 minutes / hour = 1.2 minutes,

[15] 22 minutes / 60 minutes per hour * 60 mph = 22 miles.

[16] 22 miles – 16.14 miles = 8.86 miles.

[17] 15 miles / 60 miles per hour * 60 minutes / hour = 15 minutes.

[18] 26.4 miles / 15 minutes * 60 minutes / hour = 105 mph.

[19] 6.33 miles – 4.87 miles = 1.46 miles.

Part 7 Endnotes

[1] *FBI Records: The Vault*, The Federal Bureau of Investigation, most recently accessed 12/7/2019, https://vault.fbi.gov/.

[2] Federal Bureau of Investigation, *Mississippi Burning - MIBURN*, Parts 1-9, Freedom of Information and Privacy Acts, https://vault.fbi.gov/search?SearchableText=MIBURN.

[3] Mitchell, Jerry, "Two Klan Confessions in the Mississippi Burning Case", *The Clarion Ledger*, Feb. 14, Z010,.http://blogs.clarionledger.com/jmitchell/2010/02/14/two-klan-confessions-in-the-mississippi-burning-case/

[4] Kilgore, Steve, 8th Circuit Court District Attorney, including Neshoba County, e-mail correspondence with author, 9/10/2019.

[5] Molpus, Dick, "Philadelphia, MS: A Story of Racial Reconciliation", *Mississippi History Now*, Mississippi Historical Society, retrieved 6/17/2019, http://www.mshistorynow.mdah.ms.gov/articles/389/philadelphia-mississippi-a-story-of-racial-reconciliation.

Part 8: References. Audio, Video, Newspapers

KKK References

(FBI-KKK5) Federal Bureau of Investigation, File #157-188, https://archive.org/details/foia_National_Knights_KKK-5

(FBI-KO) Federal Bureau of Investigation, *Klan Organizations*, "Section III 1958 - 1964", US Department of Justice, December, 1964, https://archive.org/details/foia_FBI_monograph-Klan_Organizations-Section_III_1958-1964.

(FBI-OK-1) Federal Bureau of Investigation, *Original Knights of The Ku Klux Klan, File Number: 173-2015*, Freedom of Information and Privacy Acts, https://vault.fbi.gov/search.

(FBI-OK-2) Federal Bureau of Investigation, *Original Knights of The Ku Klux Klan, File Number: 105-71801*, Freedom of Information and Privacy Acts, https://vault.fbi.gov/search.

(FBI-WHG) Federal Bureau of Investigation, *(COINTELPRO) White Hate Groups*, 14 Parts, Freedom of Information and Privacy Acts, https://vault.fbi.gov/search?SearchableText=White+Hate+Groups.

(FBI-WK2) Federal Bureau of Investigation, *5587102 --White Knights of the Ku Klux Klan of MS*, https://archive.org/details/WKKKKOM

(FBI-WK3) Federal Bureau of Investigation, *5587103 -- Woodrow Wilson Mathews*, https://archive.org/stream/WKKKKOM/5587103%20--%20Woodrow%20Wilson%20Mathews#page/n0

(FBI-WK4) Federal Bureau of Investigation, *5587104 -- Sam Holloway Bowers*, https://archive.org/stream/WKKKKOM/5587104%20--%20Sam%20Holloway%20Bowers#page/n0

(FBI-WK5) Federal Bureau of Investigation, *5587105 -- George Pierce -- Billy Fasano -- J. P. Moore*, https://archive.org/stream/WKKKKOM/5587105%20--%20George%20Pierce%20--%20Billy%20Fasano%20--%20J.%20P.%20Moore#page/n0

(FBI-WK6) Federal Bureau of Investigation, *5587106 -- WKKKKOM*, https://archive.org/stream/WKKKKOM/5587106%20--%20WKKKKOM#page/n0

(FBI-WK7) Federal Bureau of Investigation, *5587107 -- Plans of Klan Groups to Infiltrate Law Enforcement Agencies*, https://archive.org/stream/WKKKKOM/5587107%20--%20Plans%20of%20Klan%20Groups%20to%20Infiltrate%20Law%20Enforcement%20Agencies#page/n0

(HRC) US House of Representatives, "The Ku Klux Klan", Hearings Before the Committee on Rules, 67th Congress, First Session, Government Printing Office, 1921, https://books.google.com/books/about/The_Ku_Klux_Klan.html?id=Qg4pAAAAYAAJ

(NYW) New York World, *Ku Klux Klan Expose*, Sept 6, 1921 - Sept 26, 1921, Press Publishing Company, 1921, http://nl.newsbank.com/nl-search/we/Archives?p_product=HA-TP&p_theme=histpaper&p_action=keyword (Subscription Service).

(RKKK) Forster, Arnold. Epstein, Benjamin R. *Report on the Ku Klux Klan* Anti-defamation League of B'nai B'rith, 1965, https://archive.org/details/ReportOnTheKuKluxKlan

(WHIT) Whitehead, Don, *Attack on Terror: The FBI Against The Ku Klux Klan in Mississippi*, Funk & Wagnalls, 1970.

White Knights References

(BOWERS-O) Bowers, Sam H. Jr., *Interviews with Sam H. Bowers, Jr.*, Mississippi Department of Archives and History, 1983, http://www.mdah.ms.gov/arrec/digital_archives/bowers/.

(BOWERS-T) State of Mississippi vs Sam Holloway Bowers, Cause No. 6922, *Court Reporters Transcript of Trial*, Circuit Court of Forrest County MS, 1998, University of Southern MS, Digital Collection, https://digitalcollections.usm.edu/uncategorized/digitalFile_a55f80fd-a112-4031-b516-5ce4a0f3e7ff/

(HUAC-H1) Committee on Un-American Activities, US House of Representatives, *Hearings Before the Committee on Un-American Activities*, US Government Printing Office, Part 1: 1966, Part 2: 1966, Part3: 1966, https://books.google.com/, Book 1.

(HUAC-H2) Committee on Un-American Activities, US House of Representatives, *Hearings Before the Committee on Un-American Activities*, US Government Printing Office, Part 4: 1966, https://books.google.com/, Book 2.

(HUAC-1) Committee on Un-American Activities, US House of Representatives, *The Present-Day Ku Klux Klan Movement*, US Government Printing Office, 1967, www.archive.org, Part 1.

(HUAC-2) Committee on Un-American Activities, US House of Representatives, *The Present-Day Ku Klux Klan Movement*, US Government Printing Office, 1967, www.archive.org, Part 2.

(MCD) McDaniel, Edward L., *An Oral History With Edward L. McDaniel*, Center For Oral History and Cultural Heritage, University of Southern Mississippi , 1977, https://digitalcollections.usm.edu/uncategorized/digitalFile_55b672f7-bcdb-4a31-916a-aafeba2bd06c/.

(MSC) Mississippi Sovereignty Commission, Digital Archives, http://www.mdah.ms.gov/arrec/digital_archives/sovcom/

Mississippi Burning (MIBURN) References

(DOJ) US Dept of Justice, *Investigation of the 1964 Murders of Michael Schwerner, James Chaney, and Andy Goodman*, April 14, 2016, https://www.justice.gov/crt/case-document/file/1041791/download, http://www.ago.state.ms.us/wp-content/uploads/2016/06/DOJ-Report-to-Mississippi-Attorney-General-Jim-Hood.pdf.

(FBI-MBI) Federal Bureau of Investigation, *Mississippi Burning - MIBURN*, by page number in complete file, Freedom of Information and Privacy Acts, Files **miburnX.pdf**, https://vault.fbi.gov/search?SearchableText=MIBURN.

(FBI-MBI-X) Federal Bureau of Investigation, *Mississippi Burning - MIBURN*, Parts 1-9, by pdf page number in file, Freedom of Information and Privacy Acts, Files **miburnX.pdf**, https://vault.fbi.gov/search?SearchableText=MIBURN.

(FBI-MBT-X) Federal Bureau of Investigation, *Mississippi Burning - Trial Transcripts*, Volumes 1-5, https://www.justice.gov/crt/trial-transcripts-caseunited-states-v-price-et-al-also-known-mississippi-burning-incident-1967.

(MITCH1) Mitchell, Jerry, http://coldcases.org/articles-author/13.

(MITCH2) Mitchell, Jerry, https://www.fold3.com/page/110458148-the-mississippi-burning-case-chaney-goodman-and-schwerner/stories

(MITCHJ) Mitchell, Jerry, "Confession of James Jordan", "Two Klan Confessions in the Mississippi Burning Case", *The Clarion Ledger*, Feb. 14, 2010, pdf pp. 1-9, http://blogs.clarionledger.com/jmitchell/2010/02/14/two-klan-confessions-in-the-mississippi-burning-case/
AND FBI-MBI-4, pdf p. 66 - 82.

(MITCHB) Mitchell, Jerry, "Confession of H. D. Barnette", "Two Klan Confessions in the Mississippi Burning Case", *The Clarion Ledger*, Feb 14, 2010, pdf pp. 10-14, http://blogs.clarionledger.com/jmitchell/2010/02/14/two-klan-confessions-in-the-mississippi-burning-case/
AND FBI-MBI-4, pdf p. 44 - 50.

(RAMP) "Mississippi Eyewitness", *Rampart*, Special Edition, October 25, 1964, Edward Keating, Ed., Menlo Park, CA.

(USVG) "Case Docket No. 65", "October Term 1965: Miscellaneous Docket # 1000 to 1684 (December 10, 1965 to June 13, 1966); Appellate Docket # 1 to 299 (June 10, 1964 to October 11, 1965)", US vs Guest, US Supreme Court, US National Archives, https://catalog.archives.gov/id/82632034.

(USVG-O) "Oral Arguments", US vs Guest, US Supreme Court, Oyez, https://www.oyez.org/cases/1965/65.

(USVP) "Case Docket No. 59, 60", "October Term 1965: Miscellaneous Docket # 1000 to 1684 (December 10, 1965 to June 13, 1966); Appellate Docket # 1 to 299 (June 10, 1964 to October 11, 1965)", US vs Price, US Supreme Court, US National Archives, https://catalog.archives.gov/id/82632034.

(USVG-O) "Oral Arguments", US vs Price, US Supreme Court, Oyez, https://www.oyez.org/cases/1965/59.

(CR67H) *Hearings Before the Subcommittee on Constitutional Rights of the Committee on the Judiciary, United States Senate on the Proposed Civil Rights Act of 1967*, 90th Congress, 1st Session, August 1,8,9, and 14; September 19, 29, 21, 26, and 27, 1967.

Autopsy References

(DESH) deShazo, Richard, MD, RobertSmith, MD, Leigh Skipworth, "A White Dean and Black Physicians at the Epicenter of the Civil Rights Movement", *The American Journal of Medicine*, Vol 127, No 6, June 2014.

(FEAT) Featherston, William, MD, *Autopsy No. 64-A-82 Body No. 1, 64-A-83 Body No. 2, 64-A-84 Body No. 3, Bratley Medical Center*, August 14, 1964, provided courtesy MS 8th Circuit Court District Attorney Stephen Kilgore.

(PACK) Packer, James, MD, "Report on Three Sets of Xray Films", *Letter to Dr. William Featherston*, August 28, 1964, papers of Dr. William Featherston, provided by family of Dr. William Featherston.

(SPAIN) Spain, David M., MD, *Post-Mortem*, Doubleday and Company, 1974.

(SPAIN-A) Spain, David M, MD, *Post Mortem Examination Report of the Body of James Chaney*, August 7, 1964.

Edgar Ray Killen References

(BON) Boney, Brian, *A Race Against The Clock: The Authorized Biography of Edgar Ray Killen*, Palmetto Publishing Group, 2018.

(ELL) Ellis, Larry, *Killer Killen and the Genuine Truth About Mississippi Burning and the Three Civil Rights Murders*, independently published, October 31, 2019, e-book.

(KILLEN-1) *State of MS vs Edgar Ray Killen*, Trial Transcript, Circuit Court of Neshoba County, No. 05-CR-0006-NS-G.

(KILLEN-2) *State of MS vs Edgar Ray Killen*, Mississippi Public Broadcasting, June 16, 2005 - June 27, 2005.

(KILLEN-3) *Housing History, Edgar Ray Killen*, MS Department of Corrections, July 15, 2019, provided by MS DOC under MS Public Records Act.

(KILLEN-4) *Incident Report, Edgar Ray Killen*, MS Department of Corrections, July 15, 2019, provided by MS DOC under MS Public Records Act.

(STER) Hart, James Hart, *Mississippi Still Burning, From Hoods To Suits*, One Human Race, Inc., October 17, 2018 now

Neshoba County References

(COLL) *Oral History with Reverend Clinton Collier*, Center For Oral History, University of Southern MS, recorded 28 July 1981; 25 June 1994, retrieved 7/9/2020, https://digitalcollections.usm.edu/uncategorized/deliverableUnit_6fe55296-362a-4686-9000-de29e8972bc7/.

(GLIS) Glisson, Susan M., "Telling the Truth: How Breaking Its Silence Brought Redemption to One Mississippi Town", provided Courtesy Susan M. Glisson, published in Solinger, R., Fox, M., & Irani, K. (Eds.). *Telling Stories to Change the World: Global Voices on the Power of Narrative to Build Community and Make Social Justice Claims*, Routledge, 2008.

(GEOR) George, Carol V. R., *One Mississippi, Two Mississippi: Methodists, Murder, and the Struggle for Racial Justice in Neshoba County*, Oxford University Press, April 1, 2015.

(HUIE) Huie, William Bradford, *Three Lives for Mississippi*, University Press of Mississippi, 2000.

(LAKE) Lake, Ellen, *Cops and COFO in Philadelphia*, 10/15/1964, The Harvard Crimson, Harvard University.

(MARS) Mars, Florence, *Witness in Philadelphia*, Louisiana State University Press, 1977.

(MARS-1) Mars, Florence, *The Bell Returns to Mt Zion*, Stribling Press, 1996.

(MARS-2) Dollar, Charles, "Florence Latimer Mars: A Courageous Voice Against Racial Injustice in Neshoba County, Mississippi (1923-2006)", *The Journal of Mississippi History*, Volume LXXVII, No. 1 and No. 2, Spring/Summer 2015, MS Department of Archives and History, pp. 1-24.

(MARS-3) Healy, Thomas, "An Oral History with Miss Florence Mars, Native Mississippi Author", *The Mississippi Oral History Program of the University of Southern Mississippi*, 1/5/1978, https://digitalcollections.usm.edu/uncategorized/digitalFile_e1006458-807e-4664-b778-27201f0b45d2/.

(MITC) Mitchell, Don, *The Freedom Summer Murders*, Scholastic, Inc, 2014.

(ROS) Community Development Partnership, *Roots of Struggle*, February, 2010.

(WHIT) Whitlinger, Claire E., *The Transformative Capacity of Commemorating Violent Pasts: Exploring Local Commemoration of the "Mississippi Burning Murders*, University of Michigan, 2015.

(WISN) Freedom Summer Digital Collection, Neshoba County, http://content.wisconsinhistory.org/digital/api/collection/p15932coll2/id/43614/page/0/inline/p15932coll2_43614_0.

(ZIMM) Zimmerman, Mitchell, "Princeton Students in Mississippi", *Prince Alumni Weekly*, Volume LXV, No. 12, 12/8/1964.

General References

(BARN) Barnett, James F., Jr., *The Yamasee War, the Bearded Chief, and the Founding of Fort Rosalie*, MS Department of Archives and History, http://mdah.ms.gov/new/wp-content/uploads/2013/08/Barnett_galley.pdf.

(DOAR-O) Doar, John, *Organization, Operation, and Procedure, Civil Rights Division*, US Dept of Justice, early Fall, 1965. (after Voting Rights Act of 1965, August 6, 1965, referenced in the body of the text), p. 1.

(DOAR-W) Doar, John, "The Work of the Civil Rights Division in Enforcing Voting Rights Under the Civil Rights Acts of 1957 and 1960", FL State University Law Review, Volume 25, Number 1, Article 1, Fall, 1997.

(EJMSC) Johnston, Erle, *Mississippi's Defiant Years*, 1953-1973, Lake Harbor Publishers, 1990.

(HEWITT) Hewitt, Christopher, *Political Violence and Terrorism in Modern America: A Chronology*, Praeger Security International, 2005.

(HOLT) Holt, Len, *The Summer That Didn't End*, William Morrow and Co., 1965.

(LINDER) Linder, Douglas O., "Bending Toward Justice: John Doar and the Mississippi Burning Trial", *Mississippi Law Journal*, Volume 72, Number 2, Winter, 2002.

(MBP) *Mississippi Black Paper, Fifty-Seven Negro and White Citizens' Testimony of Police Brutality, the Breakdown of Law and Order and the Corruption of Justice in Mississippi*, Random House, 1995.

(MULL) Mullins, Andy, *Building Consensus: A History of the Passage of the Mississippi Education Reform Act of 1982*, A.P. Mullins, 1992

(NASH) Nash, Jere and Andy Taggart, "Education Transforms the MS Legislature", *The Journal of MS History*, retrieved 6/30/2019, https://www.mdah.ms.gov/new/wp-content/uploads/2013/07/reform.pdf.

(PADV) President's Advisory Board on Race Relations, *One America in the 21st Century: Forging A New Future*, US Government Printing Office, September, 1998.

(PICK) Pickett, Otis W., "We Were All Prisoners Of The System", *The Southern Quarterly*, University of Southern MS, Vol 54, No. 1, Fall, 1966, pp. 151-169.

(QCRA) Queens College Civil Rights Archives, https://archives.qc.cuny.edu/civilrights/

(REST) Reston, Jr., James, "Whatever Happened to the Southern Villains", *The Works of James Reston, Jr.*, http://www.restonbooks.com/civil-rights-and-the-south.html, retrieved 3/7/2019.

(SCHP) Scheips, Paul, *Role of Federal Military Forces in Domestic Disorders, 1945-1992*, Center of Military History, US Army, 2005

Video And Audio References

(CBS) CBS News Report, June 25, 1964, anchored by Walter Cronkite, https://www.cbsnews.com/video/from-the-archives-the-search-in-mississippi/.

(CSP-1) *1964 Civil Rights Murders*, C-SPAN, 1/13/2005, https://www.c-span.org/video/?185083-6/1964-civil-rights-murders.

(DULL) "Former CIA Director Allen Dulles Returning from Mississippi", youtube.com, 6/26/1964, newsreel footage but source unidentified, https://www.youtube.com/watch?v=sMK1xGA0XYc.

(GRAV) Graves, Matthew, *The Toughest Job: William Winter's Mississippi*, The Southern Documentary Project, 2015.

(JOHN-1) *Secret White House Tapes*, Miller Center, Univ of VA, https://millercenter.org/the-presidency/secret-white-house-tapes/research-the-tapes.

(JOHN-2) "Mississippi Burning", *Secret White House Tapes*, Miller Center, Univ of VA, https://millercenter.org/the-presidency/educational-resources/mississippi-burning.

(LEG) "Mayor James Young", *McComb Legacies on Vimeo*, https://vimeo.com/31637947.

(MBCI-1) *40th Anniversary Commemoration Ceremony*, MS Band of Choctaw Indians, 2/3/2020.

(MBCI-2) "John Lewis and Governor Winters", *40th Anniversary Commemoration Ceremony*, MS Band of Choctaw Indians, 3/17/2020.

(NESH) Dickoff, Micki and Tony Pagano, *Neshoba: The Price of Freedom*, Pro Bono and Pagano Productions, 2010.

(NNC-X) *Neshoba County - Philadelphia News Conference* $0X$, X = 1-4, William Winter Institute, https://vimeo.com/27776586, https://vimeo.com/27776600, https://vimeo.com/27776636, https://vimeo.com/27776667.

Interview References

(CB) Charles Brown, Phone Interviews, 4/20/2020, 7/8/2020, 7/26/2020.

(ET) Eva Tisdale, Phone Interview, 5/4/2020, 5/13/2020, 7/9/2020.

(MOLPUS-1) Dick Molpus, Phone interview, June 29, 2019.

(MOLPUS-2) Dick Molpus, Phone interview, July 22, 2019.

(WWAN) William Winter Institute, *Ajatha Nichols*, retrieved 7/8/2020, https://vimeo.com/williamwinterinstitute/videos/page:4/sort:alphabetical/format:thumbnail.

(WWET) William Winter Institute, *Eva Tisdale*, retrieved 7/8/2020, https://vimeo.com/williamwinterinstitute/videos/page:7/sort:alphabetical/format:thumbnail.

(WWHT) William Winter Institute, *Helen Tention*, retrieved 7/8/2020, https://vimeo.com/williamwinterinstitute/videos/page:8/sort:alphabetical/format:thumbnail.

(WWTM) William Winter Institute, *Thelma Moore Wells*, retrieved 7/8/2020, https://vimeo.com/williamwinterinstitute/videos/page:16/sort:alphabetical/format:thumbnail.

(WWAP) William Winter Institute, *Philadelphia Coalition Afterparty*, retrieved 7/8/2020, https://vimeo.com/williamwinterinstitute/videos/page:17/sort:alphabetical/format:thumbnail.

(WWNC) William Winter Institute, *Philadelphia News Conference*, retrieved 7/8/2020, https://vimeo.com/williamwinterinstitute/videos/page:18/sort:alphabetical/format:thumbnail.

Forensic References

(LATT) Lattimer, John, MD, *Kennedy and Lincoln: Medical and Ballistic Comparisons of Their Assassinations*, Harcourt, Brace, Jovanovich, 1980.

(SPIT) Spitz, Werner, MD, "Injury By Gunfire: Part 1, Part 2", in Spitz, Werner, MD ed, *Medicolegal Investigation of Death* (4th Ed), Charles C Thomas Publisher Ltd, 2006.

Specific Documents of White Knights

Constitution of the White Knights, HUAC-2, pp. 253 - 292.

WASP, Inc., HUAC-2, pp. 293 - 294.

Flyer: HUAC-2, pp. 295 - 296.

Executive Lecture of March 1, 1964, HUAC-2, pp. 164 - 168.

Imperial Executive Order, May 3, 1964, HUAC-2, pp. 169 - 171.

Secrecy, HUAC-1, p. 70.

Harrassment, HUAC-2, pp. 172, 173.

The Klan Ledger, July, 1965, HUAC-H2, pp. 2916 - 2917.

The Klan Ledger, October 21, 1965, HUAC-H2, pp. 2918 - 2919.

Civil Rights References

(BAKERF) The Ella Baker Foundation, https://ellabakercenter.org.

(BAKERP) *Ella Baker papers, 1959-1965*; Archives Main Stacks, SC 628, http://content.wisconsinhistory.org/cdm/compoundobject/collection/p15932coll2/id/18105/rec/11.

(BEECH) *Beech-- Council of Federated Organizations, 1964-1966*, from (Robert Beech Papers, 1963-1972; Archives Main Stacks, Mss 945, Box 4, Folder 5), http://content.wisconsinhistory.org/cdm/ref/collection/p15932col l2/id/ 13007.

(SPIES) Bowers, Rick, *Spies of Mississippi*, National Geographic Society, 2010.

(CORE) Congress of Racial Equality, http://www.core-online.org

(CRMV) Civil Rights Movement Veterans, http://www.crmvet.org/ Folders/Pages: mem/msmartyr.htm,/docs/, /lets/

(FBI-SCLC-X) Federal Bureau of Investigation, *Southern Christian Leadership Conference*, Parts 1-14, Freedom of Information and Privacy Acts, Files **SCLC Part 0X.pdf**, https://vault.fbi.gov/southern-christian-leadership-convention.

(MDAH) Mississippi Department of Archives and History, http://www.mdah.ms.gov/arrec/digital_archives/.

(MFDPL) *Mississippi Freedom Democratic Party. Lauderdale County (Miss.) records, 1964-1966*; Historical Society Library Microforms Room, Micro 55, Reel 1, Segment 9), http://content.wisconsinhistory.org/cdm/ref/collection/p15932col l2/id/51000

(NAACP) The NAACP Web Site, https://www.naacp.org/

(OLEM) University of MS, Archives and Collections, http://clio.lib.olemiss.edu/cdm/search/collection/civ_rights

(SCLCD) SLCC National Website, http://nationalsclc.org

(SNCCD) SNCC Digital website, https://snccdigital.org

(SNCCR) SNCC, *MS Summer Project, Running Summary of Incidents*, The Student Nonviolent Coordinating Committee Papers, 1959 - 1972, microfilm, University of Michigan

Available at various digital web repositories such as: http://digilib.usm.edu/cdm/compoundobject/collection/manu/id/8764/rec/13

and

http://content.wisconsinhistory.org/cdm/compoundobject/collection/p15932coll2/id/62581/show/62463/rec/21.

and

https://www.crmvet.org/docs/64_fs_incidents.pdf

(SVC) Student Nonviolent Coordinating Committee, *The Student Voice*, 1960-1965, Martin Luther King, Jr. Papers Project, 1990.

(WISC) Wisconsin Historical Society, Freedom Summer Digital Collection, http://content.wisconsinhistory.org/cdm/landingpage/collection/p15932coll2.

(WISC-1) "Discover Who Participated In The Freedom Summer Project", File: LIB-Freedom-Summer-Participants-List.xls, retrieved 8/2/2020, https://www.wisconsinhistory.org/Records/Article/CS3776.

(WISC-2) COFO Communications Section, *List of COFO workers for the summer of 1964, excluding reporters, visitors, and public officials*, typed by Mary A. Rothschild from files found in 1969 in the former Delta Ministry Office in Mt. Beulah, MS, retrieved 8/2/2020, http://content.wisconsinhistory.org/cdm/ref/collection/p15932coll2/id/17542.

(WISC-3) "Paid Mississippi CORE Staff As of September 21, 1964", retrieved 8/2/2020, http://content.wisconsinhistory.org/cdm/ref/collection/p15932coll2/id/16148.

(WISC-4) *Neshoba County, Correspondence, Memoranda, Reports, 1964-1965*, CORE, retrieved 8/2/2020, http://content.wisconsinhistory.org/cdm/compoundobject/collection/p15932coll2/id/43614/show/43567/rec/7.

(WISC-5) *Fourth Congressional District, Project Office Personnel, Applications and Lists, 1964-1965*, CORE, retrieved 8/2/2020, http://content.wisconsinhistory.org/cdm/compoundobject/collection/p15932coll2/id/41898/show/41889/rec/2.

(WISC-6) *Freedom Democratic Party Vote Results, Fall, 1964*, Council of Federated Organizations Panola County Office, Fall, 1964, retrieved 8/2/2020, http://content.wisconsinhistory.org/cdm/ref/collection/p15932coll2/id/8215.

(WISC-7) Mississippi Freedom Democratic Party, Memorand-Reports, 1964 – 1966, CORE, retrieved 8/8/2020, http://content.wisconsinhistory.org/cdm/ref/collection/p15932coll2/id/44803.

(WISC-8) Mississippi Freedom Democratic Party, General Papers, 1963 – 1965, CORE, retrieved 8/8/2020, http://content.wisconsinhistory.org/cdm/ref/collection/p15932coll2/id/38092.

Newspapers

(BDH) *Biloxi Daily Herald*, Biloxi, MS

(BSH) *Biloxi Sun Herald*, Biloxi, MS

(CCT) *Clarke County Tribune*, Quitman, MS

(CL) *Clarion Ledger*, Jackson, MS

(CPRT) *The Clarksdale Press Register*, Clarksdale, MS

(CPR) *Columbian Progress*, Columbia, MS

(DDT) *Delta Democrat Times*, Greenville, MS

(EJM) *Enterprise Journal*, McComb, MS

(GDDT) *Greenville Delta Democrat Times*, Greenville, MS

(GWCW) *The Greenwood Commonwealth*, Greenwood, MS

(HA) *Hattiesburg American*, Hattiesburg, MS

(LAT) *Los Angeles Times*, Los Angeles, CA

(LLC) *Laurel Leader Call*, Laurel, MS, renamed,

(LC) *Leader Call*, Laurel, MS

(MCH) *The Madison County Herald*, Canton, MS

(ND) *Neshoba Democrat*, Philadelphia, MS

(NYDN) *New York Daily News*, New York City, NY

(NYT) *New York Times*, New York City, NY

(TNR) *The Newton Record*, Newton, MS

(SMS) *Southern Mississippi Sun*, Biloxi, Gulfport, Pascagoula, MS

(TAC) *The Atlanta Constitution*, Atlanta, GA

(TPI) *The Philadelphia Inquirer*, Philadelphia, PA

(TTP) *The Times Picayune*, New Orleans, LA

(TWP) *The Washington Post*, Washington, DC

(UA) *The Union Appeal*, Union, MS

Part 9: Appendices

Appendix A: Autopsy By William Featherston, MD

Dr. William Featherston, an independent pathologist, performed the autopsies of all three victims at the University of MS Medical Center, in Jackson, on August 5, 1964. At the demand of the parents of Chaney, Dr. David Spain, also an independent pathologist, examined the body of James Chaney on August 7, 1964.

During preparation for the 2005 trial of Edgar Ray Killen, Dr. Michael Baden and Dr. Stephen Hayden of Brand, MS, examined x-rays from the original autopsy . Both of these examiners were independent pathologists.

Obtaining a copy of the original autopsy report by Dr. Featherston was necessary for this book. With an actual autopsy report, a complete forensic analysis was performed. Controversies regarding the murders and the autopsy were resolved.

Two copies of the autopsy are provided in this Appendix. The first copy is an exact copy of the original autopsy, signed by Dr. Featherston. This copy was provided by the MS Dept of Archives and History. This copy is a copy of a copy of a copy and is somewhat degraded. However, the signed copy is mostly intact and reasonably readable. And, the signed copy has the signature of Dr. William Featherston.

A second copy was provided by Steve Kilgore, MS 8th Circuit District Attorney in Philadelphia, MS. A MS Public Records Request was filed with his office. Steve responded quickly and provided a copy of the Featherston autopsy which he found in his files. This version of the autopsy was unsigned.

At the bottom of each page of this unsigned copy appears the date May 20, 2005, and the stamp MS State Attorney General, No. 4664. That stamp proves that this copy of the unsigned autopsy was provided to the MS 8th Circuit DA Marc Duncan as evidence in the trial of Edgar Ray Killen that was conducted in June, 2005. This version was retyped by the office of the MS Attorney General from the original version. A large, clear font was used. Text was broken into simpler paragraphs.

Sufficient clarity remains in the signed version to compare the signed and the unsigned versions of the autopsy report. This comparison confirms that the unsigned version is an exact copy of the signed version in every word, although better broken into paragraphs.

An unsigned copy of the Featherston autopsy was attached at the end of the publicly available FBI case files. (MIBURN-5, pdf p. 100). Only the first 4 lines of the unsigned copy appear in the FBI file. These 4 lines match the first 4 lines of the signed autopsy. These first 4 lines also match the first 4 lines of the unsigned autopsy provided by DA Steve Kilgore. All of the remaining text of page 1 was redacted by the FBI. A page appears that indicates that the remaining 4 pages of the Featherston autopsy are withheld under Exemption 67D (MIBURN-5, pdf p. 101).

This FBI redacted version was released in 2010. A Freedom of Information Act request was filed with the FBI for their unredacted copy of the autopsy report and for their unredacted copy of the complete public files. In response, the FBI claimed that their files do not contain any of the unredacted case files.

Both the signed copy of the autopsy report and the unsigned copy of the report with the MS AG markings are included in this appendix.

BRATLEY MEDICAL LABORATORY

JACKSON, MISSISSIPPI

AUTOPSY NO. 64-A-82 BODY NO. 1, 64-A-83, BODY NO. 2, 64-A-84 BODY NO. 3 (Identity not established at this time)

AUTOPSIED BY: William F. Featherston, M.D.

NOTE

These bodies were found in the vicinity of Philadelphia, Mississippi early today and were brought to the University Medical Center, Jackson, Mississippi and were accompanied by agents of the Federal Bureau of Investigation. Jay Cochran Jr. identified the remains. The examinations were begun at approximately 1:50 A.M. August 5, 1964. The first procedure was to have total x-rays performed on bodies identified at this time as No.1, No.2 and No. 3 in that order. The bodies were received in black plastic pouches closed with zippers which in turn are sealed with cotton and celluloidin.

DESCRIPTION

After the first pouch is opened, the body is found to be clad in blue denims and boots. The upper portion of the body is bare. The hands are enclosed in clear plastic with white opaque adhesive bandages sealing these. The body shows an advanced stage of decomposition. It measures 70 inches in length. The scalp hair is fine in texture and brown in color. There are some coarse black hairs on either side of the point of the chin Before any significant examination is carried out, dental examination is performed by Dr. Reuel May with careful and complete recording of his results. Following this, the body is carefully examined and a poorly defined circular wound measuring 5 mm. in diameter is found on the anterior chest to the right of the midline at the level of the fourth rib. The tissue has lost all elasticity and is plastic and crepitant. The course of the bullet transversed the pericardial sac, the left pleural cavity, and exits into the soft tissue of the left side of the chest; penetrating and fracturing the left eighth rib approximately 120 mm. to the left of the attachment of the ribs to the vertebral column. The bullet tract then pursues a slightly anterior course and is located in the soft tissues in the region of the posterior axillary fold on the left, at the same level as the ninth rib. For purposes of identification the distal two joints of each of the ten phalanges are removed for finger print study by the FBI laboratory. The clothing is removed without examination. On the ring finger of the left hand is located a white metallic ring of rather unusual design. The bullet which is removed is marked as specimen no. 1 with the initals of the examiner. It is placed in the custody of the FBI Agent Jay Cochran Jr.

Following this the second body designated at this time as autopsy number 64-A-83 is exposed. This case too shows advanced decomposition. The scalp hair is brown and fine in texture. Before any further examination is carried out dental studies by Dr. Reuel May is performed and recorded. The upper body is bare. The lower half is clothed in black pants, black slippers and black silk-like socks. Following this the clothing is removed and placed in the custody of the FBI. This includes a shirt under the shoulders. A large gapping wound is found in the region of the fourth rib to the right of the midline and a moderate amount of gray decomposed tissue is protruding from the opening. The wound measures 14 mm. in widest diameter. The chest cage is exposed

PAGE NO. 2

and there is found marked disruption of the body of the sternum with fracture of the cartilagenous portions of several ribs also. The internal organs show marked decomposition and they are dissected away free from the vertebral column. A bullet is found to lie transversely in the six thoracic interspace and with moderate difficulty it is removed from this place marked specimen No. 2 and placed in the hand of Jay Cochran Jr., agent in charge of the investigation.

Following this the third body is examined and this is designated as autopsy No. 64-A-34. The body shows marked decomposition. The upper body is clothed in a thin knitted cotton shirt. The lower body is clothed in blue jeans. The feet are enclosed in clear plastic similar to that enclosing the hands. The clothing is removed and placed in custody of the FBI. The scalp hair is kinky and dark brown. The body is in a face down position. It is turned face up and immediately there is found a crepitant fracture of the left humerus approximately 45 mm. below the shoulder. Also there is transverse fractures of both bones of the right forearm about 80 mm. above the wrist joint There is marked disruption of the elbow joint on the left. The wound of entry is found with considerable difficulty in the left upper epigastric region. The peritoneal cavity is opened and the chest cage is dissected away anteriorly. On reflecting the heart and lung toward the right and medially a bullet exit is noted in the posterior rib cage, adjacent to the attachment to the vertebral column in the region of T8. Two ribs are dissected free and a tract is found to extend into the subcutaneous tissue. A superficial skin incision is made into the back and projectile No. 3 is found, so marked and identified, and placed in the hands of Jay Cochran Jr., agent in charge. Following this the anterior abdominal wall is dissected laterally and approximately 50 mm. to the right of the midline a fourth projectile is found lodged in the anterior abdominal wall. The wound of entry cannot be located. This projectile is marked bullet No. 4, identified and placed in the hands of Jay Cochran Jr., agent in charge, FBI. Following this the skull is denuded of soft tissue and there is found a large explosive type fracture involving the right occupito-temporal area. Fracture lines extend inferiorly to involve the base of the skull as well. No wound of entry is found. The calvarium is removed with slight difficulty and the brain is found to be a very soft gray black mushy mass. After careful examination of this material, projectile no. 5 is found marked and identified. It is flattened along one surface and shows considerable distortion. The wound of entry is not located.

CONCLUSIONS

Each of the three individuals sustained gunshot wounds. While the actual damage to vital organs could not be demonstrated due to the advanced stage of decomposition of the tissues, the courses these bullets pursued from the wounds of entry to their locations in the bodies could not have resulted other than fatally.

The sequence of death of the three individuals could not be determined. Speculation of the position of the bodies at the time the gunshot wounds were inflicted would be futile.

The first two bodies showed no objective evidence of injury other than the gunshot wounds and these were sustained in the upper anterior chest.

The third body showed three gunshot wounds. Two of these definitely were sustained from the front of the body while the third wound of entry could not be located.

In addition, the fracture of the left humerus, and the right radius and ulna certainly indicated exterior force. When and how this was sustained, could not be determined. The fracture of the skull was definitely related to the gunshot wound.

William P. Featherston, M.D.
WILLIAM P. FEATHERSTON, M.D.

JN 44-1
JC:mjh
1

On August 14, 1964, an unsigned copy of the autopsy report prepared by Dr. WILLIAM F. FEATHERSTON, M.D., was received. This report covers the autopsy of each of the victims' bodies. It is set out as follows:

"BRATLEY MEDICAL LABORATORY

JACKSON, MISSISSIPPI

"AUTOPSY NO. 64-A-82 BODY NO. 1, 64-A-83, BODY NO. 2, 64-A-84 BODY NO. 3 (Identity not established at this time)

"AUTOPSIED BY: William F. Featherston, M.D.

"NOTE

"These bodies were found in the vicinity of Philadelphia, Mississippi, early today and were brought to the University Medical Center, Jackson, Mississippi, and were accompanied by agents of the Federal Bureau of Investigation. Jay Cochran Jr. identified the remains. The examinations were begun at approximately 1:30 A.M., August 5, 1964. The first procedure was to have total x-rays performed on bodies identified at this time as No. 1, No. 2 and No. 3 in that order. The bodies were received in black plastic pouches closed with zippers which in turn are sealed with cotton and celloidin.

"DESCRIPTION

"After the first pouch is opened, the body is found to be clad in blue denims and boots. The upper portion of the body is bare. The hands are enclosed in clear plastic with white opaque adhesive bandages sealing

51

JN 44-1
2

these. The body shows an advanced stage of decomposition. It measures 70 inches in length. The scalp hair is fine in texture and brown in color. There are some coarse black hairs on either side of the point of the chin. Before any significant examination is carried out, dental examination is performed by Dr. Reuel May with careful and complete recording of his results. Following this, the body is carefully examined and a poorly defined circular wound measuring 8 mm. in diameter is found on the anterior chest to the right of the midline at the level of the fourth rib. The tissue has lost all elasticity and is plastic and crepitant. The course of the bullet transverses the pericardial sac, the left pleural cavity, and exits into the soft tissue of the left side of the chest; penetrating and fracturing the left eighth rib approximately 120 mm. to the left of the attachment of the ribs to the vertebral column. The bullet tract then pursues a slightly anterior course and is located in the soft tissues in the region of the posterior axillary fold on the left, at the same level as the ninth rib. For purposes of identification the distal two joints of each of the ten phalanges are removed for finger print study by the FBI Laboratory. The clothing is removed without examination. On the ring finger of the left hand is located a white metallic ring of rather unusual design. The bullet which is removed is marked as specimen no. 1 with the initals of the examiner. It is placed in the custody of the FBI Agent Jay Cochran Jr.

"Following this the second body designated at this time as autopsy number 64-A-83 is exposed. This case too shows advanced decomposition. The scalp hair is brown and fine in texture. Before any further examination is carried out dental studies by Dr. Reuel May is performed and recorded. The upper body is bare. The

52

JN 44-1
3

lower half is clothed in black pants, black slippers and black silk-like socks. Following this the clothing is removed and placed in the custody of the FBI. This includes a shirt under the shoulders. A large gapping wound is found in the region of the fourth rib to the right of the midline and a moderate amount of gray decomposed tissue is protruding from the opening. The wound measures 14 mm. in widest diameter. The chest cage is exposed and there is found marked disruption of the body of the sternum with fracture of the cartilagenous portions of several ribs also. The internal organs show marked decomposition and they are dissected away free from the vertebral column. A bullet is found to lie transversely, in the six thoracic interspace and with moderate difficulty it is removed from this place marked specimen No. 2 and placed in the hand of Jay Cochran, Jr., agent in charge of the investigation.

"Following this the third body is examined and this is designated as autopsy No. 64-A-84. The body shows marked decomposition. The upper body is clothed in a thin knitted cotton shirt. The lower body is clothed in blue jeans. The feet are enclosed in clear plastic similar to that enclosing the hands. The clothing is removed and placed in custody of the FBI. The scalp hair is kinky and dark brown. The body is in a face down position. It is turned face up and immediately there is found a crepitant fracture of the left humerus approximately 45 mm. below the shoulder. Also there is transverse fracture of both bones of the right forearm about 90 mm. above the wrist joint. There is marked disruption of the elbow joint on the left. The wound of entry is found with considerable difficulty in the left upper epigastric region. The peritoneal cavity is opened and the chest cage is dissected away anteriorly. On reflecting the

53

JN 44-1
4

heart and lung toward the right and medially a bullet exit is noted in the posterior rib cage, adjacent to the attachment to the vertebral column in the region of T8. Two ribs are dissected free and a tract is found to extend into the subcutaneous tissue. A superficial skin incision is made into the back and projectile No. 3 is found, so marked and identified, and placed in the hands of Jay Cochran Jr., agent in charge. Following this the <u>anterior</u> abdominal wall is dissected laterally and approximately 50 mm. to the right of the midline a fourth projectile is found lodged in the <u>anterior abdominal wall</u>. The wound of entry cannot be located. This projectile is marked bullet No. 4, identified and placed in the hands of Jay Cochran Jr., agent in charge, FBI. Following this the skull is denuded of soft tissue and there is found a large explosive type fracture involving the right occupito-temporal area. Fracture lines extend inferiorly to involve the base of the skull as well. No wound of entry is found. The calvarium is removed with slight difficulty and the brain is found to be a very soft gray black mushy mass. After careful examination of this material, projectile no. 5 is found marked and identified. It is flattened along one surface and shows considerable distortion. The wound of entry is not located.

"CONCLUSIONS

"Each of the three individuals sustained gunshot wounds. While the actual damage to vital organs could not be demonstrated due to the advanced stage of decomposition of the tissues, the courses these bullets pursued from the wounds of entry to their locations in the bodies could not have resulted other than fatally.

JN 44-1
5

"The sequence of death of the three individuals could not be determined. Speculation of the position of the bodies at the time the gunshot wounds were inflicted would be futile.

"The first two bodies showed no objective evidence of injury other than the gunshot wounds and these were sustained in the upper anterior chest.

"The third body showed three gunshot wounds. Two of these definitely were sustained from the front of the body while the third wound of entry could not be located.

"In addition, the fracture of the left humerus, and the right radius and ulna certainly indicated exterior force. When and how this was sustained, could not be determined. The fracture of the skull was definitely related to the gunshot wound.

                            WILLIAM P. FEATHERSTON, M.D."

Appendix B: Chaney Autopsy By David Spain, MD

POST MORTEM EXAMINATION REPORT OF
THE BODY OF JAMES CHANEY

Report on inspection of autopsied body of James Chaney on August 7, 1964 at 2:30 P.M. at the University of Mississippi Medical School Hospital autopsy room and witnessed by University of Mississippi Medical School pathologists.

The body was in a partially decomposed state and opened from the neck to the pubis anteriorly, as a result of the recently performed autopsy. The top of the calvarium had been sawed and was independent of the base of the skull. The organs had been removed and portions of skin apparently corresponding to the entrance bullet wounds were missing. The terminal phalanges of all fingers had been removed (apparently for identification and finger printing purposes). The decomposed and partially putrified skin was peeling and the body was covered with a clay-like dirt. A circular depressed fracture - approximately 3 centimeters in diameter was present over the left fronto-parietal region. A complete through and through comminuted fracture was present in the center of the mandible. The left shoulder joint involving the upper end of the humerus was completely shattered into many fragments. The right ulnar and radius were fractured in at least two points completely across. There was no evidence of a bullet wound at this site. In addition to the fracture of the skull previously described, there was an extensive fracture extending through the base and across the occipital area. On the left of the sternum the ribs were shattered as were the ribs directly posteriorly just next to the vertebral bodies. Aside from the above, there were no other obvious injuries to the body. The state of the body at this time precluded any further meaningful examination. In lay terminology - the jaw was shattered, the left shoulder and upper arm were reduced to a pulp; the right forearm was broken completely across at several points, and the skull bones were broken and pushed in towards the brain.

Under the circumstances, these injuries could only be the result of an extremely severe beating with either a blunt instrument or chain. The other fractures of the skull and ribs were the result of bullet wounds. It is impossible to determine whether the deceased died from the beating before the bullet wounds were inflicted.

In my extensive experience of 25 years as a Pathologist and as a Medical Examiner, I have never witnessed bones so severely shattered, except in tremendously high speed accidents such as aeroplane crashes.

David M. Spain, M.D. /s/

Source: Spain, David, MD, *Post Mortem Examination Report of The Body of James Chaney*, August 7, 1964, CRMV, https://www.crmvet.org/docs/6408_chaney_spain.pdf.

Appendix C: Radiology Report, James Packer, MD

ELMER J. HARRIS, M.D.
ROBERT P. HENDERSON, M.D.

JAMES M. PACKER, M.D.
W. HOWARD COOPER, III, M.D.

RADIOLOGICAL GROUP
SUITE 318 MEDICAL ARTS BLDG.
1161 NORTH STATE STREET
JACKSON, MISSISSIPPI

354-4327

August 28, 1964

Dr. William P. Featherston
Suite 201 Medical Arts Building
Jackson, Mississippi

Dear Doctor Featherston:

The following represents a report on three sets of X-ray films, these sets being labeled No. 1, 2 and 3, all being dated 4 August 1964, being made at the University Hospital, Jackson, Mississippi.

The following general remarks are true for all sets of the films:

The films are made of bodies which are in an advanced state of deterioration, as evidenced by gases being generally distributed through the soft tissues and in the cranial cavity. They are made only in the AP projection unless noted otherwise, and many artefacts are present including metallic objects in pockets, clothing and covering material. In many instances detail is almost completely obscured by overlying grumous appearing material, apparently representing soil or rocks.

Observations made generally center around what can be seen of bullets and bullet tracts and fractures.

Re: Case No. 1

In review of the upper portion of the body the skull is turned to a lateral position, and we can see small metallic densities lying just anterior to the region of C-1 just below the base of the skull. Other fragmented metallic densities are seen superimposed over the right upper chest, scapula and right upper arm.

The films do not precisely overlap in evaluating the chest, but two bone ends can be seen which appear to represent fractured rib adjacent to the metallic fragments. Most of the left chest is obscured by grumous appearing material.

Otherwise, we see no particularly significant findings in the rest of the films made of this individual.

Re: Case No. 2

On the film covering the skull area with the skull being in an oblique position, it shows that there is a large bullet fragment

Dr. William P. Featherston   8/28/64   cont'd.

Re: University Hospital Films
Cases No. 1, 2 and 3
Dated August 4, 1964

with several minute fragments superimposed over the base of the skull posteriorly. In the chest area we can see a bullet superimposed over the mid line over the upper dorsal area with small fragments scattered to the left of this out into the lateral chest wall. A rib fracture can be seen in the mid axillary area involving the third rib with considerable offset of fragments. What appears to be a second bullet fragment is seen superimposed over the upper humerus with several small fragments in the soft tissues about this region.

No other definite abnormalities can be seen on the available films.

Re: Case No. 3

It is noted that the marker is wrong on these films as the body is stated to have been in the prone position instead of the supine position as was apparently thought to be the case at the time these films were made.

On the uppermost film, the lateral view of the skull shows a bullet fragment superimposed over the temporo-parietal area posterior to the sella. Smaller fragments are distributed anterior to this region.

A fracture of the left upper humerus is observed with multiple metallic fragments seen in the soft tissues adjacent to this fracture. A fracture of the upper end of the left ulna is observed with bullet fragments lying in the area of the fracture. There is dislocation of the head of the radius.

We see a fracture of the left 4th rib with metallic fragments in this area. A bullet is superimposed over the area of D-6 to the left of the mid line.

Another bullet is superimposed over the lower radius on the right.

On the available films no other remarkable findings are noted.

Yours truly,

James M. Packer

James M. Packer, M. D.

JMP:acb

Appendix D: Condition Of Body, Chaney, FBI

> Exhuming operations continued and at 5:07 p.m. the body of a second individual lying in a face-down position south of and adjacent to Body #1 was located. This body, Body #2, was partially under Body #1. The head of Body #2 was likewise pointed in an easterly direction with arms generally extended over its head. The left hand of this body was clenched in a tight fist. Opening of this fist disclosed a rock-like object. Body #2 was clad in trousers and shoes and naked from the waist up.
>
> No jewelry was noted on the hands of Body #2. These hands were likewise encased in plastic bags for preservation. In the right hip pocket of the trousers of Body #2 was a black leather wallet which contained among other items a Selective Service card bearing the following descriptive data:
>
> Name: ANDREW GOODMAN
> Address: 161 West 86th Street
> New York 24, New York
> Date of Birth: November 23, 1943
> Date of Registration: November 24, 1961
> Selective Service Number: 50-13-43-458 (possibly 488)
>
> What appeared to be a shirt was observed to be wadded beneath the hips of Body #2. Body #2 was not moved or disturbed in any way in order to preserve the scene.
>
> At 5:14 p.m. the remains of a third body were unearthed. Body #3 was lying on its back immediately south of and parallel to Body #2. The head was toward the west with the face turned south. The left arm and shoulder were drawn up and across the body. The right arm was lying along the side of the body. Body #3 was barefoot and clad in trousers and a "T" shirt. No jewelry was observed on the hands of Body #3. Since this body was lying on its back, no attempts were made at this time to move it to determine any contents of the trousers' hip pockets. The hands and feet of this body were encased in plastic bags for preservation.

Source: FBI-MBT-5, pdf pp. 12-13.

Appendix E: Complete Passenger List

Location	PID	Vehicle	VID	Passengers				
Several Locations	P01	1963 Ford Ranch Wagon	V1	Schwerner	Chaney	Goodman		
To Jail	P02	1963 Ford Ranch Wagon	V1	Wiggs	Chaney			
	P03	1956 Chevy Cruiser	V2	Price				
	P04	1962 Pontiac Catalina	V6	Poe	Schwerner	Goodman		
To Longhorn Drive-In	P05	1959 Chevy Bel Air	V8	Killen	Sharpe	Townsend		
To Akins	P06	Unknown	?	Killen	Townsend	Herndon	Harris	
	P07	1957 Ford Fairlane	V3	D Barnette	Arledge			
To Roberts/To Akins	P08	1959 Chevy Bel Air	V8	Sharpe	Jordan	Roberts		
To Jail, West Side Of CH	P09	1959 Chevy Bel Air	V8	Sharpe	Killen	Roberts	Townsend	
To West Side Of CH	P10	1957 Ford Fairlane	V3	D Barnette	Jordan	T Barnette	Arledge	Snowden
Location	PID	Vehicle	VID	Passengers				
Warehouse	P11	1959 Chevy Bel Air	V8	Sharpe	Roberts	Townsend		
	P12	1957 Ford Fairlane	V3	D. Barnette	Jordan	T Barnette	Arledge	Snowden
	P13	1956 Chevy Bel Air	V4	Posey				
To House	P14	1956 Chevy Cruiser	V2	Price				
	P15	1957 Ford Fairlane	V3	D. Barnette	Jordan	T Barnette	Arledge	Snowden
	P16	1956 Chevy Bel Air	V4	Posey	Roberts	Sharpe	Townsend	
To 492	P17	1956 Chevy Cruiser	V2	Price				
	P18	1957 Ford Fairlane	V3	D. Barnette	Jordan	T Barnette	Arledge	Snowden
				Posey	Roberts	Sharpe		
To House	P19	1956 Chevy Cruiser	V2	Price	Snowden	Schwerner	Chaney	Goodman
	P20	1957 Ford Fairlane	V3	D. Barnette	Jordan	T Barnette		
	P21	1963 Ford Ranch Wagon	V1	Arledge	Posey	Roberts	Sharpe	
To 515	P22	1956 Chevy Cruiser	V2	Price	Snowden	Schwerner	Chaney	Goodman
	P23	1957 Ford Fairlane	V3	D. Barnette	Jordan	T Barnette		
	P24	1963 Ford Ranch Wagon	V1	Arledge	Posey	Roberts	Sharpe	
	P25	1956 Chevy Bel Air	V4	Townsend				
Location	PID	Vehicle	VID	Passengers				
To Dam	P26	1957 Ford Fairlane	V3	D. Barnette	Jordan	T Barnette	Arledge	Snowden
	P27	1963 Ford Ranch Wagon	V1	Posey	Sharpe	Roberts		
To/From Pickup	P28	1957 Ford Fairlane	V3	D. Barnette	Roberts	Arledge		
	P29	1955 Chevy Bel Air	V5	Burrage	Tucker	Unidentified		
To Garage After Drop	P30	1957 Ford Fairlane	V3	D. Barnette	Arledge			
	P31	1955 Chevy Bel Air	V5	Burrage	Unidentified			
To Garage After Burial	P32	1963 Ford Ranch Wagon	V1	Posey	Roberts	Jordan	T Barnette	
				Sharpe	Snowden	Tucker		
To Barn	P33	1963 Ford Ranch Wagon	V1	Tucker				
	P34	Diesel Escort Truck	V7	Burrage				
To Garage	P35	Diesel Escort Truck	V7	Burrage	Tucker			

Appendix F: Specific Locations, June 21, 1964

Activity		Event	Latitude Longitude
Church Inspection	1	trio departs COFO office, Meridian	32.362302 -88.702266
	2	inspection of burnt ruins at Mt Zion Church	32.7817 -88.99128
	3	trio heads west on Hwy 16	32.75731 -88.97089
First Arrest	4	Price first sights station wagon	32.7680969 -89.0445599
	5	Price turns around at 539	32.767592 -89.04228
	6	Highway Patrol at parking spot at 545	32.768815 -89.050829
	7	Price overtakes wagon again	32.769396 -89.0596232
	8	Price starts clocking wagon speed	32.77084 -89.085152
	9	wagon passes city limit	32.7706865 -89.0936488
	10	Price turns on lights and siren	32.7710835 -89.1008593
	11	wagon tire changed, trio arrested	32.771459 -89.1034082
Lockup	12	trio locked in Courthouse jail	32.77248 -89.11035

Activity		Event	Latitude Longitude
	13	local White Knights staged	32.77297 -89.11342
Second Arrest	14	trio released from Courthouse jail	32.77248 -89.11035
	15	released trio heads towards Meridian	32.770971 -89.106105
	16	Price takes lead in chase	32.757372 -89.105220
	17	Price overtakes wagon	32.629788 -89.007777
	18	trio turns west on 492	32.62483 -88.99795
	19	WK 1956 Chevy has problem	32.628662 -89.005824
	20	trio arrested on 492	32.596151 -89.038419
Murder	21	caravan returns to and turns north on 19	32.62483 -88.99795
	22	WK picked up at 1956 Chevy	32.628662 -89.005824
	23	caravan turns west on Rock Cut Rd	32.66354 -89.03119
	24	murder trio at murder site	32.66214 -89.03410

Activity		Event	Latitude Longitude
Escape Route	25	caravan travels cross country to Hwy 21	Multiple Roads
Bury Bodies	26	caravan exits right from cross country route	32.73182 -89.19554
	27	caravan turns onto access road to dam	32.734640 -89.183410
	28	locate bulldozer operator	32.747558 -89.177210
	29	deliver bulldozer operator	32.746676 -89.192021
	30	bodies buried in unfilled excavation	32.738558 -89.192312
	31	wagon driven to garage	32.756556 -89.167893
Dump Wagon	32	wagon, truck escort travel N on 21	32.770983 -89.108342
	33	wagon diverted into swamp past 491	32.881639 -88.938096
	34	truck returns to garage on 21	32.756556 -89.167893
	35	Burrage returns to home	32.756191 -89.167035

Appendix G: SNCC Incident Tabulation

City	Beating	Bombing	Shots	Murder	Arrest	Arson	Harrassment	Total	Violence
Greenwood	8		4		14		14	40	26
Jackson	10		5	3	7	1	12	38	26
McComb	2	5			6	3	7	23	16
Hattiesburg	2	1	3		7		14	27	13
Canton	2	1	4		5		9	21	12
Clarksdale	1				10		15	26	11
Laurel	5	1	1		2	1	7	17	10
Moss Point		1	1		4		5	11	6
Philadelphia	5					1	6	12	6
Vicksburg	1	1	2		1	1	11	17	6
Columbus	1				4		7	12	5
Gulfport	1				4		5	10	5
Natchez		1	1		2	1	4	9	5
Batesville	2				2		4	8	4
Brandon		1		1		2	1	5	4
Drew					4		3	7	4
Greenville	1		2		1		3	7	4
Itta Benna	1				2	1	3	7	4
Meridian			1		2	1	4	8	4

City	Beating	Bombing	Shots	Murder	Arrest	Arson	Harrassment	Total	Violence
Holly Springs	1			1	1		12	15	3
Ocean Springs			3				1	4	3
Biloxi					2		4	6	2
Cleveland				1	1		2	4	2
Gluckstadt					1	1		2	2
Mileston		1				1	1	3	2
Raleigh		2						2	2
Ruleville	1	1					14	16	2
Yazoo City					2			2	2
Aberdeen	1						6	7	1
Amory					1			1	1
Anguilla					1			1	1
Belzoni					1		2	3	1
Browning						1		1	1
Carthage	1							1	1
Clinton		1						1	1
Collinsville		1						1	1
Doddsville				1			3	4	1
Doodleville					1			1	1

City	Beating	Bombing	Shots	Murder	Arrest	Arson	Harrassment	Total	Violence
Durant	1						1	2	1
Granada					1			1	1
Holmes County					1			1	1
Lauderdale					1			1	1
Lexington	1							1	1
Marigold				1			1	2	1
Marks	1							1	1
Mound Bayou					1			1	1
SoSo		1						1	1
Starkville					1		2	3	1
Tupelo						1		1	1
Winona County					1			1	1
Charleston							1	1	0
Fayette							1	1	0
Harmony							3	3	0
Hollandale							2	2	0
Indianola							3	3	0
Mayersville							1	1	0
Oxford							1	1	0
Shaw							6	6	0
Tallahatchie							1	1	0
Tchula							1	1	0
Toogaloo							1	1	0

City	Beating	Bombing	Shots	Murder	Arrest	Arson	Harrassment	Total	Violence
Total	49	19	27	8	94	16	204	417	213

Hattiesburg, Jackson, Laurel, McComb, Poplarville		
South Zone Total		
105	65	30.5
Incidents	Violence	% Violence
Canton, Clarksdale, Greenwood, Philadelphia, Ruleville		
North Zone Total		
87	49	23.0
Incidents	Violence	% Violence
46.0	53.5	
% Total Incidents	% Total Violent	

Tabulated From: SNCC, *MS Summer Project, Running Summary of Incidents*, The Student Nonviolent Coordinating Committee Papers, 1959 - 1972, https://www.crmvet.org/docs/64_fs_incidents.pdf.

About The Author

Bruce Krell, PhD, was born Jewish and raised in Hattiesburg, MS, about 125 miles from Philadelphia, MS.

Bruce Krell, PhD

Bruce was 15 years old at the time of the murders. Hattiesburg was one of the most-deep South of deep South cities. As a young Jewish kid in this environment, Dr. Krell regularly faced violence by redneck cops, the White Knights and the United Klans of America.

His daily life was affected by these murders of his fellow Jews, Mickey Schwerner and Andy Goodman, and the murder of James Chaney, a Black man. As Sam Bowers, Imperial Wizard of the White Knights, wrote:

> . . . *the savage Kike lust for money is destroying Christian Civilization* . . .

Violence levels increased against Blacks and Jews. Klansmen in the White Knights grew more arrogant that a white jury would never convict any Klansmen for murder of Blacks and Jews.

Dr. Krell is an independent forensic science expert who performs shooting incident reconstructions. He has evaluated over 100 shooting incidents and has testified in 10. His approach to shooting reconstructions uses math, science, physics, testing, evidence, witness testimony, and visualization techniques.

Read his insights into the murders of Schwerner, Chaney and Goodman based on his early years growing up Jewish in the deep South. See his visual reconstruction based on a decade of experience in forensic science.

www.ingramcontent.com/pod-product-compliance
Lightning Source LLC
Chambersburg PA
CBHW040748020526
44118CB00041B/2728